Barry Coulton was educated in a small village school in West Cumberland. He served a craft apprenticeship at the Sellafield nuclear reprocessing plant and was awarded a flying scholarship while training with the Whitehaven Squadron of the Air Training Corps. At the age of 24, he gave up an aspiring management career with the UK Atomic Energy Authority and ventured into the wilds of Africa.

Barry has worked on copper mines in Central Africa, gas separation plants in Siberia, sugar factories in South America and oil refineries in Malaysia. He has installed and commissioned control systems on more than 160 industrial plants in 46 different countries. He aspired to own engineering companies in Zambia, South Africa, Russia and England.

At the time of writing this book Barry Coulton was working as a Black Pearl Pirate in the Disney film trilogy, *Pirates of the Caribbean*. He is a pianist, a time-served tradesman, a chartered engineer, a commercial pilot, a blue water sailor, a background film actor and above all else, a world traveller.

BARRY COULTON

Copyright © 2007 Barry Coulton

The moral right of the author has been asserted.

Apart from any fair dealing for the purposes of research or private study, or criticism or review, as permitted under the Copyright, Designs and Patents Act 1988, this publication may only be reproduced, stored or transmitted, in any form or by any means, with the prior permission in writing of the publishers, or in the case of reprographic reproduction in accordance with the terms of licences issued by the Copyright Licensing Agency. Enquiries concerning reproduction outside those terms should be sent to the publishers.

Matador
9 De Montfort Mews
Leicester LE1 7FW, UK
Tel: (+44) 116 255 9311 / 9312
Email: books@troubador.co.uk
Web: www.troubador.co.uk/matador

ISBN 978-1905886-753

Typeset in 11pt Book Antiqua by Troubador Publishing Ltd, Leicester, UK
Printed in the UK by The Cromwell Press Ltd, Trowbridge, Wilts, UK

Matador is an imprint of Troubador Publishing Ltd

Dedicated to the memory of my great granddaughter, Mia Lucy

Contents

	Acknowledgements	xi
	Prologue	xiii
1	**The Early Years** Growing up in Cumberland after the war *Like father like son!*	1
2	**A Good Old-Fashioned Apprenticeship** Training to be a skilled instrument mechanic at Sellafield *So many people to thank!*	25
3	**Wear the Queen's Uniform with Pride** Eight years of tremendous excitement in the Air Training Corps *Venture adventure!*	50
4	**Reaching For the Sky** Earning my pilot's wings through a Royal Air Force Scholarship *A schoolboy's dream!*	65
5	**I'm the Gaffer** Leading a skilled team at the Sellafield Atomic Energy Plant *Still a lot to learn!*	92
6	**Africa Here We Come** The cradle of mankind, primitive and unforgiving *The silence of the bush is deafening!*	104
7	**Broken Hill, Zambia** Working a lead and zinc mine that is as old as the country is new *Beware mambas!*	115
8	**Living on Half a Loaf of Bread** Starting my first company and it's on the Congo border *Where is that silver teaspoon!*	129

9	**A Tough and Dangerous Year** Working a 7-day week after the Mufulira mine disaster *I hope the lights don't go out!*	145
10	**One of the White Tribe** Managing Honeywell control system projects in South Africa *Net Blankes!*	171
11	**Coulton Industrial** Working in war-torn Mozambique and South West Africa *Carry a second passport!*	212
12	**Robert Mark Brett** A new addition to our small family *Proud to be chosen!*	239
13	**Flying my Dream** Bush pilot, aerobatic pilot and then commercial pilot *Which side is up!*	250
14	**Home to Blighty** At the cutting edge of technology with Rosemount *Diogenes has the solution!*	270
15	**European Job English Salary** Working with some of the best engineers in Europe *Old frustrations re-emerge!*	284
16	**Three New Relationships** Palmstiernas, Fuji Electric and McWatters *Top hats not allowed!*	318
17	**Fall of the Russian Empire** Insider's view of those momentous years from 1988 to 1993 *Perestroika Mafia Style!*	363
18	**A Russian Misadventure** Starting one of the first joint stock companies in new Russia *Safer to stay at home!*	385
19	**Coulton Instrumentation** The last of my six companies and the most successful *Targeted by one of the big boys!*	423

| 20 | White Man's Grave
Mayan civilizations, coral reefs and a little work in Belize
Fer-de-lance, ugh! | 438 |
|---|---|---|
| 21 | Kenyan Sugar, Not so Sweet
Returning to a very different Kenya 28 years on
Death and unprecedented corruption! | 451 |
| 22 | A New Pair of Hands
Training a new manager for my succession
The market goes belly-up! | 472 |
| 23 | Clipper Round the World Yacht Race
Racing the Atlantic and following in the footsteps of Darwin
Canal, what canal! | 504 |
| 24 | Looking for Paradise
Choosing a country and finding the perfect retirement home
Retirement is hard work! | 517 |
| 25 | New Horizons to Discover
My feet are itching and I have a terrible case of islanditus
Where to next! | 541 |
| 26 | A Pirate's Life for Me
Shiver me timbers lad, it's the real thing, beard and all
A Black Pearl Pirate! | 587 |

Acknowledgements

I wish to acknowledge the tremendous encouragement and support given by teachers and lecturers at Distington Village School, Richmond Secondary Modern School, Workington College of Further Education and Liverpool Regional College of Technology. Each contributed at different levels, and in their own way, helped to change a country bumpkin who failed his 11-plus into a highly skilled professional engineer.

I reserve a very special mention for the excellent training provided by technicians and engineers at the Windscale and Calder Works of the United Kingdom Atomic Energy Authority, and in particular, I wish to acknowledge the help of Len Pearce, known to hundreds of ex-apprentices as 'Fruity'. I owe my professional career to the help and dedication of this one person more than any other. Thank you Mr Pearce, your trust in me was well founded.

I wish to thank work colleagues and customers of Honeywell, Rosemount and Fuji Electric around the world with whom I have had pleasure to work alongside on so many exciting projects. Professionally, I would like to mention officers of the Institute of Measurement and Control with whom I served for several years and I ask them to carry on their excellent work in helping young people to develop their full potential.

Finally I wish to thank Mattie, a very good companion to my father in his later years and Anne, my own very dear companion and very forgiving wife. I thank them both for their perseverance with two very difficult and stubborn members of the Coulton family.

Prologue
Never a Dull Moment

I have been fortunate to know several beautiful and graceful women in the fullness of my life. This book is inspired by one of these women; she was my first and only teenage love; Margie. When I searched through Margie's effects I found a collection of 25 handwritten pages. These pages were the beginning of her life story, 'Never a Dull Moment'. Her writing style was simple and to the point, she laid bare her innermost thoughts about those who had influenced her life. Sadly, she was only able to write a very small part of her book and now 25 years on I have decided to use her pages as the opening chapter of my own story.

And now her story……

It was even funny how we met, in a dance hall in the small steel town of Workington, Cumbria. The town had dark grimy buildings from years of billowing furnace smoke, but a short drive outside town brought me to splendid grey slate fells, sparkling lakes and lush green fields. The people in Workington were friendly but life was not very exciting.

When I was a teenager the highlight of the week was dolling up on a Saturday afternoon and getting ready for the dance that night in the Princess Hall; it used to take me three hours to get ready. The Princess band was good; very much the Glenn Miller sound. I thought that I looked splendid in my six-layered petticoat, flared skirt and tight sweater. My waist was clinged-in with a black waspie belt that was so tight that I could hardly breathe. My shoes were very high stilettos with real mink fur bows. Looking back, I must have looked ridiculous.

My best friends were Anne and Jeanie. We each backcombed our hair into huge beehives, stiffened them with lacquer and then clipped little bows in the front. When I was at school I even had a Bill Haley Kiss Curl; I used to train it with soap and water. I cringe when I look at my old photographs.

Barry asked me to dance on that special Saturday night when we first met. I thought him a bit of a square because he wore a suit and owned a scooter; I much preferred Rockers to Mods. Barry gave me a lift home afterwards, but when he asked for a date and mentioned that he was only sixteen, I stood him up. I was eighteen; I knew my friends would hoot with laughter and say that I was cradle snatching.

I remember my first dance. It was the Tanner Hop at Harrington, so called because it cost six pence, or a tanner, to enter. We all wore school uniform, short socks and long glass dangling earrings. We didn't have anything else. The last dance was always the single record, 'You are my special the angel'. The girls knew that if they were asked for that one, then they had clicked and would be escorted home.

Everyone fancied Jakey; he was slim, dark haired and dressed in jeans and a leather jacket. He looked the part but didn't own a motorbike. Strangely he had a yen for me and although he was supposed to be a bit of a tear away, I found him the perfect gentleman and rather gentle and shy. We were talking one night on a bridge when along came my mum and she clattered my ears all the way home. I thought that I would die from the humiliation of being hit in front of my boyfriend.

Mum was scared for us when we were out. She always said, 'Remember I trust you', before we left the house and she never slept until my sister and I returned and we were both in bed.

Nana

Nana, my mother's mum, lived quite close to town in a small flat. She was a wonderful old girl. I loved to watch her brush out her long hair and plait it until it hung in a long rope down her back. She wore flannelette nightdresses and had a soft wrinkled neck. I used to sit on her vast lap and cling to the folds of her neck. She was like a warm security blanket to me. I was such a timid child that I refused to go for bread to the shop unless I had one pound in my pocket because I was so scared that I would not have enough to pay.

Nana had two husbands and she lost both of them when she was very young. The first died of cholera and the second was killed in France while serving in the Highland Light Infantry. He took a direct hit from an enemy shell and his remains were never found. His name was William and he was my grandfather. He was a brave soldier with several medals to prove it and I am very proud of him.

When Nana became a War Widow she found that she could not manage on the meagre pension offered by the government; she had Billy, Maurice and my mother Minnie to support. Times were hard and she was fortunate to find work in Queen Street Mission as a cleaner. She also took washing in and forced my mother to stay at home to help. It was several years before Nana finally relented and allowed my mother to take a job in the Beehive Department Store where she worked her way up from sales assistant to manageress.

Mum eventually married my father Joe Elliot and they continued to live with Nana until I was ten years old. Then the council allocated us a semi-detached house in Salterbeck.

Whenever someone was having a baby in the neighbourhood Nana would be called to stand in as a midwife and when someone died she was asked to lay them out. I never found out if she was paid for these services but she never let her friends in the neighbourhood down. Many times in my story I thought twice about writing down all of these details, but I know that if I don't then it will be less than the truth as I saw it.

Long after my gran died and we had come up in the world, a woman who had an easy life met my mother in the street. She looked down her nose and told mum that Nana used to do their washing. Mum replied 'Yes, isn't life funny, now my husband is your husband's foreman'. My mum has a caustic tongue when she has to defend the name of her family. She was the same with us girls; in her eyes we could do no wrong.

Nana had a huge featherbed and I always slept in it with her after the Saturday night dance; I was as snug as a bug in a rug. My rude awakening always came in the morning when she called me to the kitchen table at the crack of dawn to consume vast quantities of egg, bacon, fried bread and Cumberland black pudding. Nana believed in a good breakfast but ate sparingly for the rest of the day. Perhaps that was why she lived to a ripe old age.

At the time, there was a face cream called Seafire and Nana always smelled faintly of it. Nana was quite vain and loved nice clothes. She couldn't afford them on a war widow's pension and she got them on tick at the local shop for so much a week. Nana always kept up the payments but my mother worried because she would never save a penny. If my mum saw her with something new, Nana would try to cover up and say that she had had it for ages. We always knew when she wasn't telling the truth because her bottom lip would quiver.

There was a gap between the houses opposite Nana's flat and she watched for mum or me getting off the bus. Her arms would be crossed over a vast bosom and her stout figure enveloped in an old-fashioned pinny. The tea would be massed before we got to her front door. My mother never missed a day without visiting her and she did all of her shopping. Nana never expected prices to go up and she totalled all the prices for the goods my mother was to bring. If the change was one penny out; woe betide my mum.

Mum also did her painting and decorating and when her neighbours saw how nice Nana's flat was they all wanted theirs done. Nana told her friends and neighbours that her daughter Minnie would do it for them and Mum always obliged. She never charged them but she hated her given name. When my sister and I were children we called her Minnie Ha Ha or Minnie the Mouse.

When I was in my teens I had a faithful swain called James. He was absolutely devoted to me and I was awful to him. He brought me gifts of flowers, chocolates and even a lovely pearl necklace. I use to ask Nana to tell him to go away but she thought he was marvellous. She kept telling me that he would make the perfect husband.

In the meantime, a boy called Billy was giving me the same run-around. He had black hair with big brown eyes. I would go weak at the knees just watching him across the dance hall floor. He let me down again and again. He often turned up at the dance with someone else and I would go home to sob my heart out. Occasionally he took me home in a box on wheels that he called a car. I was so in love I would cheerfully push-start it. I finally realized that it wasn't to be when he suddenly married and dropped out of sight after getting a girl into trouble.

My mother was a gentle person. She did a lot of singing as a girl and it weakened her voice, which made it difficult for her to shout when Anne and I misbehaved. When mum lost her temper she threw her shoes at us as we ran upstairs. She was a lousy shot and always missed. Afterwards mum always examined her expensive anaglipta wallpaper and then regretted her shoe-throwing episodes.

Anne and I were sisters but we had totally different personalities. I was timid, nervous and shy. She was attractive, three years' my senior, confident and a bubbly person with lots of friends. My father was proud of Anne, especially when she passed her eleven plus. I was very frightened of him and he made me even more nervous. I loved and respected him, but the more I tried to please him the more miserably I failed. I was jealous of my sister because I wanted to be like her. Money was tight and I wore all her cast off clothes, and when she got a bike, I resented it terribly.

Anne was generous and always let me borrow her bike but it could never be the same as owning one of my own. My two greatest joys were cycling across the fields and lying in bed with my nose stuck in a book. I always continued to read with a torch under the bedclothes after my mum had put my bedroom light out. This caused me to become short-sighted and I soon had to be fitted with glasses.

My father worked in the steel works where he started as an apprentice fitter in the shell shop. He eventually retired as the machine tool shop foreman in the Chapel Bank Foundry when he was 65 years old. It was dirty and dangerous work but he never earned much. I didn't really appreciate him then. I used to get mad because he always had the best food and we had to be silent while he took a short nap after eating.

My father was, and still is, a typical northern male. He expected his meal to be on the table when he arrived home, and he never did anything in the house. Like all northern men he believed housework was women's work. I know; I married one.

Barry

Shortly before my 21st birthday I met Barry again. He was more mature, and I liked him a lot better. He bought me a pretty marquisate ring and we were soon going steady. Previously I had been going out with a boy called Maurice who sadly was killed along with his three friends in a tragic car accident. It took me many months before I got over this traumatic experience and I met Barry just at the right time.

Barry was working hard, serving his time as an apprentice instrument mechanic with the United Kingdom Atomic Energy Authority. In the evenings he attended night school to get his qualifications and we would meet up after he came out of his classes at Workington College. My mother and father would go to bed early and leave us to sit on the sofa watching our black and white television in front of a huge roaring coal fire. It was on one of these evenings that I remember sitting in stunned silence beside Barry when the shooting of President John F. Kennedy was announced.

We became engaged before he left for Liverpool College. It was Christmas time and I don't remember him ever asking me to marry him. He took me into a Carlisle jeweller and asked the assistant to show him some engagement rings. I stood in amazement not knowing what to say because he had not consulted me first. He had taken me for granted but I quickly accepted and took my small three-diamond ring home to show off to everyone. It only cost 20 pounds but to us it was a small fortune.

When it was time to leave school I applied to train for the nursing profession. I passed the entrance exam, but my mother advised me not to accept their offer. I have always regretted that I did not have sufficient self confidence to go ahead and disregard her advice. Instead, I found work in a carpet factory and trained first as a creeler and then as a winder. Our foreman was like a father to us and I worked in a very friendly atmosphere. I enjoyed my work and was very happy.

After my engagement I worked very hard to earn a bonus so that I could save money to purchase household goods for my bottom drawer. It was a long two years to wait for Barry, but at last, on July 23rd 1966, we were married by Reverend Roan in Saint John's Church, Workington. My wedding day passed in a haze; it rained heavily and the taxi driver forgot to collect my Nana. No one realized that she wasn't there until after I was married and I was so very upset that I gave her my flowers in a feeble attempt to make it up to her.

Michele Julie

My biggest and yet happiest mistake was conceiving a baby on my Jersey honeymoon. Nana took one look at my face when I returned and immediately suspected that I was pregnant. She told mum that it was too soon but bought me two dozen terry nappies anyhow. Sadly, she was ill one week and died the next without ever seeing Michele. My Nana had a profound influence on my family life. I shall never forget her.

My mother and father were now living in a small terraced house that they bought from my sister in Carlton Road, Workington. Two weeks before my confinement Barry packed me off to stay with my mother. I think he was scared that I would have my baby at home. He hated hospitals, the smell alone would send him white, and he never overcame his aversion. When my time came I was rushed into Hensingham Hospital. It was 5 am in the morning and by the end of the day the sister thought that I had false labour pains. She decided to keep me in overnight and told Barry to collect me after doctor's rounds on the following day.

However, it was not false labour and I started again during the night and after 4 hours I gave birth to a beautiful baby girl. It was 5 o'clock in the morning on Sunday May 4th 1967, 39 weeks after our wedding. I remember thinking of the lines, 'But the child who is born on the Sabbath day is bonny and good and blithe and gay'. (Editors note: Margie was a little confused when she wrote her brief story, Michele was not born on Sunday but on Thursday; 'Thursday's child has far to go').

Barry rang from work at midday. His daughter was already seven hours old and I had not been able to tell a single soul. He asked the sister when he could collect me and she replied that I had given birth to a baby girl at five this morning; he was so flabbergasted that he asked her if she was sure. She hurried into the ward and then returned to the telephone to confirm that he was indeed a new father.

He dashed through to Whitehaven to visit us both in the hospital and he held Michele before I was able to. I had been given a lot of stitches and I was not allowed to hold her. I was also the only mother in the maternity ward who did not get flowers from her husband, and in addition, Barry forgot to bring a bottle of lemonade that I had asked for. This was all too much for me, and when we argued over a suitable name, I burst into tears. The sister booted him out of the ward and he sneaked back with a bottle of lemonade 10 minutes later; a sheepish grin on his face.

We were happy but broke. I had 4 pounds a week for housekeeping and with this I bought food and paid for our deliveries of coal, papers and milk. Barry paid the rest of our expenses. Just before pay day I was always skint and I looked down the sides of our lounge chairs hoping to find some silver. Ella, my mum-in-law, often slipped me a pound note without telling Barry's father. She kept Michele in little dresses that she ran up on her sewing machine and knit all her woollens.

All of our baby items were second hand, and the lady from Distington who sold us Michele's pram and baby bath threw in lots of baby clothes for the same price. My sister had a son thirteen months older than Michele called Gary Jefferson. She had a job and they were well off compared to us and she passed on lots of Gary's outgrown clothes and toys. We wanted for nothing with the tremendous help that we received from our friends and family. Everyone sticks together in the North and no one is ever too proud to accept a helping hand. We were extremely grateful for the warm offers of help that we received.

Barry always wanted to take a gamble and he decided to grow mushrooms and sell them to Covent Garden. He said that he would make us rich; I said nothing but sat back and waited for the money to flow in. His first step was to buy hay from a local farmer to make compost. He then made wood racks that reached to the ceiling in the spare bedroom. We were in a council house and I was very frightened that someone might report us to the council, and so we smuggled the compost upstairs to the wooden racks in the dead of night.

I had my orders from Barry and I tended the trays of compost and mushroom seed as lovingly as I attended my baby daughter. The hay had to be kept at a constant temperature and watered each day. It was chemical compost and I was surprised by the lack of smell. Everything that had to be done was done and we sat back to will the mushrooms to grow.

We waited and waited and long after our mushroom crop should have been harvested we could not smell a single one. In addition, something happened that made us very nervous. Barry's mum Ella had told her rent man that we were growing mushrooms in the bedroom; what she didn't know was that he was our rent man too.

Expecting to be evicted at any second we quickly dismantled everything and prepared to cut our losses. Barry sold most of the trays and compost to his workmates at Sellafield and he gave one of the trays to his Dad. They threw the compost on their gardens and used the trays to make glass hot beds.

Two weeks later Barry's work colleagues came into his works canteen and told tales of how huge mushrooms had pushed out their flowers and cabbage. I found it hard to believe until I also had some sprout up overnight in our garden; one mushroom alone weighed 3lbs. Well, we were worse off than before but at least we had tried. It was a standing joke for years to come at Sellafield; Barry and his mushrooms.

Zambia

Job wise, Barry was not getting the excitement he needed at Sellafield. He applied to Anglo American for a job at a lead and zinc mine in Broken Hill, Zambia, and his application was accepted. I hoped that it wasn't Broken Hill by name and nature. I didn't want to go, but he promised me a new house in the UK at the end of his 3-year contract.

We made arrangements to sail on the Edinburgh Castle to Capetown from where we would drive 2,800 miles through South Africa and Rhodesia to Broken Hill. However, just before we were due to leave, we saw a film in Egremont cinema about guerrillas fighting in the nearby Belgian Congo. This disturbed Barry and he decided to fly out by himself on a BOAC VC10 to check if it was safe for Michele and me to follow.

Barry left England on a cold winter's day in January 1969. The snow lay thick on the ground and Michele's nappies froze on the line as I pegged them out. Barry's father Bob and I were left to sell the furniture and to pack things that we thought that we would need in Zambia. We stored most of our wedding presents in my mum's attic and Bob's loft, then I bought a new washing machine and had it crated. I later found it to be a waste of money because our house boys preferred to tread our washing in the bath like a tub of grapes.

When the British Railways lorry came to collect my crates we had to 'knock-up' a couple of Sellafield workers who were on night shift. Only a Cumbrian would cheerfully awaken in the middle of the day and help load wooden crates onto a lorry without grumbling.

We didn't hear from Barry for quite some time. He hates letter writing but even I got worried in the end. When a letter finally reached us it explained that he had been placed in isolation following his arrival in Broken Hill. He had Hong Kong flue and the mine doctors were already struggling with a cholera epidemic and a rabies scare. They didn't want a third problem on their hands; it would be very difficult for them to separate the symptoms. I heard that police were patrolling the streets with 303 rifles and shooting any unchained dogs. What a start to our new life; reading Barry's letter I wanted to leave the UK even less.

Michele was only 23 months old and I was not looking forward to the flight. She had re-occurring ear trouble which was caused by a measles complication. After hearing about the excruciating pain that Barry suffered during his flight I knew Michele would have even more problems. The day dawned for our long journey and a hundred butterflies flew about in my tummy. We wrote Michele's flight details on a label in large block letters and tied it around her neck.

Barry's mum said that it was me that needed the label. I felt very angry at the remark but perhaps it was true. Barry's dad took us to Carlisle in his car to catch our London train. Michele looked sweet. She wore a new brown and white checked coat with a velvet collar and a white fur hat. She was car sick all the way to Carlisle and even now at 15 years old she still suffers with the same problem.

Michele carried a huge doll that I won for sixpence in a Christmas raffle, and a chap at Heathrow was quite fresh. He kept taking the doll from her; she'd run after the doll and I'd run after her. He had missed an earlier flight to Zambia and he stuck to us like glue. I must have looked confident because he seemed to think I jumped on planes every day. Little did he know that it was only my second trip to London and the first on my own.

The flight went quite well, but important dignitaries were onboard and we were kept waiting for an hour on the tarmac while President Kenneth Kaunda greeted them. The red carpet was out and the band playing while we suffered in the heat without air conditioning.

The glare of the sun was my first impression of Zambia. When formalities were over, a slim, fit and heavily tanned chap with a red beard met us. He was dressed in a blue safari suit and I admired his shorts and knee length stockings. He took my bags and I thought that he was someone sent by the Mine to meet us. Then he grinned; the upturn at the side of his mouth was unforgettable; it was my Barry. Michele took one look at her dad's beard and refused to have anything to do with him. Three months is a long time in a baby's life, I could foresee problems ahead.

It was strange to wake up on that first morning with a bright sun beaming through the window instead of the usual grey drizzle of England. Barry was up with the sun and off to work at the Mine. He and his colleagues started work early and finished early, which seemed a sensible attitude to me. They saw more of their children and their wives felt to be someone who mattered. Looking out of my window, I was alarmed to see an African in ragged shorts wielding a sharp slasher across the grass outside. I felt sure we would all be hacked to death in the near future, and heart in mouth, I wished that I was back in dear old England.

Later in the day, I was surprised to be wished 'good day' and politely addressed as 'Madam' by the murderer of my vivid imagination. Barry omitted to mention that a gardener came every day. I had to provide him with bread, jam and tea for his breakfast, mealie meal for his dinner and meat for his supper. Many people will be horrified by this, but I never saw anyone starve in Zambia. Not like many of the poor natives in countries to our north.

Barry looked the part. He fitted in and knew his way around. I felt confused, uncomfortable and apprehensive; a round peg in a square hole. It was possible to walk to the shops but the heat was incredible, and when Barry drove into town I felt the sweat trickling down my spine. I soon realized that I would have to toughen up and learn to drive. Broken Hill looked like a real cowboy town with dirt roads and high tin-covered sidewalks.

I watched an African man on his bike, his wife was sitting on the crossbar and a baby was tied to her broad back, his little nose pushed quite flat. He was tied to his mother by a brightly patterned towel. The woman had a large bundle of sticks on her head and the man carried a box of groceries in a basket that hung under the handlebars. It looked decidedly dangerous to me, but he pedalled sedately on, going about his own business.

Indians owned most of the shops and I was served personally; after English supermarkets it was great. I noticed a white girl staring at me for a long time and I wondered if it was because I had just arrived, but to my delight she turned out to be an old friend from England called Elaine; she had married a Geordie and now had two young boys. I had found a long-lost friend who had by chance arrived in Zambia only one day before me.

All the streets in the Mine compound are named after flowers in alphabetical order. The houses in each street improve as the letters become higher. When an employee had worked for a long time with Anglo American, or if he was promoted, he would be moved to a street higher in the alphabet. Barry's boss was Rhodesian. He served his apprenticeship on the Mine. Consequently he and his family lived in a fabulous house on Nerina Street. We started in humble Foxglove Street which had single bed semi-detached bungalows, and Michele had to share a small room with us; so much for a joyful reunion and not the best of starts.

We were loaned basic kitchen equipment, three of everything in our case. It was not possible to leave dishes unwashed after a meal, otherwise there were none to use for the next meal. It kept us tidy, but I was pleased when our crates arrived and so was Michele who fell on her toys with unfettered joy.

Looking back, our conditions were actually quite good. When we eventually moved to a family house in Kochia Street the Mine provided us with a new fridge, cooker, basic furniture and a loan to buy a nice second hand car. After making do with an old green minivan this was pure luxury. I had never had a nice cooker or fridge before and I soon began to enjoy cooking different recipes. Unfortunately I was still very homesick and at the time I didn't fully appreciate what the Mine had given us.

I employed my first houseboy when we moved into our house in Kochia Street. He had been recommended by his brother who had painted the house before we moved in. I learned later that the word 'brother' could mean any member of the same tribe; it did not mean that he was his blood brother. Phil was lanky, slim and very fit. His curly hair was quite light and we guessed that he was very old. Trained from a boy he had worked in Government House before independence; when Zambia was still Northern Rhodesia. He was obviously accustomed to much grander company than ours.

Michele's first words were in Bemba, his tribal language. She followed him around the house and got in his way at every turn, but he never lost his patience with her. Phil lived in a small room in the garden called a Kya. He often brought one of his wives to stay with him and one or two of his children.

Michele had a lovely time when his children visited. They would sit cross-legged in front of a picture book; Michele speaking Bemba and his children speaking English. Often she would dip her little hands in their communal bowl and relish the thick mealie-meal called Nshima which had small fish called Kapenta mixed in. She was so happy and natural in these surroundings and she learned a lot from this proud old African.

Phil soon ran our house and he was far more organized than me. He even insisted upon taking over the cooking and I became redundant but happy. I was far more relaxed and I never minded a house full of visitors or lots of children because Phil always cleaned up afterwards.

Our garden was full of avocado, banana, papaya and lemon trees. We ate the avocados the African way with salt, pepper and vinegar. We made fresh lemonade with the lemons and there was no better drink to end the day.

There was no ladies fashion as such; all the patterns and materials were the same. If one wanted a cotton dress then you had to get a dressmaker to make it. Anyone who had recently visited Rhodesia, South Africa or the UK was envied because they came back loaded down with fashionable clothes. The rest of us often found ourselves in the awful situation of having dresses in the exact copy of someone else.

We made friends with two Newcastle lads, Jim and Alan. They were both single and played cards a lot with Barry. They soon had Michele saying 'Newcastle Broon Aaale' and singing Cushy Butterfield in a broad Newcastle accent. They were mad on photography and always shared our car when we took a holiday in Rhodesia. Everyone had to pose for them at every conceivable moment. After a while this became very boring.

One hot day, when I was driving, they asked me to follow them; I had passed my test by then. They trooped off down the dirt road trying to persuade a large elephant to turn around. In the meantime they took dozens of snaps of its large backside. I was fed up and so I parked in a shady spot to snooze. They never did persuade Nellie to turn around, which was just as well. If it had charged there would have been no truck to dive into. They were quite upset with me when they returned to the truck and I had three men yelling at me instead of just the one.

Jim and Alan hated spiders and whenever they ventured into the bush Barry would flick huge ones at them. This upset them, and they knew Barry hated snakes, and so they bought rubber ones which they draped in the trees close to where he parked his car; tit for tat.

When I first arrived in Africa, I was amazed to see huge flat spiders on the ceiling of my bedroom. At first my flesh would creep, but soon I realized that these 'flatties', as we called them, were far more preferable to getting itchy red 'mozzie' bites. Barry couldn't sleep if he heard a mozzie zeroing in for a meal when we switched off the light. He had a deadly insecticide spray and by the time he finished spraying we were nearly both dead from the vapour.

I put lots of weight on when Michele was born and I tramped around the shops in Salisbury looking for something to fit. I ended up with two checked dresses, one black and white and one pink and white. I remember them well. Phil washed them so many times that the checks disappeared. Every time we went to Rhodesia, we stocked up on clothes. To avoid paying heavy duties on our return to Zambia, we stopped by the roadside just short of the Chirundu Border Post in the Zambezi Valley and rubbed dirt into our new clothes to make them look second hand.

Salisbury was a beautiful place. There was never any apartheid although British people often thought there was. If an African could afford it, he could go anywhere. The war was about majority rule. Blacks and whites mixed well, much better than they did in the UK, each respecting one another's different cultures. The colourful jacaranda trees lining the streets of Salisbury at Christmas time was a site I shall always remember. No one believed that war would eventually shatter this beautiful city.

It was a happy and full life. Miners and their families relaxed around the community pool after finishing work. Everything was dry and dusty but the fences were covered in lovely creepers with bright scarlet flowers. Michele swam at a very early age, as did most kids, and they were all so proficient; they were like small fish darting through the sparkling water.

There were lots of parties and braais. Meat was cheap and we barbecued with locally made wood charcoal to a taste never forgotten. We ate lots of steaks, boerwors, sosaties and gorgeous salads. Potatoes, carrots and green vegetables were non-existent and so apart from mealie-meal our diet was far too rich in protein. Trying to find out the special recipes was very difficult, but over my years in Africa I eventually succeeded and I kept these in a small exercise book which I still refer to from time to time.

I decided to attend a Pitman's touch typing course at the Convent. I enjoyed the course and made a new circle of friends. Many of the young women attending were Patel's, daughters of the large and very wealthy Indian shop owning community. I soon found myself getting personal treatment whenever I visited town and after Barry repaired their cinema projector they could not do enough for us.

Times get harder

Barry wasn't settled and after only one year he decided to start his own business. I wasn't certain at the prospect of having no security, but being determined he went ahead anyhow. We had to pay back the Mine for our airfares and for our car loan before they would release Barry from his three-year contract. This left as with very little money. We drove to the Copperbelt in our truck with a handful of possessions aboard and not sure if we would find anywhere to live. We finally found a huge Indian house in Mufulira. It was dirty and full of bugs and probably flees too. It took a lot of scrubbing before it was fit for us to take up residence.

Before we left, we had acquired a beige cross Labrador Rhodesian-Ridgeback puppy. A neighbour left it with us while she was on holiday. She never returned to Broken Hill and I don't think she ever intended to do so. He was a beautiful puppy and we called him Laddie. We were happy with him, but he didn't like black Africans and we were forever compensating them for their torn trousers. He was very savage with Africans and strangely gentle with Michele who rode his back, pulled his ears and even removed bones from under his nose.

Things were hard for a long time and we made many mistakes. The biggest was going into business with friends who were always busy with their own pursuits when company work needed to be done. We were forced to buy them out and this took most of our share of the first quarter's profit.

We rented two small offices above a very smelly butcher's shop. I looked after the office while Barry worked on different contracts in Mufulira and Ndola. Michele went to play group in the mornings and Phil brought her to me at lunchtime. We would have a snack in town and then she drew and painted in the office until six when it was time for me to lock up and go home. We had so little money that our supper was often half a loaf of bread and a can of baked beans.

One day Michele was sitting on our office steps and an African stole a pair of new sandals from her feet. At the time the heel on my sandals was broken and Barry was walking on his uppers. We didn't have a proper pair of shoes between us. I put my head down on the office desk and howled.

We tried to break into the retail business and bought a large selection of Sony hi-fi stereo equipment, but most people bought second hand from expatriates returning to the UK. The equipment never sold and we had to use what earnings we had to pay back the suppliers. Times became even leaner. One day Barry lost his toolkit along with hundreds of pounds worth of tools that we could not afford to replace. We were devastated and Barry was unable to work without them. On this occasion we were very lucky, a young African from the butcher's below found them and we gave him a ten kwacha reward.

In 1970, just as we thought that our luck was changing, a disaster happened on the Mufulira Copper Mine. It occurred during the night shift; if it had happened during the day then there would have been more than 2000 men down the Mine, including my husband.

For a long time the Mine had experienced several small cave-ins on the old workings. The management decided to use concentrator tailings – waste after the copper is removed – to fill in these workings. Unfortunately, while the tailings was baked by the sun on top, underneath it was a soft slurry and this slurry rushed through a large crack that had opened into the old and the new workings.

The mud rush, as it became known, trapped and killed two white men and 96 Africans; probably many more if the full truth was known. Overnight Mufulira became a ghost town; African women stood wailing in grief outside the Mine and everyone had to queue for fresh drinking water from huge tankers. Mufulira Copper Mine immediately declared Force Majeure and all contracts were cancelled, including ours.

The women and children were left in a dreadful situation. Under tribal law any monies and possessions were passed to the eldest brother and not to the widow or his children. The poor women not only had to suffer their terrible bereavement but they had to go to the bank and sign over everything that had belonged to their dead husbands. They only had two choices to make, marry the eldest brother or be destitute; they had no other rights whatsoever and this to me was so inhuman. I had to blink back the tears.

One year apart

We were finished financially. Barry decided to send Michele and me back to England to stay with my parents. He said he would work for a few months to get a little money together and then follow me to the UK. We were not to know at the time, but the management decided to recover the Mine and they found a method to extract the mud and rock. Most of the contractors had already left and Barry was awarded more work than he could handle. He employed more men and a few months turned into a year.

My parents were very good, but it was not easy living in someone else's home after having my own house for so long. The small number of traveller's cheques that Barry gave me when I left for England quickly ran out, and Barry applied to send maintenance money from Zambia. The amount was fixed by the exchange control authorities to a maximum of 10 pounds for each month. This was considered enough to buy mealie meal and any other essential items. However, Barry was so disgusted with the meagre size of the allowance that he did not go through with the hassle of submitting an application. I had no choice but to find a job.

Barry was working very long hours for 7 days a week, at the bottom of the Mine that had killed so many people, in dirty and dangerous conditions. I didn't know this and I felt so resentful and bitter. I felt that he should have stayed with his job in Broken Hill. We now had nothing; we had no house and not even a stick of furniture. As I saw it, we were going several steps backwards while everyone else was going forward.

I was lucky; I found a part time job as a waitress in the local Wimpy bar. I had no experience and I panicked at lunchtimes when it was busy and I made lots of mistakes. The owner and staff were very nice and Michele was happy and content with my mother, although she missed her daddy very much. We realized this when he sent her a soft toy lion for her birthday, called Lenny; he became her greatest treasure and she couldn't sleep until he was tucked into bed with her each night.

Living in such a small town there was the usual speculation and everyone wondered where my husband was. One old bag pushed her face close to mine and said what everyone else must have been thinking: 'Has he left you then?' I controlled myself until I got to my mother's and then my anger erupted like a volcano. Although I was depressed at times, I soon got into a routine. My work was hard on my feet, I was usually too tired to do much thinking and in this way it was therapeutic. I began to go to the pictures and occasionally I would drop into the local pub and enjoy a drink with my work makes.

I became very independent, and when Barry eventually was able to send money through the black market, I felt that I could not spend it. It had not been there when we needed it and so now I banked every penny. I couldn't see things ever getting back to normal, especially as he was such a terrible letter writer; I was lucky to receive one letter in eight weeks.

My mother in-law had been ill and she had a breast removed. She didn't want Barry to be worried and so Bob told him that it was only a harmless cyst. Ella seemed to be getting better and so I promised not to tell Barry. Michele and I visited her and Bob every Sunday. Meanwhile, I was due to go into hospital for an operation myself and I was worried how Michele and I would manage for money. Words were said between us and we had an almighty argument. I remember screaming that I had to borrow the bus fare from my dad to visit them, because their precious son could not support us.

Although we made it up, I will always regret what I said. Ella was a good-hearted person but her temper was always on a short fuse and I provoked it. Michele has inherited her Grandma Ella's temper; in fact, she is so like her in many ways that it is incredible.

When Ella found another lump in the other breast I felt that Barry should know the truth, and so I disregarded his parents and wrote to tell him. Just after writing my letter to Barry a very large bunch of red roses was delivered to my mum's door. I knew immediately that Barry was on his way home and that the flowers would be a peace offering. Sure enough, he turned up at the door as if he had never been away for twelve months. I was angry with him, but as usual he quickly talked me around.

I am pleased that I told Barry about his mother, because when we visited Whitehaven hospital that evening she was absolutely thrilled.

She didn't know that he was coming home to visit her, and looking at her happy face, I knew that I had made the right decision.

I didn't realize until Barry told me, but there were 27 red roses in the bunch delivered by Interflora, one for each year of my life. We went to the Ritz Cinema that night and my friend's mum took the tickets. When I walked in with Barry on my arm it was soon rumoured all around town that at last I had a boyfriend. No one would believe that my husband was home at last.

Footnote

I found a poem that was written in Marjorie's hand on a blank page at the end of a book that she used to read to gain inner strength during the final days of her long illness. This poem finished with the words,

'I am waiting; somewhere near, just around the corner'

I don't know how Margie knew that I would find this message. But if you should happen upon a small churchyard in West Cumberland that has a slab of grey South African Granite bearing the above nine words, then spare a kind thought for Margie and tell her that you have read her short story.

Chapter 1
The Early Years

Growing up in Cumberland after the war
Like father like son!

My father grew up in West Cumberland during the depression with one elder brother and two younger sisters. He had a difficult childhood and he suffered from terrible asthma attacks. These prevented him from attending regular classes and he left school to work in a local garage when he was 11 years old.

The first indication of his ingenuity and skills as a craftsman became apparent at an early age when he built a complete motor bike using parts from the scrap heap. He sold this to raise pocket money and then took a job selling Tognarelli's ice cream on Workington docks. Togi's, as the local ice cream chain was affectionately known in Workington, supplied Dad with a 3-wheeled ice cream bicycle; the forerunner of modern day ice cream vans. Aunt Iris told me how he would take her for rides on the crossbar and hide his Woodbines in the ice cream box whenever a bobby came around the corner.

Workington was a wealthy iron making town at the beginning of the twentieth century. Its prosperity had been assured on the 24th July 1872 when four enterprising individuals; Peter Kirk, James Valentine, Henry Kenyon and Mary Gibson formed the Moss Bay Haematite Iron Company. By the turn of the 20th century it had grown into a large operation that included four blast furnaces, a sinter plant, several Bessemer converters, a rolling mill and one of the most advanced rail making plants in the world.

The people living in and around Workington were used to the night time glow of the slag heap, sulphurous air-borne red powder from the cupolas, foul fumes from the sinter plant and white clouds of steam from the coke ovens. Housewives were always careful to test the wind direction before putting washing on the line and workers listened for the early morning horn which called them back to work. Such was life in a steel making town.

"Where there is muck lad, there is money", and this saying was so true of Workington. It had four excellent cinemas and an opera house. One of the cinemas, the Ritz, had a Wurlitzer Organ hidden below the stage at one side of the huge screen. It rose like the Phoenix at the beginning of each feature performance; an organist playing music appropriate to the film being shown.

The occupation of many individuals was described in the national census as 'Gentleman'. It is very difficult to imagine anyone having such an occupation in present day Workington. My grandfather was the foreman of the locomotive transport department. He had upwards of one hundred men working for him and he would not hesitate to dismiss a person on the spot if he did not do a fair day's work. Nevertheless he was a fair man and well respected in the local community. As a child I remember walking with him along the streets of Workington; middle aged men tipping their cheesecutters and trilbies as we passed by.

All of the industries in West Cumberland were interlinked and entirely dependent upon each other. Central to these was the Iron and Steel Works. Rich heamatite ores were mined in Beckermet, limestone was quarried in Distington, clay for the furnaces came from Mickleham, coal was mined in almost every single village and a plentiful supply of water came from the salmon-rich River Derwent.

Workington became and still is known as one of the highest quality rail makers in the world. Workington rails still join towns and cities across every country in the old British Empire and some of the very first continuously welded rails to be laid in the United States carry the Workington name. The Workington Iron and Steel Works has long since vanished but the rail making facility has been retained and steel blooms are transported from Scunthorpe to enable rails to be rolled under the Workington name.

Joining the Iron and Steel Works down by the harbour was a large foundry, the Distington Haematite Iron Company, known locally as Chapel Bank. It was named after Distington, which was five miles away, as a war time deception to divert bombing raids. U-Boat action and the capitulation of Norway starved British factories of the special steels that they needed to manufacture ball bearings and six electric furnaces were secretly built at Chapel Bank to fill this need. The only connection this works had with my home village, Distington, was the large ornate iron gates at the entrance to the works, which had been taken from Distington Hall.

The reason why the War Department chose to divert enemy bombers to Distington is a mystery to me, especially when you consider that High Duty Alloys, a factory that produced special alloy parts for the production of war time aircraft, was, and still is, located just outside the Toll Bar at Distington. The mystery becomes all the greater when you consider that a top secret factory manufactured aircraft engines nearby.

World War II

At the outbreak of war my father, Robert Coulton, worked alongside my future father-in-law, Joe Elliot, in the shell foundry at Chapel Bank. My father was too young to join-up and he was also in a reserved occupation. Undeterred he caught the local steam train to Carlisle where he was unknown and presented himself to the Royal Air Force recruiting office. Falsifying his age and describing his employment as a motor cycle mechanic he was accepted into the Royal Air Force for training as an aircraft fitter.

Because he finished school when he was 11 years old he had to work extra hours each evening to keep up with the other trainees on his wartime crash fitter's course. His instructors never suspected his real age and they gave him additional lessons to improve his mathematics. Towards the end of his very short training period he became one of the best aircraft fitters in his class.

One evening my grandfather looked through his window and saw my Dad, Sam and his cousin walking home from the local pub. They were all on leave together, for the first and only time during the war. His brother Sam was on special Dunkirk leave, he fought a rearguard action and was one of the last to be snatched from the beaches. As they walked laughing and singing down Senhouse Street in air force blue, army khaki and navy blue, my grandfather suddenly felt very proud that his family could give so much to England.

Dad was posted to 603 The City of Edinburgh Squadron at RAF Turnhouse; the squadron had just been converted from Gladiators to Supermarine Spitfires. On the 16th October 1939 they were joined over the Firth of Forth by 602 The City of Glasgow Squadron and each bagged a Junkers 88. These were the first two enemy aircraft to be shot down over British soil in the Second World War.

After a short while, Dad became lead aircraft fitter on three aircraft used by the squadron's commanding officer; the Duke of Hamilton. It was during this time that the Duke came to Dad and asked for his advice on which aircraft he should use to take Rudolf Hess, Hitler's deputy, to London. Hess had parachuted into Ayrshire to meet with the Duke who was an old acquaintance to broker an agreement between the British Empire and Germany. I can't remember which aircraft he recommended but I do recall that my father stripped it down to make it faster and more manoeuvrable.

In the summer of 1940 my father relocated to the South of England and lived in various tented camps on makeshift grass airstrips. He serviced Spitfires fighting in the Battle of Britain and as the war progressed he was seconded to the A.V. Roe factory in Chadderton, Manchester.

In the spring of 1943 he fitted special bomb slips on the Lancaster bombers that took part in the Dam Buster Raid. The idea was to use the Barnes Wallis 'Bouncing Bomb' to breach the walls of five huge dams in the industrialised Ruhr Valley. This raid did not shorten the war as originally hoped and only eleven of Wing Commander Gibson's nineteen aircraft survived the mission. However, the raid gave a much needed boost to moral and for this reason it was considered a tremendous success and Guy Gibson was awarded the Victoria Cross for his outstanding courage and leadership during the raid.

While working in the A.V. Roe factory my father met a shy young woman with curly jet black hair. Her name was Ella Mather, and she worked on the aircraft assembly lines. They were married soon after and I was born in the following year during an air raid on the factory. I was born three months premature in a large boarding house and suffered from severe jaundice. I suppose I was very lucky to have survived in such conditions.

Early childhood in Distington

My mother and father had very little to provide for me and I slept in a suitcase for the first few months of my life. As soon as possible Dad took me and my mother home to Cumberland where he rented a small house at Hayscastle in the old feudal village of Distington.

Cromwell's engineers had destroyed Hayscastle and very little remained. To one side of the moat was Brayton's farm; in front was a terrace of three old workers cottages. We lived in number one Hayscastle, Bessie Nelson in number two and the owner, old Mrs Miller, in number three. The toilet facilities were in a brick built structure across the yard and to bathe we used a small galvanised bath tub which was stored in the shed.

Mrs Miller had extensive gardens and a small orchard which I raided at will. I suppose the surrounding countryside, the primrose banks, fresh bubbling streams, bluebell woods, potato fields, haystacks, cows and sheep compensated for the lack of facilities offered by Hayscastle. We had more than most in those late days of the war and rationing only limited us to the amount of sweets that I could buy.

There were not many young Englishmen around at the time and my early years were spent with two German prisoners of war who had been paroled to work on Brayton's farm. When my father came home on leave he became very upset when I spoke German to him. He soon got to know the prisoners, one an elderly man who had not seen his own children for many years and a youngster who was little more than a boy. I think they both softened his attitude to the war and he realized for the first time that not all Germans were Nazis.

I remember sitting beside the beck that ran past my house; the two war prisoners often stopped and threw me onto their hay cart as they went to work in the fields. I must have been very young at this time but I have an even earlier memory; I remember getting off a red double-decker bus in Workington. My mother dragged me kicking and screaming into a small shop where she sold my pram; my chariot, my most treasured possession of the day.

At the end of the war my father was attached to the American Air Force at RAF Benson just outside Oxford. An American airman who was billeted with him had stockpiled thousands of cigarettes in a small storeroom and he was selling them at black market prices. My father could not afford to buy any, he was extremely upset and then one day the American was instructed to join an aircraft that was about to fly to the United States. My father padlocked the storeroom and shared out the Yank's cigarettes after his plane took off.

Dad was demobbed a few months later and he filled a small brown suitcase with his share of cigarettes; they represented the equivalent of several year's ration coupons. One afternoon Dad came home and was shocked to find me sitting on the window ledge of my second floor bedroom with this suitcase resting beside me. I had sat on my window ledge all afternoon, removed more than two thousand cigarettes from their packets and patiently broken each one into small pieces. He was heartbroken. Mum bought him several boxes of cigarette papers and for the next year or so, he rolled his own from what was left of the tobacco.

My father bought me an old army surplus tent which was originally intended for use by the Desert Rats in North Africa. I spent many an hour in this tent with Peter and Anne Leathers who lived nearby. On one occasion I dropped into Abby Gunn's little shop which she ran from her back kitchen. I bought a box of Black Magic chocolates and asked her to put them on my mother's account. We were eating them in my tent when she stormed over and dragged me home. She locked me in my bedroom and I watched Anne and Peter eat the rest of the chocolates while I suffered with a sore backside from the beating that my mother gave me. It was not so much the cost that upset her but the number of ration coupons needed.

After the war Dad was offered employment by my grandfather at the Workington Iron and Steel Works. He started by working in the railway yards as a shunter before being given the opportunity to work as a fireman and then eventually a locomotive driver.

My grandfather treated him harder than anyone else. He gave Dad all the rubbish jobs and never offered him overtime, even when it was his turn on the roster. Eventually the union intervened and forced my grandfather to treat him on the same basis as the other workers in his department. My grandfather nodded and said "fair enough". He had been waiting for this to happen and had probably even forced the situation. He did not want it said that he favoured his son above the other workers under his control.

Dad often came home with terrible stories of accidents that had occurred during his shift. He told of men who fell into ladles of molten metal and of others who were sliced into two halves while taking a short cut across the rolling mills. He described how he himself was driving a locomotive up the slag heap in winter with a ladle of molten slag up front. The wheels started to slip in the snow and he had to jump from the cabin as it began to slide backwards down the steep slope.

Several years later one of my best friends was working as a shunter in the hot mills. He was coupling a molten ingot carriage to a locomotive and the buffers trapped him. His injuries were so severe that his colleagues were frightened to release his pelvis from the buffers, but he did survive, and with time they were able to wire him back together again.

I had a cat called Smokey who followed me everywhere. I hated having my hair cut and my father used to hack it off with a blunt pair of hand shears that always pulled. He would tell me to be around when he returned from his morning shift so that he could give me a hair cut. When I knew he was due home I would run into the fields and climb a tree. I never knew how he found me until he explained in later life that he always looked for Smokey, who would be sitting patiently below the tree waiting for me to come down.

Smokey was a real terror. No dogs could enter her territory. She was ruthless and stood up to them whatever their size. Even the local sheep dogs gave her a wide berth. I did terrible things to her and yet she always came back for more punishment and she never once raised her tail to me. I threw her several times from my bedroom window to show my friends how she was able to twist around and land on her feet. Like all cats she hated water and I often stood on the small bridge beside our house and threw her into the cold beck.

Dad played rugby and was captain of the village team. I stood for many a cold winter's day supporting him on our makeshift rugby field beside Barf's quarry. Mum started a hairdressing business and set up a small salon in my bedroom. She was well liked in the village and had a strong clientele. With my father's steady work and my mother's income we soon had a good standard of living which certainly elevated us to what in the Lake District would be called middle class.

Life before television

I mixed with boys much older than myself and I spent very long hours, sometimes fourteen hours or more, in the countryside around Brown's farm looking for bird's nests. This was the main springtime hobby of youngsters in post war years. We had strict rules that we followed; never take more than one egg, don't take an egg if there are three or less in the nest, don't take an egg if you already have one in your collection. I have to admit that we did break the rules and often took more eggs than we should in order to swap for others. I stopped collecting when I became a teenager, and instead, I learned to appreciate the birds more than their eggs. I still have my collection hidden away and I hope to find a museum that can give them a home.

In 1952 we moved to 16 Coronation Crescent and my brother, Steven, was born shortly after we settled in. Our brand new semi-detached council house had an indoor toilet and a bathroom; this was sheer luxury compared to Hayscastle. My father remained in this house for the remainder of his life, and although he could well afford to buy his own home, he chose never to do so.

In the 50's most Distington folk lived in cold damp terraced houses with outdoor facilities and coal fired ovens. As children, my friends and I looked down on those who were less fortunate and still had to live in such places. Yet today these character homes are much sought after while many of the once new council houses on Flat Tops and around Hinnings Road have fallen into disrepair.

Coronation Crescent was built shortly after the coronation of our very young Queen Elizabeth II and it partly encircled a large open green where I spent much of my childhood. A lamp post stood inside a small roundabout at the end of the Crescent and this was where all the neighbourhood children gathered in the evenings to play 'Cannon', 'Jack Shine Yer Light', 'Knock a Nine Doors' and several other very simple but enjoyable games that have long since been forgotten.

'Cannon' was my favourite. This is a very simple game that can go on for hours. It only needs three pieces of firewood and a tennis ball. The idea is to set up two pieces of firewood against the kerb with a piece across the top. This is called a 'Cannon'. Everyone divided into two teams; Tony Mingins, Richard Armstrong, Christopher Charnley, Rosalind Douglas, Eleanor Simpson and Christine Halley in the red team and Ian Todd, Barry Armstrong, Alfie Mingins, Shelagh Donnelly, Maureen Simpson and Jean Halley in the green team.

Imagine that the red team is 'in'. Each person in the red team takes a turn to throw the tennis ball as hard as they can at the sticks. They scatter if the top stick is knocked off and try to rebuild the cannon without allowing the green team to hit anyone with the tennis ball. The green team is not allowed to run with the ball, they have to throw it at the red team or pass it to a member of the green team who may be in a better position. If a member of the red team is hit then they are out, if all the red team members are out without rebuilding the cannon, then they lose the game and it becomes the turn of the green team to be 'in'.

If the cannon is rebuilt, the person putting the last stick on top has to shout 'Cannon' before he is hit by the tennis ball. Sometimes one team can stay in for a long time without the other team getting a chance. The boys threw the ball incredibly hard and I was often hit in the face, but even at such a young age we behaved as gentlemen and took more care when throwing at the girls.

'Knock a Nine Doors' was also a favourite, but a little more risky. As the name implies the person who was 'it' had to knock on as many doors as possible and then run away. Those playing had to watch him very carefully because sometimes he would choose several doors in the direction that we were running. The last person then had further to run before getting around the corner and occasionally someone would get caught. In the early 50's grownups were more tolerant and they accepted that children needed to entertain themselves. I suppose this game is still played today, but with malicious intent rather than just having fun.

Our parents never had cause to be worried and even on cold dark winter nights we played outside until 11 pm and it would sometimes be so dark that we added games such as 'Jack Shine Yer Light' to our programme. Parents would begin to call for us from 10 pm onwards; 'Alfie, time for bed' or perhaps the call was 'Richard, supper's on the table'. Supper in the north was usually fish and chips from the local chippy washed down with a big mug of Ovaltine.

No one had expensive toys; we made everything for ourselves. We made pea shooters from the hollow stems of cow parsley and used hawthorn pips as ammunition. Many of us made bows and arrows from branches that we cut down in Old Cat Wood. We fashioned pieces of white cardboard into targets and erected them at the far side of the Crescent. I could shoot from one hundred yards and strike within five feet of the cardboard target. Another weapon which we used extensively, but out of sight of our parents, was a throwing stick. I was able to throw one for more than 160 yards with deadly accuracy. A misguided throw could have been lethal and so I have chosen not to describe its materials of construction.

Hide and seek was a little more dangerous than the game practised today. We were all excellent tree climbers and so we played in Old Cat Wood or the much larger Prospect Wood. We gave a long count to enable everyone to find a suitable tree and climb into a hidden position. It was on one of these visits to Old Cat Wood when I sustained an injury that still returns to plague me. I climbed into a large tree that had been felled across a small stream. The upper part of this tree still rested on the lower stump and it remained in a semi-upright position supported by other trees. I don't know what happened but I assume that the tree broke away and fell across the beck, and I fell with it.

I regained consciousness with my back curved across a huge boulder in the middle of the beck. I was in shock and couldn't breathe. My friends gathered around and I tried to signal to them to do something; I was old enough to understand that someone should press on my chest. I thought for sure that I was going to suffocate and it was several minutes before I began to take short sharp gasps of air. Eventually my friends carried me to the bank and placed me under a lean-to shelter where I lay for several hours. No one considered the possibility that I might be seriously injured. Eventually I managed to hobble back to my home which was a little more than a mile away. Even my mother treated my symptoms very lightly. I was put to bed for a few days and she never even consulted Dr Sharpe, our family doctor. No one believed that I was suffering immense pain in my lower back; I was too young to have such problems.

Our escapades continued and we devised ever more dangerous schemes. Most of these were directed towards building hideouts in the strangest of locations. In retrospect the most dangerous of these was a deep hole which we dug into a sand pit. We placed sheet steel across the top and covered it with a layer of heavy sand. After the sand had dried in the sun it was impossible to detect the existence of our hideout. It takes little imagination to guess what could have happened, but such a possibility never occurred to us.

We built a real tree house from branches and rusty tin sheeting in a huge tree beside the old Distington railway line. I have fond memories of this tree house. We built it without the farmer's permission and disguised it with leafy branches. I remember being choked by clouds of black smoke whenever a steam engine chugged slowly by; climbing the steep incline with a train of coal wagons strung out behind. This was always a good railway line for collecting a few buckets of fallen coal before venturing home.

Each season had its own ventures. In spring we continued to go bird nesting and in summer we swam in the sea around Tea Party Rocks at Mickleham. Autumn was the time to collect rose hips. We earned three old pence a pound and over several weeks I could gather enough hips to buy all of my fireworks for bonfire night. I would take four pounds at a time to the old lady that made the collections and then take my shilling to the village grocer who would allow me to buy perhaps six bangers, three roman candles or a couple of rockets.

Guy Fawkes' night or bonfire night, as we always called it, was a serious occasion in our calendar and we started to cut trees down as early as September to build huge bonfires. We built one in the middle of the Crescent and the Flat Tops gang built one on the old railway line just past the village church. Every year we cut trees down and hacked at hedgerows all across MacSherries farm.

The MacSherries were one of the better farmers in the Distington area. Unlike many farmers they never restricted access to their fields and they always welcomed help to bring the cows in for milking or to gather kale for their cattle during winter months. We used ropes to drag huge branches for miles across their fields, along old railway lines and small lonnins before finally venturing onto tarred roads for the last run along Hinnings Road and into the Crescent.

As the fifth of November came ever closer we tried to set the 'Flat Tops' bonfires alight. This was one of those occasions when the parents of our 'enemies' became very angry. While we saw these attacks as fair play, they could only see weeks of hard work going up in smoke. We had to be very careful never to be caught, and in our own case there was an additional danger; we always built our bonfire with a hideout in the centre! On one occasion several of us were inside the hideout when we were raided.

When bonfire night finally came, everyone from the Crescent gathered around and we fixed an effigy of Guy Fawkes on top. Then as darkness fell we set fire to the tinder dry branches and in minutes we had tall dancing flames reaching high into the cold night sky. Our homes encircled this huge raging fire and small burning twigs were carried towards them by the hot swirling air currents that climbed away from the compacted mountain of burning trees. The more careless of my friends threw bangers at the feet of young girls and parents scolded them, but to no avail. I threw bangers high into the air and often burned my fingers when a short fuse allowed it to explode in my hand.

Fire was something that always excited me. MacSherries cows grazed in the fields behind Hinnings Road and then the Council acquired the land for housing development. For years the grass grew long and unattended. We played hide and seek in these fields and when we became bored with the long grass we set fire to it. We set fire to long swathes of grass at a time and controlled the direction of the fire by beating along the edges and watching carefully for any change in wind strength or direction. It was obviously very dangerous and something that we should not have been doing, but this was the way that country children in post war England kept themselves occupied before the advent of television.

Occasionally, about twice every week, I visited the village cinema which was directly above Myers and Bowman's garage. 'The Enterprise', as it was called, had posh seats at the back, scruffy stalls in the middle and a large wooden floor at the front where children could sit for a penny. I never liked the floor area because it was too close to the screen; the picture was fuzzy and my neck would hurt. Instead I sat in the posh seats for a tanner.

Pathe News always opened the performance followed by a half hour short film which would often be the original Superman or Zorro. The main film normally lasted for about eighty minutes after which the lights came on and God Save the Queen resounded around the theatre. Everyone rose to their feet, youngsters shuffled impatiently and still-young veterans, not long back from the war, stood rigidly to attention. Everyone without exception showed full and proper respect to the sovereign. When the rendition stopped we all pushed and shoved our hurried way along the narrow corridor and down the stairs to the small makeshift entrance foyer. Outside, waiting for my appearance, would be Smokey sitting patiently on 'Grants Wall' across the road.

Ypres, a sniper fired at them

My grandfather on my mother's side, Jimmy Mather, had been in the Territorial Army. I am not sure if he was in the East Lancashire Regiment or the Lancashire Fusiliers, but he was on one of the first troopships to cross into France, and he never set foot again on English soil until the armistice was signed in Versailles at the end of the First World War.

He had a very bad war. When I visited my grandparents in Royton on holiday we often walked together to the fish and chip shop down Rochdale Road and he would describe terrible stories of his time in the trenches. He told how he urinated in his handkerchief and held it to his face when mustard gas drifted over their positions.

He talked about the times when he suffered trench foot and how he carried an injured friend across open ground at Ypres. A sniper fired at them, the bullet passed through his friend finishing him off and then lodged in my grandfather's spine, where it remained for the rest of his life. When my grandfather returned from the Great War he still suffered terribly from the effects of mustard gas and he had to walk twelve miles each week to collect his invalidity pension. He was very bitter towards the government and felt that he and all his comrades had been betrayed.

After the war he worked in the Cotton Mills and supplemented his meagre income by cutting hair in the front lounge of his terraced house in number 98 Rochdale Road, which he had converted into a barber shop. His only pastime was playing bowls on the crown green in Royton Park, and even at a very young age I could give him a good game. He was a staunch supporter of Oldham Athletic but allowed his temper to get the better of him. His war years had weakened his heart and his doctor eventually ordered him to stop attending their matches.

My grandmother, Lilly Mather, was almost totally deaf and I remember her by the huge chips she used to give to me. She would sit me down at the bottom of the stairs and put my plate on a wooden stool covered with an old white tea towel. If it was dinner time the chips would be served with two fried eggs and a scoop of mushy peas. If it was supper time then she would treat me with a steak and kidney steamed pudding. The knives and forks were very old and never looked to be very clean. I often spotted Dad polishing his knife and fork on his trouser leg under the table.

Their house in Rochdale Road was an end of terrace and the gable end had a large crack running down its side; it should have been condemned long ago. Outside in the yard was a whitewashed brick built toilet, a cloth bag hung on the back of its wooden door and inside were torn-up pages of the Oldham Evening Gazette to use as toilet paper. Adjacent to this toilet was a grimy air raid shelter which they slept in along with my mother and uncle during Herman Goering's attacks on nearby railway yards and aircraft factories.

My mother was an excellent swimmer and held many pre-war swimming records at Chadderton swimming baths. She also worked long hours cutting, trimming, setting and perming ladies' hair in my grandfather's converted barber shop. Dad was very upset because my grandfather kept the proceeds of her work and never paid her a salary. In her spare time she studied the piano and when I was eight years old she arranged for her piano, an upright Witton & Witton, to be brought to Distington on a lorry. She put me to the pianoforte, in the same manner that a Roman galley slave was put to the oars. My mother and piano teacher, Maisy Miller, decided without bothering to consult me that I was to become another Liszt. Before the end of my second year I played the Autumn Concerto at my junior school concert and in my third year I found no difficulty in playing the Dam Busters without music.

I took a red double-decker bus to Workington every Monday and Thursday to receive piano lessons and every evening, including weekends I was forced to practise for one hour before being allowed to play with my friends. On school holidays I received a special concession and my practice time was reduced to half an hour each day. Most of my practice was given to music written by Beethoven, Chopin and Tchaikovsky interspersed with long periods of scale playing. As a titbit I was allowed to include topical music and Winifred Atwell tunes featured along with anything that was played by Russ Conway. This included Black & White Minstrel Rag, Side Saddle, Roulette and Chop Sticks, all of which had an exciting swing to them.

After seven years of studying the piano I came to a serious turning point in my career and I had to decide where my priorities lay. I was only one examination short of my Cap and Gown, and to be able to achieve the required standard I needed to increase my practice periods to a minimum of two, perhaps even three hours each day. I had other priorities when I was fifteen years old and I could not devote such long periods of valuable time to piano playing. In addition, music examinations at this level required much more than purely playing one's chosen instrument. Recognition of different notes and humming or whistling of different tones was also required. My voice was breaking and I could not whistle to save myself. I had no hope of securing sufficient marks for the ancillary sections and my piano playing was not of sufficient standard to make up the difference. I decided that it was time to call it a day and when I finally broke my wrist during the first year of my craft apprenticeship I used it as an excuse to discontinue my lessons.

Distington Village School

I hated my first day at school. My mother took me to Distington Village School when I was five years old and left me in the infants class with several children that I had never seen before. One hour later I sneaked out and ran home to Hayes Castle. She had a terrible time for the next week trying to get me to stay put.

The infant and junior school was a stand-alone building built in a traditional style using blocks of sandstone mined in local quarries. The front of the building was symmetrical with a tall clock tower in the centre flanked by five large classrooms, two at the front and three at the back, each with a very high ceiling. Iron railings were still installed along the front of the school; most other railings in the village had been melted down and reprocessed into tanks and guns.

The front left hand side was the Infants Class. I loved to build tall towers using small wooden sticks and competed with my friends to see who could build the largest pyramid. We were often asked to express ourselves through painting and I am convinced that this was a big mistake. I hated painting and I always ended up with more paint on myself than on the large piece of rough paper we were supplied with. I enjoyed counting on large bead racks and forming characters with the lead pencils we were given. This was much more practical and I have always been a very practical person.

After two years I moved into the front right-hand classroom. This was Mrs Lawson's class and my first year in the junior school. I remember this class well; one day while sitting at my desk a large slab of masonry fell from the ceiling and hit the floor in front of me. The slab was heavy enough to kill several children, but fortunately it fell into a vacant space. The room had a wooden floor and was furnished with sixteen small wooden desks, each with a hinged bench seat, a hinged desk top and two white ink wells. Each desk was suitable for two small children; invariably we were partnered boy and girl to prevent fighting amongst the boys and to limit idle chatter amongst the girls.

I remember reading and writing and even doing very simple sums but I have no idea how old I was at the time. In the beginning we used Lakeland Pencils and then Miss Lawson filled our small white inkwells with black school ink and supplied each of us with a small pen which comprised a thin plated nib on a short white stick. This pen was a scratchy thing which cut into our rough school paper, and I found it was more difficult to learn how to use this crude writing instrument than it was to learn how to read and write in the first place.

As I scrawled across the rough white surface of my paper the pen alternated between thick black lines, little puddles of ink and scratchy sections containing no ink at all. I used a thick piece of blotting paper to soak up the puddles before they smudged into an even greater mess. I remember my thumb and second finger, the two digits used to clutch the end of the pen, were always covered in a shiny black layer of ink and the inside of my finger felt a little numb from the way I clutched so hard on the metal nib holder. I suspect I may have done better if I had used a feathered quill.

It was around this time that I remember my school taking its one and only school photograph. There were four of us lined up at the bottom of our playground. Sitting beside me was Stan Henderson, Reggie Gallagher and Bob Bennett; three of my class mates. Sadly I have no photographs of my other school friends and in particular I would like to mention Keith Wiley, Dougie Hunter, Glen 'Spuggy' Douglas and Graham 'Fargie' Ferguson.

The senior school was built as an after-thought and stood in ground extended behind the well established sandstone building of my infant and junior school. The classrooms were small stand-alone prefabricated buildings and army style wooden huts arranged around a very large tarred playground area.

Behind these wooden huts, set apart from the rest of the school in the 'boys club field', was a relatively new extension, a modern style wooden hut, slightly wider than the rest and containing large windows along the side walls. The entrance was flanked by two small rooms; one was a cloak room and the other a storage room for papers and writing materials. It was a completely self contained unit and I was fortunate to spend my last two years in this hut. My housemaster for both years was Mr Evans, an excellent teacher who flew as a navigator with the Royal Air Force during the war. I understand that he often removed small pieces of shrapnel from his legs and buttocks.

We had no playing fields and so our sports were limited to touch rugby on the tarmac playground or a game of football using our jackets as goal posts. This was not very satisfactory when one considers that our school was surrounded by some of the best and most open countryside in England. The senior school did offer two vocational classes; woodwork for the boys and cookery for the girls. The headmaster even tried to introduce the boys in my class to a brief course of cookery. We made our views clear from the outset; cooking was for sissies and we were not going to be caught in an apron. He was forced to give in.

Our woodwork teacher had a game leg and he hobbled around our benches showing us how to use our tools. Most of our teachers used a cane to maintain discipline but old man Dobbin used the nearest piece of wood he could grab hold of. I never had any problems with him, but Tony Mingins said that he was beaten so heavily that he was frightened to attend his classes. I have my doubts on the truth of this story; Tony was a good friend of mine but I suspect that he may have been given what he deserved.

Discipline was rigid and it needed to be. We had a lot of school bullies and many would take advantage of their teachers whenever they had an opportunity. Our headmaster, Mr Scott, was a rigid disciplinarian. He was ex-army and he always carried himself stiffly and very erect. He walked five miles to school and then five miles home every day, rain or snow. The women teachers never administered their own punishment; they chose instead to send offending boys to Mr Scott. He used a stiff cane to give six of the best across the boy's open palm. I was given six on one occasion for breaking a sulphur stink bomb in the classroom. I remember the knuckles of my fingers were painful for two days. It worked because I made sure that I was never sent to him again.

My birthday fell in July and because of this I suddenly found myself taking my 11-plus examination one year earlier than my classmates. It was no surprise that I failed and my mother was bitterly upset with Mr Scott who was unable to do anything to help. Distington School taught me how to read and write, how to add, multiply and divide. They drilled my times tables into me and they even taught me a little geometry. I never took any chemistry lessons and their history teaching was limited, but Mr Evans gave excellent geography lessons. I gained a very good understanding of the rest of the world and, in particular, those countries comprising the old British Empire.

In later life I found that Distington had taught me the basic necessities and I think I am a much better person for this than most. I may understand very little about the agricultural methods of North America but I know where the river Ganges is and I know the name of the capital city of Brazil. I also know how to do simple arithmetic without using a calculator. My son and daughter cannot say the same and they were both fortunate to enjoy a private education.

My mother continued to press hard for me to improve my prospects. By now she had realised that I was not going to become a concert pianist and she looked in other directions for any means by which I could obtain a better education. She discovered a number of special vocational courses that were being offered by the West Cumberland Education Authority.

Richmond School

My mother spoke with Mr Scott and everyone in my year was invited to submit an application for one of these courses. Penrith offered farming, Keswick hotel catering and Whitehaven light engineering. I took an entrance exam for the light engineering course at Richmond Secondary Modern in Whitehaven and they accepted me for their August 1958 intake; the year following the Windscale Incident.

I spent two enjoyable years at Richmond. I worked with light duty machinery, cutting machines, lathes, welding machines and metal forges. My subjects were very different to a normal school. I studied for a pre-national certificate with subjects that included technical drawing, metalwork, physics and industrial technology. For the first time I found myself being asked to do homework and I worked very hard on my core subjects. Suddenly everything started to fit together and I found myself becoming very proficient with basic subjects such as algebra, which I had never heard of before. I actually enjoyed learning these new subjects, and because I enjoyed them, I progressed faster than most on the course. I moved from perhaps being the dumbest person in my class to being one of the brightest.

During my summer holidays I joined my new school on a mixed trip to Bruges. It was my first time abroad, with the exception of a one-day cross-channel excursion to Le Touquet. We stayed in a hotel beside one of the canals. The boys shared one large room with about a dozen beds and the girls had a similar sharing arrangement. Strict supervision was needed because there were many Belgian Romeos causing problems with the girls and, to our great pleasure, the headmaster instructed that no girl could leave the hotel unless she was accompanied by one of the older boys.

What more could anyone ask, we had a great holiday and it was the girls that had to come looking for us. We spent a lot of time in the small cafes along the canal and drank copious amounts of Belgian lager. I remember a little ice cream trolley that must have realized that there was a bunch of school kids in the area, and every night I bought a cornet with three big scoops of gorgeous ice cream; ice cream that was different to anything that we could buy in England.

On one of our excursions a priest held a glass phial and we each took it in turn to kiss the blood of Christ. I don't know if this really was the blood of Christ, any more than anyone can be certain of the origin of the Shroud of Turin. On another occasion our bus driver took a comfort stop beside a children's playground. We all clambered out and joined another youngster on the swings; it was Paul Anka but his bodyguard bundled him away in a limousine as soon as we recognised him.

Discipline was equally strict at Richmond, perhaps even more than at Distington, but on one occasion I thought that I was punished without justification. I was playing the school piano during lunch break and one of the prefects, Mel Bibby, decided to be a sod. He reported me to the headmaster and I received six lashes with a leather strap. I thought this was terribly unfair. The headmaster never even allowed me to explain that I was an accomplished pianist and that I had been playing the piano correctly and not just banging around on the keys. Mel is still a good friend and I forgave him many years ago.

This was not my only visit to the headmaster. Each week the complete school visited Whitehaven sports field. Our specialist class had such large amounts of homework that many of us decided to sneak away. As we walked up Mirehouse Road we dodged into the public toilets and waited until everyone had passed by. We then took the bus home and made an early start on our homework. One day our sports master noticed that many of the older boys were missing and he made a roll call. The following morning, along with several other boys from my class, I received a lashing. It was a deterrent but our need to keep abreast of our large amounts of homework soon required us to play hooky again.

My friends in Distington finished school at the end of my first year at Richmond. Many started work on local farms or joined the armed services while Trevor Phillips and I entered our second and final year on our special engineering course. It was a difficult year and we were still considered as outsiders. We were picked on by two other boys in the school but we could not risk getting into a school fight. The more I tried to back away from my particular antagonist the cockier he became. In the end I challenged him to a fight down on the docks. I tried to keep it a low key affair but the whole class soon found out and we trooped down to a patch of land at Wellington Colliery which is high above the harbour breakwater. Everyone gathered around and formed a circle while we faced up to each other in the centre.

I found it very difficult to get my adrenalin going and I could not bring myself to throw an aggressive punch. Eventually he started to land his punches and a bear knuckle fight developed. If we had been wearing gloves we could have been following the Marquis of Queensbury rules. We slogged it out and eventually he asked if he could take a breather. I just laughed at him and then walked back to school; he never troubled me again.

Whitehaven Harbour

Whitehaven harbour nestles in a small bay and is flanked on both sides by gentle sloping hills and sandstone cliffs. These cliffs are frequented by large flocks of herring gulls that remain close to swoop on the fishing boats when they return at high-tide to land their catch of prawn, scallops, lobster, crab, dogfish, plaice and sole. In early England local fishermen used small reed coracles to fish in the bay for whiting. One line of reasoning would suggest that this is the origin of the town's name.

The Old Quay was built in 1633 to ship coal and salt to Ireland. In later years the Sugar Tongue and the Bulwark Quay were built on a foundation of squared oak with large sandstone blocks. It was built to withstand the passage of time. Whitehaven became the third largest harbour in the country and general merchandise was exported in return for tobacco, rum, sugar and slaves from the American Colonies. In 1876 the Queens Dock was built. This was a wet dock with one set of dock gates to hold the water in as the tide ebbed.

Ship building flourished and more than 1000 ships are recorded as being built in Whitehaven yards. Two press gangs operated in the town and smugglers landed contraband in nearby Fleswick Bay. One well known person to be apprenticed to a local merchant in the town was the founder of the United States Navy; John Paul Jones. On the 23rd April 1778, as the commander of a warship flying the stars and stripes of the 'Continental Navy', he sailed into Whitehaven harbour and raided the town. The harbour dredger found guns from his warship while I was at Richmond and these were placed behind the Sea Cadets headquarters on the old quay.

Whitehaven has the distinction of being one of the first planned towns in England. The Georgian town centre was built to a design by Christopher Wren and it still has more than 250 listed buildings. In my lunch breaks from Richmond several of us used to wander the streets and visit the old library, or on rough days we would walk down to the harbour and try to reach the lighthouse without being hit by the huge waves that surged over the breakwater. It was a dangerous pastime and one that we should never have been allowed to do, but no one seemed to care. Everyone was busy working harbour cranes or shunting coal wagons from the pit.

Often I stood by the wet dock with Stewart Crellin watching workmen, black as the ace of spades, offload coal wagons into the coal shoots. I was always amazed by the Coasters that visited Whitehaven to collect this coal, they passed through the lock gates with only inches to spare and then manoeuvred in such an impossibly small space.

The red sandstone cliffs of St Bees Head tower 300 feet above the waves that thunder relentlessly below. Cormorants, gannets, skuas and shearwaters skim across the thrashing waves of the cold Irish Sea. Rock pipits, ravens, peregrine falcons and stone chats can be seen flying in the huge updraft that sweeps over the cliff rim while razorbills, kittiwakes, fulmars, puffins and black guillemots lay their eggs on the narrow ledges far below.

When I was a teenager this was a bird lover's paradise that still remained to be discovered. Difficult road access and a long walk across unmade paths from the village of St Bees still afforded good protection from day tourists.

Further along the coast towards Whitehaven lay the cliffs of Fleswick, which were a little more accessible to those of us who could climb, and far below lay a small hidden bay where smugglers landed contraband in the 18th century. The mountains of the Scottish Borders could be seen across the Solway Firth and Snaefell on the Isle of Man struggled to emerge from the light stratus that drifted across the Irish Sea.

I often walked along the beach and gathered whelks, mussels and crabs which could be found around the rock pools. I didn't like seafood and never kept any for myself. I flattened the sabellaria tube worm structures which were formed in the dark coal laden sand and rummaged in the pebble banks for pieces of coloured glass. We gave these to young girls pretending that they were gemstones; many years later I found out that they really were gemstones!

After a heavy storm small shiny discs of coal gathered in huge troughs on the beaches north of Whitehaven. My father often rode down to Parton on my old bicycle and filled two sacks of coal before sunrise. In all of my father's years he never burned anything other than shore coal. It burned hot and fiercely, with small round pebbles exploding every few minutes to throw glowing pieces of slag onto our thick carpet. We always had to erect a fine mesh wire guard before leaving it unattended.

If my father could find such a supply of free coal then it will be no surprise that coal has been mined and shipped from Whitehaven Harbour since 1633. In the early 18th century Whitehaven boasted the deepest mines in the world and was proud to be the first town to cut work faces deep under the sea. More than 70 mines have been sunk in the area and several of these run as far out as five miles beneath the Solway Firth. Carlisle Spedding pioneered the use of explosives to sink several of these early mine shafts and he invented the first form of safety lamp which used a spinning cog with flints to produce a shower of sparks to illuminate the work area.

Fire damp, rock falls and underground tram accidents have caused more than 500 deaths to local miners. The largest of these disasters occurred at Wellington Pit in 1910 and William Pit in 1947. These are well remembered by the local population and almost every family has a relative who was lost in one of these two disasters. Both disasters were caused by fire damp explosions. The explosion at William Pit occurred beneath the sea and it was considered so dangerous to recover the bodies that they sealed the mine and entombed the men and young boys for the rest of time.

While at Richmond our class was invited to visit Calder Hall, the first ever Nuclear Power Station. I marvelled at huge control panels in the control centre, everything was so impressive and from that moment I determined that I was going to join the United Kingdom Atomic Energy Authority. I yearned for an opportunity to work with this futuristic equipment.

I did very well at Richmond. I gained a good sound education with a bias towards engineering and my pre-national certificate was well received by local industry. I applied for an apprenticeship with the Atomic Energy Authority, the United Steel Company, Distington Engineering Company and High Duty Alloys. To cover all eventualities I also applied to join the Army as a junior leader and the Cumberland Constabulary as a policeman. Two years earlier my best opportunity would have been in farming, now I was able to apply for a host of job opportunities.

Six weeks later, after an in-depth security scan of all my relatives, past and present, I received an official looking letter from Sellafield. I was so excited and I trembled as I cut it open with my dinner knife. Yes, it was my very first job offer. The UKAEA had invited my parents to indenture me for five years from 1st August 1960 until my 21st birthday on 30th July 1965. My parents immediately accepted and I was over the moon!

Chapter 2

A Good Old-fashioned Apprenticeship

Training to be a skilled instrument mechanic at Sellafield
So many people to thank!

The personnel department at Sellafield wrote to me and gave me information on how I was to get to work on my first day. After arrival I was issued with a special security pass that carried my photograph and a small strip of inlaid metal that could be used to determine my exposure to gamma radiation in the event of a serious incident. In addition I was given a special pass that could be used on the local steam trains and Cumberland bus services.

I was allocated a work bench in the apprentice training school that is fixed firmly in my memory. It was the first bench at the end of the workshop on the north end of the building. On my left was Rodney Campbell from Millom and on my right Stuart Crellin, who had run the gauntlet of the Whitehaven breakwater with me. There were approximately 45 apprentices in our year and around 200 apprentices across the complete works.

At the end of my first week I gave my wage packet to my mother and in a kind of a ceremonial way she handed it back to me. It contained a little less than three pounds, a meagre sum but a small fortune to me. It seemed that convention dictated that I kept my first wage packet. For the remaining five years I handed over my pay packet unopened and she gave me one pound pocket money plus my board and lodging. It was a fair arrangement and I am astounded by youngsters today who expect so much.

My mother wakened me every morning at 5 am with a bacon butty and a cup of hot coffee. Then I ran to the bus stop, usually just in time to catch the red double-decker bus as it continued on its hurried breakneck journey to Whitehaven bus station. From there I walked across to the railway station and boarded the works train that steamed its way along the rugged west coast to Sellafield. I walked with hundreds of other workers up the hill from the small station and through the main gate where I clocked on just before 7.30 am. In the winter it was cold, raining, often icy and still dark.

I toiled at my workbench, with a lunch break and two short coffee breaks, then clocked off at 5.00 pm to start my long journey home. I usually arrived at around 6.45 pm, in time to have dinner and to do homework for my day-release National Certificate Course. This was my average day, and youngsters today believe they have a right to complain! Not only did we work extremely long hours, but for the first time in my life I found that I did not have long breaks during school holidays. My holiday entitlement was only ten working days per annum!

After a short time we all started to slot into a routine. I could time my run to the bus stop in the morning with precision. We travelled in pre-determined carriages on the steam train and played cheat or 3-card brag for money. These games became very serious and we had to be careful not to bet more than we could afford. On one occasion I fell asleep and my fellow passengers sneaked out of the carriage leaving me to wake-up in the railway sidings at Seascale.

We all gathered in the same compartment again in the evening but there was a small change to our routine. Several of us continued by road to Distington but our bus departed at exactly the same time as our train was scheduled for arrival. It was a good 200 yards dash between the two and we never made it in time when we passed through the ticket barrier.

The train emerged from Bransty tunnel then ran along a section of platform that had a gate opening directly into the street. The last twenty yards of the tunnel was wide enough for the door to be thrown wide open and as we emerged into open air we jumped one after the other onto the platform. We hit the platform with our legs whirling like a windmill and headed straight through the open gate to the bus station. The bus had usually started up the hill as we jumped from line-astern onto the old style open platform.

Most conductors recognised us and didn't mind, but there was one little guy that always tried to push us back into the road. One day he confronted a middle-aged Sellafield worker who reciprocated and threatened to throw him off the bus. He never did it again.

When we jumped from the train we did it with such commando-like precision that no one checked if there was any stupid person hanging around on the platform. After all, everyone knew what happened when the Sellafield train emerged belching black smoke from the depths of the Bransty tunnel. After almost a full year with no problems the railway inspector decided to interfere and he stood waiting at the tunnel exit with several policemen.

Several of my friends hurtled straight into the inspector and as they rolled along the platform the police pounced and arrested them. I was lucky; it was my day at college. This did not deter us, we just took a little more care and in future the first jumper always checked the platform.

Our first task in the Apprentice School was to file a 4-inch square bar of steel into the shape of a scribing block. This took six working days and after the first five days the palms of my hands were covered in blisters. It would have been possible to do this work with a milling machine but I think the general idea was to break us in. The final dimensions for the block were required to be accurate to within two thousands of an inch and we achieved this by finishing off with a hand scraper, an engineering block and engineers blue. This required extreme precision, and when I finished it, it looked every bit as good as an accurately machined instrument.

We were then allocated time on engineering lathes and milling machines to manufacture our own very comprehensive mechanical engineers tool kit. This kit comprised of a large number of items. Those that I recall include an engineer's scribing block, four bell levelling jacks, dividers, clamps, engineer's squares and screwdrivers. It took 12 months for each of us to manufacture our kits and we then had to present them to the Amalgamated Engineering Union for examination; I received third prize.

After 52 weeks of hard work turning, milling, drilling, filing, scraping and polishing to achieve such a high standard I could never bring myself to use any of these tools. Instead I covered them in a thin film of oil and placed them in my attic. One day I will stay in one place long enough to display my tool kit in a glass cabinet. True apprenticeships no longer exist and these tools represent a work of art, the likes of which we will never see again.

My craft apprenticeship was all inclusive and we were each given day release to attend the Workington College of Further Education. My pre-national stood me in excellent stead; it positioned me perfectly on a course to attain the Ordinary National Certificate. This was by far the best option; many of my fellow apprentices had attended grammar schools and some were only able to enter the London City and Guilds course.

Suddenly I was on a winning ticket! I knew this and I was not going to waste my opportunity. I studied very hard through my five years and supplemented my day release with evening classes. Upon completion of my apprenticeship I was one of only two apprentices in my year to be awarded a Higher National Certificate and my certificate carried endorsements in seven additional subjects.

We were also given an opportunity to participate in physical education for one afternoon each week. Usually we ran to the sports field, which was just outside the security area and played football or took part in pre-arranged activities such as throwing the discus or long distance running. On rainy days we visited an old hanger and threw medicine balls around, lifted weights, climbed ropes and played basket ball.

It was on one of these days that I fell backwards while lifting a set of very heavy weights. I landed on my back with the bar cutting deep into my rib cage. I had a massive lump on the back of my head and my wrist was twisted into a grotesque shape. Sammy Blanche, a painter and our part time gym instructor, was rubbing my head when I came to. The works ambulance took me to Whitehaven hospital where they administered morphine and decided that I had to be transferred to Workington infirmary. The surgeons then reset the bones in my hand and wrist; I was climbing the wall by the time they administered gas and put me under.

I could not continue my training in the Apprentice School while my arm was in plaster. Sammy Blanche was also a shop steward and he reminded my parents that they could sue for compensation. Happily they declined and instead asked that I be allowed to continue immediately with my apprenticeship. A compromise was found and I worked for the next three months in the apprentice school tool store until my broken bones healed.

Every one was happy, the UKAEA was not sued, I showed willing to stay the course and my friends had someone to take their turn in the storeroom. Unfortunately the union insisted that I remain in the Apprentice School for a total of 15-months to make up for lost time. I thought this was a little unfair because I finished my toolkit on time and their action put me 3-months behind on the next stage of my apprentice training programme.

I had decided long before accepting my apprenticeship that I wanted to be an instrument mechanic, and I had to wait until the completion of my first year's general engineering course before they would inform me which discipline I would be allowed to follow. I heaved a big sigh of relief when I eventually moved to the Instrument School and started in my chosen career.

Instrument School and Central Instruments

The first year in this new school comprised of a sandwich course with three months in the physical instruments training school and three months apprenticed to a mechanic in the physical section of the central instruments workshop. The term physical instruments described mechanical type instruments such as pressure gauges, pyrometers, hygrometers, clocks, recorders with scissor type mechanisms, pneumatic type controllers and pneumatic transmitters.

In these early days most measurement and control instruments were mechanical in nature. Ring balances and similar devices that comprised an arrangement of levers, pivots, springs and bellows were used to control liquid columns in highly critical plutonium separation processes.

I was issued with a new toolkit and a new work bench. This time my tools were very intricate and included watch maker screwdrivers, tweezers of every shape and size, cutters, pliers, terry spanners, feeler gauges and Swiss files. In the school period we were issued several white cardboard backed note books which carried the name of Her Majesty's Stationary Office and we were required to write hundreds of pages of notes relating to the principle and theory of operation of different kinds of instrument.

During the Central Instruments period each apprentice worked alongside a skilled mechanic. Invariably we worked on the repair or maintenance of our own allocated instruments and the mechanic would oversee my progress and make suggestions where appropriate. This was a true apprenticeship, I was never a bag carrier; the unions ensured that mechanics mates were retained for this purpose.

Most of the mechanics that worked at Sellafield were ex-armed forces and many were in protected employment. Several had worked on the Burma Railroad or had been treated badly in German prisoner of war camps. One of my instructors in the Apprentice School was the only survivor from a submarine which was depth-charged off Norway. Local fishermen found him and managed to smuggle him back to England. He was almost deaf and he had to visit hospital at regular intervals in an attempt to fit his insides back together. As with most 'real' heroes, he never talked about his experiences and always avoided the subject in conversation.

Most foremen had been chief petty officers or warrant officers and they stood no nonsense; all-in-all, Sellafield could have been considered a military operation. This was understandable in the '50's and '60's because our sole purpose, despite all of the rhetoric, was to produce weapons grade plutonium.

In the third year I progressed to electronic instrumentation. Exactly the same routine applied, except this time one part of the sandwich course was taken in the electronics section of the Central Instruments Workshops.

In 1963 electronic technology was only just beginning to evolve; Germanium transistors were very susceptible to temperature drift and silicon was still in its infancy. Different types of semiconductor were introduced and the silicon planar transistor showed real promise. Novel concepts were used and one that I favoured had matched pairs in the same can. This helped to achieve good results in balanced circuits that provided high gain with very little temperature drift.

Elliot also introduced a range of transistor logic devices called Minilogs. We used these to build reactor shut down circuits, but they were never very successful because the transistor base connection was connected to an exposed pin. For those uninitiated, this meant that a mechanic with an unsteady hand would invariably touch this pin while testing the circuit logic and the transistor in the Minilog would immediately burn out. In retrospect, it is frightening that we even attempted to use such unreliable devices on experimental shut-down circuits.

For the most part our training in these early days was limited to equipment which used thermionic valves - an active component that was time tested and known to work within defined parameters. We worked with diodes, triodes and pentodes and applied them to electronic circuits that were particular to the nuclear industry. This included stabilised power supplies, amplifiers, counters, ratemeters, closed circuit TVs, personal body scanners, radiation detectors, alarm circuits, interlock systems and reactor shut down systems.

We continued to use pneumatic systems for control purposes and in several cases even used pneumatic logic circuits because of their reliability in a radiation environment. A very common task was to calibrate radiation detectors that had been sent in for repair. Surprisingly we did not have a suitable test area and the only location that was reasonably free of people was the entrance corridor.

We placed a cobalt source of known strength at one end of the corridor and using a tape measure placed the radiation detector at different distances to calibrate the electronic circuit. I don't know why, because there is no medical reason, but the cobalt source always gave me a headache when it was removed from its protective lead castle. Several others experienced the same symptoms.

In our practical sessions at the Instrument School we built electronic circuits on bread board and tested them before breaking them up and building something new. This was a little scary because the anode voltage of most electronic valves is around 300 volts. I reckon that I received at least three jolts in any one week when I worked with these boards.

We also worked on Geiger Muller tubes and scintillation counters that had voltages as high as 3000 volts. The circuits generating these high voltages could not supply any significant amount of current and so they were far less dangerous, but they could give a nasty little burn. Perhaps more dangerous was a fully charged electrolytic capacitor and many apprentices obtained their cruel fun by throwing a fully charge capacitor to someone and shouting 'catch'.

I was often on the receiving end of these cruel jokes and on one occasion someone flicked hot solder across the top of my work bench. It fell down the back of my neck and burned a deep hole in my back. It was extremely painful and I could not reach the solder to remove it. It goes without saying that no one rats on their work mates, no matter what they have done. So I crawled under the bench and whacked the culprit on his toes with a hammer. He never played any more dangerous tricks on me.

Unfortunately 'Sugar' Ray Wilson, the Instrument Training Manager, saw me from his office and he called for my instant dismissal. I thought this was very unfair of him because he never challenged me or asked for an explanation.

Every person needs a sponsor: someone in a position of responsibility who can look after their career prospects. Without such a person no one ever reaches their full potential. I always felt that my Apprentice Supervisor, Len Pearce, or 'Fruity' as he was better known, was my sponsor. He is a short balding man with grey hair and very stern features. He had been a Major during the war and was stereotype for the roll he played; he took his job very seriously.

My whole career, indeed my whole future, I owe to Mr Pearce and to others like him. He helped me throughout those early years of my apprenticeship. It was Mr Pearce who stood up to 'Sugar' and prevented my dismissal.

I had tremendous respect for the mechanics that I worked with, and please remember that I am describing mechanics who worked on high voltage electronic circuits. In 1963 a mechanic was a skilled artisan and an engineer was a person professionally qualified by an Institution that held a Royal Charter issued by the Queens Privy Council. This was the Civil Service in 1963, rank and position were paramount.

The mechanics that I worked with were highly skilled and I often wondered how I would cope when I became a journeyman and had to work unsupervised on such important equipment. Then one afternoon a very good friend of mine, a very likeable hard working apprentice, someone who had never upset anyone in his short life, was killed. Everyone in the instrument training school was devastated.

Barnie was working on a ratemeter with its protective panels removed. This is necessary when trouble shooting faulty electronic equipment. He put his hand around the back of the instrument and the palm of his hand touched a high voltage transformer. The muscles in both of his hands tensioned causing him to grab hold of the chassis. The instrument weighed around 44 pounds and he lifted it from the bench at full arms length; a feat normally impossible.

John Wilson, another apprentice working nearby, immediately pulled the electric plug from the bench socket and Barnie fell to the ground. It only takes 4 mA through the heart to kill a person, but on this occasion the voltage was so high that his heart burst in the first few seconds. There was nothing that anyone could do.

The inquest found no one to be at fault but the UK Health and Safety Executive issued new directives in regard to live voltage working on electronic equipment. Three years later I became one of the first examiners under this Directive. I cannot remember any specific details but I recollect that the new rules prevented any young person below the age of 18 from working on equipment with exposed live circuits exceeding 40 volts. Any person 18 and above working on live circuits had to carry a certificate indicating that he had passed an examination in safe working procedures.

I was ruthless in my examination technique and I have been approached over the years by many technicians who reminded me that I failed them for the smallest of reasons. There are three very basic safe working practices that I look for: 1. Cover floor and workbench with a suitable rubber mat. 2. Remove all unnecessary tools and debris from the workbench before, during and after work. 3. Keep one hand firmly lodged in a trouser pocket while probing live circuits. I immediately failed any person who breached any one of these basic rules.

Reactor operations

My fourth year was divided into two 6-month periods; the first period was intended to give me practical experience repairing and servicing instrumentation on a nuclear reactor installation and the second was to give me similar experience on a weapons grade plutonium processing facility. This was my first on-site experience and I was given my little blue film badge, which I carried for the remainder of my career with the Atomic Energy Authority. I entered this new stage of my training with a certain amount of hidden timidity.

These were very early days in the British nuclear weapons programme and regardless of everything said to the contrary, Sellafield existed for only one purpose, to provide Britain with an independent nuclear deterrent. Safety while paramount could never be fully guaranteed and I have always been frightened by the unknown, things that I can not see or feel; exposure to radiation or radioactive contamination fitted into this category. This fear was not helped by the many stories that were told and re-told by workers in the Pile Canteen; stories of serious incidents that were being covered-up for reasons of military security. I am unable to repeat any of these accounts and for reasons of security I have limited my description of technical subjects, or nuclear incidents, to material which I have extracted from well published articles in the public domain, from information released under the 30-year rule and to stories that I heard while I was still a schoolboy.

First I need to explain a little about the original purpose of Windscale and how it developed in the early years. In the latter part of the Second World War, Winston Churchill ordered the establishment of a top secret nuclear weapons programme. This resulted in the construction of two military reactors, Pile 1 and Pile 2, a spent fuel rod handling facility B29 and a weapons grade plutonium extraction plant B204 at Windscale. Windscale was chosen because the area was bounded by the Irish Sea and the Lake District Fells; it was remote and had a low population density.

During the war British scientists worked alongside their American counterparts in the United States on the Manhattan Project, and when they returned to the United Kingdom they were prevented from repatriating any of their technical documents. These same scientists re-invented the wheel and developed a new process for the separation of weapons grade plutonium. This work resulted in the building of what was to become the largest nuclear reprocessing facility in the world.

The military reactors at Windscale were built in a hurry. Their fuel channels were horizontal and air was used as a coolant; two bad choices that were to have terrible consequences. The third variable that would have an effect on future events was the choice of Graphite as the moderator. This moderator was necessary to slow neutrons down to the energy level at which a nuclear chain reaction could occur. The same neutrons caused a build-up of energy in the graphite. This energy had to be released during special maintenance periods by switching off the air blowers and allowing the graphite to heat up under carefully controlled conditions to give a 'Wigner Release' of stored energy.

One such maintenance operation was initiated for Pile 1 on Monday the 7th October 1957. The air blowers were stopped and the graphite blocks were allowed to increase in temperature to secure a Wigner Release. During this critical operation the temperature gauges gave conflicting information and so the operators decided to boost the release on Tuesday by allowing more nuclear heating to take place. Reactor instrumentation was very limited in 1957 and the only temperature recorder monitoring the core was a mechanical type and it was very prone to drift related problems. On Wednesday a reactor operator noticed that it showed the core temperature to be increasing at an alarming rate. He sent a messenger to advise the Reactor Manager, but the Manager assumed that it was an instrument fault and he took no immediate action.

At some time on Wednesday the air blowers were restarted in an attempt to cool the fuel rods. This was the wrong thing to do; if a fire had already started then the air coolant would have fuelled the flames. The management was in a quandary and had no idea what to do next. On Thursday the radiation monitors at the top of the stack detected high radiation levels and two senior managers stood on a portable lifting device to access a fuel channel inspection hole. When they opened the protective cover they were shocked to see cherry red uranium fuel rods and yellow flames; the reactor was on fire! Workers attempted to punch the fuel rods out of four horizontal channels in order to create a fire break but most were already wedged firmly in position.

The only solution possible was to pump thousands of gallons of water through the reactor core. No one knew what would happen; the Management was worried that an explosion could expose the complete reactor core and force the evacuation of West Cumberland. The Chief Constable of Cumberland was informed of the seriousness of the situation and civil defence organisations were placed on alert. I am told that troops encircled the perimeter fence, not to keep people out, but as one local described it, to keep the workers in. The water did its job but a substantial amount of oxidised uranium, polonium, strontium and iodine was released into the environment. National newspapers reported that most of this was carried over the Irish Sea but it was actually spread by the prevailing winds across South East England. The Government decided not to evacuate the local population and more than 1000 people died from different kinds of cancer that may have been related; I lost my grandmother, my mother, my sister-in-law and my wife. When my father was on the Distington Parish Council he tried to obtain further information. He found that West Cumberland Hospital was one of the few hospitals in the UK that did not maintain statistical cancer records; I suppose he was not surprised!

The water quenching worked and production workers used scaffolding poles to rod out hundreds of damaged fuel rods; each received his lifetime radiation dosage in only a few minutes. Workers were so contaminated that they wore protective gloves to eat their meals in the canteen and many received 150 times their maximum permitted dose. All local dairy farm production was confiscated and thousands of gallons were poured day and night into the Irish Sea; a white slick of contaminated milk drifted on an ebbing tide towards the Isle of Man.

The Macmillan Government was plunged into a sequence of events that rocked the world. Harold Macmillan was negotiating a nuclear collaboration pact with Ike Eisenhower and the incident, now known as the

'Windscale Incident', became a serious embarrassment to him. He ordered suppression of all information and even now only partial details have been released under the 30-year rule; individual witness accounts have been reclassified for a further 20 years. More than 6000 damaged fuel rods are still embedded within the reactor core of Pile 1; this is a problem that we have left for future generations to resolve.

Given the extreme circumstances of the Windscale Incident, the worst nuclear disaster ever suffered in the West, I must be fair to the management of the day and congratulate them upon the professional way in which they protected their employees during the massive clean-up operation; every single worker was properly equipped with breathing apparatus and a PVC protective suit. 29 years later when the Chernobyl reactor core was exposed in a similar accident the Soviet Government failed to provide any type of protective equipment to their workers and almost all of those who worked on the Sarcophagus died a terrible death from radiation sickness. Many of these deaths could have been avoided if the Soviets had taken their lead from the experience gained by the Management at Sellafield.

I feel obliged to pay contribute to the then General Manager, HG Davey, who along with Tom Tuohy, entered a sealed area and diverted escaping radioactive gases through the Top-Hat filter beds. Without their direct intervention the disaster would have been on a much larger scale. Mr Davy eventually died from leukaemia and the workers of Sellafield established the HG Davey Memorial Prize in his honour. This award is made annually to the best employee under the age of 21 for pursuits associated with both work and leisure. I am one of the holders of this award.

The events surrounding the temperature recorder incident is something that was never, to my knowledge, made available to the Board of Inquiry. According to an instrument mechanics mate who worked on Pile 1, the paper chart was removed from the recorder and destroyed before it could be examined. I have no idea if this is true or not but information subsequently released under the 30-year rule showed that the reactor instrumentation was very minimal and positioned in inaccessible places; those temperature gauges that were available are said to have given conflicting readings and no mention was made of the recorder chart. The Board of Inquiry recommended a huge increase in spending on instrumentation and a programme was initiated to train upwards of 40 instrument mechanics per year at the Windscale and Calder Works. I was one of the first apprentices to join this programme.

The reasons for my apprehension when I started my 6-month period on nuclear reactor maintenance can now perhaps be better understood. On my first day I was sent to the fire station for emergency evacuation training from the AGR (Advance Gas Cooled Reactor) containment area. I was trained to remove a self-air-set from a container, fit it to my face and have it fully operational in less than 25 seconds. This took considerable practice and the only way that it could be achieved was to unpack the self-air-set , open the air bottle valve, set the air regulator and then fit the mask to my face so that I could breathe. Only then did I take time to hitch the heavy steel bottle onto my back; little did I know that I would soon put this training into practice.

The Windscale AGR at this time was the only advanced gas cooled reactor in the world. It produced 30 megawatts of electric power and was the prototype for a new generation of civil reactors. The fuel was ceramic uranium oxide, enriched to just above two percent and it had a stainless steel can. The graphite was modified to overcome the cause of the fire in the Windscale Pile and it was cooled with carbon dioxide.

The reactor was controlled as before with a set of boron control rods, but in addition, there was a large number of boron balls that could be dropped into the reactor core if the channels became distorted by an earthquake. Instead of one temperature recorder there were now several thousand temperature probes monitoring fuel rod temperatures throughout the reactor core and these were monitored on data loggers as well as several high quality electronic temperature recorders. The process and nucleonic instrumentation exceeded the quantity and quality of that provided on the Windscale Piles by a huge margin.

Every critical instrument loop was repeated three times and interlocked in what we call a 2 out of 3 system. This means that every important decision is a kind of voting process. If this vote can not be realized in any two of the three systems then the reactor is immediately shut down.

The AGR reactor had one additional feature, which is why I needed my self air set certificate. The complete reactor including charge machines, discharge machines, cooling circuits and instrumentation transmitters were all contained within a secondary containment building. This containment area was maintained below normal atmospheric pressure to ensure that any leakage was into the containment.

Access was through a very large airlock on the pile cap floor, similar in principle to the escape compartment in a submarine, and in addition there was one smaller two man unit on a lower level. In the unlikely event of a radioactive leak or a break in the main carbon dioxide cooling system, then the whole of this containment area would fill with carbon dioxide gas in seconds; hence the need to find and start using a self-air-set as quickly as possible. On one occasion, during a false alarm, I saw a grown man rip a self-air-set from the clutches of a young apprentice.

There are several infra-red gas analysers installed in cells beneath the reactor core. These measure concentrations of carbon dioxide and carbon monoxide gas. In the event that a dangerous level of either is detected, then two huge air raid sirens are switched on. The intense sound in such a small containment area puts the fear of hell into anyone unfortunate enough to be caught inside.

I was working in the cells three floors below the pile cap, helping to re-calibrate one of the infra-red gas analysers, when the sirens went off. I was part of a team of three comprising mechanics mate, apprentice and instrument mechanic. At the time of the incident I already suspected that we had caused the alarm but the intensity of the sirens still frightened me. We held our breath and rushed to the nearest emergency cabinet. While fastening my mask I heard a sharp explosion and I thought that we were finished; I was convinced that we had already passed to the walking dead!

I looked down through the restricted vision of my face mask and could see my mechanic lying on the ground in shock. I held him down while the Mate replaced his air-set and got it working. The pressure regulator on the set he grabbed had released full bottle pressure into his mask causing it to explode in his face.

After we calmed him I tried to run up the stairs but was stopped by the Mate who grabbed hold of my legs. My vision was limited and I did not see the chequer plate that had been closed over the stair access; I was just about to cave my skull in on a steel girder. We retreated to the lower floor and found a steel ladder leading to the pile cap. This time the mate led the way. He was a huge kind-hearted guy. When he reached the safety rings his air bottles prevented him from passing through.

Eventually we reached the main airlock. It was no surprise that everyone had gone through without us. They are supposed to wait for stragglers, but we were more than straggling; we were a walking disaster. To make matters worse, they kept running when they passed through the airlock; no one stopped to close the outer door. Anyone who knows anything about submarines will know what that meant. We were stuffed!

We sat down on the reactor floor and panted into our face masks. My lenses were steamed up and sweat was pouring down my body. We had no idea what was happening, for all we knew we were sitting in a cauldron of radioactive carbon dioxide gas. In such terrible situations the least likely becomes the obvious. I am sure that Sherlock Holmes would have a useful catch phrase to sum up the situation.

After what appeared to be an eternity the inner airlock door opened and three health and safety guys came through wearing self-air-sets and full protective gear; three Darth Vaders in white. They stopped in surprise when they saw us sat on the floor and then helped us to our feet. For the first time in my life I knew what real fear was. My legs had turned to jelly and my whole body was shaking. The inactivity of sitting helpless inside the containment building had taken its toll on me.

The following day every self-air-set in the containment area was replaced, the floor area above the stairs was permanently removed and an inquiry was put into motion. I never received a formal apology and I was never asked to speak to the inquiry. It still remains to be one of the most frightening moments of my life.

AGR also had its funny moments. It had a very large crescent shaped control room with a picture perfect control panel about 25 yards long and containing a wide variety of different indicators, recorders, controllers and alarm displays. Most of these instruments contained thermionic valves; transistors were still unreliable and process control computers had not been invented. The panel had an excellent ergonomic design with the panel cut-outs positioned for each different type of instrument to ensure that the top of the instrument bezels lined up with one another.

It was decided that a new Honeywell electronic multipoint recorder would be placed into a spare section in the control panel. A 'mature trainee mechanic' was given the task. The trouble is that this poor chap was the butt of everyone's jokes; even the apprentices made fun of him. He always took his ribbing in good fun but if anything was ever going to go wrong you could be sure it would be with Bob.

This time Bob intended to show everyone how he could do a good job. He measured very carefully to ensure that the top bezel would line up correctly with the other instruments. He measured the recorder and cut the required hole in the control panel; then he asked someone to help lift this heavy 40-pound recorder into the panel.

His face was a picture when the recorder passed right through the hole and smashed onto the hard floor behind the panel. He had measured the outside of the bezel and there was nothing to hold it in the panel; the hole was too big! Poor guy, it was a terrible mistake. We should have taken the matter more seriously but everyone in the control room was beside themselves with laughter.

It never ceased to amaze me how engineers tinkered with active circuits to try different ideas. I suppose it was a prototype reactor and this does mean that a certain amount of experimentation was necessary. Working with us was a small number of egg-heads. Dr Don Scarratt was one; he was a brilliant engineer and he reminded me, in a kindly way, of one of those nutty professors who would not look out of place in a Disney film. Our foreman always became agitated whenever Don vanished behind the huge control panel to make new links in the reactor control circuits.

The containment area had new fangled closed circuit TV cameras and we repaired these in the shift mechanics workshop. We spent long periods of time playing cards during working hours and used one of these cameras to monitor the long corridor leading to the workshop. I don't know if the foreman had figured out what we were doing but we were always able to spot his approach in time to hide our cards and get back to work before he came through the door. Other than these brief escapades, I cannot remember very much about my work on AGR. I suppose I gained several real life experiences on survival but they are not experiences that I ever want to repeat.

Early in 1960 Sir John Hunt, leader of the Everest Exhibition, awarded me the Duke of Edinburgh's Bronze Award. I enjoyed my participation in the scheme and now, three years on, I received an invitation to receive my Gold Award from the Duke of Edinburgh in Buckingham Palace. I was one of three youngsters to receive the award, the first from Cumberland, and to mark the occasion Lord Aberdare invited me to lunch in the YMCA London headquarters. My big day was on Wednesday 12th December 1962. I was fortunate to have an opportunity to speak with Prince Philip before we were escorted into the palace ballroom. A military band was ensconced in the musical gallery and I still retain a vivid mental picture of a short guardsman beating a huge base drum. It was strapped to his chest and it threatened to pull him over the low wall of the balcony.

Plutonium separation

It was not long before my 6-month reactor training was complete, and I transferred to the Separation Group. This was again a different and rather daunting experience. Instead of entering the work area through an airlock door I was required to pass through a changing room area where I changed all of my clothing, including underwear and shoes.

I was issued with two changes of rough-cloth works clothing and one pair of black steel-toed safety shoes; each item with a personal number for identification when they were despatched to the active area laundry. The Separation Area was aptly named because it not only contained the buildings required to separate plutonium from the other fission products, but it was also an area separated from the outside world.

To gain entry I changed all of my clothing in the clean area locker room and walked in stocking feet to a bench that divided the changing rooms into two distinctive areas; clean and active. I then slid over the bench on my backside and placed my feet into active area shoes which were located in a dedicated slot beneath the bench. After collecting and donning my active area coveralls, I walked to my workshop in B209, which was about half a mile away.

The exit route was even longer; it included a long communal shower tunnel between the active and clean areas. After showering everyone had to use a 'hand and foot monitor', and if the alarm sounded you returned to the showers and scrubbed like hell. The nurses were very attractive in the works hospital but no one ever wanted to visit them for de-contamination. It was never a pleasant experience to have a young girl scrub your nose channels with a long wiry tool.

When I arrived at B209 I passed through a further gate where the safety officer recorded my entry to the building and issued me with a quartz fibre dosimeter. This dosimeter helped me to monitor my personal radiation exposure throughout the day. I prefer not to describe the purpose of B209. It was a very high risk building where criticalities could occur. I had a dosimeter, blue radiation film badge and a metal disc in my security pass. As if this were not enough, I was then issued with a small plastic bag that contained a variety of metals that absorbed gamma and neutron radiation at different energy levels.

Such a variety of detectors made me very nervous; my dosimeter was very helpful, but the remainder of the items would only help the Health and Safety Executive decide if I should be given free beer in the Windscale Club for the rest of my shortened life.

For clarification; workers who have been subjected to a criticality, or to sustained levels of high radiation, have radioactive iodine in the marrow of their bones. Small amounts pass to bone surface and this can be washed away by copious amounts of 'beer'. Hence several workers were permitted unlimited free beer in the Windscale Clubs. I don't know how medically correct I am, or of its actual benefits; but the free beer is a fact.

A criticality is when a certain amount of plutonium gathers together and forms a critical mass. There is a huge surge of neutron radiation, usually recognized by a blue flash, and anyone in close proximity will almost certainly receive a lethal dose. A huge amount of energy is released and the plutonium is thrown apart causing it to fall below the critical mass. However, there are recorded events in the United States where the criticality occurred in a bowl or cylindrical chamber. In these cases the plutonium was able to fall back to the bottom of the chamber and create a second or even third criticality.

A criticality is signalled by the sounding of the NATO attack signal and the safety instructions are to drop anything being carried, no matter what its value, and run in the direction of the green arrows to the nearest exit. I recall one story often told by the mechanic to whom I was apprenticed. One day he was servicing the criticality alarm system when the NATO attack signal sounded. He knew that he had tripped the alarm by accident and he stepped out into the corridor. Suddenly the swing doors flew open and a wall of white coats knocked him down and surged across him. He was so un-nerved by this incident that he picked himself up and ran after them.

I enjoyed working in B209. The small group of instrument mechanics were a good crowd and my foreman was very helpful. He gave me 'real' jobs to do and I repaired my first multipoint recorder without help. The self balancing circuit used high precision wire-wound resistors and these had been re-wound and connected back into the electronic bridge incorrectly. It took me a couple of days, but I cracked it and my first success gave me a mega-jump in self confidence. I learned much more than I did in AGR, and this was all down to the helpful friendly attitude of the people that I was fortunate to work with.

My wage had not increased by much in the past three years and I still earned less than four pounds for a 45-hour week, but apprentices working in the Separation Area had an added bonus. The trade unions ensured that we were paid PVC money at the same rate as mechanics.

PVC is the material used for the protective clothing that is worn while working in areas contaminated by radioactive material. PVC does not breathe and because of this we sweated profusely. In addition, we normally wore respirators with PVC hoods that were sealed to our bodies using special tape. If we were lucky 'Health Physics' allocated a Windscale Suite. This took external air in the same way as a deep sea diver and was much more comfortable; it made us look like spacemen.

Everyone hated working in PVC but, to an apprentice, a few hours each day could add thirty percent to his wage. The going rate was two shillings an hour and we would look for every opportunity to get PVC money. It sounds crazy now, but we did become very complacent with the environment that we worked in.

Whenever I entered a sealed radioactive environment, the only person with me was my attendant and he would be 50 metres away servicing my air feed and monitoring my communications. If I finished my work early, I would sit down on the floor out of sight of the attendant, and relax until I had completed the full hour. I even heard stories of apprentices sitting for a full second hour to add an extra florin to their pay packet.

My 5th and final year

During my final year I was required to work in the same department in which I would finish my time, and hopefully continue as a journeyman. Ben Cook, the engineer managing the construction department within Central Instruments, took me on board. He told me that no one else would have me and he was probably telling the truth.

Ben was an easy going person with an agreeable personality. He had a full grown ginger beard which must have caused him terrible decontamination problems. He was the only person out of several thousand who I knew who rode into work on a bicycle. On rainy days he wore an old leather motorbike jacket and with his red beard he looked like the bad guy in a Marvel comic book.

It was at the beginning of this year that I was awarded the HG Davey Memorial Prize, and I suppose this encouraged the Apprentice School to ask me to enter for the Harold Tongue trophy, which was awarded annually by the Atomic Energy Research Establishment in Harwell. I struggled to find a suitable engineering problem that would task me sufficiently to provide a winning entry.

Many test instruments and measuring circuits used in process instrument applications were based upon the Wheatstone bridge principle. This required a Weston cadmium cell to provide the reference voltage for the bridge circuit; this voltage was precisely 1.0183 volts dc. I decided to set myself the task of generating this voltage using silicon planar transistor technology. To do this I had to design several different types of electronic circuit and encase these into outer and an inner temperature stabilised blocks.

The aim was to secure very accurate temperature control of the circuit components to ensure that the voltage drift across a high precision reference resistor would be almost zero. The project required personal input at all levels; innovative thought, engineering design, manufacture, testing and final implementation. This should provide all the ingredients to give me a good chance of winning. I was disappointed when I received news that my entry was unsuccessful. I was told that my prototype instrument was damaged during transit to Harwell. I don't know what happened but when it was returned to me 6 months later it was in three pieces and the case was shattered.

Most of my year was spent manufacturing, wiring and testing prototype instruments for research applications. I needed to use all of my skills; one day I could be testing high voltage thermionic valve circuits on a measuring oscilloscope and the next I may have been working in the machine shop turning a mechanical component on one of the small engineering lathes. A true instrument mechanic is in essence a highly skilled jack of all trades who can repair a small wrist watch, manufacture a replacement component for a pressure transmitter or commission a complex electronic controller on a reactor fuel rod assembly.

My confidence was building throughout the year. I slowly began to feel that I could contribute and earn my way as a journeyman when I reached the magic age of 21. In my last three months, work study was introduced at Windscale. This was the first time, to my knowledge, that work had been studied in such a manner. I will not go into the theory and practice of work study; suffice to say that the management decided that the easiest place to start was in the construction department. I was therefore chosen as the model to be studied.

For several weeks a work study officer sat beside me on a stool and timed my every move on a stop watch. He evaluated my effectiveness, he observed whenever I had to reach or move my position to grasp a tool; he even timed any short breaks that I needed to rest my eyes or steady my hand. Other mechanics often passed by and hinted that I should slow down. Everyone knew that the information he gathered would be used to set bonus targets when the system was fully introduced to other departments.

Finally the big day came, and on 30th July 1965 I reached the ripe old age of 21, received the key to the door and became a journeyman. My next wage packet contained the enormous sum of 19 English Pounds - six times what I earned in the first year of my apprenticeship. Half a dozen friends from Central Instruments joined me for lunch at a Pub in Calder Bridge. It was the only time that I ever left the site for lunch and it is just as well. One of the old-timers had a couple of whiskies and he spent the rest of the afternoon sleeping them off behind a control panel in the Separation Area.

Later in the year I was presented with my Indentures and with the Windscale and Calder Trophy for the best 5th Year Apprentice. It was a proud moment. I owe a tremendous amount to Windscale, to all of the mechanics, foremen and managers that showed so much patience and helped to train me into the person that I now am. In particular, I remain indebted to Mr Pearce, who gave solid support when I most needed it.

Byrom Street College, Liverpool

My days as a journeyman were short lived. The Atomic Energy Authority awarded me a Scholarship to attend the Regional College of Technology in Liverpool. This award was a one-year intensive course to help prepare me for the external examinations of the Institute of Electrical Engineers.

My father drove me down to Liverpool and helped me to find digs with a widow and her young daughter in Wallasey, Cheshire. Every morning I caught a bus down to the Wallasey pier and crossed the Mersey to a landing pier in front of the Liver Buildings. From there I walked through town to the old Byrom Street College. On stormy winter mornings the Mersey was so rough that the ferry pitched 4-feet as passengers jumped ashore.

My course required lecture attendance for 35 hours in each week and around 30-hours of homework. Many of my fellow students had 3 years full time study under their belt and I had a lot of catching-up to do. My core subjects included mathematics, engineering physics, advanced electrical engineering, applied electronics and electrical measurements. I soon gained confidence and my practical experience compensated immensely for my lack of academic training.

My landlady was a terrible scrooge. She served dinner at 6 pm every day and if I was late home from college then it was tough luck. I worked every night in my bedroom and at 11 pm she rapped on my door and ordered me to knock my light out. This was totally unacceptable; I usually had a lab report to finish before morning, and so I would wait until she had retired and then switch my light back on. At the weekend she allowed me to work in her front lounge with one bar of the electric fire switched on. My feet were always freezing and I found it difficult to concentrate. Eventually I found a small flat in Kremlin Avenue on the outskirts of Liverpool. It was a difficult move; when I gave her notice she threw my belongings through her bedroom window and shouted abuse as I hurried away down the street.

Liverpool was a great place to be in the '60's. The 'Liverpool Sound' was at its height and I danced every Sunday in the Locarno Ballroom. I remember one special evening when Jerry and the Pacemakers sang 'Ferry Cross the Mersey'. It seemed so appropriate given my own twice-daily ferry crossings. The Beatles had already left their mark in the Cavern and English football was at its best. In 1966 Liverpool won the Premiership, Everton won the Challenge Cup and England won the World Cup. What more could Merseyside have wanted! The world was at its feet and I was geographically in the centre of it all. My classroom overlooked the Lions of St Georges Hall; focal point of all the famous Liverpool celebrations.

I never cooked in Kremlin Avenue. I lived on bangers and mash, mushy peas, potato pies and fish and chips; all purchased from a late night chippy. They served me in an old copy of the Liverpool Evening Echo and I ate my dinner cum supper cum breakfast as I walked back along deserted streets to my small one-room ground floor flat.

One November evening in 1965 I arranged a lift home to Distington with a Marchon tanker driver. He enjoyed my conversation and I helped him to remain awake as he drove at full speed down the fog laden M6. Fifteen minutes behind us a heavy truck ploughed into a line of slow moving vehicles. More vehicles ploughed into him and in minutes one of the largest ever motorway disasters developed. More than a hundred cars were involved and dozens of motorists were trapped in the bodies of their crushed vehicles. It was the last time that I ever hitched a lift in a tanker.

Our examinations were set in London and we had no idea what kind of questions would be asked. The advanced electrical engineering examination alone covered everything from electron ballistics to heavy transmission theory. A student in a traditional red-brick university can expect to be questioned on the core subjects of his syllabus; we had no such expectation. In one examination I only recognised three out of ten questions. I quickly answered these and then used my remaining time to develop a formula that would enable me to tackle one of the remaining seven questions. I used Einstein's basic principle, 'energy can neither be created nor destroyed' and described each of my mathematical deductions in detail. The external examiner must have been impressed because I was one of only two students to pass the examination.

Chapter 3

Wear the Queen's Uniform with Pride

Eight years of tremendous excitement in the Air Training Corps
Venture adventure!

From a very early age I coveted my father's war memorabilia; on cold winter days I wore a warm leather fighter pilots helmet, which one of his spitfire pilots had given to him. Each year we toured different parts of the United Kingdom in an old Morris Minor. We slept overnight in my desert rat tent and cooked on an old primus stove. Often we passed by an operational airfield and I made Dad park at the end of the runway while aircraft roared overhead.

One year we passed by an airport near to Blackpool and he paid 10 shillings for me to take a short flight in a Dragon Rapide. I was about eleven years old and this was long before the days of regular airline travel. My mother was very worried that I chose to fly alone, and while I was in the sky a thunderstorm passed overhead. She was almost beside herself when I returned. I thoroughly enjoyed myself and could not wait until I had another opportunity.

In the evenings I assembled Airfix models of Royal Air Force aircraft and built flying scale models from balsa wood, dope and paper. I could not afford to buy a petrol engine so I used rubber bands to power the propeller. I had several books describing different types of military aircraft and my prize possession was a wartime aircraft recognition book called 'Friend or Foe'.

Walking back from school one day I met Jim Douglas. Jim was two years older than me and he wore what I thought to be a Royal Air Force uniform.

I could not understand how he came to be wearing this and when I questioned him he explained that he had joined the Air Training Corps.

Jim scoffed that I was just a kid and that I had to be 14 years old before I could join. I was tall for my age and so one year later, just as my father did when he joined the regular Royal Air Force, I walked into the headquarters of 1030 (West Coast) Squadron and told them that I was 14 years old. It was the 23rd June 1957 and I was still only 12 years old. They wanted recruits, and when my father signed my thirty eight twenty two, no one asked any further questions.

I did not know it at the time, but this was perhaps the most important step that I have ever taken. The Air Cadets gave me confidence. Officers in the squadron helped me to establish myself as a stronger and more determined person. Most important of all, I firmly believe that it was my success in the Air Cadets that helped impress panel members in all of the interviews and boards that I attended during the early part of my career development. Without this experience to differentiate me from my competitors, I might never have travelled beyond the boundaries of West Cumberland.

My squadron met from 7 pm to 9 pm in Whitehaven every Tuesday and Friday evening. We started with marching drill for around half an hour and then moved indoors to take lessons for the remainder of the evening. The lessons followed a strict syllabus that extended from the basic theory of flight to advanced studies in jet engine design. Our headquarters also had a radio communications room, which was fitted with the same transmitters and receivers that were fitted in wartime Lancaster bombers. I was soon able to send and receive Morse code at around 14 words per minute and this helped me to obtain my Radio Amateurs Licence a few years later.

After four weeks the Quartermaster fitted me with my first uniform. It comprised a tunic, beret, greatcoat, cape and a pair of trousers. The material was very course and felt as if it was made from horsehair. The tunic buttoned right up to a full dog-collar, very similar to a Guard's uniform. It was extremely uncomfortable, but I was a very proud young boy when I marched home that first evening fully dressed in my new uniform of the Air Training Corps.

I never missed a single parade and it was not long before I was given an opportunity to visit Royal Air Force Silloth for flying experience. My first flight with the Air Training Corps was in Avro Anson UM368 over the Solway Firth. It was a memorable experience, and this was followed a short while later with a flight in an old Dakota, registration KP208. I remember walking around the airfield with other cadets and climbing into the bellies of Neptune anti-submarine aircraft that had been mothballed by the Americans at the end of the war.

Every dispersal point was crowded with these aircraft, and then, one year the Americans dismantled them. I am told that this was to prevent the Royal Air Force from putting them into useful service. I never believed this story at the time, but later revelations have given credibility to it. It would appear that our American allies were not as benevolent as I had thought in my earlier childhood.

On 8th July 1958 I was very proud to be a member of the Guard of Honour that welcomed a very young Duke of Edinburgh to Royal Air Force Kirkbride. I remember that it was a hot summer day and his arrival had been delayed; several young cadets blacked-out after standing to attention for such a long time. I was feeling terribly ill and the course hairy fabric of my tunic dog-collar rubbed against my Adam's apple until I felt certain that I would throw-up at the worst possible time. I was so relieved when he strolled quickly by me. His hands were clasped firmly behind his back and his mischievous steely gaze passed across the face of every one of us. In that brief moment he left us with a memory that we would treasure for the rest of our lives.

RAF Cottesmore, V-Bomber Command

My first camp was in August 1958 at Royal Air Force Cottesmore in Rutland. It was an operational V-bomber station equipped with Victor V-bombers. We were billeted in two huge H-blocks, which we shared with several other squadrons from the South of England. The design of these blocks was identical in almost every station that I visited during my time in the Air Training Corpse.

It was a long journey to Cottesmore. The squadron travelled under a rail warrant by steam train from Whitehaven to Oakham where we were picked up by RAF trucks late in the evening and taken to the station.

When we arrived we collected our pillows and blankets from the quartermaster and made up our beds in regulation style with hospital corners, top blanket folded back below the pillow and every wrinkle smoothed out. This was only a small taste of what was to come in the morning.

It was a horrible night. In the late '50's West Cumberland was a tough area and the older cadets, aided by many of the NCO's (Non-Commissioned Officers), encouraged an initiation procedure for cadets attending their first camp. This was a very crude and dangerous practice that involved shaving the pubic area and smearing black boot polish over the genitals. Most of the cadets ran and fought very hard to avoid such indignity, but no one ever escaped.

Our squadron quickly gained a bad reputation at Cottesmore, a reputation that would stay with us for many years. On the second night the older cadets grouped together and raided every other billet in the block. They engaged three squadrons at the same time and when the military police arrived our room was the only one without damage. The MP's (Military Police) had no difficulty in identifying the culprits and our officers seriously considered taking the complete squadron home in disgrace.

This was not the end of my own troubles. On the fourth night a group of NCOs, who had late passes, returned from town in a very inebriated condition. They wrecked our billet and one jumped on my bed while I was still sleeping. In the mayhem that followed a vein was torn open in my left foot. Fortunately one of the culprits was a first-aider. He applied pressure until the medics arrived and then two MP's took me in their Landrover to Oakham for emergency treatment. I remember the start of the journey very well. They took a shortcut across the airfield and raced down the perimeter while dodging dozens of startled rabbits.

On the first morning our flight sergeant, 'flight', woke us long before reveille. Every morning we had to prepare our billet for officer's inspection and many of us still had to be taught the ropes. The older cadets who had been troublemakers the night before changed character. They helped to make our bed-packs and showed us how to lay-out our kit for inspection. First each blanket and sheet was folded to an exact size with a smooth edge to the front. Then a sandwich was made of blanket, sheet, blanket, sheet and blanket. Finally, the complete sandwich was wrapped in an outer blanket to form a pack with no loose ends visible from any direction. It reminded me of a television set with lines running across the screen. Even the colour of the different blankets was co-ordinated with the darkest one in the centre of the sandwich. A further blanket was draped over the bed and tucked under the mattress with precise hospital corners. The bed pack was placed carefully at the head of the bed and the pillow smoothed squarely across the top.

This was a two-man job and took us almost an hour to complete. When the beds were finally made-up to 'flight's' inspection, the beds and bed packs were all placed perfectly in line with each other. Each of us was then allocated an additional job. The ablutions had to be cleaned, the floors polished, the tops of the cupboards dusted and our personal kit prepared for inspection.

Finally, after two hours we were ordered to stand by our beds for inspection. The 'officer of the day' stopped by the entrance door and ran his finger across the top sill of the doorway. It was the only speck of dust he found. His deliberate frown flinched when he saw the presentation of our beds and bed packs. We knew how to wreck billets, but we also knew how to clean them up. At the end of the week we won the best billet award!

Despite the initiations, the reckless billet fights and all of the early morning bull, I thoroughly enjoyed my week's camp. I excelled on the firing range. The 303 Lee Enfield rifles that we used were standard issue in 1958. They had a kick like a mule and their bark was deafening. When we took our turn at the butts we stuffed toilet paper into our ears and pushed our berets under our tunic shoulder. At the end of shooting practice our ears were filled with a load ringing noise and our shoulders were badly bruised. The top end of my hearing spectrum is now impaired; no doubt a result of my visits to the firing range.

The station commander was Group Captain Johnnie Johnson, the highest scoring British fighter pilot ace in the Second World War. He was credited with 38 confirmed kills against single-seat fighter aircraft. Each evening he could be seen wheeling in the sky above Cottesmore as he put his own private Spitfire through its paces. He permitted us to wander freely across most of the station and it soon became obvious, even to us young cadets, that something was amiss. Our suspicions were confirmed when several huge transporters arrived late one night. Each was loaded with a new tailplanes section for the Victor V-bombers. The cold war was entering a dangerous period and Bomber Command was doing its best to ensure that the operational status of their aircraft was kept under wraps.

Other activities at the camp included practical instruction in the operation and use of a Martin Baker ejector seat and sea survival training with inflatable dinghies in the freezing cold open-air swimming pool at Oakham. Much of our training was focused upon survival and almost every annual camp included a day when we would be divided into small groups and dropped from a blacked-out truck in a remote part of the countryside with a map and compass.

I always enjoyed this exercise. We were never told our location and we had to find our way back to the station in time for our evening meal. Sometimes 'enemy troops' searched for us in RAF Landrovers with the intention of keeping us away from the country roads. This strategy never worked because in the '50's and '60's every farm vehicle or family car would stop and give a lift to someone in uniform. Finding out where we were and getting back on time was never a problem.

RAF Regiment, Catterick

Weapons' training was taken very seriously and we were often given an opportunity to train with different types of firearm. The bren gun was commonly used for airfield defence and I could strip and re-assemble a jammed unit in less than 19 seconds. The sten gun was also an interesting weapon to use. It was standard issue in the Malaya conflict and we trained with them in October 1958 while visiting the RAF Regiment at Catterick Camp. It has a short barrel which pulls upwards and to the right if not properly controlled. I remember a very young James Pullin who sprayed half a clip across the roof of a wooden building that stood near to the butts.

Those early days in the Air Training Corps passed by very quickly and I have few recollections of the early days when I was one of the younger brats. I suppose I was fortunate because there always seemed to be someone more susceptible to bullying than me. James Pullin was a very likeable and keen young lad with a red puffy face. He seemed to take the brunt of it and was often targeted by several of the squadron bullies. I remember that he took his initiation very badly, yet he joined the army and became a tough Red Cap.

I suppose the Air Cadets prepared him well for what he would have received during his early days at Colchester Barracks. His rough experiences would have given him the edge he needed over his fellow recruits. The last time I saw James he had just come out of hospital after being hit over the head with a bottle while making an arrest outside a pub in Nicosia.

I did have my unfortunate moments. On one such occasion I was waiting for role call outside our squadron headquarters in Whitehaven. Scaffolding was erected against the wall of a building adjacent to our parade ground and a long rope stretched from a pulley at the top. Heavy cadets wrapped their hands around one end of the rope and jumped from the scaffolding while lighter ones holding the other end were catapulted upwards to take their place. I offered to lower the last person to the ground but I could not hold him and the rope burned right through to the bones of my hand. It was one of the most painful things that I have experienced.

After I had suffered my uncomfortable horsehair tunic for three years the Air Training Corps changed its standard issue for all cadets from button-up tunic to battledress. Along with this they included a blue shirt, two detachable blue collars and a black tie. This was a mega-improvement in style and comfort. With this change the only distinguishing feature that separated us from regular air force personnel was our silver cap badge and shoulder flashes.

I enjoyed many memorable flights in post war aircraft and several of these aircraft have become famous vintages. In August 1961 I attended annual camp at RAF Colerne and flew in Hastings WJ343, one of the aircraft used to airlift supplies into the Gulf during the first Kuwait Crisis. Its fuselage was stripped to maximise payload and the remaining on-board equipment was still full of fine white sand.

On the same occasion I was taken across to RAF Lyneham where I was thrilled to fly circuits and bumps for two and a half hours in the world's first ever jet airliner; a DeHavilland Comet 670. I, along with several other cadets, were very willing passengers for a Transport Command pilot who was being upgraded. In the early '60's the DeHavilland Comet demonstrated Britain's technical dominance in the aviation industry. In the sky she was incredibly beautiful; her clean streamlined body had four Rolls Royce DeHavilland Ghost 50 turbojet engines nestled neatly into the root of her low swept-back wings. The Royal Air Force roundels proudly painted on her wings and fuselage added to the pride that I felt when I climbed up into her belly.

We flew circuit after circuit and on each we touched the tarmac for a few brief seconds before her four 'Ghosts' surged with seemingly unlimited power and thrust us back into the smooth contour of our small seats. She was an exciting mistress that must have been a thrill for her pilots to tame. She gave a massive rush of adrenaline every time she unleashed herself into the freedom of the sky where she was the unchallenged mistress of all that had gone before her.

RAF Kinloss, Coastal Command

In 1963 the squadron visited Royal Air Force Kinloss for annual camp; a Coastal Command station on the Murray Firth. I was considering a career as an Air Electronics Officer in the Royal Air Force, and because of this, I was selected to join an operational patrol over the North Sea. Our purpose was to seek out and shadow Russian nuclear submarines using highly secret sonar detection buoys. Our weaponry included a full compliment of very sophisticated sonar guided torpedoes which were normally stored in secure concrete dumps on the airfield.

While I was waiting in the 'Ready Room' three armourers prepared torpedoes for an aircraft taking off later in the day. Catastrophically one of the armourers triggered a timing device and three out of the fifteen torpedoes in the dump exploded. I understand that two of the armourers ran out of the dump and were killed by flying debris while a third hid behind a rack of 'safe' torpedoes and survived. I don't know how true this version of events is because the complete episode was immediately classified.

I remained blissfully unaware of the situation as pandemonium broke loose on the airfield and the station's Shackletons, including my intended aircraft, were scrambled to a safer location. Eventually an officer explained what had happened and I walked back across the airfield to my billet and waited for the remaining torpedoes to be destroyed. This dangerous operation was carried out by a Royal Naval Officer who was later awarded the George Cross for unspecified services.

It was two years before I had a second opportunity to fly in Shackletons. This time I did get airborne and our skipper flew a training flight in bad weather over the Scottish Highlands. I spent most of my time in the bomb aimer's turret. It was a strange feeling lying on my stomach in the nose of the aircraft with nothing but glass and open sky beneath me.

When I was 17 years old and already a sergeant, I was given the opportunity to take a gliding course at Royal Air Force Kirton-in-Linsey. Travelling down on the steam train with Jim Lowther, our warrant officer, I explained how frightened I was that I may not do very well. He said something that helped me then, and has continued to do so throughout the whole of my working life. He said, 'no matter how bad you think you will do, someone will always be worse'. It is a strange kind of statement and in many ways a negative one, but it helped me to believe that the focus of attention would not be on me.

As it turned out, I was the first to go solo. I soon found myself getting into trouble for being overconfident. I often skimmed over the main road and landed short on the airfield where I would be positioned for the next winch. It was an exhilarating experience to hurtle steeply into the sky on the end of a towrope. On one occasion the rope snapped and for a moment my heart stopped beating. However, there was plenty of space to land and I quickly put it back down on the airfield.

One of my friends had a similar experience and he pulled the stick back into his stomach; the exact opposite reaction to what is needed. The glider, a Kirby Mk3 Cadet, stalled and plunged towards the ground. We were all horrified and we thought that he would surely be killed. Thankfully the nose came back a few seconds before impact. Yes, someone was worse than me! However, I am sad to say that a student and instructor were killed in a similar set of circumstances a few years later.

The Royal Air Force did go to extreme lengths to protect, as far as possible, the safety of young air cadets. However, full and proper training does require a certain element of risk and accidents did occur. In the early '60's the DeHavilland Chipmunk became the basic trainer used by the Air Training Corps. It is a single prop, low wing; fixed undercarriage light aircraft with slide back canopy and two tandem seats, each with full pilot controls.

Cadets were strapped into a standard fighter pilot type parachute, which they sat on in the rear bucket seat of the aircraft. Most cadets wanted to do a series of aerobatics, and unfortunately, the original design of the Chipmunk permitted it to flat spin. Under this condition the pilot cannot always make a standard recovery from a stall condition. This happened during a routine air experience flight and the air cadet was too frightened to jump. The Royal Air Force pilot sitting in the front seat had no way of knowing if his order to bale out had been followed, and even if he did, there was nothing he could have done; it must have been very distressing for the pilot when he later found the young cadet still strapped in the wreckage of the plane.

I had a similar occasion when I was given the controls and asked to do a loop. The G-force in a loop is very high and I did not pull hard enough back on the stick. This caused the aircraft to stall at the top of the loop and it fell inverted for more than a thousand feet. I could only see the pilot's head in front of me, just above my instrument panel, and then I saw his hand take hold of the canopy release. I suspect he was about to call jump-jump-jump, but then the nose slowly started to fall. All Chipmunks have now been modified to prevent a flat stall condition and cadets are given parachute training before each and every air experience flight.

Flying days were always exciting ones. They depended upon the weather and most particularly upon the direction of the wind. The operations centre would not allow cadets to fly in a Chipmunk if the runway crosswind component was higher than 15 knots. It was always a terrible disappointment when we approached the hangers early in the morning, ready and eager to collect our parachutes and push the aircraft on to the apron, only to find a bright orange windsock billowing directly across the runway.

Whenever Chipmunk flying was possible, I would team up with one of the sergeants and spend my day strapping young cadets into the cockpit. It was always a race to see how fast we could turn a pilot around and get him back into the air. Six aircraft would normally be flying and one would land almost every ten minutes. Our routine was well rehearsed. First of all we ensured that we always had at least two cadets standing by and securely strapped into a bucket seat parachute. We rehearsed the jumping drill with each cadet and satisfied ourselves that he knew where to find the rip cord handle.

When each Chipmunk returned the pilot turned into wind and applied his brakes. The sergeant and I jumped onto the black running strips that marked the safe area at the root of each wing. We pulled the canopy back, released the returning cadet's harness and helped him safely out of the cockpit while the second cadet clambered onto the other wing and then climbed into the cockpit to take his place. After strapping him in and checking the safety pin on his parachute harness, we placed the headset over his head and tapped the pilot's helmet to signal that everything was ok before pushing the canopy forward. As we jumped down from the wing the pilot was already taxiing back towards the runway.

This all sounds very simple, but the sound of the engine made verbal communication impossible and the cold rush of wind from the propeller seemed to make everything much more urgent. It was important to follow a strict routine to ensure that we did not forget anything. It would not have been very helpful if a cadet had come out of his harness while inverted during an aerobatic manoeuvre.

Flight Sergeant

On 17th November 1961 I was promoted to flight sergeant. This promotion made me the most senior cadet in the squadron and with it came certain responsibilities. Bullying had long since been stamped out but the initiation ceremonies still continued. These were part of tradition and so I ensured that they were carried out in a far less degrading manner. One of the most memorable was when we were on a camp that had a large contingent of 'Waff's, more correctly known as the Women's Royal Air Force. One of the young lads being initiated had his bed placed outside in the drill square. He woke up rather embarrassed early in the morning when a squad of young women marched past. I am not so sure if the former initiation ceremonies were more humiliating, or this particular one. I think perhaps that both were very cruel in their own way.

Dave Buchanan and Bill Tucker were my two sergeants; together we built up a very good drill team. We bought boots, gaiters, webbing belts and peaked hats from the Army & Navy Stores and then whitened our gaiters, webbing belts and rifle slings with blanco. After regular drill we became as good as any drill team that the RAF Regiment could muster. We represented the squadron at several local events including the annual Mayors Parade, Battle of Britain Day and Remembrance Day church parade. I enjoyed exercising our right to march on the open road and often broke the drill team away from our parade ground and marched through the town. It gave me a strange sense of importance to be able to make the cars drive along slowly behind us as we made our way down Market Street and into the square.

The squadron grew in strength and soon there were so many recruits from my home village that Warrant Officer Jim Caruthers, better known as 'Taggart', collected us every parade night in the squadron truck. Taggart was a tough disciplinarian and he was often the target of unfair ribbing. He did a great deal for the Whitehaven Cadets and we could always rely upon him. He had a tough exterior but a very kind heart.

Other officers of the day included the Commanding Officer, Flight Lieutenant George Greaves, Flight Lieutenant Walker and Warrant Officer Ron Sumpton. There were many other officers and civilian instructors but these four individuals made the greatest contribution to my training in the Air Cadets and, indirectly, to my future career. Without them the pages that follow in this book might never have been written. The content would certainly have been very different.

In 1961 we relocated into Whitehaven Drill Hall, which we shared with the Territorial Army of the King's Own Border Regiment. The senior NCOs had seen active service in the Second World War, the Korean War or Aden, and they seemed to run the show. Their officers were never in evidence. I got on very well with their sergeant major; he was my father's age and he opened the sergeant's mess to me and my two sergeants. We often drank far more than we should have done and I remember giving him a lift home on the back of my Vespa scooter. We were both fairly heavy and the scooter struggled up Bransty Hill. When he lurched to the right I counterbalanced by lurching to the left. Somehow my old Vespa got us both home.

When I was nine years old my mother bought me a Diana air rifle and I quickly developed a sharp eye with a smooth pull to the trigger. It was no surprise to anyone when I qualified as a Royal Air Force marksman. I was only 13 years old and still underage when I fired my group of 303 rounds; all six of the group sat neatly under a sixpenny piece in the centre of the bull. After moving into the Drill Hall we began to hold shooting competitions with the Terriers and they placed bets on one of their own marksmen, confident that a youngster from the Air Cadets could not beat him. I always did, and the Cumberland and Westmoreland Wing awarded me a gold medal for my shooting.

The Terriers invited us to join them on a 3-day exercise on Winscale Moor. Several army trucks carried us late in the evening from Whitehaven to the exercise area. At regular intervals the trucks stopped and everyone piled out and trudged, weapons carried at the ready, in long columns on each side of the main coastal road. We were in full camouflage with nets draped over our faces and full back-packs; it must have looked like Normandy all over again. I have no idea what the locals thought as they drove slowly by.

The Terriers took up camp at an unknown location in a wood on the Moor, and the Air Training Corps occupied a woodworm riddled hut on a nearby hillside. We were designated 'the enemy' and over the next three days and two nights we had to defend our hillside against the Terriers. I set up two bren gun teams in high positions on both flanks and issued them with wooded blanks. I then gave fifteen blank rounds to each cadet for his 303 Lee Enfield rifle and a box of thunder-flashes to each of my senior NCOs. This was a formidable amount of firepower.

On the first night we probed gingerly around our outer perimeter. There were occasional bursts from our bren gun positions as nervous cadets fired at shadows, but there were no major incursions. Then, as the sun began to rise and long tree shadows were mortally wounded with warm golden spears of light, a long line of camouflaged figures emerged from the rising vapours of sweet early morning mist. A full frontal assault was forming. The Terriers formed three long lines and strode up our lower slopes as if they were fighting a battle in the American Civil War. I couldn't believe it; if we had been firing real bullets they would all have been dead before they reached the half way mark. They covered the last hundred yards in a mock bayonet charge and when they finally reached our positions they were so breathless that they could not even shout at us. I was not at all impressed!

On the second night, a hidden Terrier threw a thunderflash into the midst of a group of cadets who were clustered and lying in a hollow behind a barbed wire fence. The cadets had no warning and it exploded in their faces. The sudden unexpected white flash on a dark and very still evening caused temporary blindness and left them in a state of shock. I was furious! I ordered that the fight be taken to them and one of my sergeants led a large forage party in search of their camp. This was not part of the game plan. The patrol found the Terriers' rifles stacked in the centre of their camp with no one standing guard. They took the rifles and returned undetected to our position where I placed the rifles under lock and key in our wooden hut.

A short while later their sergeant major stormed into the hut. He was equally furious and demanded that we return the rifles immediately. I retorted that it was a military exercise and if they were foolish enough to lose their rifles, then it was their problem and not ours. His face puffed red with anger and he was forced to explain to us the serious disciplinary action that would be taken against any infantryman who lost his rifle; particularly at a time when the IRA was known to be acquiring arms. I read the riot act to him about their dangerous use of thunderflashes and then ordered the rifles to be returned. Our joint exercise with the Terriers seemed to cool down after this incident, which was a shame because I think everyone enjoyed this weekend of war games.

My apprenticeship at Sellafield and my studies at Workington College of Further Education were beginning to occupy much of my spare time. However, the Atomic Energy Authority encouraged my activities with the Air Training Corps, and I was always given special leave to attend annual camp or any other special training course. This dispensation was important to me because I worked a full 44-hour week and I was only entitled to 2 weeks' leave per year. Nevertheless, I still found that I could not take part in as many activities as I would have liked.

When I reached 18, the maximum age for a cadet, the Commanding Officer invited me to continue for a further three years as the squadron's Cadet Warrant Officer. This was a relatively new position and I felt very privileged to be offered this opportunity.

Chapter 4

Reaching for the Sky

Earning my pilots wings through a Royal Air Force Scholarship
A schoolboy's dream!

I had every intention of joining the Royal Air Force as an Air Electronics Officer and then, in my 19th year, my sights were elevated somewhat when I was encouraged to apply for a Royal Air Force flying scholarship. I never thought that I had a cat in hell's chance, but I decided to attend my 3-day aircrew selection process at Royal Air Force Biggin Hill. On arrival I was invited to stay in the Officers Mess which I found to be rather snobbish and upper class compared to the Sergeants Mess where I had always found tradition and hospitality to be so much in evidence.

I had not had a private education, nor had I attended a grammar school, and so I fully expected to have trouble with the written tests. This was not the case; they were very simple questions and many were of a practical nature. For example, one question showed a set of gear wheels in a sketch and I had to identify with an arrow the direction in which the final gear wheel was turning. The tests were obviously intended to measure speed of response to a mental question rather than to ascertain a person's individual depth of knowledge. It was impossible to answer all of the written questions in the time given but it was essential to answer as many as quickly and as accurately as possible.

All of the aptitude tests were practical exercises, and again, they were designed to test a person's reaction time. There were no computers or complex pieces of technical equipment. Most items were wooden blocks or simple mechanical devices. One test involved keeping a ball in the centre of a circle using a joy stick and foot pedals. Strangely, I found this very difficult because the mechanical apparatus used for this test had no co-ordination between the joystick and foot pedals. In a real aircraft they both work together to give the desired result. By the end of these tests more than half of the applicants had been eliminated and sent home.

The medical examination then followed. This was very tough and the doctors eliminated a further half of those still remaining. Most failures were due to eye problems, particularly astigmatism or colour blindness. Many of the applicants were not previously aware of these problems and they found it very hard to be sent home for a reason that was outside their control. I had always been overweight and I thought that this would surely be cause for me to join those that were already treading woefully towards the railway station. I was pleasantly surprised when the medical panel explained that I would lose my excess fat after a few weeks on the officer's induction course.

On the third and final day only a small handful of us remained. I was the only flying scholarship applicant remaining and the rest were college or university graduates undergoing normal selection procedures. When I was called for my final interview I was so terribly nervous. I must have impressed the panel because when I left that room I was already flying in the air and I didn't need any wings to carry me. I was the first cadet in the Cumberland & Westmoreland Wing ever to be awarded a flying scholarship!

On 1st July 1964 I reported in uniform to the civilian management of Carlisle Airport, an old Royal Air Force station at Crosby-on-Eden on the old Roman Road that follows Hadrian's Wall. The station was equipped with six Beagle Terriers and an old Auster, which had probably been used in earlier life as an army spotter plane. There were eight of us at the beginning of the course and we were billeted in two small rooms at the end of an old single storey building that was being used as the local flying club. A really nice guy, but who was obviously gay, was assigned to be our steward and in addition there was a live-in young couple who cooked and looked after the club. The clubhouse contained a briefing room, a lounge with bar, and a small dining room. It was a cosy place and, for some of us, this would be our home for the next month.

Regrettably we still had a long way to go before we earned our 'Wings', and not everyone would make it. The Royal Air Force still wanted to weed out those that were not quick-witted enough to fly fast-jets. We were required to go solo before logging ten hours of dual instruction. Compare this to the average time a person drives a car before being allowed to drive alone. In addition, under special dispensation with the Civil Aviation Authority, we were required to take our private pilots flying examination before attaining 30 hours' experience.

During the month that we were on the course, we also had to study and take written examinations in Aviation Law, Metrology, Navigation, Engines and Airframes. Failure to complete any of the flying targets within the required time resulted in immediate removal from the course. This was a very brutal and humiliating way to shatter a young person's future.

We had four civilian instructors; I was allocated to the best, Captain White. He was a rather large well-built person who flew Lancasters during the war. He was shot down over Germany and he still carried a limp caused by the injuries he received. He told me that the Germans did not give him very good medical treatment and he suffered a rather miserable time while he was incarcerated in different prisoner-of-war camps. During my flying course he overheard two cadets exchanging a few words in German. He was extremely upset and he rounded on them in a sudden venting of verbal fury.

Master, mags, mixture

There was no hanging around on this course. Early on Sunday morning we pushed Mike Zulu, more correctly known as G-ASMZ, out of her rather large wartime hanger and pre-flighted her. On this first occasion Captain White showed me how to carry out the pre-flight with a gruff warning that I would not be shown a second time and that in future I would be expected to have her on the apron ready to fly. I did a power check on the magnetos and then taxied slowly out to runway 25 where we held, turned into wind and carried out our take-off checks.

Three M's, three P's, three T's and the rest, was how I remembered my checks. Master, mags, mixture, petrol, pumps pitch, trim, throttle, throttle nut, gauges, controls, flaps, harness, hatches, lookout and then

'Crosby Tower, Mike Zulu, request take-off clearance'. The Controller replied giving us clearance and the runway wind conditions. I took up position at the end of the runway and then, to my horror, Captain White said 'take-off'.

I pushed the throttle wide open; the canvas rippled along the length of our high fragile looking wing, and then a few seconds later, I pushed the joystick forward to lift the tail wheel off the ground. As we surged forward the nose turned slowly towards the tall field of wheat rushing past on the right hand side of the runway. I pressed hard on the left rudder peddle until I thought the control wire would snap. Suddenly White shouted 'I have control'. He pressed the left foot brake peddle as hard as he could, and skidded Mike Zulu to a shuddering halt, leaving us pointed diagonally across the left hand side of the runway. We taxied back to the hard standing and he told me to go back to my billet and put on my plimsolls.

1943
My parent's wartime wedding

1948
It must be me

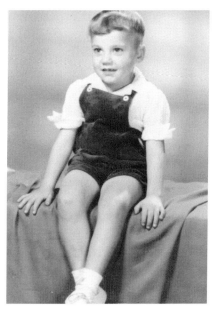

1956
And my brother Steven

1942
My mother in Royton
Ella Coulton, née Mather

1950
From left to right, Susan (Bob's mother), Sam, Bob, Connie, Iris and my grandparents, Sam and Sarah Coulton

1939
Dad with 603 City of Edinburgh Squadron, middle row 5th from right

1953
Stan Henderson, Reggie Gallagher, Dougie Hunter, me and Bob Bennett at Distington Junior School

1959
About to fly in a Royal Navy Sea Prince at Linton

1962
With Dad and Steven at Butlins, Filey

1963
Grenville Watch, Murray Firth Outward Bound Sea School, 3rd from left

1964
Pre-flighting Mike Zulu and going solo at Carlisle Airport

1963
1030 West Coast Squadron ATC at RAF Kinloss, front row 6th from right

1959
Building a PBK-20 canoe in my garden at Distington

1960
Receiving the Duke of Edinburgh's Bronze Award from Sir John Hunt in Mirehouse Youth Club, 2nd from left

Barry Coulton

The Equerry-in-Waiting to The Duke of Edinburgh is desired by His Royal Highness to invite you to attend the presentation of Awards to young people who have reached the Gold Standard in His Royal Highness's Award Scheme in Buckingham Palace at 2.30 p.m. on Wednesday, 12th December, 1962.

A reply is requested to
The Equerry-in-Waiting to The Duke of Edinburgh,
Buckingham Palace, S.W.1.

Dress: Lounge Suit
or Uniform.
Afternoon Dress.

1962
Outside Buckingham Palace before receiving the Duke of Edinburgh's Gold Award, Mr Pearce is on the right hand side

1956
Margie (Elliot) in her teens

1963
Margie paddling in Loweswater

1966
Margie and me getting into our taxi outside St Johns Church, Workington

1965
Receiving the Windscale Apprentices Cup at Sellafield

1975
Steven after receiving his PhD at Liverpool University

1968
Mam, Dad, Steven and Michele in Distington before I emigrated to Zambia

1968
Driving home to Beckermet after my last day at Sellafield

When I returned he explained the cause of ground loops in a tail dragger. A tail dragger is an aircraft with a tail wheel; when her tail swings she can get to a point where her centre of gravity causes the turn to tighten very quickly and she flips over onto her back. This happened to a student one month earlier; he was undeterred and went on to fly fast jets. Captain White explained that my thin-soled trainers would help me to get a feel for the rudder pedal pressure.

Half an hour later I was back at the end of the runway, and this time we lurched unsteadily into the sky. I juggled nervously with the joystick and pressed determinedly on the left rudder pedal to counter the strong propeller torque. As she climbed I was instructed in the correct aircraft attitude, the correct throttle position and the correct airspeed. All the time there was so much to take in and every moment there was something new to remember. I was learning by doing it the hard way. At no time did Captain White take the controls to show me how to do it. He allowed me to make mistakes and then corrected me. That is one of the good things about learning to fly. There is lot of airspace in which to make a mistake and plenty of time to correct any serious errors.

My first flying lesson lasted for one hour and when I stepped onto terra firma I became nervously aware of the fact that I had already burned one tenth of my dual instruction time. In the afternoon I did my first stalls and stall turns. I enjoyed these and I made rather fast recoveries with minimal loss of height. I eased the stick forward and used the power of the engine to hold her nose in suspension as a surge of much-needed air passed over the stalled wing surfaces. The normal procedure is to thrust the stick forward to achieve a nose down position before attempting recovery. This method sacrifices valuable height and this may not always be available. I felt that I was already beginning to get a better feel for the controls.

The real benefit of having an old wartime pilot now began to show. White was a real seat-of-the-pants flyer and on my third lesson he seized control seconds after lift off. He stood Mike Zulu on her wing tip and within two minutes he had Mike Zulu lined-up again with the runway. He called, 'Crosby Tower, Mike Zulu Finals', and gave me back control. He had broken every rule in the book, but this was not a normal air station and the rules were very bendable providing the right results were obtained.

After landing I opened up the throttle to make a 'touch and go'. As I lifted off I saw Alistair, one of my room-mates, flying downwind. He had taken-off five minutes earlier and climbed straight ahead to a circuit height of 800 feet. For every circuit that he was completing, I was making two. Alistair had a young instructor who flew and taught by the book. Learning to go solo is all about landing the aircraft. The less time that is wasted bumbling around the sky, the more time that is available to practise landing. That was my instructor's theory and he was right, I was already one third of the way through my dual time.

While on the ground I studied for my written examinations and mingled with the aircraft engineers and civilian pilots who housed their aircraft at the Crosby Flying Club. When I was not studying I visited the control tower and listened to radio communication with other cadets. I befriended a retired army major who had lived most of his life in India. He had just sold a chain-making factory in County Durham and was thinking about buying his own aircraft. He struggled with his navigation theory and I helped him while studying for my own examinations. He was twice my age and a multi-millionaire, but we got on very well together. I think this was because I never showed him any special favours and I made him do his own share of the picking and carrying. We had hoped to fly to India together, but we never got around to it.

Ten days into my course I returned to my billet and found Alistair in tears. Alistair had devoted the whole of his youth to becoming a pilot in the Royal Air Force. He had completed his ten hours of dual instruction and now he was packing his bags to go home. He was absolutely devastated; he had not made the grade and now he was being whisked away without being given a chance to say goodbye. This could have been me if I had been given his instructor.

Off you go

The following day, after receiving less than nine and a half hours of dual instruction, Captain White asked me to take him up for a round of circuit-and-bumps. For some reason he asked me to pre-flight Alpha Kilo. Mike Zulu had become an old trusted friend and it didn't seem right to be leaving her behind on the apron. After the second landing White asked me to pull across to the perimeter track. He climbed out and said, 'off you go'. He gave me no opportunity to develop a nervous reaction, I was expected to do one more circuit as if he was still sitting beside me. But he wasn't! And I could not help seeing a huge empty space in the small rickety seat beside me.

I took-off and climbed to 800 feet then turned through 180 degrees to join my downwind leg. When I finished my landing checks I found myself with nothing to do for a few minutes, and then my shakes developed. My whole body seemed to be suspended in mid-air. Somehow I didn't feel connected to the aircraft and I had to think very carefully about every action that I took. The tension and anxiety had taken away my feel for the aircraft and nothing came to me by way of instinct. I assumed that the Controller had been alerted and that he would be keeping other aircraft away from me. I told myself that all I had to do was to place Alpha Kilo on the end of runway 25 without bouncing, ballooning or entering into a belated groundloop. Not much really!

When I taxied in, my fellow cadets were waiting on the hard standing to congratulate me. I had been the first to go solo, and while I was excited, I was also disappointed that I had no friends or family present to share the occasion with me. I sat down in my billet that night and wrote to Marjorie and to my parents to tell them my exciting news. It was Monday 13th July 1964.

Weather prevented me from flying for a couple of days, and the next time I flew solo it was a much more normal event. I was told to practise stalls and steep turns in a quiet place that was north of the airfield. I enjoyed this although I felt a little strange doing stall turns by myself. My first couple of attempts did not really develop into a proper stall condition and it was some time before I gained sufficient confidence to carry out a full stall.

When I returned to Crosby a skydiver landed close to my runway forcing me to abort. On my second approach several parachutists had gathered around him and I was so nervous that I ballooned; then bumped ignominiously down the runway. I was furious and vent my wrath on the Controller. I told him to get the bloody idiots off the airfield.

The skydiver team shared our billet in the flying club for a few days.

Two of them were serving on US nuclear submarines and they flaunted bottles of whisky, rum, vodka, gin and bourbon. This collection of booze was definitely off limits to us cadets and I was reminded of my father's cigarette experience while working with American airmen at Royal Air Force Benson.

The following weekend the skydiving team was joined by a veteran paratrooper. His jumping equipment had been lost by BOAC en-route from Sydney and the other club members had loaned him what he needed for the weekend, including a main and emergency chute. As we lay in bed he told me stories of his wartime experiences. In particular, he told me of an occasion when he had cheated death. His chute had corkscrewed while parachuting into Belgium and he was fortunate to fall into a swamp. This was the last conversation I had with John.

The following morning he made his first jump. He fell for several thousand feet and then reached towards the ripcord handle on his borrowed chute. It was not where he expected it to be. He looked down for the handle and fell into what is known as a head down position. He tumbled and when his chute finally opened his legs caught in the lines and his canopy split wide open. John had no time left to deploy his emergency and he hit the ground with incredible force. John was a very lucky man twice over; he didn't break a single bone, but the intense trauma of falling to his apparent death destroyed his memory. I never saw John again and so I don't know if he regained his memory or if he ever tempted fate for a third time.

Two other cadets went solo over the next few days and I was almost as excited about their experience as I was about my own. After I had flown solo I found that I no longer suffered from the same intense pressure. As the days progressed I became accustomed to jumping into Mike Zulu and flying off to some remote area where I practised steep turns, stalls and emergency landings. I enjoyed spinning the aircraft. This gave me self-confidence and assured me that I could recover from any situation.

I had a favourite practice area over the Scottish border and I recall vividly how I would find my way back to the airfield when visibility was poor. I flew low over the open countryside in a southerly direction until I cut the river Eden and then I followed the river in an easterly direction until it made a dollar shaped bend. Runway 07 was then two minutes flying along a line slightly to the left of the direction indicated by the stroke through the dollar symbol. Not very scientific but I always found my way home.

Our small group stuck together and we enjoyed a strong feeling of camaraderie. In the evenings there was little to do on our otherwise deserted airfield. One evening we played a game of hide and seek in a wheat crop that covered the airfield. Our chief flying instructor was angry when he glimpsed an aerial view of the deep tunnels that burrowed through the wheat field. It was a very childish game but it helped to relieve our anxiety during those early days when we were under such intense pressure. I know there can be no real comparison, but like those young pilots in the early days of the Battle of Britain, we lived every single day as if it would be our last.

Crosby Airfield was no longer a Royal Air Force station and I believe ownership had been passed over to Carlisle City Council. During our course they decided to introduce a Dakota passenger service to Douglas in the Isle of Man. Commercial flights required baggage loaders and a manned fire engine had to be in attendance during take-offs and landings. Guess who became the baggage loaders and guess who manned the old open-cabin red fire engine? Yours truly and his fellow cadets! If the Civil Aviation Authority or IATA witnessed similar activities today the officers of Carlisle City Council would be thrown in jail and the key tossed away.

There was always too much baggage for the hold and so we stacked suitcases in an open space beside the main and only exit on the Dakota. Then when she was ready for departure we jumped onto the running board of the fire engine and waited with engine running until she cleared the end of the runway. The aircraft mechanic was the only regular amongst us who might have known how to operate the pumps.

Blackpool Tower this is Mike Zulu

After logging twenty five hours it was time for my first solo cross country. The route chosen for me was Carlisle, Royal Air Force Woodvale, Blackpool Airport and then back to Carlisle. My Air Ministry met forecast predicted 5/8 cloud with a 1,200 ft base covering high ground on my intended flight path through the Lake District; I decided to re-route along the coast.

I flew across my home at Distington in West Cumberland, dipping my wings and revving my engine in the hope that Mum and Dad and my old school friends would realise whom the crazy pilot was. A short while later I passed over Black Coombe where a Wellington had crashed in bad weather and then Barrow-in-Furness passed under my port wing. I could see a nuclear attack submarine being built in the shipyard and I smiled when I picked out the bridge that crossed over to Walney Island; Harry Secombe is said to have flown under this bridge when he was stationed on Walney during the war.

I felt incredibly lonely as I began to cross Morecambe Bay. I knew as a child how dangerous the currents and hidden quick sands could be. This was one place I didn't want to have an engine failure. I found myself listening to the tone of the engine and it seemed to miss a beat every second or so. Morecambe and then Blackpool passed by on my port side and then I changed direction and headed into Royal Air Force Woodvale. They were racing cars on the perimeter track and I was refused permission to land. I circled overhead to establish my presence and then set course to Blackpool.

It was Saturday 25th July 1964. It was not a good day for any pilot to fly into Blackpool, and definitely not a day for a young cadet on his first solo cross-country. I called 'Blackpool Tower this is Mike Zulu approaching from the south, request permission to join downwind'. I received a garbled response that contained more static than recognisable words. Radio communication was not mandatory in those days and so I followed the standard circuit joining procedure.

An airliner was already established ahead of me and I became even more concerned when two Super Constellations joined the circuit behind me. It was not a good sandwich to be in. Nevertheless, aviation law said that I had priority over those behind me and so I proceeded with my approach and landing. The two faster Constellations were forced to make a very wide circuit and they were not very happy.

On landing I took the very first exit from the runway and while taxiing towards the airport buildings I received my first readable message from the Tower; 'Mike Zulu; hold hold hold'. I slammed my brakes on and seconds later a Super Constellation touched down on the runway which I was about to cross. The tower had decided to bring it in on a different runway and my high wing prevented me from seeing its approach. This shook me to the core.

After securing Mike Zulu I walked into the terminal building and visited the shops. I bought a picture postcard of the other Blackpool Tower and wrote a brief message to my mother. 'Arrived in Blackpool but had considerable difficulty with the Tower'. I was careful not to drink any coffee because a Beagle Terrier does not have any facilities and I still had a long flight back to Crosby. Finally I recovered from my stressful experience landing at Blackpool and after taking a deep breath I decided that it was time to return to Crosby.

I had parked Mike Zulu on a stretch of grass in front of a fence that stood by the edge of the operational area. A café was located directly behind the fence and a group of young girls sat around one of the tables. I strutted in front of them in my smart blue uniform and proceeded to do my pre-flight, aware that their eyes were following my every move. I climbed into the cockpit, started the engine and opened the throttle. She didn't move and I was so terribly embarrassed. Aware of the backdraft hitting the girls and spoiling their tea, I climbed down and rocked the wheels until they were dislodged from the soft ground that they had sunk into. Eventually, instead of strutting like a proud lion, I scuttled away with my tail between my legs.

My return flight across the Lake District was uneventful and I enjoyed taking in the marvellous panoramic views. I looked down on places that I had frequented during my childhood and I was enthralled by the magnificence of it all. I thought about the year before when I had walked these fells with Marjorie and when I had dropped her into one of the lakes that I flew over. Wastwater, Ennerdale, Buttermere, Bassenthwaite; they all passed under my starboard wing, one by one.

It was late when I returned to Crosby and flying had ended for the day. The following morning I heard that Blackpool had lodged a complaint with our control tower. They said that it had been foolish to send a student pilot on his first cross country to such a busy airfield on a Saturday afternoon in mid-July, the height of the holiday season. I agreed entirely, I should not have been there and certainly not in a Beagle Terrier with a dickey radio.

I passed my written exams with more than 90 percent in most subjects and 98 percent in metrology. It then only remained for me to fly with the Chief Instructor, Captain Davico, and to take my final examination. Mike Zulu had almost become a part of me. Recovering from stalls and spins was now second nature and the routine climbing turns and steep turns that were part of the examination seemed to be irrelevant.

My only nervous moment was when Captain Davico throttled the engine back for a simulated forced landing. He did not order me to overshoot when I approached the field that I had chosen. For a moment I thought he was going to allow me to make a real forced landing and so I opened my throttle at the last moment. This left me a little unsure of the outcome of my test but he informed me on landing that I was now a fully qualified private pilot and that I had completed the scholarship. It was 26th July 1964, four days before my 20th Birthday.

I only had twenty-nine hours in my logbook. This was eleven hours under the legal minimum and still a full hour under the Civil Aviation Authority dispensation given for a Royal Air Force flying scholarship. To make up the difference Captain White told me to go and have some fun in the old Auster spotter plane that had stood idle since my arrival on the station. This was the first time that I had flown anything other than a Beagle Terrier. It had a large flap lever by my left hip and several small trimming levers above my head. It was like flying a real old vintage string bag and I really did enjoy myself.

Several weeks after I received my private pilot's licence from the Department of Civil Aviation, I took my driving test. I had received more than 60-hours dual instruction from my father over a period of several months, and I failed! I was able to fly an aeroplane but I was not permitted to drive a car. The examiner explained that I did not use my mirror enough. I suppose I should have explained that a Beagle Terrier had no rear view mirror and under the circumstances I should have been excused.

Dad was very nervous

My father was my first passenger. I took him for an aerial view of Distington and made several steep turns over our house. A steep turn is executed by applying full power and standing the aircraft on its wingtip. Balance, maximum rate turn and altitude are all maintained by pulling hard back on the stick. A substantial amount of G is pulled and it is a good manoeuvre to gain a full 360-degree view below the aircraft.

Dad was very nervous when I did these steep turns and he asked me not to do any more. It gave me a good feeling to be in control of the situation. For months Dad had been shouting at me while he taught me to drive and now he was in a situation where he had to sit back and enjoy the ride. There was absolutely nothing he could do, and he knew it. We flew over St Bees Head and took a distant look at the Isle of Man before flying across the Solway Firth to Kirkcudbright in Scotland. After following the Scottish coast for a while I headed back across the water and straight into a solid wall of low lying nimbo-stratus that had moved in behind me.

I reduced my altitude to 200 feet and for the first time I realised how difficult it was to judge my height when flying over water. The grey of the sea merged with the nimbo-stratus and heavy rain impinged on my windscreen to reduce my visibility even further. There was no horizon to help my orientation and with only 30 hours in my logbook I began to realise just how inexperienced I was. The rule-book said that I should turn back and land at an alternative airfield, but I knew that if I could find the river Eden and my tell-tale dollar sign, this would lead me to a safe landing on runway 07.

There was one very serious problem, my chart showed Royal Air Force Anthorn to be dead ahead and I was not certain if I was going to cut the coast north or south of the station. Anthorn was a top secret NATO communication facility that operated in the very low frequency spectrum. It had an array of wires held aloft by a large number of masts that towered several hundred feet into the air. I cannot recall the height of these masts but my aviation chart showed that I was below their height.

I circled back over the Solway Firth and called into Crosby to ask if they could get a fix on my exact position. My low altitude prevented communication and I received no response. What I did not know is that the control tower had received my call, and realising my proximity to Anthorn they had diverted a Royal Air Force Anson to look for me.

The Anson, apart from being flown by a more experienced pilot, was fully equipped to fly in these conditions. The pilot tried to make contact with me by radio but I never received even the slightest sound of noisy static. Dad was deathly quiet. He had been very verbal during our earlier steep turns, but he knew that our situation was serious and that he needed to allow me to focus on my navigation. After considering my options I decided to fly north until I knew that I was well clear of Anthorn, and then I turned back towards the coast. I made a safe landfall and found my river exactly where I thought it was. I found the dollar sign and the rest was straightforward.

After landing my father stooped down and kissed terra firma. He swore never to leave it again. Meanwhile, I was called to the control tower and scolded for not transmitting blind. The Controller explained that he had received my call and when he received no further communications he assumed the worst; he had called Royal Air Force Anthorn and asked if they had taken an aircraft impact.

I visited Crosby on several occasions that summer and on one occasion Captain White joined our lunch table. He was a very likeable person, even when I had been under extreme pressure to go solo. I was enjoying a plate of beans on toast and he stared at my food as if he had not eaten for days. He was not short of a penny or two and he certainly could afford to buy his own. Still, he persisted with his stare until I became so embarrassed that I pushed my plate to one side. He asked if I had finished and then grabbed my fork and wolfed my beans before I could reply.

Marjorie was at our table and she was astonished, but I knew Captain White; I knew what made him tick. Up there in the sky he was a damned good pilot who could still fly by the seat of his pants. On the ground he was never far removed from the reality of the German prisoner of war camp where he used whatever means he could to obtain a mouthful of food.

The local papers wrote about my exploits at Crosby, and Air

Commodore James Coward wrote to congratulate me. He invited me to take up a career with the Royal Air Force flying fast jets. I considered his invitation very carefully, but this was still too much for me to get to grips with. I was an ordinary village schoolboy who had never attended grammar school. I still had to complete my apprenticeship and I was frightened that I may not make the grade; then I would be left with nothing. I elected to complete my apprenticeship and then to reconsider his invitation.

Later in the month the Commanding Officer of Cumberland & Westmoreland Wing presented my wings at a parade in Whitehaven. I stitched them proudly onto the left breast of my uniform. My wings added to several other items of insignia. Each of my uniform sleeves carried the laurel leaves of a Warrant Officer. Above the leaves on my left arm was the insignia of the Duke of Edinburgh's Gold Award, and on my right arm, the crossed rifles of a Royal Air Force Marksman. I could easily have been taken for Idi Amin with so many badges decorating my uniform.

I finished my craft apprenticeship at Sellafield and then gave further consideration to my offer of a career in the Royal Air Force. Then the Atomic Energy Authority awarded me a scholarship to attend Liverpool Regional College of Technology. The old proverb, 'a bird in the hand is worth two in the bush', came to mind and I finally turned away from my opportunity to fly fast-jets.

Years later I discussed my situation with someone from aircrew selection. I told how I had been so frightened that only one in forty reached the end of the selection process. He explained that those who had completed a flying scholarship had effectively been through this selection scenario and that they almost always made the grade. In retrospect I might not have been as confident in my own ability as I should have been, or perhaps some would say that I used common sense and erred in favour of my long-term security. I will never know the answer to that question.

Chapter 5

I'm the Gaffer

Leading a skilled team at the Sellafield Atomic Energy Plant
Still a lot to learn!

Every morning as I walked through Liverpool from the ferry I walked past a travel agent who advertised holidays on the honeymoon island of Jersey. One day I dropped in and booked my own honeymoon for the last week of July and the first week of August. Marjorie and I had decided several months earlier that we would marry as soon as I had finished my examinations and we set the day of our wedding for 27th July 1966.

Marjorie and I were married in St John's Church, Workington. The day before the wedding we had a tremendous row about something that must have been totally unimportant. I have no recollection of what it was about. As I stormed from her parents' small terraced house in Carlton Road she threw her engagement ring after me. Marjorie had a fiery temper and it usually got the better of her. I mounted my scooter and rode away stopping only when my engine was out of earshot. I then walked back and retrieved the ring. I learned later that she and her mother spent hours looking for it and in the end they decided that it must have fallen down the storm drain.

Later, in the evening, I thought I had better make sure that I was not going to be left standing at the altar. So I dropped in to speak with her and make my peace. Marjorie had already retired and as she came down the staircase of her small cramped house her mother rushed from the lounge and told her to return to her room. Marjorie was wearing pyjamas and her mother thought that she should be properly attired. I thought this rather strange considering our impending marriage. In any event, it was obvious to me that Marjorie was very relieved that I had called by, and when I held her engagement ring up in the hall light I had to rush out of the front door before her mother hit me with the nearest heavy object.

The wedding itself appeared to go well and without incident. However, unbeknown to me and concealed from us both until after the honeymoon, my father had an accident directly outside the church. There were no off-road parking areas and the main road passed directly in front. When he stopped outside the church to pick up my mother he opened the passenger door for her and a passing motorist took the door straight off its hinges. It was the only car accident my father ever had in his whole life and under the circumstances we were fortunate that no one was hurt.

This was not the first incident to blight our big day. After a short reception we were driven to Carlisle where we boarded the Glasgow London Express. We were pulled by a famous steam locomotive whose name I have forgotten. What I can remember is the name of the hotel that we were booked into. It was the Cora Hotel; my travel agent had booked our room and paid our account several months earlier. He had told the management that we were a honeymoon couple and would arrive late in the evening.

We arrived absolutely shattered after a very long day. It was almost midnight on the 27th July 1966. I don't need to mention the significance of that date. The bloody desk staff had sold our room to the highest bidder and there was not a single hotel room to be found in London. A girl on reception left us to sit on our suitcases while she telephoned around and eventually she found a room for us. She gave me a small piece of paper with an address and brief directions. She made no effort to call a cab and she refused to refund the price of our room.

I had planned my spending money very carefully and these additional costs were not covered. Very despondent we tramped through the back streets of London carrying two very heavy suitcases. We were off the beaten track, no taxis passed by and it took almost an hour to find our lodgings. It was a dingy little terraced house that was so dilapidated that it had even been ignored by the world cup football fans. I could see the tears welling-up in Marjorie's tired eyes and so I threw our suitcases on the bed and said cheerfully, 'let's make the best of the situation; it will be something we shall never forget'.

We had not eaten since our reception twelve hours earlier and so we walked into Earls Court and found a restaurant that was still serving. It was 1 am; we bought a bottle of wine and enjoyed a candlelight meal as we started our first day together as man and wife.

The Cora Hotel never apologised nor repaid our money. Many years later I had cause to stay overnight in London and I made a point of staying in the same hotel. When I left in the morning I refused to settle my account and suggested that they called the police. Regretfully this did not help to repay those that profited from the sale of my hotel room but it gave me great personal satisfaction and enabled me to put this incident finally to rest.

Early in the morning we flew to Jersey where we lodged in a beautiful little guesthouse in Gorey. Gorey Castle stood guard high above this small fishing town and it really was a picture postcard setting. We soon forgot about our miserable start on the previous day. The other guests that shared our guesthouse were much older and we enjoyed many outings with them. One was the spitting image of Harry Worth whose series was currently running on TV. He even behaved in the same blundering manner and his smile was so convincing that I still suspect it may have been him booked under a bogus name.

On our second week we moved to another guesthouse, this time in the capital, St Helier. Our landlady told us that her guesthouse was previously the Gestapo Jersey Headquarters. She recalled how bloodstains were uncovered when her decorators stripped the wallpaper. I thought the story a little far-fetched and didn't really believe her. It was certainly not a story that I wanted to associate with our honeymoon setting.

Twenty five years later I joined my second wife, Anne, on a day trip to St Helier and we took a bus tour around the island. The island had changed substantially. It was much more commercialised and as we drove along the street where Marjorie and I had stayed so many years ago, the coach stopped to allow the passengers to take a photograph of the now famous Gestapo Headquarters!

A 'Heath Robinson' affair

Following my marriage and return to Sellafield, the housing officer arranged for me to move into a semi-detached council house in Thornhill. These particular council houses were reserved for Sellafield employees and I already knew many of our new neighbours. It was a beautiful location with the river Ehen passing through a meadow below our garden. When the salmon were running I would rise most mornings at 4 am and walk down to the river and cast fly over the shallows. I never caught a salmon but I did do very well with sea trout. It was strange beginning a normal day's work at Sellafield after spending three hours fly-fishing on the river.

Jos Thornley, the Chief Instrument Engineer, transferred me to the Pile Instrumentation Group. This was a rather isolated group, which was located in B3, the old administration building for the reactor pile that caught fire in 1957. I worked with Ken Young, the instrument engineer responsible for the measurement and control systems on an experimental reactor test rig. This rig was being constructed to test the feasibility of charging and discharging AGR reactors while on-line.

It was a direct copy of one channel in an AGR reactor. The test rig rose four floors above ground level and the equivalent of four floors deep into a pit. Two large gas compressors pumped carbon dioxide gas through the rig at exactly the same conditions as would be present in the real reactor when constructed. Our instrumentation was to control this process and in particular ensure that the compressors did not go into surge condition. This is extremely dangerous and can result in one of the huge compressors breaking from its mountings. I was very nervous when I commissioned these particular control loops.

The safety interlocks were a real 'Heath Robinson' affair. At that time, interlock systems on operational nuclear reactors were mechanical relays arranged in a two out of three system. I have described this type of system previously. As this was a test rig and not an operational reactor, it had been decided to introduce a new type of device called an Elliot Minilog. These Minilogs were the first of a new generation of semiconductor logic devices that used germanium transistors in a configuration known as an 'And' gate.

These gates were extremely vulnerable to electrical damage and one pin on each gate was connected directly to the 'base' of the germanium transistor. Whenever an instrument mechanic checked out the system with an Avo test meter he would accidentally touch one of these pins with the probe and blow the Minilog. I cut all the pins off with a pair of side cutters, but I don't think the safety interlock system ever worked correctly. Faulty interlocks were constantly short-circuited by our mechanics to enable the rig to operate.

The complete rig appeared to be a shambles and the very first fuel stringer lowered into the channel vibrated terribly and shattered into small pieces. It had taken almost two years to build the rig and it was badly damaged in only five minutes of operation. As it happened, the test was described as a huge success. It had identified a design flaw that would have cost millions of pounds to correct after the new generation of civil AGR reactors were constructed.

It was nine months before I was called to attend my Management Board at the production group headquarters in Risley, Lancashire. My previous Board, which awarded me a scholarship to Liverpool, had passed down instructions that I must get rid of my Cumberland accent. I had reluctantly worked on this but I was still aware that my remaining accent, which was still very strong, could stand in my way.

A couple of weeks later Jos Thornley called me to his office and handed me a letter which appointed me to the position of Engineer Grade E3. If I had failed then I would certainly have changed my career path and accepted my long-standing invitation to join the Royal Air Force and begin fast-jet training.

My appointment was to the Springfield Works near Preston. However, Jos Thornley needed a replacement for one of his Managers in the Separation Group. This group comprised the largest part of what is now known as British Nuclear Fuels. At the tender age of 22 years I suddenly found myself responsible for four foremen along with several teams of instrument technicians, mechanics and apprentices.

Many would expect these foremen to refuse instructions from such a young and inexperienced engineer. Not at all! I had worked under each of these foremen as a young apprentice and they were proud to have taken part in my training. They wanted me to succeed and they did everything they could to help me.

I was sensible enough to realise my limitations and I restricted myself to signing their leave applications and taking an occasional walk around the workshops. At no time did I try to force my authority upon them. I knew it would be asking for trouble and in any event the occasion never arose. Many of the skilled people working for me had served in the armed forces and had been commanded by officers even younger than me. They were not strangers to this type of situation.

While I carried the position of Shop Manager, my main task was to commission the measurement and control systems on the Head End Treatment Plant. This plant was being constructed in the carcass of the old B204 plutonium separation plant. Its purpose was to prepare stainless steel clad enriched uranium fuel rods for further processing in the more recently built B205 plutonium separation plant.

B204 had been built hastily at the end of the war to separate plutonium from the spent uranium that had been used in military reactors. The plant had been constructed behind five-feet thick concrete biological shielding. It was a maze of stainless steel pipes that linked together several tall stainless steel columns that reached through nine floors of this top-secret building. The stainless steel columns contained spent uranium fuel, nitric acid and a special liquid called 'Butex'. I will not elaborate upon the process but it can easily be understood that the level of radiation around this jungle of stainless steel was extremely high.

Over a long time period the radioactive contaminants were purged, and when safe, mechanics entered the area wearing protective equipment and remodelled the internal pipework to meet with the requirements of the new treatment process.

The old B204 process had proven so reliable over the years that it was decided to re-use the old instruments. This was not to save taxpayers' money; the Production Manager preferred to use trusted instruments that had given him years of reliable service. It was a time when new electronic equipment was being introduced in other sections of the plant. This new equipment used electronic valves and complex circuits containing electrostatic capacitors and wire-wound resistors which often failed.

To meet with his request, I removed the old instruments from their decrepit control panels, decontaminated them, and then sent them to the Central Instrument Workshops for rejuvenation. I don't use this word lightly; they really were very old. Manufacture of this type of instrument had long since ended, and while some spare parts were still held in stores, many had to be manufactured in our own workshops.

One of the most interesting control loops comprised a Kent Ring Balance, a Kent Mk20 pneumatic controller and two Wallace and Tiernan precision pressure gauges. These physical instruments were in effect an arrangement of linkages, springs, bellows, balancing arms and pivots which measured, recorded and controlled the interface between two highly radioactive liquids, Butex and Nitric Acid, in a 160ft high stainless steel column. The interface between these two liquids had to be controlled to within quarter of an inch and the specific gravity of each liquid measured. This was and still is a very demanding task, even in the 21st century!

A very novel technique was used which was very simple but classified as 'Top Secret' at the time of its implementation. Each impulse line was duplicated, one live to carry the purge-air and one static to carry the pressure signal. The purge air was regulated with a constant flow pneumercator and ninety percent of the pressure signal was backed-off with an additional fixed immersion dip-leg in a pot containing a non-evaporating liquid of known density.

This worked a treat and enabled a high degree of measuring accuracy while still working with otherwise low accuracy mechanical devices. There was one very serious drawback. The impulse tubes passed unimpeded from the radioactive area to the instrument panel. Any blowback from the active area, or even condensation, could result in the connected instruments in the safe-area becoming contaminated with radioactive liquid. Precautions were taken to ensure that most of the impulse tube had a continuous fall back into the active area. This could not always be achieved and even where a continuous fall was achieved no one could guarantee complete safety.

Two years after I travelled to Africa I heard on the news that there was a major incident on the Head End Treatment Plant. I understand that one of these tubes was unused and that it had been left open where it passed through the biological shield. A surge caused radioactive liquid to be released into the safe area and several workers were contaminated.

Seeking to increase my income

When I first started as a young apprentice I earned less than £3 for a 44-hour week while my friends earned good wages farming the land or digging for coal. They were able to buy expensive motorbikes and had plenty of spare time to enjoy themselves. My mother told me that my efforts would be worthwhile; I would learn a trade and earn a good salary when I received my papers.

I now had my papers and in addition I had been registered as a professionally qualified engineer. I was even the manager of one of the instrumentation departments that I served my time in. Yet I still earned less than £21 per week. It was understandable that my foremen were paid more than double this rate; their experience deserved it. However, I had friends who had served their apprenticeship alongside me. They were earning overtime and work-study related bonuses that also gave them much greater take home pay. Only the apprentices in my department earned less. Something was wrong!

My problem was that I was on a Civil Service age-related pay scale and I fell off the bottom of the scale. The scale gave no recognition for my apprenticeship and no provision for performance related bonuses. My management grade did not even permit compensation for the long hours of overtime that I worked. There seemed to be no way to improve my lot except to get older. Jos explained that in ten years I would almost certainly get a further promotion to Engineer Grade E2. My salary would then receive a substantial boost. I had heard this story somewhere before, about 9 years earlier.

I owed a tremendous debt to Len Pearce, Jos Thornley and dozens of other people who had helped me to get to my present position and I knew that there was far more to life than a good wage packet. However, I now had rent to pay and a wife and small baby to support. I desperately needed to increase my income.

I hit on a great idea that should help bring my cost of living down and at the same time provide a small amount of additional cash. I bought tinned food in bulk from a wholesale warehouse with the intention of selling it on to friends and family. Six months on I had not sold a single tin and I was beginning to get tired of eating tins of mandarin oranges for desert. That was the end of bright idea number one.

The next idea came from the Daily Express. The classifieds section included a small business advert for mushroom growing. The advertiser offered, at a fair price, the materials and the knowledge for commercial mushroom growing. In addition he guaranteed to purchase the total crop for onward sale in Covent Garden. I purchased what I needed and then set out to prepare the mushroom beds.

When the instructions came I was dismayed to find that the environmental conditions in my garden were not going to help the mushrooms germinate. I therefore made nine huge wooden trays and assembled them in the spare bedroom of my council house. Each tray was sized to fit the length of the bedroom exactly. I arranged them in three banks of three with a small space between each bank for access.

I bought several bails of best quality straw from a local farmer and layered the straw with quantities of chemical compost maker. Eventually I had built a huge haystack on a large groundsheet in my back garden. I watered the straw, surrounded it with plastic sheeting and then placed huge boulders on top of what I believed to be the most expensive and most hygienic compost heap in all of England.

After several weeks the straw converted into clean smelling very hot compost. I waited until the early hours and then carried this compost to my spare bedroom and layered it on waterproof plastic sheeting that I had fitted inside my wooden trays. In the morning my neighbours asked what had happened to my large heap of compost. I didn't dare tell them that it was now in my spare bedroom. I doubt they would have believed me anyhow, so I just explained that I had dug it into my potato patch.

I watered my mushroom beds carefully each day and controlled the room temperature very carefully. I even talked to the layers of compost but no mushrooms appeared. Finally I decided to give my trays of compost away: two trays to my father, two trays for my own garden and the remaining five trays to Jack Bibby and Ben Cook, fellow instrumentation engineers at Sellafield.

Three weeks later Ben launched a good-natured verbal attack upon me. He said that my compost was no good; huge mushrooms had uprooted his spring lettuce. I didn't believe him until Jack Bibby came in with the same story, and then a few days later I picked several perfectly formed mushrooms from my own garden, each weighing more than two pounds. I can only assume that the compost needed a little more fresh air than was available in my spare bedroom. My father collected mushrooms from his garden for years to come and I am still ribbed about my mushroom enterprise.

Being a young engineer in the Civil Service did have some perks. I qualified for first class rail travel warrants and enjoyed personal waitress service in the staff restaurant. I was even permitted to wear a white dustcoat instead of overalls. I always found the latter concession to be a rather comical measure of class distinction. Perhaps a good fairy had cast a spell and told the goblins that they should no longer contaminate me with radioactive particles because I was now a manager. The Housing Officer also asked me to move to a Manager's House in Seascale. I politely turned this offer down and stayed where I was in Thornhill.

This issue of class was very strong in the Civil Service. I came from a working class family and found it very difficult to deal with. One day while visiting B204 with my Group Engineer I helped a welder to carry his oxy-acetylene gas bottles into the elevator. It only took a few seconds, but as soon as we were out of earshot I was scolded and given strict instructions never to do this again.

Learning management skills the hard way

I had other problems with my senior management. I was considered to be a perfectionist. I called design engineers in Risley on more than one occasion and requested changes to their drawings. This slowed the construction phase of the Head End Treatment Plant and eventually I was called before the Works Instrument Engineer and formally requested to reduce my standards and to compromise wherever possible. Even worse than this, at the end of my first year I was called before the Works General Manager for my annual review. My report contained a 'Red Inker' which described me as being aggressive towards my seniors. This stunned me and so I decided to change my style.

I took a very low-key approach. I stayed for long periods in my office and avoided too much contact with my team. I read technical books and on more than one occasion counted the number of bricks in the wall outside my office window. I soon became bored and so I obtained a mechanical typewriter and taught myself to touch-type. My office was provided with a private change room that protected me from discovery while I thumped away on these huge mechanical levers.

At fixed times each morning and afternoon I toured the Head End Treatment Plant and asked if anyone had any problems and if there was anything that I could do to help them. Each second day I visited other areas of the plant and spent time talking with the Instrumentation Foremen on the different plants. I felt as if I was not doing anything constructive but slowly I noticed that everyone's attitude was changing towards me.

The General Manager was so impressed during my next review that he removed all references to the Red Inker. At the time I could not understand this strange accolade, I felt that I had contributed very little during the previous year. I was of course wrong. In reality I was beginning to learn the hard way how important it is to delegate responsibility. I was allowing my team to get on with their job, asking occasionally if they required my help rather than forcing myself upon them. This was a valuable lesson that was to set me up as a successful manager in years to come.

Every day I passed through my private change room, scrubbed my hands, scanned myself with a radiation monitor and then walked to the staff canteen where I joined Jos Thornley, Ben Cook, Jack Bibby, Ken Young and several other senior instrument engineers. In the beginning I felt overpowered because all of these people had been like gods to me when I was a young apprentice. This was the highlight of my long day and each day was becoming disturbingly repetitive. Our lunch breaks were far longer than would be considered reasonable and only Ken

Young ever demonstrated any kind of urgency to get back to work.

I did not like this style of working. I preferred to be heavily involved and the idea of walking around the plant with nothing more to hand but a small screw driver for tuning control loops and a pen to sign leave applications did not appeal to me. I was getting itchy feet and I wanted to see more of the world. I then decided that it was time to look for a new future with the promise of adventure in Central Africa.

Chapter 6

Africa Here We Come

The cradle of mankind, primitive and unforgiving
The silence of the bush is deafening!

It was early January 1969 and the air was crisp but not too cold as Stan Singleton and I drove out through the gates of Sellafield for the last time. Stan was a little more nostalgic than me. We had both started together as young apprentice instrument mechanics in July 1960 and he said that we must endeavour to keep in contact over the years to come. We both travelled in very difficult directions and regrettably have never kept that promise we made to each other.

I drove through fields flanked by wintry hedgerows on the small country road that would take me through Beckermet village where Michele was christened and then on to my small council house in Thornhill. I stopped when I had travelled about two miles from the security gates and took my first ever picture of the place that I had trained in for the past nine years; the largest and at that time, the most advanced nuclear engineering facility in the world.

Memories began to flood back, I looked at the AGR containment building where I was trapped as a young apprentice and the Windscale Piles with their unique top hats that saved West Cumberland during the reactor fire that became known as the Windscale Incident. I made certain that my photograph included the tall building known locally as B204: the first nuclear separation plant built in Europe and the plant which I had helped to convert into the Head End Treatment plant; my first assignment as a young civil servant with the proud title of Instrumentation Shop Manager, Separation Group.

A few days later I bade goodbye to my mother, father and brother Steven, all of whom I did not expect to see again for three years. Steven was now 16 years old and already a hardened veteran of the

Workington Grammar School rugby team. For the past four years he had been the drummer in a local pop group called the 'AC Experiment'. The group consisted of our somewhat distant relatives, Robin McNamara playing the lead guitar, Pat McNamara on the saxophone and Steven's two best friends from the Grammar School: Paul Sherwin strumming the base guitar and Peter Fagan who was the vocalist.

Steven met his future wife and my sister-in-law, Linda, in the Banklands Youth Club. I believe that Steven may have been playing in his group at the time. I met Linda very briefly outside Whitehaven Bus Station when I was travelling to Mirehouse for my Sundowner. I never saw Linda again until I returned from Zambia.

I made arrangements for Marjorie and Michele to follow me to Zambia as soon as I had established that it was safe for them. Every day the BBC reported major terrorist incursions across the Zambezi into Rhodesia. Kaunda was hosting several terrorist base camps and hundreds had been killed by Rhodesian troops in the past few weeks. All of this was happening only a hundred miles from where we would be living for the next three years and I was still wet behind the ears when it came to international travel. I was very apprehensive.

My flight was late in leaving Heathrow. BOAC invited me and my fellow passengers to the restaurant where we were served with an excellent five star meal while waiting to board the aircraft. It was the 8th February 1979. As I approached my departure point for a pre-midnight departure, a young lady stopped me and asked a series of questions from a preset questionnaire. The 'Brain Drain' was at its height and she wanted to know why I was leaving the UK.

I explained that I had served a 5-year indentured apprenticeship, been named in the newspapers as the best apprentice ever to be trained by the Sellafield Works, awarded a scholarship to attend Liverpool Regional College of Technology and promoted to a position which confirmed me to be the youngest engineering manager at Sellafield. I emphasized how extremely grateful I was to those people who had trained me and had placed me in the position where I was able to achieve so much. However, I had a young family to support and the reality of my situation in England was that my take-home pay was lower than most labourers and tradesmen of the day.

The Civil Service grading system did not reward personal achievement; my salary for the next eight years was to be determined by my age. I worked very long hours and in the same conditions as the tradesmen who worked under my guidance and yet they, rightly so, received overtime pay, work bonuses and allowances for working in a radioactive environment. I needed more; I needed to face a challenge and to be rewarded according to my efforts.

I knew that I was only one of many who suffered the same frustrations. Thousands of young engineers and scientists were voting with their feet and leaving the country, otherwise she would not have been in Terminal 3 asking these rather obvious questions. I did not tell her the real truth because I wanted to help those young engineers who were staying in Britain. The real truth was that I wanted adventure. I wanted to travel and to work in unusual places - places that I had read about in my geography lessons. I wanted to visit Kenya, Tanganyika, Rhodesia, Nyasaland, Bechuanaland, previously the British Colonies and Protectorates of East and Central Africa. The Anglo American Corporation was about to give me this opportunity and Kenya was to be the first on my tick list.

My first African sunrise

I was not feeling very well, and when our VC10 landed in Paris to take on additional passengers, I thought my ears were going to explode. I spent an hour in the terminal wondering if I dare board flight EC 719 for my onward journey to Nairobi. I need not have worried; take off and climbing to altitude did not have the same painful effect. I was later to find from experience that it is only the increase in pressure on landing that is so painful.

The flight down to Nairobi was to be the first of many, but nothing can ever compare with the first time that you fly over Africa. It was very frightening as we dodged through the Inter Tropical Convergence Zone at 33,000 feet. Lightning was dancing in the clouds around us and occasionally the plane would plummet before being picked up again by a giant hand. At times it seemed as if the wings would break off, but the VC10 was a remarkable aircraft, and I had every confidence that it would see us safely to our destination.

In the early hours of the morning I had my first sighting of an African sunrise. It is something that words can never fully describe, and even now, decades after that first flight I still marvel at the colours and the freshness of it all. It truly was the beginning of a new day. The sun was quickly lifting above the horizon and yet the ground below was still in darkness. Suddenly the rays of the sun could be seen rushing across the flat sand-coloured landscape. Mount Kenya with its snow topped peak could be seen on the distant horizon. Then the engines became a whisper and the nose dipped as the Captain came on the speaker system and informed us that we would soon be landing at Jomo Kenyata Airport in Nairobi.

On finals we passed over the Nairobi National Park and I had my first sight of Wildebeest and Springbok as they raced in different directions, frightened by the sound of our four Rolls Royce engines. There was a gentle bump as the plane settled down on the runway and soon after I walked down the gangway and stepped onto the warm tarmac; I was in Africa! Unfortunately my enjoyment was dampened by the stinging pain that I felt in my eardrums. There was something seriously wrong with me and I had so many things that I wanted to do.

It did not take long to clear immigration and customs. The airport building was basic yet very efficient and the airport officials were courteous. Jomo Kenyata ruled with the strength of a traditional African Chief and in these early days of independence there were no signs of the corruption and inherent disorganisation that would come in later years. But I will leave this part of my story to tell at the correct time, a time which even now can be described as recent history.

I took a bus into town and found the Stanley Hotel. It still had its famous thorn tree outside, but the rooms were far too expensive. I enquired at several other well known colonial hotels in the area but found them well outside my budget. I am afraid the American tourists reigned supreme. I could not afford a taxi and so I picked up my suitcase and walked out of town along a modern highway flanked with splendid flamboyant trees. I trod on Kikuyu grass for the first time and as I felt its strong spring under my feet I marvelled at the beauty of it all.

Noel Coward may comment upon mad dogs and Englishmen, but I was stepping on a new continent for the first time and I did not care.

However, after two hours I began to wilt and my large suitcase, which was packed in preparation for a new life in Africa, was getting heavier by the second. After all, it was midday and I was almost stepping on the equator. Then I came across a small cluster of buildings that lay in the shadow of several shade trees; The Equator Inn, and yes, they had a single room vacant at a price that I could afford.

I quickly changed out of my sweat soaked clothes, had a shower and then joined two Kenyans on the stoop for a freshly squeezed glass of cold papaya juice. In Africa it is so easy to make friends, no one sits on ceremony and a stranger, particularly one on his own, is soon brought into the conversation. One of my new found friends was an ex-colonial from England who chose to take a Kenyan passport on independence and the other was his partner, a young and very beautiful girl of Indian origin. It was my first day in Africa and I was already beginning to learn of the different cultures. I detected overtones in our conversation and I began to realize that not everything was as simple and straight forward as it first seemed. This was not England and the different ethnic groups were widely separated by race, religion, culture and most of all, politics.

Terrible though it may sound, as the days progressed, I began to remain within my own ethnic group and I learned not to discuss politics under any circumstance whatsoever. If you were an expatriate or ex-colonial, it was definitely bad taboo if one became too friendly with the natives. Many American tourists found this out when they were expertly fleeced by young boys who always had a sorry tale to tell. I remember a young Kikuyu trying to convince me that he was Maasai. He said that the government would not allow him to enter school because he could not afford the fees. I suppose an American tourist would have been taken in by this type of story, but you have to be pretty naive not to recognise a true Maasai.

It must be remembered that this is a time when most of Africa was just beginning to emerge from colonial rule, and indeed, several countries still had not gained their full independence. I was respectfully referred to as 'Bwana' by the Kikuyu and 'Effendi' by the Arab traders. I am rather sad to say that 'Whites' referred to them as 'Kaffirs' and 'Wogs', names they hated, and yet the origin of these names is not offensive. It is only later that their meanings and usage was twisted by a different generation of people. Take for example 'Kaffir', a name despised by all blacks. It was introduced into East and Central Africa by Arab slave traders. It describes people who are non-believers in the Koran and has nothing to do with skin colour.

Another terribly misunderstood word is 'Bantu' in South Africa. The name comes from the tribal heritage of the Zulu, Xhosa, Matabele and Shona. It means 'those people that came after the Untu'; in Zulu this is shortened to the Ba-untu. Everyone believes Bantu is a name invented by the apartheid government of South Africa.

Wog I am sure everyone will recognise as the name given by early British soldiers to describe Worthy Oriental Gentlemen, referring to the traders who bartered their goods in the bazaars of Cairo and the Middle East. Perhaps the latter does have a touch of colonialism, but it is still sad that these names have now become so terribly misused.

My new found friends were obviously nervous because they were breaking one of the unwritten rules, one which I had still not become aware of. They were partners and they came from different cultures. In England this would not have mattered, but this was Kenya! I warmed to them, they were very happy. It is many years ago and I cannot remember their names but I will always remember the conversations that we enjoyed together.

I remember that they urged me to take a freighter from Mombasa to the Seychelles where life was very simple and idyllic. He told me about all the beautiful native girls that far outnumbered the men. About the beautiful white coral sand beaches with tall palm trees and little thatched cottages which could be rented for a few rupees. I was only twenty four years old and this all sounded very exciting to me. I promised him that I would make that journey one day. Sadly they built an international airport before I could fulfil that promise. It lost its appeal to me when it was invaded by western tourists with loud clothes, big cameras and even bigger wallets. I wonder if they have McDonalds, Burger King and Kentucky Fried Chicken yet.

As the day went on my condition worsened and during the night I was convinced that a snake was in my room. I lay frozen for several minutes before I finally forced myself to switch the light on and satisfied myself that I was only having a terrible nightmare. I was covered in sweat and had difficulty getting back to sleep. I am terrified of snakes and this nightmare still revisits me from time to time. In the morning I was running a high temperature but I was determined not to miss out on my first safari.

This turned out to be a typical tourist journey into the local hills where we visited several villages and were entertained with traditional tribal dancing. Each was pre-arranged for rich camera-happy tourists but the dancing was spontaneous and big toothless smiles came from honest faces that had still not been corrupted by civilization. Hundreds of tribal dancers stomped in the dusty ground while others blew whistles and beat a steady rhythmic sound on long skin covered drums. Their attire, or in some cases lack of it, came straight out of a film set. I was witnessing scenes that had been common place in Africa for thousands of years, long before Rameses conquered the upper reaches of the Nile, long before Arab slave traders took their Kaffirs across to Zanzibar and long before the British donned pith helmets and added East Africa to Queen Victoria's Empire.

Here and there one could see the occasional headman. He would be wearing an old battered trilby and a pair of sunglasses to signify his importance. Some of the men wore tattered western clothing but all of the young women wore traditional dress and western modesty was definitely not part of their culture. I was invigorated by the raw excitement. The ferocity with which half naked warriors stabbed spears in the air made everything appear surreal.

Several young bare breasted girls in grass skirts offered bowls of warm sour coconut milk with slices of fruit and goats meat served on wooden plates. It would have been impolite, even an insult, not to accept their hospitality. It was all they had. There was no electricity to refrigerate the food and water had to be carried in gourds from a well several miles away. I eat a few slices of goat's meat and took one large gulp of the sour coconut milk. Seconds later I was racing for the privacy of a small wooded area where I was violently sick. I needed desperately to find a doctor.

The journey back into town seemed to take forever. I had a terrible headache, my stomach was retching and I had a very high pulse rate. The doctor was not able to do anything for me. He told me to stay in bed and he gave me several tablets to take. I think he suspected food poisoning. I stayed close to the Equator Inn for the next couple of days and then put on a brave face and boarded my onward flight to Zambia. I suffered a sharp persistent pain in my ears again as the plane descended from cruising altitude to land at Lusaka a few hours later.

Broken Hill, Zambia

I was met at the airport and driven up the Great North Road to Broken Hill which was about ninety miles distant. Along the way my driver explained the most basic rule of the road; if you accidentally hit a cyclist or run a pedestrian over, don't stop. Drive to the nearest police station and report the accident; even though this may be a hundred miles or so. Local justice can be very swift in Africa and if a child is involved then the driver would almost certainly be stoned to death. Stopping to take the injured person to hospital was impossible. A savage crowd would quickly emerge from the bush and such a crowd only wanted revenge.

We arrived at Broken Hill early in the evening and it was already dark. I was taken to the Elephants Head Hotel which was close to the old Ndaba Tree. This was a large and very old fig tree under which Bemba tribesmen would meet to discuss different issues. This is known as an Ndaba. Perhaps the local witchdoctor also told his stories under the same fig tree.

The hotel had seen better days and I was not very pleased with the room that I was shown into. There were holes in the mosquito netting and I was troubled through most of the night by the incessant high pitched whine as the little bastards came looking for fresh blood. They got plenty from me that night. I was not prepared for this ruthless vampire attack and I had no mosquito spray to use. I became very proficient in catching them in my hand. The secret is to leave one's fingers slightly apart while grabbing them. Air escapes more quickly from a closed hand and this rush of air allows the mosquito to escape. After catching the mosquito it is essential to crunch fingers and palm together to ensure that the mosquito is well and truly dead.

In the morning I joined a young Errol Flynn look-alike for breakfast. We compared notes, he had killed seven mosquitoes, and I had only killed five. Errol arrived two days before me and had already started his new job with Zambian Railways at their head office on the edge of downtown Broken Hill.

After breakfast I was taken to see the mine doctor who immediately placed me into quarantine. I had brought Hong Kong flue with me from England. Broken Hill already had a cholera epidemic and the symptoms are very similar to flue. The last thing the doctor wanted was a situation where he could not be certain of what he was treating. I retreated back to my horrible little room in the Elephants Head Hotel, this time armed with a large can of mosquito spray and a good book to read. I am pleased that I did not pass my Hong Kong flue on to anyone in Broken Hill because I understand that it killed thousands of people in Europe.

After five days of absolute boredom the doctor deemed it was safe to allow me a little more freedom. I moved to a small bungalow that stood alone in the bush to the north-western side of the lead and zinc mine which was contracted to be my place of work for the next three years. In Central Africa it always gets dark at around six-thirty to seven. I had very little to do in my bungalow after dark and I was very lonely. First I would listen to the crickets as they started their chorus early in the evening, then I listened to the high pitched click of Christmas beetles. A little later, when darkness was well established, frogs joined in. Frogs make a very strange noise at night and bull frogs would persist in making the loudest of noises and always right under my bedroom window.

The bush seems to be so empty and yet as darkness falls it will come to life with sounds that emanate from millions of small creatures. After a while, I became so used to this sound that it became a part of my subconscious and I found it very comforting. In months to come I was to find that the bush becomes deathly silent when there is something wrong. This could be a wild animal prowling or, much worse, a guerrilla fighter or a bandit up to no good.

I must have fallen asleep because in the early hours of the morning the whole bungalow began to shake. The shaking got stronger and stronger and then there was a strange rumbling sound. At first I thought it was an approaching earth tremor. I rushed to the window and right outside, only five metres away, a massive steam engine was rumbling by at a fast walking pace. It had a large water tender at the front with a cattle guard, a massive search light beaming down the narrow gauge track, a large log carrying tender to the rear of the driver's cabin and so many goods wagons that they trundled past for a full ten minutes. This was the Cape to Cairo railway that Cecil Rhodes dreamed about. I am afraid that it never extended beyond Ndola.

Broken Hill (now known as Kabwe) has been a focal point of events since the beginning of mankind. When Ian Smith declared UDI in the late 60's, Zambia, previously Northern Rhodesia, suddenly found its trade route through Southern Rhodesia and South Africa blocked by UN Sanctions. A new trucking industry quickly developed and thousands of lorries heavily laden with copper, lead and zinc bars began to make the perilous journey from Broken Hill to the seaport of Dar es Salaam in Tanzania. They had to follow a dirt road stretching 1,200 kilometres through inhospitable bush with no way-stations or villages in which to take respite. Those that managed to get through returned with petrol, potatoes, tinned food and electrical goods - everyday items that westerners take for granted.

Many lorries never completed this journey and they were left to rust by the side of the road. This route was known as the Hell Run. It joined the Great North Road at Kapiri Mposhi and from there the returning lorries drove north to the Copper Belt or South to Lusaka. The rear lights of these lorries were broken by stones and after dark many drivers did not see them. Cars often hurtled straight under their tailgates; roofs were ripped off and occupants decapitated. I had many close calls and my eyes were always red-raw when I arrived at my destination following a long night-time drive.

The Chinese built a railway line from Broken Hill to Dar es Salaam to help relieve the Hell Run. Unfortunately the Tanzanian authorities were not very cooperative and wagons often lay in sidings at the Dar terminal for months before beginning their journey to Zambia. Theft was rampant and perishable goods rotted. Eventually the wooden sleepers used by Chinese engineers were attacked by termites and the whole line sank into disrepair.

Broken Hill has an enormous amount of colonial history. Sir Roy Welensky worked in the Broken Hill railway workshops. A large man, he was heavy weight boxing champion of the Rhodesias. He started work at the very bottom as a steam locomotive fireman. He worked his way up to driver and then foreman, much the same as my father, except that he was then elected by his work colleagues to become one of the most powerful trade union officials in Central Africa. This eventually positioned him for high political office and he became the first Prime Minister of the now defunct Federation of Rhodesia and Nyasaland. Another famous name from the past is Doctor Livingstone. He died in a small native village, deep in the bush to the north west of Broken Hill.

Broken Hill however has a much older history, perhaps the oldest history known to humankind. Miners were tunnelling through a Kopje (a small hill) in 1906 when they intersected a limestone cave, which became known as the Broken Hill Cave. Fifteen years later, on 17th June 1921, a miner called Tom Zwiglaar found a perfectly preserved skull lying in the bottom of this cave. It had been concealed by several feet of sediment. This skull, which is known locally as 'Broken Hill Man' was eventually described as Homo Heidelbergensis, a species from which modern man is believed to have descended. Of almost equal importance were several shaped bone tools that were found near to the skull, the earliest on archaeological record. These tools have changed the view held by many scholars who had previously thought early man incapable of fashioning tools for his own use. Broken Hill Man is believed to be around 300,000 years old, possibly older.

Chapter 7

Broken Hill, Zambia

Working a lead and zinc mine that is as old as the country is new
Beware mambas!

My first day on the Mine was rather exciting. This was going to be a very different environment to Sellafield. Yet whom should I meet when I was introduced to the instrument technicians; Brian Oliver, an apprentice who had served his time at Sellafield one year before me. I slotted in well with my fellow expatriates and Cecil Armstrong, my Section Engineer, and his wife very quickly took me under their wing. Cecil was a terrific Rhodesian, very reserved and a really good person to work for. I, on the other hand, was ambitious and very impatient to impress. I still had a lot to learn but I was still too young to appreciate this.

The Chief Electrical Engineer was just about to go on long leave and Cecil arranged for me to look after his home for six weeks. It was a beautiful Northern Rhodesia home with several lemon trees heavy with fruit. I still have peaceful memories of those early days when I came home from the Mine and sat back in a bamboo chair while servants brought me cold glasses of freshly squeezed lemon juice laced with partly refined sugar from the local mills. For a young Cumbrian lad with hardly a penny in the world, this was heaven.

One afternoon after work I dropped into the Rugby Club for a drink. They were a good crowd and the new season was just beginning. Errol Flynn from the railways was propping up the bar and we both decided to join training on the following evening. I was very keen to do well and I tried my very best to keep up with the other players. The following morning I couldn't get out of my bed. Every muscle in my body had given up. The doctor declared me unfit for work and instructed me to take bed-rest for four days. I never believed that this kind of thing could happen but this was Central Africa. The ground was rock hard, the ball very fast and the altitude was 4000 feet. I trained regularly after that and soon my body hardened up and apart from the grass burns that covered my arms and legs I began to feel very fit.

Marjorie and Michele arrive

I soon decided that it was safe to bring Marjorie and Michele out to Zambia, and I wrote to her and asked if she would contact Charter Consolidated in London and make arrangements to crate our belongings, and have them shipped to Zambia. Marjorie arrived three months later and I stood in the centre of the arrivals hall, well back from the gate, and watched her walk through customs and straight past me. Michele was still only two years old and she clutched tightly to Marjorie's hand. I said 'hello' to Marjorie and she turned around thinking that I was her driver. Only after I spoke again did she realize who I was. I was in shorts, one stone lighter, very brown and sporting a strong reddish brown beard. When I tried to pick Michele up she became very frightened and cried out. We had a lot to talk about and I can well imagine how excited Marjorie must have been during these first few moments on African soil.

The housing officer relented, but only just a little. A few days before my family arrived he moved me away from my small cottage in the bush into an even smaller cottage in Jacaranda Street. On our first night Marjorie kept pressing a small button above our bed. We thought it must ring a bell somewhere, perhaps in the kitchen. The following morning we discovered that several of our neighbours had taken their guns and ran out into the street. They were confused because the person in difficulty had not used the agreed code to identify their home. They asked if we perhaps knew who it was and we both shrugged our shoulders in complete innocence; this certainly was a new kind of life!

We hired our first servant. He was a young lad and he obviously didn't have many wits about him because one morning I heard Michele screaming in the garden. I ran out and saw him pushing her on a makeshift tree swing. She was rising until she was higher than the tree branch that her ropes were tied to. I had to be very careful to allow the height of her swing to reduce slowly before I grabbed hold of her. Joseph did not last long after this frightening experience.

We were fortunate to be 'found' by Phil, an old medallah struggling to find work. He was old and thin but had a very honest face. He impressed us when he climbed to the top of our paw-paw tree and broke away some fruit for our lunch table. He used the soles of his feet against the tall thin tree as if he were a jungle ape. We started Phil as a gardener but after a short time he asked if he could do the housework and cooking. He explained that it was wrong for the Bwana's wife to be doing housework. Marjorie had been used to doing all of her own work in Cumberland and she was very reluctant to move into her new life style as an expatriate wife. It turned out that Phil had been employed as head housekeeper to the British Colonial Governor in Lusaka. We were very lucky the day that he came into our lives.

A short while later we were 'promoted' to Lobelia Street, which the Housing Manager considered more appropriate for a Senior Engineering Assistant. Cecil, a Section Engineer, was in Nerina Street which one will recognise as being much higher in the alphabet and therefore much more prestigious. Our new home in Lobelia Street had a red tin roof, painted concrete floors, several bedrooms containing army barrack style beds and a large open room surrounded by mosquito mesh. We had no air-conditioning or fans, but the rooms were surprisingly cool, and after a regular evening spray they were also mosquito free.

The garden was covered in kikuyu grass which Phil would cut with a long blunt slasher. At the back were several paw-paw trees, mango trees, banana trees and a solitary fig tree. There was also a small vegetable patch which never produced anything fit to put on the table. We liked our new home and were very happy there. As soon as we had settled in Marjorie enrolled for a Pitman's typing course at the local missionary convent. She learned a new skill and at the same time she made several new friends in the business community, all of them with the name Patel.

One day Cecil, Jacob and I drove out to Mulungushi Dam to check the recording instruments and to do some fishing. Mulungushi is not a very pleasant family posting. It is 70 kilometres into the bush and during the rainy season the dirt road is closed. During the last rains the wife of one of the engineers had her baby early and it was impossible to get a doctor through to her. All of our power was generated on hydroelectric generators downstream of the Dam. The water head was very small and the massive open rotors were made out of wood. They revolved at such a low speed that it was possible to see the individual copper windings.

Much of this equipment had been manufactured on-site or transported through the bush on makeshift wagons. I found an old steam traction engine lying in the bush midway between Broken Hill and Mulungushi. Perhaps this had been used to pull the wagons in preference to the more usual spans of oxen. I had trained as an apprentice on the advanced gas cooled reactor at Sellafield, the most advanced electrical power station in the world. Yet here I was servicing Kent Mark II flow recorders on what was possibly the oldest hydroelectric power station in the world. I was enthralled; I had not realized that such primitive technology still existed, and Mulungushi still supplies power to the Central African Grid today.

After quickly finishing our work we set about the more important task of fishing. Cecil caught a massive cat fish which put up a good fight. He gave it to old Jacob who would appreciate it far more than us. He cooked it and shared it out to his family in bowls of Nshima.

Their eyes and nostrils caked with dust

The staple diet of Zambians was Nshima and Kapenta. Nshima is mealy-meal pounded into a fine powder and mixed with water to make a very course type of porridge. Protein and flavour is provided by the addition of kapenta which is a small fish caught in Lake Victoria and then dried. Both ingredients are usually bought in two large sacks once a week immediately after payday. Money left over is then used by the men-folk to purchase chibuka in the beer halls. This is a very potent and lumpy beer often brewed illegally and almost lethal to any westerner foolish enough to try it.

Life on Broken Hill Mine was very laid back, but it could be very unhealthy, particularly for the native workers who were subjected to extremely bad working conditions. The underground workings were very cool but during one of my visits underground I was surprised when I was told that a huge underground lake was held back by the five metres of rock face that remained at the end of my tunnel. During the rainy season all of the high pressure water pumps had to be kept running to control water levels. On one occasion there was a water rush and the complete Mine was flooded in minutes.

On the mine surface half naked men, old before their time, toiled their whole working life, digging into large mounds of yellow coloured ore from the roasters; their nostrils and eyes caked in dust. I asked the bossboy why they would not wear dust masks or goggles. He just laughed and said that they didn't want to; they got in the way. I have no doubt that most would eventually die from pneumoconiosis.

Close to the roasters was a sulphuric acid plant which irritated my skin terribly. But in spite of these unhealthy conditions I have to admit that I never caught a cold. The germs could not survive in such a terrible atmosphere. The storage vessels along with several other sections of the plant were constructed entirely from African hardwood. Extremely heavy, it was harder than steel and very corrosion resistant.

The ISF was even more dreadful, and this was a place where I often worked. The Imperial Smelting Furnace melted down ore from the sinter plant to enable lead and zinc to be separated using a vapour process. One of the most hated jobs was to climb onto the furnace to change the chromite temperature wells that were immersed into the furnace. It was extremely hot and this job usually took several attempts. Strangely none of us were worried about the risk of lead poisoning even though several dogs in the surrounding area had died from it.

ISF workers always wore thick heavy boots. The idea was that it gave them time to escape the furnace area if there was molten metal runaway. I always wore sandals with loose fasteners. They tinkled as I walked and this warned the technicians in the workshop when I was approaching. They would call to each other, 'look-out, here comes twinkle toes'. I never learned about my nickname until my sundowner when I left the Mine 12 months later.

On one occasion, when I was driving down the dirt road past the instrument workshops I spotted a black mamba. I drove across it several times, each time putting my hand brake on to make the rear wheels skid over it. When I was certain it was dead I walked into the workshop and told everyone. They ran out to take a look and as they approached the mamba it reared up and lunged towards them. I reckon it takes a lot more than a car to kill a black mamba.

It was not the first time that I encountered a black mamba. A few months later I visited Lake Kariba with my family. Our friends from the Mine, Jim and Alan, were also with us. As we drove back to the border post on the Rhodesian side of the dam we saw a very large black mamba crossing the road from the direction of the lake. Black mambas are reported to move faster than a man on horseback and a bite can be fatal in less than thirty seconds. This may or may not be true but I had no intention of putting it to the test.

I stepped out of the car and Marjorie climbed behind the steering wheel. As I was taking a photograph of the snake I suddenly realized that it was attacking. It covered the first fifteen yards so quickly! I dived through the rear door and Jim slammed it shut as the snake lunged towards the window. We were terrified that the glass might break and so Marjorie drove away. Someone took a photograph of the snake lunging toward my window and gave me a print. It shows the tail of the mamba still in the bush on the opposite side of the road. We estimate that it was thirteen feet long.

I was not the only one to have these close encounters. When we were travelling up to Chibaluma to play in the rugby semi-finals, our bus ran over a python. We placed it into the luggage compartment at the rear of the coach and forgot about it until after the match. Several players had downed more pints than they could remember and they ran off to show some of the opposing team what we had brought with us. They opened the doors of the luggage compartment and were faced by this very large python with its jaws wide open, hissing and showing the most enormous set of teeth. My shell-shocked team-mates left the compartment doors open and allowed it to make its own way back into the bush.

This absolute fear of snakes that I have was shared by many of my friends, and one day I was in a meeting with Cecil and our foreman, Buster Klasse. Cecil put his hand into his desk drawer to take out a pen.

Suddenly he shouted and fell backwards on his chair; hitting his head hard against the wall. Cecil said there was a snake in the drawer, and so Buster took a stick and poked around inside, and a very large rat jumped out. It was the size of a small dog and very ferocious looking. Buster took his electrical pliers and got hold of it by the tail whereupon the rat ran up its own tail and tried to bite him. Buster dropped the rat and in seconds we were scrambling for the highest position we could find.

There is nothing worse than a cornered rat and this rather large one was, for the moment, living proof. Buster perched precariously on the filing cabinet while Cecil and I were on the table. Old Jacob came in to see what all the commotion was about and he was amused to observed three fully grown white men cowering from such a small rodent. He closed the door and returned a few seconds later with a large sledgehammer to rescue us. It was not so much the rat that really frightened us. It was the thought of all the different injections we would have to receive if we were bitten, in particular the rabies injections. These are given with a very long needle direct into the spleen for thirteen consecutive days.

Aye Zigi Zumba

These frequent visits to the copper belt where we played most of our away games of rugby were fraught with stupidity and danger. On one such occasion I was the only player who had not consumed large amounts of alcohol and I was nominated to drive the bus home. No one was concerned that the largest vehicle I had ever driven was a ford escort. I had a full team on board with their wives and children plus a small number of supporters.

We set off from Nchanga late at night and drove south down the great north road. This road cuts straight through the heart of the Zambian bush. It is badly maintained and occasionally it undulates where the tropical rains have taken away its foundations. There was never any warning and the bus would lurch up and down at speed with people bumping their heads on the roof. On more than one occasion I thought we were going to be thrown off the road.

When I had been driving for about two hours I was suddenly blinded by a searchlight. I knew what it was and I applied my brakes as hard as I could and came to a screeching stop. On each side machine gun nests were hidden in the bush, and behind were a dozen or so soldiers carrying AK-47 assault rifles. It was difficult to see them in the dark with their jet black hands and faces. They were betrayed by the whites of their eyes and their large white teeth which reflected with a blood red glow in the tail lights of the bus. Ahead of us were planks of nails which had been dragged crudely across the road.

I had already heard about these road blocks; many innocent people had misunderstood the soldiers manning the barriers for Congolese bandits. Newspapers often showed pictures of cars that had been raked by machine guns as they tried desperately to drive across the nails. The most recent person killed had been a young Englishman who had been teaching youngsters in Ndola.

I tried to behave like a real bus driver and stepped down from the coach to address the officer in charge. He was looking for Rhodesian infiltrators. There had been recent incursions by Rhodesian security forces. Several hundred of Mugabe's terrorists had been garrotted while they slept in their makeshift camps in the Zambezi Valley.

Then, to my horror, all of the players jumped out of the bus and formed a circle around the soldiers. They stooped and broke into Aye Zigi Zumba; a Zulu war dance adopted by our team, and they invited the soldiers to join in. I should mention that more than two thirds of the Broken Hill team were Rhodesian and South African origin. I was very worried that the soldiers would recognize their accents and make things difficult for us. Fortunately the soldiers found the dance amusing, realized everyone was drunk, and after a search of all of our kit we were waved on. Fortunately no one asked to see my driving licence.

Rugby was the focal point of my life in Zambia. I trained twice each week and played every Saturday. The ground was hard and the air thin. The game was very fast and visitors from the UK found it very difficult to play a full game. Grass burns were a serious problem; untreated they quickly turned sceptic. We had a very large Rhodesian player who answered to the name Jumbo. He could run reasonably fast and we would feed the ball to him as we approached the try-line. No one wanted to tackle him because of his enormous weight. He was our secret weapon but unfortunately he caused many injuries to our own players during practice games.

Jumbo was a great guy and he had the most charming and beautiful wife that anyone can imagine. All of our families supported us and the weekends were always a big social event. We entertained the visiting team and their families or they entertained us when we visited Lusaka or the Copper belt.

In Africa the strongest rules supreme

We found life to be very different to what we had been used to in England. We had to be so careful how we behaved with the local Bemba population, particularly in regard to politics. This was brought home to us when a small white child was reported to the ruling political party for drawing a moustache on a newspaper photograph of President Kenneth Kaunda. The family's houseboy reported the child and before the day was out, the complete family had been taken from their home and placed on a flight to England.

In every other African country south of the Sahara, without exception, the key jobs in government and the civil service are given to the ruling tribe. In Zambia it is the Bemba, while in South Africa, one may say that it is the White Tribe. The result remains the same, political decisions, control of the army and spending of the public purse remains within that tribe. I am sure that western Governments understand this, but their populations do not, particularly young students with strong socialist principles and 'do-gooders' who want to put the world to rights.

In Africa the strongest rules supreme and always will. Tribesmen vote according to their fears. They vote for those standing in the shadows with a Kalashnikov rifle and then the old colonial powers utter fake mutterings of surprise when brutal animals who call themselves 'freedom fighters' take office. In Africa it is what we expatriates call 'one man, one vote, one time'. This means that it will be the first and last time that the indigenous population will have a free vote.

In Zambia, while I rather like Kenneth Kaunda, his political party, the

United National Independence Party, has prevented any form of legal opposition and so it is only possible to vote for one party in the elections. It will be several generations before true democracy emerges. Britain, Portugal and France may have reluctantly given independence to their remaining colonies, but the greatest majority of new citizens belong to one of the several smaller tribes; rather than sharing in new opportunities they have everything of value taken away from them.

This is the path that Rhodesia followed after Britain, under the leadership of Harold Wilson, imposed a political solution that led inevitably to decades of poverty for its indigenous peoples. It almost made me sick to think that educated people could hold an ideology so high as to create a situation that would permit an animal like Mugabe, a terrorist of the worst possible kind, to seize control of such a beautiful and happy country.

Most people in Europe thought that Rhodesia followed a policy of apartheid. There was never any comparison between South Africa and Rhodesia. In Rhodesia the different ethnic groups enjoyed a harmonious relationship until insurgents controlled by Mugabe began to infiltrate into the farming communities. They killed black servants to strike terror into the native population and then they cut the throats of young white babies while they lay in their cots.

These insurgents were trained by the Russians to use sophisticated portable weapons and were successful in shooting down two turbo-prop passenger aircraft with shoulder-launched missiles. After shooting the aircraft down they hacked the survivors to death. Yet despite these horrors the white farmers still stood by their native workers; the farmers considered them to be part of their extended family.

I recall an incident in Trafalgar Square when some black Rhodesian students were being mistreated by local yobs. Two visiting white Rhodesians recognized the accent of the students and went to their aid. Their rather crude comment was, "they may be kaffirs, but they are our kaffirs". It is a strange relationship that exists between the different cultures in Rhodesia and one that should not be dismissed so quickly. It is a kind of mutual respect that is not enjoyed elsewhere in Africa.

On our first Christmas in Africa we drove down to Salisbury. It was a very memorable visit. The post boxes and telephone kiosks seemed so English, the streets were so clean and the policemen were courteous and helpful. Our hosts could not understand why Harold Wilson wanted to destroy all of this. We visited a large store and Michele had her photograph taken sitting on Santa's knee, and I bought my first safari suite. Then we bought all of our clothing for the coming year.

Rhodesia was under United Nations sanctions, at the request of Wilson, and so on our return to the Chirundu border post we stopped by the roadside and removed the wrappings from our new purchases. We rubbed dirt into the material, crumpled them up and then placed them into full view on the back seat.

We need not have worried because we passed into Zambia during a powerful tropical storm. Lightning was striking the ground all around us and the guards did not venture from the shelter of their small concrete building. We needed to refuel the car and I had to do everything by myself because the attendant refused to approach the pumps. With all the excitement and raw fear I forgot my passport. Later when the Immigration Officer mailed it to me he gently reminded me that he should be rewarded for his efforts.

The excitement did not end there. As we drove up the escarpment out of the Zambezi Valley I ploughed into deep water that covered the road. I suddenly realized that the car was floating, and I thought that we were going to be swept away. The only thing that I could do was to make the wheels spin. This gave us enough forward momentum to reach the other side.

This small flood saved our lives. When we crossed the crest of the next hill a flash of sheet-lightning revealed a wall of water surging across the road. Twenty more yards and we would certainly have been swept away. I reversed to the crest of the hill and we settled down to wait until morning. As the sun rose I climbed out of the car and looked down the road in both directions. There was no longer any water but I was very startled to see a very steep drop into the valley. We were lucky to have survived the storm.

Our first year in Zambia was full of excitement. Everything was so new and wondrous. It could also be very cruel. On one occasion Marjorie and I were visiting Cecil's home and while enjoying a braai, known as a barbeque in the West, we heard a high pitched piercing scream. Cecil found a praying mantis hanging by its legs from a bush. It was holding a small frog in its 'praying' hands and was eating it alive. We were all horrified and I killed the frog to stop its suffering. This was raw nature in its most brutal form. The frog was probably more than fifty times the body weight of the praying mantis.

When rugby was not in season we took every opportunity to take a long weekend out and travel somewhere different. Needless to say our first long trip was to Musy-o-Tunya, the Smoke that Thunders, better known to the rest of the world as Victoria Falls. It was a long drive and the last 100 kilometres was strip road. This is road that is only wide enough for one car. The distances are so great and the roads so straight that everyone drives at high speed. When two cars approach each other, they both move to the left, each keeping one pair of tyres on the tar road for stability. This type of manoeuvre soon develops into a game of chicken and there are many accidents.

Visiting Rhodesia was like a breath of fresh air

We drove through Livingstone late in the evening and were just in time to cross the Victoria Falls Bridge and clear immigration on the Rhodesian side before the border crossing closed for the night. The Rhodesian side was heavily fortified and the border guards were entrenched within large sandbagged fortifications. Mugabe's terrorists were encamped all along the Zambezi Valley and they had made several large incursions in recent months. We stayed in a small ranch style hotel on the edge of the rain forest which grows under the cloud of spray that billows up like thundering smoke from the falls, thereby giving rise to the tribal name of 'Musy-o-Tunya'.

Early in the evening we were joined at the bar by a group of young Rhodesian farmers who were doing their regular 6-week stint in the security forces. They were cheerful youngsters and were very eager to hear our stories of life in Zambia, while we were very interested to learn first hand what it was like to be a Rhodesian farmer when England and the rest of the world was against them. I took a short walk outside to listen to the noise of the bush. Everything felt so fresh this close to the falls, and then I heard a small almost deliberate cough. I turned around to see a young white soldier standing guard over a rifle stack. The rifles were standing with their butts in the dirt and their muzzles pointing upwards in the shape of a pyramid. Each rifle was loaded and ready for instant use.

Marjorie, Michele and I rose early in the morning and walked through the rain forest and down to the falls. We startled many different types of tropical bird which flew high into the trees as we passed by, and in turn, we were startled by two warthogs running suddenly across our path. The falls were spectacular, the rains had not arrived yet and so the cloud of spray, while very full, was not sufficient to spoil our view. Millions of tons of water cascaded over the rock precipice immediately opposite us, then fell slowly down into the deep gorge below.

Marjorie and I took it in turn to stand on a prominent piece of rock while we photographed each other. This rock jutted out over the falls and I found it very difficult not to be drawn over the edge into the billowing clouds of water spray which seemed to beckon me. The falls are about a mile long and it took us much of the morning to explore most of the Rhodesian side before returning back to our hotel.

In the late afternoon we drove along the bank of the Zambezi River and deep into the bush following a very narrow dirt track. The trees and the vegetation were very different to Broken Hill. Everything was so green and lush. We drove for an hour or so and were very excited to see our very first family of wild elephants. This can be nerve racking because a small saloon car does not give very much protection if the bull gets angry. They can thrust their huge tusks through the car window or even sit down on the car bonnet and crush it. Bush roads are never wide enough to do a three point turn and so I had been told that if I came across elephants in my path, then I should stay still and wait until they pass or if necessary reverse back down the road. They passed without incident.

Later, as it began to get dark, we were startled by a group of black soldiers who jumped out of the bush and blocked our path. They were camouflaged and heavily armed. We were very frightened and I didn't know if I should try to drive through them. We were on the Rhodesian side of the Zambezi and these looked like guerrillas. Fortunately they were not; they were the Rhodesian regular army. I had not realized until then that the greatest majority of soldiers in the Rhodesian army were Shona or Matabele, not white farmers.

Unlike Livingstone on the Zambian side, Victoria Falls only had a small number of lodges which blended perfectly into the environment. There were very few visitors to the area and it was not on any of the world's tourist agendas. Michele visited the local witchdoctor and posed for a memorable photograph, and then, after purchasing some local oil paintings and a large hide covered drum we set off to retrace our steps to Broken Hill.

Visiting Rhodesia was like a breath of fresh air after so many months working in Zambia. Everyone was getting a fair deal regardless of race, there was no repression, and it was possible to speak freely without the risk of imprisonment. The only restriction on blacks was that they were unable to vote. Smith's problem was not the colour of a person's skin but upon each voter's ability to understand what he or she was voting for. He maintained that the electorate had to be educated. True, most blacks were not very well educated, but they did have a better education than in any other central African country and they all had jobs and food in their belly. Most important of all; they were happy!

Chapter 8

Living on Half a Loaf of Bread

Starting my first company and it's on the Congo border
Where is that silver teaspoon!

While working at Broken Hill I soon realized the tremendous opportunities that existed in Zambia. Bush Africans still lived very much as they had lived for thousands of years, and yet the country was potentially very rich in mineral resources, farming and tourism. Urbanized Africans were beginning to assimilate several western trades, but they still did not have any real entrepreneurial skills. The country's mineral resources had long been exploited by Roan Consolidated Mines and the Anglo American Corporation.

President Kaunda ended this towards the end of 1969 when he declared that the underground wealth of Zambia belonged to the people of Zambia. Overnight the Government forcibly took control of all of the country's mines. The Government knew that they could not operate the mines without the support of Anglo American and Roan Consolidated, and so they were retained as management consultants.

When the Zambian government took control of the mines, the shares of Broken Hill fell overnight to around 6 pence. Alan, a very close friend in the accounts department, told me that the market had over-reacted. He explained that the 'fines' heaped in a large dump to the side of the old workings carried extractable silver that alone exceeded this stock valuation. Unfortunately I had no savings and I was unable to take opportunity of this piece of inside knowledge. Within 7 days the shares had increased forty fold to more than one pound.

Shortly after the mines were Zambianised, Cecil took three months overseas leave and I stood in as acting Section Engineer. I had discussed my plans with Cecil to start a small instrument engineering company and he was very keen to join me in equal partnership. As already mentioned, I had no disposable income and I visited Companies House in Lusaka to find out what I needed to do to form a company.

I wrote my own Memorandum and Articles of Association and registered my new company, Process Control Limited, for the price of the stamp duty. I then approached the Assistant Mine Manager and told him of my intentions. He agreed to release me from my contract providing I repaid all of my recruiting costs. These were substantial but he gave me time to make the payment. Armed with my release I visited Lusaka and secured a permit to work for Process Control Limited.

I was unable to leave my position as Acting Section Engineer until Cecil returned from leave. The Assistant Mine Manager had been very fair with me and I wanted to continue to offer my services to the Mine through Process Control. I therefore continued to work hard during the remaining part of my contract. Nevertheless, I used these three months to prepare my way forward. It was essential that I could fund the operation of Process Control Limited and still have sufficient cash left to feed my family. We were a long way from home and I had no safety net or means with which to purchase tickets back to England.

During my short period with Broken Hill I condemned several instruments that were beyond economical repair. I found that several of these were manufactured by Companies that did not have any representation in Zambia. In one notable case I condemned all eight electromechanical printers in the Assay Laboratory but the manufacturer of these printers, Addo-X, did not want to supply replacements because they could not provide technical support.

This gave me an idea which was later to change the future course of my life. I wrote to the Export Manager of Addo-X in Sweden and asked for permission to represent them in Zambia. On the same day I wrote to Honeywell in Fort Washington and asked if I could supply their products in Zambia.

I believe my background with the United Kingdom Atomic Energy Authority must have been impressive because they both came back very quickly and offered me full distribution rights. A month later parcels began to arrive containing technical information from manufacturing plants in the United States, Europe and Japan. I became overwhelmed by technical manuals and price books which had no relevance to the mining industry, but I did not care; my position in Zambia was now established with Honeywell, the largest instrumentation company in the world.

I was extremely pleased with myself, and when Cecil returned I told him the good news. He was stunned. He had spent his whole working life at Broken Hill and when push came to shove he was reluctant to take the plunge. Cecil suggested that he should stay with the Mine and use his position to channel work to me. I knew this was normal practice in the third world but it was not normal for me. I bought Cecil's shares and took full control of the company. Still only 25 years old, I was on my own in a new continent with a young family. I had no savings and I still had no work, but my optimism was boundless.

The managers and technicians at Broken Hill clubbed together and gave me 70 Kwacha to buy my own leaving present. I was pleasantly surprised; I had not expected to receive a gift after such a short time. Later in the day I emptied my post box. A scrawny ebony coloured man from the Congo was standing outside the Post Office trying to sell an elephant tusk. The tusk was solid and three feet long. It had been cut from the tip of an extremely large piece of ivory which was adorned with a near perfect carving of a young woman's face with beautifully sharp Nubian features. I added 20 Kwacha to my leaving present and bought what was to become one of my most valued possessions.

My colleagues gave me a tremendous Sundowner. We gathered at the Rugby Club following my last day at work and in true fashion everyone got rolling drunk. The favourite beverage was Lion Lager brewed by Lusaka Brewery which I had already targeted as a future customer! After the Rugby Club we moved to my home to consume large quantities of food that Marjorie had prepared for us. After washing this down with more lager we noticed that Brian Oliver had deserted us. Someone grabbed hold of the large drum that I had bought at Victoria Falls and we marched down Lobelia Street to Brian's home singing native songs to the sound of the beating drum.

Suddenly all hell broke loose. I was shot in the leg by a gas pellet gun and others were also hit and a fight broke out. Neighbours were startled by the commotion and one came running with a Smith and Wesson revolver. It seems that we had been a little too convincing with our tribal performance. The police eventually arrived at my home and even though they carried rifles they found it very difficult to quell the tempers of my colleagues who were extremely annoyed at Brian who had fired on them.

I bought half a loaf of bread

The following day I bought half a loaf of bread from the baker and with the money I had left I filled the tank of my car and drove to the copper belt. I visited Mufulira Copper Mine and secured my first order for several Honeywell Class 40 Temperature Recorders. This was followed a few days later by an order from Broken Hill to replace the Addo-X printers which I had previously condemned in the Assay Laboratory. Everything was going to plan.

While visiting Mufulira, the Instrumentation Section Engineer, John Beard, explained that they did not have sufficient skilled technicians to support a massive expansion programme recently initiated by their management. I immediately decided that Mufulira had to become my operational base. I rented a small house from the Mine and the following weekend we moved our worldly possessions to Mufulira and settled into a new and very dangerous lifestyle living only one kilometre from the troubled Congo border. This border like most in Africa had no guards, fences or natural boundaries. Incursions by heavily armed bandits were commonplace.

I took my first drive along this border following a tarred road to Ndola. I passed the place where the Secretary General of the United Nations was killed in a mysterious air crash a few years earlier. I saw smoke rising lazily towards the sky. The smoke came from the same charcoal burner's kilns that may have been mistaken as landing lights by the pilot as he returned with Dag Hammarskjöld from a brief visit to the war-torn Belgian Congo.

I stumbled across an old Sugar Refinery and they gave me a small contract to refurbish the control equipment on their steam boiler. The instruments on this boiler were electromechanical. They were extremely old, and I don't think the manager expected me to be able to repair them. The recorder was a Kent Mark II with a scissors mechanism. I had worked on these during my apprenticeship at Sellafield and I was soon able to make a new pair of scissors.

The manager was so impressed that he gave me an annual service contract. I explained my financial predicament and he persuaded his accounts department to reduce their normal terms from 30 to 7 days in return for a five percent discount. Fantastic, we only had to go hungry for seven more days.

Soon after this I began to receive regular payments for my work. I secured small refurbishment contracts for water treatment plants, steam boilers and town hall clocks. I repaired magnetometers used by diamond prospectors working for DeBeers Central Africa. There was no job too large or too small. Eventually I received my first big payment; it was for the Addo-X Printers. I used this to repay my recruitment costs to Broken Hill and with what was left I changed out my little white coloured Toyota Corona for a brand new Datsun Bakkie.

It had a long wheel base and was a beautiful turquoise blue. I made a large wooden toolbox and fitted it snugly into the back of the open truck. Finally a sign maker from Kitwe embossed two red and white triangular nameplates and I riveted these on to the side doors. I now felt that I was beginning to get somewhere and so I rented two large offices above a butcher shop in Mufulira and fitted them out to look the part. I also recruited my first employee; a young Bemba called Everest. He didn't know the difference between a spanner and a screwdriver, but he was very eager to learn.

One morning Michele, now three years old, was sitting on the doorstep of my office wearing a pretty pair of white sandals. She came running inside and told Marjorie that a lady had taken them off her feet and taken them away. I don't think she understood that they had been stolen, but nevertheless, that was the last time she wore shoes in Africa. This continued for many years and on one occasion I took her shopping in England and bought her a new pair of expensive shoes. When we arrived home, which was then in Midhurst, West Sussex, I noticed that she was barefoot and she could not remember where she had taken them off. We never found them.

We made several unusual friends in Mufulira. One was a Turkish Cypriot who I will call Altug. He was a bookie and he ran a tote on the Zambian horse racing circuit. One evening, when we were enjoying a glass of wine in his home, a top jockey visited and over a period of half an hour he and Altug fixed five out of the eight races taking place in Ndola that weekend.

They did this by asking three of the top jockeys to hold their horses back on selected races. Altug then pretended to cover bets placed on his tote by 'laying' them off with other bookies. He usually 'laid off' his bets on a third or fourth favourite that had good odds, but one that would almost certainly win when the top favourites were held back. He then divided his proceeds with those jockeys that were in on the scam.

I took note of the horses named for the day and placed small bets on each. I didn't really believe that they would come in but every one was a winner. Two years later the Wankie Coal Mine in Rhodesia had an underground fire. Several hundred miners were burned beyond recognition. Altug's name was among the dead. I know that Altug has never worked in a mine in his whole life; he was not the type. I am sure that the other bookies had discovered his deception and this was a futile attempt to cover his escape from retribution.

Marjorie, Michele and I travelled the Great North Road most weekends. I would work during the day on my different projects and Marjorie would drive our Datsun Bakkie through the night while Michele and I slept as best we could on the bench seat.

On one occasion as we were travelling to Lusaka in the early hours of the morning we pulled into a roadside bar cum hotel. I walked around the swimming pool to stretch my legs and found an African floating face down in the swimming pool. He was dressed in a dark suit and wearing a white shirt and tie. Very unusual for Zambia, even Kenneth Kaunda wore a safari suit for formal occasions. I decided not to become involved and so I quickly climbed back into our Bakkie and resumed our journey.

We moved into a large Indian-style house on the outskirts of Mufulira. It had huge rooms with lots of mosquito netting that covered the open walls of a large veranda at the front of the property. We parked our

Bakkie in front of the veranda and Laddie, Michele's Rhodesian Ridgeback, stood guard. Ridgebacks for some reason are very gentle with children and they never take any notice of white people, but they hate blacks; they are excellent guard dogs.

Late one afternoon I climbed into the Bakkie and reversed over Laddie; he had been sleeping behind one of the rear wheels and it passed over him. Laddie took it in his stride and several months later I found that he was blind in one eye. This may explain why he did not get out of my way; it certainly explains the reason why he always ran with his head pointing rather cutely to one side. We don't know how he became blind, it may have been a spitting cobra or it could have been caused by his mother who attacked him when he was only a few weeks old.

One morning I could not find my Bakkie. I looked to the side of my house, around the back, in the garage; I just could not believe what had happened. Bandits had crossed from the Congo and armed with machetes and machine guns they had raided every house in the street and loaded their plunder onto my truck.

This was not the first or the last time that one of my trucks was stolen by Congolese bandits. A few months later I gave chase to the border on a Honda 500 with Skip Wainwright, one of my employees and a motor-bike racing star. Fortunately we were unable to catch them; they had machine guns and we had pick axe handles. My Bakkie is probably still working as a native taxi in Elizabethville.

A rhino snorted in the tall elephant grass

Shortly after this incident I decided to take Marjorie and Michele for a holiday in the Luangwa Valley; tourists call this a 'safari'. We shared the long drive along dirt roads and our Bakkie ran short of water. We took a small detour and when Marjorie approached a native kraal to ask for a gourd of water the women gathered around her and rubbed their hands over her white skin. I don't think they had been close to a white woman before.

When we finally arrived at the Luangwa River Crossing it was already dark and the natives did not want to take us across on their raft.

Eventually they agreed and a guard grabbed his elephant gun and joined us on the dangerous drive through the bush to Luamfwa Camp.

On our first day we drove for several hours along dirt roads in a northerly direction, stopping at regular intervals to observe different wild animals or to allow families of elephant to pass in front of us. I was able to shoot a memorable scene of Michele with a little sun hat and wearing only a small pair of pants as she chased three very tall giraffe across a clearing. The giraffes seemed to lope gracefully with their necks swaying back and forth. After covering twenty yards or so they stopped and gazed back at this little white bundle no more than three feet tall as if to say 'come on, don't stop now, we want to race you'. The truth is that Michele was running across elephant tracks that were so deep that she may as well have been on an obstacle course.

I was always hunting for a good still photograph. I had a Praktica camera with a 40mm single reflex lens and a separate 300mm telephoto' lens. I remember one shot in particular; it was of a kudu bull standing proudly at the top of a termite hill with its head held high and its twisting horns reaching towards the sky. I have taken thousands of photographs of wild animals over the years but this is the one that I remember the most.

Perhaps the most dangerous photograph was one that I obtained later on the same day. Marjorie drove our Datsun Bakkie through the bush while I stood in the back, ducking below low tree branches that threatened to bludgeon me. I saw a movement in a clearing and jumped down to investigate. I grabbed my camera and told Marjorie to follow me with the truck.

I crossed the clearing and then to my horror a rhino snorted in the tall elephant grass. A few moments later I picked it out and in the same moment it caught my scent and turned towards me. I knew it would not see me if I stayed still and so I crouched and moved very slowly towards the relative safety of the truck, which should have been a few yards away. I was furious when I emerged from the grass and saw it 300 yards down the dirt track. Marjorie never did give me a logical explanation; I had very little money and so I don't think she was trying to get rid of me.

At noon we arrived in Lion Camp only to find it completely deserted.

The well was dry and no water could be found. This was not good news and we became very worried. We had no alternative but to drive further north until we reached the most northerly of the camps. Fortunately there was water available. After filling our water bottles and topping up the radiator we headed back to Luamfwa.

It was a very long drive and we had to cover the last twenty miles in complete darkness. This was extremely dangerous as we had no weapons and the aecia trees came right to the edge of the dirt road making it impossible to spot rhino, hippo or elephant until it was too late. We startled several elephants and were fortunate not to be charged.

The following night Marjorie and I went on a game drive with one of the Fundi. A Fundi is a native game guard authorised to carry an elephant gun. We followed a herd of around two hundred buffalo in an open Landrover. The Fundi switched our headlights off and used the moon to guide us through the bush. After half an hour he stopped and several young lions padded quietly past us. My hand was dangling down the side of our Landrover and I touched one of the lions before I realised that they were there. In all we counted about six young lions and eight lionesses; no adult lions joined the hunt. It was strange sitting motionless amongst this large group; fortunately they only had a taste for buffalo meat.

Suddenly the buffalo scented one of the lionesses that had deliberately circled to the far side. They stampeded in our direction, and as the huge terrified bellowing mass hurtled towards us several other lionesses turned them towards their leader, an old and much mangled lioness. She crouched in waiting ahead of the stampede until one of the buffalo passed close to her. She then pounced onto the poor animal's back, threw one of her paws around its huge shoulder, sunk her teeth into its neck and then used the buffalo's own weight to break its neck as it fell.

To make sure of her kill, the lioness quickly sunk her teeth into the muzzle of the buffalo to suffocate it, and then several young lions pounced victoriously onto the unfortunate beast and began to sink their teeth into its writhing carcass. It was a pitiful sight; an experience that I would not miss, but certainly one that I would not choose to repeat. I had been surprised by the ruthless agility of these lionesses and their enormous strength. Like all cats, they come to life in the dark hours and their agility should never be underestimated when found sleeping under a shade tree while the hot African sun is at its full height.

Digs discovered a large outcrop of emeralds

I had only been in Mufulira for a short time when a friend introduced me to a South African called Digs Pascoe. Digs once worked as an Instrument Engineer at Mufulira Copper Mine and during his spare time he prospected for minerals in the Northern Province. They had two beautiful children and his wife was incredibly tolerant because they spent weeks in the bush living in very difficult conditions.

Digs discovered a large outcrop of emeralds and he opened an emerald mine just before Kaunda Zambianised the mines. Digs registered his discovery but he was unable to develop it fully before police seized control and escorted him from the mine. The Government then paid compensation based upon the second hand value of his picks, shovels and wheelbarrows. They paid no compensation to cover his exploration costs or the cost of developing the mine. They did not even allow him to remove the stock of emeralds that he had already mined.

Digs needed somewhere to live and he needed a job to enable him to obtain a work permit so that he could remain in the country. I gave him both, and the following day Digs and his family moved in to share our very large Indian house. Shortly afterwards I noticed that our doors were held open by huge pieces of emerald bearing rock that Digs had taken from his mine. Each piece of rock carried tubes of at least forty emerald crystals. He spent hours chipping away at these rocks to remove hundreds of dark green crystals that he stored in old paper bags. He argued that no one would steal a worthless lump of rock that was used as a doorstop and he was proven to be right on more than one occasion.

He still had to get his uncut emeralds to Hong Kong where he could sell them to a cutting house. This was no problem to a person such as Digs; he bought his wife a very plain tight-fitting dress and then glued uncut emeralds all over the material until it sparkled like a cheap disco outfit. She then wore the dress for all to see as she boarded her flight from

Lusaka to Hong Kong for a holiday. It took Digs three such trips to externalise what he had retrieved from his emerald mine.

I often looked at the rocks and was tempted many times to chip a crystal out for myself, but this would have been a betrayal of trust. In later years I wished that I had asked Digs if I could keep a couple as a memento; knowing Digs he would have given me a complete rock and told me to chip away.

One thing that I like about my work as a control systems engineer is that I get to work on applications from gold mines to nuclear reactors and steam locomotives to jet aircraft. Every type of industrial application uses measurement and control instrumentation. I never have an opportunity to become bored.

One day I was watching a welder working high above a coal mill in Chilanga Cement, south of Lusaka. I had a contract to refurbish all of their measurement and control instrumentation. The molten metal from his welding rod was dropping onto a cable tray below him. Suddenly coal dust lying on the tray caught fire. I ran to collect a fire extinguisher and raised the alarm; not a single extinguisher in the factory worked. We even checked the extinguishers in the secretarial offices and they were also useless.

By the time the fire service arrived from Lusaka half of the factory had burned down. It was strange to watch such a small kindling flame grow within minutes into a raging inferno; we all felt so helpless. Cable trays routed the flames to different sections of the plant, and what surprised me most was the ferocity with which the cladding on the building burned. I had not realized before that galvanised sheeting was inflammable. I am now much more sensitive to the danger of uncontrolled fires and the importance of fire drills and regular equipment checks.

When I finished my contract at Chilanga the management asked me to enter into a maintenance contract to keep the measurement and control instrumentation in good working order. They were so keen to secure an agreement that they offered a very nice expatriate style home for my technician and his family. I accepted the contract and transferred Digs Pascoe to Chilanga. His wife was so thrilled, she loved the house and they became very popular in the local expatriate community.

Personally I found Chilanga to be a little more dangerous than most places in Zambia. It had a very high snake population which included the black mamba, gaboon viper and spitting cobra. They were often found inside wood piles in the garden and occasionally they entered someone's home; a resident snake catcher was on call 24 hours per day.

Digs loved to explore the bush and he took a mutual friend's children for a short outing in his Landrover. I remember how distressed my friends, Alan and June Bagnall, were when they did not return. Digs had driven deep into the bush in the direction of the Kafue National Park and his Landrover suffered two punctures. He was able to replace one wheel with the spare but the remaining puncture had to be repaired the hard way. An impossible task in the middle of the bush for any normal person; but Digs Pascoe is no normal person.

Digs removed the heavy duty tyre from its hub, repaired the inner-tube and then levered the tyre back into position. Fortunately he always carried a repair kit, full set of tools and a foot pump. He lost most of the skin from his hands but he got everyone home safely in the early hours of the following morning. If anyone has ever tried to remove a normal tyre from a car, without using special garage tools, then they will understand what Digs achieved.

No one escaped from the inclined shafts

One morning I was working in the Mufulira Municipal Water Works, when the bossboy came in and told me that I had a telephone call. It was John Beard. He told me to go home immediately and take care of my family. There had been a mud rush during the night and hundreds of miners were trapped. Ugly scenes were beginning to develop, and as often happens in these situations, the Whites were being blamed.

Mufulira Copper Mine was the second largest underground mine in the world. Two large yellow earth moving trucks can pass in the haulage ways and it is said that 3,000 workers are underground during the day shift. I don't know if this is true but the cage has three levels and 400 miners were carried in each drop.

There are several processes required to produce high grade copper. One of these is a flotation process that takes place in a plant known as the Concentrator. The waste from the concentrator is a very fine powder and this had been used over many years to fill in large areas of sinking ground above the old workings. Exceptionally heavy rains during the rainy season turned this powder into slurry which suddenly broke through a fissure into the old workings. As it gained momentum it picked up huge pieces of rock and surged with increasing force through the old levels.

At about 3 am what was then mud and rock under extreme pressure surged into the haulage ways at the 500 metre level. It passed along the haulage ways and into the three inclined shafts where most of the ore was being mined. No one escaped from the inclined shafts, but several miners were able to run along the haulage ways in the direction of the Peterson Shaft, which afforded them an alternative route to the surface. The thundering rushing sound in the hollow chambers below ground must have been terrifying to those knowing that there was no escape. Mercifully the rapidly increasing air pressure would surely have killed those at the work surface long before the mud reached them.

As the situation began to deteriorate, Kenneth Kaunda, better known as KK, arrived from Lusaka. KK may be the leader of a one party state, and I may not have agreed with his politics, but I did hold his leadership qualities in high regard. He thought on his feet which was a rare quality for an African leader. He said to the distressed and very angry relatives gathered around the mine shaft: "You blame the Whites, but I can only see white men going down the shaft to rescue your husbands and fathers. I don't see one black man brave enough to go with them". I cannot think of anyone that could have handled the situation better. The official death toll was 98 but the true figure was much higher, possibly several hundred.

As we were coming to terms with events Marjorie was horrified to learn that men were coming into town from villages all over Zambia. Tribal custom dictates that the inheritance of a dead person belongs to his brothers. These men were forcibly taking the cars, household possessions and savings of their dead brother's widow. They took her to the bank to cash-in her husband's lifetime savings and there was nothing anyone could do. She and her children retained nothing except the clothing they stood in. What absolutely stunned me is that a few months later when the mine paid widow's compensation, this was also seized by the dead miner's brothers.

This may seem terrible behaviour to those of us who were raised in a civilised society, but it is not as bad as it first appears. The eldest brother had to take his brother's wife and children into his home. She then became his second or third wife, depending upon how many he could afford. In Zambia a women had no real rights. She worked in the fields tending a few goats and chickens while her husband slept under a nearby baobab tree. But if she misbehaved and was killed by her husband then he would probably get away with a maximum of 6 months' imprisonment. If on the other hand he rustled some cows, then he was hung by the neck until dead. I think this gives a good impression of the value of women in African society.

Three weeks before the disaster I had been granted work permits for three technicians to join me from Sellafield. Unfortunately the Management of Mufulira Copper Mine declared 'Force Majeure' and all of my contracts were cancelled. My technicians had not submitted their notices and so I was able to stop them from coming to Zambia. I then had to ensure that my own family was safe and so I helped Marjorie to pack two suitcases and then placed her and Michele on an aeroplane back to England. She was very reluctant to leave but I promised that I would follow as soon as I had rescued something from the ashes and earned sufficient to make a fresh start.

I doubted that we would ever return to Africa and so I purchased two tickets with Zambian Airways which permitted stopovers in Nairobi, Mombasa and Athens. Marjorie and Michele had a fabulous time in Shelley Beach on the coast above Mombasa and did the normal tourist routine in Nairobi. But they never made it to Athens. Marjorie could not find her passport when they arrived at Jomo Kenyata Airport. Michele tearfully explained that she had tidied Mummy's handbag and placed it in the bedside drawer!

As soon as Marjorie and Michele left I began to cut my overheads. I moved out of the small mine house that we had enjoyed so much as a family and took lodgings with an old work colleague from Sellafield, Peter Fox. Peter worked at Nchanga Copper Mine in Kitwe. Phil came with me; he was now part of my extended family and I was determined not to let him go. He had travelled with me from Broken Hill to Mufulira and now on to Kitwe.

Unfortunately I had to take Laddie to the RSPA as Peter's wife did not like dogs. I paid the kennels sufficient money to ensure that they would keep him until they found a good home. This was a very sad time for me but I considered myself fortunate. So many families had been totally destroyed by the events of the past few weeks.

I was so desperate for work that I applied for six contracts in the hope that I would get one of them. I got them all. This was very difficult for me. I had stopped my technicians from coming to Zambia, and to make matters worse, the contracts were in diverse locations. I had secured orders for project work in the Ndola Copper Refinery, Broken Hill Lead and Zinc Mine and Lusaka Brewery. This was in addition to the small maintenance contracts that I already held in Mufulira and Ndola. I decided that, somehow, I was going to fulfil all of the orders.

I examined the time schedule for each project and gathered together all of my available resources, which was very little. The most labour intensive contract was to refurbish the instrumentation on the Roaster at Broken Hill. Cecil had awarded me this contract and I was pleased to have an opportunity to work with my old colleagues. I visited the labour pool in Kabwe and recruited my very first employees. They came straight from the bush and had absolutely no experience at all. They called me by the name 'Bwana Mkubwa'; which translated as Great White Chief. I suppose to them I was.

We clambered all over the Roaster fitting copper pipes, running conduit and installing new instruments. Our hair, nostrils and ears were caked with fine yellow dust. It burned our skins and itched beneath our overalls. My eyes were red raw. Everyone was very surprised that a white person could work in such terrible conditions. I began to look like the old Medallah that I described during my early days on the Mine. But I didn't care; as the old Yorkshire saying goes, 'where there's muck, there's money lad'. And I needed money!

We worked hard on the Roaster during the day and during the night I prepared for my other projects; making drawings and placing orders for equipment. Each weekend I drove to the Copperbelt and serviced my maintenance contracts in Ndola and Mufulira. I was so short of time that I always drove during the night so that I would be in position to start on-time at 7 am. In this way I was able to put in a full working day.

I had a contract with Lusaka Brewery to supply a large number of Honeywell Servotronic Controllers; it was lucrative and required very little time on site. On the other hand my work at Ndola Refinery required me to manufacture 26 electronic control units. I estimated the amount of time involved to build each unit and then I paid an engineer from Mufulira Mine to do this for me. It took 8 weeks to finish the last of my contracts and I was absolutely shattered. In the beginning I thought that my schedule would upset many of my customers. On the contrary, they were very pleased with the work that we had done and they recommended Process Control for further projects.

Chapter 9

A Tough and Dangerous Year

Working a 7-day week after the Mufulira mine disaster
I hope the lights don't go out!

I soon regretted my decision not to go ahead with the recruitment of my three instrument technicians. John Beard called me into Mufulira Mine and introduced me to Dave Agar, the Section Engineer responsible for new control system projects on the Mine. He was relatively fresh from University and was still wet behind the ears. He had not served a craft or student apprenticeship in control instrumentation but he was a good manager and he knew how to use the resources available to him.

Dave explained that the underground workings were to be re-opened and that the expansion programme was to go ahead after all. He offered me a small project on the concentrator which I gladly accepted. When I completed this he gave me another and then another. He quickly realized that I could take a project from initial design to final commissioning and handover. Not only was I able to design and commission new systems, but I could also do the welding, gas cutting, cable running and panel wiring. The training I had received in the Apprentice School at Sellafield was second to none.

Around the same time I was invited to join the Mufulira Round Table. I was immediately accepted into the local business community and I made several new friends. Our special project was to support a local leper colony. One bank holiday we organised a casino and pig-roast on makeshift benches in the middle of the African Bush. It was incredibly novel and very successful. All of our Round Table members wore a Tuxedo and served at the tables or worked one of the gambling tables. I purchased a brand new Tuxedo from Solanki's and worked a black-jack table. I still wear the same Tuxedo and have never replaced it or increased the length of its waistband; honest.

Everest was still with me. He travelled with me to all of my projects and he was very quick to learn. In only a few weeks he began to take control of individual tasks. I recruited several more locals and he passed his newly acquired skills on to them.

Very few Zambians, if any, had the skills necessary to install and commission control system equipment but they did have one very good quality. They wanted to learn, and if you were patient and taught them how to do a repetitive task such as cable running, then they would lay mile after mile without complaining; and the last one hundred yards would be laid with the same care and attention as the first one hundred. In my experience most Europeans are not able to do this; they become bored with repetitive tasks and the quality of their work soon deteriorates.

It was not long before Process Control was accepted as an extended arm of the Instrumentation Department at Mufulira Copper Mine and Dave brought in several other technicians and tradesmen to work alongside my team. I recruited two tradesmen, one from Austria and one from Wales, and poached a Rhodesian technician from a local contractor. These in addition to the local helpers that I trained soon became part of the instrumentation project department at Mufulira Copper Mine.

Dave Agar headed up the department and a newly arrived expatriate, John Owen-Ellis, became his second lieutenant. We were given a large warehouse behind the Copper Converters to use as a base and the Mine provided me and all of my employees with housing. We were allowed to use the Mine's facilities: the canteen which was excellent, the rugby club, football club, and flying club…. in fact, everything. It was as if we were mine employees but with much better salaries and with none of the formal red tape.

Mining engineers were working around the clock to re-open the underground workings. It was not a pleasant task and almost all of the workers were provided by Frazer Chalmers, a local mechanical engineering company that employed a large number of skilled expatriates. They installed specialist equipment which was used to open the haulage ways and the three inclined shafts. Millions of tons of mud and rock had to be removed. Bodies were often found encased in the mud and this served as a constant reminder to the danger they were exposed to; the danger of a new mud rush or a cave-in.

Following Zambianisation of the Mines, Roan Consolidated changed from being Owners to being Managers of the Mufulira Copper Mine. They were paid consulting and management fees, probably along with a percentage of the profits attained. It was now in their best interest to upgrade plant, improve extraction processes and, of course, to re-open the Mine. They also had several new ideas on the drawing board but no one in Europe or the United States wanted to be the guinea pig. The obvious choice for Roan Consolidated was to try out these new installations in Zambia where the financial and environmental risk could be passed on.

One such idea was a huge furnace which could melt 500 tonnes of copper bearing ore in a continuous heating process. It had six huge electrodes each six feet in diameter and capable of supplying several thousands of amps to melt the ore. The power originated from the Kariba Dam and at 40 megawatts it was equal to a small power station.

On one occasion I was working to one side of the furnace when there was a huge explosion beside me. One of the process workers was rodding out a blocked charging channel and his crowbar touched the exposed copper busbar that carried power to the electrodes. The busbar was only raised by a few volts and it had not been thought necessary to insulate it. The crowbar literally melted in the worker's hands and the resulting explosion set fire to him.

I remember the smell as I threw him to the ground and beat at his flesh with my bare hands. His black outer skin burned away and I remember seeing second layers of pink skin beneath. I was suddenly reminded of a surgeon friend who told me that all black babies are born pink. I carried him to my truck and drove him to the Mine Hospital where he received immediate treatment for his burns.

The complete project team remained dedicated to the Electric Furnace for six months. It had a very large control room and was fitted with the very latest Foxboro measurement and control instruments. We worked as a closely bound team alongside Frazer Chalmers who were the mechanical engineering contractors. The work was very hot and we consumed gallons of ice cold coke which our helpers obtained from the Frazer Chalmers compound at ten ngwee a bottle.

We worked an 80 hour week for 12 months without break, not even for Christmas or New Years day. At breakfast time we gathered in our Warehouse and sat around a collection of cardboard boxes which had been fashioned into a table. Africans collected in one group with a large bowl of Nshima and Kapenta while we Europeans consumed huge cheese sandwiches which we washed down with large mugs of coffee. It was a routine which we followed every morning seven days a week.

Each of us took our turn to drive into town where we bought a huge block of cheddar cheese and two loafs of freshly baked bread. We sliced the bread and the cheese using old hacksaw blades which had been sharpened on a grind stone and blue paint from the blade coloured the slices of cheddar. We worked rough and we lived rough. When working in such bad environmental conditions what was a little blue paint?

On one occasion someone asked each person sitting around the table of cardboard boxes to call out the name of his country. Nine different countries were called. A very proud member of our group was Atha, an elderly Greek welder who hated heights. He was seconded to me by Frazer Chalmers and I often had to climb very high scaffolding to do his welding.

I liked Atha; he lived in Zambia like a peasant. He saved his money to take home to Southern Greece where he would live like a King. En-route he bought a Mercedes in Stuttgart. Sometime later we were saddened to learn that he was killed in an autobahn accident before he reached Greece. Life can be so cruel. Other close friends gathered around the table included Bob Houghton, Colin Edwards, Bruno Tschudin, Glynn Bagott, Skiff Wainwright and two ex-Mufulira apprentices, Van and Clive.

When the Electric Furnace was finally completed we gathered together in the control room to witness the ceremonial pressing of the button that would connect power to the huge electrodes. As always on these occasions, several senior executives from head office gathered around and, to be honest, got in the way.

I looked at Gordon Patterson, an electrical engineering contractor, and he looked back at me. We were both thinking the same thing. The control room was positioned immediately below a 40 megawatt transformer which was about to take power from the grid for the very first time. Those of us who had been involved in building the control room slowly evaporated from the scene. We returned an hour later after partaking in a few slices of our cheddar cheese.

This caution was not without due cause. A few weeks later when I was working on the charge floor there was a massive blow-back. This is when the furnace is suddenly pressurised causing hot sulphurous gases to be forced into the work area. I did not have a gas mask and my eyes and nostrils burned painfully. I ran blindly towards the escape stairway stooping to gasp cold air from the concrete floor. I was four levels from the ground and as I bounded five steps at a time down the steel stairs I could stand it no longer. I climbed over the hand rail and jumped. I was blind and had no idea of what was beneath me.

I hit the ground and kept on running until I fell into a storm drain behind the Converter Isle. Two South Africans from the main instrument workshop picked me up. They were howling with laughter. They said they thought it was a Kaffir running towards them because my face was so black. I did not see the funny side, in fact, I could not see at all. They took me to the hospital and the doctor rinsed my eyes with an alkaline solution. It took a few days before they came back to normal.

On another occasion several of us were gathered in the control room and there was a runaway. Molten slag surged over the slag wagon and made it impossible to replace the plug in the slag discharge channel. The molten slag and copper crept across the rail tracks and under the control room cutting off our normal escape route. We decided to stay in the control room because we had air supplied through air-conditioning ducts, but fumes eventually started to come through the ducting. The molten river had reached the services building. Everyone except the Refinery Manager had a gas mask, we found one for him and then we ran as a group and crossed into the old works.

Four hundred tons of molten ore seeped across the floor of the furnace complex setting fire to everything in its path. Railway tracks were twisted, wagons were engulfed and the steel structure of the building was weakened. With no power for the clutches on the electrical drives, the enormous 6 ft diameter electrodes fell into the molten mass that remained at the bottom of the furnace. The damage ran into millions of Kwacha. It took months to break away the solidified slag and rebuild the furnace structure. Our team was not to participate; we were given a new project, we were to help build a recovery plant deep underground.

I dived into a 'funk hole'

The purpose of this recovery plant was to classify rock slurry which had rushed into the mine and separate it into components of rock, fine slurry and water. The water could be extracted using normal pumps while the slurry would be pumped to the surface using a large oil well pump imported from Texas. The complete idea was rather novel and had never been attempted before. A huge cavern was blasted into the rock in the old workings just above the 500 metre level and a steel support structure welded into position to carry the different vessels and associated equipment.

My job was to install the measurement and control equipment on the classifiers and to fit mass flow metering systems to the fine slurry lines just before the oil well pump. We used Ohmart nuclear density gauges, Foxboro magnetic flowmeters and analogue maths modules to ascertain the weight of solids being pumped. This was pioneering technology in the early '70's and exceeded anything being done elsewhere in the world. I became an acknowledged expert in this field and installed similar systems throughout Zambia on more conventional mining applications.

The construction methods, materials and equipment that we used were not so different to what we would have used on the surface. The main difference was that we were all contractors. Mine expatriate employees did not want to work under the conditions or risks that we were exposed to. They believed quite rightly that their remuneration package did not give them sufficient reward.

On one occasion I climbed down the shaft ladders from the old workings and I was surprised to hear the silence. It is a difficult thing to describe, but you instinctively know when there is something wrong. I dived into a 'funk hole' and a few seconds later a pressure wave flashed past me followed by a huge deep rumbling sound that echoed around the walls of the cavern for what seemed like an eternity. They were blasting and I had circumnavigated safety procedures by not using the cage which had been disabled.

This was not the first or the last time that I had such a close call. A month later I was working with my team on the rock crusher at the head of the shaft. We were installing an Ohmart nuclear level gauge on the slurries bin. Every month or so, the explosives team detonated a dynamite charge inside the bin to clear mud from the side walls. On this occasion they closed the access roads, set off the mine blasting siren and then dropped the charge into the vessel. However, they did not check if anyone was already working inside the sealed area.

We could not hear the blasting siren because of the rock being disgorged from the belt conveyer and the dynamite was only six inches away from us on the other side of the steel wall. Again, I had that feeling of silence, even though the noise was deafening. I looked outside and several workers were waving to me; then I suddenly realized what was happening. I rushed inside and told my people to run like f…k. Even as a miner I very rarely used such language, but on this occasion I had to be sure that my guys understood the urgency of the situation.

I never felt safe while I worked underground. We lived under the constant fear of another mud rush. Whenever the lights went out, the first sign of an impending disaster, everyone broke into a cold sweat and we sat down on the rock floor until the power came on again. The locals always panicked and began to climb the shaft ladders until their arms gave way. As one became exhausted the next climbed over his back and continued until he too could go no further.

Fear is a terrible thing. Not knowing what is happening thousands of feet above your head gives rise to the greatest fear of all. This intense cold nagging fear was aggravated by the occasional recovery of mud-caked bodies that once belonged to living people like us. These miners must have experienced absolute terror in those last minutes of their mortal lives. Who will ever know what they suffered.

I continued working underground in confined spaces for month after month and because of this I never drew the curtains in my small mine house. We entered the cage at 7 am just as the sun was beginning to rise and we came to the surface again at 7 pm, just after it had set. We worked these long shifts 7days per week for month after month with a short day on Friday so that we could visit the local shops.

A neighbour reported to Marjorie that she could see me working late every night on a small table in front of my lounge window, curtains undrawn. I was keeping my books in order. I have always been very careful to keep my records straight with the tax man. He is a thief that I feared even more than the bandits that came across from the Congo. The Congo Bandits may steal what you own, but the tax man steals what you own and during the same raid he lays claim to what you may own in the future.

I recall an article in the Reader's Column of the Zambian Times. It was from a Bemba in the Northern Province. He explained that he was poor and only earned a very small amount of money. He did not understand why this Company called Inland Revenue kept taking money from his pay packet. He had told his employer that he did not know who they were and he did not want to contribute to their charity. His employer would not listen to him and he was asking the newspaper what he should do.

I think this Bemba Tribesman in his innocence has summed up the feelings of many of us who work very hard to turn a dollar, only to see it wasted by highly paid civil servants who spend their days weaving red tape. I appreciate that tax has to be paid, but I object strongly to it being misused and in particular being wasted on services for which it was not intended.

All six dragons screamed in agony

When I was a child I remembered my father taking me for a walk through the Bessemer Steel Works at Workington. This was the original works where Bessemer built his world famous steel converters. These may be likened to the shape of a concrete mixer but a thousand times larger and lined with refractory brick. Air is blasted through tuyeres in the base of the vessel to remove oxygen and other impurities from the molten metal. This process creates a continuous high pitched squeal which is painful to the ears, and at the end of the cycle the converter tilts forward, erupting a shower of bright orange and white sparks that fly more than a hundred feet into the air. It is a very frightening experience for anyone and for a child it is terrifying.

Mufulira had adapted this steel making process to work with copper. They had a very long converter isle containing six Bessemer Converters. Two overhead cranes trundled continuously along this two hundred yard isle. They carried huge molten ladles of copper to and from the gaping mouths of these hungry dragons that belched huge showers of sparks every forty minutes.

All six dragons screamed in agony and no one ever dared set foot into their lairs. Even the crane driver stayed well aloft in the false hope that he was clear of danger. Unfortunately one day a pulverised coal bunker exploded and flames leaped towards his cabin. The wretched man had no alternative but to jump to his death.

I worked with my team in the converter isle for almost three months. We refurbished the measurement and control systems on two of the converters. I enjoyed the work. It was exciting but I was always frightened when I had to climb above the furnace to target an infrared pyrometer towards the surface of the molten metal. I had to time my work perfectly to ensure that I would not be above the furnace when it started to rotate.

In the early 70's no one appreciated the dangers of noise exposure and we never wore protective headgear. I found the high pitched scream to be very painful and I worked with toilet paper squeezed into my ears. In the evening my ears would sing for hours making it very difficult for me to hold a conversation with my family. This reminded me of the days when I fired 303 rifles on RAF shooting ranges, also with toilet paper stuffed in my ears.

One day while walking back to the converter isle I was hit by a sudden shockwave. A painter working on the roof of an adjacent building was knocked over. Fortunately he grasped hold of the apex before falling to the ground. My first thoughts were that a large electrical transformer had exploded; then a tall black mushroom cloud began to spread above the Kafironda Explosives Factory. The factory was about fifteen miles away and I jumped into my Bakkie and drove towards the works in the hope that I could help ferry the injured to Kitwe hospital.

The Mufulira works fire engine raced ahead of me and we were soon joined by other vehicles with the same intent. As we approached Kafironda we found every tree within a half mile radius flattened to the ground, each pointing like an arrow towards a huge crater. A steam locomotive blocked the Mufulira Kitwe road; it had been hurtled a quarter of a mile through the air.

I gaped at the terrible scene that lay before me and then the fire engine turned around and raced past me. Natives jumped into the back of my Bakkie and waved for me to follow. I did not understand what was happening but when we reached a safe distance they told me that it was an explosives train that had blown up in the Kafironda sidings. Several wagons were still intact and burning. It was several hours before rescue crews were allowed to return and when they did the scene was horrific.

The siding which was regularly used for shunting wagons from the nearby explosives factory lay beside a native village. Almost everyone in the village was killed or mutilated. Men had their clothes stripped from them by the blast and children were found running around in the bush with no arms. Doctors toiled through the night to save as many lives as possible and the newspapers carried headlines of yet another huge industrial disaster to befall the nation. The Zambian Times mentioned how the glass windows of OK Bazaars in Mufulira, Kitwe and Ndola were all broken by the shockwave. Life in Africa can be cruel but this was a genuine accident. Zambia was at least safe from the genocide being inflicted to the north in Zaire and Uganda.

Three months earlier the Management of Kafironda Explosives Factory had invited me to conduct a survey and to suggest a suitable instrument recording system that would identify the cause of an explosion. They showed me a cement mixer mixing ammonium nitrate, which is common garden fertilizer, with a fluid that I prefer not to name. The resulting mixture is commonly known as anfex and it is a very powerful explosive that we used in the mines. It was also the same mixture that the IRA used in their London truck bombs. It is a very stable mixture and needs to be detonated by a separate device. This leads to a question that I have never seen answered. The train that exploded was carrying anfex and it should have been safe; so what caused it to detonate; was the train also carrying dynamite?

I was rich in Mickey Mouse money

I visited England in the spring of 1971 and bought a small terraced house in Workington. This was my first ever home purchase and I struggled to find the money. I was very rich in Mickey Mouse money but I had no hard cash. I determined to secure hard currency using whatever means possible. I began to hoard large bundles of kwacha. Each note had a value of around nine shillings on the black market. Whenever friends had UK visitors I gave them kwacha at black market value in return for a corresponding deposit in my UK bank account. I purchased dollars, pounds and other hard currencies from Indian retailers, holidaymakers and newly arrived expatriates; again at black market values.

I mailed these bank notes in dozens of letters to different friends in Cumberland with instructions to pass the money to my father-in-law. I had to take care that if an envelope was opened, it could not be traced back to me. Still this was far short of what I needed to start a new life if my work permit was not renewed. Most company owners imported goods at grossly over-rated prices and their overseas supplier credited the difference to an overseas account. One company even imported a large crate of bricks and declared it as electrical equipment. All this was too risky for my liking; I took a more cautious approach.

Expatriates who worked for the government were entitled to a generous exchange control allowance for their annual holiday. Most of my friends could not afford to buy air tickets and so I purchased tickets for their complete family on the condition that they deposited most of their allowance in my favour. I gave them bundles of kwacha to purchase air tickets and travellers cheques; in return they deposited the traveller cheques into my account when they arrived in England or South Africa. I also opened a South African account in Johannesburg and this saved my bacon a couple of years later.

The final step in my elaborate plan to externalise money was to resign as a director of Process Control Limited and to become a contract employee of my own company. As a non-government expatriate employee I was allowed to repatriate thirty percent of my salary and to take an annual family holiday allowance. In addition, at the completion of my contract I was permitted to export personal possessions or exchange money to the value of 4,000 kwacha. This was a pittance, but beggars can't be choosers.

To put this plan into action I first had to choose a 'Paper Managing Director' very carefully. It had to be someone that I trusted implicitly, and I selected Glyn Bagott, one of my welders. Glyn was an unusual character who smoked dagga with the natives and often had furious arguments with his helpers. He had grown up in Northern Rhodesia and spoke Bemba fluently. He knew how to insult them in their own tongue and they did not like it. They complained to me and explained that he did not behave like a white bwana and that if he was not careful someone would kill him. In Africa, if someone threatens to kill you, they do mean it.

Glyn signed my annual accounts as the 'Managing Director' and I gave him a small increase in his salary. Other than that he carried on in his job as a welder and no one was even aware of the small change that had occurred in my company's legal management structure. My neighbours used to comment how Glyn would wait for me outside my house standing on his head for hours. When I eventually left Zambia he travelled to the Himalayas and studied under a guru for two years.

Early in 1972 I received a letter from Marjorie. My mother was in hospital with cancer. I purchased an air ticket to fly to England on the next flight but first I had to obtain a tax clearance certificate to board the plane. The Indian Tax Inspector in Ndola told me that I was not a government employee and so I would have to wait for six weeks while my application was processed. I threatened to hang him from the large coat hook that was fixed to the back of his door. This may sound terrible to a westerner, but anyone that has lived and worked in Africa during the 60's will know that this is the only way to obtain results. The alternative is to pay a suitable bribe and I was not in a bargaining mood.

I was very upset when I visited my mother in Whitehaven hospital but she was very pleased to see me. She embarrassed me by introducing me to all the nurses and telling them proudly that I had come all the way from Central Africa to visit her, which of course was true.

My father-in-law, Joe Elliot, was also very proud of me. He was Toolshop Foreman at the Distington Engineering Company, a division of British Steel which is known locally as Chapel Bank. Joe told me that the Chief Engineer's job was open and he wanted me to apply. I was not sure if this kind of opportunity would suit me but I did not want to disappoint him.

I visited Chapel Bank on the following day to complete an application form and the outgoing Chief Engineer afforded me a full half day tour before introducing me to the General Manager, Commander Wingate. I was only 26 years old and I considered myself far too young for such a senior position. I must have impressed them because I was the only external candidate to be short listed. The job was eventually given to an internal candidate from British Steel, Sheffield.

While I was in England I decided the time was right to invest in property. I searched throughout West Cumberland and established a potential portfolio of three properties in addition to the terraced house that I already owned. The first I targeted was the Black Bull in Cockermouth. I met with the licensing authorities and they agreed to give me an open licence if I purchased the inn from Workington Brewery. Next I made an offer on an old barn and ginnery near to Ullock. The final property was a nine bedroom guesthouse in Keswick. That guesthouse was built entirely from local Borrowdale stone.

Unfortunately I had a terrible argument with my father. He did not agree with investing in bricks and mortar. He always believed that the World would suffer another great depression and he argued that I should leave my money in the bank. I did! In years to come this was my greatest regret and one that I felt I could never bring myself to discuss with Dad. I returned to Zambia no closer to settling my future than when I first left England three years earlier.

I can't remember too much of this particular time period. I suspect my mind has blocked much of what happened into a remote inaccessible part of my memory and, to be quite honest, I don't really want to try to piece everything back together. Suffice to say that my mother died shortly after I returned to England. My father was beside himself with grief. She suffered terribly and I am not ashamed to say that I was thankful when she finally passed away in the familiar surroundings of her own home in the early hours of Wednesday 26th January, 1972.

I took care of everything for my father. There was a very ugly and long running coal miners strike at the time and the striking miners cut-up rough with me when I visited the local government offices in Whitehaven to register her death. I quickly explained the reason for my visit and they immediately opened a corridor through the crowd so that I could pass through.

I filmed troop concentrations from both sides

When everything settled down Michele, Marjorie and I returned to Zambia. I was now a valuable member of the Mufulira Project Team and they provided us with a very nice house on the edge of Mufulira. My father and my brother Steven visited us later in the year. Steven had shoulder length hair and had just finished his second year at Liverpool University where he was studying chemistry.

We decided to visit Victoria Falls and after crossing the Zambezi my father asked a garage attendant on the Rhodesian side if he would rather live across the river in Zambia. To my fathers astonishment he replied, "No Bwana, I have a good job here, I don't want to live with them Kaffirs, it is much better on this side". The following morning we took a boat trip above the falls to see the Fish Eagle and other wild birds that live on the banks of the Zambezi. We left shortly after sunrise and were surprised to see a Zambian pleasure boat beached on the Rhodesian side. It had been carrying President Kaunda on a sight seeing tour. Rhodesian soldiers had boarded it and were behaving like pirates. They hoisted the Rhodesian flag and a makeshift Jolly Roger on its stern. Several of the soldiers were waving bottles of alcohol which they had looted from the commandeered boat. All in all they were making great fun of the situation.

Sailing upriver we began to spot hundreds of camouflaged troops amongst the undergrowth on the Zambian side and suddenly we realized that we were in the middle of a major confrontation. The

Rhodesian Defence Force must have thought that the Zambian Army was preparing for an invasion because they had mobilised their reserves during the night and rushed them to the Zambezi. I filmed troop concentrations from both sides and considered mailing my spool back to the BBC. I decided that this would be too risky and continued with our holiday.

After Victoria Falls we drove directly to the Luangwa Valley, a game reserve the size of Wales and described by Peter Scott as the most natural wild animal sanctuary in the world. We had several drivers in the car and so I decided that we would travel right through the night and cross the Luangwa River before darkness fell on the second day of our marathon journey.

The tense situation made our drive rather eventful. When we crossed Victoria Falls Bridge and passed through the Zambian army checkpoint, we were ordered out of our car and our suitcases were removed from the boot. Steven had no experience of black soldiers and as they emptied his freshly pressed white shirts on to the dirt road he darted forward to pick them up. One of the soldiers covering us with his rife immediately jumped forward and held a bayonet behind his head. I told Steven to leave his clothes alone and then I shouted at the officer in charge "Zambia in the Bloody Sun". I was referring to the Zambia tourist motto, it is always a mistake to show weakness to a black. In tribal society they respect strength and take advantage of weakness.

During the night we passed through Lusaka and I rather foolishly stopped outside the House of Assembly. It was dark and there were no street lights where we parked the car. Dad and I walked up to the railings so that I could point out the different features; suddenly I heard the unmistakable sound of a rifle bolt. I looked in the direction of the sound, but black soldiers are almost invisible in the dark. Dad turned to run back to the car but I knew that would be fatal. These soldiers were on a high state of alert and were probably more frightened than us. If dad had run he would surely have been shot.

I recalled the words of my old Commodore at the Murray Outward Bound Sea School. Never swear unless it is a matter of life and death, and then never in the presence of a women. This was one such occasion and I swore at my father, for the first and only time in my life, as I told him in no uncertain terms to stand still. I had to be certain that he would listen. We both stood rooted to the spot with our hands in clear view until an officer came. I explained to him why we were outside Parliament at such a late hour and he told us to walk slowly back to our car. We complied without saying a further word. This incident changed my father's hitherto favourable attitude towards blacks. He had never understood my aggressive attitude toward them but now he began to understand.

The sun was falling as we approached the Luangwa River. I drove our car very gingerly onto the raft which comprised of wooden planks, tree trunks and several old oil drums. It was secured to a very thick rope that stretched across the river. A gang of eight then took hold of large wooden stakes which had a slot in one end. They placed the slots into the rope and pulled the raft across the river to a rhythmic chant led by the bossboy. It was a beautiful sight, these natives moving in rhythm as they pulled us across the huge river.

Crocodiles slid from the far bank and hippos peered at us through small bulging eyes that stuck just above the surface of the water. The trees were beginning to turn white as wading birds gathered to roost in the safety of their branches and a lone fisherman could be seen punting a dugout canoe through the shallows. His father and his father before him must have made their livings in exactly the same way. It looked so peaceful, yet danger was never more than a stone's throw away.

Luangwa Valley was an incredible once-in-a-lifetime experience for Steven and my father. We stayed in Luamfwa Camp again. It comprised around fourteen rondavels with a large open communal unit in the centre. All the buildings had thatched roofs and these were host to a wide variety of insects. Only the communal unit had electricity which was supplied from a diesel generator and we had to make several journeys during the day to fill our drinking water jug.

One night Marjorie asked me to refill the jug. Half way across the pitch black clearing I heard the grunt of a hippo which was foraging through the camp. Hippos are one of the most dangerous animals in the wild and so I quickly dived back into the safety of my rondavel and told my good wife to collect the water herself. Throughout the night we heard all kinds of animals. The occasional lion hunted buffalo nearby; hyenas and wild dogs scavenged through the waste bins while a lone bull elephant rubbed against the walls of our rondavel.

I took Dad, Steven, Marjorie and Michele on several long bush-drives over the next two days. It was hot and very dry but they thoroughly enjoyed themselves. Dad had one or two scares and on one occasion he ran from the bush towards the safety of our car while hurriedly pulling up his long trousers. He had been obeying the call of nature when a crocodile disturbed him. I think the crocodile was more scared of him, but he wasn't hanging around to find out.

On the fourth day we met our first white people. They belonged to a small film crew and were making a film for the Zambian Tourist Board. They tried to film a rogue elephant called Luamfwa. The old bull had been in a leadership fight with a young pretender and one of its tusks had broken. He was now an outcast suffering from the equivalent of human toothache. For some reason he was staying close to the Luamfwa Camp, hence the reason for his name.

Luamfwa had chased several camp workers over recent weeks and it was only their agility which had kept them from harm. Elephants usually make a mock charge. This involves a lot of trumpeting, spreading of ears, head shaking and trunk waving. But an elephant behaving in this way will never finish the charge. Luamfwa was different; he was a rogue!

Late in the afternoon Luamfwa approached our camp from the direction of the waterhole. He stood on his hind legs and used the sensitive tip of his trunk to break a small branch from the very top of a marula tree. Perhaps he wanted to remind us that no one could escape him by climbing one of these trees.

Two cameras were hurriedly set up on tripods and one of the cameramen asked if I could attract the elephant's attention. I was young and very prone to showing off. A very glamorous girl, presumably the presenter, was watching proceedings and so I opened the door of the nearest rondavel, walked towards Luamfwa until I thought I was still at a safe distance and then started to kick dust towards him in the form of a challenge.

He looked at me, folded his ears back, tucked his trunk under his chin and started to run at me. This was not playing the game. He had not trumpeted, waved his ears or shaken his head. He had not given me any warning at all. It slowly began to dawn on me that I should also be running.

I turned and ran across the dusty clearing and through the door of the rondavel that I had wisely left open. As I past through I slammed the door shut so he would lose sight of me, opened the window on the other side, climbed through and carried on running. I was not convinced that the rondavel would withstand the full onslaught of a fully grown bull elephant.

I walked around to the far sided of the camp and the film crew asked if I could get him to charge again. They explained that everything had happened so quickly that they had not captured the charge. The truth is that they had pressed the camera start buttons and retired to the comparative safety of a rondavel as soon as I approached the elephant.

Again I walked up to Luamfwa, who had retired to the same starting point and again he charged me when I kicked dust towards him. This time I was ready for him. I recognised the warning signs as he streamlined himself for action. I suppose it is logical that a bull elephant will not make a real charge with it ears flapping and its trunk high in the air.

It seemed to run faster than before and I could not see how fast it was gaining on me. I was too focused upon clearing every tree root that was in my path; to stumble now would be bad news. As I climbed through the rear window I heard Luamfwa bellowing at the front door; he was furious. When I rejoined the others, the manager of the camp explained that she did not want me to do it again as she was concerned that Luamfwa would damage the rondavel. I had not realised that so many of the camp workers had gathered to watch the filming. Our Fundi was also standing at a discreet distance with his elephant gun at the ready. He said that Luamfwa had only been a few feet behind me on the last charge.

I started to shake a little when I realized that I had nearly been caught but one of the camera men was determined to get one last charge. The remainder of the crew said that it was too dangerous and they refused to participate. I decided to make a third challenge and on this occasion

Luamfwa was so furious that he ran into a tree.

He circled the empty rondavel for the remainder of the day and then returned again during the night. We left the following day and returned to the Copperbelt. Marjorie drove our car while I lay on the floor; I covered myself in perfume and wore a different coloured shirt. It may have been a senseless precaution but I was so terrified that we could meet him as we left the camp. I have since met tourists who have seen the film. Oddly enough it is called 'Zambia in the Sun'.

A few days after reaching home I visited the butcher and bought several huge steaks. I gave them to Marjorie to cook for our evening meal. Everyone was very hungry and Marjorie could not understand why she had to leave the steak in the oven for so long. My father was very embarrassed; he had new false teeth and he struggled for ages to eat his large portion of meat. In the end he apologised to Marjorie and said that he was sorry, but the meat was too tough for him. Everyone else was also politely struggling with their own servings. Suddenly Marjorie set upon me with her serving spoon. She had finally realized that I had given her hippo meat to cook.

The War of Attrition

Throughout my time in Zambia a cruel war was being waged in the Middle East, it was known as the War of Attrition. The main antagonists were Syria, Egypt, 'Palestine' and Israel. This war came to a head when a group of Palestinian terrorists held hostage and killed members of the Israeli delegation to the 1972 Munich Olympic Games. The Israeli Secret Service, known as Mossad, responded with Operation Wrath of God, in which their agents assassinated most of those involved.

It was during this operation that I chanced to visit Israel. I was on one of the many stop-overs that I enjoyed while flying between Africa and England. I visited the old city of Jerusalem and found three of the Worlds most important religious structures, all within one hundred yards of each other. The Western Wall, the Church of the Holy Sepulchre and the Al-Aqsa Mosque; each representing one of the World's three great religions; Judaism, Christianity and Islam. I visited the Church of the Holy Sepulchre, King David's Tower and the place of the Last

Supper. As I walked from one place to the next I had to enquire if I should place a cover over my head, or not. The religious significance of each was so confusing.

I read a wealth of information about the history of this ancient city. Since Solomon built its first temple three thousand years ago Jerusalem had been ruled by Babylonians, Romans, Byzantines, Seljuks, Fatimids, Ayyubids, Mamelukes, Ottoman Turks and Britons. It had been conquered by many great empires since Christ walked through its narrow cobbled streets and yet I was disturbed to learn that the cruellest episode in its long history was brought about by European Nobles in the name of Christianity. When Fulcher of Chartres returned from the First Crusade in 1099 he said: "Indeed, if you had been there you would have seen our feet coloured to our ankles with the blood of the slain. But what more shall I relate? None of them were left alive; neither women nor children were spared". He referred to every man woman and child then living in Jerusalem; Muslim, Jew and even a small number of East Christians.

After Jerusalem I drove through the occupied territories of the West Bank to the lowest point on Earth; the Dead Sea. From there I took a cable car to the top of Masada, the desert fortress of King Herod where 75 years after his death more than 1000 Jewish Zealots, men women and children, took their own lives rather than surrender to the 10th Legion of the Roman Empire. Everywhere that I stepped in the Holy Land appeared to be soaked in the blood of innocent people.

The incredible ruins of Masada had been protected for two millennia by the dry climate of the Judean Desert. They were excavated eight years before my visit and I was fascinated to learn of the siege that had taken place all those years ago. As I stood looking at the huge water cisterns that were carved out of the mountain, a squadron of phantoms skimmed over my head and turned towards the Jordanian border. My ears screamed in agony and the dry sand beneath my feet danced in the cruel shock waves that trailed from the wing tips of these ominous looking birds of prey. The reality of my location was quickly brought home to me.

On my return from England I made a short stop-over in Egypt. I had visited the religious sites of the Holy Land, now I wanted to smell the spices in the old bazaars of downtown Cairo. I wanted to ride Arabian stallions across the desert and probe the innermost depths of the Pyramids of Giza. I disembarked from my airplane at 2 am. I climbed into an old banger that described itself as a taxi and set out for town. I recognized the Statue of Rameses II in the distance and it passed by me several times from the same direction on my left hand side. It was obvious that my driver was taking me around in circles and when I checked into my hotel I asked the bellboy how much it was to the airport. My taxi driver was furious when I refused to give him one penny more.

I found that my cheapest way to get around was to hire a taxi for the duration of my visit. On my first day we drove out to the Pyramid of Cheops and a guide took me deep into its interior. As we passed along one of the narrow inclined tunnels our electric lighting was extinguished and he held his hand out for baksheesh, no doubt the electricity was wired through a timer to ensure that this happened at regular intervals. After I paid him a small sum he lit a candle and then five minutes later the timer switched our lights back on again. This magnificent feat of civil engineering was the first and only remaining survivor of the seven wonders of the ancient world; yet youngsters were permitted to carve their name into its huge limestone blocks and others raced each other to its 481 ft summit.

After this brief foray into the bowels of our 4,500 year old pyramid I climbed onto a camel called 'Fantastic' and had my photograph taken in front of the Sphinx, first wearing a Fez and then a Gutrah; real touristy stuff. After our photographs Fantastic and I set out for an afternoon ride through the desert. I soon learned how to mount, dismount and ride with my feet crossed over its neck. To get it to kneel down for dismounting I made a strange sound in its ear like the snarling of a dog and pulled hard on its nose-peg, to get it to stand up I shouted Hagan and eased its rein. When my guide realized that I was getting the hang of it he bet me one hundred dollars that he could give me a hundred yard start and still beat me to the next ridge of hills. He must have thought that I was a rich American; anyhow I refused to accept his bet.

Next second he whacked my camel in a rather sensitive place and Fantastic hurtled across the desert. He trotted so quickly that I was terrified. I felt so far above the ground and the desert was strewn with huge rocks and deep holes which Fantastic navigated with surprising dexterity. I pulled on his 'nose peg' and almost had his head pointing in the opposite direction, but still he kept going. I then let him have a free rein for fear of pulling him into a hole. After a long bone jarring ride he slowly came to a stop. My guide, who had trotted alongside shouting encouragement, held a hand out for his hundred dollars and I gave him ten to show me the direction back towards Giza.

I could not pass through Cairo without visiting the Egyptian Museum. I found countless mummies, coffins, amulets, ushabtis, ceremonial boats and sculptures, many as old as 5,000 years. The bandages had been removed from several mummified bodies of women and children. Their skin was like wrinkled leather and varied in colour from dark brown to a deep purple. They looked positively grotesque and their bodies were seeping a strange kind of fluid. I don't know if this was a recently added chemical but it was my general impression that the relics in the museum were not being cared for. They may have survived the ravages of the Egyptian desert for five millennia but I doubted that they would survive the next.

I am always overwhelmed when I visit a national museum. They contain such a vast quantity of artefacts, and the Egyptian Museum was no exception. I walked past incredibly important items; a writing slate, a mortuary jar, an amulet; all stunned the World when they were first discovered; every major newspaper carried their stories and yet I never even stopped to cast a second glance. There were just too many and I was drowning in their presence, I am ashamed to say that I hurried to focus my attention upon one particular exhibit. This of course was the treasures of Tutankhamen's tomb.

There were few tourists in Cairo during this uncertain period and I had the floor entirely to myself. I knew the incredible story of Howard Carter's discovery in the Valley of the Kings and of the difficulties experienced by his multinational archaeological team, but I was still not fully prepared for the magnificence, or the enormity of what he had found in that small commoner's tomb 48 years ago. There were jewels, trinkets, caskets, boats, chariots and material possessions of every kind. Everything that Tutankhamen should have needed in his afterlife lay all around me. His famous death mask stared into open space and I remember in particular a row of intricately carved coffins which had rested one inside the other, just like Russian Matryoshka nesting dolls; the innermost of these had been crafted from 110 kilograms of solid gold.

Leonid Brezhnev was still courting the favour of Anwar Sadat and he had some 20,000 military advisors in Egypt. In the evening I visited a huge tent in the desert, I sat at a wooden bench with six young and very attractive Russian girls. There were six tables and around forty girls in all. I was the only male guest and with the Cold War at its height I found that I was in a rather peculiar situation. Egyptian belly dancers entertained us while we struggled with an eastern meal that lacked promise and the girls at my table shared their wine with me. Our hosts played Russian music and I was the only person to dance with. I had an incredible evening and then suddenly it was 12 midnight; 'Cinderellas', all forty of them, had to go home. Two KGB officers counted them as they filed out to their waiting bus. Prince Charming was left sitting in an empty tent. He nodded in the direction of his ever attentive taxi driver and set out for his palace.

I rose early at 5am and walked into the dirty restaurant of my dilapidated palace. I refused the sour milk offered with my cornflakes and pushed away my greasy bacon when a rat scuttled across the floor. It was time to leave and I grabbed my suitcase and walked out to find my taxi driver. He was twenty yards down the street sleeping under a blanket on the back seat of his taxi cab. This was probably the only bed that he had. As we drove out to the airport I could not help but notice hundreds of ill-disciplined and very demoralized troops. These troops did not know it at the time, but they would soon be fighting another terrible war against Israel. Anwar Sadat and Hafiz al-Assad of Syria had already planned this to take place on the Jewish fasting day of Yom Kippur.

I should have flown to Khartoum in the Sudan but my flight was cancelled. I had not eaten a decent meal for three days and I was determined to leave Egypt. I caught the next flight out; it took me to Nicosia where an Alitalia flight was scheduled to refuel on its route to Zambia. I managed to reserve a seat and with eight hours to kill I set off into Nicosia to explore its nightlife.

I knew absolutely nothing about the political history of Cyprus or of the antagonism that existed between Turkish and Greek Cypriots. I jumped off my airport bus at around 9pm and walked through the narrow streets of Nicosia. I walked past several sandbagged sentry posts that were manned by Canadian troops in blue berets and found a lively little bar. When I entered the bar there was a rather slim Turkish girl swirling around performing 'the dance of the seven veils'. She was much more beautiful than the rather fat, deliberately so, belly dancers in Egypt. I didn't realize until several years later that I had crossed the 'Green Line'!

They arrived in black cars wearing long grey raincoats

Early one morning I heard that several company owners in Mufulira had been picked up by Interpol. I am told that they arrived in black cars wearing long grey raincoats. Two of the owners had been taken from their beds and one from the rugby club. This story was embellished along the way but the bulk of it was true. Exchange control violation was one of the most serious crimes in Zambia and those caught found themselves incarcerated in horrible conditions. To obtain release, they were required to transfer all monies in their overseas accounts to the Zambian Government.

Rumour has it that Interpol was working with the Zambian Government to uncover large overseas accounts held by white company owners. I had never falsified my import documentation and my company accounts had always been accurate. Nevertheless, I had purchased foreign currency on the black market. I was very nervous with this development and I decided that it was time to move on.

Morris Kirby visited me in October 1972. He was manager of the Industrial Division of Honeywell Automation in Johannesburg. As one of my principle suppliers he wanted to help promote Honeywell products. Instead he spent the whole of his three day visit trying to persuade me to join him in Johannesburg. I agreed to travel to Johannesburg where I could meet with the Reg Garrett, the Managing Director, and negotiate my terms.

I travelled down to my meeting through Rhodesia and Botswana. The train comprised eight carriages, each looking like one of the old cabooses that are used in cowboy films. The steam locomotive had a huge search light and a cattle fender. As we travelled on the slow narrow gauge track through Francistown in Botswana, an old African woman, affectionately called an umfazi, was thrown aside by the cattle fender. I don't know if she lived but the fender at least gave her some protection.

The front two carriages were jammed full of blacks who were lucky if they could find a vacant wooden seat. The remaining six coaches were 'Net Blankes'; they had comfortable leather seats which folded down to make a bed in the evening and clean white linen with a pillow was provided. I was the only white passenger on the train and I felt a little ashamed that the black passengers should be crammed into two carriages while I had six all to myself. If separation was to be maintained then at least the blacks could have been given six coaches and the whites two.

When I walked around the parks in Johannesburg I was confused to see all the benches marked with 'Net Blankes'; it all seemed rather pointless. I lived in Zambia and we did not have apartheid. Even Rhodesia did not have such a pointless law. Whites drank in rugby clubs, blacks drank in beer halls. Whites ate steak and potatoes while blacks preferred Nshima and Kapenta. The truth is that European, Indian, Arab, Chinese, Zulu, Ndebele and other 'tribes' that lived in Africa during the 60's had different cultures and they reached a natural separation by choice. I found apartheid ill-conceived and unnecessary. This truth was demonstrated 23 years later when Nelson Mandela became the first black President of the Republic of South Africa. All of its citizens were integrated into one society of equals and Mandela displayed such outstanding qualities of Statesmanship that he quickly became recognised as one of the World's greatest leaders.

When I returned to Mufulira I looked for someone who would buy me out. It was very important that I secured the future for my workforce, which now comprised several well trained expatriates and a host of native Zambians. Two electricians came forward from Frazer Chalmers called Mario and John. They had very little cash available and so I accepted two thousand kwacha to cover the written down value of my welding equipment, gas cutting torches, test equipment and other tools of the trade.

Mario and John were respected in Mufulira and the Management recognised this by awarding Process Control with a large contract for the rewiring of all six converters in the converter isle. This gave the whole team the assurance of six months work before I finally packed my worldly belongings and set out for Johannesburg.

Process Control and another company called Lakeland Controls that I registered in the Channel Island are both still trading at the time of writing this book 38 years later.

Chapter 10

One of the White Tribe

Managing Honeywell control system projects in South Africa
Net Blankes!

Leaving for Johannesburg was perhaps one of our easiest tasks. We had a little red Toyota Corona Coupe, which we carefully packed from floor to ceiling with boxes that carried all our remaining possessions. These along with the Coupe were labelled, valued and listed on our export manifesto. The total value was then checked by customs, deducted from our emigration allowance of 4,000 kwacha and the balance authorised for exchange into hard currency. We had left a very small space on the back seat for Michele; we squeezed her in and drove carefully down the Great North Road for the last time.

We drove through Kitwe, Broken Hill, Lusaka and Chilanga. Passing through each of these places brought back vivid memories of the happy days that we had enjoyed in Zambia and the people that we had worked with. Not every day had been enjoyable, we had been exposed to great dangers that faced us from unexpected directions; we had learned to deal with adversity and we were much better for it. Above all else we had learned that no situation is ever hopeless; there is always light at the end of the tunnel.

I became apprehensive as we drove through the Zambezi Valley and approached the Chirundu Border Post. We always had problems when taking short holidays in Salisbury and I expected the worst. To our surprise and delight they took our documents and waved us straight through. This was certainly too good to be true. After we crossed the Zambezi the Rhodesians emptied our car and broke into our carefully packed boxes; spreading all our possessions on the roadside. I couldn't believe it.

The Captain then confiscated our sewing machine and my elephant tusk. I was furious; this was so unlike the many Rhodesians I counted as close friends. A young officer took me to one side and told me that his Captain had been in a bad mood all day; he then slipped me a piece of paper with the telephone number of their commanding officer in Salisbury.

I discussed the situation with his commanding officer on the pay phone outside the border post and then called him to the telephone. The Captain was visibly shocked when he realised to whom he was speaking. His commanding officer instructed him to return the goods and to give me a temporary pass that would get me as far as the Customs Headquarters in Salisbury.

We stayed the night in Salisbury and the following day I presented my elephant tusk to Customs and they gave me a document to take to the Veterinary Department and the Department of Game Conservation. The first department examined the tusk and declared it free from Foot and Mouth Disease and the second department gave me permission to keep the tusk and to export it from Rhodesia. Having gained three separate stamps on my now precious document we continued our long journey towards Johannesburg.

We drove along the Fort Victoria Road and stopped for a few hours at the Zimbabwe ruins. I suspect that these high stone wall fortifications were originally a fort built by Arab slave traders long before the Zulu Nation started its great trek south across the Zambezi. I recall from a passage in the book 'Ndaba My Children' written by a tribal witch-doctor, that as they journeyed south, the Zulu encountered white slave traders who came from the east and lived in a great stone lodge.

Armed convoys were still to be established on the Fort Victoria Road but we passed safely through the 'insurgency area' without incident. We arrived at the Beit Bridge border crossing just before it closed for the night. Armed with our customs documents we passed quickly through the control point and crossed the Limpopo into South Africa. This time we had problems with our car. The South African police would not let us take it into the country without paying thirty three percent deposit on its new value; we were entering as immigrants and not tourists.

We left our car fully loaded in 'no-mans land' and walked about a mile into Beit Bridge where we found a hotel and stayed the night. It was very fortunate that I had 'black' money in an account in Johannesburg. As soon as the bank opened I asked the Manager to wire funds to a local branch and I took a bank draft to the Police. By lunchtime we were back in the car and driving the final stretch to Johannesburg where Honeywell had arranged for temporary accommodation at Kings Gate in Robertsham. It was several months before I purchased my first real home in Africa, a split-level detached house in Bordeaux, which is a northern suburb of Johannesburg.

Building my team at Honeywell

My first few months working for Honeywell were different to anything I had previously experienced. It was my first time in a sales environment and everything was focused entirely upon sales volume, invoiced value and gross profit. In Honeywell, the word loss has the same meaning as 'no' in the Japanese language; it does not exist. I remember explaining on one occasion to the Contract Manager of Dowson Dobson that we needed to claim extras in order to recover our losses on a plate annealing furnace project. In reality we were making a loss, in Honeywell terms, because we were running below estimated gross profit.

Honeywell was the 50th largest company in the world. It supplied control systems for the space shuttle and high technology equipment to battle groups in the Vietnam War. Every industrial sector from steel production to oil refining used Honeywell products and to survive in such a strong commercial environment I had to sharpen my financial skills.

My predecessor had been sidelined into another role. He was a very likeable person and he enjoyed a close relationship with his engineers; too close, they were taking advantage of his generosity. There was a draughtsman who provided very detailed drawings. He was very proud of his work but he was always behind schedule. Electricians wired equipment that was mounted in wooden boxes because the control panels had not been ordered. Site foremen were driving sixty miles to work each day and then back again in the evening. Lack of on-site guidance was causing serious mistakes to be made which took longer to rectify during commissioning. Several of my new incumbents talked a good job, but when push came to shove they were unable to put their words into practice. It was painfully obvious that I had to remove the dead wood, and quickly, otherwise the Contracts Division would have no future for anyone, least of all for me.

The draughtsman was the first to go. He was the first person that I fired in my life and I found it very difficult. Next I fired one of the engineers and then two of the panel wiremen. I felt bad about these dismissals but I need not have worried. Honeywell paid so poorly that they all had another job within the week and at a much higher rate of pay. This is why I inherited so many problems. Honeywell would not pay the going rate for the job. I discovered that other engineering companies in Johannesburg paid their fitters more than I was able to pay my best project manager.

It soon became apparent to everyone in the office that I had been brought in to be the hatchet man. The secretaries took a disliking to me and put my typing to the bottom of the pile; it was several months before I was able to repair my image. This came naturally and without my intervention. As I improved profitability and the company began to meet completion dates the working environment relaxed and people began to enjoy their work. The secretaries began to appreciate that tough measures had been necessary for the common good and I was welcomed back into the fold. I had to be more careful to say 'please' to Barbara each time I gave her work, but she did start to put my typing in the proper queue again.

After making these initial improvements I set about streamlining the Industrial Contracts Division. We had around nine major projects and when I analysed each one of them I found that they all had common features. Instead of re-inventing the wheel every time it was obvious, to me at least, that we needed to engineer one project really well and then use it as a building block for the other eight. Not only would it streamline our work, reduce costs and enable us to hit completion dates; it would help prepare an accurate model which we could use as a base to prepare more accurate quotations in the future.

I needed several new people to build my team. I noticed that the Commercial Division had a very good tracer called Joanne Zermatten.

She was a young Dutch woman and could work very quickly and produce accurate ink drawings from sketches prepared by engineers in her department. It seemed to be a much better solution than employing another draughtsman. Yes I am sexist; women can work much better than men when given the right kind of opportunity!

I approached a local recruitment agency and asked if they could find a tracer for me. A few days later Joanne came to my office and asked if I would interview her sister Marion for the job. I declined and said that I did not want to employ friends or family of existing employees. I knew it would be very difficult for me to fire them if they did not make the grade. She said that she understood my problem but felt that I should at least give her the benefit of an interview.

Reluctantly I agreed. The following day our receptionist ushered Marion Zermatten into my office. My office was totally surrounded with glass windows and it was strategically positioned at the end of a large open plan office where all of the engineers, sales clerks and secretaries worked. Marion was extremely attractive and had long platinum blond hair. She was dressed in tight pink trousers and a pink sweat shirt that left nothing to the imagination. Marion looked as if she would be a terrible distraction and I made my mind up that she was un-employable. She sat down facing me with her back to the office window and I have to admit that she interviewed very well.

While I was trying to ask her intelligent questions several of the younger men were sitting up in their chairs and giving her the thumbs-up. Johann Loots, the Don Juan of our team, was even making amorous gestures in her direction. What no one realized is that Joanne, who was sitting amongst them, was Marion's sister. After such a performance from my team I felt that I had no alternative but to give her a 2-week trial. I never regretted it. She turned out to be every bit as good as Joanne.

This was not the only embarrassing incident that I had in my glass fronted office. I was the target of every sales person in Johannesburg and one day an attractive and very nervous young girl came into my office. She had just started in her new job and I was her first ever cold-sales call. "What are you selling?" I asked as Marion sat her down in front of my desk with a cup of coffee. "Screws" she blurted out.

Marion blushed and hurried out of my office as the poor girl quickly added. "I mean metal screws". Then she pushed her business card under my nose. It read: 'The Atlas Screw Company'. I never bought any kind of 'screw' from Jenny Harris but she continued to visit me for many years. She rested her feet while we enjoyed a cup of coffee, talked nonsense and put the world to rights.

Jenny and other sales reps like her became close friends and they enjoyed visiting me because they were always given refreshments and made to feel at home. In return they gave me useful information about major projects that were in the offing. They were the taxi drivers of the engineering world.

Building my control panels, boring for some

I started my work with Marion by preparing a full set of engineering drawings for control panel manufacture, panel wiring and field installation. The majority of instruments that we used were manufactured by Yamatake Honeywell and the balance we purchased from local sources in Johannesburg. This enabled me to standardise the panel cut-outs, piping layouts and wiring drawings for each type of instrument. I initiated a new drawing arrangement which combined panel wiring, panel piping, field piping and field cabling all within the same instrument loop drawing. This reduced the number of drawings needed for panel wiring and field installation. It also simplified fault finding during the commissioning period.

I sketched these different loop drawings on rough paper and Marion quickly turned them into professional ink drawings which we used as a standard. Eventually, we reached a point where I could give Marion a series of loop numbers for each section of a control panel and she would use her ink drawings to trace a complete set of actual project drawings. We even created a wire and pipe numbering system that Marion could apply without reference to any of the project engineers. These numbers followed a sequence that would quickly be recognised by a service technician during fault finding.

My intention was to reduce the need for wiring drawings as much as possible. Without deliberate intention I was applying the experience I had gained working for several years at the sharp end. I was introducing design practices which should help remove many of the maintenance problems that I had encountered in Zambia. Those technicians who have been called out in the middle of the night to find a fault on a heavily populated control panel will understand what I am talking about. In no time at all we had produced a full set of drawings for each of our nine projects and each set was perhaps the most professional and technically comprehensive that I had encountered.

My next task was to find a good sheet metal worker who could make our panels. I decided that our existing supplier was able to manufacture product to the necessary standard. Our earlier problems had been caused by our draughtsman who had never provided properly engineered drawings on time. We gave our supplier our new set of drawings which clearly stated our required tolerances, the manufacturing standards to use and the completion dates he must meet. We asked him to quote on the basis of using a standardised design with the opportunity to secure repeat work. His quotations were accepted and we were extremely pleased with the quality of his supply.

The next problem we had was to find the right people to fit instruments into the control panel, and then to wire and pipe them. Many of the instruments we used were 'huff and puff'. They were pneumatic and worked on a 3-15 psig control signal. This type of work required a very special kind of person. The instruments had to be connected together with quarter inch copper tube. Each bend had to be perfectly placed and complete sets of tubes had to run together in neat rows. Signal wiring had to be run in strategically placed plastic trunking that complemented the copper tubing. Each signal wire and control wire had to connect to field terminals clipped into rails at the bottom of the panel.

This may sound boring to some, but it is one of the most satisfying jobs that I have ever had. I loved to stand back and admire a well built control panel festooned with complex instruments that are neatly connected by thousands of colourful control wires and pipes; each run with intricate care through horizontal and vertical layers of dull grey plastic trunking. Many have photographs of beautiful new born babies in their albums; my most treasured are photographs of the control panels that I built in Johannesburg.

At home in Randburg

Dad and my brother Steven came to visit in August 1973. Steven had finished his BSc (Hons) and was about to start his PhD at Liverpool University. We visited Mafeking where Baden-Powell commanded the British Troops during the 217 day Siege of Mafeking. It was this siege during the Boer war that led to the foundation of the Boy Scout Movement. We also travelled in the Eastern Kalahari through Botswana and later to Swaziland, home of the Swazi cattle thieves who were thrown out by the Nguni during their great migration south.

Dad was thrilled when I took him to visit Rorkes Drift where 150 British soldiers defended a small supply station on the Buffalo River against an Impi of 4000 Zulu. This action earned the defenders 11 VC's and it was immortalised in the film Zulu. The battleground of Isandhlwana was also close by. This battle which started one day earlier on 22nd January 1879 is the only battle in which a modern army regiment has ever been defeated by native warriors; a defeat more deserving of infamy than Custer's last stand. More than 1,300 soldiers of the South Wales Borderers were killed and later disembowelled on the battlefield by 22,000 Zulu warriors under the command of Ntshingway Khoza.

One afternoon I asked our garden boy, Johannes, to build a new garden wall with concrete blocks. I explained to Dad that Bantu people could not see in straight lines and that he must ensure that Johannes used a piece of string to keep the wall straight. Marjorie gave Dad a pint glass of cool Lion lager and kept it filled all afternoon. Dad lost all interest in the wall and could not have seen in a straight line himself, even if he tried.

When I arrived home the wall was finished and it looked like something out of a fairy tail, it was as cockeyed as hell. I was furious, I walked up to it and kicked it over before the cement had chance to bind. Johannes looked on in dismay and my father was speechless. He sobered up very quickly but it was too late. Marjorie promised not to give Dad any lager the following day and Johannes was ready to give it another go, but I was determined that it would be done properly. As the saying goes; if you want a job done properly, do it yourself; so I did!

My home in View Road, Bordeaux was perhaps the most beautiful home that I have ever owned; it had four split-levels, each with a wealth of character. A large carpeted garage opened into the orchard; it had stairs and a strong wooden door leading to the main level where the bedrooms, dining room and kitchen could be found. The main hallway opened onto the rose garden through horsebox style doors manufactured from African hardwood. There was a serving hatch between the kitchen and the dining area that I used on more than one occasion when Marjorie locked me out. From the dining room an open plan staircase led to the lounge area which was surrounded by full length glass windows and a veranda that gave a 270 degree view across the whole of northern Johannesburg. The open plan staircase continued to a small galleried bar that overlooked the lounge area.

Outside a large walled garden contained an orchard with peach trees, apricots, nectarines, loquats and figs. Kikuyu grass surrounded the house, and cut into this were small rose gardens which I tended very carefully throughout the year. I also cut the grass using a petrol lawnmower and our garden boy, Johannes, took care of everything else. In all, it was a very charming place and Marjorie loved it.

Johannes was a minister in the local church. He held services beneath shade trees on the open veldt that lay between our house and Sandton City, a new shopping complex still under development two miles to the east. It was very peaceful to sit in our garden on a Sunday evening and listen to his Northern Sotho congregation of nannies, housekeepers, cooks and gardeners. They sang hymns and tribal songs with a zeal never heard in an English church. They harmonized together beautifully and their voices carried across the veldt until the huge red sun sank quickly below the horizon. This was their signal that it was time to return home to their kyas.

As they hurried home, in small groups for safety, a cool breeze would begin to stir and mosquitoes surged into the air to attack anyone who lingered. This was not a safe time of the day, a tsotsi might be lurking to rob anyone foolish enough to be caught alone in the early evening darkness or a cobra could be startled as it stood guard over the entrance to its nest. All three are ruthless killers but the tsotsi is the worst because he is a thief and he uses a short stabbing knife to paralyze his victim by severing the spinal chord.

This area of open veldt was a paradise for children playing hide and seek. Despite its obvious dangers Michele ran barefoot through the long grass and swam in the small stream along with many other children in the area. Over the seven years that we lived in View Road no one ever came to harm.

We did have our fair share of close calls. One evening Michele was returning from school, and as she walked through our walled garden she was challenged by a fully grown Egyptian Cobra. It reared in front of her, spread its hood and hissed in her face. It was the same kind of snake that killed Cleopatra, they warn three times before striking. If it had hit Michele in the face she would certainly not have survived. Michele stayed still and they stared at each other, as Johannes, who fortunately had seen what was happening, ran across the road to bring our neighbour Pete. Peter came running with his loaded pistol and shot the Cobra through the head. It measured 5ft 2ins.

We later found a nest of six small cobras in a crack beneath the entrance to our kitchen. This was not the last time we encountered cobras in View Road. The mother of Michele's best friend was later bitten on her hand while picking roses in her garden.

We had several maids while we lived in View Road. It was normal to have maids in Johannesburg, while in Zambia it was more common to have a houseboy. I preferred houseboys, for some reason I never really liked to have women in the house; they were too fussy. Family members were never allowed to live with servants, even for a short visit. Only servants issued with a police pass were allowed to stay overnight in a white area. This was one of those hideous laws that we had to abide by and heavy penalties were levied against any white person found breaking the rules.

Our first maid was a fat umfazi called Hannah, and we allowed her husband Noah to stay occasionally. Noah was a nice old guy and Michele liked him. One morning we were horrified to find him dead in the kya. We had to bribe the ambulance driver to take him away and to say that he had died in the ambulance. Johannes told Marjorie that Hannah was an evil woman and that she had taken bad muti from the Shaman and given it to Noah. In other words, she had poisoned him.

1969
My first day in Africa. A village somewhere in Kenya. I was violently ill while visiting the village and was later diagnosed to have Hong Kong flu. I hope I did not infect the native population

1969
Enjoying my first Braai with Cecil Armstrong, my Section Engineer at Broken Hill Mine. Notice that I am still wearing European clothing

1969
A devil tree (Baobab) on the Great North Road in Zambia

1969
Margie and Michele posing for my Praktica in the bungalow of our mine compound. Lobelia Street, Kabwe

1969
Michele talking with the Village Witch Doctor in a remote area of the Zambezi Valley

1969
An abandoned steam traction engine in the Bush east of Mulungushi Dam in Central Zambia

1969
Our first of many enjoyable Christmas holidays in Salisbury before the British Government forced Ian Smith to hand over control to Mugabe

1970
Kariba Dam from the
Rhodesian side

1970
Rhodesian border guard at the Kariba Dam. A key target for Mugabe's cut-throats who were based in terrorist camps on the Zambian side

1970
Waiting for the Pontoon to collect us and take us with our Datsun Bakkie across the Luangwa River

1970
Walking in the Luangwa Valley, North East Zambia, with a native Fundi

1972
On the Rhodesian side of Victoria Falls with Steven, Dad and Michele

1973
On Masada, West Bank, seconds before a squadron of operational Phantoms roared overhead. The Dead Sea and Jordan lies behind

1973
Posing for the camera on Giza Plateau. There were no tourists and the poor guy was desperate for custom. Notice my tie, times have changed

1974

Isn't it beautiful? One of my control panels for six continuous casting machines at the Newcastle Steel Works in Natal. The machines were manufactured at Chapel Bank, Cumbria

1975

The Honeywell Panel Shop in Johannesburg. We are nearing completion of 16 control panels for a carbon black plant

1976
Margie with her 375 Magnum. She was trained by the Randburg Police

1975
Echo Bravo Delta at Baragwanath. She was as strong as an ox and could pull more negative G than I could take

1976
Three monkeys in the Eastern Transvaal. Margie, Michele and Dad

1977
Margie and a very young Brett sitting on a robber's grave outside the old gold prospecting town of Pilgrims Rest

1977
With Michele in the Eastern Transvaal after one of my working visits to Magoebaskloof Dam

1977
Yeti, Nushka and our sledge dog team at home in Bordeaux, Randburg. From left, Gillian Knight, Jenny Knight, Brett and Michele

1978
Michele with a Rock Python in the
Snake Park at Halfway House in
the Transvaal

1978
Union Buildings in Pretoria. My nephew Garry sitting on the wall with Brett and Michele. Margie's sister, Anne, standing on the left

1979
Kruger Park in South Africa. More commercialised than the game parks in Central and East Africa but there are some fine animals

1979
The glass furnace at Companhia de Vidreira in Maputo. This was one of the factories that I helped to keep working in war-torn Mozambique

1979
Michele, Brett and Margie in a fort overlooking East London. We are about to drive down the Garden Route to Capetown

It took us some months before we found a suitable replacement, a dizzy young girl called Peggy. We left Michele with Peggy one night and visited the drive-in cinema. Just before leaving there was a water outage and I must have left the bath tap open. When we returned the house was empty. We eventually found Michele fast asleep at the home of one of her friends. It seems the water came back on and as it gushed into the bath Peggy shouted out in terror, 'Tokolosh Tokolosh', and ran from the house not to return until the following morning.

Michele realized what had happened, dressed and walked barefoot, as usual, to our closest neighbour, Kay Knight. This was the last time we left Michele at home. After this we took her to the drive-in and, if it was a restricted film, covered her with a blanket until we got past the ticket booth.

Peggy was not alone in her fear of the Tokolosh. Most of our servants were more frightened of him than they were of snakes; my worst nightmare. When Peggy eventually married and left our employment Johannes asked if he could move into our kya. The first thing he did was to place building bricks under the legs of his bed so that the Tokolosh could not reach him, and then he fixed coils of copper wire to the four corners of his roof to ensure that evil spirits were kept away.

Later in the year I removed these coils while clearing debris from the roof of his kya; he replaced them before the sun went down. On another occasion, Johannes told me that his son was ill. I gave him money with very definite instructions that he must take his son to a proper medical doctor. Even though he was a church minister he still, against my instructions, used the money to buy muti from a Shaman.

Although I employed Johannes as my gardener, I still preferred to mow my lawn and prune the roses myself. I loved the smell of freshly cut grass early in the morning and my senses were always aroused by the sight of hundreds of little sparkling diamonds as the rising sun caught small droplets of dew that still clung tenaciously to the fragrant petals of my roses.

Aeroplanes and heroes

When I finished my work I lay down on my back and marvelled at the strange shapes fashioned by wisps of cirrus more than forty thousand feet above. Hotel Bravo, the radio beacon used by Jan Smuts as a navigational point for aircraft arriving from Europe, was just to the north and I was fascinated by the Jumbos of BOAC, Lufthansa and Air France as they passed low overhead. Vapour radiated from the leading edge of their wings giving them a magical ghost-like appearance.

One morning in January 1973 the peace was shattered by Concorde 002 as she passed overhead. My windows vibrated and plates fell from the table. I had not expected her arrival and it was my first sighting of this incredible aircraft. She seemed to hover like a huge egret with her long hooked beak pointing down towards me. Deciding that I was not suitable prey she passed me by and exposed me to the huge roar of her four unmodified Olympus 593 engines.

Concorde passed overhead for the next six weeks while completing 28 high altitude high temperature test flights. Every morning the whole of Randburg was wakened by the roar of her engines as she passed overhead. Our windows vibrated so violently that it seemed as though they would break. We later learned that her Olympus engines were modified to reduce their thunderous roar but we did not mind. We were thrilled to witness the harnessing of such immense power in a supersonic passenger aircraft. This beautiful egret was going to help bring Britain back to the sharp end of technical innovation.

The following Christmas Bobby Locke, a world-famous international golfing champion, dropped in to say hello and he gave Michele a newly minted South African Rand coin as a present. He accompanied the gift with one of his short pieces of advice which he preceded with the words, "My father used to say". If one believed Bobby then he never had anything to say for himself, his father had always said it first. He once said, "You drive for show but you putt for dough". I often wonder if Bobby also credited that famous one-liner to his father.

Bobby had suffered a serious car accident some years earlier. The accident shortened his golfing career but he still played an excellent game and he was often invited to play as a celebrity in one of the US tournaments. Bobby is regarded as the best-ever 'putter' and the United States honoured him by placing him in the Golfing Hall of Fame.

Later in the year Peter, from across the road, invited Bobby and my childhood hero, Douglas Bader, for dinner. I was in Mozambique at the time and was unable to join them. I was very disappointed to miss such a fantastic opportunity. Most youngsters have football heros, mine are all Battle of Britain fighter pilots. Bobby won the UK Open four times and he became close friends with Bader just after the war when they played golf together. It is incredible that someone with tin legs actually scored 22 kills and earned the right to command a fighter wing during war time. It is even more incredible that the same person could escape from a German prisoner of war camp let alone play such a strong game of golf.

Handling contract relations

The South African economy was booming and new contracts were being won at an alarming rate. Our organisation was becoming outstretched. All of our projects were planned using techniques that might be likened to a critical path analysis. Each task had an allocated amount of resources and a time period for completion. If any one task which lay on the critical path could not be completed in the time allocated, then the whole programme fell behind and the project completion date was jeopardised. This was always very serious because if a process plant did not begin production on time, then the Main Contractor suffered huge penalties that he often tried to pass on to the offending sub-contractor.

Many of our projects were with Iscor on their South Vanderbijlpark Steel Works. A project management team discussed the progress of each individual project at a meeting scheduled every two weeks. This team comprised of a representative from each contractor and the meeting was chaired by a senior manager from Iscor. Most of the projects that I was involved in were chaired by a gentleman who was always referred to as Mr Horley; I doubt that anyone even knew his Christian name. I believe he was of German origin, he came from the old school and everyone was very frightened in his presence. He sat at the end of a very long conference table and presided over each meeting with absolute authority. No one ever dared to challenge his decisions.

Crudely speaking, any major contract can be split into four different phases; civil engineering, mechanical erection, electrical installation and control system installation. Each discipline has to complete its own work before the next can begin. There can be a certain amount of overlap but it almost always happens that the control system installation is being undertaken at the end of the 'critical path' and at a time when the project completion date is already under threat.

This means that the Contractor responsible for the measurement and control instrumentation is almost always working under extreme pressure. While the Civil Engineering Contractor may get his knuckles lightly rapped if he is a couple of months late, the Control System Contractor is kicked from pillar to post when he is only one week late.

I was tired of being kicked from pillar to post in almost every meeting that I attended, and I retaliated. It was a routine progress meeting and there was nothing unusual to create the conditions that followed. Several senior managers were gathered around the conference table, all of them at least twice my age and looking very comfortable sitting back in their large chairs sipping coffee and spluttering over a handful of cigars that had been passed around. Mr Horley started to pull Honeywell to pieces, criticising them very cruelly for not meeting his targeted completion date. This had become such a repetitive situation that I found I had no alternative but to do the unthinkable: to challenge him.

I interrupted him and told him that the targets were his targets, not mine. I told him that he always criticised Honeywell but he never held other contractors to account for their faults. I pointed out that we were working under very difficult conditions at the end of the project and that it was natural that we would be the Company to delay completion.

Everyone sat in stony silence. Mr Horley stared at me white faced and expressionless. When I had finished he stood up turned smartly around and walked out of the room. No one spoke for what seemed like an eternity and then the Lead Contractor said to me "you have done it now Barry".

I climbed into my car and drove the 60 miles back to Johannesburg. When I sat down in my office Morris Kirby joined me and asked me in his own rather crude way what had happened. The reception desk had apparently received a telephone call half an hour earlier telling them that I was no longer permitted to step foot upon any property that belonged to Iscor. In a single stroke Mr Horley had effectively destroyed my future in South Africa.

I jumped into my car and broke all the speed limits as I drove back to Vanderbijlpark. I had to get through the Main Gate before security had been informed. I was lucky, the shift had not changed and the Police let me through without any problems. I walked very nervously into the office complex and knocked on Mr Horley's door. When he answered I asked if I could have a word with him and he invited me to sit down. I apologised for my behaviour and explained the reasons for my outburst. He listened very carefully, accepted my apology and invited me to join the next meeting as usual.

I attended the next meeting and everyone must have been pre-programmed because no one was surprised by my presence, and there was no mention of anything that had taken place in the previous meeting. There was however one very noticeable difference. No criticism was made of Honeywell and in later progress meetings we were actually complimented for our work. I also noticed that Mr Horley began to treat me as a valuable member of his project team. He respected me for the way in which I had defended Honeywell and he was very pleased that I had apologised.

I believe he must have given consideration to what I said in my outburst and my apology enabled him to correct the situation without loosing face. Three years later when I started my own company in Johannesburg he called me to his office and told me to contact him if I ever needed a reference. I appreciated this very kind gesture. He really was one of the old breed.

After standing my ground with Mr Horley I had to be certain that I never gave him proper cause for complaint. It became crucial that I recruited several new people to strengthen our field engineering capability. I had severe constraints upon the salary that I was able to offer and this made it impossible to attract experienced engineers. I had no alternative but to look for young graduates or ambitious service technicians whom I could train.

Nothing can replace hands-on experience

Eventually I pulled together a project management team which included two young Afrikaaner technicians who had relevant experience and two new immigrants who had each recently graduated with a masters degree in engineering. I allocated projects to each of them and then worked carefully with each one in turn, giving encouragement and advice wherever it was needed.

Over the years I have trained a great many engineers, all of whom have served a craft or a student apprenticeship and a very small number have also been professionally qualified. I feel rather proud to mention that five of these project engineers became company managing directors within six years and one of these, Martin Muller, eventually became the Managing Director of my present employer, Honeywell South Africa.

The highest qualified of my new recruits, Christos, had been awarded a masters degree in control systems engineering by an American University. I gave him our most important contract to commission. This was with the Distington Engineering Company; the same company that short listed me for a position as their Chief Engineer two years earlier. We were contracted with Distington to supply and install the measurement and control instrumentation on three new continuous casting machines at the Iscor Steel Works in Newcastle, Natal. His task was to commission 144 identical flow control loops on these three machines. Two weeks after he began, the Chief Engineer from Distington complained that Christos had not been able to get the first machine working.

When I visited the site I found that Christos was trying to calculate the controller settings. In real applications, there are always far too many unknown variables to achieve an accurate calculation. I tried to help Christos to understand the difference between theory and practice but he could not make the adjustment. I took over from him and commissioned the first machine.

I don't want to go into too much technical detail but you could say that I entered provisional values, watched the process dynamics and then, after a lot of thumb sucking, made the appropriate adjustments. This took about 24 hours and then in the remaining 12 hours I worked with the Process Operators to check that the process alarms were correctly set and that the safety systems functioned. Only then did I consider it safe to leave the control room and return to my hotel for a well earned sleep.

I don't want to knock academics, I believe that a good well-rounded engineer should have a strong theoretical foundation, but this must be coupled with real hands-on experience, the kind that can only be obtained through a Craft or Student Apprenticeship. Nothing will ever change my view on this.

When I returned to Johannesburg I fired Christos and replaced him with Frik Eloff; a huge Afrikaaner who was gentle and well mannered. He had the sweetest young wife who was very homely and behaved as if she had just climbed off the back of a voortrekker wagon.

Frik had no formal qualifications but his personality and ability to obtain the very best from his workforce more than compensated. I remember well how Dr David Lewis, the man who got the Chief Engineer's job at Distington Engineering, asked Frik to address him by his Christian name. Frik could never bring himself to do this; he met David half way by addressing him respectfully as Dr David. It seemed so strange coming from a giant of a man with a deep Afrikaans accent. Frik was well liked by our Customers and I safely left him to handle all of our projects in Newcastle.

Shortly after this incident we were approached by Kawasaki Heavy Industries to bid for the installation of process control instrumentation on three large basic oxygen furnaces that they were building for Iscor at Vanderbijlpark. They issued detailed installation drawings and hundreds of material lists that described every component to be used. This is when I began to realize that Japanese engineers were not as meticulous as I once thought. Their documentation was presumably based upon designs already implemented in Japan and their engineers had not transformed these correctly into working documents that were suitable for use in South Africa.

Most of Central and Southern Africa had already metricated; hardware including all electrical fittings and pipe fittings could only be purchased in metric sizes. These material lists not only described a mixture of imperial and metric threads but the lists also mated BSF bolts with BSW nuts.

I used these documents to prepare our quotation knowing that if we won the project we would have to fall back on the old fashioned system; buy a few thousand of each metric size and top-up on our shortfalls. It was the largest quotation I had ever prepared. It included several miles of conduit tube, ducting, piping and electrical cable.

I was very excited when we won the contract and I immediately starting to purchase the materials we needed. Only then did I fully appreciate how big the project was. I found that my purchasing engineer had to travel all over Transvaal and even into the Free State to procure the quantities required.

I gave this contract to my youngest project manager, Johann Loots; he is a bit of a Don Juan and could never resist a pretty face. I was always jealous of the girls that he gathered around him but this never seemed to distract him from his work. It was his first major project and he rose to the challenge. What he could not buy he would beg, what he could not beg for he would steal. He would do anything to keep the project on course and he used all of his influence with fellow Afrikaaners to get out of trouble when he was caught 'borrowing' a welding machine or pipe threading machine from one of our fellow contractors.

The truth is that in a contracting environment everyone 'borrows', and if you don't, then you are the loser. I heard of an offshore contractor that borrowed several large diesel generators from his Customer, a well known oil company. Several years later his Customer needed five diesel generators and the Contractor sold them back to him. It is incredible what goes on!

I learned a tremendous amount while supporting Johann on this large project. We purchased large quantities of materials that were not specified in the Customer's schedules. I submitted a claim for extras and the General Manager of Kawasaki Heavy Industries called me to a meeting. I found myself sitting at a large conference table along with Johann and six senior Japanese managers. Each of the managers discussed a section of my claim and they never once used the word, 'no'; this was considered impolite. If someone did not agree with me he lowered his head with much mmm-ing and ahhh-ing, and a general reluctance to carry on with the conversation.

It soon became apparent that each of the six managers had to secure a small reduction in the claim otherwise he would lose face. However, he had to secure the reduction in an agreeable way that would not upset me. I came away from the meeting feeling as if I had been outmanoeuvred on all sides. I had an agreed claim that was promptly settled but it was substantially lower than what I had wanted.

I learned quickly from this experience and the next time that I submitted a claim for extras I ensured that I had included sufficient 'padding' to allow each of the participants to secure their required reduction. Everyone saved face and I achieved fair compensation for my claim.

Working with the Engineers and Management of Kawasaki Heavy Industries put me in good stead for my work in later life. I learned how to negotiate at a very high level and to secure the confidence and trust of senior managers. I learned how to work with Japanese companies; companies that were no longer the copy-cats, but companies that were now beginning to lead the world in technical innovation. Most important of all, I learned not to be confrontational - one of my largest failings as a young engineer in the United Kingdom Atomic Energy Authority.

My work at the end of this project was rewarded by the receipt of an excellent gift and a letter of thanks from the President of Kawasaki Heavy Industries. I have no doubt that many other managers received a similar acknowledgement, but I appreciated this kind thought.

Western companies have much to learn from their Japanese counterparts; very few senior executives in the West show formal appreciation to their customers with a small gift and a few words of thanks, even fewer show appreciation to their own sub-contractors. In the United Kingdom the government discourages this by taxing gifts to customers and in recent years they have even been so short-sighted as to impose corporation tax on the entertainment of foreign guests.

Eventually we suffered our worst nightmare

The Industrial Division went from strength to strength, and as our level of competence increased, so did our list of customers. We diversified into several new areas of work which included the breweries in Durban, fruit refrigeration facilities in Capetown Docks, coffee roasters in Brackpan and air refrigeration units one mile deep in the bowels of the Orange Free State gold mines.

We installed refrigeration systems on both President Steyn and President Brandt gold mines. They were very different to anything that I had worked on before. They were large industrial units mounted on skids and assembled in chambers one mile beneath the surface. The mines in the Free State are so deep that the rock surface is warmed by the earth's molten core and workers collapse from heat exhaustion. These refrigeration units are an attempt to improve these terrible working conditions. Not only are the conditions very hot but they are extremely dangerous. The rock is under such tremendous pressure that pressure bursts are common. The rock literally explodes killing anyone in close proximity.

Between shifts the main cages are used to haul rock to the surface and entry to the mine must be made by travelling in the Maryanne which is usually built to carry a maximum of two people. It is a wet and very lonely journey as one bounces around in a cage descending in freefall more than one mile into the bowels of the earth. As the cage gets deeper the shaft water seepage increases until it can be likened to riding in a bird cage that has just passed over the edge of Victoria Falls. I am very pleased that I did not have to visit our projects on the Orange Free State Gold Mines often, and when I did, I kept my inspections below ground as short as possible.

Installing our control equipment in dangerous and volatile environments was bound to lead to a serious incident, and eventually we suffered our worst nightmare. Sixteen process workers were killed in an explosion on a carbon-black plant in Vereeniging. I had supplied the instrumentation and built the control panels only two months earlier. A board of inquiry was set up and the control system was examined to establish if there was any design or manufacturing faults.

The examiners discovered that the controllers were in manual control at the time of the explosion and operator error was blamed. This did nothing to console the poor families affected by this terrible accident, so yet again, I was witness to a tragic event that took so many lives in horrific circumstances.

I have always been aware of the dangerous consequences that can occur if an operator does not respond correctly to a dangerous situation, and this tragedy caused me to be more creative with my control system designs. I began to incorporate new safety features that would help to protect against human error. These designs increased the total project cost and I listed the safety element separately to ensure that we did not lose the customers order in a competitive bid process. I have very rarely found a customer who will refuse to pay a little extra to ensure the safety of his workers and my designs became widely accepted. Moreover, when I was called upon to commission a new plant, I felt much more assured in regard to my own safety.

Early in 1974 Morris Kirby, my mentor in Honeywell, was appointed to take over from Reg Garrett as the new Managing Director of Honeywell South Africa. Morris came storming into my office one day muttering verbal abuse in all directions. He said that he was unable to get a clear understanding of what was happening in the Commercial Contracts Division; the department responsible for control equipment on high rise buildings, hospitals and large commercial enterprises.

Commercial development was at an all-time high in Southern Africa and this division had a massive order backlog which he believed was being mishandled. Morris was a strong manager who had worked at the sharp end for many years; he always wanted results, not explanations! He asked if I would take over the Commercial Division in addition to my existing responsibilities. I accepted and he created the new position of National Contracts Manager with total responsibility for more than sixty projects that were in various stages of completion.

The Commercial Division Manager, Piet van Schaardenburg, was an old-world Dutchman with a very black neatly trimmed beard and shaved upper lip. He wore spectacles and was always in deep concentration when I approached him. He bore no grudge when I was placed above him and we worked well together. I could easily understand how Morris had difficulty in obtaining information from him. He was not the kind of person who would respond to the foul language that Morris always used when he became impatient.

South Africa was preparing for a war with the Cuban forces in Angola and the Government awarded us a contract to supply and install the heating and ventilation control systems on two very large military hospitals. These hospitals were to be built secretly under military restrictions and then mothballed. Each hospital had more than two thousand control points and we elected to use the new Honeywell Delta

2000 control system. This was the first system of its type which was fully integrated and provided access to control parameters through a centralized video display unit in a remote control room.

When war did break out in Angola the South African forces advanced quickly through South West Africa and deep into Angolan territory. They enjoyed overwhelming aerial superiority. Cuban Mig 15's and 17's were no match for French-built Mirage jet fighters, and I was later told by one of the Cuban Commanders who flew and survived two tours of duty in Angola that his instructions to 'green' pilots were always to avoid a direct one-to-one confrontation with a South African pilot.

The South African forces advanced to a point overlooking the capital city of Luanda and then suddenly, with no explanation, they turned and rushed back into South West Africa. Their retreat was so rapid that they left heavy military equipment behind and several of my friends in the Air Commando had to abandon their aircraft. The grapevine said they were acting under instructions from the United States. Perhaps the Soviet Union had warned the incumbent President of their intention to intervene?

I needed to gain a better understanding of the new projects under my control and so I flew down to Capetown to inspect one of our largest contracts. This was to supply and install building automation controls on the BP Centre. This new commercial development was being built on land reclaimed from the sea in front of the Capetown business district. It contained shops, offices and a cinema complex that was already complete and operational.

When I arrived I found our workers engaged in installing air supply headers in the lift shafts at a height of about twenty floors above ground level. When installing controls on a high-rise building it is necessary to work on a building shell that has no walls, ceilings or elevators. It is essential to work at a steady pace on the floor levels that have been completed by the civil engineers, while keeping just ahead of the people who fit the basic fabric of the building. This can be hazardous and it certainly requires a good head for heights.

I asked the Bossboy where the Baas was and he refrained from answering me. Eventually I was able to ascertain through a question and answer routine that he was in the cinema watching the afternoon matinee. The Bossboy was very loyal. He didn't want to tell me any lies but he did not want to rat on his white foreman. After I met with him later in the day, I left the Baas in no doubt as to what would happen if I ever again caught him leaving his workers unattended.

My reputation working in the Industrial Division had preceded me and I did not find it necessary to make an example of him. Instead, I gained the respect of our black workers who saw that I was treating everyone equally, and the white foreman accepted that it was a fair 'cop' and was pleased to be able to keep his job.

Time for a holiday

I yearned to visit the more interesting areas that South Africa had to offer, and whenever I had an opportunity to take a holiday we jumped into our brand new company car, a Triumph 2000 saloon, and left the Reef (the gold reef of Johannesburg) to explore. I liked my Triumph; it was the only British-built car that I owned in Africa and the only car that let me down many times. It simply wasn't built to drive in the African Bush.

One Easter weekend my fan belt broke while driving through the Drakensburg Mountains just below the magnificent amphitheatre of the Royal Natal National Park. Marjorie had no nylon stockings and I rather foolishly forgot to pack a spare belt. The garages were closed and so we stayed in a farm-cum-hotel at the foot of the mountains. This was opportune because the school of the Drakensburg Boys Choir was nearby and their founders, the Tungay Family, gave a special Easter performance for local people and we were invited to join them.

The sound of so many young voices singing high in the sharp clean air of the Drakensburg Mountains was breathtaking. Their voices harmonized beautifully in a fashion which can only find its equal among young girls of the neighbouring Zulu Tribes. The performance was given in an old farm building where a stage had been improvised.

As we left the building we stopped for a moment and looked up to the Amphitheatre which towered in front of us. I imagined the soft voices of the boys whispering back to us from the mountains. Their voices mingled with the soft lapping sound of a small river which glistened in the moonlight as it meandered slowly towards us. Suddenly, in my mind's eye, I could see Michael Caine struggling across the river in his smart red army tunic. He shouted to Stanley Baker who was stripped to his waist and struggling with a large piece of timber. I realized that the scene before me was one that I had seen so many times before in the film 'Zulu'. This was Paramount Pictures' version of Rorkes Drift.

Living on the backbone of such a vast continent we often felt the need to swim in the ocean and this involved a long drive to Durban on the Natal Coast where we would normally stay in town or at Umhlanga Rocks. Michele loved our stays in Durban, and she enjoyed her colourful rickshaw rides along the Golden Mile pulled by Zulus in large feathered headdresses.

This part of the Natal Coast is notorious for shark attacks and nets are stretched at intervals along the main bathing beaches. On one of our visits I swam in very large seas and a rip tide swept me past the nets. I am terrified of sharks and I swam desperately towards a breakwater further down the beach. I was too exhausted to pull myself out and the waves pounded me relentlessly against the rocks. Eventually a large wave threw me out of the water and I lay gasping for several minutes before I could stand again.

My body was covered in deep cuts and I was embarrassed as I walked down the Golden Mile past hundreds of gaping holiday makers. A trail of blood marked my passage from the breakwater to the place where I had left my clothes. Marjorie seemed un-concerned; it was not the first time and would not be the last. She took me to hospital and they treated my wounds; I still carry scars to remind me of my Durban swim.

While I had been in Durban I noticed the wide range of trinkets on display for tourists. I always thought there was a strong overseas market for African novelties and so I decided to set up a small business manufacturing and selling different tribal items through mail order to the United States. My first items included a lion's tooth charm capped in sterling silver, an elephant hair fertility bracelet and an Ndebele love necklace. I had a complete Ndebele village making my necklaces and I soon gathered a stockpile of almost a thousand pieces.

My items were priced so low that I was convinced they would sell in huge numbers. I placed a full-page advert in the Woman's Day magazine and registered a private mail sack at the Randburg Post Office. My advert cost 10,000 dollars which at that time was a fortune. If I remember correctly the Woman's Day magazine had a circulation of 4 million across the United States; I received all of eight orders. One of my customers wrote saying that she was surprised with what she received for her money. A marketing guru later said that if I had multiplied my prices by a factor of ten then I would have obtained a good sales volume. This showed just how little I knew about marketing.

Time to move on again

Both the Industrial and Commercial Divisions continued to win major projects throughout South Africa and I was able to achieve reasonable profit margins on every single contract. I had always prided myself as a good hands-on engineer but the number of contracts under my control required me to become more and more of a cost accountant.

In 1975 Honeywell secured the contract to supply measurement and control instrumentation for the largest single project in the world. The Shah of Iran had been forced into exile by the Islamic Revolution and Ayatollah Khomeini cut off the supply of Iranian crude oil to South Africa. The South African Government had to find an alternative source as quickly as possible. They elected to build a massive refinery to extract oil from coal using a process developed during the Second World War.

The project was given the name Sasol II and the first phase was to be fitted with upwards of 8000 control loops each wired back to 32 separate control rooms. The control equipment selected was a new distributed system known as TDC-2000. Sasol II was about to become the guinea pig for the largest and most successful control system ever developed.

I had given five years of my life to Honeywell and much of this time had been spent in Newcastle, Vanderbijlpark, and other remote industrial areas which were devoid of wildlife or any of the other features that one associates with South Africa. Sasol II was also located in the middle of nowhere and I desperately wanted to spread my wings. I decided that this was the right time for me to move on.

Chapter 11

Coulton Industrial

Working in war-torn Mozambique and South West Africa
Carry a second passport!

I started my third company, Coulton Industrial, a few weeks before I resigned from Honeywell and opened an office in Randburg Five, a new office complex in the northern suburbs of Johannesburg. I recruited a very attractive young German girl called Friga and trained her to do my engineering drawings. She was a likeable young girl with a fresh face and a pleasing personality. After Friga I recruited David, a Welsh Technician who claimed to have several sales contacts in the area, and then I stole Steve, the best sales engineer working for Honeywell.

I was careful to pave the way before leaving Honeywell and I soon closed several orders with large engineering companies. The first was with Iscor in Newcastle. They gave me a small order to measure and transmit the flow of several different process fluids as part of an energy management scheme. Honeywell transmitters were specified but the sales manager, an old friend called Harry Viljoen, refused to supply the transmitters to me. He believed that he could make more profit by supplying direct.

Harry misjudged the situation and my contact, an Afrikaaner engineer in Newcastle, promptly gave me permission to use Hartmann & Braun transmitters. This turned out to my advantage, Hartmann & Braun were looking for a way to break into Newcastle and they gave me a 60 percent discount. In addition, they awarded me a large contract to provide hundreds of engineering drawings for South African Railways on their huge electrification project. By default Harry did me a favour.

I enjoyed working in Randburg Five, my offices were very plush. I had sun filter curtains, comfortable chairs, office desks, typewriters and a large drawing board for Friga. This cost more than most of the furniture combined but then we had the South African Railways project to pay for it. It was a pleasant change from my facilities in Zambia and I felt that I had earned it. I enjoyed being able to walk through Randburg during my lunch break and do a little clothes shopping or enjoy a milk shake in the Café directly below my window.

I became friendly with Paul Hopwood, the charismatic Managing Director of Combustion Engineering; a small company that occupied offices directly opposite and on the same floor. Paul once had a stand on Oldham market and he was every bit the salesman as he was a good engineer. He won a contract to provide burners on nine curing furnaces at Coverland Tiles in Vereeniging and he sub-contracted the electrical switchgear and the control equipment to Coulton Industrial. We worked together as a team and worked day and night for weeks until the project was finished. It was very profitable for both of us and neither of us ever looked back.

Paul and his wife Maggie became very good friends and later Marjorie and I were pleased to be able to help them to adopt two babies in Johannesburg. Another good friend was Walter, a Swiss Travel Agent who organized charter flights to Europe. He occupied the remaining office on our floor in Randburg Five, and one day I came in to find that his office was full of police from the serious fraud squad. Walter had decided that it was time to leave South Africa and the maximum emigration allowance for a full family was the equivalent of $10,000. This included the value of furniture and any other personal effects that he wanted to take with him. He felt that this was not a fair amount and so he made alternative arrangements.

Walter made money from booking large charter flights to Europe. He filled Boeing 707 aircraft with around 160 passengers and each time he obtained exchange control approval to pay for the overseas arrangements. This was around a quarter of a million dollars for each charter. Eventually the transfer of this quarter of a million dollars became routine and Walter's bank manager no longer took care when examining his exchange control documents. Walter created an imaginary charter flight and transferred a quarter of a million dollars of his own money out of the country.

Walter had paid his taxes and he worked hard for most of his life, so why should he not be free to take his retirement money and spend it as he pleases? We never heard from Walter again, but Paul and I wished him well and congratulated him on his brilliant deception plan.

Bangkok and Hong Kong

I had always wanted to visit the Far East, and then one day, I spotted a 14-day air package to Bangkok and Hong Kong. The United States was not doing too well in nearby Vietnam and accommodation was reasonably priced. I jumped at the chance and immediately applied for my annual exchange control allowance.

Bangkok was still untouched by modern civilization. There were no high rise buildings and the incredible living wealth of this historical city of ancient Siam was outstandingly beautiful. Ancient palaces, temples and shrines glistened in the sunlight as yet another flake of gold was impressed upon a thousand Buddhas in the city. An impoverished peasant hoped that Buddha would look favourably upon him and reward him with a good crop while another hoped that her son would soon be well again. Bangkok was not overshadowed by any of the ugly new developments so evident in London. The yob-like culture of Western Europe was still not in evidence, traffic congestion was not a serious problem and pollution was within acceptable limits.

I was enthralled by the temples, palaces and shrines that I visited. They were living monuments to the beauty and fascination of Siamese culture and tradition. Tuk-tuks were the main form of transportation; a cross between a 3-wheeled motor scooter and a rickshaw. Traditional massage parlours, as opposed to brothels, were common place and I am told that Pat Pong thrived for those who are aware of that particular area.

I re-visited Bangkok on several occasions over the next 30 years and I was deeply disappointed by the exponential increase in traffic and pollution that was causing serious chemical damage to the surface of many old buildings. But most of all, I was deeply upset by the government's reluctance to prevent indiscriminate construction of ugly modern high-rise buildings only feet away from the foundations of once beautiful historical and religious structures. I believed that the architectural heritage of Bangkok was being compromised, possibly forever.

My travel group included half a dozen very straight laced South African doctors. They wanted to visit a traditional massage parlour, purely for professional reasons of course, and so I hunted one down for them. We set out after our evening meal and I took them to a place with a window 30 feet long. We were the only Europeans and so it must have been a genuine place. On the other side of the window there were 36 young and very attractive women with long jet black hair, dark complexion and huge genuine smiles. Each wore a smart long dress and carried a number on their chest.

I chose a girl for myself and the attendant called out her number on a loudspeaker. I imagined that we were at our local boating lake; "come in number 26". She took my hand and went to a booth where she collected a basket containing a towel, bar of soap, comb and the key to a room. Inside the room I was directed to undress and climb into a bath while she rolled up her long sleeves. She then gave me the bar of soap and indicated that I was to wash my own head; the rest of my body was not a problem.

The massage was somewhere between a full body oil massage and a treatment session with an overzealous osteopath. She rocked my head gently from side to side, placed one foot on the end of the table, and then jerked my head back with all of the strength she could muster. There was a loud cracking sound and I thought she had broken my neck. She shifted her stance and put her other foot on the end of my table and started to rock my head in the other direction. This time I knew what was coming and I was so terrified that I held my head absolutely rigid; she had to give up.

After my session I collected my charges and led them back towards our hotel. It was almost 9 pm and the army was already clearing the streets. There had been another military coup, one of many, and Bangkok was under a very strict 9 pm curfew. My South African friends were understandably more sensitive to this kind of situation than me and they became very agitated. I decided to have some fun with them.

When we were within five minutes of our hotel entrance I circled a neighbouring block and told them that I was lost. They were beside themselves, we were the only ones remaining on the street and they started to run in the wrong direction. I called them back and exactly on-time we rounded the last corner and walked into our hotel foyer. They were furious when they realised what I had done.

Our Cathay Pacific flight from Bangkok to Hong Kong was much longer than expected. The skipper, Jules Brett, knew several of my friends who flew with East African and South African Airways. He allowed me to fly in the jump seat and I was intrigued by the huge dog-leg that we had to fly around the Vietnam War zone. There were no navigational aids and we used a Doppler Navigation System. It was incredibly accurate; after a flight of several hours, which involved two major changes in direction, we arrived at our destination less than 5 miles east of our intended track.

Our approach into Kei Tak, Hong Kong airport, was rather unusual. We approached from the seaward side and on finals the control tower called in and said "the runway is obstructed by a junk, be ready to abort". I can't think of many airports where one would receive this kind of call on finals.

Hong Kong was everything that I expected it to be and much more. I visited the Royal Navy dockyard, Victoria Peak, Repulse Bay and all the normal tourist places. My lasting impression was one of desperation; mega-rich financial tycoons living in denial of the absolute poverty around them; large ugly tenant buildings festooned with washing lines and television aerials, bedraggled people trying to etch a meagre existence out of a small piece of British occupied land.

Most of these unfortunate people had climbed wire fences and sailed treacherous waters to get into the British Crown Colony from neighbouring China. A guide told me how a new water line feeding Kowloon from mainland China had been blocked by dead bodies when the authorities first opened the gate valves. Refugees had been walking through the pipeline when the first rush of water passed through. It sounded like a Hollywood movie, but sadly it was all for real.

So many people had died trying to enter Hong Kong that those who succeeded placed no value on another person's life. I suspect that if someone dropped dead in the street, then the mass of heaving pushing struggling humanity would just pass right over him. It was the only place in the world where I had ever felt uncomfortable and unsafe.

RMS Queen Elizabeth could be seen lying on her side in Victoria Harbour. She had caught fire two years earlier in mysterious circumstances and then capsized during fire fighting operations. Launched on the Clyde in 1938, she first served as a troopship and then as a luxury liner. Cunard retired her in 1968 and at the time of the fire a Hong Kong Business tycoon was converting her into a floating university. She was the largest steam passenger ship ever built and was certified to carry 15,000 troops during wartime operations. The James Bond film 'Man with the Golden Gun' was in production and the MI6 Headquarters were constructed beneath her partially submerged decks. Years later I was to stay on board her companion, RMS Queen Mary, who had been retired as a hotel ship in Long Beach California.

Business was growing steadily in Coulton Industrial. Friga and I had plenty of contracts to keep us busy but David and Steve, try as they might, were unable to bring in any new business. The projects that I closed in the first few months of business were directed towards me by former customers of Honeywell and this included my old friend Mr Horley. I had no need for an expensive sales office and a team of sales engineers; I closed down my sales office in Randburg Five and asked for the resignation of David and Steve. It was a major step to take, but it was the only sensible thing to do, and I moved into the garage of my split level home in 75 View Road, Bordeaux.

Working in Communist Mozambique

Shortly after moving out of my offices in Randburg Five I received a telephone call from Bill McDougall, the workshop foreman at Honeywell. Companhia de Vidreira wanted Honeywell to refurbish their glass furnace in Maputo.

Portugal had recently lost a long guerrilla war in Mozambique and Samora Machcl, the leader of Frelimo, now headed a communist government that controlled the southern part of Mozambique. A separate group of rebels supported by South Africa was still fighting against Frelimo in the north around Beira. Honeywell were not permitted to supply high technology services to Mozambique and Bill asked if I would like to take the project.

I gave him a positive answer and two weeks later I received advance payment from the Bank of Mozambique. It was a crazy kind of deal, these people were so desperate to get their glass furnace operational again that they were prepared to pay hard currency, up front, to a company that they had never heard of, and in a country that was effectively at war with them.

Bill took two weeks holiday and we boarded a South African Airways flight to Maputo. After landing our Hawker Sidley aircraft was immediately placed in one of the hangers so that the South African Flag could not be seen by a delegation visiting from Eastern Europe. We were quickly cleared through customs and given special permits for our tools and test equipment. It was all rather disturbing when we were interrogated by ex-guerrilla fighters carrying AK-47's. They were undisciplined, could not speak a word of English and they were very authoritarian in their attitude. Even the lowest private wanted to demonstrate his elevated importance as an airport security guard.

We were taken in a beaten-up old Fiat to the Polana Hotel; a magnificent hotel in beautiful surroundings on a cliff overlooking the Indian Ocean. Our rooms were excellent and the large hotel foyer was a hive of activity. Late afternoon tea and cakes were served at dozens of small tables placed randomly across the large marble floor. It seemed that every Portuguese colonial who had not fled the country was taking tea in the ambience of this large meeting place.

Large groups of young Portuguese girls huddled together sharing news of their parents who were trying to start a new life in strife-torn Portugal. These girls were second or third generation Portuguese and had never known any other home. They were all childhood friends and were desperately trying to cling together in this beautiful city that use to be known as Lourenco Marques, regarded by many as the most fashionable city in all Africa.

I spent many evenings in the foyer of the Polana Hotel and I soon became well known by the local diplomats who sipped tea and nibbled at small cakes after a long hot day in the office. The girls eventually plucked up courage and asked me to join them at their tables. They wanted to practise their English while listening to me about life in South Africa, England and the rest of the western world. They told me incredible stories that only those who have lived in Africa would believe.

They explained how they were able to walk around Maputo at any time of the night without danger of molestation. After Samora Machel gained power a young white girl was raped on the beach. No one could be certain which soldier was guilty and so Machel ordered every soldier in the platoon to be lined up against a wall and shot in public. This was very brutal but it had the desired effect; imagine the outcry if this had happened in White South Africa.

There was also a negative side to this rigid moral code; a man and woman could not walk down the street hand in hand unless they were able to produce a marriage certificate. No one was allowed to play western music in public or in the privacy of their own home. My young Portuguese friends told how they would hold parties late into the night with their record players set at the lowest volume level. Life was very difficult and yet exciting.

After our evening meal we walked in large groups to the Italian Ice Crème Café and sat on the pavement; still hot from the afternoon sun. This café would serve the most incredible concoctions that excelled far beyond anything available in the proprietor's native country. We could not understand where he obtained his basic ingredients, there were no cows or goats to provide milk and the different flavourings that he used must have been obtained from hidden stocks secreted into his cellar long before the communists took control.

Sometimes I just stayed in the Polana and propped up the bar in true colonial fashion. With the exception of locally brewed beer and poor quality wine, Pimms Number 2 was the only alcoholic beverage available. Hundreds of crates were found in a cargo ship that was trapped in Lourenco Marques harbour at the start of the Portuguese Revolution. I didn't like beer and so Pimms, along with a very special kind of Sangria, became my two favourite drinks. It took me several visits to Mozambique before I finally learned the ingredients that the barman used to make his version of Sangria and I have since served this refreshing but lethal concoction in a large punch bowl at many parties in South Africa, England and the Bahamas.

When I entered the country I was forced to change a small amount of foreign currency into Mozambique Escudos. I didn't need this money because my customer met all of my expenses. I walked around town trying to find something to spend my Escudos on and found hundreds of assistants standing behind empty counters, bored to tears. All of the stores had been taken-over by the government and they were unable to make their staff redundant under the new communist system. Not only the stores had been seized but every building, factory and piece of land in the country was now government owned. One of my young friends explained that her family owned a large house which she still lived in, but all her unused rooms were allocated to African families. This was communism Lenin style.

At the end of my visit I thought I had given away all my remaining Escudos but I was mistaken. When I arrived at the airport I was searched by one of the ex-guerrillas and he found a few Escudos in my trouser pocket, the equivalent of two shillings. He arrested me and filed a criminal report. I thought for a moment that I was in big trouble but my host was able to explain that I was a guest of the government. The soldier allowed me to board my aircraft on the condition that I returned to Maputo the following month and reported to the police station. I did return but I was not foolish enough to report to the police.

Bill and I worked fourteen hours a day for two weeks at Companhia de Vidreira refurbishing the glass factory control room and all of the field instrumentation associated with their huge glass furnace. This furnace used several oil burners to raise the temperature of a continuous feed of silica sand, pre-mixed with feldspar, dolomite, limestone and soda ash, to a temperature of 1460 degrees centigrade, at which point it became molten glass. The molten glass was then tapped off to bottling machines which moulded beer bottles and coca cola bottles.

Repairing and refurbishing the pressure, temperature, flow and level transmitters on this furnace was incredibly hot work. The water was polluted and so we drank huge amounts of warm coke to prevent dehydration. Sweat poured from our bodies and ran in small rivers to fill our boots. The temperature of the molten glass was measured by platinum thermocouples that dipped at regular intervals into the surface of the glass. I volunteered to repair and calibrate these probes, and to do so, I had to walk across the roof of the furnace.

Imagine a self supporting arch roof approximately 100 feet long and 30 feet wide that has been built with refractory brick by persons of unknown skill. The surrounding air temperature is in excess of fifty degrees centigrade and beneath the brick roof is several hundred tons of molten glass. This is not Pilkington's in Lancashire where the environment is controlled, it is war torn Mozambique in mid-summer.

I wore a dust mask, placed a wet towel around my neck and used boots with extra thick soles. Gingerly and very nervously I walked across the roof and worked on each probe for a couple of minutes until I could feel the heat burning through the soles of my boots, then, like a cat on hot bricks I ran for the safety of the service floor where I could throw my boots off and dance around until the pain subsided. I repeated this activity for most of the day until I finished my work with the temperature probes. After this the pressure, flow and level transmitters were child's play.

Whenever someone comments upon the relatively small amount of wealth that I have been able to accumulate for my retirement years, I think of these times and of the times when I worked down the copper mines in Zambia. I worked hard for my money. It is on occasions such as this that I baulk at the fat lawyers who have no moral standards and who use their positions to fleece unfortunate clients of large sums of money. I am professionally more qualified than any barrister and yet I earn perhaps less than one tenth of a percent of what they can take from a simple libel action with minimum effort on their part. It is no wonder that hard working people get so upset when the people who make our laws use the same laws to feather their own nests at the expense of others.

Shortly after Bill and I returned to civilisation, albeit Johannesburg, I received a telephone call from the accountant at Vidreira. He and his family had escaped through the bush into neighbouring Swaziland to escape Samora Michel's henchmen. It seems that he had fallen foul of one of his Lieutenants, the head of the Frelimo Security Police. He needed money to buy air tickets to Brazil where he hoped to start a new life; bang went the greatest part of my profit from our short venture into Mozambique.

Nevertheless, word spread quickly in Maputo that we had done a very good job and for an honest price. No other western companies were prepared to work in Mozambique during the early days of independence. Payment was uncertain, the conditions were terrible, Frelimo styled communism had taken away personal liberties and a civil war was waging.

I was asked to re-visit Vidreira a few weeks later and when I arrived two other Companies were waiting to meet with me. When I returned to Johannesburg I held maintenance contracts for the four largest industrial companies in Mozambique. They produced glass, cement, steel and sugar. I was also offered contracts with the army to repair communication equipment but the South African Government was secretly supporting the Renamo rebels around Beira; I thought it was safer to decline.

I made several good friends in Maputo. Most were born in Mozambique to colonial parents; however, I should give particular mention to Joachim Duarte, an expatriate from Oporto who is an expert in glass production. Joachim raised several of my contracts with Companhia de Vidreira and on more than one occasion he extracted me from extremely dangerous situations.

I returned many favours to Joachim and one of my most memorable was to help repatriate his tools to Portugal. First he telefaxed a list of his tools and specialist equipment to Johannesburg and then I included this list with mine when I took my own personal tools through customs. The Frelimo Soldiers had no idea what my tools were, they just counted them and then rubber stamped my papers. When I returned to Johannesburg I replaced my junky decoy items with Joachim's tools to make the same count, and then shipped them on to Oporto. I was committing a serious criminal offence, but they were the tools of his trade. I could not see why Joachim should return to Portugal after ten years with no more than the clothes on his back; who are the real criminals?

I established a regular routine and flew into Maputo every two months for a two week period. With time I learned the ropes and became expert in dealing with difficult Frelimo soldiers at the airport until an arrogant upstart stamped my passport for four days. I explained as best I could that his government issued my visa for two weeks and that he had no right to disregard the instructions given in my official letter. He rudely explained that Mozambique was a communist country where everyone was equal and that he had decided I could only stay for four days; the miserable little sod!

The Johannesburg flight was weekly and I had no opportunity to comply with the bastard's ruling. On day five the soldiers placed me under hotel arrest and took my passport from me. This was very bad news; there were people in Mashava prison who had been left to rot without trial and I was very concerned that I would become one of them. On day seven I took a dangerous chance and visited the immigration office where my passport was being held.

I stood outside the entrance with Joachim and he asked every person passing by if they would look for my passport, explaining that I would reward anyone who could find it. Eventually a young soldier came out brandishing it in his hand. I went straight to the airport and boarded my plane before anyone realized what had happened. When I reached Johannesburg I wrote to the British Passport Office and they issued me with a second passport. From that moment I always carried a reserve passport to get me out of such dangerous situations.

My friendship grew with the Portuguese girls that I met every evening in the foyer of the Polana Hotel. They gave me large bowls of mango fruit and boxes of frozen Lorenzo Marques prawns which I packed carefully and took back to Johannesburg in my carry-on bag. One evening they invited me to a farm barbeque where we had to catch the pig, which ran squealing into the bush, kill it and then place it on the spit. The mosquitoes that gathered around us were dreadful. It was not my idea of a fun evening but it was an interesting experience.

The same girls gathered around the hotel pool on Sundays where we had a beautiful view over the harbour. The gardens surrounding the pool were perfect for them to stretch out and add more tan to their already dark skins. One of the girls that befriended me was a very attractive coloured girl; my host warned me that she was the niece of the Security Minister and I decided to give her a wide berth. A short while later she was relocated to a labour farm in the north; apparently to facilitate her re-education.

My main contact and friend at the Cement Factory was Ferdinand Bruheim, an engineer who trained in Eastern Europe during the days of revolution. He kept me informed of my political environment and ensured that I remained clear of those people that could endanger my safety.

Ferdinand offered me an unlimited quantity of cement in trade for the supply of industrial equipment required to effect repairs on his factory. I gave serious consideration to this offer because Saudi Arabia had a massive civil works programme and they were only a couple of thousand miles up the East African coast. The Saudis were able to purchase anything that I could ship to them. I serviced and repaired the measuring and control equipment on his cement factory, Companhia de Cimentos. I was confident that his cement was cured under the precise conditions required to achieve the highest quality. However, I was not confident of the loading facilities in Maputo harbour, and I visualised a concrete laden hull arriving in Jeddah. I decided to stand back from Ferdinand's offer.

Perhaps my fears were well founded. Several years later a retired sea captain in the Bahamas told me of a similar story which occurred off the Mozambique coast. A young inexperienced captain agreed to accept a shipment of polished rice and when he arrived at his destination the humidity had reduced his cargo to a rotten consignment of sake wine.

Life was exciting and stories abounded in the Polana bar. I heard of a man who was returning from a small island in the bay when a storm struck. His boat sank and rescuers found him lying unconscious on a marker buoy in the channel. The buoy had smooth vertical metal walls and he was lying face down on the rim five feet above the water. Everyone believes that he was thrown to safety by one of the porpoises that frequent the bay.

I also shared stories with British crews that flew a Boeing 707 charter flight every night to Angola. This was the first leg of the departure route for ex-colonials starting a new life in Portugal after the coup in Lisbon. I had just completed my senior commercial pilot's written examinations. These were based upon the 707 and I saw this as an opportunity to get some hands-on experience. One of the pilots gave me a shirt, another a pair of trousers, another a cap; before long I had a full uniform. They assured me that the soldiers in Luanda never asked for their passes and that I would have no problem in joining them for a round trip on the crew deck.

This all sounded rather crazy. Both Angola and Mozambique were in the middle of a brutal civil war and I was going to travel between both countries without a crew pass. Perhaps it was fortunate that on the day that I was about to leave I received a call to fly to a sugar factory east of Beira. To alleviate my disappointment, my host arranged for me to fly on the flight deck of the Mozambique Airlines 737 that took me to Beira.

I enjoyed the flight and it was my first ever opportunity to fly a Boeing jet aircraft. I found the controls incredibly easy to handle; it was certainly easier than flying a light aircraft. The co-pilot was converting from a small turbojet aircraft and he took over the controls for our landing. I am sure that I could have done much better. He rounded out too soon and the strong crosswind in Beira carried him off the runway with 86 passengers on board.

We were met by the maintenance foreman of the sugar factory. As we drove quickly through Beira I noticed how deserted the streets were. Small groups of blacks stared at us from street corners as we passed by. I did not see a single white person. Only then did my host explain that the area was controlled by Renamo rebels.

The sugar factory was a long drive out of town, and when I arrived, I was given a large house to use for the length of my stay. The kitchen was full of crockery, the bedroom had children's toys in the cupboard, clothing was hanging in the wardrobes and my bedside cabinet was full of stamp albums. The owners had literally walked out of the house with nothing but the clothes they were standing in.

I looked around several other houses and they were all exactly the same. This was not a place to be in. I slept very lightly that night and after a very brief inspection of the factory I elected to get on the next flight back to Maputo. I thought about taking the stamp albums with me but somehow it just didn't seem right. I left them where they were and I guess they have long since been destroyed by the savages that were brutalizing this part of the country.

I attended the Maputo theatre one evening for a gala performance in honour of Frelimo. At the end of every isle a sentry stood guard with an AK-47 assault rifle and along the main corridor between the upper and lower stands were several soldiers with machine guns. Just before the curtain rose Samora Machel entered and everyone in the auditorium jumped to attention. I followed suit, not in respect of Machel, but for reason of self preservation.

My reputation continued to grow and soon I even began to give credit to my customers. This was something unheard of when dealing with a third world country, but my trust paid off and I received large orders for SKF ball bearings, bottle moulds, electrical motors; everything that was needed to keep their factories working.

Frustrated by incompetent Banks

My problems in servicing my orders came from an unexpected quarter, I had a serious altercation with an over zealous bank manager in Johannesburg. I presented a letter of credit for settlement by the Bank of Lisbon. They refused to make payment because the goods had been shipped from Kaserne Railway Station and not from Johannesburg Railway Station. Kaserne was the name of the Railway Station in Johannesburg and the manager knew this. I was furious. I wrote to the newspapers and only then did the manager capitulate and made payment.

It is a sad fact that in Africa I always found that it was necessary to resort to aggressive behaviour before a satisfactory conclusion could be reached. Banks were my biggest problem. My customers paid on time but the banks never honoured their obligations. They always found a small clause or a very minor discrepancy to avoid payment. On one occasion the Bank of Mozambique refused to settle a bank transfer. This was because the number of cents in the purchase order had been rounded down to the nearest dollar. The difference was even in their favour.

These problems are not unique to banks in Central and Southern Africa. US banks think that the whole world shops with dollars; they are helpless when presented with Sterling, Deutschmarks, Yen or any other of the major world currencies.

As my work developed in Mozambique I decided that it was foolish to transfer my earnings to Johannesburg where they were locked into unconvertible South African Rand. My long term plan was to re-settle in Arizona and so I opened a bank account with Chase Manhattan in New York and arranged for all my payments from Mozambique to be transferred direct to this account. Even though I was a British Subject, I was also a resident of South Africa and as such I was not permitted to hold a bank account outside of South Africa; I had to keep this account secret.

After I had built up a sizeable sum the Chase Manhattan Bank telexed my bank in Johannesburg and asked them to inform me that they had just received a further transfer from Mozambique; they gave my South African bank full details of the transaction. Can you believe it, how naïve can someone get, what happened to bank confidentiality? The bloody idiots!

My Johannesburg bank manager showed me the telex message and told me that I must close the account immediately and transfer the funds to South Africa. I had no choice but to follow his instructions; 51 percent South African corporation tax was deducted on arrival of the funds and the balance was locked into unconvertible South African Rand. Stuff it and stuff the Chase Manhattan Bank for their ignorance! My work in Mozambique came to a grinding halt after this. I saw no point in working in such a dangerous environment if the South African government was going to be the largest benefactor.

This event precipitated my departure from South Africa. From that point onwards I decided to take every opportunity to externalise my funds; funds which had been stolen from me in the first place. I could have understood if my money had been earned in South Africa but the bulk of it had been brought into the country from England seven years earlier. At that time there were no exchange controls. They were introduced after the Yom Kippur War to prevent the outflow of Jewish money to Israel.

I had always been uncomfortable with the legalised practice of racial segregation in South Africa and had always believed that this would eventually lead to serious unrest in the country. Anti-apartheid demonstrations were taking place around the world and Honeywell was being targeted by protestors in the United States. It was obvious to any reasonably intelligent person that a white government would not survive much longer.

The Afrikaaner, oppressor or the oppressed

I have a soft spot for the way in which many Afrikaaners look after their native workers. One day while I was working at a water treatment plant in the Northern Transvaal, a Boer called Jan invited me to his home for lunch. I sat quietly with his wife while he said a prayer over a table of well prepared fresh farm food, and then shortly after we had eaten our fill, he went out and found his bossboy sleeping in the orange grove. He chased him with a big stick, threatening to kill him if he ever caught him sleeping again. Jan would not have hurt his bossboy but it was necessary to assert his position of authority; remember that the Chief is always the strongest and usually the most ruthless person in the tribe.

Three months after this incident the same bossboy came to Jan and explained that he needed to go home to his village because his father had died. The bossboy's village could only be approached by Landrover and it was a full day's drive deep into the Bush. Jan's wife packed sufficient food for a three-day journey and Jan took the bossboy to his father's funeral and brought him back two days later.

This would never happen in Europe or the United States; the relationship between a Boer and his native workers was very special. This same relationship existed in Rhodesia where there was an even stronger bond between the 'White Baas' and his native farm workers. The farmer was always firm with his workers but they were part of his extended family. He looked after them and their children; he fed them, clothed them, provided healthcare and took care of all their basic needs.

Before any clever do-gooder throws a stone in the direction of a South African or Rhodesian farmer he or she should first look at what has happened in those countries where radical black governments have taken control. (Editors note: this is written from the perspective of a person living in Southern Africa before Mugabe ravaged Rhodesia, now known as Zimbabwe)

Much of what has and is happening in Southern Africa stems from the migratory patterns of native tribes, colonial powers and white farmers over the past hundred years or so. Vusamazulu Credo Mutwa, a Zulu Shaman and custodian of Nguni lore and custom, states clearly that the Ba-untu, or Bantu as they are now known, migrated south from an area close to the Luangwa Valley. The Bantu tribes are therefore not the original inhabitants of South Africa; the indigenous people are the Khoikhoi and San, better known as Hottentots and Bushmen who today are close to becoming extinct.

In the early part of the 18th century there were around 2,000 white people living in Cape Colony. These were largely servants of the Dutch East India Company plus a small group of 200 French Huguenots. This number increased over the next 100 years and in 1836 around 12,000 white farmers known as Afrikaaners or Boers, trekked north east from Cape Colony to escape the influence of British Colonial rule. 5,000 of these 'Voortrekkers' gathered in the Orange Free State and then travelled on towards Port Natal where they met with the Zulu Chief Dingaan and engaged in the Battle of Blood River. This was on 16th December, 1838.

The Afrikaaner believed that he had just as much right to South African land as the Bantu; he fought hard to establish his farms in the Orange Free State, Natal and the Transvaal Republic. He then had to fight even harder to protect them when Lord Kitchener and the British Army began a scorched earth policy and herded his women and children into concentration camps during the Boer War.

I abhor apartheid and its policies can never be excused, but we have to ask who the oppressed people really are. I believe that the Afrikaaner has been given a raw deal over the past 200 years. British colonial power, and more recently the United States, is largely responsible for the problems that have been created in South Africa and the United States certainly is not in a position to set any kind of an example on race relations.

Regardless of who is to blame historically, the Afrikaaner Government was handling things rather badly. They continued to persist with apartheid and in one last desperate attempt introduced a Homeland Policy which western governments had no intention of recognizing. Perhaps if the Afrikaaner Government had been more realistic in their division of the available land they would have had more chance of success.

The Homeland Policy was never accepted by rest of the world and yet it is now this very policy that the United Nations has supported in Iraq, Israel and Yugoslavia. It would appear that segregation is acceptable on religious grounds but not on tribal grounds; strange! I suppose many will argue that there are only four tribes involved; black, white, yellow and mixed. Anyone that believes this to be the case has no real understanding of Africa. There is more hatred between different black tribes than has ever existed between those segregated by colour. This applies equally in India, Burma, Sri-Lanka and many other third-world countries. The Middle East is boiling with hatred and much of this is directed against fellow Arabs who follow different paths in Islam.

Now I will talk about the United States. The American Government, not its people, has always annoyed me with its hypocrisy. They don't have a problem with natives because they massacred a large part of their indigenous population. In South Africa the Boers co-existed with those natives that were peaceful and recognised their tribal customs. I have never witnessed an Afrikaaner treat another human being in the same way as I have seen prejudiced white people treat 'Niggers' in the United States.

The political situation in South Africa was brought to a head on 16th June 1976. The children of Soweto refused to attend school because of the implementation of a government decree that had been issued two years earlier. This decree stated that fifty percent of the children's lessons must be taught in Afrikaans.

Riots broke out in Soweto and Alexandria, a black township very close to my home in Randburg. Very soon armed police and soldiers were dispersed right across Johannesburg. I had to escort my daughter to school and collect her again in the evening. People who had never owned a gun in their lives were hurrying to the local gunsmith.

I was working in Mozambique when this occurred and I was very worried about leaving my family at home unprotected. I asked the police for advice. They told me to buy Marjorie a magnum 357 revolver. It would not jam, it would penetrate the door and it would stop the assailant with the first bullet. This all sounded rather terrible but hopefully she would never need to use it and if she did, then at least she and Michele would stand a better chance of survival.

We bought a 357 and the police trained Marjorie how to use it at the local police shooting range. In particular, they trained her how to shoot from a defensive position while lying in her bed. Her training made Starsky and Hutch look like rank amateurs. I never liked the idea of my wife sleeping with a loaded magnum under her pillow and I insisted that she locked it in our safe when I was at home; I had a nasty habit of sleep walking.

In Africa water is life

I continued to win new contracts for Coulton Industrial and I worked with one principle in mind; 'the quality of a good company can be recognized by its percentage of repeat business'. Once I gained a new customer, I made sure that I never lost him. One such customer was Reunert and Lenz, a Johannesburg engineering company that built water treatment plants in South Africa and South West Africa. I secured the measurement and control instrumentation for every water treatment plant that they built in the late '70's. This included plants in Mafeking, MarientaI and Karesburg which were located in remote semi-desert locations.

I enjoyed working on these projects. It was peaceful to sit outside the treatment plant late in the evening for a sundowner. I sipped cool glasses of brandy and coke with fellow contractors and watched the blinding sun change to orange and then blood red as it grew in size before being swallowed by the blackness of the desert. Even though I had seen it a thousand times, I was held in awe by the incredible hues of blue, pink and then purple which swept across the sky.

As the colours darkened Venus emerged from its slumber followed by Sirius, the Dog Star, and then slowly millions of small diamonds began to sparkle as the Milky Way splashed across the southern sky with a brilliance that is eluded in the murky skies of industrialised Europe. A beetle began to chirp, several answered his call and then hundreds of crickets joined in the chorus. They announced that the Sun God Amen-Ra had given the desert over to them. Amen-Ra was making his underground passage to the East where he would rise again in the morning to retake his domain.

Getting to Karesburg and Mariental in the old German Colony of South West Africa was always a problem. It was a two-day drive from Johannesburg. The roads were empty and there were long stretches passing through Cape Province where not even a small farm could be seen for hour after hour.

The Shah of Iran had just been overthrown and he had supplied South Africa with most of their energy needs. Draconian speed restrictions had been introduced across South and South West Africa to conserve fuel. Even in these remote areas policemen hid in culverts beneath the road to trap speeding motorists. A typical punitive fine was equivalent to 200 US dollars for driving in the desert on a perfectly straight road at around 60 mph. This was more than a week's wage and a fellow contractor from Austria arrived in Karesburg carrying speeding tickets equivalent to two months pay. He would have been better off if he had stayed at home.

The small hotel where I stayed in Karesburg offered lamb for both lunch and dinner; they had no alternative food on offer. Local farmers searched the desert before sunrise and bludgeoned newly born Karakul lambs to death. They then removed their unblemished black skins and sold them to Scandinavian fur dealers. I had never heard of this barbaric practice before.

The same hotel displayed dozens of German miniature liquor bottles. These bottles reminded me that South West Africa was a German Protectorate before it was annexed by the Union of South Africa in the First World War. I purchased many of these miniatures and they became the beginning of a large collection that is now occupying a display cabinet in my home.

I soon built a strong reference list for the water industry and I decided to trespass into the government buildings of Pretoria. This is an area where only fluent Afrikaans speakers dared to tread. I visited the Department of Water Affairs and was pleasantly surprised when I was received by a middle aged German engineer who offered me tea and made me feel completely at ease. His name was Jens Brehm. He and his wife Gisela had immigrated to South Africa when Germany was still recovering from the post war depression. I still keep in contact with Jens and received a letter from him only yesterday.

Jens introduced me to the Chief Engineer and he invited me to write a specification for the upgrade of measurement and control systems on all government owned water treatment plants. This was the break that I had been looking for. I always strove to provide my customers with the very best that I could offer, but this came at an increased price, and if my competitors did not do the same, then I would price myself out of the job. Writing the specification gave me an opportunity to level the playing field.

I prepared a detailed specification for the supply, installation and commissioning of new equipment. I gave a generic description of the type of equipment that would be acceptable but took care to ensure that a reasonable level of standardisation would be achieved. Most important of all, I described carefully the workmanship standards required and the manner in which pipes, cables and wires must be laid, secured and identified. As-built documentation including maintenance manuals, wiring and piping schematics and instrument calibration certificates were also all properly addressed in the specification.

Most of the Department's plants were badly maintained. They had no idea what was installed and in many cases they did not even know the correct calibration details for important pieces of metering equipment. My specification was very specific to their needs. It was a breath of fresh air and they clutched it eagerly and immediately circulated it to all of their suppliers.

Vince Pinnock, one of the sales managers at Kent Instruments, a British Company which was one of the big three instrument companies in the world at that time, telephoned me and in his gruff Lancashire accent said that I had 'stitched them up good and f……g proper'. Vince was a real down to earth guy who had helped me on many occasions in the past and I was sure he would continue to do so.

Six weeks later the Department of Water Affairs issued a tender calling for quotations against an enquiry document covering water treatment plants and water dams in every region of South Africa. They were seeking companies which would enter into bi-annual maintenance contracts for measurement and control instrumentation, chlorinators and dosing equipment on seven different plants. All the bidders recognized that the Department's enquiry was written around my specification and no one, but me, was surprised when Coulton Industrial won all seven contracts.

None of the larger companies were concerned. They realized that I had to buy my equipment from them and the last thing they wanted to do was upset me. After all, the specification which I wrote was generic, and I was free to choose from several manufacturers.

Every two months I toured all seven plants. This involved several flights out of Jan Smuts Airport and more than 1,400 miles driving in hired cars, a substantial part of this on dirt roads. I always hired cars with front-wheel drive, usually a Volkswagen Golf. I used the front-wheel drive to pull me straight whenever road corrugations caused the car to drift sideways. I became expert at driving on bush roads and quickly learned how important it was to maintain certain speeds for different kinds of road condition, particularly if the road was heavily pot holed. I never hired a four wheel drive vehicle; apart from being costly they were real bone shakers and much of the territory was semi-desert, so the possibility of getting stuck in a mud hole was very small.

During the first few months I had to work extremely hard to bring the equipment on these plants up to scratch. I replaced several items, refurbished others and established a calibration programme. Where appropriate I trained the native operators to use the equipment correctly, and with time, I earned the trust of the Afrikaans-speaking plant managers who were often local farmers supplementing their income. They invited me to their homes for lunch and whenever I visited they gave me produce to take home. I brought home prickly pears from the Transkei, gemsbok biltong from the Orange Free State, bananas from the Eastern Transvaal, oranges from Northern Transvaal and wine from the Cape. Marjorie had one of the best stocked larders on the Reef.

The treatment plants covered by my contract were mostly downstream of large water dams that had been built in some of the most beautiful parts of Africa. I was extremely fortunate; I worked where most people took their annual vacation; I was almost on a perpetual holiday. My favourite was Magoebaskloof Dam that lay above the farming community of Tzaneen in the Eastern Transvaal. The plant itself was located just beneath the dam wall, which I am told is one of the largest earth walls in South Africa. I am not sure if this is true, but I enjoyed climbing to the top where I would eat my lunch and count the different kinds of bird that visited the water's edge.

I liked Magoebaskloof so much that I often brought my family with me. Michele loved to play on the hillside where she picked wild flowers and chased butterflies. This place was so beautiful and the flowers, birds and butterflies were much more prolific than anything I had ever seen in the Cape or on the Garden Route. We stayed in a picturesque camp that enjoyed a magnificent view across a vast sub-tropical rainforest. The forest spread its lush green canopy far below and across the valley to distant hills where prospectors scrambled for gold in years gone by. The camp consisted of several rondavels with thatched roofs, a small restaurant and a few braais which had been spread around for guests who wanted to prepare their own evening food.

All of the places that I visited while working for the Department of Water Affairs were incredible. Each place was a distant cry from the industrialised areas that I frequented while working for Honeywell. Another of my favourites was Tulbach. It rested below a ridge of high mountains north west of Wellington in the Cape. It was a wine growing region and many famous estate wines were produced in the area.

My work was varied and interesting. During one of my visits to the Cape, I was asked to intercede in a disagreement between the Government and the City of Capetown. Three huge Kent magnetic flowmeters were being used as fiscal meters to measure and charge for the water supplied by the Department of Water Affairs to Capetown. These meters were connected in series and in theory they should have always read the same. Instead the three meters had demonstrated a random discrepancy of up to seven percent since the day they were commissioned.

This represented a considerable sum of money underpaid or overpaid by the City of Capetown and no one, including the manufacturer, could establish which of the meters was correct. Over a period of 7 years a number of consultants were brought in to investigate the problem but no answer could be found. These magnetic flowmeters are based upon the latest metering technology and with the possible exception of several similar flowmeters installed on the Hong Kong water supply, they are the largest that I have ever seen.

I noticed yellow stakes were driven into the ground at regular intervals. They followed an imaginary line running parallel to the water pipeline and 20 feet distant. The resident engineer explained that these poles marked the position of a high voltage cable that supplied power to three high voltage pumps at the start of the pipeline. I asked for the operational logs for the pumps and it only took a few moments to establish that the flowmeter discrepancies were directly proportional to the current taken by these water pumps. The water pipeline was lying within a magnetic field generated by the high voltage cable, and after all, these were 'magnetic' flowmeters.

It is on such occasions that I become terribly frustrated with large organisations who pay incredible retainers to 'big name' consulting companies and then haggle over a couple of hundred dollars when a small guy like me comes along and solves their multi-million dollar problem.

Later in the same year I was asked to upgrade a flowmeter in the goldfields of the Orange Free State. On this occasion I encountered one of the oldest forms of 'industrial age' metering technology. This flow metering system was precision engineered by George Kent Limited, the grandfather of the company who made the magnetic flowmeters used in Capetown and Hong Kong.

This particular flow element was a 5-foot diameter short venturi tube, cast and precision machined in gunmetal. It was installed in the water pipeline at the bottom of a brick-walled 30-foot deep pit. Two float chambers were flanged to the venturi tube; one to the upstream pressure tapping and one to the downstream pressure tapping. These chambers were six inches in diameter and approximately sixty feet high with the top thirty feet protected by a brick tower. Two wires connected the floats through a system of pulleys to the flow meter, which rested in a glass case on a wooden table in the centre of a purpose built meter house.

The flow meter was hand machined from brass, gunmetal and phosphor bronze. A recorder pen was linked to a mechanism of gear wheels, levers and pivots that in turn linked to a mechanical integrator which calculated the total amount of water supplied to the gold mines. The recorder charts were fitted to a circular drum which was driven by a spring wound clock and each chart carried the name of the meter house. The complete instrument had been manufactured by a skilled instrument maker who had engraved his name on the base plate in the manner of a true craftsman who takes pride in his work.

I served five years as an indentured apprentice instrument mechanic and this was one of the first times that I had an opportunity to use my original skills. The metering installation was as reliable and as accurate as the day it had been installed. I felt guilty that I should be the one to de-commission such a work of art. The small electronic flow transmitter that I put in its place looked petty and insignificant and it made the large brick built meter house totally redundant. What had I done!

I was convinced that the complete flowmeter system should be given to a suitable museum. I offered to buy the metering mechanism at a price that probably exceeded its original cost and the cost of the electronic transmitter that replaced it. Unfortunately government red tape prevailed and I was told that it would be transferred to a government surplus store where it would eventually be auctioned to the highest bidder; no doubt a scrap metal merchant. I was terribly upset and I even considered stealing it, no one would have known but my conscience did not allow me.

With my work now extending right across southern Africa my purchasing power increased and Coulton Industrial became a valued customer of several large instrumentation companies, including Taylor Instruments, Honeywell Automation, Hartmann and Braun, Kent Instruments and Foxboro Yoxall. I demanded significant resale discounts by forcing them to compete for my business and this helped my profit margins to increase significantly.

I had gone a long way since I won that first contract with Iscor in

Newcastle. In 1978 my old friend, Harry Viljoen, had to stand up in his annual sales meeting and present a league table to the senior management. This table listed Honeywell's best customers and I was in their top ten! Ken Pearson, one of my closest friends, said that Harry almost choked when he read out my name. This gave me a real feeling of pride and at the same time a certain amount of cruel satisfaction.

Chapter 12

Robert Mark Brett

A new addition to our small family
Proud to be chosen!

When Michele was six years old Marjorie and I were no longer short of a penny or two and finally, with some stability in our lives, we looked towards adding to our family. Unfortunately nothing seemed to happen, and try as we might, Marjorie was unable to conceive. We both visited family clinics and tests showed that there was no evident medical reason.

Eventually we decided to visit the Johannesburg Children's home where we befriended two blonde haired brothers around three and four years old. We arranged to take them home every second weekend and they soon became part of our family. I remember vividly a photograph that I took of them sitting on the wing of my Airtourer at Baragwanath.

Unfortunately I could only see heartache for us and for the two little boys. They were in the Children's Home by court order to protect them from their parents who were mistreating them. Under these circumstances the boys could never be adopted and home visits had to be kept to a minimum to prevent any kind of connection developing. Sadly this also applied to all of the other children in the Home, and so we decided to take another approach.

A friend told us of a Child Welfare Society in Hillbrow where arrangements could be made to adopt a child. Uncertain of the procedure, Marjorie and I obtained an appointment to meet with a very official looking South African woman who looked sternly over us and asked the simple question, 'Why do you want to adopt a child?' This approach threw us off guard and we explained our reasons in great detail. She delved deeply into every aspect of our lives and then suddenly terminated the interview and told us that she would be in touch.

It seemed that nothing was going to happen. Perhaps we had failed the verbal test and had not come up to scratch. Perhaps it was the old Afrikaans thing again. Fourteen months went by with no word, and then we received an invitation from the University of the Witwatersrand to attend an evening course. This course was directed towards parents hoping to raise an adopted child. Of course we attended, we had to show willing, but we did not really believe that it could teach us anything useful. After all, we had raised Michele successfully; what could they possibly teach us that we did not already know?

How wrong we both were. Raising an adopted child was so different to raising our own. There were numerous pitfalls for the child and for the parents. The course brought all of these to our attention in such an illuminating way and using real examples. Three key recommendations deserve special mention because they worked for our adopted son, Brett. If any potential adoptive parent by chance reads this book I suggest that they make a mental note of these recommendations:

* * *

An adopted child enriches the adoptive parents' lives and therefore the child should never feel that he has reason to be in debt emotionally or otherwise to his adoptive parents.

From the moment that he begins to talk, make him aware of his adoption. Let him know that you chose him. Don't keep any secrets from him. Encourage him to grow up feeling proud that he was chosen.

When he begins to mix with other children and they tease him cruelly and say that he is adopted, tell him to respond by saying 'I know I am adopted. I am more fortunate than you because my parents chose me.'

* * *

After we had completed our course at 'Wits', the name used by Jo'burgers to refer to this prestigious South African University, we again entered a long period of inactivity where nothing seemed to happen.

Other prospective parents who we met at Wits told us that this was normal and that we were being tested; they explained that applicants who were not suitable to adopt usually dropped out on their own accord long before they were selected.

We were also told that the Child Welfare Office was taking its time to ensure that we were carefully matched to suitable birth parents. Their officers considered race, nationality, personality, physical features and even professional or vocational backgrounds. Financial considerations were the only item not taken into account; the only pre-requisite in this regard was a family's ability to provide a stable and loving family home with reasonable amenities.

It became apparent to Marjorie and me that we were dealing with a very professional organisation that knew exactly what it was doing.

A new baby for breakfast

Six months later I was disturbed by the telephone ringing at six o'clock in the morning. It was mid-winter and the telephone was located in the dining room on a large wooden table which was cut from African Hardwood. The corridor between our bed and the dining room had a cold stone floor. I didn't want to rise so early but the ringing sound appeared to be urgent and something said to me that I had to answer its call.

"Hello is that Mr Coulton, is Mrs Coulton with you? I want you to look at a baby in the Queen Victoria Hospital". Mrs Verwood, the rather official looking women in the Child Welfare Office who said that she would get back to us, had kept her promise. She asked if we could both be in her office at 7.30 am.

From that moment we seemed to be travelling within the clutches of a whirlwind. Everything seemed unreal, it did not seem to be happening and yet it was, and very quickly. I shaved hurriedly, dressed and then joined Marjorie to drive through the early morning traffic down Jan Smuts Avenue and into Hillbrow.

We were only with Mrs Verwood for 20 minutes. In this time she told us that the baby's birth parents were English and that they had met on a Union Castle Liner from Southampton to Capetown. The mother was the daughter of an English Vicar and a member of the Salvation Army and the father was a civil engineer travelling to start a new career in South Africa. Both were well educated and in excellent health.

Mrs Verwood went on to explain that the baby had been born two weeks earlier, but an infection in the maternity unit had caused his adoption to be put on hold. His mother had named him Mark and under South African adoption law this information was all that we could be given.

Mrs Verwood arranged for us to visit Mark in the Princess Alice nursing facility at Queen Victoria Hospital in Johannesburg. We had to check him out and return back to her office and give our answer. We knew what our answer would be but we had to follow the laid down procedure.

After returning hastily with our answer we were despatched to the Crown Court in Central Johannesburg where an elderly Judge, who was extremely kind and very pleased for us, signed papers which gave us permission to take Mark from the hospital.

Still this was not enough. We were then given a list of items that we had to purchase before collecting Mark. This list was several pages long and it covered everything from a pram to several cartons of nappies. Fortunately I had my cheque book with me. We drove to the Rosebank Shopping Mall, grabbed hold of two store assistants and walked through the babies section buying everything on the list in less than 30 minutes. The staff were perplexed and we didn't even attempt to explain the reason for our mad and very extravagant behaviour.

Finally we took our consent papers and our very long till receipt to Queen Victoria Hospital and presented it to the staff nurse. She wrapped Mark in a shawl and placed him in the carry cot that we had just bought. Thirty minutes later we lifted Mark from the back seat of our car and took him into our home at 75 View Road. It was 1 pm; only seven hours had passed since we were awakened by the urgent ring of our telephone on that large heavy wooden table.

We needed to give him a name. I had always liked Brett; I took it from

Brett Sinclair, a name used in a television series a few years earlier. This by itself would perhaps be a little simple and I wanted to give him more choice for when he grew up. Robert, my father's name, seemed to be appropriate and the two names went together well. Meanwhile his birth mother had already given him the temporary name of Mark which we wanted to leave in place. So it was decided; he would be christened Robert Mark Brett Coulton.

For the remainder of the afternoon our friends knocked on the door and asked to see Brett, who was sleeping peacefully in his carry cot. He had a chubby face, as most babies do, and high on his cheek was a large strawberry birth mark.

Anne Smith from across the road was the first. She visited with her two girls, Susan and Sharon. A little later Mary, Lorraine, and then Kay arrived, each a neighbour and all very close friends. Everyone was so excited, and then the servants who worked in our neighbourhood started to walk past our front gate, each stopping to peer through our window for a short while.

Johannes asked me for the name of the Shaman that Madam had seen. He explained that he must have given very powerful muti to Marjorie; she had left home early in the morning and returned 6 hours later with a baby. Johannes had been asked by the other servants to explain how the White Madam could give birth to a baby boy without being pregnant. Nothing that I said could change his opinion that Marjorie had visited a Shaman.

Brett changed our lives overnight. Michele rushed home from school every day to see him. She doted on him and showed him off to her school friends. She loved the idea of having a small baby brother.

As soon as it was reasonably safe for Brett to fly, Marjorie decided to take him home to Cumbria so that our parents might be given the opportunity to spoil him. Before she could take him to England we had to obtain his South African passport and to do this we needed a birth certificate. We applied to the appropriate department in Pretoria and a full birth certificate was forwarded by return mail. To our surprise this certificate described Marjorie and me as his birth parents. It gave no indication that he had been adopted. This again demonstrated the care that the South African Government was taking in the application of their adoption procedures.

As soon as Brett had his passport, Marjorie and Michele flew with him to England where he was christened at Distington Church in West Cumbria. Everyone from both of our families was present except yours truly, who had to remain with his company in South Africa.

After two years we attended the High Court in Johannesburg and appeared before a Judge to have Brett's adoption finalised. It was a strange and sombre occasion full of the normal pomp and ceremony that goes with all legal occasions. The judge and the legal people all wore their wigs and black gowns. Everything seemed so inappropriate but they were friendly enough and they did have a smile for Brett.

The South African courts had given very specific guidelines to protect adopted children. These guidelines prevented, rightly or wrongly, the divulgence of the names of birth parents and adopted parents. Up to this point, the name of Brett's mother had been closely guarded. It therefore seemed rather strange that the Clerk should read her name out in court. I made a mental note of her name so that I might repeat this to Brett when he grew up; I had no intention of keeping any secrets from him.

Michele had many really good friends in Bordeaux and I want to mention their names so that they will never be forgotten. There were six girls all around the same age called Kim, Susan, Sharon, Paula, Jennifer and Louise, and four brothers from across the road called Malcolm, Derrick, Gregory and Richard. Kimie was Michele's closest friend and she was almost a second daughter to Marjorie and me. If Kim was not in our house then Michele was in hers. They were inseparable and were always closely guarded by Brutus, Kimie's huge Great Dane who was never far away.

Barefoot in Mauritius

Michele had gone barefoot since her very first days in Zambia and Brett followed suit until we visited Mauritius for a short holiday in 1978. It was a very beautiful island almost totally encircled by a pristine coral reef that protected bathers from huge sharks that scoured dark waters plunging deep beyond its rim.

We stayed in La Piroque which had only opened the previous year. It comprised of around eighteen thatched cottages built in the shape of a traditional fishing boat called a Piroque, and in the centre was a large communal building, built in the same style and containing the reception, bar, restaurant and dance floor. The area was surrounded by tall trees which shed sharp thorns and beyond these trees lay sugar plantations that almost covered the total island.

Shortly after our arrival Brett ran barefoot from our cottage and across an area of short grass towards the white coral sand beach. He covered a good fifteen yards before he stopped dead. It looked as if his feet were frozen to the ground and he was screaming with tears rolling down his face. I hurried out and carried him back to a chair on the wooden porch. His feet were full of long sharp thorns. I used Marjorie's eyebrow tweezers to pull them out one by one. Fourteen in all; fourteen loud screams interspersed with frightened calls of "no daddy, no daddy, no daddy". Brett never went barefoot again.

Michele and I spent hours swimming in the warm waters of the Indian Ocean. The reef supported all kinds of colourful fish and the living coral carried perfect formations of every kind. We were occasionally startled by a sea snake and I disliked being encircled by the strange looking caterpillars that were almost four feet long. I never knew if they were living creatures, sea anemones or just pieces of seaweed.

One morning I decided to go deep sea fishing with a friend from the next cottage. He brought his daughter, Christine, with us and together we hired a local fisherman complete with his small fishing boat. The boat was so small it could have been described as a rowing boat with a single outboard motor attached. We left at five in the morning so that we could cross the reef on high tide. It was still dark and we motored out into the Indian Ocean until the island of Mauritius fell below the horizon and only the mountains could be seen.

I became concerned that we had no food on board, no water except the personal bottles we carried, and only one small can of spare fuel. We were 16 miles offshore from a mid-ocean island in a small boat, with only one outboard motor, and with no communication equipment or emergency rations. This was not a very safe situation; I thought we were only intending to cross the reef, not the Indian Ocean! Nine hours went by and the midday sun almost burnt us to a frazzle. The open boat had no bimini and we urged our fisherman friend to take us back to La Piroque. He explained to us that we could not return until late in the evening when the tide would be high enough to cross the reef.

Through the whole day not one of us detected the smallest of nibbles on our bait, and then late in the afternoon I saw a whale blowing only 20 yards in front of us. I was terrified that others may surface beneath our boat and turn us over. If that happened, we would be goners. I shouted "whale, whale" to the fisherman, but he ignored me. Everyone thought that I was joking because we had not caught any fish. Then Christine began to scream. This left no one in any doubt and the fisherman turned us away and finally we headed home.

Later in the evening, as we approached La Piroque, our next great hurdle became apparent. A large swell was breaking over the reef and the sharp ragged rim was breaking surface between each wave. Swiss Family Robinson came to mind and I wondered if we were going to be shipwrecked. It was a good three hundred yards to shore and I did not want to swim the rest of the way.

Our fisherman held off the reef for several minutes and he watched the incoming waves to gauge their speed and interval. Then he selected a large wave and gunned the outboard. We surged forward on the crest of the wave, across the dangerous rim of the reef, and into safe calm waters that stretched towards our own little stretch of beach. As we motored slowly in, we could smell our evening meal being cooked in preparation for our return. No one ashore had been concerned that we did not return until late in the evening; it was if it had been a normal day.

I still have vivid memories of Marjorie and Michele standing on the white coral sand at La Piroque, each in a Sarong that Marjorie bought from a beach trader. I suspect that they both enjoyed one of their most memorable holidays during that short week. Yet my original intention when I visited this remote island had been to externalise South African Rand.

The South African Reserve Bank permitted four thousand Rand for each adult and two thousand for each child when taking an overseas vacation. Mauritius was the nearest overseas place that met this criteria. We took 12,000 rand in travellers cheques and mailed almost all of them to my father in England. Our holiday certainly was a bargain in more ways than one.

Yeti and Nushka, white balls of fluff

Our lives were enriched by Brett, and one day I saw this little ball of white fluff in the Randburg Pet Shop. I could not resist it and I bought Yeti, our little Samoyed puppy which was soon to grow into a very large and disobedient ball of white fluff. He was a perfect Samoyed and would have made an excellent show dog; he had sharp pointed ears, long white hair, deep black eyes with long black eyelashes and a jet black nose.

The only problem with Yeti was that he was totally un-trainable. He pulled on the leash like a sledge dog and one night he 'killed' my Serval Cat and tore it into small pieces. Perhaps I should point out that my Serval Cat was already dead, it was the skin of a cat that was killed several years earlier by a car while crossing a road through the Zambezi Valley.

One year later I bought a female Samoyed puppy which Michele named Nushka. She took her name from the Samoyed dog which was launched in a Russian Sputnik just before Yuri Gagarin made his historical space flight. Nushka followed Yeti everywhere. She idolised him. One day Yeti escaped from our high walled garden and headed away from our house before passing through a very heavy tropical storm. A short while later Nushka escaped; we were devastated and thought that we had lost them both.

Two days later I received a telephone call from someone who lived several miles to the north of us. Yeti had turned up at his front gate looking for food and the caller had taken our telephone number from his tag. I collected Yeti and took him home. We were now even more dejected because we were sure that Nushka would be lost without Yeti to look after her. We need not have worried, five hours later we received a further call from the same person. Nushka had followed Yeti's scent right to his doorstep. It seemed impossible that she could have done this for so many miles and after such a heavy rain storm, but she did, and that is all that mattered.

It was not long before Nushka gave birth to six more small balls of white fluff. Five were dogs and the sixth, the weakest of them all, was a female; I refrain from calling her a 'bitch' because she really was a very likeable little creature. She immediately became Michele's favourite and she named her Shanseau. They all had pedigrees and were worth a considerable sum of money but we could not bring ourselves to part with any one of them and for a long time we had a family of eight Samoyeds; our very own sledge team.

Brett continued to have small accidents. When he was still learning to talk we explained to him the meaning of the word hot. This was to prevent him touching the braai which was always in constant use. One day while I was emptying grass from the bin of my petrol mower I heard Brett screaming. I ran back and found him stooped over the mower with his hand glued to the engine cylinder. The palm of his hand was badly burned, but he had learned the meaning of the word 'hot', and I never had to worry about fires, pans or hot water again.

Another 'teach yourself' situation was with an African bee. He called creepy crawlies 'Haw Haw's' and he chased them around the garden trying to capture them in his cupped hands. He often came into the kitchen and opened his hands to allow a butterfly to fly away unharmed. He was very fast and could catch almost anything that rested on a flower. That was until the day he came into the kitchen crying 'Haw Haw'; but with tears dripping from his eyes. When he opened his cupped hands I saw an African bee and what was left of a sting lodged into the palm of his hand. I had been stung myself a few years earlier and I knew the extreme pain he would be suffering.

African Bees kill more people in Africa than snakes and I was pleased that he only received one sting. A nest was lodged in our neighbour's chimney and if the bees had swarmed on him he would certainly have been killed.

When Michele was in her final year at Bordeaux Primary School we signed indemnity papers to allow her to undergo jungle survival training. She was ten years old and this training was the real McCoy, not a school outing in the English Lake District. This was four days of real tough training in the rainforests of the Eastern Transvaal. They were provided with none of the normal camping facilities and what little food they had was taken from the forest. Michele and her classmates thought that it would be fun but they had a real and very unpleasant surprise.

At the end of their three days of rigorous training they were split into groups of three. Each group had to go independently into the forest, build their own shelter from whatever they could find and then stay in it overnight. The rain, mud, mosquitoes and risk of snake encounters were too much for some of the children and several ran away. Two of Michele's friends were found in the morning hitch hiking along the Johannesburg road. I am terrified of snakes and I think I would have been with them.

When Michele returned home Marjorie made her strip at the kitchen door. She looked as if she had been mud wrestling. Her clothes including those in her rucksack smelt absolutely foul. Many English immigrant parents lodged a complaint, but this was South Africa, not suburban England where society became soft after the war years. Schooling in South Africa was very different. Discipline was extremely tough, even for a girl. One morning Michele was five minutes late for roll call and her headmistress gave her three lashes across her backside with a split leather strap. I can't say that I agreed with Michele's punishment but South African children do seem to be tougher and much better behaved than their British counterparts.

Chapter 13

Flying My Dream

Bush pilot, aerobatic pilot and then commercial pilot
Which side is up!

I had not been in South Africa very long before I learned that Baragwanath, one of the best flying clubs in Africa, was no more than half a mile from my office in Robertsham on the edge of Crown Mines. At my earliest opportunity I visited the clubhouse and signed up for a flight test with Jim Galway, one of the instructors. It had been many years since I had last flown at Crosby Airfield in England but flying an aeroplane is like riding a bicycle. After only one hour with Jim I checked out on a Cessna 150. This was on 14th October 1973. All that remained was for me to retake an examination in aviation law and the Department of Aviation in Pretoria issued me with my South African private pilot's licence.

I found the clubs Cessna 150 underpowered for the Highveld, where airfields are more than 5,000 ft above sea level. I quickly upgraded with the Chief Instructor, Mike Schumann, to a Cessna 172 and then on 19th March 1974 to a 182 which had a variable pitch propeller. This was a beautiful aircraft and one of my favourites to fly. Still, I wanted more, and so I asked around and found a 10-way syndicate on a Victa Airtourer. I bought into this aircraft for only 500 Rand and after a short check-out with one of the syndicate members, Dave Collins, I was airborne in GS-EBD.

Echo Bravo Delta had short stubby wings and a very strong undercarriage. She was built in New Zealand and had a 110 hp Lycoming engine. It had low wings giving the two pilots who sat side by side an excellent view through the sliding canopy. Used primarily as a military training aircraft it could withstand tough punishment and was stressed for aerobatic use in excess of 6 positive and 3 negative G; far in excess of what I could stand without a G-suit. It was fun!

I found that it was very strange flying aerobatics without wearing a parachute and none of my fellow syndicate members really wanted to teach me anything beyond the occasional loop or barrel role. I learned most of my manoeuvres by talking to other pilots in the clubhouse and then I just went up and tried them out. I had three basic rules of self preservation; never start a manoeuvre below 2,000 feet, never remain in a nose-down attitude above 160 mph and never allow the plane to slide backwards. Following these three rules I found that I could recover from any situation.

Foolish escapades with experienced pilots

I soon began to develop a full programme of exciting manoeuvres and other pilots gave me tips on how to make them more attractive to onlookers from the ground. These were small things, such as giving a little opposite stick before kicking the rudder over in a stall turn, or lifting the nose high and to the right just before going into a left handed barrel roll.

I lived for my aerobatic flying and soon I had friends asking me to sit in the right-hand seat while they learnt to do aerobatics. On one occasion a far more experienced pilot than me put the aircraft into a negative spin during a badly executed stall turn. Everything hit the canopy and he lost his nerve.

I had never been in a negative spin, but I remembered a brief moment with Captain White during my Royal Air Force flying scholarship training. He told me in an anxious moment that a well balanced aircraft will recover itself if the controls are left alone. I took over control, relaxed my grip on the joy stick and after less than a full turn the Airtourer flipped violently into a positive spin from which I executed a normal text book recovery. I was rather pleased with myself and enjoyed the experience.

On another occasion I was flying in the right hand seat with an ex-glider pilot who had several hundred hours' experience. We entered a barrel role, which is a very simple and comfortable manoeuvre. To maintain the impression of flying 'around the barrel' it was necessary to give a lot of opposite stick to keep the nose high while inverted.

For some reason this very experienced glider pilot, who should have known better, pulled the stick back into his groin while we were inverted. We dived inverted towards the ground and it was all I could do to take control and complete our roll so that I would be in a position to pull the nose up and arrest our steep descent. By the time that we had levelled the ground was just below us and trees were rushing by our canopy at an alarming rate. This was an experience that I did not enjoy.

Dave Collins imported our small Airtourer, Echo Bravo Delta, from the manufacturer who was located in New Zealand. He also imported a slightly more powerful Airtourer which could be distinguished by the blue flashes along its side. It had a variable pitch propeller which dramatically increased its performance in aerobatic manoeuvres. Dave checked me out on India Golf Delta and allowed me to fly it at cost, which was 15 Rand per hour; peanuts!

Dave was a Londoner who had lived for many years in South Africa. He hated blacks and with good reason. He flew an aircraft down from England on a delivery trip and was forced to land in Nigeria with engine problems. The Nigerian Army seized his aircraft and threw him into a hell hole for 6-months. Several times he was taken into the yard with several black prisoners, blindfolded and tied to a post. Those beside him were then shot and he was taken back into his cell until the next time; never knowing if it would be his last moment on earth. I came across many people with similar stories and even have some of my own which have remained untold.

As the months and then the years went by we got up to all kinds of foolish tricks at Baragwanath. We always wanted to go one better and try something new. One evening Mike Heaton, a good friend and ex-spitfire pilot, suggested that we take one of the planes at our disposal for a night time flight. We had both been drinking, which was very stupid and something that I am not proud of. It did not help that the runway lights were out of service and I suggested to Mike that it would not be a good idea. He explained how he had been trained to land on aircraft carriers when lights were not permitted because of the proximity of U-boats.

We took off with no problems and flew over Soweto before returning to line up on an imaginary line 300 yards to the left of the clubhouse lights. This is where he expected the runway to be. The runway was only a strip of tar about 12 feet wide and one mile long. Mike found the end of the runway but his direction was wrong; we touched down smoothly on a short stretch of tar before the aircraft hurtled through tall grass towards the hangers and control tower.

To be fair, Mike kept his head and opened the engine to full power, and in the blackness of the night he stood the aircraft on its wingtip and executed a maximum rate turn away from the hangers. It was a brilliant piece of flying; he could have played safe by cutting the engine to reduce his speed before hitting the hangers, but this would have written off our aircraft.

We were now safely back in the night sky but we still needed to land on this narrow piece of unlit tarmac. As Mike came around for a second attempt I looked at our magnetic compass and realized that he was following the same track. We were trying to land on runway 03 which would by convention have a magnetic bearing that lay between 025 and 035 degrees; we were flying 045 magnetic. Mike was obviously a seat-of-the-pants wartime pilot who had forgotten how to use his instruments. I asked permission to take control and I made my first and last night time landing with no runway lights or visual aids. It was a sobering experience for someone who had recently downed three brandy and cokes in the clubhouse.

This was not the only time that I had a close call with a pilot older and far more experienced than me. One evening I was returning to land at Baragwanath with an Afrikaaner friend called Toby Boshoff. Toby had been showing me his favourite pastime which is following farm tracks at 4 feet and hopping over farm gates. A very strong wind was blowing straight down runway 21 and I could see that we were going to suffer at least 15 knots of wind shear. Toby was in the left hand seat which gave him control. I explained to him that his approach speed was too low and that he was not making proper allowance for the wind shear. He reminded me that he had landed hundreds of times at Baragwanath and I had no choice but to tighten my harness and sit back.

Twenty seconds later we passed through the wind shear and our aircraft stalled out of the sky. Fortunately the wheel struts held and our nose stayed high long enough to avoid the propeller ploughing into the runway. The only thing that was hurt was Toby's pride. He kept apologizing all of the way back to the apron for nearly killing us both. The date recorded in my logbook was 10th August 1975. When we reached the apron he pleaded with me not to tell anyone in the clubhouse of what he had done. Sorry Toby, I had to include this story in my book!

Some of my own mishaps

There are so many instances when I, as a young and rather foolish pilot, went beyond the bounds of sensibility. There was the time when I strayed close to a restricted area and the South African Air Force dispatched a Harvard to escort me into Dunnottar airbase. I managed to outfly the Harvard pilot and escaped to continue my journey to Newcastle. On another occasion I ran out of fuel passing over Ladysmith, and there was the time when I could not find the airfield at the Pongola Sugar Plantation in Zululand because I only had a road map. Both rather foolish events would not have happened with proper pre-flight planning; such is the stupidity that comes with youth.

I always seemed to run out of fuel when on long cross country trips. Sometimes I carried a drum of fuel behind the passenger seat but this was never a good solution. On 12th March 1974 I landed at Newcastle to refuel only to be told that the pumps were dry. Volksrust would be a good bet I was told. I climbed the escarpment with only vapour in my tanks and landed on the deserted airfield. A young woman came out to ask what was wrong; no one had landed for the past 6 months.

She took me into town where the regional manager for BP authorised the attendant at one of the stations to fill several small drums with ordinary leaded petrol. There were fuel restrictions in force and it was unlawful for car drivers to use petrol containers, but then I was not a car driver. The manager took me back to the airstrip and stood with an unbelievable look on his face as I filled my wing tanks with low grade leaded fuel. There was very little wind and the field gradient forced me to abort my first take-off run. I turned around and took-off in the opposite direction towards a line of electric pylons. I remember the worried look on the BP manager's face as I raced past him.

On 12th November 1974 I was flying Dave's Airtourer down to Durban on a business trip. I lost three cylinders while over the Drakensberg mountains and only just managed to reach Virginia Airport; a small airfield north of Durban. Dave flew down the following day and helped me to effect temporary repairs. It was early summer in South Africa and the escarpment was covered in thick orographic cloud. Dave bought a ticket with South African Airways and left me to fly his plane home.

India Golf Delta was not equipped for instrument flying and I had to find a way through the mountains in rather bad flying conditions while still maintaining visual contact with the ground. Just before climbing the escarpment she began to sound rough and I decided to make a precautionary landing at Newcastle. The oil rings were passing oil and I had to fit a new set of spark plugs; the last hundred miles into Baragwanath were the longest I have ever flown.

I loved aerobatics but my second best thrill came from low flying. Everything passed by very quickly and the secret was to maintain high airspeed with plenty of reserve power so that it would be possible to pull the stick back and gain height if something went wrong. India Golf Delta with her variable pitch propeller was perfect!

I often flew down the Vaal River just above the water line with trees rising high above me. One day I climbed India Golf Delta slightly to clear a road bridge, and then I was shocked when I suddenly realized that I had not allowed sufficient height for the power lines that followed the road. It was only by good luck that I cleared them. This was a dour lesson to me and I never flew low again without first over-flying the route to check for obstructions.

I suppose the funniest occasion was when I decided to do a touch and go just after completing a Piper Cherokee conversion. I landed well down the runway and opened up to take-off again but then realized that I was not going to make it. I cut the power and slammed my brakes on. Everything seemed to happen in slow motion. It was as if I was in a dream as I watched the end of the runway slowly coming towards me.

My brain began to race, and like so many other occasions when the cards were on the table, I started to look for my way out. I decided that the proper course of action was to head in any direction other than that of the main road, which passed by the end of the runway. I waited until the last moment and then took my foot off the left brake peddle. This caused the plane to slew off the runway before coming to rest in a cloud of red dust.

Cars came rushing to my aid and I climbed out of the cockpit to tell everyone that I was OK. I must have been suffering from a mild form of shock because my legs turned to jelly and I fell flat on my face. I was so embarrassed.

A Johannesburg doctor had a similar experience. His was much more serious and certainly more embarrassing than mine. I was in the Baragwanath Control Tower on voluntary air traffic control duty and the airfield was very busy. I had several aircraft in circuit waiting to land while three or four others were waiting their turn at the holding point to take-off.

I cleared the doctor to take-off in his Cessna while an Aztec was on long-finals. I moved my attention to the Aztec and then my father, who was in the tower with me, pointed to a cloud of dust at the end of the runway. He said that he had not seen the doctor's Cessna rise above the tree line. Sure enough, the Cessna had ploughed into trees at the end of runway 03. The doctor and his passenger were both unhurt, but I was told later that he had some difficulty trying to explain why his servant girl was flying away with him for the weekend.

I suppose that I enjoyed more than my share of good luck. When I was young I took a lot of very silly chances, but everyone recognized that I had a good basic instinct, and I was never short of friends or colleagues who would ask me to sit in the right hand seat as a safety pilot while they took their family on an outing or if they wanted to practise aerobatics or instrument flying.

I carried a type rating on almost every kind of single-engine aircraft and this was perhaps fortunate because our Airtourer was eventually written-off by one of the syndicate members. He was flying aerobatics with an ex-Red Arrows pilot who was not accustomed to flying aircraft with normally aspirated engines. We were all pleased that they were unhurt and accepted the sad loss of our little workhorse that answered to the radio call sign Echo Bravo Delta. My logbook gives the date of my last flight in her as 23rd May 1975.

Aspiring to become a Commercial Pilot

I regretted my decision not to fly for the Royal Air Force, and by way of compensation, I elected to join Dave Collins in the South African Air Commando. I thought that my experience would qualify me for immediate acceptance but I had not reckoned upon the Commandant, a rather dour-faced Afrikaaner who did not like Englishmen. He deliberately placed obstacles in my path and he insisted that I made my own aircraft available whenever the squadron was called for duty. Afrikaaners often complained that British immigrants were happy to live in South Africa but were never prepared to fight for it. I wonder why?

To compensate for this disappointment I signed-up for a very intensive Commercial Pilots course at the Aeronav Academy in Johannesburg. I worked a full eight-hour day for Honeywell and then at 5 pm I grabbed a sandwich and headed for Rand Airport where the Academy was based. Classes ran from 6 pm until 10 pm five nights a week. The studies were very intensive and I found it was difficult to concentrate after a full day's work. Every night when the classes finished I drove to the night club district in Hillbrow and grabbed a late meal before driving home to Randburg for a well earned rest in preparation for another long day.

I found all of my technical subjects relatively easy and I thoroughly enjoyed the meteorology course. I remembered that I had obtained 98 percent in this subject when I took my flying scholarship examinations and I obviously had not lost any of my skills. I was so pleased with my results that I elected to go straight from my Commercial Pilots examinations to my Senior Commercial. To give some idea of what this involved; a Senior Commercial Pilot, with the appropriate type rating, was qualified to fly a Boeing 747 Jumbo-jet as pilot-in-command. This was a mega-jump for me and I had nothing like the number of flying hours required in my log book, but to hell with it; I decided to have a go!

It was easy to adjust to my new course and this time I was joined by a very different group of students. All were very experienced commercial or military pilots. They came from far afield. I had a friend who flew for South West African Airways. He was based in Windhoek and was a true bush pilot. He flew in adverse weather conditions with very little in the way of navigational equipment and he often had to risk terrorist groups who were trying to target his twin engine turbo-prop aircraft with stinger missiles. Another friend flew Britten Norman Islander STOL aircraft between Mahe and Praslin in the Seychelles. He was young and single. He led an idyllic lifestyle and he was always surrounded by a throng of young female tourists. I could not understand why he would change such a job; others would have died to take his place.

Both of my pilot friends were looking to get their senior licence so that they could move to one of the large carriers such as East African Airways, British Airways or perhaps Lufthansa. However, many on the course were Captains and Majors from the South African Air Force. They had a few thousand flying hours on military aircraft and were looking for retirement and subsequent employment with South African Airways. It may well have been one of these pilots who tried to force me down a couple of years earlier when I was flying to Newcastle.

Apart from me, we had one other odd-ball on the course. He was a Czechoslovakian fighter pilot who had just escaped from behind the Iron Curtain. He had taxied his single-seat Mig 21 fighter aircraft to the end of a Soviet operational runway where his wife and small child were hiding. He then opened his canopy so that they could climb in and sit on his lap. After tying his harness the best he could, he roared down the runway and flew south through the mountain valleys of Eastern Europe, keeping below radar, until he entered Austria where he asked for political asylum.

His was a remarkable escape and his story hit the front page of newspapers throughout the free world. Unfortunately our course at the Aeronav Academy was difficult for most of the South African Air Force pilots and this poor guy could barely speak English; I have no idea if he ever graduated. What I do know is that the United States Air Force gained a wealth of knowledge from his Mig 21; much to the dismay and embarrassment of the Soviet Union.

I suppose my career in measurement and control helped me to stay ahead of my colleagues and I continued to find the technical subjects relatively easy. As before, I thoroughly enjoyed the meteorology subjects, and we had an excellent teacher who was the head of the South

African Meteorological Institute in Pretoria. All of our lecturers were employed in full time jobs related to their area of expertise, many with South African Airways.

One day I was working in Newcastle, Natal and I arranged to fly direct into Rand Airport. I took-off from Newcastle just before dark and encountered a wall of cumulo-nimbus storm clouds, Charlie Bravos, as I climbed over the escarpment. I had no weather radar to help me find a way through the strongest cells. Lightning was striking all around me and my small plane buffeted violently as I tried to find a break in the clouds.

It was already dark and I could not return to Newcastle. There were no night landing facilities and high obstructions surrounded the airfield. I listened to several commercial aircraft in the area. They had weather radar and were reporting a belt of Charlie Bravos right across the Reef. I was breaking every rule in the book. I should not have been flying on such a night with the limited equipment that I had on board.

Recriminations were not going to help me. I could see headlights beaming through heavy rain on the Newcastle Volksrust road. I had driven this road so many times that I knew the approximate location of nearby mountains, and so I dived to a very low altitude and followed the lights of these cars. A deluge of water covered my windscreen as I passed beneath a storm cell and I broke into a cold sweat as fear gripped hold of me. I knew that I had to maintain visual contact with the ground and, if necessary, make a forced landing on or as close to the road as possible.

It was a frightening few minutes but eventually I broke through the wall of storm clouds and a faint orange coloured horizon beckoned me to safety. Half an hour later I called Rand Airport approach control and made a smooth landing just in time to taxi across to the Academy buildings where the first lecture was about to begin.

As I entered the lecture room our instructor for the evening wrote a message across the blackboard which read, 'Beware of Charlie Bravos'. It was the Head of the Meteorological Institute and he swore blind that the message was not directed at me. He said that it was just a coincidence that hurricanes and tornados were the subject of our lesson that evening.

I left my Airtourer at Rand Airport for the night and took Michele with me to collect it on the following morning. It was the first and only time that I ever took her flying. She told me afterwards that the mother of one of her friends had taken her up in their Tiger Moth, an open cockpit stringbag. It must have been a memorable experience for an eight year old girl.

When I finished my course I joined twenty other nervous pilots in Pretoria and took my examinations. I received my results on 31st December 1975 and immediately arranged to meet with the Personnel Manager of South African Airways. South African Airways offered an unusual career path for young pilots. They had just introduced the first non-stop flight from Europe to Johannesburg using a shortened version of the jumbo-jet; a Boeing 747-SP. This particular aircraft no longer had to make a re-fuelling stop in the Cape Verde Islands and it carried three pilots who were rotated to keep below the legal maximum of 8-hours' flying duty.

The third pilot was usually a junior pilot who had just started his career, and because of this, South African Airways was the only airline where a young commercial pilot could obtain his first rating on a Boeing 747. I already had several friends flying as a third pilot and I intended to join them.

I was very excited when I entered the Personnel Manager's office; but, just as with my interview for the Air Commando, I was again over-optimistic. He explained that I must attain standard-7 in Afrikaans conversation, hand in my British passport and become a South African Citizen. I had not expected these particular barriers and, yet again, I felt so deflated. A South African passport closed more frontiers than it opened and I had no intention of going down that particular route. I comforted myself in the knowledge that I had obtained my airline pilots qualifications and then continued in the career that had served me well for so many years.

This was the last time that I would pursue any thought of a flying career; either in the armed forces or with a civilian airline. Woe betide anyone that should suggest that I was a Soutie with no interest in doing my bit for South Africa!

A long goodbye to Africa

I was still smarting over the manner in which our Afrikaaner-led government had locked my foreign earnings into South African Rand and it was increasingly obvious that South Africa was heading towards international isolation over its policy of apartheid. Marjorie was continuing to have problems with her health and Michele had just finished her four years at Bordeaux Primary. The writing was on the wall; it was now time to move on again!

I gave serious consideration to moving to Tucson, Arizona. I sat beside an engineer from Tucson while flying in the Far East and he told me about the beauty of the Arizona desert and how he could drive a couple of hours into the mountains and fish for trout at the weekends. It sounded like my kind of place. I contacted the US Immigration Service and they told me that I had to invest 50,000 dollars in a small company and employ two US Citizens. If I did this then I would get an immediate green card.

This all sounded very simple except for one thing, I had to transfer my money before leaving South Africa. The South African Reserve Bank only permitted each family an emigration allowance of 10,000 rand and this was not even sufficient to make the down payment on a small house. While I had saved sufficient funds in the Channel Islands I was not prepared to transfer any of this to an American bank and risk another breach of confidentially similar to my experience with Chase Manhattan. I never really understood whether the previous breach was downright stupidity on their part or simple ignorance. In any event, after an absence of 12 years I elected to play safe and return to the United Kingdom.

Once Marjorie and I had made our decision, we sold 75 View Road and rented a small bungalow a few blocks away. We found it very difficult to move out of our house; it was the first real home that we had enjoyed together as a family. Michele was distraught; she had grown up in Africa and did not want to leave her friends. Brett was very young but I sensed that he was not so happy about our decision either. Indeed, I think I was the only driving force behind our decision to move. I was convinced that it was an important decision for our long term future and one that could not be delayed any longer. So move we did!

I had worked in every corner of southern Africa but I never carried a movie or still camera. I realized too late that I had seen and done things that many normal people could only read about in travel books. I had never taken any photographs of the lead and zinc mines, copper mines or gold mines of Africa. I had never even carried a movie camera while performing aerobatics in my little Victa Airtourer.

This was a terrible disappointment to me and I decided that we had to take one last rush around the perimeters of South Africa and capture what we could on film. Marjorie, Michele, Brett and I jumped into our faithful white Mercedes Benz 220 diesel and started our long drive south in the summer of 1979. Our first stop was Oudtshoorn in the Klein Karoo where Michele jumped up and down on a clutch of ostrich eggs in a futile attempt to break them, at the guide's request, and then we visited the Kango Caves. Marjorie and Brett stayed at the entrance while Michele and I walked deeper and deeper into the cave with other tourists. As we progressed with our guide the less adventurous gave up until eventually the guide told us that only experienced potholers should continue.

He told us that if we went through the next tunnel it would not be possible to return. From that point we would have to crawl on our stomachs and then exit by climbing a chimney. He warned that we must start our climb with our hands stretched in front of us because the chimney was very narrow. I turned back with everyone else and then Michele shot forward and dived through the tunnel. She left me with no choice, I had to follow. It was a terribly claustrophobic experience and I was terrified that I would get jammed in the chimney. I am not exactly thin and my shoulders only just squeezed through the narrow space. When I eventually emerged my elbows and knees were skinned and extremely painful. Michele thoroughly enjoyed her experience and was thrilled that she had pulled such a fast trick on me.

We continued our journey down the Garden Route, past Plettenberg Bay and on to Capetown where we enjoyed a fabulous time visiting several old Wine Estates and my old haunts around the water treatment plant outside Wellington. I bought five boxes of 1973 vintage Backsburg estate wines for crating and shipment to England and then we drove back to Johannesburg, visiting Kimberley diamond mines on the way where we finished off our last role of film.

Moving from View Road to our rented Bungalow was the only time that I ever carried Marjorie's 357 magnum revolver. I had to transfer everything from my old safe to a hiding place in our rented bungalow. I stuffed my pockets full of our safe's contents and walked the short distance to our rented bungalow. I complied with South African law and kept the revolver in full visibility by carrying it in a low slung holster. I looked and felt like John Wayne.

As with Process Control eight years earlier I ended up selling Coulton Industrial for a very low price in order to provide my customers with continuity. I sold to a small company called Fala Services which was owned by an Afrikaaner and a Welshman, both instrument technicians. They bought Coulton Industrial for only one reason, and that was to gain access to the ongoing long-term contracts that I held with the Department of Water Affairs.

I spent a month with them doing their first round of maintenance visits, introducing them to the site managers and showing them how to carry out their maintenance routines. I eventually handed over to them on the strict understanding that I would transfer my shares and the company documentation after the company's accounts had been finalised and they had complied with all of the requirements of our written agreement.

There is always a certain amount of trust required in such transactions and goodwill is needed from both parties. Marjorie had a bad feeling about one of the purchasers and she told me that I needed to be careful. How right she turned out to be!

The big moment arrived and it was time for Brett and Michele to say goodbye to Africa. We arranged for a young nurse, herself returning to England, to accompany them on their long flight to Heathrow. I stuffed Brett's socks full of hard currency, gold necklaces and emerald bracelets and placed the socks amongst his clothing in a small suitcase. This sounds rather crazy but it was the only way I could think of to get Marjorie's jewellery back to England.

Our first ever visit to the Americas

The following morning Marjorie and I boarded a Varig flight from

Johannesburg to Rio de Janeiro with a short stop in Capetown to pick up passengers. The short stop changed into a long one when the airline found that it had seriously overbooked and the airport officials would not give permission for the flight to resume.

It was the same aircraft type and the same route from Capetown to Rio that I had been given for the plotting section of my Senior Commercial Pilots written examination. I found our flight very interesting from that point of view, but I never witnessed any star shots being taken and this was a small disappointment. I suppose the Captain was very certain of his Doppler Navigation System.

For me, Rio closed a triangle; a triangle of three cities divided by three great oceans and yet all three very similar. Each city was incredibly beautiful and surrounded by warm blue seas with a back drop of uniquely shaped mountains; the Sugar Loaf, Table Mountain and Victoria Peak.

Each city had two very distinct population groups, the incredibly rich upper class and the terribly poor who lived in abject poverty. In Rio many of the inhabitants lived in shanty towns called Favelas. These towns did not enjoy the supply of basic utilities that most of us took for granted. They had no electricity, water or even basic sanitation. This did not trouble the richer inhabitants who lived in leafy suburbs and shopped in large well-stocked stores that were protected by guards carrying a selection of revolvers, shotguns and machine pistols.

There was no middle class in Rio and we decided from the outset that we could not afford to stay more than five nights. Our hotel was on the Copacabana and we enjoyed our early morning and late evening walks along the mosaics of its long tiled promenade. I looked for the girl from Ipenema and all of the other beautiful girls that should be walking alongside us or sunning themselves on the sandy beaches, but I never saw any of them. Brazilians are very proud of their image and believe they have the most beautiful girls in the world. I am afraid that none of these girls came out to see me. Clifton beach around the corner from Capetown had a much greater selection of bathing beauties.

We visited all of the usual tourist places, travelled in a cable car to the top of the Sugar Loaf, bought a plate with our photograph imprinted on its enamelled surface and took a bus to Serra de Carioca where we marvelled at the huge Statue of Christ who immersed his head and shoulders deep into an isolated patch of low lying cumulus.

The view from the top of the Serra de Carioca was incredible. There were spectacular mountains with Favelas on their lower slopes and long sweeps of yellow sand which separated communities of modern high rise buildings from the deep blue azure seas of the South Atlantic. Nothing could match the sheer physical beauty of this magnificent panorama. My triangle of beauty, wealth and poverty really had been closed.

Will future generations ever change this? Probably not, if anything this divide will continue to increase. The rich will get richer and the poor will get poorer. Third world governments will favour their own electoral elite and European governments will be too tied up in their own political problems to care.

Regrettably, the world's new superpower will not have sufficient foresight or the will to accept those responsibilities that go with its new crown. No doubt it will continue to pander to the selfish whim of rich industrial lobbyists to the detriment of those less fortunate. And as for the Soviets, well, Stalin killed more of his own people than Hitler killed in the whole of the Second World War. Do I need to say anymore?

The next part of our journey took us to Brasilia and then on to Manaus deep in the Amazon Rainforest where we made a night-time landing. On finals we flew low over a moonlit river that was so wide that it appeared as though we were landing upon a silver ocean. This turned out to be the deep waters of the Rio Negro winding its way down to join the highest navigable point of the much narrower 'white' river of the Amazon.

While our McDonnell Douglas DC 8 refuelled, we walked around a hot, humid and dimly lit transit terminal where we fought off squadrons of huge flying insects that wanted to refuel from our own plentiful supplies of fresh European blood. Small pygmy-like Indians gathered around us and offered numerous artefacts which included what I hope was an imitation shrunken skull, bows and arrows, water gourds and a hideous face mask. I bought the facemask.

We were pleased when the call came to re-board our aircraft; this was a place where we were very likely to catch malaria, dengue fever or any of the other diseases that mosquitoes carried in this part of the rainforest.

Our next refuelling stop was made directly into a bright golden sun which was beginning to rise quickly above the eastern horizon. It was as if an Amazonian Witchdoctor had thrown the sun before us to blind our flight crew during their attempt to set us down on terra firma. Perhaps the Spirits had taken offence against our long night-time flight across the jungles of South America. This time our finals carried us across a different kind of ocean; an ocean of rusty tin roofs that gave way eventually to the high rise buildings of oil rich Caracas. We were not allowed out of our aircraft on this occasion and a short while later we took off to fly across the Gulf of Mexico before landing at our final destination, Miami International Airport.

Pleased to turn our backs on New York

It took some time before we cleared customs and set foot on American soil. This was our first time in the United States and my first memories were of tall palm trees swaying in the afternoon breeze, long chauffer driven limousines, petrol guzzling cars with huge engine compartments and tiny cramped passenger seats, wide multi-lane highways and short dangerous off-ramps. This was indeed a strange but fascinating place.

Marjorie and I spent several days in Miami and then took the Greyhound Coach along the eastern seaboard to New York. Our journey took about ten days because we took short breaks in Disneyworld, Charleston and Washington.

Disneyworld was fascinating and I marvelled at the new technologies displayed in Tomorrow's World. Disney was relatively new and the giant Epcot Centre was still under construction. I visited the Kennedy Space Centre and was pleased to be able to tour the Apollo Mission Control Centre and the Shuttle Launch Pads which were still under construction. In Washington I spent hours in the Smithsonian Institute and we were very fortunate to be able to join a guided tour of the White House which included a rare and very brief glimpse of the Oval Office.

Until this point in our visit we had really enjoyed the generous and welcoming hospitality of the American people. We were impressed by the accessibility of government institutions, presidential offices and, in particular, anything related to the space programme. We still had to reach Manhattan, New York.

Manhattan was a totally different story from the moment we arrived. Our pre-paid hotel was overbooked and the management refused to find or pay for alternative accommodation. I was furious. We were given our rooms the following day but we were not offered any compensation for the huge rack fee that we had to pay to the second hotel. When we came to leave I stripped our bedroom of all the towels and bed linen. We had no space to carry them in our suitcases and so I gave them to a tramp in the street. I don't think this really achieved anything but it did give me a little personal satisfaction.

The second major problem in New York occurred with my old enemy; American banks. I only had Sterling traveller cheques and these useless institutions did not even know how to change foreign currency. I couldn't believe it! After visiting several different banks I was eventually recommended by one teller to visit a commercial bank located in a block about two miles away. I had no dollars left and had to walk the total distance. By the time I arrived I was in no mood to listen to their usual rhetoric. When the commercial bank told me that they also had no facilities to exchange foreign currency traveller's cheques, I stormed into the manager's office and vented my wrath upon him.

"You Americans travel the world buying your big fat cigars and expect every small shop and hotel to accept your payment in dollars and yet here in Manhattan you are totally incapable of even changing a traveller's cheque. Why is it that you expect so much from others when your own institutions are so useless"?

He apologised and repeated the rhetoric given to me by all of his minions before him. I was so frustrated. How could these large American banks be so unworldly! Why should Americans be so ignorant as to believe that theirs was the only currency in the world? I was becoming desperate, we had no money to buy even a cup of tea, and then I had a brainwave. The account that I used while working in Mozambique was a dollar account with the Chase Manhattan Bank.

This had to be somewhere in Manhattan. I had been forced to transfer most of my funds back into South Africa following their breach of confidentiality, but I knew there was still a small amount left.

I visited Chase Manhattan and arranged for a withdrawal, it was a real lifesaver. Finally we were able, and pleased, to turn our backs on New York. We continued our journey across the North Atlantic to London where we took an express train to Carlisle and then on to my father's home in West Cumberland where we had a lovely reunion with Brett and Michele.

I left Marjorie with Michele and Brett and returned to Johannesburg four weeks later to finalise the company's accounts, withdraw the company's cash assets and, providing all aspects of our written agreement had been complied with, transfer ownership of the shares to Fala Services. However, I was surprised to find that none of my customers had settled their overdue accounts. When I approached several of them they explained that they had made full payment and that their cheques had been paid into a well known bank, which for obvious reasons I will not name.

I took my problem to the Company's Auditors and they found that a second bank account had been opened without presentation of the company's certificate of incorporation or the signature of a Company Director. I can only guess at what the intention of the new owners may have been, but in any event the Auditor took a very serious view and recommended that I seek counsel. Before taking this advice I met with the Department of Water Affairs and asked for their opinion. The main reason for selling Coulton Industrial had been to provide continuity on my long term contracts with the Department.

My meeting opened a complete can of worms. One of the new owners had made a complete tour of the contracted sites and submitted several invoices for work that he had not done. The Department made it very clear that they did not trust him and that they were going to cancel the contracts. I then recalled Marjorie's comment that she had a bad feeling about the same person. I had been blinded by my own urgent desire to secure continuity and I was the only person who had not seen them for what they were.

My attorney took immediate control of the situation and worked with such incredible speed that Fala Services could barely find time to issue revised instructions to their own Counsel. We terminated the agreement on default and I took back total control of Coulton Industrial and then closed it down. I lost the money already diverted but I protected my good name and prevented the possibility of any future fraudulent use of Coulton Industrial.

Fala Services lost their opportunity to acquire Coulton Industrial and they were furious. I was equally upset with the un-named bank that broke banking regulations and allowed my funds to be diverted. My Counsel advised me not to implicate this bank or to attempt to recover my funds. He advised that the incident was so serious that the bank would be forced to bring a counter action which I could not afford to fight. I thought that it was so unfair that my financial position prevented proper recourse to justice.

Chapter 14

Home to Blighty

At the cutting edge of technology with Rosemount
Diogenes has the solution!

I arrived at Heathrow early in the summer of 1979. The English newspapers were still carrying stories of Margaret Thatcher's huge election victory. My tasks in order of priority were to buy a car to secure immediate mobility, buy a house for my family to live in and then to find a job to pay for it all. My legal emigration allowance from South Africa was such a pitiful amount and only a small portion of what I had originally taken in to South Africa. It was so pitiful that I did not even bother to apply for it. Instead I relied upon what I had moved on the Black Market, this was easily sufficient to make a fresh start.

I hoped to secure a management position working on the Zakum Field offshore from Abu Dhabi. The position had been advertised as two weeks on and two weeks off; it was therefore logical that I should buy a house near to Heathrow.

I took the airbus link to Woking Rail Station, placed my baggage in the left luggage office and started walking. After two hours I passed a garage near to Bagshot which had a beautiful white BMW 520 with low profile tyres standing on the forecourt. It only had 12 thousand miles on the clock. After a short test drive and the normal formalities I drove the car away and started my house hunting. This took a little longer. Two days to be precise. I bought a small two-bedroom house a couple of miles from Woking Station in a small village called Knaphill.

My job hunting did not go to plan. BP Offshore were Management Consultants for the Zakum Field, and instead of giving me the position I applied for, they offered me a senior position with their own company on the BP Fortes Field in the North Sea. They offered an excellent remuneration package, but it had one drawback, I was expected to live in Dyce near to Aberdeen.

BP were very keen to get me on board and they paid for me to take my family to Dyce where we spent four days at their expense, checking the area out. The countryside was beautiful, just as I remembered from my teenage years. However, I had lived in Africa for the past twelve years. The cold damp wind cut right through me and it was the middle of July. What would it be like on the North Sea platforms in the middle of winter?

Rosemount, Bowater Scott and Steam Boilers

When we returned to Knaphill I decided that I should find employment as far south as possible, and then I remembered Rosemount Engineering who were based on the South Coast in Bognor Regis. I telephoned late in the evening and spoke with Paul Bass, the engineering manager responsible for aviation products. I explained who I was and he arranged for me to visit their factory the very next morning.

My telephone call had been opportune. The Company had signed a major contract with Bowater Scott in Barrow-in-Furness to upgrade their high-pressure steam boiler from oil to North Sea gas. There was one small problem, Rosemount was an instrument engineering company and they knew absolutely nothing about high-pressure steam boilers. It was not so much a matter of me being interviewed for a job, but me interviewing my new boss, Norman Geldard, the marketing manager responsible for control systems. I wanted to understand exactly what I was letting myself in for.

Rosemount offered me a position and I started on 20th August 1979. After twelve years developing my career I was right back where I started; a project manager installing and commissioning new control systems. This time, however, the systems were intriguingly different.

Rosemount Engineering was a small subsidiary of a North American company that manufactured pressure and airflow sensing devices for high-speed aircraft. It had a small research facility in Bognor Regis that was staffed by only three people. One of these was a person called Romilly Bowden who had earned a doctorate in radio-astrology.

Romilly was a brilliant engineer who had no practical knowledge of control system engineering, yet he had just developed one of the first medium sized industrial computer based control systems in the world. He used the same Texas Instruments 550 computer as was used by the telecommunications industry and engineered a pin-board matrix to interconnect the required process control algorithms. Only three systems had been installed to-date. This appealed to me as a tremendous challenge and I was excited to work with a small company that showed so much opportunity for growth.

Romilly called his new control system 'Diogenes' after a Greek Philosopher who lived in an apple barrel and found simple solutions to complex problems. The pin-board matrix was used with a selection of coloured plug-in wires to inter-link 'blocks' of memory in the Texas Computer which had been programmed to represent mathematical formulae, logic functions and complex process control algorithms. It looked rather like an old-fashioned telephone switchboard. It was extremely easy to use. Any one with a basic understanding could configure a 50-loop control system using a simple control schematic.

This was not the only feature that set Diogenes aside from its competitors. Each critical control loop could be connected with the real world through a process interface module, which contained sufficient functionality to take over in the event of a catastrophic computer failure, or on demand, by manual intervention of the process operator. These unique features are now common place but in the late '70's they were cutting edge technology.

The engineers and technicians working for Bowater Scott paper mill were mostly Cumbrian. I knew several from my earlier days at Sellafield and they provided me with all the facilities that I needed. The contract had been awarded to Norman under the condition that the complete conversion could be done during their four-week annual shutdown. He had committed Rosemount with no idea if this could be achieved. There was no room for error. If we did not meet the deadline then the complete paper mill would be unable to operate and one can easily imagine the losses that would build up for each additional day of lost production. This was the first time that this type of oil to gas conversion had been done and the engineers of Bowater Scott were concerned and rightly so.

I prepared a work schedule and the shortest critical path realisable was seven months. Three months were needed to manufacture the burners, burner management panels and the boiler control panels. I placed the order for the gas burners and their associated management panels with Hamworthy Engineering in Poole, Dorset. They completed their part of the project on time and to a very good standard, which pleased me because my experience in this area of work did not qualify me to challenge any technical problems.

To meet the required time schedule I had to do three months' on-site work while the boiler was in full operation; not an easy task and one that required very careful supervision to ensure that no one was injured. A steam boiler is a notoriously dangerous piece of industrial machinery. New cable trays, cables and pneumatic signal lines were installed throughout the structure in extremely difficult working conditions.

I built a control room on the second floor level and lifted the control panels in through a hole cut into the external wall. The crane was unable to extend its jib into the control room and we had to attach ropes to the panels and swing them through the hole. It was a very risky operation. My rigger had to guess the exact instant to drop the main control panel otherwise it would have toppled back and crashed onto the road below.

When it was time for the shutdown everything was in place. All of the control room equipment was installed and fully tested; the field equipment had been installed, pre-wired and piped. All that remained was for the impulse tubing to be fitted to the transmitters, the gas trains to be installed and the pneumatic control actuators fitted. This was the work that I understood and could easily deal with. The rest was new to me and thankfully was undertaken by Bowater Scott and by a number of experienced engineers that I was able to engage for the duration of contract. This work was the repair of the water tubes within the boiler, re-bricking the furnace walls, and finally the installation of the new gas burners.

During our cold commissioning trials I damaged the Texas Computer. This was a disastrous situation. My electrical foreman agreed to drive with me to Bognor Regis where I could take parts from our sales demo unit and effect emergency repairs. We shared the driving and made the entire return journey in a time that would have placed both of us behind bars if we had been caught.

Repairing my first ever computer without help in such pressing circumstances gave me added confidence. Eventually we finished our cold commissioning trials and connected the North Sea gas main to the burners. This was a stressful time for everyone. The Hamworthy engineer admitted that this was the first time he or anyone had commissioned this type of burner. It was a new experience for all of us and we were fearful of the consequences if we unknowingly permitted a dangerous build-up of unburned gas.

Everything went well from that point onwards. We commissioned the boiler and I set about training the shift operators. I enjoyed being the key person and the centre of attention in this type of operational environment. It was not long before I began to appreciate the power of Diogenes. The accuracy of process information gathered by the system and calculated in digital format enabled me to develop new strategies to improve boiler safety management and combustion efficiency.

Over the Easter weekend I was alone with the shift operators and I spent hours observing the colour of the combustion flame. We were running the boiler at four percent oxygen and I was certain that we could get our excess-air much lower. I believed, rightly, that the Hamworthy engineer was erring too much on the safe side. Slowly I began to reduce the oxygen content and at half a percent the flame shape and colour appeared almost perfect.

To ensure that I was not creating a dangerous condition I borrowed a gas sampling kit from the laboratory and found that I was producing a very high level of carbon monoxide gas. I charted these levels against excess air and oxygen for different boiler loads and different burner conditions. The increase in carbon monoxide production was exponential and the starting point of each curve depended very much upon the condition of the burner.

By the end of the weekend I was convinced that I had to introduce a new control strategy for gas fired burners that would include a continuous input from a carbon monoxide analyser. Bowater Scott agreed to purchase a Land Infrared Carbon Monoxide Gas Analyser and I introduced the first of what was to become a world-wide strategy for the control of gas fired boilers.

Six months later a senior executive from Rosemount in the United States visited Bowater Scott and checked the results. The reliability of my control strategy and the resultant increase in combustion efficiency impressed Corporate Headquarters and Rosemount Minneapolis subsequently purchased all intellectual rights to the Land Infrared Gas Analyser. Ron Stacey, the Chief Engineer of Bowater Scott, was very upset when he found out that the Rosemount executive had visited his facility without my knowledge; he only permitted the visit because he thought that I had made the arrangements. I don't know why Rosemount kept their visit secret from me; I suppose someone wanted to steal the credit.

Bowater Scott estimated that the savings in both fuel and operational costs paid for their conversion project in less than six months; Norman had only guaranteed two years. The Management were so pleased that they immediately placed an order to fit Diogenes to all six of their low-pressure shell boilers. I had won my stripes, and our huge success with Bowater Scott enabled my project team in Bognor Regis to go from strength to strength. In a short time Norman secured orders for several new control systems. Almost all of these were for steam boilers and I quickly became recognised as a leading expert in the field.

I developed several new control strategies to improve operational safety and total boiler management. All of these strategies were made possible by the powerful features contained within Diogenes, which was also being developed to provide even more information to the operator. This was realised when a powerful visual display system, VDS-25, was introduced to replace the small black and white television-like screen and the pin-board matrix. I was reluctant to witness the passing of my favourite pin-board matrix. It gave a real-world feeling to the task of control scheme configuration.

I drove the wrecked car back to the showroom

Around this time I decided to upgrade my Company Car and I visited a main Vauxhall dealer in Worthing. They had the very first show room model for a new range of sports car and the salesman persuaded me to take it for a test drive. It was a cold dark and very wet night. As we drove along the A27 from Worthing towards Brighton there was a sudden loud crunch. I braked heavily and then we were shunted from the rear. I jumped out and found a huge black Labrador lying by the side of the road. It had been completely invisible on such a wet and dark wintry night. I was devastated. I lifted it gently and placed it into the boot of the car, which was already swinging wide open in the heavy rain.

After gathering my breath I took a look at our car. It was crushed into a concertina shape, both front and rear, but the radiator was intact and it was driveable. It occurred to me that the salesman should have been doing all this, but he remained sitting in the passenger seat staring at the floor in a total daze. He was suffering from shock, not because of the accident, but because of the damage to his brand new showroom car. It only had sixty miles on the clock and he knew his employers would not be able to replace it for several weeks.

I climbed into the cab of the large lorry that had crashed into the back of us and wrote down the drivers details so that he could continue with his journey and then I took the Labrador to a veterinarian's surgery. He must have known that I was helping him because he allowed me to carry him into the surgery and he offered no resistance. I then drove to the local police station and reported the accident.

The policeman took a very strange course of action with me. He kept me at the station and would not allow me to leave until the officer on watch had decided if any charges should be pressed. I was rather surprised that the police would even have considered such a possibility. He explained a whole series of factors that they had to take into account. First of all the Labrador carried no collar, and as there was a farm nearby he assumed that it was a farm animal and therefore had the right of way. Then he pointed out that I had braked for an animal which put the lorry following me in jeopardy. One argument seemed to contradict the other and in any case, the lorry driver should not have been tailgating me. I was convinced that he was having fun at my expense but I could not be sure and I had to take him seriously just in case.

The salesman meanwhile was sitting in a corner chain smoking. He had given up smoking under a New Year's resolution and this was the first time he had touched a cigarette in twelve weeks. By now his manager would be wondering what had happened to this bright young salesman and the brand new sports car that should be decorating his showroom.

Eventually the police station received a telephone call from the Vet. I was amazed; the Labrador had totally destroyed the front of the car and yet he appeared to be in good condition. He had no broken bones, no internal bleeding and he was not even in shock. I was overjoyed. No one could have believed that I had just destroyed a brand new car with 60 miles on the clock. Satisfied that the dog was safe I left the policeman to muddle over his papers and drove the wrecked car back to the showroom. I gave a brief explanation to the manager and then jumped into my own car and left the poor salesman to face the music.

Diogenes helped me to discover easy solutions

Norman eventually resigned and moved on to join our agent in Johannesburg, and surprisingly, against my best advice he purchased a large house in a suburb close to where I had previously lived in my Jo'burg days. My managing director, Bill Yates, added control system marketing to my responsibilities and within a few months I was successful in recruiting several new and very experienced project engineers.

We were growing so fast that it was difficult to keep pace with the skill requirement. On each project Diogenes helped me to discover easy solutions to hitherto complex problems. The system was certainly living up to the origin of its name. At Wiggins Teape in Fort William they had a problem with steam blowing off during the night. At Bowater Scott in Gravesend they were unable to prevent water carry-over when additional burners were fired.

All of these local problems and many more were easily resolved by introducing simple control strategies that were not previously possible in analogue type control systems. I wrote several articles in technical journals, and professional institutions in many overseas countries invited me to speak at their professional meetings. My favourite subject was controlling steam boilers using energy balance techniques. It was such an important area. An area where significant cost savings could be achieved while simultaneously improving both operational safety and product quality, and as almost every type of process plant had one or more steam boilers, the potential was enormous.

Whenever I came to the final task of commissioning a new control system on an operational steam boiler, the Chief Engineer always became very nervous. After all, if steam was lost then production was usually lost and then heads began to roll. One of my most memorable incidents occurred when I was commissioning a new steam boiler control system for Wiggins Teape in Fort William; a beautiful old town below Ben Nevis in the Scottish Highlands. The Chief Engineer was a real down to earth dour Scotsman who knew his job well but was terrified of new-fangled ideas.

When we installed Diogenes on his high-pressure steam boiler he demanded a switching unit between the old and the new system. During the day I switched loop by loop from the old pneumatic controllers to Diogenes. During the night his operators switched back from Diogenes to their old pneumatic controllers, and I had to begin all over again. I found that he had left a written instruction in the Operators Shift Log; 'Diogenes is not to be left controlling any part of the boiler while Barry Coulton is not present'.

It was obvious that if I was to succeed then I had to find a way around this problem. I therefore stayed on-site for a full four days; ate in the control room and slept behind the control panel. Eventually I commissioned the complete system and then so many loops were under Diogenes control that it was impossible for the operators to switch back. The Chief Engineer finally began to trust his new system and he used my stubborn performance as a measure for future contractors. Some six years later I stumbled upon a Contractor who had experienced similar problems while commissioning a paper machine gauging system at Wiggins Teape; he said that he had been instructed to sleep behind the control panel.

Solving control problems on different types of plant was an exciting experience. The results were immediate to see and, of course, getting it wrong had serious consequences which added to the flow of adrenaline. Whenever I introduced a new strategy I also implemented new safety interlocks to help protect against any mistakes. After all, the first person to be hurt would probably be me.

Family life in West Sussex

When we returned to England, Marjorie was still suffering from the after effects of two very painful operations. The first was to remove cartilage from her left knee and the second was a hysterectomy. She was having a very rough time but still she kept on smiling and braved everything in a way that I never could.

Despite her excellent medical treatment in South Africa she developed yet another problem and her doctor in Knaphill referred her to a specialist in one of the local hospitals. For six months she was under the care of this specialist and during this time we came no closer to knowing the reason for her problem. No explanation was given for her condition and no tests were ever made for cancer. I prefer not to mention the name of this hospital or of the specialist. Her treatment was not bad; it was criminally negligent.

We soon adjusted to our new life in England. However, the location of our home in Knaphill no longer served the purpose for which it was intended. I was not using Heathrow on a regular basis. Instead I commuted three hours each day to Bognor Regis. I drove different routes, sometimes through Petworth, sometimes over Goodwood. I had at least five different possibilities and each within five minutes of the other. Nevertheless, it became tiresome.

Eventually we bought a renovated house in Midhurst, West Sussex. When we applied for our joint mortgage a strange thing happened. The mortgage was turned down on the basis of Marjorie's medical report. I could not understand this because the specialist had not been able to find anything wrong with her. I asked to see the report but was told that it was confidential. At that time medical records were not freely accessible and so I had no way of finding out what the specialist had said. I had no choice but to exclude Marjorie and take the mortgage on my life alone.

Midhurst is the ancestral home of Lord Cowdray. He maintains a large number of polo fields in the area and an excellent golf course that nestles amongst the South Downs. It is one of the most attractive settings in all England. Small cottages cluster together, some built from brick, some stone, many are flint with thatch, but almost all have yellow painted window frames; the trademark of Midhurst.

I joined Cowdray Park Golf Club and was astonished by my membership fee. My house in Carron Lane was within the boundaries of Lord Cowdray's Estate. I am not sure of the technicality of this or if I paid any ground rent, but I was classed as one of his 'Serfs' and as such was entitled to preferential membership for only £100 per year. This was incredibly cheap for West Sussex and an unexpected perk for living in such a beautiful area.

Michele was experiencing problems at school. Her history, languages and geography subjects had all been based upon the tribal peoples of southern Africa. Almost every subject in England was a new beginning and her classmates were streets ahead. We decided to place her in the Midhurst Convent School where she could receive more attention and, in particular, the strong discipline that she had been accustomed to. Many young teenage girls in Midhurst, regardless of religion, attended the Convent and Michele soon made several new friends whom she retains to this day.

Brett started kindergarten, and with our house suddenly very empty, Marjorie felt a need to do something that would get her out. She searched the local newspapers and found that a Care Assistant was needed to work with old people in Petworth. Marjorie saw this as a tremendous opportunity to contribute in the local community. The council provided her with training and she soon became fully immersed in her work. She became attached to those people that she cared for and this was the cause of many tearful occasions, but she loved her new vocation and would not have changed it for the world.

When we arrived in Midhurst the very first thing we did was to register Marjorie with a new GP. He was a good doctor and very professional. On Marjorie's very first visit he referred her to a top surgeon in St Richards Hospital, Chichester. Within one week Marjorie was given a biopsy and the following week she had part of her colon removed. The surgeon told me that this type of cancer could normally be removed with a high degree of success, but in Marjorie's case her treatment had been left for far too long. All we could do was to carry on with our lives and hope for the best.

I took Marjorie for a well-needed holiday to the ancient fortified town of Dubrovnik. The local people talked incessantly about the strength of Marshal Tito and how he had held Yugoslavia together through difficult times. I recalled these conversations when civil war destroyed Yugoslavia eighteen years later. Democratically elected governments do not always like strong dictators, but often they are the best option. Yugoslavia was one such example.

The Falklands War broke out just before we left for Dubrovnik. We visited the fleet in Portsmouth Harbour as they prepared to sail south. I was surprised to witness hundreds of naval ratings transferring munitions from barges that were moored in the harbour. Invincible, the Royal Navy's most modern aircraft carrier, and her attendant escort ships had no mechanised facilities to help prepare them for war.

Shortly after our arrival in Yugoslavia the British Expeditionary Force arrived off the Falkland Islands and we heard from news reports that the Argentine Air Force had sunk HMS Sheffield. The Ardent and several other ships followed in quick succession. Media information from Moscow indicated that the Royal Navy was losing Harrier Jump Jets at an alarming rate. It soon became apparent, to us, that Britain was fast losing the war.

I booked a telephone call home and asked my brother how everyone was taking the bad news. He was surprised by what I had to say and he told me that there were no reports of Harriers being shot down. The Soviet propaganda machine had been working very hard. This was my first experience of media manipulation and I had been proved a gullible recipient.

When we returned from Dubrovnik my father visited Midhurst to help convert our large vegetable garden into a lawn. My father always was a hard taskmaster and even though he was 25 years the elder he soon put me into bed with a slipped disc. My doctor prescribed bed rest. This was the worst possible recommendation and two weeks later I was carried from my bedroom on a stretcher. The specialist placed me in traction at the Bognor Regis War Memorial Hospital and for the first few days I climbed up the wall with pain.

I was in hospital for four weeks and my office was only a short walk down the road. It was not long before I started to receive regular visits from my engineers and the matron was forced to place a ban on them to prevent work being brought to my bedside. I disliked being in hospital and the traction did nothing to help me. Two weeks after my release I was again in terrible difficulty. This time I visited an osteopath and by my own decision I forced myself to remain active. I set myself a fitness regime and kept my back mobile. It worked; I found the correct medication for back pain and at least fifteen years before the medical profession began to play catch-me-up. Continued mobility was the key!

Marjorie's medical problems refused to go away and eventually our worst fears were realised. While on a River Thames boating holiday she suddenly experienced terrible pains in her lower abdomen. She was rushed back into hospital and the surgeon immediately removed her ovaries. He placed her on a course of chemotherapy and then followed this up with radium treatment. Eventually she became so ill that she refused to continue. The next few months were absolutely terrible and impossible to describe. She eventually died at home in her own bed and with her family close by. I was so terribly upset that I could not bring myself to take legal action against the specialist responsible for her negligent treatment. I suddenly found myself a single parent with two children, a large mortgage and a very demanding job.

Because of the earlier report given by the same person, the report that I had already been refused access to; I received no insurance settlement of any kind. How could the specialist have given a bad report to the insurance company and yet tell me that there was nothing wrong with her. Something was terribly wrong and I am very pleased that the government has now passed a law which gives patients access to their medical records. This may help others to identify and avoid incompetent medical consultants of the kind that Marjorie was referred to.

Less than one year following my promotion to head up the United Kingdom systems business, I was approached by our Holding Company to do the same for Europe. The Company enjoyed luxurious offices in a large chalet on a mountainside overlooking Zug, a very beautiful town near to Lucerne. They wanted me to take over as European Manager with responsibility for the total control systems business. I refused the position.

A few weeks later I attended a European control system conference in Switzerland. Everyone present knew that I had been offered the European Managers position, even the incumbent manager. It was very difficult for me. All of my friends and work colleagues urged me to accept the offer. On the last evening, after consuming a large meal with copious amounts of alcohol, the vice president, Larry Soule, pulled a hand written contract from his pocket. My colleagues began to chant heavily and he presented the document for my signature. Everyone had been in on the plan; how could I refuse to sign under such conditions!

Chapter 15

European Job English Salary

Working with some of the best engineers in Europe
Old frustrations re-emerge!

The holding company, Rosemount Zug, wanted me to keep my home in Midhurst and work from their research and development office in Bognor Regis. They reasoned that Heathrow was the most versatile airport for me to access the Company's subsidiaries and agents in East Europe, West Europe, the Soviet Union and Africa. I was pleased with this arrangement because I did not want to uproot Brett and Michele a second time.

Unfortunately I was stabbed in the back. My old managing director, Bill Yates, hated the Holding Company. He had no respect for many of its employees and considered them to be overpaid for what little they achieved. Bill convinced 'Human Resources' that I must not be paid a European salary and I found myself back in the same situation as when I worked at Sellafield. I was again the lowest paid employee in my section. Yet my predecessor, who had been removed from his position, was retained by the Holding Company on more than double the salary that they had offered me.

The old excuses of Sellafield no longer applied. I was now a chartered engineer, fully experienced and successful. In my new position I was expected to review and recommended annual salary increases for persons on a higher salary scale than mine. This made me feel like a second class citizen. I found that I had to continue to count my pennies while those working under my direction enjoyed a more affluent lifestyle. Why should being English set me aside from mainland Europeans who worked alongside me? It seemed wrong!

My new boss, Mogens Ronberg, was extremely angry when I accepted the salary package. He was convinced that they would have no alternative but to pay me the salary for the job. However, I wanted the challenge and my recent bereavement had made me realise that money was not as important as I had once believed.

I found myself flying out of Heathrow on a regular basis, sometimes twice in the same week. My company car spent more time in the car park alongside runway 27R than it did in my garage. Occasionally I drove down to Dover and crossed by hovercraft. I was a member of the executive club and as such could drive straight onto the first available flight without having to pre-book or even queue.

It was a good arrangement and on one occasion I took my father with me. We drove all through Western Europe giving him the opportunity to see many of the places that were still vivid in his memory from the darker days of World War II. The most poignant moment was when we visited the war graves at Oosterbeek, Arnhem. He had many friends in the Border Regiment who never returned from the airborne assault of September 1944, known to most as Market Garden.

Hein Van Marwijk, the Managing Director of Rosemount Benelux invited my father to an excellent meal in the old part of Brussels. I had always been impressed to observe how European people, even those from West Germany, held my father's generation in such high respect. Unlike our own youth, they remembered the tremendous sacrifice our parents made during the Second World War.

Later in the week we drove south to Wessling where Bernie Kirner, the Managing Director of Rosemount Germany, also invited us to dinner. Bernie was a very interesting person. I had known him for several years but had never realised that he was once a very young prisoner of war in a camp close to our home village in West Cumberland. He described to my father how one day his cell had been left unlocked. He walked into the local town and the police found him sitting in the park. He said that a Cumberland housewife brought him fresh eggs and bacon while he waited for the prison camp to send a car to collect him. He knew that she had given him her full week's ration and found his escapade to be an unforgettable experience.

This was the first time that my father had visited West Germany and it was obvious to me that he was finding his visit very difficult. This became all the more evident when we were invited to the home of one of my work colleagues in Munich, Diethelm Platte. We were joined by his parents who unlike Bernie were much closer to my father's age. Dad was very reserved at first but he soon warmed to them both and he was terribly impressed with their hospitality. After we left my father said to me:

"Son, I have hated Jerry's all my life for what they did to my mates in the War. I enjoyed the company of your friend's parents. For the first time I realised that the majority of Germans are decent ordinary people. This has been the best evening of my holiday and it has helped me finally to put the past to rest."

The Holding Company shared a large office with the employees of Rosemount Switzerland and every year we were invited to join their staff on a skiing weekend. This was always a major event for me because I could not ski. To make matters worse there was no ski school; all of the participants had grown up with skis glued to their feet.

At the end of our weekend in the mountains my confidence increased enough to enter the cross country race and I came sixth out of thirty two. I was very pleased with my result and I put it down to my high level of physical fitness rather than my skill as a cross-country skier. After the race everyone gathered in the sauna. I found this to be a little embarrassing; everyone was naked!

I had been in similar positions before, but this was different; the sauna was occupied by secretaries and receptionists that I worked with. Obviously realising my predicament, one of my colleagues, a very attractive young woman with long black hair, wrapped herself around me and jumped into the ice plunge pool. I was surprised that the iced water was so cold that I could not feel it; instead my whole body tingled as if hundreds of small needles were pricking me.

The following year was equally eventful. This time I plucked up courage and decided to learn the downhill slalom. The ski lift was the first thing to frighten me. I was terrified that I would not get seated properly on the tee-bar before the winch whisked me away. In the beginning I skied down the beginners slope until I reached a dangerous speed, and then I deliberately fell onto my side to slow down. I then picked myself up and started all over again. It was not long before I learned to copy other skiers and I began to plough and make small turns to slow me down.

Mogens had a delightful daughter who could not have been more than eight years old. She elected herself to be my official instructor for the weekend. She was very good and I did learn a lot from her. However, she was also very mischievous, and she enjoyed a considerable amount of fun at my expense. On one occasion she asked me to follow and she deliberately went across a very small jump. I ended up in a heap with my skis twisted around my neck and her standing above me in a fit of laughter. She knew that I would not make the jump successfully but by the time I realized what she was doing I was committed.

This particular year I decide to enter the downhill slalom race instead of the cross country. The first three to finish were army instructors and they had times of around eighty five seconds. Then there was a mix of times with most being around twelve minutes. The final person on the race board was Barry Coulton, number 26, not arrived yet! I had missed the flags on the mountainside and ended up at the wrong finishing point.

The difficulties of being a single parent

Raising two children as a single parent required careful organisation when I travelled overseas. I was determined not to place Brett or Michele into a boarding school, so I wrote to an Au Pair Agency and they forwarded details of suitable girls. I chose an older girl who appeared to be more mature than the rest, and then asked the agency to make my situation clear to her parents. Her name was Waltroud Dembinski.

Waldi joined us in Midhurst a few weeks later and stayed for ten months. She enjoyed an excellent relationship with Brett and Michele and was the perfect answer to my problems. We continue to maintain contact with Waldi and have visited her and her husband Robert in Frankfurt on more than one occasion. She and Robert now have two beautiful young children of their own, Oliver and Clarissa.

Michele reacted very badly to the loss of her mother and she became impossible to discipline. No matter what I asked her to do, she deliberately defied me and did exactly the opposite. When she was young I placed her over my knee and spanked her until my hand was sore. She always told me that it didn't hurt; meanwhile the tears welling in her eyes told me a different story. However, she was now too old for physical discipline, and I had no idea how to regain control of her.

I often waited for Michele outside the Midhurst Youth Club and on one occasion I looked for her in the local pub and found her sitting at a table with her school friends. I tasted Michele's drink and it was lemonade, but all of her friends were drinking alcoholic beverages. She was only fourteen years old and when she refused to return home I telephoned the police. When I explained my situation to the sergeant on duty he told me that she was over 14 and because she was not drinking alcohol I had no right to prevent her from remaining in the pub. I had not expected this kind of response. I was legally responsible for her behaviour and yet I had no right to prevent her from entering a public bar? Something was cock-eyed with our legal system!

Meanwhile, the government had refused to recognise Brett's South African adoption under English Law and they refused to give him a passport. When I decided to apply to adopt him a second time in England they placed him under the supervision of a young girl from Social Services. I suppose this was because I was a single male parent. How sexist can you get! The young girl was so shy that I often had to telephone her and asked her to visit so that she could prepare her report. I knew that I would have a problem when my case came to court if I did not have the paperwork to back me up.

I also had to be careful that no one accused me of mistreating Michele while Brett's adoption proceedings were underway and she used this to maximum benefit. I often tried to prevent her from going to the late night disco but again I was told that I had no right to stop her. It appeared that everyone was conspiring against me to ensure that Michele could behave in any manner that she chose. I even discussed my problem with a manager from Social Services and he recommended that I punish her by confining her to her bedroom. It seemed that no one was listening to me; that was my very problem. I couldn't have kept her in even if I chained her to her bed. One of her friends would have given her a hacksaw. In desperation I asked my father to help. He drove down from Cumbria and we physically forced her into the backseat of his car and he took her home to Cumbria where she stayed for several months before I allowed her to return.

It took two years before Brett's adoption was brought before Chichester Crown Court. We sat around a very large wooden table with several official looking people, including our young social worker. The Judge had a kindly demeanour despite his long grey wig and he quickly announced the reason for our long delay. It seemed that the Crown Court had written several letters to the South African Embassy asking them to confirm Brett's original adoption papers. The Embassy had not even acknowledged the Crown Court's letters. The Judge therefore took the view that if they chose not to respond, then it would be reasonable to assume that my South African adoption papers were correct.

The Judge turned to Brett and said "Youngster, I am going to set a Court Precedent. Do you choose this person, Barry Coulton, to be your legal adoptive father?" Brett brightened up and with a cheerful smile said "Yes Judge." The Judge hit the table with his gravel and asked Brett if there was anything else that he could do for him. Brett then asked the Judge if he could have his English Passport. I was horrified but everyone laughed and took it in good spirits.

I slowly began to get my personal life organised, I had many friends in and around Midhurst who were very happy to help me and I was never short of baby sitters when they were needed. Michele eventually took her GCE 'O' Levels and secured nine very creditable results, which really pleased me. I then helped her to secure a place on a private secretary's course at Chichester College.

Unfortunately after six months the Principle asked to meet with me and she explained that Michele could not be expected to take her examinations and look after her young brother at the same time. It appeared that Michele had only attended forty percent of her classes and had used baby sitting as her excuse. When I checked into this I found that she had been at her boyfriend's home for much of this time; I was absolutely furious.

Michele was not allowed to continue her course and I became very despondent; I didn't know which way to turn. My friends tried to console me, they explained that she was not taking drugs, refrained from smoking in my presence and never came home drunk. By today's standards she was extremely well behaved. Regardless of my friend's kind words, I remained very concerned that Michele continued to turn her back on the educational opportunities available to her.

Six crazy Englishmen in Minnesota

I continued to fly out of Heathrow on a weekly basis and on one of these occasions I travelled to Haifa on the Lebanese border. There was a war in Southern Lebanon and Moshe Lorber had asked me to give a lecture on the features of using digital equipment to control large chemical plants. It was very hot and I found it a rather novel occasion when Moshe's customers provided a large and cool bomb shelter for my presentation. We were not in any kind of danger but later in the week I was lying on the beach and an Israeli coastal defence battery opened fire from the cliffs above me. Now that was a wake-up call!

Sometimes I stayed for extended periods at our headquarters in Minneapolis. On one occasion I arranged to host a delegation of engineers from Bowater Scott. I knew these engineers well and I really enjoyed their company.

I hired a very large sedan and collected them from Minneapolis St Paul Airport on a very cold winter's day. It was dark and there was light snow falling as we drove down the ramp and joined the highway into town. There were six of us in the car and five very large suitcases. Everyone was making the normal raucous noises about driving on the wrong side of the road and how they were going to be killed when suddenly, after driving for several miles, I saw a car coming towards us on our side of the dual carriageway. We really were on the wrong side of the road, the left hand side. I quickly stopped the car and did a three-point turn.

I can only assume that my brain had slipped back into English mode when I collected such a large group of Englishmen. Can you imagine the crescendo of voices that followed? Mike Stewart, as always the comedian sank down into his seat and groaned "We are all going to die," while Tony Seal sat on the edge of his seat and nervously rubbed the sides of his greying beard.

This was not the only incident that we had in this very large sedan. The following week I decided to take them to an ice hockey match. Unfortunately we were not able to purchase tickets and so we drove to Duluth on the Great Lakes. This was unplanned and I did not take into account the atrocious weather conditions. As we drove north the snow drifted deeper and eventually we were following a narrow track that stretched relentlessly before us.

Determined not to turn back we eventually reached a large lake that was completely frozen over. A fisherman was sitting in the middle with a pole suspended over a hole that he had cut into the ice. A small tent was erected beside him and I suspect that he intended to spend his whole weekend on the lake. I knew that the ice on Minnesota lakes was able to carry heavy vehicles at this time of the year and I swung off the road and started to drive out to the fisherman. Suddenly all three passenger doors were flung open and Englishmen were spilling out in all directions. My car must have looked like an SAS vehicle despatching troops on a secret mission.

We arrived in Duluth a few hours later and found that there was so much to see that we forgot all about the ice hockey match. We walked around town and booked into a small hotel for the night. None of us had packed an overnight bag and so the first task had been to find a late night store so that we could at least buy toothpaste, toothbrush and a disposable razor for the morning.

After breakfast we visited the railway museum and marvelled at the many different kinds of steam engine. There was one that came straight out of the old western movies; indeed, it had been used in many of the films that I had seen as a child. One of the most impressive locomotives was a massive beast that was reported to be the largest in the world. Two of these had been used to haul iron ore from mines in the north down to the harbour in Duluth. Each train had been more than two miles in length. Tony was our in-house locomotive fanatic and he climbed eagerly onto the footplate while I did my duty as a good host and took lots of touristy type photographs.

Keen not to miss anything we tramped through the freezing cold streets of Duluth with our duffle coats fastened tightly and our woollen pompoms pulled hard down over our ears. In the distance we could see a strange looking bridge crossing the waterway. Certain that this must be a feature of some importance we wanted to capture a few photographs.

It turned out to be the grandest and largest aerial lift bridge in the United States, and when I explained who we were the manager gave us a guided tour. The control room was located in the centre of the bridge span which weighed 900 tons and was lifted by four 95 horsepower dc motors. I think the manager was pleased to have an opportunity to show his bridge to engineers who were able to understand the technical features that he so eagerly described.

My engineers from England had not flown across the Atlantic to throw snow balls at each other or to take photographs of historical exhibits in Duluth. They had travelled to Minneapolis to learn how to repair and maintain their new Rosemount control systems. Bowater Scott had issued the largest single order ever placed upon a Rosemount Company. This order was for equipment to control machinery on their huge paper mill in Gravesend, Kent.

1980
Back in England after 11 years in Africa. Showing Brett and Michele the area in which I spent my childhood; the lakes of West Cumbria

1984
Christmas Dinner with members of the Rosemount (England) Control Systems Group. Peter Barnett is at the head of the table

1984
Engineers from Bowater Scott, Barrow-in Furness, taking a weekend out in Duluth during a Diogenes training course. Mike Stewart is on my right, Ted Hodgson and Tony Seal on my left

1986
The Ratty at Eskdale in West Cumbria

1981
Margie's parents on holiday in Switzerland. Joe and Minnie Elliot

1986
The first European Distributors Meeting at the Fuji Electric Factory in Tokyo. Gen Katsumata is in the centre and Noboru Majima on his left

1986
Fuji pressure and differential pressure transmitters (FC Series) being assembled and tested in the Fuji Electric Tokyo Factory

1987
European Distributors at the annual Fuji Electric Sales Conference. This year it was held in Holland

1988
Dinner with Fuji Electric in The Hague. Anne with Magnus Palmstierna on her right, Vita and Mogens Ronberg on her left

1991
Yngve Svensen and John Southam after a good meal and too much hot Sake on a boat in Tokyo Bay

1991
Winchester Cathedral Close. David, Norma, Phillip, Brett, Chris, Dad, me Anne, Steven, Linda, Paul, Toni, Stevi, Michele and Mattie

1960
Anne with her mother, Mary. Keate House, Eton College

1984
Anne's father, Stephen McWatters. Pilgrims School, Winchester

1990
Coulton Conference Room in Christchurch. Engineers from Tula Chermet discussing our blast furnace re-instrumentation project

1994
Freezing to death after flying a MIL-5 at Beligorsh. Alexander Skormin from the Tula Chermet steel works is on my right

1991
With Bob Eades after closing a contract for instrumentation on a huge asbestos factory in the Ural Mountains

1991
Possibly the largest open cast mine in the World. The dark clouds are asbestos rock following routine blasting near the city of Asbest

1991
Make-shift barriers erected around the White House by Yeltsin supporters and some of my Coultech staff during the August Putsch

1995
Mobbing a Russian Tank during the 50-year victory parade outside Moscow. Marina Tauschkanova in front

1993
My grandchildren in my Christchurch garden which overlooked the River Stour. Clockwise from far corner; Hayley, Fiona, Stevi and Toni

1983
Michele has been practising her hairdressing skills on Brett

1994
Toni and Stevi looking rather innocent for the photographer

1992
Coulton staff gathered around Marina during her visit to Christchurch

1996
Instrumentation staff gathered in the Cane Yard of Mumias Sugar, Kenya. I was running a training course on my control systems equipment

1994

Coulton staff and Coulton distributors (still called PMV) gathered outside our Christchurch factory. Bryan Maddock is stood between Katie and Mandy on the left. Peter Roberts is fourth from the right

1997
Anne's parents' Ruby Wedding at Fairy Hill on the Gower. From left; Johnny, Mary, Anne, Cathy, Stephen, James and Henry

2002
Presentations of Coulton Medal to Engineering Officers at HMS Sultan

2001
Dad about to fly over Cambridge in a Tiger Moth on his 80th birthday

2004
Flying over Bristol Harbourside with Anne on my 60th birthday. It was also Brett's 28th so he and Julia joined us

2002
Brett in the workshop of my Christchurch factory being filmed by a BBC camera crew for the BBC Best Inventions Programme

2006
Brett and Julia in Schladming, Austria, two days before their secret wedding in the Schladming Rathaus

The new Rosemount control system was best described to the layman as a unique selection of distributed control components that utilized the latest semiconductor based technologies. These new technologies had been proven in several small configurations but the most important operator interface, the main operator's console, was still on the drawing board. My guests kept asking for further information on this console and our development engineers avoided their questions.

I became very concerned and when I made my own enquiries I found that the project was running over budget and the Rosemount Board of Directors were seriously considering a reduction in the total project scope. This would have been the death knell for our Bowater Scott contract and the long term implications for the Control System Division were extremely serious. I put my job on the line and telephoned Jim McConnell, the most senior Vice President, and demanded that he come down to Burnsville where the Control Systems Division was located, and tell my guests face to face that the main operators console was dead.

Jim McConnell is a tall very straight speaking Texan and I decided that it was time for him to do some straight talking. A few minutes later, Ron Ward, the vice president responsible for international operations, telephoned me and told me that Jim was on his way and he forewarned me, in as polite a way as possible, that my job was on the line. When he arrived he told my customers face to face that there had been some concern in regard to the total project cost but that he would give his personal assurance that the operators console would be completed.

My customers flew home to England re-assured and Jim McConnell kept his word. Funds were made available, the operator console was completed and several units were installed on schedule at the Gravesend Paper Mill. The rest is history and the new, still unnamed control system went on to become a world leader. In the years that followed many have said that the development of this system was never in doubt. I know this is not the case; a good friend on the Board of Directors told me that the additional development funds were only sanctioned after my intervention with the Bowater Scott engineers.

I hope they don't shoot the messenger

Several months after this extended visit to Minneapolis, Bob Britton asked me to join him for a meeting of the Board of Directors. Bob was the Vice President responsible for control systems in Rosemount. He was a huge and very likeable Texan and if Romilly Bowden was the father of Diogenes then he was most definitely the son. Bob and I had become very close friends over the past couple of years. We were both experienced control system engineers and held a good deal of respect for one another's abilities.

A few weeks earlier I had written a memo to Bob explaining that their decision to name the new Rosemount control system 'Vanguard' was a mistake. I pointed out that this new name could not be correctly pronounced in any of the Scandinavian languages, Dutch, German or even Afrikaans. It seems that several of the Vice Presidents agreed with me, but they had chosen not to make their feelings public. I flew to Minneapolis and found that the meeting was to be held in the Emerson Box at the home ground of the Minnesota Vikings.

The football game started shortly after we gathered. Around twelve of us were present in the Emerson Box. The front of the box had three rows of comfortable chairs and to the side were several video displays. These were used to show re-plays from different angles. Several comfortable armchairs occupied the central area and a table was laid with a large selection of canapés, cold meats, salmon and salads. The champagne was flowing freely and catering staff stood discreetly in the background awaiting the smallest hint that further service might be required.

In the first time-out everyone gathered around the table and Jim McConnell announced that I had put forward a number of objections to the name chosen by Vern for the new control system. I shrank back in my seat. Now I knew why several Vice Presidents had been afraid to voice their own opinion. Vern Heath was the principle founder and original co-owner of Rosemount. He remained on the Board as the Company's Chief Executive and he was also a very active member of the Emerson Board of Directors. No one wanted to tell him that his choice of name was unsuitable. They had brought me across the Atlantic to inflict the death blow. Hopefully Vern had no intention of shooting the messenger.

The game lasted for several hours and every time the referee called an interval or a time-out we gathered around the table and discussed the pros and cons of different names. Vern was determined that we would not use the name of a star, a letter in the Greek alphabet or a number. Polaris, omega and combinations such as TDC-2000 were all fully played out and he wanted to be different.

The San Francisco 49'ers gave Minnesota Vikings a hiding. Vern is an avid supporter of the Vikings and this left him in a foul mood. He did not accept any of the suggestions put forward and he told everyone to write two names on a piece of paper and to place the pieces of paper in his hat. He said that he would browse through the names and inform us in the morning of his decision. The following morning he informed Bob Britton that he had chosen Rosemount System 3. A quick telephone call to each of the Vice Presidents established that none had written this name down. Vern must have become so discouraged that he probably said to Bob, it's the third system and so you can call it that. I doubt we will ever know what really happened.

I kept my personal life very separate from my work. I never dated anyone from my work environment and I was always very careful not to date anyone in England; I preferred to spend my free time gardening or visiting the cinema with Brett and Michele. Never once did I invite anyone other than work colleagues to my home in Midhurst.

However, these rules did not extend to the United States and I met several very attractive young Minnesota women whose company I enjoyed. Some I met through work colleagues and others I chanced upon in restaurants. My single male American friends often told me that they would love to have an English accent because in the Mid-West my voice behaved as a magnet for women. I had to agree and I certainly did meet some very beautiful women.

I always kept these friendships under control. I was never in any mind to form a permanent relationship and as soon as they began to dig their hooks into me I ran as quickly as my legs could carry me. On one occasion a millionairess employed an intermediary to try to entice me to visit her home in Chicago. This was the worst thing that she could have done and I gave her a very wide berth.

I took Michele and Brett on several beach holidays and on one occasion we visited Tunisia. This was the venue for my 40th birthday and I was disappointed when no one remembered to wish me many happy returns. We took dinner at our hotel in the evening and still no one remembered. Then to my surprise, at the end of our meal, several waiters marched in with a huge birthday cake covered in candles. Everyone sang happy birthday and I have to admit how astonished I was that Brett and Michele had been able to keep their secret for so long. There was not even the slightest hint or even a sly smile from either of them during our meal. Michele explained that they had sneaked into the hotel kitchen and made their arrangements while I was learning to windsurf earlier in the afternoon.

Earlier in the year I had joined an organisation for single parent families in Bognor Regis called Gingerbread. Most of the members were women who had been treated badly by their husbands and they had an inherent dislike of men. Fortunately they held me in a different kind of category and promoted me to the rank of Honorary Woman. It was a strange situation to be in, but a very helpful one for someone in my position. The Bognor Regis group was a particularly good group because several of the members were professionals and I was able to relate to them more easily.

Gingerbread organised special holidays for single parents and one of these was in a large Caravan Park perched on cliffs east of Bude in Cornwall. Gingerbread commandeered the camp each year for the last three weeks of the season. During this period the caravan rentals were very cheap, but most important for me, the members gathered together and arranged baby watches in the evening and group outings during the day. It was perfect and both Brett and I enjoyed our visits year after year.

Brett will remember visiting fishing villages in the area and the huge pasties that I warmed up in a small gas oven, but most of all, I am sure he will remember it as the place where he had mumps. My memory will always be of a small restaurant where I took him and two friends for an evening meal. I told my friends that I had forgotten my credit card and we would have to wash the dishes. Later when I returned from the bathroom everyone in the restaurant looked in my direction and giggled. I couldn't understand what was wrong, were my flies undone?

Then I noticed that Brett was not at the table. I walked bemused into the kitchen and saw Brett at the sink with a towel in his hands drying dishes. He had told the waiter what I had said and the rest you can guess.

It was while we were on one of these holidays in Cornwall that I made the mistake of telephoning my office to check if my secretary, Patsy McDuff, had any messages for me. My telephone call brought our holiday to an abrupt end. Emerson Electric, the Parent Company of Rosemount, had just purchased the industrial business of Beckman for 193 million dollars.

Flying with Mohammad Ali

This acquisition brought into doubt the future intention of both the Beckman and the Rosemount control system groups. Beckman had a large process instruments and controls group which manufactured a competitive control system in Fullerton, California. Customers of both of our Companies were now concerned that they might have invested heavily in a control system that might not survive a merger between the two groups, and they wanted to know our corporate intentions regarding the two control systems, Rosemount System 3 and Beckman MV-8000.

I visited Larry Soule in Zug for a full briefing. The itinerary that he planned for me over the next ten days required me to spend most of my time trying to sleep on an aeroplane. I had to remain coherent enough to attend several meetings in different cities on different continents and so it was agreed that I would purchase a first class air ticket. The equivalent price of this ticket would have enabled me to fly bucket seat around the world each year for the next ten years of my life.

I did have some compensation for taking on such a heavy itinerary. Flying first class on a British Airways 747 can be extremely comfortable; the meals, the service and the in-flight entertainment are second to none and I also got to meet Mohammad Ali on the flight. When we arrived at Los Angeles airport he shuffled down the walkway and an old and very bedraggled white porter called after him. Mohammed turned around, shuffled several yards back along the walkway and stuttered a few well meaning words to him. Most famous people, even those in the best of health, would not have acknowledged the porter. I was very impressed and surprised that his fame had not caused him to lose his common touch. There are many people in this world that could learn from his example.

I also stayed on board the Queen Mary for three days. She lay in retirement as a hotel ship in Long Beach Harbour and was accompanied by the Spruce Goose which many will remember as the huge wooden aircraft built by Howard Hughes towards the end of the Second World War.

The purpose of my visit to Los Angeles was not to visit Universal Studios or to tour Hollywood, all of which I did, but to examine the Beckman manufacturing facility and then recommend a course of action to the Rosemount Board of Directors in Minneapolis. My schedule was very tight and after three days preparation I flew the 'Red Eye' into Minneapolis and drove straight to the Board Meeting. Half way through my presentation I fell asleep at the conference table. I was very embarrassed and the Chairman called a break until the following morning so that I could catch up on my sleep.

When we resumed I explained that DuPont was the only Company using Beckman Control Systems in Europe and it seemed logical that we should continue to support the Beckman systems owned by DuPont and kill all further marketing activities. I proposed that Rosemount System 3 should be the only product marketed in Europe and that this decision should be conveyed immediately to the customers of both Companies. My proposal was accepted for the European Market. Several years later the US Marketing Director confided in me; he told me that the Board had made a terrible mistake when they did not adopt my recommendation in the United States.

After meeting with the Board I prepared for an onward flight to Johannesburg where I was met with senior engineers from my old stamping ground at Iscor Vanderbijlpark. The South African Iron and Steel Corporation had placed a very large order for two Rosemount Control Systems and they needed personal assurance that System 3 was going to survive the merger. This was more easily said than done. South African Airways had overbooked and they failed to honour my first class air ticket across the South Atlantic. There were no alternative routes available through South America. In the end I travelled through Boston and into London where I had managed to obtain a first class reservation with British Airways on their overnight flight to Johannesburg.

This gave me a few hours to kill and I grabbed my car, which was in its usual parking place beside runway 27R, and drove to Midhurst where I was able to enjoy a full hour with Brett and Michele. When I returned to Heathrow I found that Minneapolis had not confirmed my reservation in London and again my seat was not available. I was furious; it was unbelievable that I had a first class ticket costing several thousands of dollars. However, British Airways has always been my favourite airline and they quickly came to the rescue with a special seat; they always excel when others fall flat on their face.

I continued to work well with the Rosemount companies in Europe and our installed base increased rapidly. Rosemount became one of the world leaders in measurement and control technology and those that helped create this success were targeted by head hunters to take leading roles in competitive companies. I was happy with my role in Europe and never responded to any of these approaches but many of my friends soon became Managing Directors in their own right.

I could not do much about my salary but my expense account was unlimited. This was fortunate because I had some very wild nights in Brussels, Paris, Copenhagen and many of the other cities in which we held our conferences. The standard gag amongst English salesmen was to leave the restaurant one by one and leave me, the Holding Company guy, to pick up their very heavy restaurant tabs. On other occasions Mogens would be generous and order a bottle of champagne in the wrong kind of place and leave me to pay the corkage of around 140 dollars. I was caught in these situations as regularly as clockwork but Mogens signed my expense account and I never had a problem in being refunded.

Everyone but Mogens was surprised

Eventually Mogens was head-hunted to take over as the Managing Director of Procos Control Systems in Copenhagen, a company owned in equal shares by two of the largest industrial companies in Denmark, Novo Industries and Superfoss. Procos manufactured a range of control system products and Mogens wanted me to join him and establish a subsidiary company in England. I had always enjoyed working with Mogens and we had a good understanding of one another's strengths and weaknesses.

While I was considering the suggestion made by Mogens I received a telephone call from Minneapolis advising me that the Board of Directors had decided that I should replace Mogens as the new European Marketing Director. Then a few days later I learned that Hans Christian Anderson, the Managing Director of Rosemount Denmark, had been given the position and that he was to be my new line manager. Hans spoke several European languages and this was cited by Larry Soule as the reason for his appointment. I don't know what actually happened to change the decision of the Board, but Larry must have asked Mogens for his recommendation, and under the circumstances I doubt that Mogens would have shot himself in the foot and put me forward as his replacement.

I had always worked well with Hans Christian and I would have enjoyed working under his direction, but Mogens was very persuasive. I therefore put together a proposition for Mogens to consider. The key feature of my proposition was that he should secure a distribution agreement for the Fuji Electric range of instrumentation products.

To understand my reasoning for this, one needs to understand that the bread and butter business of Rosemount was their range of pressure and differential pressure transmitters. Rosemount held 60 percent of the world market and I had identified the Fuji range of transmitters to be the only products with stronger technical features. The reason that Fuji had never been successful in Europe was that they were represented rather badly by one of their co-founders, Siemens. Siemens manufactured their own range of products in Europe and always kept any Fuji offerings on the back-burner.

I had learned that Siemens and Fuji Electric were about to separate their operations in Europe and I saw this as a golden opportunity. I studied the portfolio of the Fuji Electric Instrumentation Division and prepared a comprehensive marketing plan for him to present to the Fuji Board of Directors. Mogens travelled to Tokyo with the Engineering Director of Novo Industries and together they secured distribution rights for our respective territories. I was good to my word and I submitted my resignation the same day that I received the news.

Everyone was very surprised in the United States. I received a call during the night from Bob Britton and he asked if there was any job he could offer in the United States to keep me in the family. I explained to Bob that I had given my word and it was now too late to for me to change my decision. Bob was a very honest and straight forward person; he respected my position and wished me well.

When a Senior Manager resigns he or she is normally required to leave immediately. I suppose my integrity was solid with Rosemount because they asked me to work three months' notice. Given such a long period to occupy I decided to go out in style. I organised my last control systems conference and located it in Rome during the most beautiful time of the year. It turned out to be the largest and most successful conference that I ever held. Even Bill Yates attended!

Steve Krebs, a good friend and work colleague who had worked on the development of System 3, was transferred from the United States to replace me. I had the highest respect for Steve; he was a good engineer and being American he received a United States salary for the job. Nothing ever changes!

Chapter 16

Three New Relationships

Palmstiernas, Fuji Electric and McWatters
Top hats not allowed!

I finally left Rosemount on 31st May June 1985. I was very sad to leave so many good friends and work colleagues behind me. In only five years the European Control Systems Division had grown from a small number of technicians into a very large Group with an installed base that reached into every corner of Europe.

Procos Control Systems was the fourth company that I had started from scratch and I was not at all daunted by what lay ahead. After all, I was using funds supplied by the two largest companies in Denmark.

While working with Rosemount in Bognor Regis I had quickly realized how badly the Company was located. Bognor had very poor communications with the industrial heartlands of England, Scotland and Wales. There were no good airports nearby, the rail service was terrible and the closest motorway was the M25 which struggled on its circuitous route around London. I did not want to move too far from Midhurst because Michele, Brett and I had grown very fond of the area.

I used my notice period with Rosemount to draw up an action plan. The first serious item was to find a suitable location. It had to enjoy good communications by road, rail and air, and above all else, it had to be a place in which I wanted to live. I examined several small towns in the South West of England and contacted all of the regional development services to examine what start-up grants were available. In comparison to the grants available in rural France, the offerings in the United Kingdom were abysmal, and what was available required such a large amount of paperwork that I decided to give that route a wide berth.

Eventually I found a very attractive historic Georgian building overlooking Winchester Cathedral. The building was owned by a small company that operated a business service for small start-up companies. They offered furnished office accommodation, secretarial services and a telephone answering service for a small monthly charge and they required no long leases. It was perfect.

I shared the building with several other small Companies, all of them professionals in their own field and very successful. There was an office staffed by a very motivated team of attractive young women who placed highly recommended nannies, butlers and other key staff with prominent households in London. There was also a two-man operation that bought and sold the contents of oil tankers while they were still in transit on the high seas. I enjoyed short coffee breaks while I dared to share my own experiences with them and I marvelled at their own determination to succeed. They were a great inspiration to me.

The building had a magnificent location and my old sash window framed a beautiful view of Winchester Cathedral. To the front was the Peninsular Barracks, previous home of the Rifle Brigade, the Kings Royal Hussars and many other fine Regiments that had earned their place in the annals of British military history. The present incumbents, the Royal Green Jackets, often marched down Southgate Street and into Main Street, bayonets fixed and drums beating to exercise their freedom of the City.

HRH Diana the Princess of Wales was their Colonel in Chief and whenever she visited, the Royal Protection Squad searched my office for bombs. Our building had several locked rooms and police dog handlers forced windows open and pushed their charges inside to check out the contents. My storeroom had several hundred transmitter boxes and the dogs would sniff every single box before giving the all-clear. I was amazed at the methodical way in which these dogs would move from one box to the next without missing a single container.

The Peninsular Barracks houses one of the most impressive military museums in the world. This was not surprising because the Rifle Regiments were at the forefront of every campaign fought by the British Army in the 18th, 19th and 20th centuries: the French and Indian Wars, the American Revolutionary War, the Peninsular War, the Waterloo

Campaign, the Crimean War, the Indian Mutiny, the Boer War and the First and Second World Wars. It is a terrible shame that recent Governments, Tory and Labour alike, have chosen to disband or integrate the names of such fine regiments that served our country so well over the past three centuries.

After establishing my office, I focussed upon recruiting two people whom I had already identified as key individuals for my new Company. The first was Phil Fathers, a rough looking individual, a womaniser with long wispy hair and a course tongue, but one of the best and most likeable sales engineers in Rosemount. The second, Terry Minns, was the exact opposite. He was very tall with jet black hair, very well spoken, a gentleman and an excellent engineer whom I had been fortunate to recruit three years earlier into the Rosemount Control Systems Group.

Both agreed to join me but Phil had a very unfortunate incident. On the very day that he accepted my offer he was attending a meeting in Bognor Regis and he went out for his customary drinking session with other visiting sales engineers. At six in the morning he climbed into his car and started his long drive back to his home in the North East of England. After a short distance he was stopped by the police and breathalysed. We both thought it best that he remained with Rosemount because they agreed to provide him with a chauffer for the twelve months that he was without his driving licence.

I no longer had my Rosemount company car, and so I looked for something reasonably priced and found a sporty little MGB-GT coupé which I drove along the A272 each day from Midhurst to Winchester. It was a beautiful drive and my low seat gave me the feeling of driving at incredible speeds while still remaining well within the defined speed limit. It was a driver's car but not a very safe one. It had no crumple zones and no hardened protective side walls. It had none of the safety features that were inherent in modern cars, but it was fun.

I employed a young girl called Alison Price who worked as a receptionist cum secretary. Her secretarial skills were not brilliant but she had a very good telephone manner. She held several long telephone conversations with a contract engineer working with Thames Water. Her technical knowledge of our products was limited but he always asked for her by name. They never met each other and we teased her relentlessly about their telephone relationship. Alison had the last laugh on us all because she became the first person to close an order in our new venture. It was for eleven Fuji differential pressure transmitters that were to be installed on an upgrade at the Hampton Court water purification plant in London. This was a good sized order and it laid the foundation for several huge contracts that were placed by Thames Water in the years to come.

Over the next 12 months I established a small, but well focused team in Winchester. Each member of our team took ownership of a particular task and contributed significantly to our success in those early months of formation. Our team in the first year included Terry Minns, Peter Webb, Trevor Ginn, Jozanne Penfold and Alison Price. I am deeply indebted to each one of them for their hard work.

Winchester, the most beautiful city in all England

We had always loved our home in Crosswinds, Carron Lane. It was only a short walk from the Spread Eagle Hotel, a 14th Century coaching inn which is described by several writers as the finest in the world. In the other direction at the top of Carron Lane was open woodland and on more than one occasion a deer had strayed into our garden.

Midhurst was a neighbourly market town which nestled in the foothills of the South Downs where famous people were able to walk peacefully and in total ignorance of the locals who honoured their privacy. Because of this the town's restaurants were frequented by show business celebrities while members of the Royal Household supported first father and then son on the world famous polo fields.

Regrettably, house and town both carried sad memories of Marjorie's last days and I wanted to put these behind me. We therefore sold Crosswinds and bought a three-story town house in Hyde Church Path, Winchester.

Hyde Church Path lies within the grounds of what used to be Hyde Abbey, the last resting place of King Aelfred the Great. What are believed to be his remains were moved a few years ago, during road works, and placed beneath an unmarked stone slab twenty paces from my front door. I often took guests for a walk in the evening and informed them that they had just walked across Aelfreds grave.

The area was in a peaceful backwater of Winchester which has been described as the most beautiful city in all England. It was very small in ground acreage and untouched by modern industrial development. A tourist could not be blamed if he thought that he had entered a small market town and not the ancient capital of England. Yet so much history could be found within its city walls.

William the Conqueror built the King's Castle which was home to the Domesday Book and the bones of his son William Rufus lay in a wooden mortuary chest above the Choir. Alongside were several other mortuary chests, one of which held the remains of King Canute who ruled England, Denmark and Norway but still managed to get his feet wet at Bosham. On a serious note, it is not commonly appreciated that Aelfred and Canute achieved more for the common people of Wessex and England than perhaps any King or Queen that followed. They are the only Kings of England who ever earned the title 'Great'.

Regrettably Michele refused to move with us to Winchester and she found a small room to rent overlooking a pond that lay below the Spread Eagle Hotel. Meanwhile Brett transferred to a primary school in Winchester and on his first day he was asked to describe himself to his new classmates. He stood up and said, "My name is Brett Coulton and I have been adopted twice". When Brett told me what he had said I quickly explained to his teacher that he had indeed been adopted twice, but on both occasions by me. I needed her to understand that he had been brought up to be proud of his adoption and that this was why he had reacted in the way that he had.

Each day I helped Brett with his breakfast, made arrangements for him to go to school, and then walked briskly to my office. It was a walk that I enjoyed even on a cold frosty morning and I always arrived refreshed and ready for a full day's work. I had never worked in such pleasant surroundings before. I had always been used to an industrial environment and this was the first time that I had been able to enjoy a magnificent view from my office window.

Every lunch time I walked through the old town and discovered something new. I always took my overseas guests to visit the Cathedral and occasionally I would take time to walk by the Winchester Castle Great Hall, home of the mythical King Arthur's Round Table. As I walked back to my office I ordered a specially prepared sandwich from a nearby shop. My favourite was banana and bacon on toasted wholemeal bread with sunflower spread. People started to ask for my order to be repeated and eventually it became so popular that the owner turned it into a menu item.

I had no Au Pair in Winchester. My replacement for Waldi needed more parental supervision than Michele and I decided that it was safer to send her back to her home in Finland. Without Michele to help me I had no alternative but to consider a boarding school for Brett. I was told that Stroud in Romsey was an excellent day school with two rooms for weekly boarders; eight boys and eight girls. This was ideal. I preferred mixed to non-mixed schools; they give a balanced upbringing and the number of boarders was small enough to ensure that Brett received personal attention.

Stroud School was based in an old country house. It had extensive grounds with well established trees, a rugby field, football pitch and cricket field. Fortunately they had a bed available and I had no hesitation in placing Brett into their care. The matron and staff were very likeable people with a homely demeanour and Brett soon settled in. I collected him after lessons every Friday afternoon and returned him again early on Monday morning. Brett made many good friends at the school and he still retains fond memories of his days at Stroud.

My first visit to Tokyo

Two months after Procos commenced business I flew to Tokyo with Mogens and together we briefed 18 of Fuji Electric's best development engineers about the European Market. I had worked with Japanese companies for many years, particularly Yamatake Honeywell, but this was the first time I had ever visited Tokyo. We were hosted in the New Otani by Gen Katsumata San, the International Director of the Instrumentation Division. I took an immediate liking to Gen; he was a gentleman in the true sense of the word and he demonstrated a good understanding, and tolerance, of western behaviour.

I appreciate that many Europeans will take exception to my use of the word tolerance, but one has to travel extensively to understand the strong difference between our two cultures. There have been many occasions when I have been deeply embarrassed by the drunken behaviour and foul language of well dressed Europeans in the bars of foreign countries. I can never tolerate this kind of behaviour and am deeply offended when women are present. On the other hand, Japanese people demonstrate deep respect for their elders, for their guests and for each other. They have traditional values which they still live by and they don't even have a word in their language that means 'no'. By comparison we can be so vulgar in our ways.

Working in a Japanese factory was a very interesting experience. Everyone worked very hard and they really did have exercise breaks. Those with the slightest hint of a cold wore a white face mask and each person to whom I was introduced first made a polite bow and then shook my proffered hand. I noticed the depth of the person's bow increased with the seniority of the person being addressed.

Our meetings were always well organised. Six engineers from the Temperature Controls Product Group would enter and we would conduct our exchange of information, and then six would enter from the Pressure Transmitter Group, and so it would go on for around three days until there had been a full dissemination of information in both directions.

In the evenings Gen entertained us in different locations and on one occasion we visited a hillside restaurant where we were required to remove our shoes and sit on the floor. It was a traditional restaurant with paper walls, and geisha's kneeled beside us to prepare our food and serve hot sake. I believe Gen paid more than one thousand dollars per person for our meal. I will always remember this evening as Jacques Hammers, the Managing Director of Van Hengel Instruments, was with us. He had huge holes in his socks. Poor Jacques, he took our heckling in good fun, but I cannot understand how he could have made such a mistake. He knew that we were visiting a traditional Japanese restaurant.

Every evening Mogens and I visited an amusement arcade and raced computerised motorbikes. This was long before similar machines arrived in Europe. We both became quite expert and it was not long before our two names were vying for leadership at the top of the scoreboard.

Mogens commented upon his meals and would eat a pizza every evening to settle the Sashimi, slices of raw fish that were still swimming around in his stomach. I rather liked Japanese food and I even had occasion to partake in the swallowing of half a dozen live fish but I don't think I will repeat this delicacy. For me it is like eating frogs' legs or snails. I will try it once to suffer the experience but only once.

I think that most people in the West have tasted Sushi, which is raw fish sliced and served on rice heaps or fried fish known as Tempura. I prefer Yakitori chicken or Sukiyaki boiled beef followed by Gyoza dumplings.

After only ten months Mogens resigned from Procos Denmark and the joint owners, Novo Industries and Superfoss, decided that they would curtail future development of their control system business. This did not fit my own business plan for the United Kingdom, and because the owners' prime interest lay in Denmark, they agreed to sell their shares to me at an affordable value. Unfortunately my relationship with Fuji Electric was still in its early stages and they were reluctant to allow me to keep my UK distribution rights while I still had such a small operating capital.

PMV buys Procos

I therefore looked for a company that would form a partnership with me, and I found PMV Sweden, a company that had began operations by manufacturing microtomes for the medical profession 50 years earlier. PMV was owned by Magnus Palmstiernas, a Baron by birthright but no longer permitted under Swedish law to use the title. Magnus had developed his Company in recent years and it was now one of the largest manufacturers of valve positioning equipment in the world.

My relationship with Magnus was facilitated by Rolf Sundvisson who had previously worked with me when he was the Managing Director of Rosemount Sweden. The Rosemount old boys' network was working in my favour and it continued to do so for many years. Another person closely involved in our first meeting, which was at a tennis tournament somewhere in the West of Sweden, was Goran Folke. All three of us worked as a close knit team for the next seven years.

We decided to start a new UK subsidiary which we called PMV Instrumentation and I negotiated an option on 26 percent of the shares. PMV Instrumentation purchased the assets of Procos, provided substantial working capital and secured the distribution rights for all PMV valve positioner products marketed in the United Kingdom. In return I helped PMV to secure the distribution rights for Fuji instrumentation products in Sweden. Rolf then squared up the package by joining PMV along with the total sales force of Rosemount Sweden!

Fuji Electric signed up to both agreements and the stage was set. I had a good operational base in Winchester and two excellent product ranges in my portfolio, Fuji instrumentation and PMV valve positioners. Rolf had the same portfolio and an excellent operational base in Karlstad, Sweden. This arrangement enabled us to pool our technical and logistical resources, a benefit that we both used to maximum advantage.

Terry Minns moved on to take a senior position in the development team of the Eurotherm Control Systems group but before he left he prepared a strong technical quotation structure for the Fuji range of pressure and differential pressure transmitters. He prepared several standard documents and he helped structure a very detailed quotation for the renovation of nine British Gas compressor stations that were positioned throughout the United Kingdom to facilitate the distribution of North Sea Gas.

The engineers in Hinckley remarked afterwards that this quotation was very professional and surpassed anything offered by the large multinational instrumentation companies that we were bidding against. These Companies included Rosemount, Honeywell, Foxboro, Kent, Taylor, Siemens and Hartman and Braun. We were thrilled when we won this contract; it established us in a single stroke as one of the UK market leaders.

We were a small organisation but we focused our activity into a very small niche market that required accurate high quality process transmitters to measure pressure, differential pressure and flow. We won major projects with Amoco, British Petroleum and the CEGB. Within two years Rosemount described PMV Instrumentation in their annual review as their most serious competitor and we were shown to hold a UK market share that exceeded ten percent.

Our range of PMV valve positioners was also enjoying tremendous success. I had employed a young engineer relatively fresh from University where he had studied electronic engineering. His name was Nigel Chant. Nigel enjoyed a high closure rate in selling process transmitters and so I divided the Company into two divisions and I gave him total responsibility for the positioner business. Within three years Nigel secured agreements with more than sixty percent of the process control valve dealers in the United Kingdom. In this particular field we were unquestionably recognised as the market leader. It was not long before the two divisions were vying with each other for market volume and profit contribution.

It was around this time that my professional status was upgraded by my two professional institutions and I was made a Fellow of the Institution of Electrical Engineers and a Fellow of the Institution of Electronic and Radio Engineers. I was very pleased with this achievement. I was still only 44 years old and there had been a time when I thought that I would never have been in a position to achieve this level of recognition. Shortly after this I was also given the title of European Engineer with the right to prefix my name with the letters EurIng.

Only an engineer could come up with such a bizarre title and I certainly never had any intention of using this questionable inscription before my name. Mr would continue to suffice. No wonder engineering has become one of the least attractive professions in the United Kingdom. Not only do we pay ourselves very badly but we can't even find a suitable title to honour those who have achieved a creditable standing in the engineering profession.

Dad, you are about to become a grandfather

In the summer of 1986 Michele telephoned me and asked if she could live with me in Winchester. She sounded very subdued and I suspect that she had learned her mistakes the hard way. Her first words asked me not to say 'I told you so'.

She had large debts. I decided to settle the rent with her landlady and clear the outstanding amount on her Barclay's credit card. I was annoyed with her landlady because she should not have offered Michele accommodation when she knew that it was against my wishes. As for the bank; why on earth they agreed to give her a credit card when she had no income was a complete mystery to me. I was strongly tempted to tell them both to get stuffed but that would not have helped and I was pleased to have Michele home again.

Michele was back to her normal self again. I think she had recovered from the shock of losing her mother when she was at the most influential part of her young life. She soon obtained employment with an old people's home in Winchester. She was accepted and trained as a Care Assistant; the same kind of work that her mother opted to do in the years before she died. Michele loved her work and continued for a short time until she found out that she was pregnant. Michele had known Paul for six years and in the very week that she finally broke away from their relationship she became pregnant.

I was opposed to Michele's relationship with Paul when she was a child. Michele was only twelve years old when Paul, already an adult, stood outside school waiting for her to finish class. This was something that no sensible parent would accept. Nevertheless, the situation was now different. Michele was eighteen years old and I suggested that they should make arrangements to be married as soon as possible.

Michele retaliated against this and said that she would not get married under such circumstances. Instead she moved into council accommodation with Paul and gave birth to my first granddaughter, Toni-Louise, on Monday 9th February 1987. Seventeen months later they married in West Lavington Church. Yet again Michele demonstrated her determination to do exactly the opposite to my wishes. In later years she admitted that it had been her deliberate intention to oppose me.

They moved to a very nice terraced home in Boxgrove; a beautiful medieval village just outside Chichester. On 8th December 1988 Michele gave birth to a son. Sadly Nathan was born before his time and he only lived for a few hours. He now lies beneath the branches of an old Yew tree in the grounds of Boxgrove Priory.

Three weeks later Michele, Paul and Toni were involved in a terrible accident. Paul was driving home across Goodwood and their Volkswagen Beetle veered off the road into a huge tree. Paul and Toni were saved by their seat belts but Michele was crushed into her seat and the fuel tank ripped open spilling fuel across her. Fortunately the idiot who arrived on the scene with a cigarette hanging from his open mouth did not rush to her aid. She lay drifting in and out of consciousness for almost two hours while firemen cut her free from the wreckage. She had a serious head injury, broken teeth, broken pelvis, crushed knee and a badly scarred leg. Michele was lucky to be alive and the insurance company insulted her by offering a pitiful settlement of £13,000.

Her solicitor seemed to be out of his depth and so I joined forces with Michele and we retained a Barrister in London. We fought the insurance company for several months and a few days before the court hearing they raised their offer to £98,000. We had no choice but to accept the offer. If the judge had awarded even two pounds less, then we would have had to pay the court costs, which might have exceeded the value of the settlement. Rather disgusting really; only the rich can afford to pay for justice in an English Crown Court.

My second granddaughter, Stevi-Lianne, arrived on Saturday 13th January 1990. Michele burst into tears when I visited her in St Richards Hospital. I told her that I was pleased that she had given birth to another daughter; God was giving her my revenge for all those difficult years that she had given me. In retrospect I suppose I was being a little unfair, but then she had given me a really tough time.

It took several years for Michele to overcome her disabilities, but when she did, her caring nature began to re-emerge. She returned to her vocation and became a senior nursing auxiliary. Even for a fit person it was a real challenge. Michele cared for her family during the day and then worked night shift in a nursing home for the elderly and mentally infirm. Not an easy job but one that she dearly loved.

Unfortunately her marriage to Paul did not last. They separated and Michele married a youngster who had served his country as a signalman in the Royal Navy. Ian Simms was at that time a hard working and very ambitious insurance salesman. His was not my most favoured of occupations but he was very clean cut and his naval service onboard type-42 destroyers impressed me.

Michele and Ian married at Diani Reef in Kenya on 22nd April 1994. Ian had two lovely girls by his previous marriage, Hayley and Fiona. They became my ready made granddaughters and took on the job as elder sisters to Toni and Stevi. Theirs was a model family and Michele used her insurance settlement to purchase a four-bedroomed family home on the old Tangmere Airfield outside Chichester.

History was coming around to repeat itself. This was the same airfield from which Douglas Bader flew from during the Battle of Britain and the place where the Royal Air Force High Speed Flight was based when Squadron Leader Neville Duke captured the world airspeed record in a Hawker Hunter Mk3. This was on 7th September 1953 and at that time 727.63 mph seemed to be an impossible speed. Yet 16 years later the Americans would send a man to the moon.

The runways sweeping past Michele's new home brought many old memories back to me and I enjoyed visiting her new family in Tangmere. I had four grandchildren, all girls, and I jumped at every opportunity to be in their company. Michele and Ian invited me to join them for a holiday in Florida and I faithfully escorted the girls on every one of those crazy rides at Disney until we came to Space Mountain. I chickened out on this one; I had ridden it with Marjorie when the park opened in 1979 and that was enough for me. I sat on a very hot bench with Stevi and ate an ice cream while the other girls rode it several times.

My biggest memory of this holiday was being lured onto the Stuka Dive Bomber at Wet and Wild. I must have been the only grandfather stupid enough to hurtle down that 250 ft near vertical water slide.

The following year I collected the four girls in my car and drove them to Euro Disney just outside Paris. They thoroughly enjoyed themselves but I found the park to be a terrible disappointment after Florida.

I talked to a slip of a girl at the barbecue

When I moved to Winchester I visited the local Gingerbread Group and found that the members were not really my type; they were very different to those whose company I had enjoyed socially for many years in Bognor Regis. I needed to find friends away from my work environment and one day I noticed a small advertisement for the Inter-Varsity Club in Southampton. It was advertised as a social club for young active professionals and boasted several weekly events that included board games, badminton, country walks and dance evenings. This sounded right up my street and I decided to join them at my earliest opportunity.

My social life centred on IVC for the next few years and I acquired many new friends. Each member took it in turn to organise an event and I began a tennis group which met every Saturday morning at the sports centre in Winchester. I enjoyed board games and I met Ken Phillip who became my close friend and chess partner. We continue to play chess whenever we are in the same country. In recent years this has included China, the Bahamas, Spain and even England from time to time. Ken, when you get around to reading this book, remember; he who wins the last game wins the night!

One of our members organised a barbecue evening at his home and I chanced to talk to a young 27 year-old slip of a girl from Southampton University where she worked as an academic administrator. She had been invited to the barbecue by one of her friends from Voluntary Service Overseas. Her name was Anne McWatters; she had lightly permed dark brown hair and wore a thick yellow pullover with light brown corduroy trousers. She had a bright smile and spoke with a cultured voice free of accent but without the slightest hint of pretence. I warmed instantly to Anne and invited her to join me for dinner later in the week.

Anne and I continued to date for several years. Our relationship lasted because we enjoyed each other's company without allowing it to restrict our own personal freedoms. I knew very little about Anne or her background. She never talked about herself or her family. Then, one evening, as we walked through the Winchester Cathedral Close, I commented upon the rustic features of Cheyney Court. This is a well known Elizabethan building that stands against the ancient walls of the Close. It is often painted by local artists and can be seen on more picture postcards than any other Hampshire scene. Anne replied that it was the oldest inhabited building in England and that one of the walls dated back to Roman Winchester.

She surprised me when she told me, almost as an afterthought, that this had been her home for many years. She told me how she carried a huge metal key under the seat of her Austin Mini to open the huge ancient doors of the Close when she arrived home after 10.30 pm. My mother often locked me out but this was a first for me. I pictured a similar situation for Michele but I am sure she would have found a way to scale the walls.

Anne's father, Stephen, had been the Headmaster of Pilgrims School which provides choirboys for Winchester Cathedral and Winchester College; hence the reason for living in the Cathedral Close. It was not until he died many years later, and I arranged his Memorial Service in Winchester Cathedral, that I uncovered much of his background. Even now I only know a very small part.

Stephen returned from India as a child to the Dragon School in Oxford where he studied extremely hard and won a scholarship to Eton. He excelled in both classical music and sports; his Eton School long jump record stood for 30 years. Stephen then went on to Trinity College Oxford and gained a First in Classical Moderations before his studies were interrupted by war service in the King's Royal Rifle Corps.

He crossed into France as part of the second wave during the Normandy Landings and was engaged in some of the fiercest fighting of the War. His Company was among the first to enter the Arnhem battle area and what he and his comrades found was so distressing that it deeply affected him for the rest of his life.

He achieved the rank of Captain and when the war ended he resumed his studies at Oxford securing a First with a distinction in Greats. He was then targeted for a return to Eton where he soon became Master in College. It was here that he met Anne's mother Mary, an Oxford Graduate and language teacher. Together they brought my wife Anne, Cathy and then Henry into the world. Anne was born in Windsor on 6th January 1959.

From Eton he was appointed Headmaster of Clifton School and after 12 years he moved to Pilgrims where he remained until his retirement; a remarkable career and one which Anne strived to live up to. Anne attended school at Wycombe Abbey and then went on to achieve a 2:1 in

Classics at Girton College, Cambridge. Her grandmother, Gillian Nairn, also studied at Girton and was the first women ever to be awarded the Cambridge Chancellors Medal.

Anne's family owned a tract of land on the nature reserve at Llanmaddoc on the Whitford Estuary. This land had two old white-washed stone cottages, Pill Cottage and Pill House. The small cottage was owned by her father and the larger house by her uncle, William Wilkinson. Stephen and William both had a very strong interest in wild birds and the salt marshes surrounding Llanmaddoc provided an abundance of expectation of wild life in early summer and they were never disappointed with what it brought to them year on year.

I had a tremendous admiration for William; he was an extremely intelligent person and one-time President of the Cambridge University Pitt Club. Every time that I met him he would ask me a very simple and different question about my recent activities and then he would just sit and listen. And I mean listen. He digested and mulled over every single word before making a very intelligent and informed comment.

William tragically lost his eyesight during a surgical operation. This would have deterred most people of his age but his inner strength came to the fore and he worked even harder to fulfil his duties as Chairman of the Nature Conservancy Council. His tremendous determination was rewarded by the Queen when she dubbed him Sir William, a Knight of the Realm. William now lies along with his parents in the grounds of Cheriton Church at the other end of the village of Llanmaddoc, and a bird hide on the Whitford Estuary stands in memory of his significant and lasting contribution to nature conservation. Anne's father Stephen lies nearby.

We continue to use Pill Cottage. Anne loves to take long walks through Cwm Ivy and around the Estuary. In 1992 we returned from the Worms Head and I was shocked to find a spring tide rushing across the salt marsh. My precious new Mercedes Benz was slowly sinking beneath the rising water. It took me several minutes to find my car keys and our retreat to higher ground was quickly cut-off. The exhaust pipe was already submerged and I was extremely fortunate to be able to recover my car to the safety of a nearby grass bank. We remained marooned in the cottage for the rest of the night and in the morning the water was so high that it covered the top post of the wooden farm gate that stands outside the cottage.

Anne lived in a terraced house in Southampton close to the University. It was in a poor state of repair and I helped her to make substantial improvements which culminated in Paul replacing the roof and converting the attic to an additional room. This enabled Anne to sell for a reasonable profit and with my help she bought a semi-detached house in Christchurch. It was in Riverside Road, Tuckton, and was one of only a handful of houses that benefited from a garden on the banks of the River Stour. The river had navigation through Christchurch Harbour and across the lake to Mudeford Quay before passing into the English Channel off Hengistbury Head, the first known landing place of early Roman Legions.

Shortly after buying this house, Anne made a career change that was to have far reaching consequences. She joined the Winchester Regional Health Authority. This also created a very unusual logistical situation. I owned a house in Winchester but by this time worked in Christchurch while Anne owned a house in Christchurch but worked in Winchester. We therefore swapped homes during the working week and got together in our waterside home at the weekend. This arrangement continued until I eventually sold my home in Winchester and then, a short while later, the Government closed down all the Regional Health Authorities and Anne was transferred to a new job in Bristol with the Department of Health. All rather complicated!

One morning as I walked through Hyde, along the West Wall and past the Theatre Royal, following my usual and direct route into the office, I noticed that the streets were absolutely empty. It was as if Winchester had suffered a major nuclear incident, the type of incident that involved the use of a neutron bomb rather than the destructive power of a hydrogen device. When I eventually arrived at my office I sat down and waited for my staff to arrive. No one came and I waited for the telephone calls that would indicate that they had all gone down with radiation poisoning or something of the like. Then when no telephone calls came I started to make serious enquiries.

A nuclear bomb might well have been dropped as far as poor old Michael Fish, the BBC weatherman, was concerned. It was Friday 15th

October 1987. Fifteen million trees had been lost and ninety percent of the forestation of Southern England had been destroyed by the Great Storm. Not only had the met office failed to predict the storm, the worst to hit England in 300 years, but I had slept through it all. Winchester was cut off from the outside world. The telephone lines were down and trees blocked all roads and railway lines.

London was also hard hit and power failures in the City prevented the London Stock Market from opening. By coincidence, worldwide markets began to fall on the same day and the City was unable to react for a full three days. Then on Monday 18th October 1987 the stock index fell by the largest amount ever. The value of Companies listed on the London Stock Market fell by 50 billion pounds in a single day. What a week that was!

Anne and I eventually came under pressure from both of our families to get married. Anne's family in particular had very old fashioned values and they wanted to see her married in church. I had never been placed under pressure by Anne and therefore I decided to go ahead and pop the question at the moment of my choosing; I suppose it must be obvious who gave Michele her stubborn streak.

Meanwhile, I had three half-carrot investment diamonds that I had bought several years earlier from Mannie Judin of the Lustre Group in Johannesburg. I selected one of these and asked a jewellery manufacturer in Southgate Street to make a solitaire engagement ring to my very specific design. I gave him an old ring for sizing information.

Saga of the three loose toes

A suitable opportunity occurred two months later when I attended a conference in Tokyo. I took Anne with me as far as Thailand where we enjoyed a few days in Bangkok before flying on to the island of Phuket, which was still untouched by the ravages of commercial tourism. Our hotel lay in tranquil surroundings on the shores of the Andaman Sea and we appeared to be the only guests.

The rainy season was about to start and so we quickly took a long-tailed boat to the mainland. After a brief visit to Ko Khao Tapu, better known as James Bond Island from the film, Man with the Golden Gun, we headed for the Phi Phi Islands. As we zipped along the mangrove swamps of Phang Nga we passed fishing villages which were perched on wooden stilts far from land. Young children waved happily to us and I gasped in awe at the stunning scenery that rushed by. Colossal limestone monoliths rose from the emerald green sea and soared five hundred metres into the azure blue sky to complete what could have easily been a movie scene in the fantasy dream world of Walt Disney.

That evening on 4th May 1988, we returned to our hotel and I booked a very special meal in a small restaurant overlooking the sea. We were the only customers as we sat on the terrace and burned sticks of incense to keep the mosquitoes at bay. The moon reflected from ripple free waters that stretched before us and the chorus of a million crickets chirped in the background. The venue was perfect. When our dessert was ready to be served I poured two fresh glasses of white wine from our cooler, took a little red box from my pocket and placed it in the centre of the table.

Anne stared at the box not daring to believe what was inside. She opened the box very slowly. Her hands trembled and her fingers struggled with the clasp. She was still uncertain of its contents and tried unsuccessfully to look calm and unperturbed. When she finally opened the box she stared at the solitaire ring in absolute silence. In her normal annoying fashion she sat speechless for several seconds. I could almost hear the gears grinding as her brain spun around trying to select the appropriate response.

The following day we decided to swim by the hotel and we took a short boat trip to a nearby island. On our return I jumped into the water and while wading towards shore the sea suddenly turned red. I have no idea what happened. I crawled onto the beach and watched blood gush from my foot. Three of my toes were almost severed. Two Thai boys picked me up and carried me quickly to the hotel surgery. A doctor arrived within minutes and she managed to stem the flow of blood. I lay on a bed while two people held my foot secure. Then without administering any painkillers she scrubbed my wounds clean. She repeatedly poured copious amounts of iodine into the open wounds. After doing this for about twenty minutes she then bound my toes roughly into the correct position using pads and bandages.

This was one of the most painful experiences that I have been forced to endure. Every day for a whole week this exercise was repeated. She removed the bandages, opened the wound and scrubbed it clean while pouring even more iodine over the flabby white flesh that clung to three small exposed pieces of bone.

For the rest of the week I was unable to walk and I lay on my bed watching dozens of in-house movies. The doctor obtained a crutch for me and I started to hobble around the hotel grounds. I protected my foot from the monsoon rains with a polythene shopping bag which I taped tightly around my ankle. I still wanted to see something of the island; Anne hired a small car and we set off into the interior. We were warned to stay off the forest roads and my experience in Zambia should have taught me to stay away from dirt roads in the rainy season.

Nevertheless, I persuaded Anne to leave the main road and take us to a remote area in the centre of the island. As we followed the dirt road it narrowed and began to wind deep into hilly rainforest, more commonly referred to as Jungle. We knew long ago that we should have turned back but we could not find anywhere to turn. As always in such conditions we believed that there would be a turning point or clearing around the next corner.

Suddenly the skies opened and the dirt track turned into a mud bath. We were following a steep gully and I became concerned that we could slide over the edge and into the fast flowing stream beneath us. Anne became frantic and her knuckles whitened as she clutched at the steering wheel. She had never experienced such horrendous driving conditions.

There was no alternative, I had to drive. I could not climb across to the driver's seat and I had to hop around the car in deep mud. I began to wonder how we would get out of the forest if I could not find a turning point or if we sank deep into the mud. Walking was out of the question with my bandaged foot and it was beginning to get dark. How could I have been so stubborn and get into such a ridiculous situation? Yet again Michele came to mind.

I drove for another 100 yards before coming to a steep incline where the wheels spun viciously and the rear of the car slowly moved sideways towards the precipice. There was now a shear drop of thirty feet to the stream gushing below us. I could not risk going over the edge and so I took the car out of gear and allowed it to roll back down the hill. At the bottom I placed it into reverse and considered the possibility of reversing to the main road. It was several miles and the track conditions were now so atrocious that I thought my best option was to attempt a three point turn.

I asked Anne to step out of the car, partly for her safety but also to watch my rear wheels. I reversed as close as I dared to the soft crumbling edge of the gully. A small bush pushed against my bumper. This gave me a little moral support but no actual physical support. I yelled at Anne to give me more clear instructions. We had no room for error. What if we slipped over the edge, would I get out, how would I walk back to the main road with my three toes hanging off? What would the Owner say when I told him his car was five miles from the main road at the bottom of a gulley? All of these thoughts raced through my mind as the soil subsided beneath my rear wheels.

Eventually after several hairy manoeuvres I managed to turn the car. The return track was downhill and Anne sat quietly in the passenger seat praying for her safe return to civilization. Then my worst and most secret fear was confirmed. As we rejoined the tarred road a snake hastened across our path; what if?

This was not the end of the 'Saga of the Three Loose Toes'. Anne waited for me in Bangkok while I flew to Tokyo and attended my conference. Noboru Majima, one of the senior Fuji engineers organising our conference, arranged for my dressings to be changed by their factory doctor. The doctor was horrified when he removed my bandages. He told Noboru that I must visit the hospital immediately.

I had already suffered enough humiliation and pain and I told Noboru that I would wait until I returned home. He refused to be deterred and he surprised me later in the morning when he stopped beside me in a taxi. He and one other person took hold of me and forcibly guided me into the taxi. He took me to the hospital where I was registered and given a plastic identity card in Japanese. I was really impressed by the efficient way in which I was processed.

First of all an elderly nurse came to remove my dressings. She could not speak English and I am certain she must have worked in field dressing stations during the Second World War. I tried to warn her of my predicament but she pushed my hands to one side and quickly ripped the bandages from my foot. I fully expected three toes to be contained in their wraps. When the doctor came he examined my foot and explained that there was nothing he could do for me. He said that my toes should have been stitched within a few hours of the original occurrence.

When I eventually returned to England my own doctor took a totally different view. He explained that my Thai doctor had done the correct thing. By repeatedly cleaning my wounds and soaking them in iodine, she had ensured that I did not get any gangrene. My toes may have taken a long time to heal and they may not look very pretty but I am very thankful for the excellent treatment I received.

We move to the old Christchurch Naval Airbase

Our business was growing so quickly that I had to increase the number of rooms that we rented from Hampshire Business Space. I arranged to consolidate my deliveries by sea-air from Japan. I shipped containers from Yokohama to San Francisco and then flew the containers for the remainder of the journey into Heathrow. This created additional problems. Containers arrived outside our offices in Southgate Street. The road had double yellow lines and traffic was backed-up into the centre of Town while we formed a human chain and passed hundreds of transmitter boxes across the pavement and into the front window of our office.

Eventually our offices started to resemble an industrial facility and I had to find alternative accommodation. I scoured the light commercial areas but they were totally unsuitable. They comprised a ramshackle collection of metal-clad storage sheds that were poorly insulated against heat loss, extremely expensive to rent and in addition required a 21 year lease. I calculated that our accommodation costs would increase by more than two hundred percent and our budget could not withstand such an impact.

I was left with no alternative but to look further afield and eventually I purchased the empty shell of a large building on the old Royal Naval

Airbase at Christchurch. The building was part of a refurbished hanger which had previously been used by DeHavilland to assemble Vampire and Venom jet fighters.

I converted this empty shell into a high-tech facility that would meet my demanding specifications. Nigel Chant helped with my design and we used local engineering firms to fit an additional floor, insulated walls and ceiling, lighting, plumbing, computer wiring and everything essential to facilitate our special requirements. The building included a reception, two offices, conference room, workshop, a very large storage facility and an environmentally controlled calibration room.

Eventually on 1st January 1990, after four enjoyable years in the centre of Winchester, we moved into our own facility on the Christchurch Airfield. I had agreed a reasonable rent with Magnus and PMV Instrumentation gave me a 21 year lease. In addition I claimed an industrial business allowance from the Inland Revenue and I registered myself with Customs and Excise for value added tax. This arrangement was perhaps one of the best financial decisions that I ever made. It provided PMV Instrumentation with an excellent and affordable facility while I secured a very tax effective source of income which still continues today.

Many of my employees lived in Southampton and they found it was much less tiresome to travel through the New Forest each day, and so I was able to retain almost all of my staff. Even our accountant, Judy Cassells, elected to travel each day from Winchester and she remained with PMV for several years. Our salaries were decided by profitability and even my salary was maintained significantly below industry average. However, all of our employees enjoyed their work and related very well with each other and, most importantly, with our customers. Because of this we had a very low staff turnover and many stayed with me until my retirement.

Ionians traded with the Doric Greeks

My first overseas visit after moving to Christchurch was to give further support to Entek, our agent in Istanbul. Anne was very keen to visit classical sites on the coast of Ionia and so we flew to Dalaman airport in the month of August, which was rather a hot time of the year. This unfortunate timing was necessary to discuss ongoing projects with state owned oil refining companies in Ismir and Ismit.

We collected our hired car and headed westwards along the coast. As we left the Dalyan delta we saw some extraordinary rock tombs carved into the side of the cliffs. Our journey continued along hilly coastal roads until we arrived at Marmaris. I was frightened at almost every corner as a crazy lorry driver hurtled towards me on the wrong side of the road. Turkish drivers drive with such senseless bravado; I imagine they believe that they are protected by some divine power. Sadly their bravado often results in the untimely death of an innocent person.

From the distance the bay of Marmaris looked very picturesque, and it was described as an attractive local coastal resort in the guidebook. In the event it was quite disappointing with little of interest to see and so we did not linger. We stayed overnight in a comfortable hotel just outside Bodrum. The following day we climbed to St Peter's Castle which gave a good view across the mountains and out to sea.

We continued our journey westwards through marshland where the sea had penetrated in earlier days. Anne identified several stopping places with historical names that she recognised from her classical literature. We investigated all of these places; they were established during the period when Turkey was occupied by the Ionian Greeks. Anne gave me a running commentary and informed me how Ionians traded with the Doric Greeks who inhabited Greece during the classical period. We visited the theatre buildings of Miletus and the famous temple of Apollo at Didyma, where Ionians once consulted the oracle.

Finally we arrived at Kushadasi, where we based ourselves for the next few days. It was a large city with a modern shopping area and good access to reasonable beaches. Most importantly for Anne it was the main starting point for our visit to the ancient city of Ephesus. Ephesus was amazing but for me my main memory will always be the incredible mid-summer heat. It was in the middle of a plain and its arid harbour lay many miles from the coast. The site has surviving remains from seven civilisations.

There is an old library and the huge stone building blocks look as if they are about to fall onto the tourists below. In particular I remember walking down the old roman forum. A roman theatre is on one side of the site, and further on, there is a freeze reconstructed to its original appearance, which was the façade of another library in the time of Alexander the Great. Anne told me how St Paul of Tarsus preached to the Ephesans from one of the Roman buildings, telling them that their altar to 'the unknown god' was the God whom he and other Christians worshipped. His epistle to the Ephesans is one of the books in the New Testament bible.

After visiting Ephesus I flew to Istanbul to conduct my business and Anne enjoyed the 'Ladies Beach' just outside Kushadasi. When I returned our motel had been taken over by three families for a Circumcision festival. That evening three young boys were circumcised and laid out for all to see on separate beds in the middle of the lawn. Young girls looked under the boys sheets and teased them. They sniggered at the boys' obvious embarrassment which was tinged by the lingering pain of their very public ordeal.

We were invited to join in the celebrations and we feasted, danced and drank copious amounts of raki into the early hours of the morning. Anne dislikes aniseed and she gave the raki a wide berth. I suffered immensely and remained motionless in my bed through the following day and night. I have never touched it since.

Our hire car period expired and we had to rent an old banger at an extortionate cost. It was the only one available at short notice and when we had driven sixty miles into the middle of nowhere, the tyre burst. This was when I discovered my first big mistake of the holiday; I had not checked my spare and it was as flat as a pancake. I had to remove the wheel and take it to the nearest garage for repair.

After Kushadasi we headed back to Dalaman via some other interesting places. We diverted to visit the thermal springs at Pamukkale where crowds of Turkish families bathed in crystal clear pools on the hillside beneath cascades of solidified white travertine. Our final stop was close to Fethiye harbour. We swam in the blue lagoon off Olu-Deniz beach. It was blissfully warm and its colour was a most spectacular, deep blue, almost too blue to be true. It also had a strange taste, not salty, perhaps even a little stagnant.

We arrived at the airport a few hours after our swim, and by then I was extremely sick. It was just after midnight, and after we checked in we were told that our flight had not even left Gatwick Airport. I was sat miserably on the floor of the airport departure lounge and my de-arranged brain cells began to suspect that Saddam Hussein had dropped chemical weapons on Dalaman; American forces were stationed nearby and they were soon to launch Desert Storm. We ignored instructions from the airport staff and booked into a nearby hotel where I could suffer in private until our aircraft arrived. It was one of the most horrible periods of my life.

Brett replied nervously and said 200 ft

I never took Michele to Disney while she was a child. We lived in Africa and the Florida version was still under construction. I became concerned that my opportunity to take Brett would also pass. The years were unfolding so quickly and I decided to book a charter flight to Orlando in the summer of 1990. When we arrived we collected a compact car from Budget and drove to our small hotel on the Orange Blossom Trail. We climbed out of our car into the parking lot at 4 pm on a sunny Saturday afternoon.

Two weeks later another father arrived with his small boy on the same flight from England. He also hired a compact car from Budget and climbed out into the same parking lot at 4 pm on a sunny Saturday afternoon. A drug addict shot him dead and robbed him before his feet touched the tarmac. How place and time can change events so tragically; this could so easily have been us.

Brett could not get enough of the wild rides in Universal Studios. The queues were very long and yet he insisted that we visited 'Back to the Future' three times. I don't think there was a single attraction in Universal Studios, Disney or Warner Brothers that we did not enjoy. Still Brett wanted more and eventually he plucked up enough courage to ask if I would let him do a bungee jump. I could not understand why he would want to do such a crazy thing. He was terrified of heights and I instantly recalled how many times that I had to carry him screaming up the steps of the concrete car park in the Portsmouth Tricorn shopping centre.

We set out early in the morning and drove to one of two high-lift cranes. We were the only customers. 150 feet or 200 feet, which do you prefer? Brett grinned nervously and replied 200 feet. Could I be hearing this correctly? No, he was not going to go through with it; I was absolutely convinced that he would back out at the last moment.

A full team of people looked after him. Straps were fitted tightly around his ankles and he was weighed and tagged before the correct bungee was fitted. Everything was checked and double checked. It all looked super professional and finally, before he stepped into the cage, a further person checked all of his equipment against the tag wrapped around his wrist. No, there was still time, surely he would refuse to get into the cage.

While this was happening I waded through a thick wad of indemnity forms. Brett was under age and I was required to sign his life away. The more documents that I had to sign the more nervous I became. When I emerged from the control shack I was visibly shaking. I wondered if I was making a mistake in allowing him to make such a dangerous jump. I assured myself that hundreds of people jumped safely every day. Why should I worry, it would help him to master his fear of heights once and for all.

Brett was already being winched high into the air. It was at this point that someone said to me, "Do not be concerned sir, we do things properly here; the people on the other crane did not check and double check". I then wondered why we were the only customers and so I asked him to explain. "Oh, did you not hear about the accident last night, the bungee broke and a young man was killed".

Brett was almost invisible to my naked eye but I could see that he made a clean dive from the cage. He fell towards the ground, yes the ground, this was not above water, and then the bungee stretched to its limit and catapulted him back into the sky. His shirt wrapped around his shoulders and he wailed like a banshee. I am sure there could have been an easier way to overcome his fear of heights, and a far cheaper one. Perhaps not! Anyhow, I have always been one for a challenge and I pondered carefully. Should I give it a go?

The whiplash effect worried me and I decided that it would be very stupid for me to jump given the condition of the three lower discs in my back. This was one of the few occasions in my life when I showed good sense. I climbed into my car and drove one very excited youngster back to the safety of his hotel.

Rabat, it's only a short drive

We managed to sell several Fuji single-loop process controllers to a power station in Morocco. This was a very difficult situation for us. The Fuji CC-S controller was way ahead of its time. It was the first single loop controller that gathered several function blocks into a standard sized controller case. Fitted with conventional operator controls and a manual override for emergency conditions it could be used to replace outdated controllers manufactured by Foxboro, Honeywell, Taylor, Kent and Fischer Porter.

A single-loop control strategy could easily be configured by a trained instrument engineer from a library of function blocks contained within its built-in software package. Creating an application specific 3-element boiler level control loop or a burner fuel/air ratio control strategy was relatively easy.

Single loop controllers and their eventual replacements, multi-loop controllers with trending, have been an integral and very import step in the rapid evolution of control systems in the second half of the 20th century. They are the first real attempt to utilise powerful new features made available by recent step-by-step developments in silicon advanced manufacturing technology; the first attempt to step back from the practice of miniaturisation and to give the operator a conventional interface to the process, which he understands and can use to control the process in the event of a plant malfunction.

While the configuration of this type of controller was easy, many of the larger companies were over ambitious and wanted to integrate groups of controllers into a plant-wide scheme that could be monitored from a centrally located control room. This was achieved by using RS-232 or, in later models, RS-485 communications with Modbus protocol. To the non-technical this sounds a mouthful and in real terms it was. This is because the communication standards and protocols were often interpreted in a different way by different manufacturers of control hardware. In other words, getting our controllers to talk to other devices was always a very difficult task, even for those with the technical know-how. Selling the latest technology single-loop controllers to Morocco was, we thought, a big mistake.

We had already established an agency in Casablanca with a company called Relec that was owned by an electrical engineer called Abdiljilil Benemar. I decided to visit Casablanca to give him help with a large quotation that he was preparing for a sugar factory and to examine his capability in writing supervisory software for the CC-S controllers.

It was mid-July and I arrived in Casablanca on an Air Gibraltar flight at 1pm. Abdiljilil met me at the airport and after transferring the contents of my suitcase to a wardrobe in my hotel, he rushed me to his office in the backstreets of a Casablanca suburb. His office was an empty shop with a long glass window fronting a dusty and very dirty street. Two young women with long black hair and typically long very attractive Moroccan noses sat at a single desk, one of them typing the initial draft of our quotation on an old mechanical typewriter. They were shy, extremely polite and both were dressed in an attractive blue caftan. Their heads uncovered; one was Abdiljilil's wife, the other, his sister.

We worked as a team stopping only to sip mint tea from a small glass. After several hours I was satisfied with what we had prepared and instead of driving me back to my hotel he suggested that we should deliver our quotation, now sealed in a tender envelope, to the sugar companies head office in Rabat; "it's only a short drive".

It was late; I was hot, hungry and covered in dust. I wanted to take a cold shower, change my clothes and sit down to an enjoyable meal in my hotel. Instead I found myself driving with Abdiljilil in a beaten-up car along the Atlantic highway to Rabat. We arrived just before midnight and handed our tender envelope to the night guard. "We are almost at the sugar factory, why don't we carry on and visit them first thing in the morning". "Oh hell, OK Abdiljilil let's get going" I replied.

It was a long hard drive along the Atlantic coast in the direction of Tangier and we arrived at the remote sugar factory a couple of hours before sunrise. We met with shift technicians in their workshop and sipped mint tea while waiting for the engineering manager to arrive. I was dog-tired; I hadn't slept, washed or eaten since leaving Winchester in the early hours of the previous day.

Our meeting went very well and I was confident that our commitment had impressed our host sufficiently to win the contract; I was already confident that our price was right. Unfortunately he wanted us to meet the works manager; he was in Rabat and was not expected to return before Monday morning.

Red eyed and feeling very scruffy, we retreated to a small hunting lodge nearby, and after a huge lunch of roast boar we slept for the remainder of the day and through to the early hours of Sunday morning. I was ready for a relaxing day on the beach and then Abdiljilil suggested that we should drive over the Riff to a small village on the Mediterranean coast. He explained that it was only a short drive and that it was such a beautiful place, we could relax for the day and then return refreshed for our meeting first thing on Monday morning.

It was a very hot and difficult drive over the dry rugged mountains and we didn't arrive until 5 pm, far too late to enjoy any of the many beach facilities. I handed in my passport for checking by the security police and then bought a razor and other essential items from the porter. Unfortunately there was no shop in the village where I could buy a change of clothing.

I showered and sprayed deodorant all over my body but I still felt terrible. My shirt was soaked with sweat and it clung to my back like a wet unwashed lettuce. As for my socks! Well do I need to say any more? I felt like a leper when I eventually sat down in the restaurant and ate my evening meal among a dozen well dressed French families who were enjoying their summer vacation.

By now I was furious. We had driven the whole day across the Riff only to sleep the night and drive back again. I just couldn't see any point in what we were doing. We could have been relaxing in a small fishing cottage on the Atlantic coast. I had long since given up on my clothing and toiletries which were hundreds of miles away in Casablanca. Abdiljilil's wife had collected them and taken them home for safe keeping.

After our meeting at the sugar factory we drove south to a shanty town and visited the home of a young graduate from Rabat University. She lived alone in a small two-roomed brick building with a tin roof. One room contained a single army-type bed and the other a very powerful desk top computer which rested on a wooden table. A single uncovered light bulb glared above her head and I am reliably told that she worked on this computer for 18 hours each day. There was no other furniture in the building.

She asked if I would sit with her for a couple of hours and help her with several technical problems that troubled her. I was astounded by her in-depth knowledge of process control engineering. She not only had a strong grasp of her subject but she was writing an interface for the supervisory software that we needed to work with our CC-S controllers. I certainly had no need to worry about providing technical support for my products in Morocco. Before leaving, I asked Abdiljilil to ensure that she was properly remunerated for her valuable work.

It was almost midnight when we reached Casablanca and I found that I had been transferred to a different hotel. When I tried to check in I was shocked to discover that I had left my passport with the desk of our hotel on the Mediterranean. She explained that all occupants, including foreign nationals, had to lodge identification cards or passports for inspection by the security police. Any person unable to identify himself was immediately incarcerated in a rather horrid Moroccan jail.

I was dirty, tired and very hungry and now I had no bed for the night. This seemed to be the continuing story of my first visit to Morocco, but instead of being annoyed, I was filled with admiration for Abdiljilil's commitment to his company and to the loyalty of those young women who worked so very hard for him.

I telephoned Anne and explained my predicament. She contacted the night desk of the Foreign Office and the person on duty knew her uncle Dick very well. A short while later I received a telephone call from the British Consul in Casablanca. The receptionist relented and allowed me to stay while Abdiljilil drove back to the Mediterranean for my passport. Abdiljilil returned the following day. He had driven his car and himself for 36 hours without a break, including three crossings of the Riff. His eyes, if I may use a rather crude expression, were like piss-holes in the snow.

I tried to make things right for my incredible stupidity and offered him monetary compensation. This only made matters worse; he brushed my hand aside and told me that I was his guest and that he was responsible for my safety. I could not thank him enough and my view on the honour and integrity of at least one Moroccan individual knew no bounds. When I returned to England I gave instructions that whatever technical help Relec may need in the future, then they were to get it. I also instructed June, my company's Accounts Clerk, to provide commercial credit terms equal our domestic UK customers. It was the very least that I could do.

My second and third discs were ruptured

Shortly after moving into our new facility on the Christchurch Airfield I slipped a second disc and I suffered so badly that I prepared a makeshift bed on the floor of my lounge in Riverside Road. Apart from being very bored, I needed to contribute to the growth of PMV Instrumentation and I searched for a useful project that I could work on.

Quality assurance was becoming the in-thing in Britain and many large organisations were pro-active in selecting bidders from a list of ISO-9002 approved suppliers. We were a very small Company but this would catapult us into the big league if we were able to obtain approval. I selected this to be my target and for the next six weeks I lay on my makeshift bed and wrote our Company Procedures.

Approval required far more than a set of procedures but this positioned us to apply to Lloyds Register Quality Assurance and eventually these procedures, written around our purpose-built high-tech unit, enabled us to become one of the first instrumentation companies to obtain ISO-9002 quality approval.

I may have helped secure the Companies quality approval but the quality of my back deteriorated rapidly. I found a pretty young osteopath practising only three hundred yards from our home in Tuckton. She had recently qualified and her approach to my treatment was very different to what I had received for the past twelve years. She arranged for my spine to be x-rayed at the Southbourne Chiropractic Hospital. The films showed that my first disc was very thin and my second and third discs were ruptured. The prognosis was not good. She said that my stomach muscles were much stronger than my back muscles and this was contributing to my problem. My muscles were not in balance. I was not surprised by this because I focused upon exercises that would limit the size of my oversized paunch.

She showed me a series of exercises that I should complete every morning and these helped but they did not resolve my problem. Then during one of my frequent visits I took hold of a skeleton that was hanging in the corner of her surgery and placed it face down on the massage bed. I propped it up on its elbows in a similar position to what I had taken while working on my quality procedures. The spine of the skeleton flexed across the first three vertebrae. Yes, my osteopath agreed, this was the root cause of my problem. I began to sleep on my back and continued to exercise my back muscles each day. Touch wood, I have not had a serious problem since.

We were after all, the main tourist event of the day

As our wedding day drew nearer I began to get cold feet. Anne had the right to be married within Winchester Cathedral and her mother Mary was determined that we were going have a wedding to remember. The Dean wrote to the newly appointed Archbishop of Canterbury to request our special licence, but he was still waiting to be enthroned, and so our licence was granted by the Lord Bishop of London. Meanwhile, Trevor Beecham, the Dean of Winchester gave Anne and me special instructions upon how we should respond to our vows; he explained that we must speak loudly in order that we could be heard clearly throughout the stone-built Cathedral. This unnerved me somewhat and only helped to make me even more apprehensive.

My slipped-disc was also giving considerable pain. Anne's mother had been terrified that it would prevent me from standing during the wedding ceremony. She joked that she might have to place a small chair at the altar. Anne tried desperately to persuade me to wear tails and when I learned that her uncles intended to wear top hats I drew the line and attempted to withdraw. Anne was horrified when I suggested that we travel overseas to get married. She explained that her mother would be terribly upset. In the end I gave an ultimatum. We would wear tails but no one from the immediate family, including myself, was to wear a hat. The compromise was agreed upon by everyone except the uncles who presumably were not informed.

My brother Steven was Best Man, and Brett, along with Anne's brother, Henry, served as ushers. When I arrived at the Cathedral on our big day I was surprised by the large congregation that was already gathered in the stalls. It was late morning on Saturday 27th April 1991 and the town was full of tourists from the United States and France. Many had gathered discreetly in small curious groups to witness our marriage ceremony. We were, after all, the main tourist event of the day.

I had expected Anne to enter from the side door of the Cathedral. I had never seen the huge main gates opened in all of my days in Winchester. But on that warm spring day they stood wide open. Canon Job welcomed Anne before she took her long nervous walk down the longest aisle in all Europe. The Organ played 'lead us heavenly father, lead us over life's tempestuous sea'; a hymn which would realise true meaning in later years. On that momentous occasion Anne followed in the footsteps of Joan of Navarre when she married King Henry IV on 7th February 1403 and Queen Mary who married Prince Phillip, later King Phillip of Spain, on 25th July 1554.

The wedding procession was unusually impressive. Canon Job set the pace followed by the Dean of Winchester and the Provost of Portsmouth, all fully robed in their best attire. The Winchester Cathedral Choir attended as did Rufus who lay entombed before us and King Canute, the most senior of them all, rested in his little wooden casket above our heads and cast his royal approval upon the proceedings. Trevor Beecham invited David Stancliffe, the Provost of Portsmouth and an old family friend, to give the address.

After the ceremony Anne and I joined both of our families on the lawn in the centre of the Close. I could smell freshly cut grass as we stood to have our family photographs taken and then we received our guests in the Pilgrims Hall. Pilgrims Hall boasts one of the best hammer beam roofs in England and is second only to the Great Hall in the Palace of Westminster. It was full of charm and crates of champagne were broken open to make the reception a very forgettable experience.

Yes forgettable, the champagne flowed so freely that most, including my father, became very intoxicated; so much so that he danced with a policewoman outside the Buttercross in the middle of the afternoon.

We flew to Paphos

Steven and Anne's uncle, Sir William, gave excellent after dinner speeches and then Anne and I quickly hurried across to the Dean's house where we changed before driving in the direction of the Dorset coast. After the debacle of my first wedding, when the Cora Hotel sold our room to the highest bidder, I had no intention of making any prior reservations. Yet we almost suffered a similar disaster when we drove for two hours before finding a vacancy. We eventually checked into a small hotel in Lyme Regis which gave us a good base for visiting some attractive places in this area of Dorset. Four days later on Wednesday morning we flew to Paphos in Cyprus and enjoyed a fabulous honeymoon.

During our honeymoon Anne decided to try parasailing. When I helped fasten her into her harness her slender figure had no contours to bond with the rough heavily-worn fabric straps. Her crotch strap locked into the last hole and there was still sufficient slack to fit a second Anne. It seemed certain that she would slip through its bonds. When the tow boat raced away Anne was snatched into the air without having to run even two paces. The speedboat raced past the town quay and she was so light that her parachute carried her across Paphos. I could see her discomfort. She sat awkwardly in the harness with one leg cocked up to keep her in position but she enjoyed the thrill and I wanted to follow her example.

My slipped-disc was still giving me some discomfort but I needed to take some risk if I was to enjoy my honeymoon. I was determined to parasail, if Anne could do it, then I could. I noticed that the hot Mediterranean sun was beginning to heat the land and a strong sea breeze had developed. This would enable the speedboat driver to pick me up from the beach and put me down again with a very soft landing. This whole thing was an insane idea for someone who, three weeks beforehand, had struggled to walk more than twenty paces without stooping in absolute agony.

The harness had no difficulty in locking onto my very ample frame. I lifted off as planned and glided down the beach, over the historic harbour of Paphos and across a small army camp. I carried a video camera and filming from my precarious position I imagined myself to be James Bond. Would the guards shoot me down? Perhaps not. Then I came back into the real world and saw the real-life guards on the perimeter fence; I quickly pointed my camera in a different direction. The shore breeze was even stronger when I returned and the parachute placed me down so softly that I might have been on an afternoon stroll.

We jumped on the Bullet Train to Kyoto

In October 1991 Fuji Electric hosted their annual distributor conference in Tokyo. I took Anne with me and she was terribly excited. To her it was a journey to the far side of the world; to a culture and a people so steeped in history that she could barely contain her pent up anticipation.

We flew Malaysian Airlines via Kuala Lumpur. It was a long 32-hour journey that was made surprisingly short by the smiling service provided by our ever attentive flight hostesses who were dressed in their traditional Malay costumes. When we arrived we took the Narita Express into Shinjuku. The carriages of this train were so technically advanced that it seemed that we had been time-warped into the 22nd century.

Our hotel in central Tokyo was extremely luxurious and equalled the best that could be found anywhere in Europe. We found a welcoming letter on our bedroom table from Fuji Electric along with chocolates and a beautiful spray of flowers. Fuji Electric appeared to have no financial limitations when it came to the accommodation and entertainment of their guests. This no doubt was subsidised by the Japanese business system which encourages money to circulate within their own closed group of sister companies and organisations.

In the morning I joined my fellow distributors in the conference room of Fuji Electric and for three days team after team of highly skilled development engineers presented their new instrumentation products. These products were innovative, technically advanced and used the very latest silicon manufacturing technologies. They established performance specifications that far exceeded anything currently available in Europe or the United States. But, and it is a big but, many of the items were technically complex, over-specified and overpriced.

European customers almost always buy on price and having the best product in the world does not necessarily make it the best seller. We, the European Distributors, could never get this message across to Fuji Electric. Try as we might, on this occasion and on many others, we could never change them into a market driven company; they were and always will be engineering driven.

We felt that we were beating our heads against a brick wall. The innovative and technically advanced capabilities of the Fuji Electric development team were outstanding. If they had only fine tuned their design criteria with a little marketing input then they would have outstripped all of their competitors. I still wonder how many more people will bruise their heads on that brick wall before the message finally gets through.

While I was immersed in this informative but deeply frustrating conference, Anne joined Miriam Southam and together they explored the downtown areas of historical Tokyo. They walked through the outer gardens of the Imperial Palace and gawped back at the huge carp that threaded their way through a gorgeous display of white lilies that gave beauty to the huge palace moat.

They found their way into centuries old and very colourful Nakamise Street where they found small food markets and stalls selling fans, kimonos and Japanese curiosities. This opened out through Kaminarimon, the Thunder Gate, into Sensoji Temple. Legend says that in the year 628, two brothers found the statue of Kannon, the goddess of mercy, in the Sumida River. Every time they threw the statue back into the river it returned to them and so Sensoji was built to house the goddess and it is now the oldest temple to be found in Tokyo.

As Anne and Miriam walked through different areas of old Tokyo they could not fail to notice the Pachinko Parlours where young men sat in a trance for hour after hour punching hundreds of steel balls into a pinball machine. Their obvious addiction seemed pointless as the only prize was even more steel balls. However, the punters were able to exchange these for simple prizes such as pens or cigarette lighters which in turn could be sold through a Yakuzi controlled shop for cash. Cash gambling was illegal in Japan but the authorities always turned a blind eye towards this type of activity.

On their second day Anne, Miriam and Rolf Sundvisson's wife, also called Anne, were taken by our hosts to a Chashitsu; this is a small building that lies within the grounds of a traditional tea garden. Here they took part in the traditional team ceremony known as Chaji. This was the first time that Anne had tasted green tea and she and her two newly found friends thoroughly enjoyed their long and very intricate experience.

Afterwards they were entertained at a Kabuki theatre where the actors painted their faces white, spoke in a monotonous voice and were accompanied by traditional Japanese musical instruments. It seems that the plays were for common people and were about historical events, moral conflicts and love relationships although she had no way of knowing this at the time. Her impression was that of several painted men acting out different charades.

Anne was terribly impressed with the variety of clothing available in the Ginza shopping area and they were fully stocked with sizes that fitted her rather diminutive frame. Her excitement turned to disappointment when she converted their price tags into pounds sterling. In the end she settled upon a silk housecoat to place in her wardrobe as a souvenir of what could have been, if she had been a wealthy tourist.

After her expensive visit to Ginza she visited the Meiji Jingu Shrine and paid her respects to the Kami who dwelled there and wondered at the difference between Shinto and Buddhism; it seemed that many Japanese paid equal respect to the shrines and temples of both religions. I asked Gen Katsumata this begging question and he replied that many Japanese people have learned to take the best from each of the three main religions; they are purified after birth at a Shinto Shrine, married in a Christian style ceremony and then buried or cremated at a Buddhist Temple. This would appear to be the logic of Diogenes; a simple solution to a complex problem. Would it be that other peoples could one day apply the same logic and put an end to the religious hatred that so often erupts between communities and nations?

The evening entertainment provided by Fuji Electric was so impressive that it is difficult to find the right words to give full credit. On the first evening the President of Fuji Electric hosted a huge banquet in the ballroom of our hotel while a young and very attractive concert pianist played classical music on a grand piano. I could have killed John Southam when he stood up and announced that they had another accomplished pianist in their midst and that he would be pleased to accompany the young lady. I knew that he was going to announce my name and when everyone applauded my introduction I had no alternative but to join her on her rather small stool.

The ivory keys were moist and very slippery and the young girl was unable to move enough to allow me to take a central position at the keys. This placed me at an immediate disadvantage. Nevertheless, I played Lara's Theme from Doctor Zhivago without making any noticeable mistakes, and the applause I received helped to quell the tremendous embarrassment that I felt.

Gen Katsumata and Noboru Majima, still a young engineer with his first foot on the executive ladder, were as always the perfect hosts. Gen hosted our party at a traditional paper-walled restaurant in the hills outside Tokyo, the same one that I first visited with Mogens Ronberg and Jacques Hammers in 1985. On another evening he and Noboru entertained us on an old Japanese ship in Tokyo Bay. We all got absolutely smashed on warm Sake while sitting on reed mats singing karaoke style. I hate karaoke but after half a dozen cups of Sake who cares. When we walked home in the evening Anne was brought down to earth when she found dozens of homeless tramps sleeping on cardboard boxes outside the metro station. Tokyo was not so different to the other major industrialized cities after all!

As soon as the conference was finished we were on our own, and we jumped on the Bullet Train and hurtled down to the nation's original capital city, Kyoto. We stayed in a traditional Japanese lodge known as a Ryokan. The 'shoji' sliding paper doors opened into a small unheated room covered with 'tatami' reed matting. Two very thin futons were stored in a closet called an 'oshire' and several 'zabuton' sitting cushions were scattered near to a low wooden table. Our only separation from the couple next door was a thin paper wall and it was possible to hear them breathing during the night; we could have been sharing the same bed. Slippers and robes were standard issue on arrival and a large communal bath served everyone.

Anne, as usual, set out to visit as many historical sites as possible. Our most memorable visit was to Kiyomizu, where we found a spectacular collection of temples and pagodas from which we enjoyed a beautiful view down a picturesque valley and across old Kyoto. Wooden plates called 'Ema' were available to write down our wishes and hundreds of 'Omikuji' paper slips fluttered from the branches of small trees. These slips had fortunes written on them to bring someone good luck or, in many cases, to help them to avert bad luck.

I watched large groups of well behaved school children as they were shepherded around. They were all so happy and extremely polite. None were overweight and I guess Sushi, raw fish sliced and served on rice heaps, must be a good alternative to hamburger and chips.

The British Crown Colony of Hong Kong

These few days that we entertained ourselves in Japan soon began to eat very deeply into our pockets and we were relieved when it was finally time to fly to our next destination, the British Crown Colony of Hong Kong. I was rather annoyed with the expensive airport tax that we had to pay to cover the poor facilities available at Narita Airport. Narita was not the kind of facility one would expect after disembarking from the luxurious and very modern Narita Express.

We flew Nippon Airways to Hong Kong in an aircraft that was fitted with a pilot's view camera. This was the first time that I had experienced one of these cameras and I was surprised when the pilot allowed passengers to follow his approach into Kei Tak. Hills surrounding the airport prevented a direct approach from the landward side. We passed very low through a corridor of high rise buildings before turning through 90 degrees to land on a short runway that jutted out into the sea. I was in the cockpit on my last flight into Kei Tak, which was 17 years earlier, and had felt much more comfortable; following events on a large wall screen was too much like being a back-seat driver.

I was very impatient to replace my super-8 movie camera with one of those new fangled things that used something called a video tape. We took the green Star Ferry across to Kowloon where I found little had changed since my visit in the early '70's. A line of Rolls Royce cars still stood outside the Peninsular Hotel and, if anything, the divide between the mega-rich and ultra-poor seemed to have widened.

We walked into the downtown shopping area which was festooned with gaudy bright lights. There were people jostling, pushing, shoving, juggling, haggling or simply just trying to get in one's way. It was vibrant and full of life; all kinds of life. It was seedy, sordid, select and agreeable all at the same time. The 'Bottoms-up Bar' was on one side of the street and an up-market exclusive restaurant on the other.

I dragged Anne protesting from shop to shop, up one street, down the next, and then back to the beginning again. It took a dozen shops before I decided which video camera to buy and then another dozen to find the best price. After finding the shop with the right camera at the best price I told him a white lie. I told him that I had been offered the same camera for six hundred dollars, a lot of money at that time, but still far below market price.

He matched my price and included several cassettes of tape only to realize afterwards that he had sold below cost. His original price of 1,400 dollars was daylight robbery. He deserved to lose money, but I relented, and gave him an extra 20 dollars knowing that I had played the game better than him.

We made the must-do journey up the funicular railway which had been trundling up and down Victoria Peak since 1888, and marvelled at the dazzling panorama across Victoria Harbour and the romantic South China Sea. Later we boarded a picturesque tram that could have been used as the model for a Dinky toy. We rocked, rattled and rolled our way along streets in the business district and then took lunch on a boat in the Aberdeen Typhoon Shelter where people lived in terrible poverty on crowded sampans gathered together in a gypsy-like community. The Stanley Market was nearby and I purchased two suitcases at a bargain price. I still use these suitcases and they have circumnavigated the world seven times.

After enjoying the scenic coastal beauty of Repulse Bay and Deep Water

Bay, Anne took a taxi through the New Territories to the Chinese border. My back was giving trouble and I elected to have a couple of days' bed rest. I had fond memories of my first holiday in Hong Kong and in particular my visit to the border town of Lok Ma Chau. An old Chinese woman dressed in black sold me the 'Little Red Book' which contained the thoughts of Chairman Mau Tse Tung.

Hong Kong had changed considerably since my first in 1973. A new airport was under construction to replace Kai Tak and the wreck of RMS Queen Elizabeth had now been folded into the landfill used to provide the foundations of one of the new runways. A fantastic aquarium had been built where the most incredible killer whale demonstrations took place and a huge net enclosed a butterfly sanctuary that provided beautiful photo opportunities.

We took a ride on a modern cable car and I could see how the Bank of China Tower now dominated the Hong Kong Skyline. In all directions there were dozens of new high rise buildings shooting into the sky. Anne was fascinated by the bamboo scaffolding poles which festooned these structures to the highest floor. I explained how conventional metal scaffolding corroded in the high humidity salt-laded atmosphere of the South China Sea.

A dozen pit vipers around my neck

Our epic journey continued to the island of Penang, which lies in the Andaman Sea just off the mainland of north western Malaysia. When I flew this route in 1973 our aircraft took a huge dog-leg around the Vietnam War zone. This time we flew directly over Vietnam and Cambodia.

The beauty of the landscape overwhelmed me. Columns of granite burst high into the sky as we approached the coast and then a vast lush rainforest stretched across undulating hills and semi-rugged mountains. A cold shudder ran down my spine as I remembered the thousands of American and Australian soldiers who died fighting an invisible and extremely resourceful enemy in such beautiful terrain. Suddenly the landscape did not look so beautiful after all.

We stayed in the Palm Beach Hotel on Batu Ferringhi Beach, and Anne practised her waterskiing. She had learned to ski during our first holiday together on the Mediterranean Coast of Tunisia. I went paragliding instead. We needed our time in Penang to relax after rushing around Tokyo, Kyoto and Hong Kong. I certainly needed time to get my spine straight before our long flight back to the UK.

We made friends with a retired Royal Air Force wing commander who was teaching Royal Saudi Air Force pilots to fly the BAC Lightning, a point defence interceptor which was the only aircraft capable of overtaking Concorde on a stern intercept or reaching the height of a U2 spy plane. With its two piggy-back style Avon 302 turbojet engines it could climb at an incredible 50,000 feet per minute. It was the most incredible aircraft of its time but sadly lacking in fire power and operational range. The Wing Commander earned his wings through a Royal Air Force Scholarship around the same time as me and I imagined myself to be in his shoes if I had taken up my own offer of a commission all those years ago. I will never really know if I made the right choice.

The Temple of the Azure Cloud, or the Snake Temple as it was more commonly known, was one place in my tourist guide book that I did not want to visit; just its name was enough to make me shudder. Of course Anne dragged me there and I was horrified when my eyes got used to the darkness inside and I spotted several snakes moving slowly across the altar. There was a very strong smell of incense and I guess this is what caused them to be docile.

I sensed a quick movement behind me and someone draped half a dozen pit vipers around my neck. He did it so quickly that I had no chance to prevent him. I froze in horror. This was my worse possible nightmare and I could do nothing at all about it. I was even to frightened to speak; one of the snakes sensed my Adams apple with the tip of its flickering and very forked tongue. It tickled my throat and my skin shrivelled as the blood drained from my face.

The other snakes, dry and warm, slid along my bare arms while another turned around to stare right into my glazed eyes. I wanted to tell the bastard to get the bloody things off me but I was still too frightened to speak. Do you want a photograph ferengi, cheap very cheap?

Every major city seemed to have a Little India or a China Town and nearby Georgetown was no exception. It was time for the festival of lights, or Deepavali as it was known. The streets of Little India were covered with large and very beautiful floral patterns, which had been painted using thousands of different coloured flower petals. Different sections or areas of Hindu society celebrated Deepavali in different ways and one of the local customs in Georgetown was to invite strangers into their home.

Six young foreign women were volunteered by their husbands to become guests of the Diwali festival and they were each dressed by local women in the finest of Indian costumes. They became honouree Indian women for the day. When the celebrations finished, Anne and her five companions were allowed to keep their very attractive and colourful costumes. This occasion was a fitting conclusion to our long business-cum-tourist excursion in South East Asia and Anne's costume still hangs in her wardrobe as a reminder of her big day.

We divided PMV into two companies

PMV Instrumentation was well organised and everyone worked together to create a solid well oiled operation. Everything had its place in the scheme of things and every member of staff knew exactly what to do. My favourite expression was; 'look after your customer, give him the service that he expects and our success will be measured by our level of repeat business'. We had secured an excellent customer base and most of the large process engineering companies in the United Kingdom were using our products. It was at this point in time that I approached Magnus and asked if he would sell his share of the business.

Magnus was a pragmatic person and always more than fair in his dealings with me. His main interest lay in the PMV valve positioner business and we reached a mutual agreement to divide the Company into two separate units; PMV Valve Products Ltd and PMV Instrumentation Ltd. I had generated substantial profits over the past seven years and the agreement required that one hundred percent of these retained profits, along with Nigel and the remainder of my valve positioner staff, be retained by Magnus within PMV Valve Products. In addition I had to purchase the assets of the instrumentation business.

The arrangement worked well for Magnus. It helped to strengthen his bargaining position five years later when he sold the PMV Group to Worcester Controls. Two years after this Worcester and PMV were acquired by the Invensys Group of Companies, one of the largest engineering groups in the world.

From my point of view, I had to relinquish my 26 percent option on the substantial profits that I had generated and I had to take out a huge mortgage to purchase the assets of the instrumentation business. Financially, I found myself even further back than when I returned from Africa. However, I now had total control of a well structured company that enjoyed a huge high quality customer base within the United Kingdom, Russia, Turkey, Romania and Kenya. The future was now up to me! My new company started trading independently on April Fools Day, 1st April 1993. Perhaps this was a sign, but I never regretted my decision to become fully independent.

Chapter 17

Fall of the Russian Empire

Insider's view of those momentous years from 1988 to 1993
Perestroika Mafia Style!

Ronald Reagan was a mediocre movie actor but he played his part well when he became the 40th President of the United States. With a huge boost in military spending he convinced the Soviet Union that the United States had a credible Star Wars programme. The Soviet Central Committee ploughed more and more money into their military programme but they could not match the huge financial reserves made available to Reagan. Gorbachev brought a new and more conciliatory form of leadership to the Kremlin and while he wanted to reconstruct the Soviet Union, 'Perestroika' in Russian, he found that he indeed had no alternative. The Central Committee no longer had the financial capability to match United States' spending in the arms race.

I was fortunate to work in Russia during a time of momentous change, and during my very first year, I witnessed events that happened so quickly that it was difficult to keep pace. The year was 1989.

The Soviet Military received a sound thrashing in Afghanistan. They eventually suffered the same fate as the Americans in Vietnam. For some reason the leaders of these mighty nations could not begin to understand that you can never fight and win against a hidden enemy on his own turf. The last Soviet tanks left Afghanistan on 15th February 1989 and on the same day a rally was held in Budapest calling for democracy and the total withdrawal of Soviet troops from Hungary. A similar rally in 1956 was violently crushed by Soviet tanks but this time there was no military response. Times were definitely changing.

On 9th April, Georgians clashed with Police and called for independence from the Soviet Union. Georgia had been a strong member since 1921 and was the home country of Joseph Stalin, the most ruthless leader the world had ever known. Stalin murdered more than 40,000 of his own people and this dwarfed the crimes of Hitler by comparison. Around this time Gorbachev visited Windsor Castle and invited the Queen to visit Moscow. Gorbachev was playing his cards well on the international scene, but Perestroika was not providing the results he needed and the Russian economy was fast collapsing.

Students of Communist China climbed onto the bandwagon and demonstrated in Tiananmen Square, Beijing. Chinese leaders saw this as a serious threat to their own power and quickly moved against these rebellious students. On 9th June they ordered tanks of the Peoples Liberation Army to move into the Square and several hundred were killed.

On the 10th November thousands of East and West Germans converged on the most oppressive symbol in the Soviet Union, the Berlin Wall. They tore it down piece by piece with their bare hands. Brett visited the remnants of the Berlin Wall a short time later and he brought me a small colourful piece to add to my collection of memorabilia.

Ronald Reagan having laid the foundation stones had already left the playing field and the two big players were now Mikhail Gorbachev and George Bush Senior. They held a shipboard summit in ferocious storms off Malta and at 11.45 am local time on 3rd December 1989 the leaders of the two world superpowers declared the Cold War to be ended.

There have been many large Empires throughout history but none have fallen as quickly as the Soviet Empire did in 1989. This momentous year started to draw to a close when Christmas Day was marked by the execution of Nicolae and Elena Ceausescu by firing squad in Romania. Only the home country of Count Dracula could commit such a violent act on Christmas Day. This execution was considered by many nations in the Western World to be the final death throes of Communism. This was not to be the case.

On 20th June 1991 Moscow Mayor Gavril Popov warned the US Ambassador of an impending coup attempt against Mikhail Gorbachev. Bush passed this message on to Gorbachev who dismissed the warning.

On 18th August 1991 the Putsch went against Gorbachev who was held at his holiday home in Forus on the Black Sea. Boris Yeltsin organised resistance in the streets of Moscow and following his famous stand, when the world witnessed him climbing onto the turret of a Soviet tank, the coup was overthrown.

Gorbachev finally resigned on Christmas Day in 1991 and the Russian Flag immediately replaced the Hammer and Sickle over the Kremlin Ramparts. Finally, on New Years Eve 1991, the USSR ceased to exist under international law. However, this was still not the end. Even as late as 4th October 1993 the Communists rose against Boris Yeltsin and made one last, almost successful, attempt to regain power.

I witnessed these frightening events first hand. For me it all began in 1988 when the USSR Academy of Sciences invited me to bid for the supply of process transmitters on a large district heating scheme in the Ural Mountains. My customer, Asbest Kombinat, was a city organised and run as a communist community of 50,000 inhabitants whose sole purpose was to extract asbestos from the largest open cast mine in the world.

Eleven miles in length and eight hundred metres deep, this enormous man made ravine cut through the grey featureless landscape as far as the eye could see. It was a long cruel jagged scar with enormous yellow earth movers weaving along crude tracks cut into the side of the chasm. These monsters could be mistaken for soldier ants carrying their burden back to their nest if it were not for their bright yellow colour. They did not even stop when the siren sounded late in the afternoon to announce the daily round of blasting that would throw large dust plumes of white asbestos bearing rock into the sky. This asbestos would eventually settle to add a soft white velvet carpet across the city that bears both its name and its legacy.

First impressions of Moscow

I visited Moscow early in spring. I was met at Sheremitivo Airport by Dr Zinovi Chernyak, Technical Director of the Centre for International Cooperation of the USSR Academy of Sciences. I soon found that everyone that I was to meet in the Soviet Union would have a very long and very impressive title. As Zinovi drove me into downtown Moscow he pointed out several large tank traps that marked the point where the German advance was stopped in the Second World War. In later years I was to learn much more about these events.

As we arrived outside the Russian apartment block that contained the office where he worked on his private projects, Zinovi carefully removed the windscreen wipers from his old car and put them into the pocket of his scruffy old raincoat. He explained that it was much safer to drive in a battered old car and to wear clothing that was more in keeping with the poverty that was so apparent during the early days of Perestroika.

The communal entrance of his building smelled terrible; it was dirty and disgusting. No one wanted to take ownership of the building's maintenance and there was no sense of community spirit among the incumbent residents. The apartment that Zinovi used as an office was guarded by a solid sheet of steel with two large padlocks. Inside everything was very basic. There was a small kitchen with a stove and a few kitchen utensils, a lounge with an old sofa and a bedroom that had been converted into an office. I knew it was an office because it contained a rusty old filing cabinet and the Russian clone of an IBM PC.

Primitive though it may have been, this office was the proud possession of two enterprising Russian Entrepreneurs who presumably still worked for the Soviet Academy of Sciences. I felt proud to be their guest.

Zinovi booked me into the Sebastopol Hotel, a twenty minute ride on the Metro from his office. After an excellent meal of 'Shchi' cabbage soup followed by a large selection of different meats and well presented Russian salad, I invited my waiter to change my US dollars into Roubles. He followed me at a discreet distance until we reached a deserted corridor and there we conducted our clandestine negotiations. I received an excellent rate which was around seven times the official exchange available at the airport.

My waiter was not permitted to travel and I have no doubt that he already had a buyer lined-up who would offer him an even higher rate of exchange. The movement of Moscow residents was restricted to an area that lay within a 40-mile radius of the city centre. To travel outside this perimeter they required a travel pass which they had to obtain from one of the five railway stations. Travel on the road network was extremely difficult because special passes were needed to get past the security check points. Travel outside of Russia, even to one of the neighbouring Republics, was only an impossible dream.

On my first morning I ventured into the metro system. I stared in absolute astonishment. How could I find words to describe the incredible feat of civil engineering that lay before me? With the exception of the Kremlin and a few other notable buildings that have survived the destruction of Stalin's henchmen, the architecture of Moscow truly lay deep below the surface. The metro stations were enormous. It is difficult to believe that such large caverns could exist without structural support. In every tunnel or underground hall there were enormous reliefs sculptured out of granite, each depicting feats of Soviet heroism.

The metro system was also very efficient and easy to navigate once I had learned a few basic words of Russian. The architects who designed these stations were indeed masters of their trade and such people were hard to find in Russia. Communism had reduced the working classes to a common level where individualism was frowned upon. I enjoyed many evenings travelling on, and admiring, the Moscow metro system over the next six years.

My agent employed a very attractive young girl who had just graduated from Moscow State University with the highest mark in her class for French. Marina was her name and she was proud to tell me that her grandfather was the architect of the best designed metro station in all of Moscow. Marina Tauschkanova, little field mouse in Russian, was tall with waist long black hair and high cheek bones of the Tartar tribe who migrated north from the Steppes centuries before.

All Russians have to offer themselves for military service if they are to obtain a privileged education. Marina was no exception to this rule. She was a skilled linguist with more knowledge of French weapons systems than most of the French Officers whom she was trained to interrogate. She had already received her call-up papers for the GRU and was quietly ignoring them. The Russian military was not very efficient and she reckoned that it would take them some time to catch up with her. In fact, they never did.

Marina's parents invited Zinovi and me to dinner. They lived in a beautiful apartment on the second floor of a classic Russian building only a stone's throw from Red Square. It had a wooden floor and a huge indoor balcony with high ceilings. Most Russians would die to live in such an apartment. I was met at the door by a large old ginger Labrador called Patrick and Marina's mother Alla. They welcomed me as if I was a long lost friend returning home from Siberia.

Marina's father, Yuri, was an enormous yet very gentle man. Like his father, he was also an architect and he had chanced upon this apartment through his work. Later when communism collapsed and tenants were given an opportunity to buy their homes, Yuri and Alla bought their little jewel in the old district of Moscow for less than a thousand US dollars. Today it must be worth a small fortune. Marina's grandmother joined us for dinner. She was held in great respect by the rest of the family and I warmed to her from the outset. We both got on like a house on fire and yet we could not speak a word of each other's language.

The following morning I visited the International Oil and Gas Industry Trade Show at the Exhibition Centre. Marina translated for me and I was fortunate to meet several potential customers who were visiting from Asbest in the Ural Mountains. We had an excellent meeting and Marina translated very proficiently.

In later years when I had improved my knowledge of Russian I found it necessary to scold her from time to time. I had to ask her to translate precisely what I had said and not what she thought the customer wanted to hear. Marina was incredibly quick in learning the most important technical details that related to my products and often, if she knew which features the customer required, she translated my sales pitch in a slightly different way and I needed to be careful that I could fulfil the promises that she made on my behalf. She never liked to translate bad news!

After the exhibition, I joined Marina and Zinovi with two other work colleagues, Aleksander Kotliyarski and Victoria Perepeleyatnik, for vodka and caviar in a small open air café. We talked about our future plans and how we would best progress our potential project in Asbest. Suddenly my colleagues changed the subject of our conversation and started to talk about my dinner the previous evening with Marina's parents. Sitting just to my right was a person in a scruffy raincoat reading his copy of Pravda upside down. Our unwanted eavesdropper was obviously KGB and so we decided it was time to move on to my hotel. My room in the Hotel Sebastopol was actually a large suite comprising a lounge, television area, bedroom and kitchen. It was a good place to hold a business meeting and much better than the dingy little office in Prospekt Mira.

When we returned to my hotel Marina was pushed back into the street by a person in a scruffy raincoat. Victoria was allowed to pass but Marina was very young and she had not paid a 'fee' to the appropriate person. I was furious; I grabbed hold of the offending KGB officer and held him by his collar against the hotel wall. Everyone was stunned. Marina explained that I must let him go or she would be punished when I returned to England. He didn't trouble us any more and we all proceeded to my room where we were able to conclude business before partaking in another excellent meal in the hotel restaurant.

This was the first of several brushes that I had with the KGB. Their junior officers are so arrogant and yet there are those, usually of high rank and well educated, who are friendly and can be helpful from time to time.

When I was preparing to return to the UK, Marina met me at the entrance to Sevastopolskaya metro station and gave me a small gift for Brett. It was a miniature book that contained photographs of several medieval Russian buildings. It can't have cost more than a few roubles but to Marina this must have been a small fortune. I am afraid that I didn't give the book to Brett. It remains to be one of my most treasured possessions, a reminder of my first visit to Moscow.

His contact in MI-5 checked my file

A few months later I received my official contract to supply process transmitters to Asbest Kombinat. This was followed in March 1990 with an invitation to meet the Kombinat's senior engineers in the city of Ural Asbest.

Ural Asbest is 100 miles from the closed city of Sverdlovsk. Nearby is

Chelyabinsk, the top secret centre for nuclear weapons production in the Soviet Union. In the '60's there was a huge outcry when Gary Powers was shot down while over flying in a U2 spy plane. Normally it would have been impossible for me to access this restricted area but Zinovi had contacts at the highest level and he arranged for a colonel in the KGB to issue me with a pass.

I asked Zinovi how the KGB Colonel obtained sufficient information to check my security profile. I was concerned that he might learn of my earlier work with the United Kingdom Atomic Energy Authority. He laughed and explained that his contact in MI5 had checked my file; I am absolutely certain that he was telling the truth.

I flew with Marina to Sverdlovsk in a huge Antanov aircraft. Marina boarded through the domestic gate and a service bus took her and her baggage straight to the aircraft. Meanwhile, I was directed to the special 'foreigners' gate which was supposed to have more comfortable facilities and tighter security. There were no facilities, only a gate sign. A woman pointed urgently to a distant aircraft and I hurried unescorted across the operational area dragging my suitcase behind me. I climbed unchecked into the belly of the aircraft and placed my suitcase onto a wooden rack; a rather strange security arrangement for foreigners.

I climbed a further set of stairs which were within the belly of the aircraft and found myself in a cabin that carried around 16 passengers in each row. The front row seated several high ranking army officers; each had a chest so full of medal ribbons that there was no place left to stitch on the buttons. A large screen placed in front of these officers completed my scene; I imagined that I was in a cinema with a captive audience waiting for the film to start.

I knew the Soviets had large aircraft, but this was far beyond my expectations. When we trundled down the runway I had no sense of acceleration. I thought that we would never achieve rotation speed, and when we did, we climbed away from the ground ever so slowly. I breathed a great sigh of relief when we finally landed in the snow covered Ural Mountains later that evening. We were supposed to report to the local KGB headquarters in Sverdlovsk but it was late and we still had a three hour drive on snow covered roads to Ural Asbest. The KGB would have to wait!

In the morning I visited my first ever Soviet factory. What an experience! The entrance to every building carried instructions on what to do in the event of nuclear attack. These instructions gave a drawing of the mushroom shape for each type of nuclear bomb and a description of the type of fallout that could be expected. I had the distinct impression that the message being given was not 'if' a nuclear bomb was dropped, but 'when'. The asbestos factory that I visited was processing fibres from the largest open cast mine in the world. I am sure that the workers and their families were already experiencing far greater problems than could be visited upon them by enemies from a distant land.

After dinner our party took a short walk into town. The roads were covered in a thick sheet of ice and the pavements were hard packed with snow. It was minus 17 degrees centigrade, the air was still and the stars shined brightly. All in all, it was a very pleasant evening and Victoria linked arms with Mikhail, one of the instrument technicians, to steady herself as it began to snow. It was rather quaint to see people in the Ural Mountains behaving just the same as those in rural England.

I was beginning to have a deep affection for the Russian people that I knew. They stayed close to their immediate family and to their small circle of friends, but once I was admitted to their inner circle, then there is no limit to their generosity. It was a shame that such a rich and diverse people should have been ruled by so many tyrants over the past five hundred years. It was because of their necessity to survive in such adverse political and environmental conditions that they have become so insular.

A full moon guided us on our way and it illuminated two KGB officers who were following at a discreet distance. My hosts felt uncomfortable but they explained that a mining town such as Ural Asbest had many dangerous criminals and it was probably to our advantage that officers from the KGB were in attendance. The snow began to fall very heavily and we retreated to my hotel suite where a chess board was quickly laid out and we drank vodka and played chess until the early hours. I had brought several presents with me and had already given these to my hosts. This included bottles of whisky, digital wrist watches, jeans, perfume and nylons; all luxury items that could only be bought in 'Berioskas' by a privileged few.

Misha and Sasha, the two instrument technicians accompanying me, were each the proud owner of a new digital wrist watch. I was very mischievous, and cruel. I let each of them win several games and then I made a bet that I would play them both together for the last game of the night and win. The bet was a bottle of whisky against their wrist watches. I have never seen anyone take a game so seriously and of course, I had set them up and I won. The following morning I returned their watches and added two bottles of whisky. It was a delight to see both the excitement and the relief on their faces.

Our early morning breakfast was interesting. We gathered around a long table where we enjoyed a large selection of meats, breads, cheeses and boiled eggs. Our hosts appeared one by one and each produced a milk bottle from his jacket pocket. Each in-turn proceeded to pour a large swig of home distilled vodka into everyone's milk glass. This vodka normally had different flavours and it was absolutely lethal. The flavoured variety produces the most terrible of headaches. Guests are obliged to down their glass in-one or the accompanying toast will not be realized.

We discussed our plans for the day while a television that was ensconced on the end of our table dished out many hours of useless patriotic information. My Russian hosts found this to be a normal distraction but I considered the television to be a rude and unwanted intrusion upon my own private thoughts. The additional lubrication afforded by my large glass of home distilled vodka didn't help.

During the long tedious day that followed, we visited different sections of the Kombinat. Each time we were taken into a meeting room that contained a large table with a samovar boiling in the middle and plates of dry biscuits distributed around the periphery. Representative of the workers committee would be patiently awaiting our arrival, these committees almost always comprised of huge robust Soviet women that I would never want to cross. We each gave welcome speeches and talked about all kinds of nonsense that had no bearing on the work in hand.

I became very confused and could not decide who really made the purchasing decisions. My first impression was that the 'Party Apparatus' controlled everything, but then I began to believe that these committees had a 'spoiling influence' and therefore had to be kept on-side in any new developments. To be honest, I was never able to find the answer to this question; events were soon to be overcome by the birth of a new and very ruthless force in Russia, the Russian Mafia.

I only worked for a short period of time in the production area. Perhaps this is just as well. When I examined the evaporation chambers my nostrils caked with white asbestos fibre in less than ten minutes. Several years later I helped Brett to dismantle an old asbestos garage. Brett and his friends could not understand my lack of concern. After all, I have worked in plutonium separation plants, lead mines, copper converter isles and in asbestos production plants. I might glow in the dark, have a bad memory, be hard of hearing and cough a little, but I think that I am still fortunate to be healthier than most at my age; touch wood!

I never visited the KGB office in Sverdlovsk and no one seemed to care. The KGB has many things in common with the UK National Health Service. Both are by far the two largest employers in the world and, despite their enormous technology budgets, they are still unable to communicate effectively. No doubt their paperwork will catch up eventually.

I returned to Ural Asbest six weeks later, in May. On my earlier visit the conditions had been extremely cold and my hosts disapproved of my clothing. I had worn several pullovers covered by a western style anorak, two pairs of long johns and a borrowed Ushanka. They were very worried because I did not wear a long thick woollen overcoat similar to what my grandfather wore in the trenches of Flanders. So when I returned in May, I was fully prepared and my suitcase bulged with warm practical clothing.

On this occasion when I walked down the streets of Ural Asbest the mosquitoes were so thick that I couldn't breathe and I quickly realized how little I knew of this part of the world. The Ural Mountains border the huge Siberian land mass and the conditions had changed in the space of only six weeks from a severe winter climate to something that was hotter than the Sahara desert in mid-summer. The air temperature exceeded forty degrees centigrade and I only had winter clothing!

I was so hot that I grabbed the opportunity to visit a water works which channelled raw water from a source fifty miles distant. This appeared to be unnecessary as there was substantial water in the region. When I made enquiries I discovered that a fierce reactor fire had contaminated the local water table. This same fire prevented local people from collecting forest mushrooms, a favourite delicacy in the Ural Mountains.

I also visited Sverdlovsk, later to be renamed Yekaterinburg, and was surprised to learn that it was the home town of Boris Yeltsin. When he was party leader for the region he had destroyed a potential rallying point for those opposed to communism. This was the building in which the Romanov Tsar and his family were brutally murdered. I visited the site with Marina; a simple wooden Russian Orthodox Crucifix stood impaled in the ground where a bulldozer, on Yeltsin's instructions, had levelled the building. Around the Crucifix lay several bunches of fresh flowers laid by visitors who wished to acknowledge the Romanov memory.

Marina was surprised by what we found. She explained that she had not known that the Tsar and his family were murdered by the Bolsheviks. It was a subject that was never discussed in her school and she assumed that the Tsar and his family had left Russia at the beginning of the Revolution. I was surprised by her lack of curiosity. She pointed out that Russian children grew up to accept what they were told and not to question.

I never had an opportunity to visit Ural Asbest again. In my short time in the Ural Mountains I had grown to like these tough hardy people. They lived in such a terrible environment and suffered a very short life expectancy. Yet they were wonderful, hospitable people. Victor Stepanov, the Director General, was trying his level best to improve their quality of life. It seemed that he had a hopeless task and events elsewhere in Russia were leaving their plight to pale into the darkness of their polluted forests.

The small city of Ural Asbest lay at a point in the Ural Mountains that had created a natural divide between the vast continents of Europe and Asia. It was positioned on the notorious one-way route to the horrendous Siberian Gulags. Many of these unfortunate workers in Ural Asbest were the children of those same political prisoners that had tramped that desperate path only a generation ago. I am afraid these children were destined to continue the struggle of their parents and their struggle was only just beginning.

Half a million marched through the streets

I was in England when Mikhail Gorbachev was overthrown in the first Putsch. In the early hours of the morning I received a telephone call from Victoria Leva, a Russian freelance photographer. Victoria was very excited and she explained that army tanks were rolling through the streets of Moscow.

I later learned that Zinovi and several of my friends rushed to the White House and helped erect barriers in front of these advancing tanks. Eventually Yeltsin joined my friends and that was when he was filmed taking his legendary stand in front of a CNN camera crew. He mounted a stationary tank and asked the commander to stand down. I found out later that the officer leading the armoured group had been ordered to open fire, but this was not Budapest. This was Moscow and Russian people were manning the barricades, not nationals of an occupied country.

Later in the same year while Yeltsin was still trying to establish his leadership, the people decided to demonstrate their support by marching through the streets of Moscow. Several friends asked me to join their march and I found myself walking through the streets in an old raincoat waving a new Russian flag alongside more than half a million ordinary Russian people.

There was an over-riding fear amongst those taking part that their Leaders would return to communism. As we walked passed the Lubyanka I spared a thought for those thousands of political prisoners who had suffered within its stone walls and for the German prisoners of war who perished working as slave labourers on the huge buildings that lined our path. I wondered how the KGB would react to this march; would they try to break it up or would the size of the rally deter any formal response. Slowly our long procession snaked into Red Square and everyone started to chant for Yeltsin. No one had any idea what would happen next. The political situation was still very tense.

Eventually the big wooden gates of the Kremlin swung open and Yeltsin walked out to join the enormous crowd. He crossed the Square in front of St Basil's Cathedral and climbed onto a small wooden platform. I have no idea what he said but a hushed silence spread right across the square and TV cameras carried his message live to hundreds of millions across the world. I felt a shudder go through me and I began to suspect that the Communists would soon make their own bid for control.

It was very difficult to break into the Russian market, but Russian customers are extremely loyal to Western Companies who have a good track record in the Soviet Union. News of my work in the Urals spread very quickly and it was not long before I was approached by a team of engineers from Tula Chermet, a large steel complex situated 120 miles south of Moscow.

The next time that I visited Moscow I stayed with Zinovi's parents in a protected building just off Oktyabrskaya. Aleksander Chernyak and his wife Raisa were devoted to each other. Aleksander's claim to fame is that he survived Stalin. This may be a strange thing to say, but he was one of Stalin's ministers and very few people who were close to Stalin survived his reign of arrogant terror.

Aleksander served under Stalin, Khrushchev and Brezhnev, three of the most feared communist leaders of the cold war. In return for his loyalty and lifetime of service to the Soviet cause he enjoyed a pension of around $80 per month plus free accommodation in a small three roomed apartment in a secure building. Stalin's daughter-in-law occupied a similar apartment on the floor directly above.

Raisa prepared my meal every evening. It was typical Russian fare that usually began with borsch, a thick potato and cabbage based soup. The second course would normally be a stewed meat with Russian salad and a mixture of vegetables. Desert was often rhubarb from his own allotment and a strange kind of custard. While vodka was always to hand in most Russian homes, Aleksander had made several bottles of very sweet orange wine. It was his speciality and we drank it every evening as if it were lemonade. However, the effect was not the same. Invariably it ruined my evening because it caused me to fall asleep soon after we had eaten.

Aleksander played a good game of chess and we played whenever we had the opportunity; this was usually in the late afternoon. He slammed his pieces down on the board making all the others jump into the air. If I made a silly move or one that was not necessarily the best, he pointed at the threat and insisted that I changed my move. He usually had a strategy in mind and he didn't want me to spoil it. In the beginning I could never beat him but my game improved over the next two years and I started to win some games. He was such a dear old man that I always made sure that he won the day. We both got so much pleasure from the thrill of our intense competition. For a person in his late 80's he had such an active mind.

Aleksander's head was still turned by a pretty Russian girl and Marina, who had known him for many years, was always teased by him. But she took it in good fun and admired his spirit. As we played chess, Aleksander told me stories of the 'good old days'. He explained how he always avoided a game of tennis with Stalin because he knew he could never win the 'real game' no matter how he played. So many ministers displeased Stalin and they were taken into the forest with their families never to be seen again. It was a 'no win' situation.

We talked about the tank traps at the outskirts of Moscow, near to Sheremetova airport. I had never realized that German forces came so close to Moscow. Aleksander explained how difficult those days had been and he shocked me when he told me that he had dinner in the Kremlin with Churchill and Stalin during the worst days of the Second World War. I was stunned; I have never heard it said that Churchill had visited Moscow during the war, let alone at such a precarious time.

Aleksander was kind enough to give me an old book describing those early days. I identified him in one of the group photographs and asked him to sign it for me. We enjoyed a close friendship for 4 years until sadly Raisa passed away followed by Aleksander two years later.

They were Chernobyl children

During our first long stay with Aleksander we were collected by a worker driven car from Tula Chermet and taken to accommodation within the grounds of Yasnaya Polyana; the home of Count Tolstoy. His estate was preserved as a living museum. At breakfast time I was joined in the dining room by 60 children. At first they looked as if they were perfectly normal children; playful, laughing and yet so well behaved. I was saddened when someone whispered to me that they were

Chernobyl children, many of them already orphans, many of them still to become orphans. This became even more tragic when I found that they also had varying degrees of illness that resulted from their unnecessary exposure to radioactive pollutants.

We all knew how tragic the Chernobyl disaster was. We also knew how the Central Committee had sat on their big fat backsides, as always, and had done nothing to help the local population. These children, many with their hair already falling out, were brought in groups to Yasnaya Polyana by a foundation that enjoyed no government funding whatsoever. On the Tolstoy estate they were able to play in open unpolluted countryside without fear of further contamination. Unfortunately this freedom was short lived as all of these poor children had to return to their new homes which was in an area surrounding the Chernobyl exclusion zone.

Early each morning and again in the evening I walked through the forest that is encompassed by the estate of Yasnaya Polyana. My hosts spoke of the serenity of the forest and how they loved such a natural environment with so much wild life. I found the area to have a special feeling but this perhaps came from the knowledge that we were walking in the footsteps of Count Leo Tolstoy.

We sat on a wooden bench amidst the Berioska trees and a Scarlet Rosefinch called "pleased to meet you" from high above in the leafy branches. This was the favourite place of Tolstoy. He sat on a bench in exactly the same place and gazed across the same water meadow that lay before us. This place was said to have inspired him when he wrote Anna Karenina, perhaps his most famous book, second only to War and Peace. It truly was an enchanting place.

When I returned to the main building I was met by Yalina Alexeeva, the senior curator of the museum, and she kindly took me around Tolstoy's home. It was exactly the same as the day he walked out and took his fateful train journey south; he died alone on a remote railway platform two days later. No one knows why he made this sad journey. His bedroom, his small office with writing desk, pen and ink are all preserved in his memory.

Yalina explained to me that Tolstoy commanded his own regiment in the Crimea. When he returned he was so upset with the carnage of war that he sold his mansion and gave everything he owned to help treat his wounded soldiers. The peasants who lived on his estate were allowed to live in his outbuildings and to farm his land to their own benefit. It was this generosity that protected his estate from being ravaged during the Bolshevik Revolution.

I tried to explain to Yalina that I lived in Bournemouth and next door to my home on the river Stour was the water treatment plant where Tolstoy's works were originally published. My words fell on deaf ears. I don't think she grasped what I was trying to say. When I was about to return to my room she asked if I had ever heard of a place called Christchurch.

I couldn't believe what she had just said, and then I remembered that the town of Bournemouth did not exist at the beginning of the century. Her records would show the water treatment plant to lie within the jurisdiction of the medieval town of Christchurch. Finally I was able to explain what I had been trying to tell her. The following morning I was invited to a special meeting of the managers of the Tolstoy Foundation. They wanted to know all about this famous place called Christchurch. I promised that I would find out what had happened all those years ago.

When I returned home I visited the Red House Museum in Christchurch and the curator kindly gave me several newspaper cuttings that he found buried in the archives. These cuttings referred to a strange community of Russian revolutionaries living in the Tuckton Water Works. They were printing the works of Count Tolstoy and mailing leaflets worldwide from the small post office in Southbourne. Countess Chernyak, the mother of Tolstoy's friend and publisher, Count Chernyak, also lived in Tuckton with the revolutionaries. She remained in Tuckton and now lies at rest in Southbourne Cemetery.

Following the Revolution, Lenin sent a ship to England to retrieve the original manuscripts of Count Tolstoy. The Captain came ashore at Keyhaven, a very small harbour at the west entrance to the Solent. He took the manuscripts from the water works, placed them in a large metal container and took them back to Russia. They remain in the Kremlin to this day. None of this was known by the Foundation and they grasped eagerly at anything that I could tell them.

In recent years I have toyed with the idea that Christchurch should 'Twin' with the village of Yasnaya Polyana. Perhaps if anyone from Christchurch Town Council should ever read this book they might decide to give my trivial thoughts more serious consideration.

I visited the steel works of Tula Chermet and again went through the ritual of meeting representatives from the different workers committees. Again we munched dry biscuits and drank tea from huge colourful samovars, except on this occasion I was in Tula, the town which was famous for its samovars. Every samovar was different and had its own special design. Tula was also famous for the AK-47 assault rifle which was being used with terrible effect against South African, British and American Forces. Marina, normally very reluctant to talk about her military connections, told me how she had been trained at school to dismantle and re-assemble an AK-47 blindfolded.

As on earlier visits to Asbest Kombinat, my on-site visit was kept very short and again I was very pleased that this was the case. I had worked for several years on steel factories in South Africa but I never experienced such terrible conditions as I did on the Tula Works. The pollution was horrendous and the working environment around the blast furnace where my transmitters were to be installed was extremely dangerous.

I invited my hosts to visit England for training. In reality, this was just an excuse for an overseas jolly. I arranged for their visas and booked them into a hotel in Bournemouth. I took them to Stonehenge, Windsor Castle and London. They found it very difficult to take everything in; the freedom to travel, the freedom to communicate and the freedom to shop; freedoms that we take for granted in the West. Roads in the Soviet Union had a control point every 40 miles, private telephone conversations were monitored by KGB spies and only foreigners or party members could shop in Berioskas. Yes, we did take our freedoms for granted in the West.

I provided a substantial allowance to each of my guests; they were extremely proud and at first declined my offer. Aleksander Skormin, an elderly control systems engineer, whom I liked immensely, continued to refuse my offers of 'spending money'. I noticed his admiration for my Harris Tweed jacket and so I bought one and presented it to him when he was about to return to Russia. He was over the moon.

Later in the week my Tula guests joined me at my home on the river Stour in Christchurch. Another of my favourite guests, Valerii Kulichkov, said that he had not been able to talk with his son for more than 6 months. His son was a naval officer based at the top secret nuclear submarine base in Kamchatka, a volcanic region in eastern Siberia. Security restrictions made it very difficult, if not impossible, for him to telephone Kamchatka from Moscow. I asked Valerii for his son's telephone number and then dialled him on my Christchurch telephone. In 60 seconds Valerii was talking to his son and we all laughed at how unbelievable the situation was.

Several of my office staff joined us later in the evening for dinner and we consumed copious amounts of wine, whisky and vodka. To say the least, we were happy. At 10 pm we transferred to my small eight-seat power boat. We motored down the river Stour, across Christchurch harbour and into the Mudeford run. At the Mudeford sea wall the girls in our party jumped ashore and quickly visited the Ship Inn for a comfort stop.

After they rejoined we applied power and raced out to sea. Despite being overloaded we were able to plane across Christchurch Bay. A heavy sea was running and I began to appreciate the absolute stupidity of our situation. The only thing that I can say in mitigation is that I gave everyone a life jacket. After gathering my senses I turned around and immediately headed back into harbour. I am afraid to say that this was not the first or the last time that I behaved so irresponsibly while under the influence of alcohol.

In the morning I walked my guests along my river bank and stopped opposite the old water works. I had not told any of them of the significance of these works or of my discussions with the managers of Yasnaya Polyana. I just simply said 'This is where the works of Leo Tolstoy were printed and distributed to the world'. I already knew that Valerii was a member of the Tolstoy Foundation and that he would appreciate the significance of what I said. He was so thrilled. He took several photographs and I have no doubt that at least one of these captured images has been enlarged and placed in the Tolstoy museum.

Our helicopter skis settled into the deep snow

When I next visited Russia the bitter cold winds of early January were sweeping through the streets of Moscow. I drove south and stayed in Velligozh, the summer holiday retreat for steel workers from Tula Chermet. Velligozh is 100 kilometres from Tula and positioned in a remote berioska forest on the banks of the river Oka, one of the largest inflows of the mighty Volga.

Perestroika was now firmly established and ordinary people were starting to go hungry. The armed forces had not been paid for 6 months and yet their discipline remained intact. The Kremlin repatriated their air force from East Germany and the Government of Helmut Kohl paid several million Deutschmark into an unknown bank account to pay for their re-housing in the Soviet Union. Meanwhile these same air force pilots and their families took refuge from winter's subzero temperatures by living in their helicopters. No one knew where Kohl's money went. I blame the German government for their lack of proper control on these funds more than I do those corrupt Russian party officials who most probably secreted the West German tax-payers' money into their own personal accounts.

I stayed in a large log cabin on the edge of the forest. In the evening the men in our party enjoyed a traditional sauna while we hit each other with the leafy branches of a berioska tree. After sweating in the sauna I rolled naked in the deep snow. It was about 15 degrees below zero and it was so cold that it was impossible to feel the pain. In the morning I found that my hosts had provided a pair of skis, a snowmobile and a Russian MIL-5 military helicopter. Now that took some beating.

Marina and I put our skis on and set out along the forest tracks, taking care not to lose our direction; it would be very dangerous to get lost and spend the night outside during a Russian winter. While we were in the forest our pilot took his batteries to a local farm and recharged them. His helicopter had twin jet turbines and he needed fully charged batteries to get the engines started in such cold conditions. After lunch Marina and my hosts climbed into the back of our helicopter and I climbed into the right-hand seat. Our pilot knew that I held a fixed-wing licence and he let me take the controls after take-off.

As we warmed the engines several children gathered to watch and so we invited them to join us. The helicopter was only rated for 12 passengers but we filled all of the seats and the floor as well. We certainly had more passengers than seat belts. Our pilot gunned his turbines, gathered the collective and up we went. Russian pilots certainly don't follow the book. He handed over to me and I followed the Oka River southwards. The scene beneath our pulsating helicopter was absolutely beautiful. Berioska trees drooped under the weight of glistening snow and the river changed to large expanses of whitened ice wherever its waters slowed into a wide sweeping curve. Here and there, large wooden dachas could be seen and an occasional group of farm animals gathered around small heaps of fodder.

When I returned our helicopter to Velligozh, our pilot regained control and brought us down to land in front of my log cabin. I noticed how he waggled the control column to allow our skis to settle in the deep snow; if one ski had settled deeper than the other then our rotor would have touch the ground and sent us cart wheeling. After we climbed down he offered me a helicopter conversion course for 2,000 US dollars. He assured me that his course would entitle me to an international rating for twin jet turbine helicopters. I was not convinced that this certificate would be recognised in the United Kingdom and chose not to take him up on his offer.

When we visited Tula Chermet I found that Dick Cheney, the United States Defence Secretary, had just finished an official visit to the works and during his visit he was presented with a special dagger. A second identical dagger was given to me. It is now part of my growing collection of most treasured possessions. The handle is carved from rosewood and inlaid with silver filigree with a semi-precious stone at the hilt. It has an extremely sharp blade which was forged from approximately 80 layers of steel. This technique is known only to a small number of craftsmen and the skill needed to beat out the steel has been handed down from father to son from the days of Peter the Great. Layered steel forged in this fashion is very special because it will cut through body armour. The blade carries two stamps, one for each of the craftsmen who made the dagger. Even the rosewood box, also inlaid with silver filigree, is a work of art.

By now I realized that doing business in Russia was all to do with relationships. Make no mistake, the equipment had to meet specification and the product support needed to be in place. But once I had supplied my transmitters the customer took over. Russian engineers knew how to get the best out of our Western products. All they needed was the personal assurance that I would be around if they needed help with spare parts or additional supplies.

On this particular visit we did not even make the usual round of samovars and workers committees. Aleksander Skormin told me that he was exceptionally pleased. He had not even found it necessary to re-calibrate any of the hundred or so transmitters that I supplied for his blast furnace. By comparison, he had to re-calibrate his Russian manufactured transmitters almost every week. When I returned home I received a further large order for transmitters on the continuous casting plant at Tula Chermet and the following year Aleksander placed a third order for transmitters on a Vanadium plant.

I hold my friends in Tula in very high regard. I have an open invitation to join them on a canoeing holiday down the Volga. I hope that one day I will be able to take them up on that invitation. As they do not speak English the experience will certainly help to improve my Russian language skills.

Chapter 18

A Russian Misadventure

Starting one of the first joint stock companies in the new Russia
Safer to stay at home!

As Perestroika became firmly entrenched I grew confident that a whole new market was about to open in the Soviet Union. I rented an apartment above the newly opened Macdonald's in Mayakovskaya. This fast food restaurant was the first in the Soviet Union and beyond doubt the largest in the world. There were more than 40 serving tills working flat out to satisfy a queue that stretched for more than half a mile past the square. It featured on the BBC news and my apartment could be seen on television in England.

I never enjoyed hamburgers but food was in very short supply. Most of my day was not spent working, but searching to find a square meal. While holding business meetings one of my secretaries would sit on the windowsill. Occasionally the queue would shorten for no obvious reason and she would rush down to buy a couple of dozen Big Macs. We would have half a dozen for lunch and then place the remainder into the refrigerator to keep us going for a day or so. It was not safe to re-cook meat, particularly hamburgers, but it was better to risk food poisoning than not to eat at all.

I have to say that I was very impressed with the Macdonald's operation. Their meat was flown in, probably from South America. Yet a Big Mac, with French Fries and a large Coke, cost less than a dollar fifty in Roubles. The management sold at a fair price in local currency. A hundred yards down the road in Tverskaya, known to many as Gorky Street, was the only other restaurant in downtown Moscow where food could always be found. It was the Pizza Hut. At this place a Pizza cost much more than in London and only US Dollars was accepted.

One evening I was having a meal at the Pizza Hut when two young Russian soldiers came in. They were probably on leave from one of their regiments and struggling to find an evening meal. It was extremely cold outside and they were shown the door because they only had Russian roubles. If this had happened in Colchester England, our soldiers would have broken the restaurant up. I was absolutely disgusted and it was the last time that I ate in a Pizza Hut. Three cheers for Macdonald's. The following year when the Russian Mafia began to divide Moscow into territories, Pizza Hut was one of the first to place gun-toting security guards on their door.

Mikhail Gorbachev was very well liked in the West. While striving to modernise the Soviet market economy he slowly eroded the roots of communism. However, in doing so the Soviet food distribution chain failed and millions of people went hungry. Civil servants, teachers, hospital workers and more importantly, the military, were not paid for several months. This was a frightening situation. Despite all of this, I still couldn't understand why the people disliked him.

Then one afternoon I switched the TV on. Gorbachev was talking in a fast monotone voice telling everyone what had to be done to improve the economy. Four hours later I switched on the TV and he was still talking in the same fast monotone voice. My guest explained that this was normal; all he did was talk, talk and talk, but he never did anything. I suppose there were two sides to the story. After all, the Russians worshipped the Iron Lady, Maggie Thatcher, and yet our own politicians couldn't wait to stab her in the back.

Seven missile sites in Cuba were armed

I began to meet several influential people from the Central Committee. I was never sure of the source of my introductions. For a long time I suspected that Victoria's husband, Sergei Perepeleyatnik, had stronger connections than at first appeared. He claimed that he was nothing more than a retired Mig-15 pilot and yet he had access to the inner sanctuary of the Kremlin. He must have been a senior KGB Officer but he always smiled and denied it.

Sergei introduced me to Igor Senchilo who was a member of the

Executive of the Council of Ministers of the USSR State Commission. Igor was a very likeable person. He explained that the Duma had passed new legislation which would enable Westerners to form a Russian limited company in partnership with Russian nationals. He explained that with the right contacts I would be able to secure very large contracts in the oil industry.

Two days later I had a business dinner in a small select restaurant in Moscow. Joining me were three people who were to become directors and shareholders in my newly proposed company, Coultech Limited. The first two I have already mentioned, Sergei Perepeleyatnik and Igor Senchilo. The third person was Yuri Kharchenko, a senior government minister in the USSR and a Deputy Prime Minister of the Russian Federation.

Yuri was the person who negotiated the repatriation of 10,000 Russian technicians with Saddam Hussein at the outbreak of the first Iraq war. More importantly, he had strong contacts in the oil and gas fields of Northern Russia and Siberia. As we enjoyed our dinner Igor and Yuri told me many stories from the cold war years. I was amazed and, at the same time, shocked, when I listened to the Soviet side of many of the cold war incidents that had rocked the world in earlier years. I was particularly horrified to learn how close we came to nuclear conflict during the Cuban missile crisis. It was much closer than appreciated by western intelligence services.

I thought that the Russian nuclear warheads were on cargo ships that turned around in mid-ocean and returned to Russia. In reality, Yuri told me that there had been 40,000 Russian soldiers in Cuba and they were armed with mobile tactical nuclear weapons. He also told me that seven of the MRBM sites had been armed and that Khrushchev had already authorised his commanding general in Cuba to launch if an American invasion force set sail from Florida.

I don't think that anyone will ever know the full story of what happened on that frightening morning; the morning of Sunday 28th October 1962. Kennedy ordered his generals to cancel their invasion of Cuba and he gave no explanation for his decision. A new moon had kept the World in darkness that night and few of us ever appreciated that the World had been less than two hours from full scale nuclear conflict.

I didn't want to sound entirely dumb while discussing these mind-numbing subjects, and so I casually mentioned the Urals reactor fire and asked why they had not been able to protect the water table. All three of my guests looked at each other in absolute horror. They didn't know what to say because this fire was one of their most closely guarded secrets. The world had only ever known about Sellafield, Three Mile Island and Chernobyl. How could a Westerner possibly know about such a closely guarded secret? What else did this person know that could cause embarrassment to the old guard of Soviet Russia? Yet again I found it very interesting that Sergei shared in the stares of amazement that crossed the table. He obviously held higher station than he allowed me to believe.

The following day we all visited a rather disorganised government building in the centre of Moscow and we each signed the Russian equivalent of the Company's Memorandum and Articles of Association. I suspect that our new Company, Coultech Limited, was the first of its kind to be registered in the new democratic Russia.

I was so excited by the opportunities that I now had. When I returned to England I set about obtaining the Fuji Electric distribution rights for the Soviet Union. I knew that the only way to do this was to show absolute commitment to the senior management of Fuji Electric. I therefore telephoned Gen Katsumata, the director of the International Instrumentation Division, and asked if he could join me for lunch in Tokyo. I explained that I would be flying out to discuss an important matter and that I would be returning to London on the same day.

It was not often that someone flew to the other side of the world, enjoyed lunch, and then flew back on the same aircraft a few hours later. I knew this would demonstrate my commitment and my shortage of time would circumnavigate the long series of meetings that a Japanese company often needed to reach a decision. My strategy worked; Gen pulled his team together; we reached an agreement and I flew back with a contract in my pocket.

Sergei helped me to pull together our new company and we employed four highly skilled engineers. All, except a young girl called Tanya, had worked with me on earlier projects. Tanya often recalled her childhood days in Kabul where she was the daughter of a Russian technical specialist. She travelled to school in a Russian tank every day and enjoyed a very unusual upbringing. Tanya was the only girl amongst her circle of friends and she quickly learned to take care of herself in an all-male environment; she impressed me as a real tomboy.

Tanya told me a very tragic story of how a young Russian guard offered her best childhood friend an AK-47 assault rifle to play with. Her friend did not know the difference between a real gun and a toy; he pointed the rifle at the young guard and shot him dead. Tanya never heard from him again and understood that he was returned with his family to Moscow.

Within a short space of time my new engineers translated all of our product brochures into Russian. Demonstration products and office computers were shipped out from England and work began in earnest.

How not to fly into Siberia

Our first target was the gas separation plants on the Samotlor oil field in Siberia. There were 27 of these plants in the region and we were given permission to install demonstration equipment for fiscal flow metering on the newest of these plants, Belozerny, which was about 40 kilometres from Nizhnevartovsk. I obtained help from a specialist company that provided similar equipment for the North Sea oil production companies and designed a system suitable for the extreme weather conditions in Siberia. My system required significant up-front investment.

When I was confident that I had everything working I packaged it into several cartons and took it with me as additional baggage on a Lufthansa flight to Moscow. The baggage was lost and eventually it arrived two days later. This worked out rather well because it was delivered to me and I didn't have to pay any duties. The following day Marina and I took a taxi to Domodedova Airport which operated Aeroflot flights to Siberia. The extra baggage charge was only a few roubles but I had to pay 200 US Dollars to the baggage attendant. This purchased his 'assurance' that my equipment would be loaded onto the aircraft and not into the back of his friend's truck.

Marina headed off to board our flight through the Domestic Gate which was only a few yards away and I tramped across the airfield through the deep snow to the foreigners terminal where I had to wait to be taken to the aircraft. I have no doubt that this may have been a good system some years earlier, but I was not provided with any transport and I had to walk across the airfield with aircraft movements all around me. This was not the first time that I had suffered this kind of treatment at Domodedova. Anyhow, I was the only foreigner, no one bothered to collect me and the flight left.

I knew that poor Marina would arrive in the middle of the night in Nizhnevartovsk, she would have all of my heavy equipment to carry and no one to help her. I was absolutely livid. I tore into the controller's office and almost broke her door from its hinges. Even in Russian I found the right words to tell her what I thought of their cock-eyed system. When I asked what I had to do, she said that I should go back into Moscow and buy a new ticket for the flight leaving on the next day. I couldn't believe what she was telling me. I had to buy a new ticket!

I stormed back across the snow covered airfield half hoping that a security guard would challenge me. I needed to vent my wrath on someone other than a fat Russian woman who was ensconced behind a large empty wooden desk. I took a bus into Moscow where I visited Yuri and Alla, Marina's parents, and explained what had happened in the hope that Marina would be able to telephone from Nizhnevartovsk. I left them with a message that I would join her the following day.

In the morning I visited the Aeroflot Office and they issued me with a new ticket. I was pleased that they did not ask for payment as I was in no mood to negotiate. I took the bus to the airport, and I ignored the airport staff when they told me to go to the foreigner's terminal. I walked across the airfield from aircraft to aircraft asking if they were going to Nizhnevartovsk. Eventually I found the right one. I was very surprised at the lack of security; no one challenged me. I suppose that if you were bold enough, then everyone assumes that you have a right to be there.

After I settled down our Russian passengers boarded from the domestic terminal. My flight was obviously overbooked because there were more passengers than seats. No problem, they just brought a dozen wooden chairs from the airport terminal and placed them in the isle. Safety discipline was non-existent, and to make matters worse, the hostesses continued to smoke cigarettes during take-off. Every month there would be a newspaper report of an Aeroflot flight that had crashed because of serious overloading. British Airways became so concerned that they prevented their staff from using Aeroflot for crew positioning.

I heard so many stories of flying incidents in Russia. One of the saddest was of an airbus that crashed under bizarre circumstances. The investigation team only found the Captain's teenage son in the cockpit. The airbus had dived 35 thousand feet to impact the ground with explosive force while the Captain and Co-pilot struggled to get back to the flight-deck. The youngster who was sat at the controls must have disengaged the aircraft's autopilot. The craziest story, but very believable, was of an Israeli businessman whose flight was late returning from Siberia to Domodedova airport. He allegedly paid the Captain 100 US Dollars, equal to a months pay, to declare an emergency and divert to Sheremetova airport where he could catch his onward flight.

During my long flight to Nizhnevartovsk I became friendly with the Chief Engineer and Captain of a Canadian flight crew. They were positioning for their first ever flight over Russia, from Calgary to Tokyo. For future flights they intended to use their own aircraft for positioning, but as this was the first one, they had no choice but to use Aeroflot.

When we arrived at Nizhnevartovsk it was late at night, snowing, 25-degrees centigrade below zero and there was a thick layer of ice on the tarmac. The terminal building was closed and there was no one to meet the Canadian crew. Nikolay Polychuk, the Chief Specialist for Metrology and Instrumentation for the Ministry of Oil and Energy Industry, another long title, and Marina were at the airport to meet me. We didn't have space for the Canadian Flight Crew and the young hostesses became frightened and one sat down on her suitcase and began to cry. We took the Chief Engineer into town where he was able to make arrangements for a bus to collect the rest of his crew. It must have been a terrible eye opener for them.

In the morning Marina and I were taken in a four-wheel drive army vehicle to Belozerny gas separation plant. The snow was very deep and yet our driver drove as if we were on a normal road surface. He was obviously experienced with driving in these conditions and ignored the possibility that he might need to stop or make a sudden change in direction. I was not surprised when we passed a dead pedestrian lying by the side of the road. I was very pleased when we finally arrived and at the same time disturbed in the knowledge that we had to make this same journey for several more days.

Senior management was blatantly corrupt

I used my first two days learning to appreciate how the operators ran the Belozerny plant. I had commissioned many hundreds of control systems over the years, more than most people, and I had always been questioned upon my apparent inactivity for the first day or so. I always maintained that a good engineer should not begin to implement a new control strategy until he fully understood how the old system worked, and I would never change my view on this.

I believed it was important to observe the way the operators and the management inter-react with one another; to observe how the process reacted under different conditions and with different types of disturbance, deliberate or otherwise. I needed to question both operators and managers so that I could learn what they hoped to achieve with a new system. What system reports do they want and how frequent? Where can the largest cost savings be achieved? What process conditions can give rise to life threatening situations? These were all important issues that had to be addressed before a new control system strategy could be implemented.

A good control system would increase operational efficiency, increase throughput, improve product quality, reduce production costs, reduce environmental pollution, reduce wastage, increase management data and most important of all, increase operator safety. A rather big mouthful, but so much could be achieved if control systems were properly applied. It was no wonder that many governments were introducing legislation to compel large industrial concerns to introduce proper measurement and control systems in key areas of safety management, energy conservation and environmental pollution control.

I was very impressed by the knowledge of Nikolay's on-site instrument technicians. Their enthusiasm was contagious and I had not experienced such a desire to learn new ideas since my early days as an apprentice in the United Kingdom Atomic Energy Authority.

Belozerny was the latest and the most modern of the 27 gas separation plants that served the Samotlor oilfield. Yet the equipment by western standards was primitive. Fiscal metering of the gas transported through the natural gas pipeline was calculated and summated using a mechanical device that traced the area lying beneath the pen mark on a strip chart flow recorder. We had not used this method in England for thirty years. I was astounded that the gigantic Soviet military complex was able to put men into space but it was unwilling to share new technology with its own industrial sector. In the end, this lack of foresight helped to contribute to the decline of the Soviet economy and eventually to the downfall of the Soviet Empire.

When I had gathered sufficient information I very quickly installed and configured a new instrumentation system that would gather quantitative data from all key areas of the plant, control the important parameters, provide full management information and give accurate fiscal data for the different gas separation lines. I had the full system working within one day and the operators were impressed by the accuracy with which I could achieve a balance between the fiscal inputs and outputs of the process plant.

Unfortunately, the operators became dismayed when my equipment showed that the gas separation plant was not as efficient as they had been reporting to their political masters for the past five years. Each separation plant had to achieve a predetermined level of efficiency and each plant always achieved target. No one could explain why the gathering plant a thousand miles down the pipeline always had a large shortfall. I suppose the management put this down to pipeline leakages.

I was not prepared for this kind of problem. The management was not going to purchase a metering system that uncovered misreporting of production volumes; not in a communist society where everyone was perfect and no one ever accepts responsibility for their mistakes. So I did something that I have never done before; I put a multiplying factor of 1.16 into the calculation programme in order to give an artificially high totalized flow reading that was close to what they had been reporting.

I believed it was very important that Belozerny did not feel threatened. With time they would become comfortable with the new technology and if an agreement could be reached to install my equipment on all 27 plants, including the gathering station, then a balance could be obtained and everyone would be happy.

Alexander Varioshkin, the Chief Engineer of the Samotlor Field, would have to be informed of the true situation; it would have been very unprofessional and dishonest for me not to do so. As it happens, events took a much more serious downturn. Dishonesty at the highest level of management was already becoming evident. The workers had not been paid for several months and funds allocated to new projects went astray. Samotlor was the 7th largest oil field in the world. It was pumping 7 million barrels of oil each day and yet the senior management was so blatantly corrupt that it could not even pay its own workers.

This was the beginning of the debacle that was about to engulf new Russia under the pretext of democracy. The free market economy being espoused by an enlightened Kremlin was a farce. It was free for everyone in a position of influence, but paid for by every peasant farmer, soldier and industrial worker in the new Russia. No wonder peasants in Siberia longed for a return to the good old days of Communism. They had food in their bellies when Khrushchev was in power. Don't get me wrong, I don't agree with communism, but what was happening in Russia during these early days was intolerable and the wrong people profited from such an uncontrolled and cataclysmic change.

The funds for my project were never recovered and I decided to move forward with much more caution. I had learned a very expensive lesson. My next foray was into the steel industry at Novokuznetsk, a steel works that prided itself upon its contribution to the Second World War by producing an astonishing number of Soviet Tanks.

Novokuznetsk lies north of Mongolia on the Tom River in the Kuzbass Region. The Altai Mountains form a distant backdrop and the region was home to the indigenous Teleut, who were close to extinction, and the Black Siberian Bear. The writer Fyodor Dostoevsky was once a reluctant resident of the town; he served four years' hard labour in a stockade with his feet fettered in chains.

I was only exposed to snipers on the rooftops

My luck was not to change in Novokuznetsk. Everyone gathered in my hotel room to watch a movie. I could not follow the sound track and my concentration slipped until suddenly, without announcement, someone started calling for help on the TV screen. I thought this was part of the film until I noticed that my guests were in a state of shock. The person was desperately frightened and he shouted that his TV Station was under attack. Then the screen went dead. We quickly switched to the Moscow radio station and that was also dead. It was Saturday 2nd October 1993; the Second October Revolution had begun.

The following morning the Kuzbass Peasants were ecstatic. Communism was returning to Russia; they would lead a good life again and have food to fill their empty bellies. I switched the TV on to see if I could obtain any news and I was surprised to capture raw unedited CNN transmissions. An American CNN reporter was transmitting blind. She had coverage of hand-to-hand fighting in central Moscow and her US networks were refusing to cut into their scheduled programmes. They were unable to grasp the significance of what was happening; she was fuming. She cursed like a trooper and swore profusely at her network controllers.

I expected the worst, and so I searched for a route through the mountains into Mongolia. Perhaps I could fly home from Ulaan Bataar. The maps that I had were printed in Soviet Russia and my hosts quickly explained that they were deliberately misprinted to confuse American spies. I found this to be the most stupid thing that I had heard all week. Nevertheless, the map depicted several Siberian towns more than 1,000 miles from the position that I knew them to be located. Perhaps there was some truth in my hosts' warning. In the end I decided that I had return to Moscow; this was the only semi-reliable connection that I had with the outside world.

When we arrived at Domodedova Airport, I had a terrible argument with Marina. The two engineers accompanying me wanted to take a bus into Moscow. I was not prepared to do this because of the risk of becoming entangled in crossfire. I told Marina that I was responsible for her safety and that she was to take a taxi with me to the nearest metro station from where we would proceed underground to her parents' home. This was just across the river from Red Square and very close to the White House where the fighting was taking place.

After leaving her with her parents I hurried back to my apartment. I left the metro at Mayakovskaya and walked up Tverskaya, the old Gorky Street, taking care to stay very close to the nearside buildings. In this way I was only exposed to snipers on the rooftops of the buildings on the other side of the street. It was after curfew and not a single person could be seen; normally Tverskaya was one of the busiest streets in all Russia. A police car came screeching to a halt beside me; I ignored it and kept walking. After I had walked twenty yards it reversed at high speed and came to another screeching halt beside me. There were four policemen inside; all except the driver had sub-machine guns pointed at me. I still kept walking, I was absolutely petrified. Then suddenly they were gone.

In the morning Tanya turned up at my apartment, which now also doubled for an office. I was surprised when she told me that she came to work on the first day of the Revolution and taped my windows to prevent them from shattering during the battle for Byelistancia, a huge railway station which was just across the road.

The International Media were confined to their hotel on the river bank opposite to the White House, home of the Russian Parliament. Because of this the world was never made aware of the fighting that was taking place in other parts of the city. Communist supporters had overpowered the guards at all Communication Centres, Mainline Railway Stations, the Mayor's Office and the Russian Parliament. Trucks circled the city and distributed AK-47 assault rifles to anyone who answered the Communist call to arms; Tanya's husband collected one of these rifles along with three clips of ammunition and hid it beneath his bed.

The KGB, re-named the Border Guard, remained loyal to the Mayor's Office but it was over-run by the sheer weight of Communist supporters that were bearing arms. The Russian military was extremely well trained and their discipline on this occasion was outstanding. The army had no clear orders and so their regular soldiers remained confined to barracks. In truth their Commanding Officers did not know if they should obey the legitimate Russian Parliament or if they should take instructions from Yeltsin.

There were several accounts of what actually happened during those few days early in October 1993. As far as I can ascertain, Yeltsin was trying to impose so-called unpopular reforms on the Russian People and Parliament stood against him. Yeltsin had two strong opponents: The Vice President, General Aleksander Rutskoi, born in the Ukraine and highly decorated for his service in the Soviet Air Force during the Afghan Conflict, and a Chechen called Khasbulatov who was Leader of the House.

Yeltsin dissolved Parliament and Parliament, supported by the Constitutional Court, declared Yeltsin's Presidential Decree null and void. Parliament then proclaimed General Rutskoi as the new President. Rutskoi took oath on the Constitution and then immediately dismissed the Ministers for Defence, Security and the Interior. This was Rutskoi's mistake. Until then, Pavel Grachev, the ousted Minister of Defence, had remained uncommitted. Now he came down firmly on the side of Yeltsin.

Pavel Grachev knew he could not be certain of the regular army. Instead he mobilised young conscripts who were training with the tank regiment in Tula. These youngsters had families in Moscow and he knew they would not turn their guns on the local population. It took a full night for the tanks to travel up to Moscow. They arrived in the morning and mustered on the bridge in front of the White House. Western reporters wondered why there was no activity for several hours; the tanks were waiting for ammunition. Eventually a lorry loaded with high explosive shells arrived and one by one the tanks opened fire on the White House.

Hundreds were killed within the parliament building, but many more escaped through the secret network of tunnels that lay beneath the streets of Moscow. Those that did escape spread across central Moscow and sniped from the rooftops of prominent buildings until they finally accepted that their revolution had failed. With the Russian Government destroyed, there was no central control and it was then relatively easy to remove all further opposition. Through all of this there had been no sign of Yeltsin. Boris Yeltsin had gone to ground. As far as I can ascertain, he played absolutely no part in the final outcome.

It was never generally appreciated in the West just how close the

Communists were to regaining power and in my opinion they would have done so if Rutskoi had not made the mistake of firing Grachev. This changed the political future of Russia and of the free world. Yet very few people have ever heard of Pavel Grachev. Will history be more kind and give him credit for what he did in those crucial hours on 8th October 1993?

I was obviously not going to get any sensible work done during the next few days and so I decided to return to the England. I was surprised to find that British Airways was still flying into Moscow. There were no 'Peaked Hats' at the airport and I walked straight past the immigration cubicle, through the customs check point and onto my aircraft without even showing my passport. I had never enjoyed such an easy departure and this was very unusual for Moscow where little men normally revelled in their brief moment of power as passengers stood nervously in front of their shiny glass cages.

On arrival in London I was equally surprised to learn how little the rest of the world really understood about what had just happened.

Russian Champanski at a dollar a bottle

I continued to be hopeful that my new Russian Company would flourish. I loved my visits to Russia and took every opportunity to learn more of their history and culture.

Their behaviour was so very different to anything in the West, largely because they had lived in isolation for the best part of the twentieth century. The Russians that I encountered were very indifferent towards people they did not know. It was as if people outside their own little circle of family and friends did not exist. Storekeepers never looked me in the eye and commuters always let the metro entrance doors swing back into my face; even when I had a suitcase in each hand. These were the things that I hated about Russian people, but they also had many strong features in their personality. When I entered that circle of friends there was no limit to their warmth and generosity.

During my earlier visits I produced my passport and bought my essential items in the Berioska. When food began to trickle back into the supply chain I became adventurous and purchased my food in the rather grandiose stores of Tverskaya. These stores had very high ceilings sculptured and painted in a manner that would compete with the Sistine Chapel. To make a purchase was in itself an adventure. First I selected which loaf of bread I wished to buy, then I paid for it at a rather ornate glass enclosure, then I took the receipt back to the counter where I had located my loaf of bread and gave the receipt to the woman who then gave me the loaf. I then repeated the same process to purchase my butter, and then my cheese and then all of the other goods that I needed. It was a very lengthy and frustrating shopping excursion, one that I decided not to repeat.

I met with many interesting people and often visited Yuri's dacha in the countryside north of Moscow. It was always an interesting day. We joined neighbours and barbecued until late in the evening while drinking lots of home made vodka. In particular I enjoyed black caviar layered thick on brown bread with an equally thick layer of real butter. It was only two dollars a tin and we washed it down with Russian Champanski which at only a dollar a bottle was every bit as good as the real thing.

Travelling on trains within Russia and the old Soviet Republics was even more dangerous than flying by Aeroflot. The trains were very long and travelled at surprisingly high speeds for such poorly maintained tracks. The corridors were patrolled by armed soldiers, but they often slept or took bribes and so I bought a lock and chain from the guard and wrapped it around the door handles of my compartment. I found this to be a life saving precaution when thieves tried to break into my compartment during one of my overnight journeys to Leningrad.

On another occasion, when returning from Leningrad, the train stopped at a small village hundreds of miles from nowhere. There were only a few wooden huts protruding from the deep snow and somebody in one of them began to serve hot cups of tea. The guard told me that he would be stopping for ten minutes to take on water. Marina and I jumped down into the snow and hurried across to join other passengers to make our purchase.

Suddenly the train started to pull away. It was freezing cold, and my passport and all of my winter clothing was in my compartment. I was horrified. Everyone was trying to get back onto the train and it was gaining speed every second. I was, as always, the perfect English gentleman and could not bring myself to fight my way through. Eventually there was only Marina and I running desperately along the track. I managed to lift her up to the guard who grabbed hold of her and pulled her through the door which was a good four feet above the snow. I then grabbed the freezing cold steel rail and hauled myself in as my feet finally gave up the chase. Never again will I leave a train to buy a cup of tea.

One of my most memorable journeys ever was a boat journey from Leningrad along the inland waterways and into northern Karelia. Marina's mother booked the cruise through a Russian tour group in Moscow. It was for Russian people and so only cost the rouble equivalent of 80 US dollars. When I boarded in Leningrad I had to be very careful to speak as little as possible. While my Russian was improving it was still very patchy and foreigners were supposed to take the special cruise at 1,800 US dollars. I wore my dirty raincoat reserved for such occasions. It helped me to look the part.

It was late evening when we began to cruise up the Neva River. I lay in my bed and watched the river bank slowly glide by. As we travelled further north the countryside changed and soon I was able to see small villages that appeared to come right out of a medieval film script. Peasants tilled their fields using old ploughs, and horse drawn carts rattled along old dirt roads. There were no modern vehicles or implements and there were no young people to be seen. The buildings were all built out of wood and I am told that for 6 months of the year they were totally cut off from the outside world. It was so peaceful but I don't think that I could stand to be isolated in such extreme winter conditions.

For safety we were joined by another cruise ship as we crossed Lake Ladoga to the beautiful island of Valaam. This ozera was more like an inland-sea than a lake and many similar flat bottomed ships had been wrecked in violent storms. Inland water captains had long ago chosen to sail in pairs whenever they crossed a vast expanse of northern water.

Valaam was part of a picturesque archipelago that consisted of 50 individual islands. We left the boat and walked through never ending forests of berioska until we reached a medieval monastery where we received food and drink from a group of Monks, the only residents on this peaceful island. As we cast off in the late evening our ship played Tchaikovsky on specially installed loudspeakers and coloured searchlights weaved amongst autumnal trees casting shadows in harmony with the music. I remembered Maisy Miller trying to teach a young pianist to play this same music half a century ago. When taking my lessons with Maisy I didn't even associate Tchaikovsky with Karelia, let alone appreciate how beautiful his music could sound in such a natural setting.

We passed through several more rivers and canals, and then crossed Lake Onega to Petrozavodsk where we stayed for a short visit before sailing to the island of Kizhi. As we approached Kizhi, we were buzzed by a very noisy helicopter with counter rotating blades. It was a strange contraption that looked as if it had been designed by HG Wells. It could well have been his time machine paying me a very brief visit.

We visited several old wooden buildings that preserved the heritage of Karelia. I was held in awe by the incredible wooden architecture that lay before me; it was so different to anything that I had ever seen before. The Kizhzky Pogost Ensemble was the main feature in this complex of wooden buildings. It consisted of the Transfiguration Church, Pokrovskaya Church, and a bell ringer's dream: the incredible Bell Tower.

Karelia was undoubtedly a beautiful and remarkable place. It remained untouched by the ravages of the 20th Century. When we left Kizhi our short northern day was already drawing to a close, and as we passed by these old wooden churches their bells peeled in honour of our visit. It was late September and, as if by intention, the first winter snow flakes began to fall across our bow.

He thrust a revolver under my nose

Every day I walked along Tverskaya to Mayakovskaya Stancia. It was a long walk and I was fascinated to observe the changes taking place as, season by season, and year by year, Moscow shed its communist past and entered a new era that more resembled a cross between Monte

Carlo and 1930's Chicago. The only thing that never changed was the length of the very short miniskirts that street girls wore in Tverskaya. These short skirts accentuated their 'ochen glinia nogi' as they walked Tverskaya late in the evening; the length of their skirts even remained the same when temperatures fell to thirty degrees below.

One hot summer's day I walked out of Gorky Park and headed in the direction of Oktyabrskaya. I was immersed in a jostling crowd with people hurrying in every direction. Suddenly I felt a hand in my back pocket. I grabbed hold of it and spun around to confront the person. The gypsy was part of an organised group and he thrust a revolver under my nose. I quickly let go and backed away from him. As expected, not a single person came to my aid. This was the second time in as many months that I had been robbed and I began to feel like a character from one of Ian Fleming's novels.

On the previous occasion I had just boarded a midnight train from Bucharest to Bacau in Romania. Five ruffians trapped me in the darkened corridor of my carriage and robbed me of my money, credit cards and air ticket. It was 18 degrees below and twelve homeless tramps had already frozen to death outside the railway station. I was concerned that I might become one of them and so I stayed on the train until I reached Buhusi, a small village near to Bacaau. Then I struggled through five feet of snow to reach the house of a friend, Carmen Capata, who I knew would be able to help me. Carmen was only 27 years old and yet she was already one of the most highly qualified Judges in Romania. Carmen attained her remarkable position in the wake of the Romanian Revolution.

This particular incident was a big eye opener for me. No one except Carmen was prepared to give me any kind of help. Even the airline that held my reservation refused to talk with me. I had no money and I was treated like a tramp. My insurance company offered to help but they had no method to get new airtickets, cash or credit cards to me. I may as well have been at the South Pole. Carmen and her mother gave me shelter for five days and eventually help came from an unexpected quarter; a taxi driver. When I eventually got home to England I swore never to place myself into this predicament again. From then onwards I always dispersed cash and credit cards in different places when I travelled. Carmen is now President of the Court of Iasi in the north of Romania.

On 8th May 1995 I visited the Cherkizovsky Meat Processing Plant in the southern suburbs of Moscow. They bought high quality meat from the European Community surplus meat pile in Brussels at giveaway prices and then processed this meat into what had to be the best quality sausage in the world. It was a very important weekend and I was surprised that the factory was still working. It was 'Pyat Lyet Pabyedi', which translates to 'Fifty Years since Victory'; the Second World War had finished fifty years earlier.

I joined the Vice President, Albert Miroshnikov, in his office and found that we both had much in common. I was born three months premature during an air raid and he was badly injured in an air raid at about the same time that I was born. Out came a bottle of vodka and we toasted our good fortune, our fathers, our mothers, our wives, our girl friends; we toasted until we could barely stand up.

After this we set out to inspect his factory, which incidentally had a strict ban on alcohol because of rotating machinery. Whichever direction I looked, there were very attractive young girls in short white dust coats, hundreds of them. I vaguely remember staggering around with him commenting in my best Russian, "ochen glinia nogi, krasivi, krasivi"; which translates to 'very long legs, beautiful, beautiful'. Marina was very embarrassed and kept telling us both to behave ourselves.

All veterans had been given an army flask full of special 50 Year Victory Vodka'. When Marina finally bundled me into the back seat of our chauffer driven car he presented me with his own hip flask as a memento of my visit.

The following morning I nursed my monumental headache; I hate the after effects of vodka, and set out to join the military celebrations taking place on the outskirts of Moscow. The roads were blocked by thousands of people converging on the same area. It was a surge of humanity at least a hundred times larger than the approaches to Wembley on cup final day.

Soldiers, sailors and airmen were gathered in small groups, dancing and singing Cossack style while balalaikas were strummed in the background. Old soldiers walked along arm in arm with their young families, medals stretching across their chest, row after row after row. I joined them at one of the many army field kitchens and a soldier served one ration of black peas and rice, a reminder of the siege of Stalingrad. Various field weapons from the Second World War lined the streets and I joined several youngsters to climb the turret of a Russian tank where we posed together for that 'once in a lifetime' photo opportunity.

In the centre of this huge gathering was a very long and wide road. I believe it was the ceremonial approach to a city gate built to commemorate the defeat of Napoleon. The victory parade started with a large number of tanks racing down this wide concourse. There were tanks of almost every size and description followed by mobile guns, rocket launchers and weapons that I never knew existed. A thousand or so soldiers followed, goose stepping in columns twenty abreast and then helicopter formations began to fly overhead supported by squadrons of fighter aircraft. Several aircraft were connected, four at a time, to massive refuelling tankers.

This victory parade was undoubtedly the largest display of military might ever witnessed. There were military vehicles and aircraft so large that they took my breath away. The enormity of it all far exceeded the smaller victory parade attended by foreign heads of government in Red Square.

When I registered Coultech one year earlier I appointed Sergei as the Managing Director. He had negotiated an interesting deal with a large school in one of the Moscow suburbs. They allocated office space and we in return helped with technical equipment for the school. The headmistress invited me to Paslednizhvanok, which translates to 'Last Bell'. This was a traditional gathering at the end of the school year when graduating pupils made speeches and offered small gifts to their teachers. I was also asked to give a short speech to the pupils. It was a very moving experience for everyone and most of the girls were in tears when they walked through their school gates for the last time.

The school was a rather grandiose looking building with a dozen classic columns supporting the front of the building and it stood in grounds that contained a varied selection of oak, maple, ash and chestnut trees. Later in the year I reached an agreement to purchase the school and its grounds. Unfortunately I was sidetracked by a Town Hall official who refused to rubberstamp my purchase; I understand that he may have stepped in and purchased the property himself.

The company did not survive long after. Corruption was rampant and this was only one example of what was happening in Russia. When I started my company I had to transfer a substantial amount of hard currency into a Russian bank account. This was required to formalise the share capital requirement. After making arrangements for the transfer I found that the certified copy of my Memorandum and Articles of Association had been changed using snowpake to give the Russian Rouble one for one par with Pound Sterling. If my Russian shareholders decided to withdraw then I would have had to purchase their Rouble shares at several thousand times their face value. I don't think that this was their intention, but I decided not to proceed.

While corruption was already a very serious problem in the corporate world there was an even more serious threat emerging. One evening as I walked back to my apartment in Tverskaya, a car stopped just ahead of me and a youngster was bundled out onto the pavement. Three well dressed thugs jumped out behind him and beat him with pickaxe handles. My first reaction was to help him and then I noticed that two policemen with submachine guns were deliberately looking in the other direction. This was my first experience of a Mafia beating.

A few days later I visited Yuri's for dinner. His pavement was blocked by several new Mercedes cars and none of them were fitted with number plates. As I waited for Yuri to open his door, I listened to a group of youngsters in the adjoining apartment. The door was wide open and I could hear them dividing the various districts of central Moscow into territories.

I could not understand how these youngsters came to form the core body of the new Russian Mafia. Yuri explained that when young people previously finished university they were conscripted into the armed forces. Now these same youngsters had nothing to occupy them and many were inspired by old American films that now flooded into new Russia. Al Capone was their hero and Moscow was fast becoming a modern day Chicago; protection rackets, drinking establishments and prostitution was the name of the game, at least for the moment. The larger institutions were soon to follow.

Organised crime strengthened and different groups looked for new avenues to enrich themselves. They placed their own people into key positions in the banking system. If a bank manager said that his bank had no vacancies, then the Mafia shot one of his managers and created a position. This new style of operation was very different to their original model; the American-Italian Mafia. These new operators gave no warning and killed with impunity. They had absolutely no regard for human life. The year was 1984 and unlike the Sicilian Cosa Nostra, Japanese Yakuza or Hong Kong Triads, the Russian Mafia displayed no obvious code of conduct.

Eventually I decided that it was too dangerous to work in Russia. Huge profits could be made by anyone ruthless enough to do what was necessary but the stakes were far too high for me and the potential rewards were not worth the risk. At the very heart of it all, I preferred to do an honest day's work for an honest dollar; I did not like to profit from the misfortune of others. I pulled out!

1983
Sledging a frozen river through Tornado Alley in Minnesota

2001
Riding a class 5 rapid on the While Nile in Uganda (centre front)

1989
Kho Kao Tapu where the
'Man with the Golden
Gun' was filmed

1989
A fishing village on stilts off Phang Nga, South Thailand. This village was destroyed in the Asian Tsunami of 2004

1982
Brett overcoming his fear of heights by jumping from a 200 ft crane in Florida. The person who jumped before him was killed

1984
Michele and Brett at El Gem in Tunisia. *Gladiator* was filmed here in 1998

1990
Anne cooling off in the thermal springs of Pamukkale in South Turkey

1991
Sailing through the Aberdeen Typhoon Shelter in the British Crown Colony of Hong Kong. My first visit was in 1974

1998
Visiting Chichen Itza in Mexico, en-route home from Belize Sugar

1998
I was snorkelling off the Yucatan Peninsular when a Mexican Gunboat intercepted these drug runners. The boat caught fire and sank

1998
Kaieture Falls deep in the Amazon Rainforest during a short break from my work at Guyana Sugar. It is 5 times the height of Niagara

1999
Breakfast in the British Ambassador's Residence in Caracas, Venezuela

2000
Our annual Fuji Sales Conferences were always held in exquisite locations. This year the Dolomites were nearby

2000
Anne, Dad and Mattie in Mijas, Andalucia. Two days earlier I had made the dreadful mistake of buying a property 'off-plan' in Spain

2000
On one of my visits into the Amazon Rainforest I stayed alone in this stilted hut. It had no windows and monkeys raided me each night

2004
The largest footprints in the World. On the dinosaur trail in Asturias

2001
Walking a narrow path on a wooded hillside in Northern Thailand

2001
Riding a long-tailed boat up the Mekong River from the Golden Triangle with Burma on the left and Laos on the right

2002
Sailing the Nile in a Falucca
south of Luxor

2002
Overlooking Naqsh-e-Jahan Square in Esfahan following a sales visit to the
Iranian Oil and Gas Exhibition in Tehran

1995
Hayley, Michele, Toni, Fiona and Stevi (front) during our holiday at Disneyworld in Florida

2002
Port Lucaya in Grand Bahama, my home while writing this book

2002
Racing Hong Kong into Colon, Panama, after 1000 miles of open sea

2003
Helming Bristol in the Pacific during the second leg of the Clipper Round the World Yacht Race

2002
Mid-Atlantic with Jeremy Waite following a haircut

2003
A giant Galapagos Tortoise on Santa Cruz in the Galapagos Islands

2003
Sea Lions on Espanola. Wild life in the Galapagos has no fear of man

2004
Cuba leads the world in the reduction of greenhouse gases

2004
A barrel of 60 year-old port in an Oporto cellar. My birthyear; can I have a bottle for my 60th please?

2005
Iguaçu Falls. Brazil is on the left and Argentina on the right

2005
Anne would not let me travel to Chile without taking her to the Concha y Toro wine estates

2005
My brother Steven,
Linda and Katharine in
Horsham

1998
Katharine Ella age 5

2005
Christopher Thomas age 24

Chapter 19

Coulton Instrumentation

The last of my six companies and the most successful
Targeted by one of the big boys!

Our separation into separate business units on 1st April 1993 was far simpler than I had hoped and I received excellent support from everyone concerned. Magnus allowed me to retain our well recognised name, PMV Instrumentation, for three years and then he asked for it to be changed in line with our agreement. Robin Nixon, my bank manager, convinced me that I should change to Coulton Instrumentation. I had a secret fear that many would believe that I was on an ego trip, but Robin was confident that my customers would rally around and take the new name as an expression of my own personal commitment to the Company. His assessment was correct and our sales activity increased dramatically from day one.

I decided that we needed a sales engineer to replace Nigel who had assumed responsibility for PMV Controls and my recruitment agency head-hunted Mark Dutton from Delta Controls. Mark was selling pressure switches. He was very successful in closing orders but he was young and his experience in process measurement and control instrumentation was still limited at that time.

Mark was a very confident person and a strong supporter of Leeds Football Club. His brashness gained him access to engineering accounts that had long eluded Coulton. He was very ambitious and it was not long before he asked me to promote him to Sales Manager. He was an excellent sales engineer but I felt that he had not yet earned this responsibility; he had still to gain the confidence and support of several of his work colleagues, particularly those in the accounts department.

Meanwhile one of my competitors and Fuji's old parent, Siemens, had fallen flat on its face with its range of differential pressure transmitters. It had expended substantial funds in developing a new range of transmitters that suffered terribly from temperature drift. Fuji Electric came to its rescue and supplied a superior product to it under a badging agreement. This was not a problem to Coulton. We had a strong installed base in the United Kingdom and our marketing ability far surpassed anything that Siemens had previously demonstrated.

This was the second time that Siemens had tried to sell Fuji transmitters in the United Kingdom and yet again the huge Siemens conglomerate had fallen flat on its face. It failed to make any substantial inroads into the UK market. I was told that the senior management of Siemens held their UK marketing team to account and questioned their inability to compete with such a small company as Coulton. I don't know if this information was true, but a short time later Mark Dutton received a substantial offer from Siemens to join them as the UK Sales Manager for their Instrumentation Division.

Siemens told him to target my customers

Mark gave me the opportunity to better their offer and to give him the position that he had requested some months earlier. I have never permitted myself to be blackmailed and I chose not to do so on this occasion. Mark took great pleasure in my discomfort and then he said something that hit me like a pole axe. I can even remember that I was standing on my office stairs when he told me. He said that Siemens had instructed him to target my customers immediately.

I could not believe what he was saying to me. Mark was under a contract of employment which required him to work one month's notice. He had not even submitted his resignation and yet he was, in effect, telling me that Siemens had instructed him to work against the business interests of his current employer.

I had no alternative but to pay Mark a full month's salary and I asked him to leave the building immediately. This did not help because he already had copies of our outstanding quotations, price lists and a copy of our customer database in his home-based filing cabinet.

It was not long before we were contacted by several long standing customers who had received unsolicited quotations from Mark with prices for Siemens transmitters which were way below market. He told me that he had been authorised by his head office to make an operational loss during his first year. This enabled him target my customers at a price that I could not possibly match.

Mark rubbed it in; he revelled in his strong position and repeatedly reminded me that I should have made him my UK Sales Manager. I could not even understand the position of Fuji Electric in all of this because he was not creating additional business for them; he was simply changing the supply route.

I was so upset with Mark's strategy. I was more than upset, I was absolutely furious and I had sufficient evidence to hang him out to dry. I explained to him that I was considering legal action and he simply laughed and told me to go ahead. He said that he had the full support of Siemens management and that they would throw so much money behind him that I would be bankrupt before the case came to court. I knew that he was right and I had no alternative but to back down.

I soon lost several of my larger customers. Most of these had short-sighted purchasing managers who were unable to look further than the bottom line. I also had many loyal customers who understood the importance of long term support. One of these, Spirax Sarco, was repeatedly approached by Mark but their purchasing manager refused to be tempted. Spirax had long been one of Coulton's best and most loyal customers and in return we moved heaven and earth to ensure that we supplied them with the excellent service they deserved.

In time Mark had to return his prices to normal so that he could report a sensible profit margin to his head office. Several of his newly acquired customers then returned to Coulton but the damage had already been done. Our hard-won market was seriously damaged and Coulton suffered a fall in turnover and operating profit that was difficult to recover. I could never forgive Siemens or Mark; what they did to Coulton was unethical and, in my considered opinion, downright illegal.

Mark continued his fight to get to the top and two years later one of my old friends at Rosemount recruited him. Mark became the Sales Manager for Pressure Products at Emerson Rosemount, the largest instrumentation company in the United Kingdom. I may not have agreed with Mark's methods but I had to take my hat off to him; he targeted the top job and he got there.

I realised that I had to find someone that I could trust; someone who could share my responsibilities and take a pro-active role in the further development of my Company. This time my head hunter found Bryan Maddock, a regional sales engineer working for Druck, the largest manufacturer of pressure transmitters in the United Kingdom. Bryan had a solid engineering background and he consistently achieved sales targets which remained year on year to be one of the three highest in his company. I had high hopes for Bryan and together we put together an action plan which we believed would take us towards my ultimate target of four million pounds turnover.

To better explain this turnover target, I maintained that a self-financed company had to break through four fiscal barriers during its early years of growth. Coulton broke through the first three barriers in its first two years of operation, but I was never able to approach the fourth, four million pounds sterling.

I might have been able to achieve my target by acquisition but this would have required a bank loan. I was never willing to operate on borrowed cash and this sound principle has sustained me through several recessionary periods. I had no cars on lease-hire or equipment secured through hire-purchase schemes. I owned everything. This rigid financial regime had enabled me to tighten my belt on several occasions when the going got tough, while competitors with fixed monthly overheads went to the wall.

I used my Rosemount marketing skills to maximum effect and ensured that we created a strong market image. I invested heavily in our attendance at the bi-annual measurement and control exhibition at the Birmingham International Exhibition Centre. I experimented with different advertising techniques but I did not have sufficient funds to change the subject of my advertisements or to spread them across several journals. Instead I designed a simple full-colour full-page multi-product advertisement and placed this in the Measurement and Control journal on exactly the same page every month. This was very cost effective and it gave the impression that we were a large international company.

I created a full range of marketing letters and developed a matrix from our database to ensure that each target received a different letter from Coulton every two months. I believed strongly in the principle of brainwashing. I never expected my letters to be read, but I did expect that the first letter would inform my target that there was a company called Coulton. The next letter would get the message across that we sold pressure transmitters. Perhaps when the reader next wanted to buy a pressure transmitter he would be sufficiently brainwashed to remember the name of a company called Coulton who sold pressure transmitters. It was very important that each letter was no more than a third of a page and very presentable. This was my basic principle and it worked.

It was important to add value to our products wherever possible and one of our greatest achievements was to obtain a licence from the European Explosion-proof Certification Service. This licence enabled us to assemble Fuji process transmitters at our facility in Christchurch. This Certification was then ratified by a team from the Russian Goss Standard Commission. The team visited our facility for 10 days and conducted a full series of intensive tests under different environmental conditions. At the conclusion of these tests we were awarded pattern approval to supply fiscal metering transmitters under a Coulton label throughout the Russian Federation. This was a real brownie point for Coulton because Fuji did not have this approval and they had to supply their own customers under a Coulton label.

I ate with my fingers

It was about this time that Abdiljilil Benemar secured a good contract with the Moroccan sugar company that I had visited a few years earlier, and he invited me to visit again, but this time he insisted that I brought Anne with me. I was still trying to repay him for the incredible journey that he made across the Riff to retrieve my passport and so I accepted without hesitation.

We flew to Tangier and based ourselves in a hotel on the harbour front.

This was not the best choice. We had to walk down a steep hill from the Medina and then along a promenade to reach the hotel grounds. In the daytime young boys pestered me to buy cheap trinkets; after dark they offered different goods.

One night I walked back alone. There were no street lights and the same boys pestered me to buy hard drugs; then they changed tack and offered me a young girl. They were convinced that I must be looking for something or someone, because no normal person walked the promenade at night. They then decided that I must have wanted a young boy, and when I continued to ignore their offerings they became aggressive and pulled at my clothing. Fortunately I reached my hotel with pockets and money intact.

I hired a car and we drove down the Atlantic coast to Casablanca where I met up with Abdiljilil. We visited a number of customers for the next three days while Anne took the overnight train to Marrakech. I dropped her at the station and found that she was booked to share her sleeping compartment with a young Moroccan family. I thought this was strange arrangement for a Muslim country but they took very good care of Anne and shared their food with her on what turned out to be a very slow and long train journey.

Anne stayed in a small hotel just outside the walls of the Medina. The stench of sheep dips pervaded the area. Silks, spices, jewels, skins, trinkets, crafts and trade goods of all kinds covered hundreds of market stalls. She imagined camel trains of old heading across the Sahara desert to this ancient capital city. The old square was full of atmosphere and she hired a personal guide to escort her around the Souks and through the summer palace with its superb coloured mosaics. Her guide was for protection; his job was to keep the hawkers at bay, not to lecture on the various buildings they found. Anne always preferred to use one of her 'Eye Witness Travel Guides'.

I was very surprised with the change in Abdiljilil since my previous visit. He told me that his wife had encouraged him to become a better Muslim. I suspect that he was forced to blend into the general flow of fundamentalism that was sweeping Morocco. We entered a restaurant near to the Kasbah and he heard the call to evening prayers just before taking his seat. He faltered and struggled between his responsibility as my host and his need to obey the call; he reasoned that Allah would want him to attend to his guest.

The following day Abdiljilil invited me to his home for dinner. His hospitality epitomised everything that I had grown to like about Morocco; with one exception. His wife covered her hair completely and remained in her kitchen. She did not socialise or eat with us as she did on earlier meetings. I sat with Abdiljilil on a carpeted floor and leaned lazily against huge fringed pillows as she brought several meat dishes and plates of spiced vegetables to our low wooden table. Each time she shuffled into our 'Salon' on her knees and never once did she look either of us in the eye. I questioned Abdiljilil on her behaviour and he insisted that his wife was a devout Muslim and that it was her decision that their family should revert to traditional Moroccan values.

I ate with my fingers and used my napkin to gather bones, skin and other leavings. Suddenly Abdiljilil leaned over our table and threw my napkin across the floor, allowing my scraps to scatter alongside his own. "It was bad manners to leave your refuse on table; you must throw it on the floor". This was rather a shock to me and a little embarrassing. I thought that I had a reasonable understanding of other cultures, obviously not. Suddenly I realized why the streets of Arab towns and villages were always so disgustingly dirty.

Apart from this small insight into Moroccan culture, I found Abdiljilil, as always, more than the perfect host. After eating we retreated to the huge and very long sofa that surrounded three walls of his traditional Salon and lay down to allow our food to digest. We drank tea and talked of the resurgence of traditional Islam in North Africa. I referred to traditionalism rather than fundamentalism because Abdiljilil holds high his Muslim values; he was not a radical using the Koran for political purposes.

After our business visits were over Anne and I drove inland to Fez, which she described as a smaller version of Marrakech. We arrived late in the evening and struggled to find our hotel in rush hour traffic. I have no idea how my hired car survived the melée without suffering any noticeable loss of paint. A policeman on point duty directed me the wrong way down a busy one-way street. He explained in faltering English that my hotel was a short distance down the street and on the left-hand side. When I said that it was a one-way street, he shrugged his shoulders as if to say, 'who cares'.

Fez had several huge tanneries that must have dated back into the middle ages. Ancient skills were used to tan thousands upon thousands of dirty stinking hides. Mud-built living quarters, work sheds and hide soaking pits crowded together in horribly close proximity. A group of Japanese tourists clenched their mouths and nostrils as they hurried along behind a flag waving guide, terrified that they might get left behind. For once, not a single tourist stopped to take a photograph.

On our long journey back to Tangier we met with Abdiljilil for lunch at a roadside barbecue. I preferred roadside eating, the meat was fresh and unlike a restaurant in a dirty suburb, one could see how it was prepared. Slivers of meat were cut from a bloody shank that hung from the branch of an old thorn tree and placed on a grill above a huge charcoal fire. Any bacteria that might have been present were barbecued with the meat and greens were added to prepare a huge and very authentic mutton kebab. Vultures circled overhead and after enjoying our meal we threw our remnants into the road knowing that nature would take its course. I cheated a little and pushed our dirty napkins into my pocket. I still could not bring myself to comply fully with Moroccan custom.

Driving along the Atlantic coast I saw a fleet of open fishing boats standing off a small inlet. Atlantic rollers thundered against a long breakwater that jutted deep into the ocean. They were waiting for the sea to reduce in ferocity before entering harbour to offload their overnight catch. I knew this would be a perilous time and much to Anne's chagrin I parked our car and waited.

One hour later the first boat made its run. It was amazing to watch. The skipper positioned himself one hundred yards off the breakwater and studied each wave as it surged towards him. He picked his moment and gunned his powerful motor to race for the protection of the breakwater, knowing that if the following wave broke over his stern he would immediately broach and sink.

He made it, but only just. The next boat followed 15 minutes later, and then it was another 10 minutes before the next, and then they all started to make their run, one by one. This was obviously a well rehearsed event; their anxious families watched from the safety of the quay and two smaller rescue boats stood outside the reach of breaking waves ready to pull their comrades from the huge rip that would surely take them to a watery grave.

Two of my earlier apprentices did well

Brett worked in our Christchurch facility during his summer, Easter and Christmas school breaks. He packed boxes, cleaned our workshop and helped Mick to calibrate transmitters. I did not want him to become father's little boy and so he was always given the dirty work to do. My staff liked Brett and if he had decided to remain with Coulton they would certainly have accepted him as the future owner and managing director. Unfortunately this was not to be. Brett was determined to make his own mark in life and he set his target on becoming a product design engineer. I respected this and I worked with him to ensure that he studied the right subjects at school.

Brett transferred to Winchester Sixth Form College for his final two school years. He studied maths, computer graphics, and other design related subjects. After securing a commendable set of A-levels he signed-up with Coulton as a student apprentice. We already had two other trainees on our books. Richard Burt was serving three years as a 'Modern Apprentice' and Kim Seward was on a government youth opportunity scheme to train as a secretary.

The subject of government sponsored training was a sore point with me. So much red tape was involved that it was much easier to employ youngsters, take them under your own wing, and tell the government officers to get stuffed. Coulton had already trained two university graduates and three young school leavers. Two of my earlier apprentices did well and entered university while one transferred to the Army Corps of Engineers. I gave each of my trainees paid day-release to attend Southampton College and the Government helped by charging me for this facility. They even charged me for the services of a so-called training officer. What morons! I feel that I have to expand a little on this pet subject of mine and explain the reason for my comments.

Each month a woman visited Kim Seward, my trainee secretary, and ran through a check list with her and her supervisor. I paid the government training initiative a substantial sum for this service and so one day I decided to check what I was getting in return. I was shocked to find that Kim, who was extremely bright, could not take any shorthand and had very limited typing skills, on the other had she knew where everything in the office was filed.

The next time her training supervisor visited I discussed this with her and asked what Kim had been studying for the past year during her day release. "Oh, she has been studying office organisation". Does this mean that she has been learning how to file documents? "Weeeeeell, I suppose you could say that". What secretarial training has she received? "Oh, we don't do that". Well what do you do? "We check to see if your Company has a fire certificate and we provide the necessary records for her training".

I couldn't believe the way this conversation was going. She was a middle aged woman and I knew that she would have received excellent training when she started out 30 years ago; I knew what the government had on offer in the '60s. I asked her if she knew shorthand. "Yes", she replied. Do you know how to type? "Yes", she replied. And who taught you how to do this? She knew where my questions were leading and she then admitted that the present day government training syllabus was totally inadequate.

I asked her not to take what I was about to say as a personal attack, but an attack upon her position within the government training initiative. I told her to leave my office immediately and never to return. I told her that I would take over total responsibility for Kim's training and that she must instruct her organisation never to seek false training fees from Coulton again.

I believed that our youngsters deserved better! It appeared to me that this whole affair was simply a scam to keep the old boy network in jobs using my good money and an equal amount from the tax payer. The following week Coulton registered Kim for her first Pitman's typing class at our local college and we paid for it by diverting those funds originally used to pay the Government's Training Officer.

Our training was not as good as I would have liked. It fell far short of what I had received as a young craft apprentice but it was much better than what was on offer in most other private companies, and certainly, better than any scheme supported by the Government. Perhaps if the Government had offered a tax break more Companies would have followed my lead and we might have increased the number of youngsters in skilled employment.

Training young people to become craftsmen, technicians and engineers was the responsibility of every skilled person and certainly the responsibility of the Government of the day. Everyone has a responsibility to pass on his own area of expertise to the next generation. After all, this was how we attained our own very valuable skills.

I was terribly concerned with the way our country was ignoring this important subject. Successive governments made the right noises but that was all they ever did; make a noise. There seemed to be no one left in government that understood the importance of craft and student apprenticeships. The old guard was dying or passing into retirement. Before long this would also happen to our experienced teachers; teachers with craft, technical and engineering skills and with real hands-on experience in real industrial companies.

Before long we would need teachers to teach our teachers. We would be forced to recruit these people in Japan, Taiwan or South Korea. What a terrible legacy our political elite have left us. Successive governments have presided over our industrial decline with total indifference. They have insulted a once proud nation whose forefathers created the industrial revolution. My great grandfather must have been turning in his grave.

Perhaps he played tiddlywinks

I discussed my concerns with Richard Carborn, the UK Minister for Trade. Richard served a student apprenticeship and he understood exactly what I was talking about. Did he do anything? Did he hell! He made all the customary noises and then was moved on to become the Minister for Sport and Tourism. Perhaps he played tiddlywinks at college. He probably stood at the end of a famous race track with Stephen Byers and held a rather large piece of Labour red tape across the finishing line.

Joking aside; I thought that Richard Carborn was the perfect man for the job. I just could not understand why Tony Blair had to move him away from Trade and Industry and put him into a job which bore no relevance to his training. This happened so often in government; no private company would work in such an unprofessional manner and survive to tell the story.

The European Community sponsored an apprentice exchange scheme called the Petra Exchange Programme, and Dorset Business Link invited Brett to apply for participation. Brett joined Deutsche Aerospace in Munich where he spent 2 months in a German language school, 4 months in the Spacecraft Quality Control Division and 2 months in the Graphic Design Publicity Department. It could not have worked out better for Brett because Waldi and her husband Robert lived in Munich and they were pleased to look after him once again.

As part of this exchange we had the additional benefit of receiving a very good student from West Germany who made a strong contribution during his six months with Coulton. This exchange worked so well that Dorset Business Link set up a similar but private arrangement with Danfoss in Denmark and we exchanged apprentices very successfully for the next 5 years. It was very noticeable that the Danfoss apprentices were well trained and they contributed far more to Coulton than they received. Nevertheless, Danfoss valued our arrangement and when we had no apprentices left to exchange they continued to send their youngsters to us.

When Brett returned to England he was visibly more mature in his outlook and reasonably fluent in German. I was immediately reminded of a furious argument that I had with Brett's language master at Westgate School in Winchester. Brett was refused permission to study German at school and instead he was forced to study French. I tried to explain to his Language Master and then to his Headmaster that German was more appropriate for Brett because he intended to become an engineer and not an artist. Perhaps I was being rather simplistic, but when I was told that French was more appropriate because it was a pretty language, then I began to wonder.

Following his return to England Brett began to consider his university education. At first he targeted universities in cities where he wanted to live, but it soon became apparent that Bournemouth was the highest graded University for his chosen discipline. He therefore made this his first choice. This resulted in several unexpected fringe benefits for Coulton. We developed several new products within our product range and Bournemouth provided a ready supply of eager young product design engineers to help us. They wanted projects and we wanted products. It was an excellent combination and the Head of Department gave full access to the university's latest computer aided design equipment and modelling facilities.

Our relationship with the Product Design Department of Bournemouth University became very strong, and in return for their help we provided placements for several third year honours degree students and offered openings to two of their final year graduates.

Brett's 'Halokettle'

Brett progressed well at Bournemouth, but when it came to his third year placement he did not want to return to Coulton. Instead he chose to go to Strix in Chester where he worked on the design of thermal switches for electric kettles. One of his designs was used by a manufacturer in Hong Kong and this provided him with an excellent idea for his fourth year design project; a halogen heated kettle.

He found an old coffee jug and whacked it on a halogen ring. Sure enough his idea worked, although it took about ten minutes to boil. Turning it from this crude prototype into a gently glowing, practical object of desire was the hard bit. He used 3D computer graphics to design a sexy looking transparent jug with plenty of smooth curves and a clean Sauvé looking handle.

After making a polystyrene model to test the shape of his design he downloaded his drawings to computer disc and set about finding those companies which would be willing to manufacture prototype components free of charge. A glass blower on the Isle of White moulded three prototype containers from a special preparation of borosilicate glass, and a plastics company in the Midlands manufactured his polycarbonate lid, handle and base. Brett's greatest challenge was provided by the halogen elements and he eventually found a specialist company in

South Korea which was able to manufacture prototype elements to his very tight specification.

Brett had several hurdles to overcome. His first elements were the wrong shape and the next batch did not provide sufficient heat to boil water within his target of two minutes. The first polycarbonate handles were also a few thousands of an inch too small and they caused the borosilicate glass to crack and spill hot water during a design exhibition at Bournemouth University. This happened just before a Sunday Times photographer was scheduled to take a photograph; sod's law I am afraid!

Brett's final working design had a warm orange glow and boiled water very efficiently in less than 3 minutes. It could even be used for soups or pre-mixed drinks and it definitely had a sexy shape that would not look out of place in any designer kitchen or yuppie class office lounge. It featured in a special article in the Sunday Times and Brett received two requests for permission to use his 'Halokettle' in TV commercials. One of these was a Powergen commercial promoting the use of energy efficient home appliances.

Free promotion of this kind soon generated even more possibilities and Brett received a telephone call from Trevor Bayliss of the BBC Tomorrow's World team. He wanted to include Brett's Halokettle in a new mini-series called The BBC's Best Inventions. Two weeks later a BBC production team arrived at our Christchurch Workshop and over a period of two days they filmed several sequences that covered different stages in the manufacture and testing of Brett's kettle. These film sequences provided free advertising for the staff of Coulton who were filmed in conference while taking a serving of tea from the kettle.

Brett took a very active part in the BBC programme and was filmed alongside Kate Hill and Trevor Bayliss on location at a Victorian Pump House near to Sunbury. The programme was aired worldwide and Brett received several enquires from potential manufacturers. He patented his design and then awarded limited rights to Morphy Richards who carried out a full investigation into the cost of high volume manufacture.

Unfortunately Morphy Richards found this to be a little too high for their traditional market and they did not proceed. This was a shame because Brett always thought his Halokettle would appeal to a special group of people who wanted something different. Nevertheless, he retained the patent on his innovative design in the hope that one day a forward thinking company would bring his product to the production line.

The Halokettle project gave Brett a high profile and he found no difficulty in securing an excellent job as a product design engineer with Dyson in Malmesbury, a leading manufacturer of vacuum cleaners and household appliances. Sadly this was the end of his short career in process control instrumentation and I was left with no family member willing and able to take over my business. Brett progressed well with Dyson and a couple of years later Ron Dennis of the Maclaren Formula One racing team offered him a position in their new product design offices in Woking. This was a fantastic opportunity for Brett and I must admit that I was a little disappointed when he did not grasp it with both hands.

Chapter 20

White Man's Grave

Mayan civilizations, coral reefs and a little work in Belize
Fer-de-lance, ugh!

A large boiler engineering company based in Birmingham, Thorne International, learned of our expertise in boiler control, and in November 1994 they awarded Coulton a large contract to refurbish the instrumentation and controls on two bagasse fired steam boilers at Belize Sugar Factory in Orange Walk. This was the first time that we had been required to design, manufacture and install a turnkey project. Orange Walk was located in one of the most inaccessible regions in the Americas; all trans-Atlantic flights into Belize City were routed through the United States.

When we requested Belize technicians to visit England for training they had to obtain US visas to transit Houston airport terminal. The not-so-clever US immigration authorities refused a multiple entry visa to cover the return portion of their tickets. Instead of training in our Christchurch facility they spent half their allotted time queuing outside the US Embassy in London for a return visa. Almost every backward country in the world has a transit lounge to overcome this problem. Not the United States!

This visa situation became even more difficult and after the terrible events of 911 the American authorities became so paranoid that they were unable to gain a sensible degree of control over the situation. They grasped in every direction and achieved nothing except to increase the length of their already overburdened security channels. Everyone with any common sense knew that the efforts of Homeland Security were just window dressing for the American public. A fully trained terrorist could obtain everything that he needed from the duty free shops that were located within their own security barriers.

I was even refused a glass of wine with my meal in an Atlanta downtown restaurant. The girl had been instructed by the local police to identify everyone regardless of age. I told her that if I was a Muslim extremist then I certainly would not be asking for an alcoholic beverage. Eventually I pulled my passport out and threw my civil liberties through the window. I felt as if I was in pre-glasnost Soviet Russia.

Eventually we managed to get the Belize Sugar technicians back home and I flew out to join them. When I arrived I saw a Hercules transport taking Ghurkha soldiers deep into its gigantic hold. They had completed jungle training at the local British army camp and were preparing to travel back to England. They carried full equipment and had no seats worth a mention. I did not envy their upcoming ordeal.

British troops had been positioned in Belize by Margaret Thatcher to give a clear signal to Guatemala that this was still British Overseas Territory. Guatemala believed they had a historic right to rule Belize. Again we have an example of colonial enforced borders, except this time the line was not drawn in the sand. It was cut deep into the lush vegetation of a thick, impenetrable rainforest. Jaguars stalked its depths while on hot humid nights small groups of British Commandos cut through thick undergrowth and cursed the insects that drew blood from their unprotected skin. Belize was once the Crown Colony of British Honduras, better described by Anne's elderly and very well travelled Aunt Marjorie, as 'The White Mans Grave'.

Despite its terrible mosquito ridden climate, Belize is an incredible country with a lot to discover. There are ancient Mayan Temples that remained hidden deep in almost every area of the rainforest and incredibly beautiful string-of-pearl coral islands make up the second longest barrier reef in the world. The natives of Belize are a mixed but fully integrated population of less than 280,000 people. They comprise several ethnic groups including Mestizo, Creole, Ketchi, Yucatec, Mopan Mayas and Garifuna.

English and Spanish is widely spoken but the ancient Mayan and Garifuna languages still existed in outlying areas. This very low population was all the more surprising to me when I discovered that more than

2 million Mayan Indians were believed to have occupied Belize during the days of Mayan Civilisation.

More than 33 percent of the country's export revenue was earned from the export of refined sugar, and this refining process was 100 percent dependant upon the successful operation of the measurement and control system that I was about to install. I only had four weeks until the 1995 sugar campaign started. The importance of my work was driven home when the President of Belize visited to examine my fabulous new control room. Following his public relations visit the government hailed my work as a prime example of industrial excellence in the new Belize.

My control panels fell far short of industrial excellence; when I tried to commission my analogue inputs to the supervisory system I found that I had significant measurement errors. This was caused by a badly designed multiplexer which used a common ground for all 4-20 mA input signals. This kind of problem would have been difficult to locate in ideal working conditions; here in Belize with no air-conditioning and mosquitoes buzzing around my ears it was a miracle that I ever found the problem.

I could not replace the multiplexer and so I changed the arrangement of the input circuits and rewired both control panels. I worked day and night in hot humid conditions for almost a week. I only had a small portable light hanging behind my head and to make matters worse an Indian found a fer-de-lance outside the control room door. This was a very poisonous snake which could jump into the air and bite a person's face. It frightened the hell out of me.

I was staying in the Chief Engineers house and I walked home most evenings in the pitch dark, always terrified that I might step on a snake. One night at 3 am, I was so intent upon looking for snakes that I walked straight into the night watchman. He was doing the same as me, but walking in the opposite direction. I don't know who got the biggest fright; the old Indian with his rusty shotgun or me. It didn't help when he said that he had seen a coral snake in the middle of the road fifty yards ahead. I didn't have a torch and so I stamped heavily with each step as I walked towards the house.

The Chief Engineer and his wife, Alan and Josie Sharpe, were the most gracious of hosts; Josie made me feel very much at home. Her elderly father was also visiting from Corozal and while neither of us could speak each other's language we still had a unique way of communicating with each other.

It was extremely hot and humid and I consumed large amounts of liquid. My favourite drink was diet coke but the diet version was not available in Belize and for some reason importation was banned. Josie decided that it was time to visit Chetumal in Mexico where she could do her monthly big shop. Good produce was not readily available in Orange Walk and she invited me to join her. We bought two crates of diet coke and re-packed them into flat cardboard containers. Josie then lifted the bonnet of her Range Rover and placed the cartons on her engine block.

It was six hot and very bumpy miles to the border and I was terrified that the cans would start bursting. I could already read the headline story. "The Chief Engineer's wife of the Belize Sugar Company and her accomplice, Barry Coulton, Managing Director and Owner of Coulton Instrumentation, were detained on Tuesday for smuggling. They were arrested after several Border Guards dived for cover behind protective sandbags when several cans of Coca Cola exploded under the bonnet of Mrs Sharpe's car".

Shark Ray Alley, Ambergris Caye

After two weeks of solid work I decided that I would fly to Ambergris Caye. This caye was situated on one of the longest unspoiled barrier reefs in the world. Alan was very reluctant to allow me to leave the factory. I had been imprisoned within the boundaries of the outer perimeter fence for two weeks and had worked even longer hours than Nelson Mandela in his rock quarry on Robben Island. I was determined to have a break and I told Alan that it was his choice. He could arrange for his company driver to take me to the local airfield or to the international airport in Belize City where I could make arrangements to fly home.

I don't think Alan expected me to stand up to him and he relented. Josie, who was the main driving force behind my visit to Ambergris Caye, quickly made the arrangements and told him to behave himself. Alan is a very hard taskmaster, but he also drives himself very hard and he always leads by example.

It was a short flight to Ambergris Caye, my light aircraft only had half a dozen seats and most were filled with school children returning home for the weekend. When we landed I was taken on an electric cart to my small wooden guest house which lay on the edge of crystal blue-green waters that lapped up onto the white sands of the Caye. I wondered how these shacks would survive the hurricane season. The highest point on the Caye could not have been more than a few metres. There were no concrete floors and most buildings had a sand floor.

I was only able to visit for a couple of days and so I wanted to maximise my time. An open wooden boat was beached in front of my lodgings and the Indian owner advertised Shark Ray Alley on a heavily weathered piece of wood that rested against its bow. He was about to leave with a small party of American youngsters. On a wild impulse I gave him forty dollars and jumped into his boat before I had an opportunity to get cold feet. We motored out to a shallow part of the reef and he fitted us each with fins, goggles, air bottles and lead belts. I had never dived before and so the Indian stayed close to me and showed me all that I needed to know.

He taught me how to buddy breath and how to clear water from my face mask. The rest he said I could learn as we dived on the reef. I learned quickly; it was much easier than snorkelling because the pressure prevented water from flooding my mask and I didn't have to worry about a rogue wave filling my breathing tube. There was also another very strong advantage. I was able to see what was around me and this removed much of my fear of the sharks that I knew were nearby.

My Indian host stayed very close to me for the first ten minutes. We swam amongst delicate sea fans that waved casually in the warm sea breeze. All movement seemed to be in resonant harmony with the passage of delicate waves high above our head. Huge shoals of rainbow-tinged fish engulfed my very presence and purple coloured parrot fish kissed the water in front of my nose. Evil looking moray eels caught my attention as they eyeballed me from crevices in the coral wall. In every direction there were coral gardens, majestic and full of colour. They were heavily populated with perfect examples of stag and elkhorn coral which in turn hosted small groups of tiny angel fish.

Suddenly my host tapped my shoulder and then he left to help another diver who was having trouble with his ears. Only then did I realise that we had slowly followed the contour of the seabed down to forty feet. I carried on by myself and marvelled at everything before me. Everything was so colourful and crystal clear. It looked so different to anything that I had previously observed when looking through the wall of a glass bottomed boat. Eventually my Indian returned and signalled that it was time to return to the surface. We all gathered together and after making a brief decompression stop he took us safely to the surface.

This dive gave me tremendous confidence for what was to come. We motored down the reef to an area known as Shark Ray Alley. This was where the locals fed reef shark and sting rays to keep them in a pre-defined area for the pleasure of adrenalin-seeking tourists such as myself. I intended this to be a once in a lifetime, never to be repeated, shark experience.

The sharks were much larger than the young Americans in our party had expected and they were cruising all around our boat in expectation of the fish scraps that were about to be thrown to them. The Americans were in the company of several girls and I am sure they all wanted to demonstrate their male bravado, but one of them refused to budge from his position where he had lodged himself firmly in the scuppers of the boat. I assumed that if these reef sharks and stingrays really were dangerous then we would not have been allowed to dive with them. My only prayer was that no strangers came to feed on that day.

I sat on the edge of our small boat and fell backwards into the water. I felt more than water when I plunged into the sea. I landed across a reef shark and it must have been more frightened than me because it quickly rushed away. After a few seconds the air bubbles cleared away and I could see sharks all around me. They were circling around waiting to be fed. We were in a large valley of sand that lay between distant walls of coral. I swam deeper so that I could look upwards and more easily spot the sharks and then I began to feel as if I was the predator.

Two dozen large stingrays swam slowly by. They moved gracefully through the water and several brushed along the underside of my bare belly. Their long barbed tails swayed in the moving water and I stayed as still as I could to ensure that they did not feel threatened in any way. They didn't maintain their distance like the sharks and appeared to be a much greater threat. This was confirmed 12 years later when Crocodile Hunter Steve Irwin was killed by the stabbing barb of a stingray. Despite this my confidence was growing rapidly and then, in the distance, I saw a diver desperately waving me off. As I backed away, wondering why he should be so concerned, chunks of bloody red fish started to hit the surface and suddenly three dozen reef shark went into a feeding frenzy. Yes, it was time for me to rejoin the boat.

The other divers told me about the Blue Hole which lay 80 miles off the coast. It is supposed to be one of the most famous dives in the world. As soon as we returned to the beach I visited a guide who advertised that he was organising a trip to the Blue Hole on the following day. He was an Englishman who previously served with the Royal Marines at the Belize Jungle Training Camp. He liked Ambergris Caye so much that he returned after being de-mobbed and married a local girl.

He refused to allow me to dive the Blue Hole and when I told him that the Indian further down the beach had taken me diving without a paddy certificate he was furious. In the end we reached a compromise and he said that he would arrange for me to snorkel around a small coral atoll which was close to the Blue Hole.

The power boat that took us out to Lighthouse Reef was operated by a shifty looking character and the boat itself resembled a very powerful drug runner. It had three large outboard motors and we soon clocked up the miles. Amongst our party were four young girls in very skimpy bikinis, and two very experienced guys who looked as if they were diving in a James Bond movie; one even carried a cruel looking dagger. Then there was the dive master, an Indian fisherman and me. The sun was still very low on the horizon and we all huddled together to keep warm; all except Scaramanga, who kneeled by the rail and wished that he had stayed at home. His face was as white as a sheet and he struggled to overcome his terrible seasickness.

We sped past two remote coral atolls and gazed through squinted eyes at scenery which could only be described as out of this world. It was absolutely stunning. The sea was crystal clear and carried a tint of blue which swiftly changed to emerald green as we passed across the shoals. Several sand banks emerged without warning and our experienced skipper navigated through the quebradas with a skill that was probably used for more than 'diver' running.

We raced across a deep channel and then passed through further shallows close to the Lighthouse Reef. A large fish resembling a swordfish began to follow us. It was incredibly fast. It darted through the shallows beside us and occasionally jumped high out of the water or simply skipped along on the surface of our wash. It followed for several minutes before breaking away and diving back into deeper water.

As we approached the Blue Hole our skipper stopped the boat and gave me my snorkelling equipment. Without a second thought I jumped into the water and the dive master threw a yellow buoyancy bag behind me. The Indian fisherman followed to keep me company and then the boat motored away. We had been left to snorkel over a totally submerged atoll. The clarity of the water was unbelievable. I could see lobsters, a dozen large kingfish, an eagle ray, and shoals of different coloured tropical fish. I had never witnessed such splendour and probably never will again. The fisherman dived 25, perhaps 30 feet to a sand bed that lay below the coral wall and he brought a huge living starfish to the surface. Then he stiffened and pointed towards several huge barracuda.

He was not very happy, and if a fisherman is not happy in the water, then I decided that I should not be happy either. I looked around for the dive boat just in case we needed an escape route. It had passed over the horizon and there was no land or even a sandbar anywhere to be seen. It suddenly dawned upon me that we were swimming in tropical waters more than 50 miles from the mainland and our boat had left us to fend for ourselves with nothing more than one buoyancy aid. What if the barracuda attacked, or worse still, a bull shark or some other nasty predator turned up. I began to believe that I would have been safer diving the Blue Hole.

The fisherman continued to watch the barracuda and the barracuda continued to watch him. My fear of sharks did not extend to barracuda. I had encountered them on many previous occasions and they had never troubled me. But the fisherman was very frightened; he said that I must not turn my back on them. He said that he had fished these waters all of his life and barracuda were his worst and most distrusted enemy. I ignored the barracuda and carried on searching through the stag horn and brain coral that lay deep beneath us. They didn't bother us but the concern of my Indian friend did make me aware of our vulnerable situation. If a shark did come I would have no escape route and this was unacceptable. I always had a plan and I lived life on what I called the 'What if Scenario'. On this occasional the only answer to my scenario was to pray.

The Blue Hole is a cavern that was formed long before water covered this part of the Central American land mass. It is a 120 ft dive straight down the centre of the hole and then a further 100 ft horizontally beneath the cavern ceiling. This is a very serious dive by any standards and I was deeply impressed that four young girls made this dive and lived to enjoy the experience. When they eventually returned to pick up two very tired and badly sunburned bodies from the middle of the Caribbean Sea they were bubbling with excitement.

Three of them were eager to tell me about their incredible experience while the fourth huddled in a corner with a towel wrapped around her shoulders. She had found the water in the cavern to be extremely cold and suffered some kind of panic attack which prevented her from breathing correctly. She couldn't swim to the surface because she was deep inside the cavern and even then she had to observe at least two decompression stops. The dive master detected her condition and knew how to deal with it. He had managed to calm her and they both returned safely to the surface. He saved her life.

We settled down in the boat for the long ride back, and again, we huddled together for warmth. This time we were both wet and cold and, instead of rising, the sun was falling slowly out of the sky. After an hour we noticed that the skipper had been watching a small blip on his radar screen. His boat was surprisingly well equipped for a dive boat. He passed a powerful pair of binoculars to the dive master and asked him to identify the boat that was bearing down on us. It was a US Coastguard Cutter. After a positive identification the skipper, to everyone's surprise, opened his throttles wide and we surged ever faster across the smooth surface of Belize territorial waters.

We matched the Cutter's speed and together we raced through seas slowly darkening as the sun fell quickly and more urgently towards the horizon. In a last show of defiance the sun god Atum turned blood red and surged across the sea before Osiris took reign. The Skipper used his experience to find a quebradas, a narrow break in the reef. He raced through fully expecting the Cutter to follow. It was at this point that the Cutter turned broadside and dropped a rubber dinghy into the water.

The dinghy was extremely fast, just like an inshore lifeboat. It hurtled after us and cut our escape by crossing the reef. Our Skipper pulled into a small wooden quay on a nearby coral island and quickly left the boat. The complete chase had been around sixty minutes. We remained in the back of the boat and behaved as dumb as possible. Six fully armed marines climbed out of the dinghy and stood-to while their Commander interviewed our Skipper who was enjoying a rum and coke at the Sand Bar.

The Skipper obviously knew the shallows very well and he knew that he could make this wooden quay before he was caught. I guessed that this was not the first time that he had out-run the US Coastguard and it would not be the last. We were in Belize territorial waters and he knew that the US Coastguard could not arrest him unless drugs were actually found on board. I don't think that the Skipper was having fun at the expense of the Coastguard. I am convinced that this was part of a deliberate plan to make it very difficult for the Coastguard to know when he was carrying divers and when he was carrying drugs. After a short time he rejoined us and we put back to sea and returned safely to Ambergris Caye with one more exciting story to tell our grandchildren.

Yucatan Peninsula, Mexico

Two months later, January 1995, Anne and I took a holiday in Cancun on the Yucatan Peninsula in Mexico. Our holiday was most enjoyable. We visited the El Castillo Pyramid in Chichen Itza and walked around the barbaric walled ball court where Spanish Conquistadors once found a kind of netball being played. Three small differences were recorded to the English game; there was only one net, the game lasted several days and the losing team was beheaded.

We also visited Xcaret where a Mayan seaport existed for more than a thousand years. Mexican authorities had developed the area into a fantastic nature reserve which afforded a totally different kind of experience for those who wished to enjoy a fantastic holiday in complete touch with nature.

We swam half a mile through an underground stream and stayed late into the evening to watch a light and sound extravaganza that was presented on water in front of a vast cavern. Scores of singers, musicians and actors portrayed the history of Xcaret from the early days of Mayan Civilization. The singers had magnificent voices which rebounded from the walls of the cavern. I felt as if I had been warped through time and that I was actually witnessing real events as they occurred. I was witnessing the death of a once proud civilization. It was an emotional evening and I am sure the lead singers, of which there were many, would have raised several encores in the Albert Hall.

The following day I left Anne to soak up the sun on the beaches of Cancun and I flew in a light aircraft to the Mexican border town of Chetumal. From there I was able to walk across the Rio Bravo and into Belize where I had arranged for a Sugar Company driver to take me to Orange Walk. This was a much more sensible route into Belize. It avoided all the hassle of passing through the United States airport border controls.

The control system was working very well and I commissioned various pieces of equipment that had been ordered as extras. However, the real purpose of my visit was to look after the workers; to give them a little extra training and to take them for a night on the town. And what a night out it was!

We piled into two old cars and set off for Chetumal, the Mexican border town that I had just left. We arrived late in the evening and enjoyed a meal of enchillados and huachinango in a small tavern overlooking the Caribbean Sea. Then these crazy guys that I was with, and they really were crazy, took me to a cantina on the edge of the rainforest. It looked like and was a real cantina; just the same as a movie set in one of John Ford's films. It had a very large square bar where Mexican beer and tequila was served by girls with large bosoms and low cut dresses.

Loud Mexican music played while naked girls danced on the bar and solicited peso notes from my open mouthed hosts. Needless to say all of the peso notes had all been provided by yours truly. Behind and above our heads was a balcony that surrounded the inside walls of the cantina. There were several doors leading to private rooms and scantily clad girls beckoned to us from the balcony rail. They tried to encourage my hosts to participate in the obvious pleasures that were on offer but I made it very clear that I was prepared to pay for the meals, for the drinks, even for the girls dancing on the bar; but no more than that. To be fair to my hosts, they had a lot of fun but none climbed those sixteen wooden stairs.

Horus had taken control of the rising sun by the time we emerged from the cantina and everyone decided that they were hungry again. Nothing ever seemed to close for the night in Chetumal and we re-visited our tavern on the beach where we filled our stomachs with tostas. This helped to absorb the alcohol we had consumed and after two huge cups of coffee we set off for Orange Walk. We were stopped several times by heavily armed soldiers but they were not too bothered with us. If we had been drug runners we would have been driving north. The fact that both of our drivers were stoned was of no concern to them.

It was only a short distance to the Rio Bravo and when we arrived at the border posts both the Mexican and the Belize border guards were fast asleep; we raised both barriers and passed through unhindered. Two days later I returned to the Rio Bravo and the Belize border guards would not let me through. I had not entered the country so how could I possibly leave? I explained that I had entered during the night and that everyone was fast asleep. They realised that I was telling the truth and so they came up with a logical solution. Even Spock of Startrek fame would have been proud of them.

They held my suitcase while I walked across the bridge to obtain an exit stamp from bewildered guards on the Mexican side. I then returned and they stamped my passport with a Belize entry stamp. "Now Gringo", they said in a good natured way, "we can now see that you have entered Belize so we can let you leave, here is your suitcase". The Mexican guards were in stitches by the time I had tramped back across the bridge and obtained my fourth and final stamp.

I flew back to Cancun and rejoined Anne. From there we drove down to the island of Cozumel where we suffered an interesting but very uncomfortable 'gee gee' ride through the rain forest. I spent most of my time ducking under branches; my horse refused to follow directions and kept leaving the track to beat a new route through the undergrowth.

Our working holiday was drawing to a close, but my brief adventure in drug running territory was not quite over. On our last day we sailed past a drug runner's boat that was about to be boarded by the Mexican Coast Guard. The skipper set fire to his boat and we watched as the boat and its cargo of evidence burned. The charred hulk finally gave way and an hour later it sank to join Davey Jones's locker. This was a fitting climax to my adventures in Central America.

Chapter 21

Kenyan Sugar, Not so Sweet

Returning to a very different Kenya 28 years on
Death and unprecedented corruption!

I had a fortunate break with an engineering company called Booker Tate, and with their help, I won a series of contracts to design and manufacture new control panels and instrument calibration workshops for the Mumias Sugar Factory in Western Kenya. These orders were later repeated for the Nakambala Sugar Factory in the Zambezi Valley and this opened up a totally new area of business for Coulton; sugar refining.

When I visited Mumias Sugar for the first time in 1995 I found that 40 thousand people lived or worked on the sugar plantations and around 12 thousand died each year from aids, typhoid or malaria. I found these figures difficult to comprehend and suspect that they may be exaggerated. However, from a percentage perspective, I can say that I trained sixteen people to operate my boiler control system and four years later they were all dead or dying.

I knew that these terrible conditions existed in remote areas of Africa but this was my first personal experience. The native population, many skilled workers, accepted fate as a normal part of their short existence and every day a friend told me that one of his children had passed away during the night. What did she die of? "I don't know baas; she was just tired and I didn't have any money to buy medicine".

I hated mosquitoes at the best of times. Their bites itched like hell and they carried so many different diseases. An infected mosquito could carry malaria, heartworm, dengue fever, encephalitis, yellow fever and possibly even aids, although this is denied by the medical profession. A new kind of drug resistant cerebral malaria was sweeping through the sugar plantations and every expatriate in Mumias had contracted the disease. The Mumias factory doctor had cured them with a powerful Chinese drug which offered a good, if not a complete lifetime cure. These drugs were not approved in the UK and so the same doctor gave me a supply to take home with hand-written instructions on how my wife should administer them.

While I worked in Mumias I smothered myself in mosquito cream during the day and then retired to the safety of my mosquito net when it became dark. Dawn and dusk are the periods when these winged vampires hunt for fresh blood and I was determined not to give them more opportunity than absolutely necessary. As soon as my work in Mumias was finished, I was gone! Fortunately I never had cause to use my supply of rather powerful drugs.

A pink haze spread across Lake Nakuru

The following year, in October 1996, I rented a car and returned to Mumias with Anne. It was a dangerous drive. There were bandits in the suburbs of Nairobi and overloaded taxis careered recklessly down both sides of the road. I may have survived a direct hit by one of these dangerous rattletraps but I could not avoid the numerous potholes that hammered at the poor shock absorbers of my hired car.

Kenya had been the safest and most visited tourist destination in Colonial Africa. Westminster once showcased the government of Jomo Kenyata as the model for all newly emerging independent countries within the British Commonwealth. Such things dreams are made of! Kenya had deteriorated enormously since my first visit 28 years earlier. President Daniel Arap Moi replaced Kenyata on his deathbed and bled the country dry through corruption and criminally bad governance. Almost all United Nations aid had found its way into the wrong pockets and the country could no longer maintain the most basic of services.

As we drove through the Rift Valley the sun sank below the escarpment and then in its last dying moments we were surprised by a pink haze that spread across Lake Nakuru. We turned back and checked into a small roadside inn. The following morning we rose early and drove around the lake. Half a million lesser flamingos were illuminated in the fresh beams of the early morning African sun. They stained the shallow soda lake a bright shade of pink. Pelicans and the occasional marabou stork waded close to the shore and when they took to the air a thousand followed; wing tips gently disturbing the smooth water as their huge bodies rose gracefully into the shimmering horizon.

In the background a totally unexpected collection of wild animals gathered. There were buffalo, lion, white rhino, giraffe and several species of antelope; all co-existing in a very small area. As we drove around the far shore a giant tortoise lay on its back, legs flailing in the air. It had somehow rolled down a bank and ended the wrong side up. I considered the possibility of making a large cauldron of hot tortoise soup, but relented and rolled it carefully back onto its feet.

After working for a short time in Mumias we enjoyed a plate of tilapia from Lake Victoria and then set off for the Maasai Mara game reserve. Unfortunately the rains had already started and it was not long before we had to turn back. We drove overnight and most of the following day back to Nairobi and boarded a light aircraft which flew us straight into our camp at Mara Serena.

This was Anne's first visit to a game reserve of this size. We spent several days driving along the Mara River looking for glimpses of the wild animals that drank from its waters. There were huge herds of wildebeest and zebra; black-maned lion unique to the Maasai Mara, buffalo, rhino, crocodile and the most dangerous of them all; the bad tempered hippo.

On one hot afternoon we stood for hours waiting for a leopard to emerge from a reed bed. Eventually Anne spotted it running through tall grass and I pointed my video camera in the general direction. My eyes were better than Anne's and I was sure that she was mistaken. When we replayed the video in slow motion I had to apologise for having doubted her.

We passed several small herds of elephant, but these were not the magnificent beasts that I remembered from my earlier days in Africa. They were small and timid and their tusks were underdeveloped. Our guide explained how the bulls that carried large tusks had been killed by poachers or by white hunters in the '60s and '70s. This reduced the breeding stock, and just as with dairy cattle, fine bulls were needed to strengthen the herd.

I could understand how over-hunting, or even culling, could reduce the size or number of herds. But this was one aspect that I had not considered before. Selected hunting of the larger and stronger animals damaged the breed. It is logical that this should happen but to witness a real example before, and then 28 years after, is something that very few people have done.

The Great Rift Valley is the cradle of mankind where human form began to develop four million years ago. Yet here on its high escarpment still lives a group of unique people who are finally beginning to lose a long battle to retain their identity. These are the proud peoples of the ancient Maasai tribe. The unique identity and ancient culture of the Maasai will eventually be the cause of their inevitable demise. Jet travel enables tourists to visit Africa in ever increasing numbers and the lifestyle of the Maasai herdsmen is being corrupted as they leave their Enkangs to dance in the plush lounges of tourist lodges in the many game reserves. This problem is exacerbated by the technocrats in Nairobi who have taken away their right to use ancient salt licks or to graze their well-tended long horn cattle across the great Mara plain.

One evening we spotted a huge glow on the horizon. The following morning Anne and I drove southwards to investigate the source of the fire, which was very close to the border with Tanzania. We found that Maasai herdsmen had stolen secretly across the valley to allow their cattle to use a salt lick in the game reserve. When they drove their cattle back to the safety of their Enkang, which was high on the escarpment and overlooking the Mara plain, they burned the long dry grass behind them. This drives snakes away and encourages the growth of fresh green grazing grass for their next visit to their life giving salt lick. Park Rangers had already been deployed to intercept these Maasai Herdsmen, but the Rangers were sympathetic to their plight and I suspect that they turned a blind eye.

After witnessing this timeless event we drove to the invisible border between Kenya and Tanzania. We searched for the line which had been drawn into the sand by civil servants at the Berlin conference of 1885. Perhaps these minions did not know of the Mara plain or of the Maasai tribe that had lived there since ancient times. Now and for all time the Maasai, like so many other African tribes, have to live in two countries and under the influence of two separate western-style governments. No one bothered to ask them if this was what they wanted. Yet Britain still elected to follow this old colonial example as late as 1980 when it gave independence to a ruthless Shona dominated government in what is now called Zimbabwe.

Our guide took us to a small concrete marker post. I very much doubt that the Maasai could have read the small notice inscribed on each side, and if they could, they would not have taken any notice of it. I stood nervously on Tanzanian soil and proudly announced that I was now in the Serengeti National Park. I looked cautiously around for a Customs Officer, worried that he might seize my camera, but the only primate interested was a small inquisitive vervet monkey.

During my next visit to Mumias Sugar I drove south to Kisii and purchased three huge stone sculptures; an elephant, a rhino and a giraffe. I had no idea how I was going to get them back to England. One piece alone weighed fifty pounds. My agent in Kisumu solved my problem by bribing the porter to place my heavy boxes into the aircraft hold without passing them through check-in. I was very unhappy with this arrangement. I was flying in a light aircraft and every piece of excess weight should have been carefully weighed to ensure that we were within maximum take-off weight.

When I arrived at the British Airways desk in Nairobi I thought that the check-in girl would refuse to accept my stone sculptures; she could not even lift them from the weighing scales. I decided to take a chance and slipped a fifty dollar bill into my ticket holder. No problem sir! She weighed my boxes, recorded the correct weights on her computer and then asked a porter to take them to the loading area. Good old British Airways!

White water rafting in Uganda

I continued to win small orders in Western Kenya and each order usually required a visit to Kisumu. I continued to be very cautious in my short visits to Mumias and on my last visit the Chief Engineer and the Electrical Engineer were both undergoing treatment for re-occurring malaria. I stayed two nights and then visited the Kigali Sugar Factory in nearby Uganda.

This short visit gave me a golden opportunity to go white water rafting on the upper reaches of the Nile. I thought the chances of ending up in the river were extremely small and our helmsman assured me that the large crocodiles we observed earlier in the day could not be found below the hydro-electric dam. Still, my host refused to join me, and after a short training period I set off down the river with a small party of youngsters who were working with Voluntary Service Overseas.

Never ending up in the river; what a stupid expectation! The very first rapid was only rated class 3 and yet the raft turned over and dumped us into a volatile fuming churning white surge of water that seemed to have no interface with the world of the living. I rolled into a tight ball, just as we had been trained; my head was rammed tightly between my knees and I prayed that a jagged rock would not lunge out and tear at my exposed spine. My lungs were already bursting and the boiling water contained thousands of entrained air bubbles which destroyed my buoyancy. Not even my very substantial life jacket could pull me to the surface.

When I thought that I would surely die I unfurled my body and looked through the murky swirling water for a glimpse of the sun. I saw it six feet above my left hip and I struck out for the surface in a last fit of desperation. I had barely cleared the edge of the rapids, and when I looked around, I could see our helmsman counting each colourful helmet as it burst from the depths of despair. It took several minutes to get everyone back into the boat again. We almost suffered a mutiny because several wanted to put ashore. I took one look at the riverbank. It was impenetrable rainforest and I knew there was no alternative. We had to carry on.

The next set of rapids was the highest survivable grade, a class 5. We each took tight hold of our wooden paddle and thrust deep and hard into the wall of fast flowing water. Our helmsman, a lithe muscular New Zealander with long brown hair and very dark sunburned skin, yelled instructions above the thunderous roar of the river. He used his small oar to keep the raft astride a ridge of smooth water that ripped through the centre channel. Huge boulder formations punched in our direction; first from the right and then from the left. A southpaw caught us unexpected and then suddenly we were in clear water, shouting and waving our paddles in jubilation. We had lost the first round but the second was ours. We each suffered a massive rush of adrenalin and relief was evident on more than one strained face.

Seven more were to go before the day would finish. Four were class 5 and we ended up in the river on three separate and very desperate occasions. At the end of our enjoyable but very frightening day we gathered on the river bank and each of us, including non-drinkers, downed a huge plastic cup of locally distilled fire water. It was extremely potent stuff but essential to kill the dangerous bugs now swimming around in our gut. No one argued, and to be absolutely certain, many of us enjoyed a more leisurely sip from a second cup.

A mega-jump in our engineering capability

The control panels that we manufactured for Mumias Sugar occupied a large section of our store room and it was obvious that we needed to increase our factory space. We decided that the time was right to make a mega-jump in our engineering capability and we began to manufacture our own range of primary flow devices, thermowells and valve switch boxes. At the same time I rented an additional unit on the Christchurch airfield and fitted it out for the assembly and wiring of control panels. With the purchase of software design tools and recruitment of qualified project engineers, Coulton was then able to assume total responsibility for the engineering and supply of complete process measurement and control systems.

This capability was swiftly recognised by the British Steel Corporation and they awarded Coulton a very large contract to supply all field instrumentation and primary elements for the Queen Bess Blast Furnace. One year later they awarded a second contract for the Queen Victoria Blast Furnace. These contracts signalled our entry into a new field of operation. Large process engineering companies were now beginning to recognise Coulton as a major contractor with the ability to provide single source responsibility for the supply of all field instrumentation products.

Several large companies added Coulton to their approved vendors' lists and awarded us major contracts. This included BP, Esso, Glaxo, Nestle, Bechtel, Foster Wheeler, British Nuclear Fuels, Rolls Royce and Severn Trent. Our specialist skills even helped to add our two biggest competitors, Honeywell and Fisher Rosemount, to our customer data base. I was thrilled to become a supplier to my competitors and one time employers.

It was during this stage of our development that we bid Able Instruments for the field instrumentation on the Azerbaijan Oil Pipeline. This was the largest single project in the world and we were on cloud nine when we were included in the approved list of qualified vendors. The political climate was very tense because the pipeline was being routed around those territories controlled by Russia, and in particular, Chechnya.

Bidding for a project of this size did have mixed blessings. It was very costly and several of my engineers would be occupied for many weeks in each of the bidding processes. This removed valuable resources from our bread and butter work. There were sometimes as many as sixteen companies in the first round and this was usually reduced to the three strongest technical bids. The Purchasing Manager then took over and he often tried to make a name for himself by pressurizing the three remaining companies into reviewing their prices. This made a mockery of sealed bids and often the Company who reduced his price would win. This process of squeezing the last three was not only unfair but it reduced the successful bidder's ability to provide good after sales support.

I have seen suppliers accept orders with less than sixty dollars profit per unit on fiscal metering transmitters that measured crude oil throughput of several million dollars per day. This margin is much to low for suppliers to provide the level of technical support necessary for such important instruments. The Buyers Purchasing Manager may have saved a few dollars by squeezing the Seller but he passed a serious support problem to his Production Manager who stood to lose millions if his new transmitter failed to work correctly. I was always distressed when Companies took this short-sighted nit-picking approach and I am certain that I am not alone in my view that the Senior Executives of these companies need to redefine their purchasing standards to ensure that a more equitable balance is achieved between cost of purchase and cost of ownership.

We had just finished another good year and 1997 looked even better. I even began to hope that our target of four million could be achieved within four years. Even perhaps before the end of the millennium. Wouldn't it be great? I looked for new markets to develop and Pat Gilbert, a Londoner, approached me at exactly the right time; or so I thought!

Pat enjoyed tremendous success while representing engineering companies in the Tiger Economies of South East Asia. This was an area where we thought we could succeed and so I signed an agreement with Pat in February 1997. I had every confidence in Pat's ability to find us business. He reminded me of a Cockney that once sold me a load of wafer-thin blankets in Covent Garden. With his help we put together an ambitious marketing plan for Thailand, Malaysia, Singapore and the Philippines.

I visited Thailand and Malaysia with Pat and we travelled extensively throughout both countries. We visited his excellent range of personal contacts and secured interest at the highest level. Pardon the pun, but this included a meeting at the top of the Petronas Twin Towers, the highest building in the world. Pat and Shahrul Zain of Mafira Energy Resources, our agent in Kuala Lumpur, got us onto the bid list for a large oil refinery project with the Malaysian oil giant Petronas. We put in a strong technical bid and the Lead Engineer informed Shahrul that we had been selected by Petronas to be the preferred supplier for process transmitters. He explained that the Main Contractor was the Toyo Engineering Corporation and he arranged for me to meet with one of their purchasing managers in Tokyo.

I flew the following day to Tokyo and met with Hiroshi Kato, one of their senior purchasing executives and Satoru Suda, a senior instrument engineer. Then my problems started; problems that only a person with an intimate knowledge of Japanese business would understand. Companies in Japan are bound together in groups and each member in that group has a symbiotic relationship with the other. For example, a large engineering company in one particular group will always do business with the same bank, the same instrument manufacturer, the same shipper, even the same geisha house. Unfortunately it appeared that Fuji Electric were not a member of the group that Toyo Engineering belonged to. My host in Tokyo had never been visited by a sales representative of Fuji Electric and any hope of closing my first ever multi-million dollar order slowly slipped from my grasp.

A few days after my return from Tokyo I found that someone had leaked information about my bid and Rosemount reduced their own pricing by such a huge amount that Petronas had no choice but to withdraw their support. I was told later that Rosemount considered my threat to their traditional market in Malaysia to be so serious that they intended to prevent me from gaining a foothold, no matter the cost. There is no honour in business and I lost the project.

Shortly after this escapade the Asian financial crisis took hold and my brief foray into South East Asia came to an abrupt close. I drew back to lick my wounds and again turned my attention towards Central America and the Caribbean.

I forgot about the piranhas

Thorne International was extremely pleased with our work in Belize and they retained my personal services as a consultant to prepare a report for the Guyana Sugar Corporation. Guyana Sugar had placed an order with a well known process automation company to supply several new control systems for the high pressure steam boilers on their Albion Works. These systems did not function in accordance with the original design parameters and I was asked to provide a report on the system design and recommend a course of action to make their steam boilers safe.

I found this to be a ridiculous situation. Guyana had paid six times the price they would have paid if they purchased a working control system from Coulton. Now Coulton was being asked to recommend a course of action to make these systems work. The facts were very simple. The system was extremely expensive and terribly over-designed. I don't know who prepared the enquiry specification but the strategies employed were extremely complex and very difficult to implement in a remote industrial environment. In addition the control algorithms were configured within a single control module which made it hard for their commissioning engineers to isolate individual problems. I was convinced that the system must have been designed by engineers who had never worked in a third world environment.

While I was on-site I noticed that several of the critical control loops were not operating correctly and the operators preferred to leave these loops in manual operation. On several occasions the boiler water level fell to a dangerous condition and the operators had to respond quickly to correct the situation. To be blunt, these control systems were downright dangerous! I completed my work and left the operational area as quickly as possible.

When I returned to England I produced a very comprehensive report and recommended a course of action to Thorne International. Unfortunately, there was no senior decision maker at Guyana Sugar who would take ownership of their control system problems, and to the best of my knowledge no corrective action was ever taken. I would have loved to have picked up the baton but Guyana Sugar had burned their fingers once and it was unlikely that they would ever upgrade any of their remaining factories. Coulton could have upgraded the steam boilers on every sugar factory in Guyana for the cost of the one system installed at Albion. And our control strategies would have worked!

I was not upset by the lack of interest shown by my otherwise generous hosts. Guyana is a country of exceptional natural beauty. The picturesque capital and Caribbean port of Georgetown has an abundance of fine colonial buildings, broad tree-lined boulevards and a system of narrow Dutch-built canals. Most of the striking wooden architecture is reminiscent of Guyana's centuries as a Dutch, and then a British colony. The most imposing of these is St. George's Cathedral and the Dean remarked during my brief visit that it is reputed to be the tallest wooden building in the world.

I enjoyed several days absorbing the atmosphere of this old town. I walked through the smelly fish market on the side of the Demerara River and rummaged through artefacts in the old market hall. As I walked along one of the un-tarred streets a large black guy came hurtling along the sidewalk on a bicycle and he called to me "get out of my way white boy". I had travelled in hundreds of ex-colonial towns and this was the first time that I had ever been on the receiving end of racist taunts. It was funny in a strange kind of way.

Life in Guyana is dominated by mighty rivers, including the Demerara, the Berbice and the Essequibo, which provide essential highways into the rain forests and jungles of the interior. I didn't have sufficient time to set out on such a journey and I elected to take a light aircraft. Our first landing was at Kaieture falls. We flew for several hours over a solid never-ending canopy which lay like a bright green shroud over the Guyana Rainforest. I became concerned that we should fly over such densely wooded terrain with only one engine. When I discussed this with my pilot he said that they had only suffered a couple of engine failures in recent years. This did nothing to improve my confidence level.

After a couple of hours we landed on a small dirt strip that had been cut into the forest. I disembarked and joined an Indian Ranger who eagerly awaited our arrival. He took us to a small ledge that jutted out from the Pakaraima Plateau and we watched the mighty Potaro River plunge 800 feet into a witches' cauldron that lay precariously before us. The old wench herself tried to pull us from our perch as we took dozens of photographs while standing dangerously close to its slippery edge.

Kaieture is reputed to be the highest single drop water fall in the world, five times the height of Niagara. However, Angel Falls in nearby Venezuela is the true holder of this title; a much smaller volume of water falls 3000 ft from the Auyantepuy Plateau; a lost world made famous by Sir Arthur Conan Doyle. Nevertheless, the magnificence of Kaieture stands beyond any comparison in its majesty and sheer size.

I walked along a narrow jungle trail which weaved through the rainforest and marvelled at the different hardwood trees that reached high above me. I tasted liquorice and smelled incense. The Ranger pointed out dozens of trees which Shamans had used to produce raw medicines long before any modern chemist discovered their true healing powers in refined form. Occasionally I caught a glimpse of the sun breaking through and flashes of scarlet, yellow and blue burst through the forest's intense green as Macaws flew like arrows across clearings in the canopy. I never saw any Toucans but I did see the awesome Harpy Eagle and I was continually haunted by the wild unearthly cries of Howler Monkeys as they chased across the canopy; nature's highway in the Amazonian sun.

"Shsssss"; the Indian Ranger signalled for me to join him. He crouched below a small tree and pointed in the direction of a dead tree stump. It took some time for me to realize what I was looking at; a small orange coloured bird with a large fan shaped crest. It was the Cock-of-the-Rock; a very difficult bird to spot in the wild.

I spent a considerable length of time in conversation with my Indian Ranger and he invited me to return for a much longer period; preferably two weeks. He said that he would take me deep into the forest so that I might meet people who had never seen a white man before. I thought carefully over this invitation, but the thought of sleeping rough on the forest floor with snakes for company, and no access to medical attention, did not appeal to me. On this occasion my fear of snakes overcame my spirit of adventure and I have not, as yet, plucked up enough courage to accept his kind invitation.

Our next landing was at Orinduik Falls where the Ireng River thundered over steps and terraces of solid jasper, a semi precious stone. We were served a late afternoon lunch by several young Indian girls. With the rolling grass covered hills of the Pakaraima Mountains as a backdrop, this was truly one of the most beautiful places in all of Guyana. After lunch I relaxed beneath a cool shower provide by the Orinduik Falls as they tumbled all around me in a small Jacuzzi like pool beneath the steps of Jasper.

Guyana, while firmly on the continent of South America, was still part of the Caribbean and just a few yards from my present position, across the Ireng River, was Brazil. I was never up to swimming the English Channel but I thought that I could better this feat by swimming from the Caribbean to Brazil. I waded into the fast flowing water of the Ireng and looked across to the other bank to ensure that no giant Anaconda was slipping into the water. I gave no consideration to the real threat; piranha. However, I was alone and eventually common sense prevailed. I gave up my foolhardy 'marathon' swim and returned to the Caribbean.

On our long flight back to Georgetown I was distressed when suddenly we emerged from the rainforest. It was not a slow process where the tree density diminished. It was crude and sudden. One moment we were flying across a continuous green canopy, a canopy which provides 20 percent of our oxygen supply. The next minute we were passing over a desert of arid khaki coloured land. Totally devoid of all vegetation, the ground was rocky and without water, not a single tree was standing.

Then I saw the loggers at work, they were raping the land with large yellow bulldozers. They ripped and gouged until every root was pulled from the ground. Anything that was of no use to the loggers they burned. The devastation was so great that a heavy pall of smoke filled the sky and followed us as far as the mighty Demerara River. Why could they not leave tree barriers to prevent soil erosion? Why could they not leave sufficient trees to re-seed themselves? Why could they not leave the trees alone all together? These were the burning questions that future generations will ask.

The Amazon Rainforest has long been a symbol of mystery and power, a sacred link between humans and nature. It is also the richest biological incubator on the planet. It supports millions of plant, animal and insect species. Chemists have extracted secrets that have led to the refining of quinine, muscle relaxants, steroids and cancer drugs while more importantly, new drugs are still awaiting discovery. So alluring are the mysteries of indigenous medical knowledge that over 100 pharmaceutical companies were funding projects to study specific plants used by native shamans and healers.

At the present rate of deliberate destruction the Amazon Rainforest will cease to exist in 50 years. Our oxygen supply will be greatly diminished, carbon dioxide levels will increase, global warming will accelerate and the knowledge of native shamans will be lost forever. World leaders must take corrective measures immediately. Indeed, I suspect that it is already too late.

My pre-paid hotel room is given away again

I routed my return flight to England through Barbados and used this as an opportunity to visit the Barbados Agricultural Management Company (BAMC) outside Bridgetown. When I arrived at my hotel I found that my prepaid room had been given to the highest bidder. How many times has this happened to me before? The receptionist avoided direct eye contact and told me that my name was not in his register; then he quickly turned to his next customer. I asked for his manager, and of course, he was not available. Wherever I stood I was unable to get the receptionist's attention and I wanted to throttle the little rat. I wish I could remember the hotel's name so that I could name and shame its management.

It was the 12th of March 1998. Cricket fundies will recognise this as the first day of the 5th Test Match between England and the West Indies at the Kennington Oval in Bridgetown. Brian Lara and Mike Atherton were kings of the day, depending of course upon one's point of view. The only bed that I could find was shared by sandflies on the beach, and as cricket was the most boring game that I have ever had the misfortune to watch, I decided to re-join the next flight onwards to London.

This gave me half a day to quickly visit Portvale Sugar Factory. I met with the works engineer, John Hepburn, and the production manager, Paul Trayner. It was a pleasure to be received by these two engineers. They gave me a full tour of their bagasse fired steam boilers and explained what measures they wanted to take to increase the quality and reliability of steam supply to their sugar production facility. Afterwards, Paul's gorgeous Australian wife, Monica, took me for a quick swim in the local marine park and then drove me directly to the airport for my overnight flight to England. I remember that we were startled by two sea snakes that swam close to us and for those who are interested, it was a draw, but the West Indies won the series and retained the Wisden Cup.

This was to be the shortest and most successful sales visit that I ever made. It was a breath of fresh air meeting with good engineers who knew what they wanted and had the determination to make it happen. John asked me to provide a full quotation for the design, supply, installation and commissioning for the two bagasse fired boilers at their Portvale Factory. While I was preparing my quotation the purchasing department of BAMC secured two competitive bids and secured references for my work from Alan Sharpe in Belize. The old boy network in the international sugar industry worked for me again. One month later I received a huge order to refurbish the two bagasse fired boilers at Portvale and a further two at their Andrews factory.

The Portvale and Andrews factories were very similar to those that I upgraded in Belize, and I used my earlier experience to be more selective in my choice of instrumentation. I refused to consider the installation of another multiplexed supervisory system and, fortunately, Paul preferred paperless recorders. I also made several other small changes which gave significant improvements to the cost of ownership.

Paul and John accepted my recommendations and they built a large air-conditioned control room to house my equipment on the main operating floor. I then built four identical control panels in our new panel shop in Christchurch and shipped them to Barbados where they arrived in good condition and on-time. I could not believe how smoothly everything had gone.

I shipped one of my young engineers, Chris Merritt, to supervise the installation work. It was his first on-site assignment and his first trip to the Caribbean. I threw him in at the deep end but we all have to start sometime. Chris has one strong advantage; he is a likeable and very easy going person. This is essential when working with Caribbean nationals and the Baijan workers accepted him and made him their own. Chris liked it so much in Bridgetown that he over-ran his schedule and I was so concerned that he would never return to England that I flew out to join him just before the beginning of the 1999 sugar campaign.

I found Chris lying on a hammock and reading a book in John Hepburn's beachside house. His legs were heavily bandaged. Chris had worked late one evening and he cooled off with a few bottles of Banks which he chased down with a sniff of Mount Gay Rum before falling asleep on the beach. The sand flies took one look at his virgin white flesh and feasted on the exposed portion of his legs while he slept as soundly as a new born baby. Three days later Chris was on the verge of septicaemia and the local doctor had to dress his swollen legs and administer a very heavy dose of penicillin.

Anne and I made several visits to Barbados during the construction period and also during the early days of the 1999 sugar campaign. On one of my visits a local fisherman invited me to join him for the day. We loaded my friend's small open boat with a large plastic drum of fresh fish which he had caught the day before, and then we motored out to a position 12 miles offshore, which he said would take full account of wind and tide. John had a very experienced eye and he seemed to be able to smell where the shoals of fish would be. It was around 6 am.

We pounded his dead fish in the open plastic drum and added sea water until they were mashed into a kind of cold fish stew and then stuffed five miles of hemp rope into the drum. This rope absorbed the flavour of the fish; it is known by local fishermen as a trash line. Five miles before we reached his targeted fishing area we started to throw the trash line into the water and when it was all paid out we stopped the outboard and allowed ourselves to drift.

First we deployed seven small drift nets and then we seeded the water around us with what was left of the fish stew. After enjoying a short breakfast we started to fish with hand lines and in seconds we were pulling fish aboard. They came in all shapes and sizes. John was very concerned that a shark might follow the fish towards our boat and damage his nets; he said that this often happened, but not today.

One hour later John decided it was time to recover the drift nets. One by one we pulled them in and removed hundreds of flying fish that were trapped in the small mesh. After clearing all seven nets we cast them back into the water and started to recover the 5 miles of trash line. This was a real eye opener for me. As we pulled the hemp rope towards us several hundred flying fish followed and swam straight into the drift nets. This provided a further and very substantial bonus which almost doubled the days catch.

After sorting the catch into different drums we estimated that we had around 2,300 flying fish and 60 mixed tropical fish, which we had caught on lines. We then set out for shore but still John had not finished. Every minute and every mile travelled was a valuable opportunity to be exploited. He fixed one of his tropical fish onto a huge barbed hook and threw it off the back of his boat on a short heavy duty line. We were not lucky that day but later in the week I saw him return with a 7 ft shark tied to the side of his small boat.

When we returned to the rickety wooden pier close to John's home in Speightstown I was burned to a frazzle and salt was making my skin uncomfortable. I stank of fish and I needed to have a shower. Before I could do this I had to help John carry his catch to the fish market where he received 10 dollars per hundred flying fish. Two days earlier I had paid nine dollars for a plate of two flying fish with peas and brown rice. It was obvious that commercial fishermen were getting a raw deal.

After ridding ourselves of our catch John invited me for a Banks in a small wooden bar and we talked about his unusual fishing methods. He told me that HMS Invincible visited Bridgetown two years earlier and he had to call them on his marine radio to warn them that they were bearing down on his trash line. The Captain, not wanting to cause a diplomatic incident, immediately followed 'International Right of Way Rules' and changed course to pass around the trash line and John's fishing boat.

After establishing his right of way over the Invincible, John then passed his regards through the Ship's Radio Officer to the Flight Deck Chief using terminology that only he would recognise. John received an immediate and very respectful reply. It turned out that this scruffy little barefoot Baijan fisherman, with grey woolly hair and wearing torn shorts and a frayed tee shirt, was the last serving Chief Petty Officer on the flight deck of HMS Ark Royal. This was a strong lesson to me of how a person's appearance can be very deceiving.

My exciting adventures on and beneath the waters of Barbados were still not finished. A few days later Anne and I paid a small fortune to explore the deep water reefs. We didn't have paddy certificates and so there was only one way to do this and Barbados was the place. We bought tickets to join a special submarine which had large and very strong transparent reinforced windows. The submarine sailed to a point off the west coast of Barbados and then dived to a depth of 120 feet. Everything was carried out very professionally and a support vessel tended our position on the surface.

The dive took around forty minutes and we cruised along the wall of two separate coral reefs; one at 40 feet and the other at 80 feet. Fan corals in shades of blue, purple and gold waved gently in the water and hundreds of tropical fish darted by. Occasionally a parrot fish or a puffer came up to one of our windows and ogled at the strange people encased in such a huge plastic cage. The pilot of our submarine sat within a plastic bubble which amplified and distorted the fish that passed before him. He had a large selection of instrument gauges and I enjoyed watching how he used a joystick to guide him through the water in the manner of an aircraft flying through the sky.

A large rusted hulk stretched before us and small fish darted through the many doorways and broken portholes that lay along its heavily barnacled hull. This was the climax of our short adventure in the land of Captain Nemo and we made our way slowly towards the surface where our pilot checked with our tender before breaking surface into a choppy rain-swept Caribbean Sea.

Glasses of sherry and humming birds

We used Bridgetown as a base to visit Venezuela and several of the Caribbean Islands. Anne's uncle Dick was the British Ambassador to Venezuela and we enjoyed the comfort of his elegant yet relatively modern residence in Caracas. We were hosted in the manner fit for a king. Indeed, this was not unexpected because several members of the Royal family and Her Majesty's Government had already signed the guest book. Signed photographs were also in evidence and HRH Diana, Princess of Wales, held pride of place on the grand piano.

Several members of Household were instructed to look after us and it was rather grand when, in the morning, we found that Dick and his wife Angie had already left for work. We entered the huge dining room and found a very long 24 seat solid wood dining table set for two people at one end. We felt terribly important and the service was impeccable. Our places were set with solid silver cutlery and bone china; each piece carrying the Royal Crest of King George VI or Queen Elizabeth II.

The huge gardens displayed an abundance of flowers and we enjoyed our evening glass of sherry while humming birds collected pollen from around our carefully selected position on the porch. Most evenings, as the sun began to fall, two parrots roosted and a woodpecker hammered on an old tree stump that had been left deliberately on the green croquet lawn. Not that it would have been possible to play croquet; Angie had invited the Brownies to set up camp.

While we enjoyed being treated as Royalty, we soon got a hankering to explore Caracas. Unfortunately this was not possible. The residence was heavily guarded and we were not allowed outside the gates. This was understandable; we were only able to visit town on one occasion and that was when Dick and his driver took us for a brief excursion.

After returning to Barbados I worked for a short time and then we travelled to St Lucia, Granada and the Commonwealth of Dominica. We didn't care for the attitude of the people on St Lucia and this suppressed any feeling we had for the natural beauty of the island. We loved the scenery and colour of Granada, otherwise known as the Spice Island, but nothing could match the simple grandeur and beauty of the Commonwealth of Dominica. Tree covered mountains rocketed 5,000 feet into the sky, and hundreds of small crystal clear streams gushed through narrow ravines towards the ocean, with swathes of bright coloured vegetation on all sides. Macaws swooped across deep valleys early in the morning while Dog-head Boas coasted through long sweet smelling sedges that sparkled in the early morning dew. I know, I hate snakes, but at least Boas are not poisonous!

The people of Dominica are among the friendliest in the Caribbean and it is the only island where native Carib Indians can still be found. We spent several days walking in the mountains, looking for Macaws and enjoying the cool crisp air. We climbed Morne Plat Pays to examine the volcanic vents which spew hot water and sulphurous fumes into the air. The Valley of Desolation and the world famous Boiling Lake were five miles away but we were discouraged from making the long trek when we heard of a huge steam explosion. Volcanic activity was high and several minor earthquakes were being felt each day. When we returned from our climb we had to avoid several rocks that were blocking our road.

The owner of a small coffee shop told us that Morne Plat Pays was expected to explode in the near future and I wondered how we would escape if this was a pre-curser to the real thing. I decided to do a little research into local events. The last major cataclysmic eruption was Morne Pelee 30 miles away on the island of Martinique. On the 8th of May 1902 it exploded violently sending a pyroclastic flow of super-heated gas surging down the mountainside at over 100 mph. In less than 3 minutes the lungs of 29,000 people were scorched in the small French colonial city of St Pierre. Only two people survived and one of these was a convict who was incarcerated deep in the prison cells.

This was one of the most catastrophic events in recent history, but I was assured by a vulcanologist that modern technology would give several days' warning of a similar event; just as it did in Montserrat. He told me that six seismographs had been installed around the Morne Plat Pays region and he was monitoring them on a continuous basis. I have to admit that I breathed a sigh of relief when my aircraft flew southwards and the beautiful emerald green mountains of Dominica finally slipped over the horizon.

Chapter 22

A New Pair of Hands

Training a new manager for my succession
The market goes belly-up!

Brian and I worked well together and in 1997 we achieved our highest ever profit margin. We had a mutual understanding that he would eventually move with his family to Christchurch and become my General Manager. Unfortunately when I offered him the position his family was unwilling to move from their home town and again I had to start looking for Mr Right.

This time I decided to target someone that I had known for many years. Coulton had become one of the most respected companies in the supply of measurement and control equipment for specialized applications in steam production and distribution. Our expertise was already to be found on steam boiler applications as far afield as the Ural Mountains, Romania, East Africa, the Caribbean and Central America. There was only one other Company who could better this experience; Spirax Sarco, our largest customer. I therefore targeted Malvern Jones, their steam metering product manager.

I could not simply walk up to him and offer him a job. This would have been very unprofessional and I would have lost the confidence of my best and most valued customer. I approached Peter Michael Smith, the Engineering Director of Spirax, and asked if I could make a formal approach. Peter was pragmatic and he realized that he could not keep hold of Malvern indefinitely. I suggested that it would be more appropriate to lose him to one of his major suppliers rather than a competitor. Peter agreed.

I started Malvern in December 1998 as my General Manager, just in time for our Christmas festivities, and gave him responsibility for all UK operations; I retained control of our export market. Shortly after his recruitment Dorset Business Link invited Coulton to become a member of their Premier Club and they appointed a business consultant to work closely with Malvern. Together they put together a detailed business plan that we hoped would help us to achieve our four million pounds target. Malvern re-allocated our financial resources and the additional investment immediately tugged hard on our bottom line.

We had fourteen international distributors, and with more than five hundred major customers we were strongly represented in almost every industrial sector. Nevertheless, our turnover did not increase, and try as we might, we could not begin to approach our four million pounds target. On paper we looked like a major international operation, but we were not. We were a small but very specialized engineering company that survived by providing excellent customer service.

It took me 32 years to reach Lake Como

Fuji organized their 1999 annual sales conference at Stresa on the western shores of Lake Maggiore in Italy. It was June and the weather was fabulous. Malvern joined Anne and me for his first ever Fuji conference. Our venue was a beautiful old waterfront hotel overlooking the picture-postcard Borromean islands, the most famous of all being Isla Bella with its sumptuous palace and ten terraced gardens created in the style of the Hanging Gardens of Babylon. While we engaged in technical debate Anne took herself into Milan where she was excited to find the newly restored 'Cenacolo' on display in a small monastery. This is better known as 'The Last Supper' by Leonardo da Vinci.

Our conference followed the same routine as we had already followed for so many years in the past. Design engineers from Tokyo explained the advanced features of new innovative products while we tried desperately to explain that we wanted less functionality and more simplicity. As usual our arguments did not sink in.

Young sales engineers that had not taken part in earlier conferences went over old ground and tried to beat the drum on so many subjects that we had raised many times in the past. They showed frustration when their arguments fell on deaf ears and were even more annoyed when the old hands proffered no support. The sad fact was that we had been down the same road so many times before and to no avail. To be fair to Fuji Electric France, they were suffering even more from these problems of communication than we were; their entire bottom line depended upon Fuji manufactured products. Increasingly we found a strong ally in Michel Narche, the General Manager of Fuji Electric France. He and his excellent team from Clermont Ferrand brought a new sense of purpose to our annual meetings.

After the conference finished we travelled across northern Italy to Lake Como. It had taken me 32 years to complete this drive. In my mind's eye it began in 1967 when Marjorie and I drove our little green minivan through France on our first ever holiday. Our target had been Lake Como but our minivan broke down in the Swiss Alps and we never did reach our destination. I was determined to see what we had missed and so we took a ferry along Lake Como to the beautiful town of Bellagio.

Malvern had joined us on the first part of our journey and after leaving Bellagio he returned to the Company's helm in Christchurch. We then continued on our own to Venice and visited the Duke's Palace, enjoyed a romantic gondola ride and took coffee in St Mark's Square. We had both visited Venice in our youth, but never together as a couple. Unfortunately my never-ending back problem re-emerged and I soon found it was very difficult to climb into the boat which passed between our hotel and the ferry landing. Therefore, after doing all of the things that one does when visiting Venice, we set out in the general direction of Malpensa Airport. As always, we had absolutely no idea where we would stay the night. The only fixed item on our agenda was the day and time of our flight back to England.

As we drove westwards Anne recognised the names of several old towns and villages from Shakespearian plays. We decided to stop for the night in a place called Mantua; it has a small historic centre with several medieval buildings and another Duke's palace. We found a bed in an old hotel opposite the palace and Anne, who very rarely enjoys meat, ordered grilled donkey steaks for her evening meal. The following day we drove to Verona where we had a wonderful time. Anne had not realised what a huge and visible legacy the Romans had left behind. She was drawn immediately to the huge arena where operas are now performed. Petite actors have replaced fearsome gladiators of times gone by and penguin breasted musicians play Mozart where lions once roared.

The season was about to open with Tosca in three days' time and this fortuitous opportunity was too good to miss. I booked two stone ledges on the outer lip of the arena; the same parapets that were used by rabble from the lower quarters of the city in Roman times. It was not by accident that I chose the cheapest and most available 'seats' in the arena. My back was still hurting and I intended to convert my stone ledge into a comfortable bed.

Lake Garda stretched far to our north and beyond its northern tip a valley reached high into the Dolomites. I could see on my map that it would be a huge diversion from our route, but I just had to see this spectacular mountain range, and we had three days to kill. We stayed the night in a small guest house on Lake Garda, our third great lake, and then we drove north along its banks and then up the Adige Valley to Trento.

I was very intrigued when the owner of our guesthouse told me how American pilots from a local airbase had often dropped their bombs into the lake after their return from aborted missions over Iraq; one clutch almost hit a small fishing boat. I could understand why they would do this and I sympathised with the pilots, but surely there must have been a more appropriate dumping ground.

As we drove north the scenery changed and then the language also changed. This part of Italy was annexed from Germany at the end of the First World War and everyone preferred to speak German. Anne was reasonably proficient in Italian and she became very frustrated when the locals ignored her; I eventually persuaded her to revert to English.

The backdrop of the Dolomites from the small wooden chalet that we discovered was absolutely stunning; well worth our long diversion. The early morning was pleasantly disturbed by cow bells on the hillside and the air smelled of freshly cut grass. Dew still glistened on low lying branches that framed the pinkish coloured mountains and their jagged peaks exploded into the pale blue sky.

A Frenchman called Dolomieu discovered that these mountains were formed with a chemical composition of stratified calcium magnesium carbonate. This is why they radiate with a gentle pink glow when the sun begins to set. We were determined to catch this colour at its best and found a really good photo opportunity in front of a small lake called Lago di Carezza. I captured a stunning photograph to remind us both of our fabulous day in the Dolomites.

On returning to Verona we walked the walls, visited Roman fortifications and then headed for the arena. The atmosphere on opening night is something that I will always remember. Only a few adventurous backpackers had ventured into the dark unlit areas of the arena. When the opera started we looked down on the orchestra and performers. They were illuminated in a ring of light, and with excellent acoustics, their voices passed to us high in the heavens. We were Roman Gods looking over them and surely they were performing for our pleasure alone.

Re-building to save the future

During the 45 years that I have been pleased to work in the measurement and control industry, first as a young craft apprentice and then as a chartered engineer, I have belonged to several professional organisations. All of these served me well and I would like to mention their names: the Amalgamated Engineering Union, the Nuclear Engineering Society, the Institution of Electronic and Radio Engineers, the Institute of Electrical Engineers and the Institute of Measurement and Control. All were dedicated to the training of young people in their own areas of influence, and I was pleased to make my own small contribution through the organisation that best served the interests of Coulton Instrumentation: the Institute of Measurement and Control.

I have long been a Fellow of the Institute and Coulton enjoyed equal recognition as a Companion Company. In 1998 the local Wessex Section was in such rapid decline that the Section almost closed. I picked up the reins and was soon elected Chairman of the Wessex Section and I became a member of the Institute's Council. This was not a very difficult accomplishment; I had no contenders. I rebuilt the section and four years later I was awarded the L.B. Lambert Diploma for meritorious service to the Institute. When I was presented with my certificate I recalled my humble beginnings at Distington Village School and suddenly felt tremendously proud to receive such an honour. It was the crowning of my professional career and I wished that my mother had been present to witness the fruits of her labour all those years ago.

While re-building the Section I used the Institute as a vehicle in my efforts to further the skills training of youngsters in the Wessex Region. I wanted to return something to the profession that had given me so much over the past 40 years. I sponsored a medal which was awarded annually by the Institute to a student of science and engineering in the Wessex Region. The principles of the award were loosely specified to enable the selection panel to use their discretion. The only proviso I made was that the award should be given to the student that made best use of the basic principles of measurement and control in his or her final year project.

The medal is cast from bronze and it carries the Institute's Logo on one side. The Institute elected to name it the Coulton Medal and with the award is a cash prize of 200 pounds sterling. The Institute has awarded medals to final year students at Southampton University, Southampton Institute and a Secondary Modern School in Milford-on-Sea. I was rather pleased when I heard that a young girl in a Secondary Modern School had received the award; it showed that we were identifying with younger members in our region.

One of our most interesting awards was to three engineering officers at HMS Sultan in Portsmouth. This project was a team effort, a very important feature of naval training, and so we decided to strike three medals in that particular year. When we were ready to make our presentation the recipients had already been posted to active sea service. When they eventually returned to Portsmouth the commanding officer of HMS Sultan, Commodore Peter Kidner RN, invited me to present our medals at a special gathering of newly qualified engineering officers in their main training facility.

I knew that I would be called upon to give a very special talk, and so I decided to visit my good friend and old neighbour, Ali Baghei. At that time Ali was the Director of the Future Aircraft Carrier Programme and I asked him if there were any titbits that he could give me to use in my talk. We chatted over a glass of wine and he gave me a wealth of un-classified information. This enabled me to give a very interesting and detailed talk about the design philosophy of the Ministry of Defence Procurement Team in Bristol.

During my talk I noticed that many of the senior officers were taking as much interest as were the young graduates. It appeared that I had pitched the technical level of my talk at the right level to hold the attention of everyone present. The Wessex Section Education Officer, Don Bullen, accompanied me on my visit. He administered the award and it was a very proud day for him. I gave my talk to a smartly dressed group of young engineering officers and after fielding a host of questions I presented the medals to our three young officers; Laura Dodd, Rob Satterly and Peter Buckenham. Don and I were both pleasantly surprised to find that each had been promoted within the past week and they were already wearing the second gold band of a full lieutenant.

We toured the weapons and aviation training facility at HMS Sultan and then joined Commodore Kidner for a formal lunch in his home. Laura Dodd was a very smart young woman and she, along with her two colleagues, was very proud to sit at the Commodore's table and drink port. This must have been a first for Lieutenant Dodd and certainly a break with Navy tradition; I refer to the drinking of port while ladies are still at the table. In fact it was a very special day all around because we learned unofficially that our host had been informed of his promotion to Vice Admiral earlier in the day.

The award selection panel was very impressed by the professional and business-like approach taken by these three fine young engineering officers and I am certain that they will go far in their future naval careers. From a personal perspective, I was encouraged to find well equipped training facilities at HMS Sultan. These facilities are staffed by seasoned instructors who impart their knowledge in a skilful manner and maintain an incredibly high standard of training, a standard which I have not witnessed in the United Kingdom for decades. I was reminded of the excellent training that I received 42 years earlier at Windscale. I would certainly commend the armed services to any youngster who aspires to be a professional engineer.

Bid-bonds, nepotism and political ineptitude

I will now return to our commercial problems. At the beginning of the new millennium we were finding that our success ratio on major project bids was much better than our competitors. This was not because we were better then them, it was because we selected our projects very carefully. We simply did not have the resources to waste on bids with a low probability of closure. On small projects we achieved around one in eight while on larger contracts we closed one in three.

Of course this whole bid process was thrown into disarray when we tried to sell our products in the Middle East. Our Arab customers normally asked for a bid bond to be established before they would consider our quotation. These bonds often carried conditions which enabled our Customer to delay his decision on the award of a contract; if we withdrew then we lost our bond. The last time that I was involved in one of these bid processes it transpired that the Customer never had any intention of placing an order.

Perhaps my most frustrating bid was in connection with the European Union Tacis Programme in 1999. This programme followed the Chernobyl disaster and our offer was to supply, install and commission instrumentation metering systems that were required to upgrade the safety of several nuclear reactors in Central Europe.

We were very excited when we were informed by telephone that our bid was competitive and that an order would be placed with us in due course. But first we had to incorporate several additions for the project consultant. This was not easy to do because the documentation package was extremely complex and we had to comply with so many different requirements to satisfy the European Union bid process. This occupied a significant part of our engineering resources.

While we were waiting to receive our order a well known UK newspaper ran an article on the Tacis programme. It criticised the programme's consultants for charging substantial fees while placing very few orders for 'real' work to be done. I assume that my potential contract fell into this category. Shortly afterwards, in January 2000, Romani Prodi was installed as the new Commission President and at the same time the project consultant informed us that our project had been put on hold.

Nine months earlier Jacques Santer and his entire European Commission had rocked the world when they resigned in response to an independent report that described fraud, mismanagement and nepotism within the Commission. Our project consultant carried the same family name as the new President and I could not help but wonder if there was some link which caused her to withdraw from the project. If there was a link then it was commendable that she withdrew before Mr Prodi was installed.

I have no idea if the project was ever brought to a satisfactory conclusion. If not, then perhaps someone should have asked the European Commission a number of very serious questions. After all, serious money was paid by taxpayers of the European Union to carry out a very serious task, and that was to upgrade the safety of Soviet-built nuclear reactors in Central Europe.

In January 1999 Malvern was invited to bid for the supply of several control valves in Iran. I was not happy with the political situation and I instructed Malvern to stand back. Unfortunately the Department of Trade and Industry encouraged him to bid the project and I relented. We won the contract and shipped our control valves only to have them seized by Customs and Excise. When we contacted the Department of Trade and Industry everyone went very quiet. No one would respond to our telefaxes or telephone calls.

I wrote to the Secretary of State for Trade and Industry, Stephen Byers, and he never acknowledged receipt of my letter. In desperation I wrote to the Prime Minister and I was very surprised to receive a reply from his private secretary, Mr Copeland. While his ministers further down the pecking ladder in Westminster did not bother to give me the time of day, Tony Blair showed a genuine interest in my problem. I was terribly impressed and he passed immediately to the top of my all-time list of favourite Prime Ministers.

I received Mr Copeland's letter on 13th October 1999 and when I telephoned the DTI two days later they jumped to attention. I was asked to submit a formal application for export approval and they informed me that the application would be considered at the next interdepartmental committee meeting.

Several meetings occurred over the next few weeks but I never received any news. I then decided to contact Peter Reed of Dorset Business Link and Peter spoke with the head of Licensing at DTI export control. She advised that the application had to go before an interdepartmental committee consisting of representatives from the Department of Trade and Industry, the Foreign and Commonwealth Office and the Ministry of Defence. I now began to see a muddy picture emerging. For the first time the Ministry of Defence had been mentioned; perhaps we had some 'Spooks' in the background.

Three meetings occurred and still I received no news. In desperation I wrote again to the Prime Minister and explained that my problems had increased since I had last written. I said that in my opinion the Department of Trade and Industry was unable to meet its obligations to exporting companies and I again asked for his personal intervention. I received a further letter from Mr Copeland but still the Department of Trade and Industry did nothing to process my application.

My Member of Parliament, Mr Christopher Chope, then picked up the baton and he tabled four parliamentary questions to the Department of Trade and Industry. He received no satisfactory response to any of his questions and this finally confirmed my suspicion that MI6 was involved.

Christmas came and went, and we entered a new millennium. My letter of credit expired and my customer transferred his order to a German company who delivered within four weeks. All I wanted now from the Department of Trade and Industry was full financial compensation and several heads rolling down the corridors of that huge glass fronted building in Victoria Street. Number one on my list was Byers.

Chris Chope was also on the warpath because he was unaccustomed to his parliamentary questions being ignored. Towards the end of January I received a surprise telephone call from Christopher Booker of the Sunday Telegraph. He asked me for further information on the Small Firms Debate which had taken place in the House of Commons on 20th January 2000. I had no idea what he was talking about and he told me to obtain a copy of the Hansard parliamentary record for that day and to read pages 289WH through 305WH.

Christopher Booker said that the largest part of the debate had been in relation to the terrible service rendered to Coulton Instrumentation by the Department of Trade and Industry. He said that it was the first time he had found several pages of the Hansard given over to the problems of a single company. He was honest and told me that he could smell a good story and he wanted to meet me straight away. I suspect that he had grown to dislike the rat pack in the lower ranks of the Labour Party as much as I did.

I read the transcripts and found that Chris Chope had held the floor for a considerable length of time. He had the bit between his teeth and he had climbed into the Department of Trade and Industry and Stephen Byers. Regrettably he also criticised Tony Blair for not achieving any results. I was a little disappointed about this, but Chris was a member of the Conservative Party and so I suppose this was to be expected. Chris requested that the Department of Trade and Industry provided financial compensation but I suppose the only way I would have secured this would have been to take my case to the European Court.

Patricia Hewitt, the Minister for Small Firms and E-Commerce, was in attendance at the debate and she was one of the few Ministers in the Labour Party whom I considered to be capable and deserving of high office. I was pleased to find in the Hansard that she had given me a formal apology from the floor of the House of Commons. This helped to cool the raging anger inside me.

Christopher Booker did not interview me because all the information he needed was carefully detailed in the Hansard. I was pleased about this because I knew how journalists could make a small quotation into a big story. I didn't want to go down that road and I had to consider the best interests of Coulton Instrumentation. He just clarified a few small details on the telephone and then his photographer, Les Wilson, visited my office and took about 80 photographs.

On Sunday 6th February 2000 I was featured in the news section of the Telegraph. The article ripped Stephen Byers and the Labour Government into shreds. I was pleased that I had not offered any quotations. All of Booker's information had been taken directly from the Hansard and any colouring came from the Telegraph's own editorial staff, not from me. After reading the article I almost felt sorry for Stephen Byers.

On Monday the Head of Export Licensing telephoned Malvern and asked if we could join a meeting in Victoria Street. It was obvious that the DTI had switched to 'damage control mode'. Malvern and I caught the train to Waterloo and took a taxi across town to Number 1 Victoria Street. We arrived in good spirits and in eager anticipation of what we hoped would be an interesting meeting. For the first time we felt as if we were in the driving seat. Tony Blair's government was hyper-sensitive to media coverage; the newspapers were on our side and they were printing our story.

We were invited to sit in the centre of a very long wooden table. At one end was the Head of Licensing and at the other was a senior government press officer. Several other people were gathered around but it was the Press Officer who seemed to be leading the meeting. I allowed Malvern to field all of the Government's questions while I sat back and figured out what was really happening. I remained passive and eventually I was totally ignored in the meeting; which was what I wanted.

It soon became apparent to me that the whole meeting was a sham. It had been called because the Press Officer was under instructions to prevent any follow-up to the damaging article in the Sunday Telegraph. Eventually the Press Officer said to Malvern. "Good then, you agree that the matter is now closed and that you will have no further discussions with the press".

"Excuse me Malvern". I said in a raised voice. "I will take it from here". Suddenly everyone's eyes shifted to me. I could almost hear the guy directly opposite me groaning, "Christ, we have been talking to the wrong person". I had been watching him and his side-kick for the past half hour and I decided that he was the person who was really calling the shots. Like me, he was staying quiet, but I had figured him out for what he really was and it was not what was written on his business card.

I looked him straight in the eye and shouted, "And what will you give in return. I know exactly who you are. I pay your wages. I don't have my own private team of spies. That's your job. You knew exactly whom we were doing business with and you didn't tell me. I pay your salary and you didn't tell me. And now you want me to agree to your terms without offering anything in return".

He was stunned and he realized that there was no point in continuing to deceive us. The conversations that followed are confidential. The only comment that I am permitted to make is that the control valves were never released for shipment to Iran and I never received any financial compensation. I was not happy about this but there comes a time when one has to stop fighting with the big boys and I decided that I had reached that point. We certainly cleared the air, and following our meeting in Victoria Street we received excellent cooperation from the Export Licensing Section.

Stringfellow's and scantily clad girls

I have already mentioned our largest project; this was the Azerbaijan Oil Pipeline. I was very confident when I bid for this contract. We knew that our products were technically the best for the job; we were prepared to outsource to ensure single point of supply and our documentation was second to none. The other reason that I enjoyed a reasonable level of confidence was that the final selection was being made by an instrument engineer who was qualified to recognise the technical value of our bid. For once the tender process was on my side. My main concern was that the main contractor, Kaeverner Offshore, traditionally bought Rosemount transmitters and this was a very difficult hurdle to overcome.

Fortunately Rosemount stabbed themselves in the foot. They were overconfident; one of their engineers told me that my bid was on the top of the pile but Kaeverner intended to place the order with them. I was furious. Without hesitation I telephoned the engineer handling the contract and read the riot act to him. I knew that he was on contract and that he would be looking for another job when this one was finished. I told him that it was companies such as mine that employed experienced engineers when they reached the end of their career, not large organisations such as Rosemount. I told him that he knew my bid was the best one and that he should give us his support and not take the safest option by staying with Rosemount. Everyone who overheard my conversation was shocked, but I had nothing to lose. The next day Coulton received its largest ever order!

Later in the month Tim Gibson of Keystone Valves invited me and several of his customers to the annual dinner of the Energy Industries Council. I was delayed by a telephone call and I grabbed my tuxedo before rushing to the railway station to catch my London train. I checked into my hotel and quickly changed only to find that my trousers were three inches short around the waist band. I had taken Brett's tuxedo by mistake.

My situation was desperate and so I improvised by tying the top button holes together with a piece of string. It was raining heavily and my raincoat did not look out of place when I walked into the Grosvenor Hotel. I walked past the cloak room and straight to my designated table where I sat down and passed my dripping-wet raincoat to a waiter. My fellow guests looked a little surprised at my cavalier attitude until I explained my embarrassing predicament.

A few minutes later the toastmaster asked us to be standing while our top-table guests entered the room. About a dozen foreign ambassadors, mainly from the eastern bloc countries, and a few of our own hangers-on from the department of trade and industry marched across the room. In accordance with tradition we slow handclapped in recognition of their high status and on this occasion I think a slow handclap was more than appropriate because they really were a waste of space. Of course my handclap was slow for a different reason; I was trying to hide the huge gap in my flies.

After a rather excellent dinner and a lot of pomp and ceremony Tim decided to get down to the real entertainment for the night. And if one thought that my predicament had already been embarrassing enough, then wait for it. Yes, we jumped into a couple of taxis and Tim shouted "Stringfellows". I almost jumped out of our taxi in shock, but I had heard so much about this den of iniquity that I had to stay the course. I suppose the copious amount of wine and port passed around the dinner table had loosened my inhibitions.

We pulled several small tables together and gathered around in a group. The whisky started to flow and it was not long before a string of scantily clad girls joined us. Tim paid several of the girls to perform lap dances and I will not issue any prizes to those that can guess the amount of fun the guys had at my expense.

Only the filthy rich

Shortly after this saga a sequence of events unwittingly changed my life. These events laid the foundations for my eventual exit from my lifetime's work in process measurement and control. Anne and I were walking alongside the Bristol Floating Harbour early in March 2000. We loved the area and we spotted a Beaufort Homes billboard that had just been raised in front of a new harbour side construction site. Anne and I tried hard to get our names on the viewing list, but had no success. Then out of the blue we were asked if we would agree to be interviewed by Malcolm Frith for BBC Television News.

Our interview took place in the show house and after several sensible questions Malcolm suddenly threw the gauntlet down. "There are those who believe that only the filthy rich can afford to buy a house on the harbour side". I was furious and forgetting that I was on camera, I yelled at him, telling him that I damn well deserved to buy any house that I wanted. I had earned my money by working in dangerous conditions down copper mines on the Congo border when I could only afford to buy half a loaf of bread, and yes, "I damn well deserve a house on the harbour side"! I barked the last few words at him; he smiled and said "that's a take". Later in the day my outburst appeared on both National and World BBC Television News; Malcolm's rather clever taunt had been edited out.

During a short camera break I made an offer to purchase the best apartment at the full asking price. It enjoyed a 270 degree panoramic view that extended from the Industrial Museum, across the full length of the Floating Harbour, and down to the SS Great Britain. The Sales Manager refused to accept my offer and then I suspected, rightly or wrongly, that something was afoot. I decided to use my interview with Malcolm Frith to maximum advantage and repeated my offer on camera. She had no alternative but to accept, and I signed my provisional contract early next morning. It was the first contract to be signed for an apartment in the new harbour side development programme.

A few months later Beaufort invited Anne and me to join them on a Floating Harbour champagne cruise aboard the Bristol Clipper with Sir Robin Knox Johnston, the first person to sail around the world single-handed non-stop. The Bristol Clipper was about to set out on the Times

2000 Round the World Yacht Race, a race designed entirely for amateurs who had never sailed blue water before. Sir Robin was the Chairman of the Clipper Race, and I told him that I would love to participate, but that I was much too old and would never be accepted. He said that I was talking nonsense and that no one was ever too old to take on a new challenge in life. He asked me to submit my application for the 2002/2003 race without delay. And so it was that our sighting of a Beaufort Homes billboard on the Bristol harbour side changed our life.

A very special day

Friday 5th May 2000 was a very special day; it was my father's 80th birthday. Dad and Mattie were staying with Steven, Linda, Christopher and our most recent addition to the Coulton family, my niece Katie. They lived in a beautiful house with a noisy washing machine on the edge of the small village of Linton, near to Cambridge. On the morning of his birthday, Linda took Katie to school as usual and Mattie and Dad joined them at St Mary's Church for what they thought was to be the weekly church service for the children of Linton Primary School.

Linda welcomed everyone by ringing the church bells, and after the service started, Katie escorted her grandfather to the front of the church where she and Father Julian lit a candle 'for a very special person on a very special day' and all of the children sang a special birthday song to him. Dad was taken completely by surprise and felt very honoured! After the church service, Linda and Mattie took Dad for a trip to Anglesey Abbey while Katie and Chris prepared a surprise tea with champagne, presents and his favourite chocolate cake.

On the following day Steven took Dad for a long walk whilst Linda, Chris and Mattie decorated their house with banners and streamers in preparation for his surprise party. Steven had pre-arranged for everyone to arrive while they were on their walk, and in a short space of time I arrived with Anne, Brett, Michele and the remainder of my family. When Steven returned with Dad we consumed in Dad's words, an 'ample sufficiency' of tea, pastry and sandwiches before setting out for Cambridge Airport.

Steven told Dad that he had arranged for a bungee jump as a special birthday treat. Not knowing what to believe he was very relieved when he found that Linda had arranged for a flight in a Tiger Moth. This is a pre-war biplane trainer with open cockpit and a voice tube for communication, better described by my father as an old canvas string-bag.

Dad entered the small briefing room on the airfield and came out a short while later wearing a leather helmet and a large pair of flying goggles. He looked the part and would have put Biggles to shame. He was surrounded by four grandchildren and four great grandchildren, six of them girls, and they poked fun at him while Linda took dozens of photographs. Eventually Dad climbed into the cockpit and after a short pre-flight check his pilot climbed onboard and they had a memorable flight over the Cambridgeshire countryside. He later recalled his route and described how he had flown over the Ancient Colleges of Cambridge, Newmarket Racecourse, Ely Cathedral and Madingly American War Graves Cemetery.

Combining old memories with new in Scotland

A couple of months later Anne and I made our usual summer visit to Dad and Mattie in Maryport, Cumbria. After a short stay we headed north across the border into Scotland. As always I had no fixed plan in mind, only a map and a credit card. After a short drive we entered Gretna Green and for the first time since my childhood, I stopped outside the old blacksmiths shop for breakfast. It was very different to what I remembered, much larger and adapted to meet the demands of modern day international tourists. There were no runaway brides so early in the morning and so we resumed our journey north until we reached the whisky distillery in Dalwhinnie.

Lying deep in the Scottish Islands, this distillery held fond memories of a similar rainy day 37 years ago. I was one of 24 boys from the Murray Outward Bound Sea School on a forced march across the Cairngorm and Grampian mountains. We had to join the Prince Louis Schooner off Ballachulish, exchange crews and sail the Hebrides. An endurance exercise designed to strengthen our character under extreme conditions; as the outward bound motto goes, 'to serve, to strive and not to yield'.

It had been a dark forbidding night on Monday 15th July 1963. We trudged down the mountainside into Dalwhinnie. Exhausted, hungry and soaked to the skin, the villagers took pity on us and allowed us to bunk down in the distillery. I can still recall the rich musty and rather pleasant smell that filled my nostrils as I enjoyed my first real sleep for several days. The distillery is now on the Highland tourist route and, as with Gretna, it has changed to accommodate the flood of Sassenachs who seem to be more interested in taking photographs than partaking in a good sip of malt.

On our last day of sea school, the Warden had urged cadets to return one day with their families. I therefore decided that our next stop would be the Murray Outward Bound Sea School in Burghead. It was late evening as we passed through Forres, and several surveillance aircraft of Royal Air Force Kinloss stood at their dispersal points. It had been almost 40 years since that terrible day when the torpedo dump exploded. Even more memories flooded back. I looked for the operations room where I had been at the time of detonation, and for the Astra Cinema which stood opposite the main gate. Neither was there.

A few minutes later we entered Burghead and parked on the old fishing quay beside the small stone built harbour. One evening on high tide, all those years ago, ninety six of us were marched down the hill in our course navy blue merchant marine uniforms and ordered to jump from the highest part of the harbour wall. The nearest ladder was on the far side of the harbour and those who were unable to swim were fished out by instructors in canoes. There were many who went under and outsiders who had never witnessed this ritual were horrified. Those who were rescued were subsequently identified as non-swimmers and prevented from taking part in seagoing canoe activities.

This had been a swift eye opener for what was in store for us. Over the next month we crawled commando ropes, climbed rigging and crossed the yardarm without harnesses, jumped high waterfalls in the Grampians with full back pack and rafted canoes in rough northern seas.

This kind of activity may sound astonishing in the 21st century, but one needs to understand that the first Outward Bound Sea School opened in 1941 to help prepare young merchant seaman for service in the North

Atlantic convoys. The cruel ocean had already claimed thousands of lives and the founder of Outward Bound, Kurt Hahn, believed that many young men could be saved if they were given the strength of will to survive. My own particular group was told that our instructor's main task was to develop our state of mind to enable us to overcome any dangerous situation by sheer courage and determination.

Kurt Hahn also founded the Salem Schools, Gordonstoun Public School, the Duke of Edinburgh's Award Scheme and the Atlantic Colleges. All five institutions had a common thread that extended beyond the individuality of purpose for each, and that was to develop character and a sense of public service in young people through energetic participation. My own participation in two of these schemes had a profound affect on my life, and I believe that I owe Kurt Hahn and the Duke of Edinburgh a great personal debt.

We walked up the hill past a small café where I had tasted my first ever pepsi-cola. Council houses stood where wooden barrack rooms had once been and a children's play area replaced the huge and very challenging commando course. There was no one to welcome me back! A young woman standing in the doorway of a nearby house told me that the school had been knocked down long before she was born. Suddenly I felt very old. Her mother had been the cook and she explained how the school failed to attract support after several boys were killed in a sea-going accident. I was deeply saddened to learn of the accident and of the school's demise.

Memories of the warden's dog, Tramp, sneaking into our group photograph lingered and I imagined Mr Macgregor driving poor Alistair Macdonald harder and harder to overcome his fear of heights. I could see the other members of Grenville watch in my mind's eye as if it were yesterday. Chris Miller, Hugo Boyd, Dennis Jones, John Aliston, John Bingham, John Lockhead, Bill McDermott and Raymond Rennie; I wonder what life has brought to them since we all embarked on our separate journeys?

After staying our first night in Inverness we shot up to John 'O' Groats. I had expected our drive to take most of the day but a new 'oilmans' highway had been constructed along the North Sea coast to Thurso.

A ferry was about to set sail for the Shetlands

We parked our car and set out, baggage free, for a one day tour of the Orkney Islands. I wanted to see the huge natural harbour of Scapa Flow, which was the wartime home of the British Grand Fleet. My wife has a family association with Scapa Flow. Her aunt, Lady Kate Wilkinson, is the granddaughter of Sir John Jellicoe who commanded the British Grand Fleet in the Battle of Jutland, the largest engagement ever of big-gun warships. His adversary was Vice Admiral Reinhard Scheer in command of the German High Seas Fleet.

The British Grand Fleet included 28 dreadnought battleships, 9 battle cruisers, 8 armoured cruisers, 26 light cruisers and 78 destroyers. Sir John, later to become Admiral of the Fleet Earl Jellicoe, surprised Scheer and succeeded in crossing his line of advancing warships in a classic 'T' before unleashing a deadly broadside from his dreadnoughts. Scheer realised his tactical dilemma and ordered his destroyers forward in a suicidal torpedo attack. Sir John took the less hazardous option and turned his dreadnoughts away from these torpedoes. Many foolhardy people have since said that in doing so he denied the Empire a greater victory than Trafalgar. The truth is that it could so easily have gone the other way. Sir John achieved his ultimate goal; the German High Seas Fleet never put to sea again and our Atlantic trade routes remained open.

After the battle Winston Churchill said that Jellicoe was the only man on either side who could have lost the war in an afternoon. Kate's grandfather now stands in Trafalgar Square under the watchful eye of that other great Sea Lord; Nelson.

Apart from the remnants and memories of enormous and very tragic events that occurred in and around Scapa Flow during two world wars, the islands themselves offer a considerable number of well preserved Neolithic remains. The islands have never been ploughed or heavily farmed. This has left much of its unique heritage undisturbed for 5,500 years; there is just so much to see and because of this UNESCO has granted the Orkney's World Heritage status. Our tour took us past Skara Brae, an extremely well preserved stone village thought to have been inhabited around 3,200 BC. We stopped at the magnificent Ring of Brodgar and the strange but very lonely Standing Stones of Stenness.

We stopped for afternoon tea in Stromness and noticed that a ferry was about to sail to Lerwick in the Shetland Islands. On the spur of the moment we told our tour guide that we were not rejoining his bus and then jumped onto the ferry. I thought the journey would be a short crossing and we were both very surprised when we found ourselves committed to an all-night sailing with no return passage for four days. We were pleased that we had not known this before boarding in Stromness because our three full days on the Shetland Islands were the best mistake we ever made.

From our first moment of arrival in Lerwick we were astonished by the rich variety of wildlife. The bitterly cold sea, the grey rocky beaches, the steep cliffs, the soft peaty heather and the slate grey skies all supported fish, mammals and birds in such overpowering numbers and diversity that I found it difficult to comprehend.

Even the huge Sullom Voe oil terminal surged with wild life. Birds and mammals have adapted and even taken advantage of what this monstrous eyesore has to offer. Common seals bathed in warmer waters surrounding the pipeline jetty and an otter zigzagged back to shore. Our bus driver was unable to use the oil workers' car park because it had been commandeered by several dozen artic terns; clutches of undisturbed eggs lay all over the parking area.

I was encouraged by the way in which wildlife could adapt when pollution was kept under control and humans learned to co-exist. One night as we walked along the cliff tops, in the middle-light of a northern summer, we heard grey seals singing. Further along two huge males had beached themselves on isolated rocks in the middle of the bay and several females had gathered in small rocky coves where they could protect their pups from predatory killer whales.

The following evening Anne and I joined a group of ten people on a boat trip around the steep cliffs that surround the small island of Noss. Great Skuas dived on our small boat and tens of thousands of Guillemots, Razorbills and Puffins crowded high rocky ledges while even more Kittiwakes and Fulmars wheeled and dived around us. Gannets returned from their long day of fishing far from shore and we all huddled beneath oil skins to protect ourselves from the small messages they sent us.

Sullom Voe was one of my many customers in the North Sea, and as we left Lerwick on our return journey I caught sight of another; Shetland Fisheries who used our miniature temperature controllers. Their factory was surrounded by hundreds of seals that presumably feasted on factory left-overs.

We eventually arrived back on the mainland and found our car safe and with no parking ticket. On our return journey we headed for Urquhart Castle on Loch Ness. From there we drove down the more difficult and slower west coast roads to memorable places where I had camped in the 50's with my parents and baby brother.

The old buildings and scenery around Fort Augustus are incredibly beautiful and we walked along a string of old locks before crossing the Caledonian Canal. Our next stop was Ben Nevis. We climbed to a vantage point which gave us an excellent view of Fort William and the Wiggins Teape Pulp and Paper Factory where I had installed a Diogenes control system back in 1982. From there we drove through Glencoe over the Bridge of Orchy and down to the banks of Loch Lomond where we stayed the night. The whole day had been filled with memories of my childhood camping holidays and those later years when I crewed the Prince Louis through Loch Linnhe and out to sea by way of the Sound of Mull.

This had been a very different holiday to anything we had done before; full of unexpected adventures, combining old memories with new. It had been a holiday full of rich surprises but also tinged with a little sadness. Our last stop on our long journey home was at the Lockerbie memorial where Pan Am Clipper 103 had been destroyed. This was the single most disturbing event ever to occur in British airspace. We were very moved by our visit and my subsequent interest and examination of events distressed me even further. I remain convinced that the real culprits have still not been brought to trial and probably never will be.

Building the Company's corporate image

In January 2001 I decided that it was time to hand the reins over to Malvern. I made him the Managing Director and then stepped back for the first time in my life. It was not easy. I kept my position as Company Chairman and set about building our corporate image.

Coulton held a wide selection of certificates and approval ratings. We were registered on the Utilities Vendor Database and on the Oil and Gas Vendors Database. We were approved by Lloyds Register, British Gas, ICI and the Russian Goss Standard Approvals Commission. I had to get this information across to our customers if we were to succeed in our task and this signalled the need to review our method of presenting information.

I worked hard to pull together a shortform brochure that sold Coulton and Coulton's products to our worldwide customer base. I used all the presentational skills that I learned while working in the corporate marketing team of Rosemount. The end result was, in my opinion, a brochure that surpassed anything available from the largest of our multi-national competitors. It contained information on everything that a customer would ever want to know about Coulton. It included a full profile of the Company, a technical description for every product the Company sold, copies of the Company's certificates and, in addition, several engineering tables and conversion factors. It was, and still is, a very attractive and a very practical document in every respect and I am very proud of it.

Malvern and I worked with Brett to build an excellent website for Coulton. We used our new brochure to develop the structure and Brett added buttons to enable customers to download instruction manuals in pdf format. We included customer reference lists, examples of our engineering drawings and technical details for our primary devices. The website along with our new brochure portrayed Coulton as a large and truly international instrument engineering company with real professional capabilities.

Malvern helped considerably with all of this work and his in-depth knowledge of our software was instrumental in us reaching such a high standard. With everything in place we hoped that our new corporate image would provide the growth that we so desperately wanted. But this was not to be. England was teetering on the brink of a recession and several customers re-located their manufacturing facilities to low cost areas in Taiwan, South Korea and China. We had never looked more professional and yet our turnover and profitability started to fall.

Golden Triangle and black gold

I was deeply immersed in my problems at work and Anne suggested that it was time that we re-visited Thailand. We both loved the area, and after all, it was the place where I proposed to her. Anne wanted to visit Chiang Mai Hospital where a systems procurement team had just installed a new computer system; she viewed this as a good opportunity to visit the hill tribes of Northern Thailand.

We flew to Thailand in February 2001 and a senior consultant at Chiang Mai hospital treated us to a tour of the building where the new system was installed. He explained the Hospital's Information Technology Strategy and Anne was impressed by his enthusiasm. I was equally impressed by the high level of patient care in Chiang Mai and I recalled the excellent treatment that I had received on my earlier visit to Phuket.

After this brief visit to Chang Mai Hospital, and no Mr Gordon Brown, we did not charge our visit to business expenses, we donned our tourist hats and set off into the mountains. Our first port of call was the orchid farm outside Chiang Mai and then we took an elephant ride through the mountains; a rather nerve racking experience but one that every tourist has to include on his must do list.

We visited several hill tribes in the area and I recall with affection our encounters with women and children from the Lisu, Karen, Palong, Akha, Hmong and Yao tribes. The women of these hill tribes are characterised by their extraordinary and brightly coloured dresses. The men and women produce various decorative items of bamboo and seeds. The men make crossbows, musical instruments, a variety of baskets, and other items of wood, bamboo, rattan and even silver. Almost all have teeth blackened by betel nut which they chew for its stimulant properties. Several, such as the Hmong and Yao, originate from the Yunnan province of China while others migrated south from the steppes of Tibet.

Several remnants of Chiang Kai-chek's Nationalist Army settled in the hills around Chiang Mai as they retreated from the Chinese Red Army in 1949. They continue to live under the protection of the Thai Government on hill territory where they are permitted to build their own villages and to perpetuate their way of life under the prime condition that they grew vegetables and not poppies; a condition that is often flouted in their desperate attempt to scratch a meagre living from the soil.

From Chiang Mai we flew to Chiang Rai and then we drove a considerable distance to a fabulous hotel where Anne's brother Henry had stayed earlier in the year. It was five-star and reasonably priced, yet it remained devoid of guests. Our room crowned a small hill from which we enjoyed a magnificent view across the Mekong River into Laos on the one side and across the Ruak River into Burma on the other. The junction of these two infamous rivers created a triangle of three countries; Thailand, Laos and Burma. Gold was prevalent in the area, not the yellow metallic kind; black gold taken as seed from the mature red poppies which were being cultivated in nearby jungle clearings.

We were in the Golden Triangle; an area controlled until recently by General Chao Khun Sa, King of Opium and known locally as the Prince of Death. Khun Sa established the Mong Tai Army, a private army of 20,000 people who were responsible for the poppy plantations and heroin refineries located along the Burmese, Laos, Thai borders. Following his demise in 1996, the area transferred to the control of the United Wa State Army, which is divided into several regional commands. Each command is funded by a different organisation whose roots are in China, Taiwan, and Thailand. Each command is headed by a different General and funded by a different organisation.

The Wa is allied to the Burmese Military Junta and enjoys substantial logistical support from the Burmese Army. They are opposed by the Shan who have their own rather depleted army, the Shan State Army; and if my informant was correct, the Shan State army occupied several hill camps on the Thai side of the border around Mai Sae. Confused! Well I am as confused as hell.

This is complicated by the fact that there are also ethnic groups, the Kerenni in particular, who are fighting for full autonomy in the western region. Meanwhile the Burmese Military Junta and their Generals continue to reap substantial rewards from the opium trade. They maintain control of the region by burning the villages of opposing ethnic tribes and sowing mines in rice fields along the border region with Thailand.

A border war was being fought along the Ruak River and this was why our hotel was almost empty. Three weeks earlier the Burmese Army had crossed the Ruak and captured a Thai Rangers camp on Bang Pang Noon Hill. They then set up an artillery position which was in turn destroyed by Thai Artillery. In retaliation the Burmese shelled Mae Sai which is only 5 miles from our hotel, the Baan Boran. Then the United Wa State Army crossed the Friendship Bridge from Tachilek and took control of the Mae Sai town centre. This was one day before we arrived. They were driven back by light armoured vehicles from the local Thai Garrison but then the Shan issued a warning that the Burmese Army might decide to use chemical bombs, a tactic used earlier against the Kerenni.

All of this was very confusing to me. I thought these battles were being fought to establish political control of the region but I was reliably informed that the United Wa State Army, with logistical support from the Burmese Army, was re-establishing control of their heroin and methamphetamine supply route across the Friendship Bridge and into Northern Thailand. The Shan State Army were opposing this and of course the Thai Army had been drawn into the conflict to protect the integrity of their borders.

I was very disappointed that this region was in turmoil because I wanted to visit a number of interesting places in South East Burma. Not only were we prevented from crossing the Friendship Bridge but we now found that our holiday might be cut short. The Thai Government had despatched re-enforcements from Chiang Rai to prepare for a possible mass evacuation of the area if chemical weapons were used.

Anne and I were determined not to have this small border incident interfere with our holiday and we paid a young Thai villager to take us in a long-tailed boat up the Mekong River in the general direction of the Chinese border. There were colourful little fishing villages on both river banks. On the left there were bamboo houses erected high above the flood level on long bamboo stilts, and Burmese women in bright blue sarongs kneeled beside the river washing clothes that were stacked in large wicker baskets.

The right hand river bank was less populated and the Laos jungle came right down to the waters edge. It was strange motoring up-river with Burma on one side and Laos on the other while our passports remained within a third country which was now five miles downstream. As we came in close to the river bank to photograph the Burmese women I wondered how we would extricate ourselves if a soldier from the United Wa State Army challenged us.

Still determined to secure a legitimate entry into Burma, we took a taxi into Mae Sai and found the Friendship Bridge blocked by a huge steel gate and reinforced against ramming by several army vehicles. Three hundred yards back along the main street, in a strategic position, was a Thai armoured vehicle with its gun trained on the bridge. Market stalls erected around the vehicle gave a non-intentional but very effective camouflage screen.

The local people were very appreciative of the protection afforded by the armoured vehicle and it was covered in a carpet of fresh orchids. The Thai soldiers were part of a very professional army which showed a genuine determination to protect all ethnic groups on their side of the Ruak, unlike the private armies allied with the Burmese Junta who only had their own self interest to heart.

I walked up to a very young Army Lieutenant who appeared to be directing operations in the main street. He was able to speak fluent English and, unlike many foreign soldiers that I had met in earlier years, he was very receptive to conversation. He answered all of my questions without reservation and gave me a general description of the border situation. Unfortunately I struggled to retain any sense of what he told me and so I decided instead to have my photograph taken with him in front of his armoured vehicle.

On a normal day in Mae Sai there would be dozens of Burmese traders crossing the Friendship Bridge each day. These traders sold bags of uncut gem stones and boxes of intricate jade artefacts to the Mae Sai stall owners. The stall owners graded the gemstones by size and arranged them into suitable lots of 500, 1000 and 10,000 Baht and displayed them on their open stalls in little stone pots. Professional buyers would scan these open market stalls for suitable purchases to take back to their cutting houses in Bangkok and Hong Kong. This was the way trade was conducted in this part of the world.

There were no Buyers today and would probably be none for some time. There were terrific bargains to be had and I bought a 'lot' of sapphires and a 'lot' of emeralds. Then Anne and I visited an up-market shop and selected the most attractive jade vase to be found in Mae Sai.

Our visit to the Golden Triangle took a further twist when a Boeing 737 blew up on the apron at Bangkok International Airport. It was the same flight that we had taken one week earlier from Bangkok to Chiang Mae. Thaksin Shinawatra, the Thai Prime Minister, was about to board the aircraft and our Opium Generals in the Triangle were immediately included on the list of suspects.

Our return flight came under extreme scrutiny and getting our vase back to England was an adventure in itself. It was too precious to place in the check-in luggage and I packed it very carefully in three boxes; each one inside of the other with individual stuffing between each layer. When our jade vase passed through the x-ray machine we were immediately surrounded by soldiers who painstakingly dismantled our carefully packed container. Eventually they allowed us onto our plane and we flew to Bangkok in our Boeing 737-400. We were the only two passengers and I have never been so nervous in my whole life.

Our priceless jade vase, at least priceless to us, now stands in pride of place resting on the sideboard of our home on the Bristol Harbour side.

I flew to Esfahan with Babak

In April 2001 Coulton received an invitation to join the British Pavilion at the Tehran Oil and Gas Exhibition. I was still very reluctant to commit resources to an exhibition in Tehran after the disgraceful behaviour of the DTI. I therefore elected to visit as an observer and refrained from taking part in the exhibition.

Tehran is a surprisingly modern city that has been pulled back into the middle ages by the Islamic Revolution. It is not a very attractive city, it lacks character and the traffic congestion is continuous. I found that it is almost impossible to cross the road. There are no pedestrian traffic lights and I could only cross by following another person step by step. Many streets were three lanes in each direction and one had to walk very slowly and allow the cars to pass on each side. I disliked this so much that I refrained from walking around the town as much as possible.

Women are a very integral and important part of the workforce, yet they are often humiliated by overzealous religious bigots. On more than one occasion business women in my company were accosted by men who had noticed a wisp of hair protruding from beneath their headscarf. I had to be very careful not to react in the same manner as I had several years earlier with the KGB in Moscow. These people are totally unpredictable.

My Iranian hosts were kind hospitable people who contrasted starkly with the religious fanatics who stalked parks and meeting places looking for innocent young people to hassle. Unmarried people of the opposite sex were not allowed to mingle unless they were escorted and my taxi driver told me of a terrible incident. A man was driving home late one evening with his wife and the police stopped him. He didn't have his marriage certificate and so they arrested his wife. The man was so worried that he had an accident while hurrying home to collect his certificate. By the time he returned to the Police Station an Islamic Court had executed her.

I don't know what she was accused of but what I found to be particularly disgusting was that the Islamic Court automatically considered guilt to rest with her and not with her husband. The Cleric who sentenced her to death told her husband not to worry because she was now with God and Allah would know that she was innocent. I hope that Allah has taken a careful look at the terrible guilt that now rests upon the Cleric's shoulders!

I flew to Esfahan with Babak, one of my agent's sales engineers. He is a native of Esfahan and he welcomed an opportunity to visit his family. His mother invited me to join her with Babak and his two sisters at a traditional tea house in the old part of Esfahan. It was an old military barracks during the Saffavid era and we sat in a group eating gaz, which we warmed over hot coals while his mother and two sisters smoked a qalyoun; better known in the West as a water-pipe. His mother was accosted by the doorman who told her to tighten her head scarf, otherwise no one troubled us.

Afterwards we returned to her home to meet Babak's father, and as soon as we passed through the door his mother and two sisters removed their drab outer robes to reveal an under layer of smart western style clothes. His youngest sister removed her head scarf and brushed her long black hair over her shoulders. I almost felt as if I was intruding. They were still heavily dressed and yet it was as if they were naked.

In the morning I visited the world famous Naghsh-e-Jahan Square which is totally enclosed by several buildings of incredible beauty. It is very difficult to describe the Imam and Sheikh Lutfallah Mosques, or the Ali Qapu Kings Palace that together form three walls of the square. I had never before seen buildings of such splendour. They were built with such keen attention to artistic detail, and one of the domes is a masterpiece in Persian architecture with perfect structural clarity and geometric balance. It had been built with such perfect acoustical properties that the walls amplified sound to the extent that one could hear a piece of paper hit the floor ten paces away.

The fourth side of the square is enclosed by Esfahan's huge covered bazaar. This bazaar sold Persian carpets, silver inlaid goods, gaz and all kinds of local produce. I was impressed by the intricate detail of the camel-bone ink engravings. The detail on several of these was so fine that I had to use a magnifying glass to recognise each individual pen stroke. I chose a very fine engraving which depicted Persian horsemen playing polo in the centre of Naghsh-e-Jahan Square.

The square is only one of the many fine historical sites in and around Esfahan, and I visited as many as possible before returning to London where I had an important date with Anne and her family at the Opera in Covent Garden. It was Stephen's 80th birthday and Henry had obtained tickets to Verdi's 'Othello' . For the second time in as many years I had a problem with my tuxedo. This time it was in my suitcase, which was still flying around the world courtesy of Iran Air. I had travel insurance and so I paid a quick visit to Jermyn Street and bought everything I needed.

What I had not known during my visit to Esfahan was that the arid mountainous terrain around this beautiful ancient city was probably under the ever watchful eyes of an American spy satellite. Four years later the world discovered that the Iranian regime was enriching uranium. This technology along with other plants that they had constructed in the Esfahan area would give them the ability to manufacture nuclear weapons. It is very possible that the equipment that I had been prevented from supplying to Iran in 1999 had been intended for one of these plants.

Considering retirement

Dad had another go at me about my retirement. He said it was time to let the Company go and he reminded me about his father who died of hard work in his 50s. Yes it sounds crazy, but there was nothing wrong with him and that was his doctor's diagnosis; he never stopped working and he simply just died. This had encouraged my father, who had replaced his father at the steelworks, to take early retirement. My father now believed it was time for me to follow suit.

I lived for my work and I enjoyed visiting remote locations in third world countries to commission new plant. I thrived on it, but the last plant I commissioned in Belize had taken its toll. When I returned home my doctor was shocked with my blood pressure readings and he placed me on tablets and ordered me to slow down. Perhaps my father was right. I didn't want to step down but Brett had moved on and I had no one to take over the business. I knew that I would never be able to stand in the background and allow Malvern to run the Company unhindered; it was not my way. It was time to think about selling the Company!

I had received regular enquiries from Companies wishing to purchase Coulton when my profits were high. Now my margin was on a steeply falling curve and I knew that it was not going to be easy to find a buyer. We continued to get hit by costs that were not covered in Malvern's budget and eventually I had no alternative but to instruct him to seek redundancies. This was the very last thing that I wanted and it was the straw that broke the camel's back.

In March 2002 I approached one of my Customers and told him that I was interested in selling my Company. He made a formal approach with backing from a large electrical engineering company which was based in the Midlands. I made it very clear to him that any prospective purchaser must have a structure that was complimentary to Coulton's existing products; they had to agree to leave the company base in Christchurch, guarantee continued employment for all my staff and bring added value to the business. The prospective buyer was able to meet all of these criteria. Unfortunately he started to haggle over the price and this was not my way of doing business. I withdrew from the negotiations.

Chapter 23

Clipper Round the World Yacht Race

Racing the Atlantic and following in the footsteps of Darwin
Canal, what canal!

On the 11th December 2000 I was invited to attend the Mariners Society in London where Tim Hedges, the Race Director, interviewed me for a crew position in the 2002/2003 Clipper Round the World Yacht Race. I had to wait until the London Boat Show in Earl's Court to learn if my application had been successful. It was, and later in the year I flew down to Clipper's winter training headquarters in Vilamoura on the Algarve for 14 days of intensive sail training. It was an incredible experience and I made many good friends, all of them much younger than me, but the age difference and the physical and mental abilities of each one of us did not matter. I found sailing to be a huge leveller and everyone worked together as a team to achieve one goal; to sail safely and to win. I trained on Glasgow and our competitor in training was London.

Those two weeks were magical; they were in many ways far more enjoyable than the real race. I so much admired those who had physical limitations and yet strived harder than anyone else to prove their worth as a competent crew member. There was one person who was a diabetic. Our variation in energy requirements while sailing an ocean racer was enormous and he struggled to maintain his blood sugar levels. He collapsed on the foredeck and the race director decided that he could not be allowed to continue. We were all so terribly disappointed for him but his problem would have worsened on the race itself; our boats had no refrigeration facilities to carry his insulin.

And then there was Iain Cook. Iain is a very successful businessman who was born with no lower limbs and with several fingers missing from one of his hands. Iain raced across the deck on short wooden stumps and heaved on the rigging lines with impossible strength. He set us all an incredible example, one that was difficult to equal. It would be unfair for me to even suggest that he had a disability because his performance was far beyond my own. Iain was also tremendous fun. One night we all went on a Vilamoura pub crawl. There was a lot of heavy traditional downing of beers followed by lethal chasers. I struggled back to my bunk on Glasgow and an hour later I heard a commotion as Iain returned with two of his drunken shipmates.

Iain was wearing his long wooden legs which fastened to his torso and made him more than 6 ft tall. He fell into the harbour and his two mates were so drunk they could not rescue him. Eventually two policemen ran down to the pier and when they fished him out he came in two halves, upper and lower. One can imagine the look of horror on their faces. This was not the end of this rather hilarious episode. Iain fell, literally legless, down the gangway into our main cabin. Under normal circumstances he would have been in agony, but he never felt a thing. We put him to bed in his own bunk and put his other half, his legs, into bed with one of the girls. The poor girl, also inebriated, woke up in the middle of the night and yelled out when she though that someone had joined her. We all suffered the following day as we sailed into a heavy Atlantic swell for another day of training.

I returned to Vilamoura on 29th April 2002 and crewed London back to Plymouth with Simon Rowell. Simon skippered Leeds in the Times 2000 race. He is an excellent skipper and he taught me much during those 8 days of sheer hell as we sailed up the Portuguese coast and across the Bay of Biscay. Almost immediately after rounding Sagres we headed nose-on into a force 8 storm. The waves were huge, for hour after hour and day after day we climbed their steep walls only to plunge down into the chasm that lay just beyond. Each sickening crash threatened to split our thin hull from stem to stern. But it never did, and with time I began to develop a strong trust in both skipper and boat; a trust that is so essential for anyone about to embark on a round the world yacht race.

One of our crew members became dehydrated and Simon put into La Corunna so that she could be hospitalised. The sailing club in La

Corunna was so typical of many such establishments. Their members wore smart white caps while they wined and dined their guests; they had probably never put their boats to sea. We were very wet and had not slept for several days, yet the sailing club would not allow us to use their showers or restroom facilities. I suppose we were only sailors; ah well, it takes all kinds!

We were allotted our boats later in the year and then the final stage of our training took place in coastal waters around the British Isles. I joined Bristol skippered by Richard Butler and took part in several training races between Bristol, Southampton, Cardiff and Cork before our boat, alongside those of our competitors, was established in a boatyard on the Merseyside for final boat preparation. Our competitors were to be London, New York, Capetown, Hong Kong, Jersey, Liverpool and Glasgow.

A hurricane delayed our departure

The race was scheduled to start from a point off the Liver Buildings in the River Mersey on the 27th of September 2002. A hurricane swept up the Irish Sea and Winds of over 100 mph battered us overnight, and our escort, HMS Edinburgh, slipped her moorings and deserted us. We were berthed in Albert dock and the high buildings surrounding us afforded reasonable shelter. Thankfully the lock keeper refused to open the lock gates which would give us access to the Mersey and we had no choice but to ride out the storm. We eventually started our race on the following morning. It was a working day and despite this tens of thousands of well wishers thronged both banks of the Mersey to wish us God Speed. Our stormy weather continued unabated for the next 9 days as we raced down through the Irish Sea, across the Bay of Biscay and down the Portuguese coast into the port of Cascais, just outside Lisbon.

I had the honour of our first 24-hour mother watch. I had to prepare meals and hot refreshments with the boat heeled over at 45 degrees, bucking and kicking in steep 20-ft waves. I had to wear full oilskins to protect myself while boiling large pans of spaghetti on the gimballed gas stove. Occasionally the boat heeled to the full limit of the stove's gimbal and boiling water spilled over me. I was clipped in position with a harness and couldn't escape the front of the cooker whenever this occurred. Cooking at the beginning of a race is the worst duty possible for anyone and it made me seasick more than 16 times; it was the worst 24 hours of my life.

This was the second time that I had sailed the Bay of Biscay in an Ocean Racer and on both occasions I experienced terrible conditions. We had many occasions when "all hands on deck" was called, usually to take in a reef or to tie down equipment that had broken loose. We lost several items overboard and halfway across we were called by race headquarters to check if we were still afloat. Our emergency radio beacon had been washed overboard and this had alerted the international rescue services; rather embarrassing but good to know that the rescue services were doing their job.

I slept in cold wet clothing in a forepeak bunk that was heaving and pitching. I had to tie myself into position with a lee cloth. Seawater gushed through a vent hole above my head, and at best, I managed 2 hours sleep before being called back on deck. Many have asked if I was scared. The truth is that the conditions were so bad below deck that I was pleased to get back on watch where I could be occupied helming, winching or changing the sails. I had no time to be scared and I was too wet and tired to care. After a while I became confident in both the boat and my crewmates; I learnt to appreciate, and to accept, the punishment that both could take.

About half way across Biscay I took a really bad fall. I was struggling through the bowels of the boat in complete darkness, trying to get on deck at the start of my watch. I had just grabbed hold of my harness when a huge wave hit our boat. I was thrown across the full width of the cabin and landed headfirst in one of the 'coffins'. I seriously thought that I had broken my neck. In any event, I damaged my ribs and this caused me extreme pain for the next ten days. I managed to hide my injury from my crewmates and we were off Casablanca before Matt noticed my bruised ribs.

The race into Lisbon was eventful for all clippers. Two had to put into other ports to effect emergency repairs and one had to have a crewmember taken off for hospital treatment in La Corunna. The race result was not very good either. We came fifth, which was a poor start for our first leg. Nevertheless, it was good that we experienced such bad conditions early in the race. It prepared us for what was to come.

Surfing gigantic Atlantic waves under spinnaker

After Lisbon we raced south, down the African coast as far as Mauritania, picked up the trade winds and then turned west to cross the Atlantic. From then onwards we sailed downwind under spinnaker. Under normal conditions this could have been an enjoyable holiday. However, we were racing, and racing meant that we had to fly spinnakers when any sensible sailor would have taken them down for safety. We had to push to the absolute limits and beyond. Five times we ended up with our medimum weight spinnaker in the sea.

Our first broach occurred while I was at the helm; our medium weight spinnaker sank beneath the waves and pulled our port winches deep into the ocean. Suddenly a thunderous crack split the air; the spinnaker halyard had snapped cleanly at the winch and in doing so it released us from the clutches of hell. Bristol came back to an almost upright position and after a brief 'all hands on deck' we were able to fly the heavyweight and get back to racing. We continued time after time to tempt the wind gods and during one of our many tropical squalls our anemometer registered 65 mph and yet we maintained a full spread of sails.

It could be very demanding in the middle of the night, especially when we had no moon to illuminate our foredeck; fortunately we usually had a star to place above our masthead for guidance. As we progressed towards the Windward Islands we all became more experienced and soon our individual helming records started to shoot up. We surfed larger and larger waves and everyone was excited when I beat big John and set our Atlantic record at 14.4 knots. Sometimes we achieved a daily run of more than 200 miles. Riding a gigantic Atlantic wave was akin to surfing a 35 tonne boat across a playground covered with ten thousand glass marbles. The whole boat seemed to vibrate with excitement.

Not everything was so easy. We had many frightening moments when the boat came close to broaching in heavy seas or when we broke halyards in the squalls. Our skipper had never sailed the Atlantic; it was the first time for all of us, but he was a very experienced sailor and he always seemed to be there to save the day. It would seem that he never slept; none of our crew had much opportunity anyhow. For much of our Atlantic crossing we were only 17 degrees north of the equator and the sea temperature was constant at 31 degrees centigrade. It was incredibly hot and sticky below deck.

The whole crew was interested in wildlife, except the Skipper who was totally focussed on racing. Whenever we spotted a new type of bird, fish or whale, I rushed to our collection of books to make a positive identification. We spotted a pod of nine or so Pilot Whales and several groups of Minke Whales; the first group of Minke Whales passed several times beneath our bow.

I identified many new birds, at least new to me. I spotted Madeiran Storm Petrels, White Bellied Storm Petrels, Cory's Shearwaters, Magnificent Frigate Birds and Red Billed Tropic Birds. I felt sorry for the Storm Petrels, they swept in a zigzag direction over the surface of the sea, dodging waves and taking no notice of our boat. They were always alone, living in the middle of the ocean with no companion to share their lonely existence. The Tropic Birds were usually in pairs or even threes and always circled our boat a couple of times, as if to say hello, before flying off in an easterly direction.

One morning I spotted a once in a lifetime phenomenon; the rising sun was blocked by a very small cloud and beams of golden light radiated outwards like a fan from the eastern horizon. Not unusual? Well on the opposite and rather dark western horizon, these same beams radiated inwards, like a reverse image from the sky and back into the ocean; a total 180-degree refraction of the sun's beams from eastern to western horizon. Absolutely incredible! We also witnessed several silver rainbows that were refractions of the moon's rays and on one occasion a tornado reached down from one of our nearby clouds. What incredible things the Atlantic Ocean has to offer!

Earlier in the crossing I was pressured into having a haircut. Polly, one of our three watch-leaders, lost her shear guard and accidentally, she swears, shaved the top of my head. My boat name then changed from 'Big Bad Baz' to that of a cartoon character called 'Big Vern'. Later in the race it changed again to the 'Smash Kid'. While I was making coffee under red lights I mistook Cadbury's Smash for milk powder and I served four cups of coffee flavoured mush to the night watch. It didn't go down too well!

Every week the Skipper gathered his crew together on deck and we ate lovely warm freshly baked bread while discussing our race tactics. We always had something to celebrate; a birthday, a long daily run, the halfway mark from Africa to the America's. Baking birthday cakes and fresh bread in a gimballed gas oven is a skill that we are all very proud to have acquired. No landlubber can have any idea what hot fresh bread tastes like after several weeks at sea. The remaining fruit and vegetables had long since turned rotten and much of the dried food was beginning to taste mouldy.

The trade winds were very kind to us and we made good time across the Atlantic. For almost two weeks we never saw another boat, or even an aeroplane in the sky. We felt very lonely and then a blue heron suddenly joined us. The poor hapless bird was exhausted but there was not much we could do to help him. He flew away on several occasions and each time he came back to crash-land on our deck until eventually he just ran out of steam. So sad!

Shortly afterwards we made landfall off Antigua. From then it seemed to take forever as we raced around the outer perimeter of the Windward Isles passing the British Virgin Islands, the Dominican Republic and Haiti. We passed five large cruise ships and one of them, the Carnival Princess, turned her searchlights onto us. We must have been a fabulous sight under full spinnaker with our bow cutting firmly into the heavy Caribbean swell. Her duty officer was kind enough to relay a message from London Clipper who was having difficulty with her satellite communications.

We rounded the south-easterly tip of Quantanamo Bay and the US Coastguard buzzed us several times in their reconnaissance aircraft. I suppose they were rather excited to have something interesting to disturb their otherwise monotonous routine. After this we sailed through a very narrow channel between the Great Bahamas Bank and the northerly coast of Cuba. To us seasoned sailors the ocean appeared calm, and yet a trawler sailing in the opposite direction bucked wildly as she ploughed into rather heavy seas. We had definitely won our sea legs!

As we sailed majestically under the guns of Castillo Del Moro and into the Port of Old Havana we could hear Bristol Clipper supporters cheering us from the ramparts. Sky Sports filmed our arrival and photographs of Bristol Clipper passing beneath the Old Castle appeared in newspapers right across the United Kingdom. New York had won our Trans-Atlantic Race but they arrived in the early hours during a tropical storm and so we stole their media coverage and took consolation in receiving the pennant for second place.

When we entered the Hemingway Marina we had to stand-to while the Cuban Customs Officers inspected our boat. We had all lived together in close proximity for the past five weeks. The only water that we had on board came from our water maker. This water was more valuable to us than gold and very little could be spared for personal hygiene; most had to be used for cooking and drinking purposes. We had become accustomed to sleeping in a bunk that stunk to high heaven and we had long since become immune to any peculiar body odours. Suffice to say that our customs inspection was completed in record time.

Entering Havana was like travelling back 50 years in time; to the days of big chrome plated cars and Al Capone. Every street corner had a small cafe with live bands playing Latin American music and ballads about Che Guevara. The buildings had incredible character and the square adjoining my Hostel was straight out of a Hollywood film set, but all I wanted to do was soak in a huge cool bath and sleep in a bed that didn't bludgeon me against the bulkhead every five minutes. It was so good to sleep for more than two hours without having to respond to 'all hands on deck'; life was suddenly very normal, so normal that it didn't seem real anymore.

Christmas Eve transiting the Panama Canal

The race from Cuba to Panama was not what I expected. Everyone had difficulty in adjusting to the new watch system and we were hot, wet and very tired for most of the time. The weather was very unkind to us. We were hit by several squalls each day and everyone became uncomfortable and irritable. When they came they often trashed our spinnaker or forced us to divert from our intended course. It was hot and humid below deck and the stormy conditions prevented us from opening any hatches. Sleep was impossible and no one, not even a seasoned sailor, can imagine what the conditions were like.

After rounding the western tip of Cuba the fleet headed for a waymark south east of Jamaica. Clipper established this waymark to ensure that we didn't try to take a short cut through the coral reefs lying off the coasts of Yucatan, Belize, Honduras and Nicaragua. The danger of these reefs crystallised into reality when we passed a large ocean going freighter sitting high in the mist shrouded water, hundreds of miles from land yet obviously lodged firmly on a coral bank.

Richard was highly strung when we made our final run into Colon. Hong Kong had been on our port beam for the whole morning and as we approached the finish line they crossed our bow and took the lead by only 2 boat lengths. This was incredible close after racing in open seas for more than 1000 miles. For the next 20 minutes we fought like hell to pull in the difference. Richard yelled furiously at our ship's photographer and told her to stop taking photographs. The rest of our crew who didn't have a job to do sat on the port rail and tried to make what difference they could to the trim of our surging 32 ton ocean racer.

Here is an entry in 'real time' taken from my diary:

……..The trimmer stood below the shrouds and called "trim trim, ease, trim". The grinder grinds in the sheet and then, oh hell! A turn crosses on the winch. A few seconds is lost on the trimmer's last call and Richard is beside himself. Now we are drawing alongside and for the first time in the race we eyeball the crew of Hong Kong across fifty feet of churning water. The crossed turn is released and the trimmer's call becomes even more urgent. John has been at the helm all morning and his arms are aching; Richard wants him to stay, and John wants to stay, but the pain is beginning to tell on his face as he tries to concentrate on his elusive heading. The spinnaker pulls to port; she tries to head starboard. The spinnaker starts to collapse and John over-corrects. Every small turn of the helm is crucial and the concentration on John's face deepens as Hong Kong starts to draw clear again……….

Everyone held their nerve, and in the next few minutes we reeled them back in, and as we took the lead the skipper of Hong Kong changed to a slightly higher heading. He signalled that we were low on the finishing gate, but Richard told John to hold firm to his course, and we crossed the finishing line correctly and only seconds ahead of Hong Kong. We finished 5th in the race but our extra point gave us 3rd overall. The adrenalin rush and tremendous excitement of our fight with Hong Kong helped to compensate for our miserable passage through the stormy grey waters of the Caribbean. It helped to cheer us up for what was about to come; three days of absolute boredom anchored in the sweating heat off Colon waiting for permission to enter the Panama Canal.

As we lay at the canal entrance we watched many of the world's largest vessels pass by. Several acknowledged our presence including the P&O Cruise Ship Princess Royal from Southampton who gave us a long blast on her horn. To our enormous relief our pilot boarded in the early hours of 24th December. We then spent Christmas Eve motoring through the Panama Canal. This in itself was very interesting. We saw a lot of wildlife including a crocodile at the entrance to the first gate of Gatun Lock and a sloth hanging from a nearby tree.

Jim Malcolm, the British Ambassador to Panama, joined for the transit. He is a very likeable Scotsman and he interfaced very well with our crew. With his daughter's help, he became the boat cameraman for the day. We rafted with Capetown and New York to join the Panamax container vessel Pearl Queen. She was our companion in all three sets of locks and paid around 48,000 US dollars for her transit compared to our 800 US dollars. Eight huge 'mules' pulled Pearl Queen into position and her 'Panamax' hull cleared the side-walls of the locks with only inches to spare. We followed closely behind her huge slowly churning propellers and struggled to hold our position when water gushed in from side channels to raise our position to the next level.

On entering the huge Gatun Lake, we realised that we were now geographically speaking at the highest point of our race, 80 ft above sea level; rather a strange place for an ocean racer. I was amazed by our surroundings as we passed through the divide that separated two huge continents. Car transports from China, bulk carriers from Canada, container ships from Korea, massive ships from all over the world were sitting at anchor in this beautiful lake, which was surrounded by low lying mountains and a huge tropical rainforest; everything was so unreal.

Gatun Lake gave way to a long meandering waterway which eventually entered the Culebra Cut, a huge man-made scar carved through the smallest mountain on the Isthmus. Late in the evening we passed through the Miraflores Lock and sailed quietly down the remaining stretch, under the Bridge of the Americas and out into the Pacific Ocean, just as the sun began to set. Meanwhile, England was already celebrating Christmas Day!

After a short stay in Panama City to effect repairs and restock our food supplies we started our race to the Galapagos Islands. We knew this was going to be a very different race. Not only were we in the Pacific Ocean, but we were racing close to the equator in an area of low and uncertain winds. This could be very stressful for crews trying to win a race. Lying dead in the water on the equator with no way to keep cool and sleeping in a hot wet sticky and smelly bunk is mind destroying. I hated having to struggle into stinking clothes in the middle of the night; clothes that were already soaked in salt water and sweat from my previous watch. These conditions are difficult to describe. Whatever anyone can imagine; it was much worse; fighting to change sails in a squall was easy by comparison.

We celebrated New Year's Eve at midnight English time and later at boat time. We were racing and so our celebrations lasted for all of two minutes. Crossing the equator on the following night was pretty much the same. We sacrificed a cup of cornflakes to Neptune and then got back to trimming the sails. Perhaps this was why we were not getting better winds; our sacrifice had not been to Neptune's liking.

Following in the footsteps of Darwin

I gathered our weather faxes every night from the United States Coast Guard in New Orleans. Every night I looked for a few isobars that might indicate a pressure gradient that would give us some wind. It never came and southerly boats that stayed close to the Bolivian coast forged ahead to take the first three places. Our approach into the islands was overwhelming. Blue-footed and masked boobies flew overhead, two white tipped sharks cruised by and a sea lion poked its head up to take an inquisitive peek at us.

How can I begin to explain the tranquil environment of the Galapagos

Islands and the ancient creatures that inhabit its shores? Every island had its own charm and I could easily recognise the unique features of the different types of giant tortoise and of the colourful land iguanas. I struggled to recognise the thirteen types of Darwin finch but the thousands of blue-footed boobies, frigate birds, shearwaters and swallow tailed gulls were easy to distinguish.

Our racing fleet anchored off Puerto Ayora, a small town on the southern tip of Santa Cruz. I was keen to explore the interior, and as soon as I finished my deep clean duties on board Bristol I joined three friends from other boats and set off into the Highlands. Ankle deep in mud and wearing only trainers, we trudged through lava tunnels, up volcanoes, through deep undergrowth and eventually found what we were looking for, giant tortoises living in the wild. We found several that were around 96 years old.

The following day I joined a boat sailing for Espanola, one of the southern group of islands. I hoped to see an albatross but was terribly disappointed when my guide told me that they had already flown south for the season. It was a very rough crossing and my five fellow tourists had a terrible time. I was the only person able to enjoy my meals and I even had a good night's sleep. This was luxury for me!

When we arrived off Espanola I had to brush several sea lion pups to one side so that I could wade ashore. The bulls were defending their harems against all-comers but they ignored me as I walked through their colony. There were sea turtles and iguanas everywhere. They had no fear of man and I was amazed by their absolute indifference to our presence. Well almost, two mocking birds took an interest in me and swooped down to drink water from my outstretched hand.

I sat on a rocky ledge while a friend took video footage of me sitting beside two masked boobies that were feeding their young chicks only inches away. Then I stood mesmerised by hundreds of frigate birds and swallow-tailed gulls as they soared high above the cliff tops. Suddenly my guide called me to a small rocky clearing. There to my absolute delight were two large albatross chicks, and hiding in long grass near to them were two very shy adults. This alone made the whole trip worthwhile. It was a bonus that I had not expected.

My race from Liverpool to the Galapagos Islands was a tremendous challenge; it filled two of my greatest ambitions. One was to race the Atlantic in an ocean racer and the other was to follow in the footsteps of Charles Darwin; even if I did cheat a little and pass by way of the Panama Canal. And to boot, the Lord Mayor of Bristol presented me with a runners-up silver medal. I was fortunate to be able to participate in the 2002 Clipper Round the World Yacht Race and I know that I will treasure memories of this adventure for the rest of my life.

Chapter 24

Looking for Paradise

Choosing a country and finding the perfect retirement home
Retirement is hard work!

Anne and I were determined to find a second home in a warmer climate. I had worked overseas for most of my adult life and it was very unlikely that I would be able to retire in England; a second home would create a good stepping stone for both of us.

We visited Anne's sister Cathy in Johannesburg early in February 1996 and enjoyed a casual drive through the Little Karoo and then down the Garden Route before ending up in one of my old haunts at Haut Bay in the Cape. It is a gorgeous place and we considered buying a five acre plot of land beneath the 12 Apostles for only 50,000 pounds. I liked the beauty of the area and we loved swimming with the Jackass Penguins on Boulder Beach near to Simonstown, but I was very reluctant to bring good money into South Africa a second time around.

After South Africa we started to look at other possibilities. We considered many locations and investigated them all. There were several attractive locations in Eastern Europe that were opening up and they were extremely cheap. Budapest is incredibly attractive and it has an excellent National Opera House with easy connections from Bristol, but again, it has a vicious winter. We even visited Madeira and we loved its wild beauty and colourful flowers. It has long walks along a strange network of hillside irrigation water canals, but we preferred easier access to mainland Europe.

Malta had favourable tax and immigration rules and it was soon to join the European Union. It had an incredible history but for me it was much too dry in the summer months. Cyprus had similar characteristics but I thought that it was too cold in the winter; as was Italy, Greece and France. We drove the length and breadth of Europe and no matter how hard we tried, everything pointed towards the coastal areas of Andalucia or the Algarve as being the most suitable place.

Our biggest mistake, buying in Spain

In March 1998 we flew to Alicante and hired a car. Anne was keen to drive and she took the wheel all the way from Alicante on the Costa Blanca to Sagres on the south western tip of the Algarve. It was an incredibly long journey and we followed the Mediterranean Sea and Atlantic Ocean along the whole route. Anne took no short-cuts; we examined every small village and town en-route. Eventually we reached the fortified school of Henry the Navigator at Sagres and we then made our way back to Alicante using inland roads so that we could check out the attractive old Moorish cities of Andalucia. Anne loved Seville but it was too commercial for my liking. Granada had enormous character but it was too hot and dry.

Eventually we decided that Fuengirola offered the best combination of local life with a coastal frontage for our grandchildren and a mountainous backdrop to provide a cooler refuge for me in the warm summer months. The main benefit for Anne was that there were real Spanish people living in the town. The centre and its environs were not overly swamped by foreign tourists and it enjoyed excellent communications with Bristol through the airport at Malaga.

We returned to Fuengirola in April 2000 with Dad and Mattie and searched the area carefully. I wanted an apartment with a balcony where I could take a sundowner while watching the setting sun. The apartment had to be high in the hills overlooking the ocean so that the warm sea breeze from the African continent would be cooled adiabatically before reaching our position.

My specification was met perfectly by a development called Bonita Hills which lay in a perfect position high above Calahonda. It had local access to the motorway which connected to Granada, Cordoba, Seville and Gibraltar; all within a maximum driving time of two hours. The development was being constructed to a high specification by a German architect and it had been awarded the best development award in Spain by Jaguar Cars.

Anne and I met with the sales agent and I studied the plans very carefully. There was a duplex penthouse that provided well balanced rooms on the corner of the development. It was in a high position that could never be overlooked from any direction except the northwest, which was where the entrance door was located. Fearful that such an excellent location would be snapped up by someone else we bought it immediately.

The following day I borrowed the plans and measured out the exact position where our apartment was to be built and I placed a boulder on the spot. We enjoyed a panoramic view of sea and mountains through a full 270 degrees. Even North Africa and the Pillars of Hercules could be seen through the shimmering haze of the late afternoon sun. Dad, Mattie, Anne and I stood on muddy ground surrounding my boulder and took photographs of each other to remind us of this exciting day.

We were the first to purchase in Bonita Hills and our salesman treated all of us to an excellent meal in a fish restaurant on the Cabopino harbourside. It was a wonderful day and I was so pleased that Dad and Mattie had been with me to witness our purchase and to share in our celebratory bottle of champagne.

With the purchase behind us I drove Dad and Mattie down to Gibraltar. This was to be the first of many such trips and Gibraltar later became our main shopping centre. On this occasion we left our hired car in La Linhia, walked through the border posts, across the main runway of the Royal Air Force station and through the heavily fortified gate of the South Ramparts. This was a proud moment for my father. In all his years he had never had an opportunity to visit this remote bastion of the British Empire. For the rest of the day we toured the underground hospital, the siege tunnels, the Trafalgar cemetery and several other historical sites related to the Rock's prominent military history.

After paying one third of the total purchase price to Bauer Hagel, the developer, we stood back and I waited for our retirement home to be built. I contacted our Spanish attorney at regular intervals to check on Bauer Hagel's progress and I found that it was increasingly difficult to get information. After nine months my contract with the developer expired and I asked my Attorney to return my funds. He shocked me when he said that he had granted them a 12 months extension. I could not believe that he would have done such a thing without consulting me first. Then suddenly a 'For Sale' sign appeared on the hill top. Bauer Hagel reported that her Spanish accountant had stolen her funds and that she had no choice but to sell the land.

I resigned myself to losing my deposit of around 50,000 pounds and got on with life. Then six months later the bulldozers moved in and began to level the hilltop for the first phase; Bauer Hagel had found financial backing from an alternative source and she was making a fresh start. Slowly the main structure began to take shape and I waited eagerly to see the beginning of my own foundations. Eventually these were dug deep into the bedrock at a position some 15 yards northeast of my boulder and 16 feet lower that the crest of the hill. I was so pleased that everything had restarted that I chose not to complain about the new location.

Several months later the basic structure of the building was complete and I then found that the orientation of my building had been rotated anticlockwise by 90 degrees. My balconies now looked towards the mountains and I had lost my coveted view of the sunset. I tried again to withdraw from my contract but my Attorney reminded me that I would lose my deposit. I began to wonder what kind of legal system operated in this remote outpost of the European Community.

At this point it sounded as if nothing further could go wrong; but it did. Eventually I was called to make my next payment and I yet again I was reminded that none payment would put me in default and cause forfeiture of my deposit. In for a penny in for a pound; I paid a further 50,000 raising my total exposure to 100,000 pounds.

Our apartment was finally completed two years after signing my original contract. At the time I was in the Pacific Ocean sailing towards the Galapagos Islands and so Anne travelled down and took possession for me. It was touch and go for a while because our attorney discovered that Bauer Hagel had borrowed additional funds from her Bank using my apartment and several others as security. My attorney came into his own at this point. He used my payment to clear the bank charge and then hurriedly placed my name on the Land Register.

Four years later several owners discovered that their properties were owned and registered in the name of Bauer Hagel's bank. They had to pay huge sums to clear her debts, not only on their own properties, but on others in a different development. This could so easily have been me. I was utterly disgusted that the Spanish Authorities not only permitted this kind of trickery, but in many instances had been part of it!

Later in the Summer Anne and I loaded her Volkswagen Golf to the ceiling and set out for Andalucia. We crossed the channel from Portsmouth to Saint Malo and drove through the Loire, Cognac, Bordelaise and Armagnac wine regions before taking a short break in Basque country and then on down through Navarra before setting off on the long trek across central Spain towards our final destination, which was just west of Fuengirola. Those who are connoisseurs of fine wines will have recognized that Anne had planned our trip to pass through five very famous wine growing regions. Needless to say we spent several half days diverting to different vineyards along our route and at the end of our long journey I was so pleased to find that her Golf had not been emptied of our possessions.

When we arrived we soon made friends with several people who had also retired to Bonita Hills. I was pleasantly surprised to find that an old university friend of Gen Katsumata had moved into a neighbouring apartment. His name is Saki Kurukawa and he had just retired from his position as the President of Maxell Europe. Saki and his good wife, Musse, became very close friends. We no longer had any view of the sun setting from our apartment and so we spent many enjoyable evenings taking a sundowner and sipping green Japanese tea on their balcony instead. I remember with affection the chocolates and other calorie laden goodies that Saki always asked Musse to tempt me with when I was trying to lose weight.

Rock carvings and dinosaurs

One really great feature of Andalucia is that it is so perfectly positioned to take motoring holidays in one direction and fly in the other. We often took the ferry from Plymouth to Santander and drove through Spain to

Fuengirola, taking short breaks in different towns on the way. Sometimes we would drive northwards instead and along different routes; one of our most enjoyable trips was through the wine regions of Penedas, Prioral, Languedoc, Bourgogne, Jura, Alsace and Champagne. It was a circuitous route that allowed us to visit Barcelona, Fuji Electric in Claremont Ferrand and to visit the European Parliament in Strasbourg.

Anne always did the driving, she enjoyed sitting behind the wheel and I hated it; I always struggled to stay awake. Over several seasons we explored almost every region of France and Spain and on the last occasion we made two surprising discoveries. The first was in the Douro Valley, Portugal and the second was in Asturias, Spain.

We enjoyed a long drive through Extremadura which by now was becoming very familiar to us both and then we branched off into Portugal and spent a few enjoyable days in Oporto. We visited an old cellar which had casks dating back for almost 200 years. Marshal Soult's soldiers had drunk everything during the Peninsular War and there were no casks pre-dating the 12th May 1809, which was the day when Sir Arthur Wellesley, later the Duke of Wellington, crossed the Douro in several wine barges and liberated Oporto. We spotted several barrels carrying my birth year, 1944, and Anne paid a small fortune to secure a bottle which had been taken for a 60 year sample.

After this short enjoyable stay in Oporto we headed up the Douro Valley. I was following in the footsteps of Bernard Cornwall's fictitious Napoleonic hero, Major Richard Sharpe, and Anne was back again on her never-ending wine trail.

At the end of our second day we stumbled upon a prehistoric site where thousands of examples of rock carvings had just been discovered. The carvings were found by an archaeologist during the construction of a huge hydroelectric dam across a near vertical ravine in the Côa Valley. His find received enormous publicity and huge public support forced the Portuguese Government to suspend construction of the Dam. Eventually the civil engineering project was dropped altogether and 17 kilometres of the Côa River Valley became a World Heritage Site.

We arrived in the Côa Valley late in the evening and stayed in a small hotel. At 7 am the following morning we visited the archaeological office; there was a notice on the window explaining that reservations to visit the valley had to be made several weeks in advance and that only 8 persons were able to join each group. A young ranger arrived a few minutes later and she checked her computer, it was time to leave and two people had not arrived; we were in luck!

Anne and I climbed into the rangers Landcruiser and she drove us along a dirt track that followed steep contours high above the rock strewn valley. It was a very difficult drive and one that I would not have wanted to make. There were steep hairpin bends with absolutely no margin for error. A small wheel slide in the loose dry sand would have put two wheels over the precipice and we would have bounced from rock to rock like a dinky toy in a Steven Spielberg movie.

The Valley was a deserted inaccessible place and we were shown outstanding examples of Upper Palaeolithic rock-art that lay in dry snake-infested open terrain that had been protected from the ravages of mankind for 20,000 years. Our guidebook pre-dated the Côa Valley discovery and I later managed to gain more information from the internet. The writer explained that the Côa Valley carvings presented outstanding examples of creative intelligence at the dawn of human cultural development. He went on to say that they were by far the best examples of their kind anywhere in the world and they threw light on the social, economic, and spiritual life existing when mammoths and aurochs walked the ice cold wastes of Western Europe. I am sure that he was right!

It was difficult to believe that I was standing in open sunlight and not in a cave. I dragged my fingers gently across these fine lines that had been stippled into stone by my ancestors; prehistoric man. I struggled to understand how these subtle traces had withstood erosive sand storms and the ravages of warming ice for 20,000 years. Yet I remain saddened in my belief that modern man will soon accomplish what nature has been unable to do, he will surely vandalise this priceless rock-art with crude carvings or destroy it in a more subtle way. He, with my help, will burn huge quantities of fossil fuels and drench the Côa Valley rock art in corrosive acid rain.

Sustained by our fortuitous find we travelled along the back roads of

Portugal and Spain until we arrived in an area known as Cordillera Cantabrica. This ridge of high rugged mountains gives refuge to wolves, bears and eagles. It looked totally impassable as we approached its steep slopes, and then a fast modern road took us through a succession of long tunnels. When we emerged on the other side we were immediately blinded by the red glow of the setting sun, and when our eyes recovered we were further dazzled by the beautiful panoramic view that stretched before us; the rich green pastures of Asturias. In the distance we were beckoned by the deep blue hues of the Cantabric Sea. Perhaps other secrets were awaiting our discovery before our journey came to an end in the bowels of a large ugly passenger ferry in the nearby seaport of Santander.

It was late in the day and we rushed east and then west along this narrow corridor of land. We couldn't find a hotel for the night and then when all seemed lost our searching headlights picked up a small stone-built hostel on the cliffs before us. It was perched precariously on the edge of high cliffs overlooking the small fishing village of Lastres. We were given a quaint little room with picture windows on three sides and all opened above a sheer drop to the rough thundering sea which lashed against jagged rocks far below. I could imagine Long John Silver sitting in the far window with his peg-leg resting on the deep wooden sill. Lighting flashed in the distance and three fishing boats struggled passed the outer harbour light. It really was an eerie-creepy kind of place.

The following morning we happened upon several signposts marking the Route of the Dinosaurs. One of these indicated that footprints could be found on La Griega beach which was a short walk from our hotel. A cold sea breeze caused Anne to lose the blood circulation in her hands; this is a problem that she has lived with for most of her life and the reason why she was unable to join me on the Clipper race. Despite this, Anne found a small three-toed print in a rock that lay just above the high water mark.

While I was taking lots of photographs of this small imprint Anne called to me from a large grey body of flat limestone rock. This rock was partly covered by grass banking and it could be seen that its surface had been uncovered in a recent storm. She had found several different groupings of dinosaur footprints. I made out three very distinct types, many were tridactile, although there were others which were more difficult to identify. The largest appeared to be a complete set of four prints from a sauropod of colossal dimensions; these deep rounded depressions had a raised outer edge and measured 130 cm across; I understand that they probably came from a dinosaur weighing more than 100 tons. They were the largest footprints ever found anywhere in the World.

I hate visiting museums because the artefacts on display have almost always been taken from their original location. In some cases, as with the Elgin Marbles, they have been taken under suspicious circumstances. On the other hand, if they had not been removed to a safer environment, then they would have been looted or ravaged by the sands of time. These footprints from the Jurassic Age were scattered all along the Colunga Coast and I was immensely privileged to find them in their natural surroundings. There were no warning signs, railings or protective buildings to spoil my moment of absolute awe. However, I do believe that something should be done to prevent the ocean laying claim to what the green pastures of Asturia have held secret for the past 160 million years.

In the spring of 2004 I arrived at our apartment to find Saki throwing stones in the general direction of Spanish workers who were building the second phase of Bonita Hills. The developer had obtained planning permission to add three further floors to the original design. I guess money had passed under someone's table in the Town Hall. We considered taking legal action against Bauer Hagel but she formed another company to build the second phase and with her first company teetering on the verge of bankruptcy there appeared to be nothing we could do to stop her.

This was the final straw in regard to my own very beautiful retirement home. It had marble floors, luxury on-suite bathrooms, piped music in each room, wall air-conditioning units, a laundry and a fully fitted kitchen with German built stainless steel appliances; but not one of my five Andalucian style balconies enjoyed a view of the sunset. And now that the second phase was being built high above me and in the position previously occupied by my boulder, I was about to lose 100 percent of my sea view. The spawn eating six-eyed toads! Small stones; Saki should have been throwing cluster bombs.

I decided that I should sell 50 Bonita Hills at my earliest opportunity.

Anne, Brett and Michele loved the area and they were very upset at my decision but I no longer felt that my investment in Spain was secure. I had originally thought that I would be safe buying a property in the European Union; what a mistake that was! It took some time before I found a buyer and when I did everyone wanted a last piece of the pie; my deductions and selling charges were enormous. The final slice was taken by the Bank of Andalucia who deducted 700 euro for transferring my money to another euro account. I would have been charged 40 euro for the same transaction in England. In the end I was just relieved to have put Spain behind me.

Freeport, Bahamas

When everything went belly-up in Spain I started to look further afield. I considered Barbados and I even took a second look at the Commonwealth of Dominica. Then at an opportune moment Anne's Aunt Marjorie offered to give us two plots of land in the Bahamas. We often took Marjorie and her son John for a pub lunch in Chobham at Christmas. It was great to listen to her fabulous stories of life in the Far East during those glorious days of Empire before the Japanese invasion forces arrived.

Her father was the Chairman of the Peninsular and Oriental Steam Navigation Company better known today as P&O, and her husband Alfred headed up the Oriental side of the business. She had wonderful stories to tell and she was such a jolly person that it was always fun to listen to some of her wicked tales. There were always famous characters in the background. On one occasion while she was stranded in the Suez Canal none other but Howard Carter took her on a guided tour of the Egyptian Museum. She played a good game of golf with the senior ladies at Wentworth and put me to shame with my miserable stroke.

Anyhow, getting back to the Bahamas; I could not possibly accept these two plots as a gift and so I insisted upon paying fair market value. When I flew out to Grand Bahama to view my new acquisitions I found them both deep in the forest. Anne's uncle Richard had described their disposition to me, but I had hoped that he was exaggerating a little. I am afraid he wasn't! I was otherwise impressed with the island and with its friendly people. The white sand beaches and crystal clear blue waters were more attractive than anywhere I had visited in my 40 years of globe trotting. The banks were filled with coral formations and incredibly large shoals of every kind of tropical fish. I even had an opportunity to swim with wild dolphins on my first ever visit to Dead Mans Reef. The International Hub of Miami Airport was only 90 miles away and communications were reputed to be as good as anywhere in the United States. I am afraid this turned out to be untrue, but I was still very impressed. It only took me five days to decide that this was going to be my retirement island. I visited Thompson Estate Agents in the Port of Lucaya and gave them the task of finding a suitable apartment for me to buy.

A really friendly salesman called Robert escorted me to dozens of places but none seemed to be just right. As we drove around in his old Buick Robert told me stories about the golden days when the Rat Pack hung out on the island and Howard Hughes owned and lived as a recluse on the top floor of nearby Xanadu. Drug running boats brought hidden wealth to many islanders and high speed chases through the canals around Lucaya were common place until helicopters of the United States Coastguard gained the upper hand.

I was beginning to despair and I thought that I would not find a suitable purchase. Then on the last day of my visit I noticed a photograph in Thompson's reception room. It reminded me of the view that I enjoyed each morning from the balcony of my rented apartment. It turned out to be a photograph taken from my next door neighbour's balcony; Robert had not told me that my neighbour's apartment was for sale. I suppose he was frightened that I would arrange a private deal and cut him out of his commission. This was not my way of doing business and we closed a deal before the day was out.

The apartment that I bought is in Harbour House Towers and it enjoys a fabulous position on the foreshore of Port Lucaya. Beyond the waters of this picturesque harbour, which once played host to Hemingway, stretches a narrow strip of land where colourful wooden buildings and an artificial lighthouse still stand having defied hurricanes long past. Flashing red and green lights mark the entrance channel for Bahama Mama as she returns each evening with her cargo of rum laden American youngsters bopping to the sounds of very loud Bahamian music.

My apartment on the 8th floor enjoys a fabulous uninterrupted view of all of this and my rear window gives a perfect view of the sun as it sets over the western horizon. Only the forces of nature can ever take this away from me; a tsunami, tornado or perhaps a category 5 hurricane. All are possible in this part of the world, but at least I don't have to worry about the 'Spanish Factor'.

Harbour House Towers became my new home and I applied to the local immigration department for a residence permit. I was lucky to have several sugar companies in the Caribbean who were prepared to write testimonies on my behalf, and armed with a police certificate from Scotland Yard, a medical certificate from my doctor and a financial appraisal from my accountant I was able to convince the authorities that I was an upright citizen worthy of living amongst the best of the Freeport Drug Barons.

2005
Cap'n Jack Sparrow and his Black Pearl Pirates. From left; Brad Fox, Barry Coulton, Johnny Depp, Skip Hunt, Lawrence Lafond, George Jarolim, Bobby Stone, Michael Gabor, Barry Thorpe and Jim Pappas

2005
At the helm of the Black Pearl off Grand Bahama

PIRATES OF THE CARIBBEAN II & III. 2005/2006

DATES	NAME OF VESSEL	DETAILS OF VOYAGE	DAYS ON BOARD	DISTANCE LOGGED	NIGHT HOURS	SIGNATURE OF SKIPPER
12/10/05	BLACK PEARL	GOLD ROCK CREEK GRAND BAHAMA	1	N/A	NIL	JACK
13/10/05	BLACK PEARL	FIGHTING THE FLYING DUTCHMAN	1	N/A	NIL	JACK
15/10/05	BLACK PEARL	FIGHTING THE FLYING DUTCHMAN	1	N/A	NIL	JACK
17/10/05	BLACK PEARL	FIGHTING THE FLYING DUTCHMAN	1	N/A	NIL	JACK
18/10/05	BLACK PEARL	RUNNING FROM DUTCHMAN UNDER FIRE	1	N/A	NIL	JACK
19/10/05	BLACK PEARL	RUNNING FROM DUTCHMAN UNDER FIRE	1	N/A	NIL	JACK
30/10/05	BLACK PEARL	KRAKEN ATTACKS SEVERAL PIRATES KILLED	1	N/A	NIL	JACK
31/10/05	BLACK PEARL	KRAKEN ATTACKS JACK SPARROW TAUNTS KRAKEN	1	N/A	NIL	JACK
4/11/05	BLACK PEARL	FIGHTING THE KRAKEN CANNON FIRE	1	N/A	NIL	JACK

PERSONAL LOG OF CRUISES/RACES

DATES	NAME OF VESSEL	DETAILS OF VOYAGE	DAYS ON BOARD	DISTANCE LOGGED	NIGHT HOURS	SIGNATURE OF SKIPPER
6/11/05	BLACK PEARL	FIGHTING THE KRAKEN LOADING CARGO NET WITH POWDER	1	N/A	NIL	JACK
7/11/05	BLACK PEARL	FIGHTING THE KRAKEN CANNON FIRE	1	N/A	NIL	JACK
20/11/05	BLACK PEARL	FIGHTING THE KRAKEN CANNON FIRE	1	N/A	NIL	JACK
21/11/05	BLACK PEARL	HEAVY WEATHER SAILING HELICOPTER SHOTS	1	N/A	2	JACK
22/11/05	BLACK PEARL	GOLD ROCK CREEK TO FREEPORT 30 KT WINDS	1	N/A	6	JACK
6/12/05	BLACK PEARL					
7/12/05	BLACK PEARL					
8/12/05	BLACK PEARL					
9/12/05	BLACK PEARL					

PERSONAL LOG OF CRUISES/RACES

2005

Closing page in my Ocean Racing Logbook which includes my sailing record as a Pirate on the Black Pearl. It is signed by the Ship's Captain; Captain Jack Sparrow (Johnny Depp)

2005
Lobsters gathered during a dive on the Lucayan Reef

2005
Reeling in a 50 lb Wahoo which we consumed at a 'Pirates Meeting' at my home in Port Lucaya

2005
Wilma battering my home in Port Lucaya, Grand Bahama

2005
The day after Hurricane Wilma. She hurled a wall of water through the coastal settlements of Grand Bahama

2006
A modern day camel train in Rajasthan

2006
Another misty day at the Taj Mahal

2006
Kathmandu. The Civil War re-started two days earlier. Our flights were cancelled and there were few tourists

2006
Perhaps the most beautiful view in the World. The Annapurnas from Fishtail Lodge in Pokhara, Nepal

2006
I visited Singapore Airport many times over the past 30 years but this is the first time that I have travelled downtown to this incredibly modern city

2006
Another visit to Thailand, my most favoured destination. This photograph was taken on Koh Samui

2006
Anne helping me to discover the redwood forests of Oregon and Northern California

2006
Monument Valley. A visit to the West Coast would not be complete without walking in the footsteps of John Wayne

2006
The Great Wall of China shrouded in mist and pollution

2006
Terracotta Warriors guarding the mausoleum of the first Qing Emperor outside Xi'an. He built the Great Wall!

2006
Riding beside Qinghai Lake on the Tibet Plateau

2006
Climbing above the Yellow River in North West China

2006
Giant Pandas near Chengdu in Sichuan Province, China

2006
My great granddaughter Mia Lucy at 3 months

2006
My granddaughter Sadie Josslyn at 3 months

Chapter 25

New Horizons to Discover

My feet were itching and I have a terrible case of islanditus
Where to next!

Malvern was encouraged by the new level of cooperation that he received from the DTI and he carefully nurtured our business with Iran. He focused our efforts on the Iranian Oil and Gas Company where he could be certain that our products would not be diverted for military purposes. He visited Tehran to help close these orders and was taken by a very attractive young Iranian girl who worked for our agent, Rye Pala. Her name was Vina Varzandeh. She is a tremendous girl with a really nice personality and a homely manner. Malvern looked for every possible excuse to spend time with her, usually under parental supervision, and 14 months later they were married. Vina filled a huge cavern in Malvern's personal life and they are very happy together. I am very pleased for them both.

Word of my retirement spread and Coulton soon received two further offers. I agreed to one of these. It was from Flowmax Holdings, a South African group who were looking for a base to develop their instrumentation business in the United Kingdom. Coulton had the infrastructure they needed and our negotiations moved forward with incredible speed. Graham Nel, the Chairman of Flowmax, knew exactly what he wanted. I shook hands on our deal and returned to my home in the Bahamas with every confidence that Graham was a man whom I could trust.

Luxor

I was not able to spend as much time as I would have liked in Freeport during my first year because the Clipper Race kept me at sea for several months. In addition, I had just retired, and I wanted to begin my travels to those places that I had not been fortunate to visit during my working career. My first target was Luxor, Karnak and Thebes.

There were not many tourists visiting the upper Nile and we were able to visit all of the temples that we wished and at our leisure. This gave me ample time to study and learn the meanings of several hieroglyphics which I noticed were repeated at the entrance to several of the better known tombs in the Valley of the Kings. Anne and I were incredibly impressed by the wall paintings and colossal stone statues that we found. We travelled across the Nile from our hotel close to Karnak and visited several ancient sites in the land of the dead. One evening we took a Falucca and sailed into the sunset; I am afraid that I behaved like a typical tourist and wore a bright green coloured Dishdasha for the occasion. I found it incredibly cool and a very sensible garment for such occasions.

We tried to immerse ourselves in the overwhelming amount of ancient history which was ever present around us. However, no matter which direction we turned we could not help but be affected by the abject poverty that had been visited upon the local population. Recent acts of terrorism had totally destroyed their local economy.

Anne's parents had visited a few years earlier and they were in Luxor when a terrorist machine gun attack killed 62 people outside Hatshepsut's Temple in the Valley of the Kings. This barbaric incident had frightened tourists away from the Upper Nile. The Egyptian Government was making a valiant attempt to prevent any further attacks, and this was most evident on our full day cruise to the Dandera Temple. A navy detachment mounted two machine guns on our foredeck and a gunship escorted us along the more remote stretches of the Nile. When we arrived in Dandera two buses transported us in convoy to the temple with armed military vehicles front and rear. Unfortunately this extra protection frightened many of the tourists.

I was deeply saddened to observe hundreds of idle Faluccas and Hantour's. Wretched horses stood by the roadside with protruding rib cages; their owners unable to buy straw to fill their nosebags. Everywhere honest hard working Arabs sat by the roadside starved of American tourists to bargain for their alabaster bowls. Young shoeshine boys hardly bothered to grab their toe rags as we approached; they knew half a dozen others had already vied for our custom. It really was a heart rending sight.

Several of the lieutenants who organised these barbaric acts of terrorism were Egyptian and many religious clerics chose to give them verbal support. These clerics needed to grasp an understanding of the long term poverty and hardship that the effects of terrorism were inflicting upon their own congregation. I doubt that any of them ever had a heart, and their soul was probably condemned to lasting damnation by Allah long ago.

Many Americans that I met on my travels believed that the rest of the world hated them. This is not true; Americans were welcomed and treated exactly the same as any other tourist; it was the Bush Government that everyone hated. George Bush Junior and Dick Cheyney used the threat of terrorism to further the interests of powerful American corporations, not the American people as a whole. What I could not understand was why ordinary voting Americans could not see through this façade. Perhaps this was because the Democrats were unable to offer a viable alternative. I hope upon hope that the American electorate will show a little more common sense next time around and put another Clinton back into the top job.

Dublin

Our next trip was to Dublin in the spring of 2004. Grandiose buildings are in evidence throughout this beautiful city; buildings very similar to those found throughout England but unspoiled by the ravages of the Second World War. Dublin is a vibrant city filled with friendly people and yet it has suffered so much political turmoil over the past 200 years.

We started with a visit to the Guinness Storehouse where Anne and I enjoyed a cool pint in the Round Tower. My last visit was in 1982 when Guinness invited me to recommend control system improvements on their steam raising plant; it was interesting to see the changes that had taken place over the past 20 years. After the Storehouse we browsed through the exhibits of Trinity College Library and found the famous Book of Kells. This is a 1,200 year old illuminated manuscript of the Gospel, and it is in pristine condition.

One of the historical places on our tourist agenda was Kilmainham Gaol. I was very disturbed when I visited the Gaol; not because of the atrocities committed within its stark walls, but because of the way in which tourists are being misled into the belief that several of the leaders of the 1916 uprising are martyrs. I never had an opinion on this before visiting the gaol but something seemed terribly wrong; the year 1916 was right in the middle of a world war. And so I returned to Trinity College Library to do some research.

First of all I should mention that I am a staunch Royalist. I have always believed that the Monarchy has contributed substantially to the benefit of the peoples of Britain and the British Commonwealth. So my research started with the Kings and Queens of England. My first discovery was that Ireland and England were united as far back as 1199 when John, of Norman lineage and Lord of Ireland, succeeded his brother Richard to the English Throne. This was 337 years before Wales was annexed by Henry VIII and 404 years before James VI of Scotland became James I of England. Subsequent marriages within the Royal Families of Europe further added to this melting pot, and any argument that the Irish people may have had against an 'English' crown are totally invalid; Ireland and England were united under one Crown for 717 years and the person wearing this crown had more European ancestry than English.

I decided that the real objection of the Irish people must not have been against the Crown, but what it represented; the aristocratic class, wealthy landowners and Lords of the Manor who annexed vast quantities of feudal land. These individuals massed great personal wealth and paid subsistence wages to those workers who tended their needs. However, the Irish people should understand that this problem was not unique to Ireland; it was a problem that existed throughout the British Isles and, for that matter, throughout Europe. One prime example was the Tolpuddle Martyrs in Dorset England.

Now back to my original point: I do not condone execution as a humane form of punishment, but the fact remains that a traitor, or a soldier who deserted or showed cowardice in time of war was usually executed by firing squad. I would suggest that under these circumstances that it is no surprise that the leaders of the 1916 uprising were executed when they allied themselves to the German High Command. Barbaric though this punishment may have been; English, Welsh and Scottish nationals were executed by firing squad for lesser crimes.

I like the Irish people, they have a beautiful country and the Taoiseach had done much for Eire within the European Union. But after my research in the Trinity College Library I concluded that the trustees of Kilmainham Gaol should divert the attention of visitors and tourists to the thousands of proud Irish Volunteers who were killed each week fighting on the Western Front for their country.

Cuba again

One month after visiting Dublin I arranged to meet Anne in Cuba. I took a short flight from Freeport and arrived a few hours before her Air France long haul from Paris. I arranged for us to stay in the same hostel as the one I used during my Clipper Race. This was the Hostel Tejadillo in La Habana Vieja, which is just off Plaza de la Catedral de San Cristobal; the most beautiful square in Havana. Colourfully dressed old mamas smoked huge cigars and vibrant musicians competed against each other for the attention of tourists who dined on wooden tables arranged in the centre of the old cobbled square.

I took Anne to my old haunts and showed her Hotel Ambus Mundos where Ernest Hemmingway began to write his book, 'Where the Bell Tolls'. We both enjoyed our first cool Mohito, a blend of rum, mint and honey, and then settled down in one of the many bars where authentic impromptu flamenco was danced by local afro-Cuban enthusiasts.

On our second day we crossed the river to Castillo del Moro. This castle is the backdrop in the newspaper photographs taken of me when Bristol Clipper crossed the finish line on the Transatlantic leg of our Round the World Yacht Race. It is also the location where Halle Berry dived from the ramparts in the James Bond Film, 'Die Another Day'. We spent a full day visiting this castle, the fortifications overlooking the Harbour and the rockets and ballistic missiles that were left over from the Cuban missile crisis.

Anne needed time to soak up the vibrant never ending pulse of Cuba. There was no better place to do this than the World Heritage Site of

Habana Vieja. However, we needed to see the rest of Cuba and so we hired a car and set out early in the morning for Cayo Coco. It took us all morning to find the main highway leading to the South East. Three attempts left us driving down the wrong road against the morning rush hour traffic. Old lorries loaded with people and buses with huge trailers, best described as people movers, competed with us for our piece of tarmacadam. No matter how hard I tried I could not find our highway; signposts just did not exist. This reminded me about my visits to Siberia where maps and signposts had been falsified.

When we did eventually find the correct road it was like driving down one side of a never ending runway; it was so straight and wide and totally devoid of traffic. We passed a lorry after 20 miles and it was 3 hours before we passed a private car. I swear that we must have been the only foreigners using the highway and the only Cubans were riding horses. I wondered why the CIA had not used transport planes to land their invasion forces on this highway instead of making a futile attempt to put troops ashore in the Bay of Pigs.

We followed our highway past Sancti Spiritus and then later in the afternoon we started to make guesses at which road we should take towards the sea. We got it wrong again. I made several attempts to follow different roads and in the absence of a magnetic compass I tried to maintain the sun behind my left shoulder. This didn't work very well, and after more than an hour we arrived back where we started. Eventually, when the sun was falling towards the western horizon I stumbled, more by accident than by good intent, upon a guard post. We showed our passports, paid a small fee in American dollars, and then drove onto a 27 km man-made causeway that led us across shallow pink flamingo infested waters to Cayo Coco.

The narrow strip of sand that we found at the end of the causeway was a holiday resort littered with western decadence. Rum, whisky, vodka and gin were served in unlimited quantities on presentation of a reasonably priced coloured wrist strap. Half naked foreign women sunbathed in landscaped tropical gardens and everywhere one looked there was an ambience of relative wealth. Hobiecats fringed long white sandy beaches and a formation of three crazy looking rubber dinghies with huge hang-glider wings flew overhead. I took several photographs of these strange flying contraptions and I swore to Anne that the topless girl lying on the beach was caught in my lens by accident; three times! Cayo Coco and other tourist hot spots are essential to the Cuban economy and I can understand why Fidel would not want his people to witness such opulence; I kind of agree with him.

The mountains known as Sierra de Trinidad were our next destination. We arrived in Trinidad during a tropical storm and the streets were awash with surging rivers of muddy mountain water. The following morning a freshly washed golden sun brought life to the brightly coloured houses of Trinidad de Cuba; another World Heritage Sight. Mamas sold huge cigars on each street corner and tourists, all two of us, visited a small street bar for the best Mohito in all Cuba.

Horse drawn carriages were the only form of transportation; passengers sat on two long benches that ran sideways above a set of four wheels and a canvas cover screened their heads from the scorching sun. An old steam train chugged along a narrow gauge track each day and passed through beautiful valleys where sugar cane was once harvested by black African slaves. It stopped below a tall look-out tower in front of the overseers office; now a tourist store where memorabilia could be bought for a couple of US dollars. We climbed the tower to gain a splendid view across the lush green countryside and were startled by a huge hornets' nest that was attached to the tower beneath one of the long rickety ladders. From the top we could see black smoke billowing from the old sugar train as it approached.

The Sierra de Trinidad beckoned to us and we hired a guide to take us into these densely forested mountains to look for the elusive Cuban national bird, which we understood could be found resting in tall hardwood trees. We heard the strange unmistakable call of the Tokororo on several occasions but never managed to spot him. We did stumble across a Pileated Woodpecker which thumped relentlessly into an old tree and called to its mate with a loud shrill hacking sound. It was a very invigorating day, the forests were fresh with early morning dew and the fresh mountain air cooled me as I burned off hundreds of extra calories in pursuit of Anne who swept through the green undergrowth, ever anxious to see what lay in wait over the brow of the next hill.

It is not often that I dance with Anne; she always follows the beat of music with the same precision that she used when she played her violin in the Southampton City Orchestra. On our last evening in Trinidad I took her to a place where Cubans gathered in the evening and we sat with them on stone steps and listened to the vibrant beat of afro-Caribbean music. We sipped a few Cuba-libres and then moved into a small tavern where several locals were dancing Salsa. No one knew me from Adam and so I decided to teach Anne a few Ceroc moves which could be adapted. I am hopeless at Salsa; my hips refuse to gyrate in time with the music, but on this occasion we both danced well together and we had a tremendous evening.

We next drove from Trinidad to Cienfuegos. It was a nightmare, our map bore no resemblance to the actual terrain that we were driving across. On several occasions our dirt road just stopped in the middle of the countryside. Anne struggled with her Spanish and tried to secure directions from people who we passed, but every time we came to a dead end. Eventually a peasant directed me to a young girl who needed to get to a village which was in our general direction. She climbed into our car and directed us along farm tracks that we would never have considered using and at one point we even passed through a deep stream. Without her help we would have been forced to return to the main road and take a 100 mile detour.

Our next accommodation was near to Playa Larga in a small cottage on a stretch of sand known to the American CIA as Red Beach, Bay of Pigs. This beach has many old machine gun fortifications and on the road leading between Red Beach and Blue Beach are dozens of stone memorials indicating where a Cuban soldier had fallen. This is the place where Fidel Castro humiliated the American CIA on the 17th April 1961.

We visited a small museum in Giron and I was surprised to find a Hawker Sea Fury in excellent condition. This British aircraft is arguably the fastest piston driven aircraft that has ever flown. It was used with devastating effect against the American sponsored invasion and was a contributing factor towards the eventual capture of all 1,300 invading mercenaries. Thucydides said of the Peloponnesian War, "it is always the victor who writes the history" and I am sure that Castro ensured that his own little piece of history read very badly for the so-called Imperialist forces of the American CIA.

Castro may have restricted civil liberties, but he kept the two promises that he made to his people during the revolution; he provided universal education and free healthcare. Neither was available to peasants under the Batista government and I can vouch personally for the Cuban healthcare services; I needed treatment when I arrived in Cuba during my Round the World Yacht Race and they gave me excellent treatment free of charge. Unfortunately US sanctions has destroyed what could be a beautiful and rich country; rich in humanity and culture if not the monetary kind. True, Castro was once a threat to the security of the United States, but Germany, Japan and Vietnam gave the United States a much bloodier nose, and the US Government buried the hatchet with them a long time ago.

I suspect that the leadership of the United States is more concerned with the Cuban vote in Florida than it is with the welfare of the Cuban people as a whole. The White House is also influenced by the CIA whose officers still refuse to forgive Castro for the many times that he has pushed his thumb up their nose. In my opinion it is time for the United States to grow up and behave like a mature nation. Castro has proven himself to be a survivor and they need to find a way to work with him!

My main reason for visiting the Bay of Pigs was to obtain a permit to enter the Swamps of Zapata. I had read that it was a naturalist's paradise and I was determined to see for myself what it had to offer. Early in the morning we collected a guide from his home and set off into the swamps. It was already hot and putrid steam could be seen rising from the still water of the salt marshes. Small armies of land crabs scuttled across the dirt road in front of us and occasionally our guide signalled for me to slow down as he spotted movement in low stumpy trees far to our right and then to our left. Whenever I stopped and peered through his binoculars I struggled to define whatever he was trying to point out to me. This was not helped by the absence of any common language between the three of us.

First I picked out a small Cuban Pewee on a branch beside the bonnet of my car and then a Yellow Canary which was easy to pick out against the green background of the swamps. Several times he pointed out a Tri-coloured Heron but it was only on his third sighting that I managed to see one on a mangrove tree in the distance. A Blackhawk rested defiantly on a dead tree that stretched above the road and try as I might I could not frighten him from his perch. Suddenly our guide whispered

'Tokororo, Tokororo'. This time I was determined to find it and I walked deep into the swamp following the direction of its strange call as it moved silently from tree to tree. I scanned with my video camera and suddenly I spotted a glimpse of its strangely proportioned body with green, blue and orange plumage.

Mosquitoes took blood from my legs, my arms and the back of my neck. They savaged me like a shoal of hungry piranha and took more blood than would have satisfied the bride of Count Dracula. Later, when I reviewed my footage to see if I had captured the Tokororo on camera, I could hear the high pitched whine of these hungry bloodsuckers. Still, at long last I had found my Tokororo.

We carried on driving until we reached the very end of the Zapata Peninsula. We spotted several other birds but these were similar to what I could find in any normal location; terns, flamingos, blue herons, storks, egrets. Anne was scheduled to join her flight back to Paris on the following evening and so it was time to head back to Havana. Then disaster struck! The oil gauge light came on and we were 25 miles from the nearest tarred road. It was impossible to walk that distance in the swamp and I could find nothing wrong with the car; perhaps the large potholes that we had been driving over had damaged the pressure switch. I took a chance and did my best to keep our speed high enough to stay in top gear. At least this kept the engine revs as low as possible and maintained a high airflow over the radiator, but it did knock the hell out of our car because we were on a very poorly graded dirt road.

We were absolutely terrified that we would be trapped in the swamp for the night. It would have been extremely uncomfortable, the mosquitoes would have eaten us alive and Anne would have missed her flight home. We were all sweating profusely when we eventually emerged from the swamp and it was not the putrid heat that was responsible. After tipping our guide we dropped him by the roadside and headed for Havana. We were not out of the woods yet; there were no garages near to the Bay of Pigs. Fortunately our oil pressure returned to normal and later in the evening we checked into the Havana Hilton for our last night in Cuba. All that remained was to buy a good supply of black market Churchill Cigars.

I returned to Freeport and then flew to Bristol for my 60th birthday, which was on the 30th July 2004. It was Brett's birthday on the 31st and so we had a joint party. Anne surprised me with an evening balloon flight over Bristol. Brett and his partner Julia joined us, but I was a little disappointed when Michele had to remain on terra-firma to take care of our other guests.

We took off in Butler's Balloon from Ashton Court and flew straight across Landmark Court on the harbourside and then across the city centre towards Bath. It was a calm evening and we could hear voices carrying from the ground as we floated along in the evening breeze at around 1,000 ft. Our pilot guided us towards his chosen landing field by increasing and decreasing his height to pick up the different wind directions. His method of finding the wind direction below our balloon was very technical; he spit over the side and watched his spittle fall towards a point on the ground.

He called his retrieval team twenty minutes before we landed and told them which field he had chosen. Five minutes before touch-down he pointed his landing spot out to me. It was a narrow field with electrical pylons one mile short, a hawthorn hedge on the left hand side and conifer trees on the right. The field sloped upwards and at the top was another hawthorn hedge. It was impossible! There was no way that he could land in such a small space; we were not in a helicopter that could be guided to left or right. Just before touchdown the pilot shouted to us that we were going to make a rough landing. We held tightly to the edge of our basket and leaned against the wicker walls as it hit the ground. The basket rolled onto its side and we were dragged for a few yards before coming to rest in the very centre of his chosen field. Unbelievable!

My birthday and my visit to England was not a happy one. My father's eyesight had started to fail him two years earlier and now his medical condition had begun to deteriorate rapidly. Mattie, Linda and Steven kept his spirits up until the very end, and he passed away in his sleep on the 26th of November 2004.

Hurricanes hit Grand Bahama

While I was in Europe two powerful hurricanes ripped through Freeport. The first was Frances, a category 2, which made a direct hit on

Friday 3rd September 2004. The eye stalled directly over Freeport and the on-island residents felt her fury for almost 3 days. During this time the villages of West End and East End were wiped from the face of the earth. Trees were snapped throughout this serenely beautiful little island, houses were torn apart and the airport was submerged beneath a huge tidal surge.

In her wake Frances left more damage than any other hurricane. Over 1,200 power poles were broken and many miles of transmission wire that once looked down from lofty heights now lay on the ground. Almost all large condominium complexes lost their roofs, including Harbour House Towers. The roof that once kept the elements out of my 8th floor apartment was found on a very flat Mercedes in our parking lot.

The airport was closed, cruise ships bypassed Freeport, communications were down, power was down and there was very little water or food left unspoiled on the island. The situation was desperately uncomfortable for those who lived on-island or had been trapped by the passage of Frances. Many of the homeless lived in village halls and schools. Those in condominiums bathed in their communal swimming pools. Water was supplied in tankers and then, without any warning, Mother Nature decided to vent her wrath once again on this poor little island.

On 25th September 2004, exactly three weeks after Frances, hurricane Jeanne moved over the east end of Grand Bahama and skirted the north shore with category 3 winds. Because the island had no communications many of the islanders were caught unawares and they had no time to prepare. Jeanne dumped thousands of gallons of salt bearing water into those homes that had already lost their roofs in Frances. My furniture, ceilings, interior walls, doors and kitchen were totally destroyed.

At the time of the storms I was a director of Harbour House Towers and I, along with my fellow directors, had the unenviable task of affecting repairs to the structure of the building. We had sufficient funds to rebuild the security walls, gates and ground floor offices but we didn't have funds to replace the roof. This was estimated to cost half a million dollars. We raised an assessment against the other 122 owners and with a small advance from the insurance company we made a start.

However, at the time of writing, the roof was still not finished and no insurance funds had been made available to repair individual apartments.

We submitted an insurance claim in excess of 2 million dollars, but the insurance company came up with so many different clauses that our first offer was very little more than our annual premium. Needless to say, everyone in the building was rather disgusted with this offer and we are still pursuing our claim against the insurance company, who continues to duck and dive.

I counted myself lucky to have several really good friends in Freeport. Two of these are Nick and Jackie. Nick is a crazy kind of guy who was born within the sound of Bow Bells and he is proud to call himself a genuine real McCoy Cockney. Jacky hails from the Potteries; she is a stunner and was Miss United Kingdom in 1962 and a runner-up in the Miss World Contest. They lived in South Florida for many years and eventually decided to up-roots and move to Freeport. They arrived along with their worldly possessions in a motor yacht and tied up against three plots of land, which they purchased on the bank of a canal just west of Port Lucaya.

They lived in their yacht and built a wooden gazebo over their canal to house a washing machine, kitchen and large bar. This became home for several years while Nick built a large house fit for a king in gardens landscaped by Jackie, alias Capability Brown. She planted trees, shrubs and plants native to the Bahamas and caged several large areas to house love birds, cockatiels and parrots. Peacocks and even more parrots are free to fly around Jackie's gardens while about nineteen Chihuahuas and five cats live together in total harmony with each other. The cats stalk small wild birds that frequent her garden but for some reason they ignore the domesticated ones, even when they are not in their cages.

Nick doesn't like to cage his birds and he gives them as much freedom as possible. His youngest cockatiel was a proficient talker and one day it flew away and it never returned. I am sure that it was not lost; if it wanted to return home it would have asked for directions. One of his blue parrots, another good talker, sank its teeth into my finger while I was feeding it and a few days later a red one gouged my shoulder. It was extremely painful and I swore I would ring its bloody neck. The following morning it was found lying dead in the garden; no Nick, I swear that it wasn't me!

One afternoon, to be more precise, Saturday 5th February 2005; I thought I would call around to see Nick and Jackie. Nick announced that he was taking his granddaughter Georgia and her friend Kayle for a sail in his Hobiecat. It was extremely cold for the Bahamas and a fresh wind was blowing from the North. We sailed down the canal and out into the ocean with Georgia and Kayle sitting astraddle the two hulls forward of the mast. After heading south to ensure we were clear of the reef I turned across wind and pulled the sails in to maximise our performance. The ocean was carrying a heavy swell and we quickly picked up speed and started to knife through the waves with impunity.

It was such a thrilling experience to race across the ocean in a small catamaran with the wind filling tightly stretched sails and the windward hull pitching gently out of the water. Waves surged across our starboard bow, adding to our excitement, and Nick politely asked Georgia to move back to the trampoline. Suddenly his call became more urgent and then I realized that the watertight seal on our starboard storage compartment was missing. I turned into the wind and put Nick's Hobiecat 'In Irons', but it was too late. Water gushed into the open compartment and our hull thrust deep into the waves that were now washing right across us. As we came to a halt our starboard hull was already sinking deep into the crystal clear waters of the Grand Bahama Reef.

The mainsail enveloped Georgia as it sank below the surface and I called to Nick to help rescue her. We need not have worried; Georgia was wise to the situation. It was not the first time that Nick had capsized his Hobiecat, but it was certainly the first time he had sunk it. When we were satisfied that both children were firmly ensconced astride of the port hull, which was still floating, Nick and I attached a rope to the mast and righted the Hobiecat.

I was the first to clamber onto the trampoline and I quickly tried to release our halyard so that I could drop the mainsail. Nick meanwhile called to me and asked me to grab the children and pull them back onboard. This was a critical mistake. The wind caught our sail and within seconds we were all back in the water. This time the mast also filled with water and there was nothing else that could be done.

All four of us climbed onto the port hull and waved towards a boat gathering lobsters nearby. Try that we might, we could not attract their attention. I suspect that they were deliberately ignoring us because they looked briefly in our direction and then headed for shore. I was extremely annoyed at their callous attitude. We had two children on board and I don't think they had given any thought to our predicament. It is extremely rare that I want to punch someone on the nose, but this was such an occasion.

We sat astride our life saving hull for a long time and the girls began to get very cold. The sky appeared drab and featureless. The sun was hidden behind a low layer of strata-cumulus that added to the general misery of our situation and it became apparent that we were going to have to affect our own rescue before darkness descended upon us. I suggested to Nick that he should swim to the shore and bring his boat to take the girls off. Meanwhile, I would stay with them and help to keep their spirits up.

Nick made very slow progress against both wind and tide. It took him almost an hour to reach the rocky breakwater that guarded the canal entrance. Meanwhile the girls were beginning to get very cold. Kayle was already shaking rather badly and her lips turned blue. I tried to reassure the girls that we would soon be rescued and we shared different jokes about our situation. Georgia pointed out a small cut on my leg and I explained that it was only a small cut and that she should not worry about it. She replied in a slow very deliberate way, "Yes, but it is getting towards that time"; meaning that it was getting dark and this was when the sharks from Pier One would begin to feed.

The remains of Pier One were only a short distance away. This is a restaurant overlooking the ocean where the owner fed Bull Sharks and Yellow Fins every evening. Pier One had been destroyed by the recent hurricanes and I told Georgia that I did not want to be reminded of these sharks, I knew that they were looking for new food. The chance of a shark attack was almost negligible but I was not going to take any chances. I told Kayle to move closer to the centre section of the hull and I asked both girls to keep their legs out of the water.

As time dragged by I could not help but notice that the remaining hull was slowly sinking into the water. I didn't like the thought of a shark taking a piece out of my backside and I began to wonder what had happened to Nick. Then we saw a large power boat surging down the canal at high speed and we prayed that it would turn in our direction. It did, and a few moments' later, Gary Simmons and Nick pulled alongside in a rescue boat. A fisherman had called Bahamas Air Sea Rescue and Gary, a close friend of Nick's, had fished Nick out of the canal on his way to rescue us. Unfortunately the rescue boat holed the remaining good hull and as we powered towards the canal entrance our Hobiecat could be seen sinking slowly below the waves and then, as it vanished from view, total darkness finally descended upon us.

After dropping Georgia and Kayle at Nick's home we took a warm shower, put on dry clothing and went back out in a small power boat to make the wreck safe. It took several hours to drag it to a safe position clear of the navigation channel where we anchored it and attached a large marker buoy. Then disaster struck again. The gear mechanism on Nick's power boat broke and we could not engage forward gear. Afraid that we may have to alert the rescue services again we reversed all the way home with the waves doing their very best to ride over our transom and sink us for a second time in the same day.

At daybreak on Sunday morning we repaired Nick's boat and returned to the wreck with ropes, diving gear and a selection of salvage tools. We recovered various pieces of equipment from the Hobiecat and separated the mast and sails from the main section of the catamaran. Both hulls then came to the surface and we attached a tow line and dragged them slowly back to the pontoon by Nick's dock.

We returned and after a short search found the mast and sails, but try as we might we could not recover them. The swell had increased and there was an increasing danger that we could be swamped. In addition we had a further scare with the engine; the fuel line had broken away during our salvage efforts and it took some time before we located our problem. Nick decided that we had tested our luck to its limit and that it was time to throw down another anchor buoy and wait until the weather improved.

That evening as I mulled over my glass of red wine and looked at the crimson skies turning to a deep colour of purple over Port Lucaya, I wondered how I should explain our little escapade to Richard; my skipper during the Clipper Round the World Yacht Race. I could picture his reaction; he would look me in the eye then grit his teeth and turn away before muttering a few select words to himself. Never mind, it takes all kinds to make the world go round.

Santiago and Valparaiso

When Dick was on his final overseas posting he was the Ambassador to Chile, he invited Anne and me to stay at his residence in Santiago. We visited during the second week of March 2005 and found that Prince Edward had been using our room for several days prior to our arrival. Our stay in Santiago was very much the same as when we visited Dick in Caracas except this time his resident birds were different. Instead of Woodpeckers and Humming Birds he had a pair of Andean Plovers. They strutted around Dick's huge gardens and uttered shrill calls whenever we invaded their territory.

His grounds had several mature hardwood trees and hundreds of fresh chestnuts were falling around us as we walked through the rose gardens. The fresh petals released an exquisite scent in the gentle evening breeze, and the Plovers flew around angrily as we assaulted their croquet lawn with a couple of wooden mallets. I felt a real Charlie when I hit out at the ball, I couldn't get it to reach the hoop, let alone pass through the middle.

One advantage of Santiago is that it is extremely safe and Dick did not feel that his guests were threatened in any way. We were able to leave his Residence and take long walks into Santiago. We enjoyed cable car rides in the hills and visited local restaurants and cafes in the downtown area. Good natured student demonstrations were being held outside the American Embassy but they left the British Embassy alone. The Manageress of the Residence was also very kind to us and she arranged for us to visit the Concha y Toro wine estates.

Each evening Anne and I joined Dick on his patio where we enjoyed a glass of Chilean wine before retiring to our large dining room for dinner, which was served with the same elegance as on earlier occasions. However, the quality of our food was second to none; it was the best that I had ever tasted. The fish filets were extremely thick and succulent; there was not a single bone to be found and it melted in my mouth. Dick's chef and the members of his household had worked in the Embassy for many years and I had to say that I had never enjoyed such excellent service, even in the very best of Milanese restaurants. This really was a very special experience for Anne and me.

The following day Dick had some free time and he took us for a drive into the High Andes where we hoped, but failed, to spot any Condors. Anne and Dick are very close, Dick is more like an elder brother than an Uncle and she was very pleased to have an opportunity to visit him on his last posting. She had visited Dick on every single appointment during his diplomatic career with one exception; Mexico City.

When it was time to leave Dick we hired a car and drove down to Vina del Mar on the Pacific coast where I had booked a hostel. It reminded me of Bournemouth and so we climbed back into our car and drove north along the rugged wind swept coast looking for a more characteristic place, but we found that all of the remaining hostels were full. Late in the evening we sat down on the beach and watched thousands of Humboldt Penguins returning from the ocean to roost on a small rocky island. We became worried as Anne watched the sun fall below the horizon. It was the first time that she had seen a Pacific sunset and we thought that we might have to join the Penguins.

The Pacific Coast was stunningly picturesque and untamed. High in the background the snow capped Andes fell to a narrow strip of green hills before one last rocky plunge into the wild white crested waters of the Pacific Ocean. Early in the morning small open deck fishing boats could be seen emerging from a rolling bank of fog that stretched like a cloak along the edge of the cold Humboldt Current. Every ten miles or so high granite cliffs gave way to a small sandy beach where pelicans, gulls and terns waited patiently for these colourful fish laden boats to return safely from beneath the cold shroud of Neptune.

We were fortunate to find a small hostel in one of these inlets and we enjoyed an early breakfast in a café overlooking the beach. Shore helpers ran out to the returning boats and attached strong tractor lines which dragged them above the high-water mark. One of the boats attracted a large group of local people and a Naval Officer hurried towards it with a battered old camera. When I joined the throng of excited onlookers I was amazed to see something that I had previously thought only existed in the imagination of a Jules Verne novel: a giant octopus filled the boat. The fishermen had to cut it into several large pieces before they were able to pull it onboard. Other boats were filled with conger eels, anchovies, sardines and mackerel.

The cold Antarctic water flowing up the coast of Chile, known as the Humboldt Current, causes deep nutrient-rich water to rise along the coast and this upwelling brings with it thousands of tons of plankton which is the beginning of the food chain for an extraordinary variety of fish, marine mammals and seabirds.

Chilean Dolphins, Burmeister's Porpoises, Humboldt and Magellanic Penguins, Hawksbill Turtles, Southern Sea Lions and South American Fur Seals lived at the top of this food chain, and we saw many of these during our long drives along the rugged coast. When we walked along the cliff tops our ears were constantly filled with the sharp call of Wilson's Petrels, Sooty Shearwaters and Inca Terns. It was a thrilling place to observe such a wide diversity of life and I determined that I would return to study this coastline and Antarctica itself in more detail at the earliest opportunity.

We both hope that this will be soon because Anne's uncle, Johnny Wilkinson, has just retired from the House of Commons where he was one of the longest serving Conservative Members of Parliament. Johnny and his wife Cecilia are close friends and they are building a hacienda in a remote area 140 miles south of Santiago. Anne is the legal guardian of their son Alexander and Johnny has invited us to spend quality time with them.

Johnny once flew fast jets in the Royal Air Force, including the legendary Hawker Hunter, and he was the Parliamentary Private Secretary to the Minister of Defence, John Nott, during the Falklands Conflict. He is notorious as one of the Maastricht Rebels who lost the Tory whip for opposing John Major on the ratification of the Treaty for European Union; after my problems in Spain I have to agree with Johnny on his stand. He often arranged for us to attend Prime Minister's Question Time in the House of Commons and on one occasion we were pleased to dine with him in the Churchill Room where we met several prominent politicians of the day.

After several exciting days we visited Valparaiso and then drove directly to Santiago Airport where we joined an Air France flight across the jagged peaks of the High Andes to Buenos Aires. Fifty years earlier this had been a very hazardous route for the pilots of British South American Airways. They flew Lancastrians, a civilian version of the world famous Avro Lancaster bomber. We had the comfort of a pressurised cabin while the passengers of BSAA had to wear oxygen masks. Our pilots used a satellite GPS navigation system to fix their position to within a few metres while the Lancastrian pilots used star shots and dead reckoning to estimate an approximate position which on more than one occasion proved to be disastrously incorrect. I reflected upon the changes that had occurred in civil aviation over such a brief period of time.

I was held in awe by the range of mountains that lay below. Our wings flexed as we passed over turbulent air which had been thrust upwards by the huge wedge of granite that extended below us. My admiration was mixed with pangs of fear as these rising air currents interfered with the jet stream. I recalled my lessons in the Johannesburg Aeronav Academy when we were told of crashes where 'clear air turbulence' had caused structural failure. Knowing too much does have its disadvantages!

Somewhere far below lay 'Stardust', a Lancastrian that never made it from Buenos Aires to Santiago. She is embedded somewhere deep in a glacier high on Tupungato. In her belly rests a King's Messenger who was delivering a top secret message to one of Dick's predecessors. The location of her crash was not discovered until the summer of 2001. An expedition from Mendoza discovered one of her Merlin engines and a fully inflated wheel at the foot of the Tupungato glacier, where they had been disgorged after 53 years of concealment.

Buenos Aires and Iguaçu Falls

Buenos Aires is a vibrant modern city full of beautiful people who value their European heritage. English and Italian architecture predominates and one of the world's finest opera houses, the Teatro Colon, flourishes in this seductive port city that lies on the south bank of the Rio de la Plata. Portenos, as the multinational people of Buenos Aires are known, are friendly, very polite people who always make visitors welcome in their proud city.

Many compare Buenos Aires with Paris, Madrid or Rome but I thought this to be a very unfair comparison. Buenos Aires was much better. Each neighbourhood had its own very personal atmosphere. The ones that Anne and I had the pleasure to enjoy were Palermo, Recoleta, San Telmo and La Boca. We stayed in a small friendly hostel right in the City Centre, just off Florida Avenue. It was within easy walking distance of Puerto Madero and with a little extra effort we could easily walk to most of the other districts.

On our first day we walked through Plaza de Mayo and admired the exquisite Casa Rosada from where Evita Peron made her passionate speech during the final days of her life. On the other side of the Plaza was the Catedral Metropolitana. It is a magnificent Cathedral but today it was surrounded by TV camera crews who were monitoring special prayers for Pope John Paul who was in his last moments. This plaza is so beautiful; it represents the aspirations of all Argentineans and yet it has witnessed so much tragedy. Portenos are wonderful people but they are not strangers to political turmoil; this is the place where they demonstrate and, if necessary, die for their political beliefs.

We entered Puerto Madero and enjoyed our first glass of Argentine sparkling wine and followed this with a Mendoza malbec. The sun was falling over this new world harbour and yet it looked so much older and far more characteristic than many harbours of the old world. The malbec was one of the finest I have ever had the pleasure to taste and it was incredibly cheap. I was surprised to find that, unlike France and South Africa, Argentina reserved the best of its wines to be tasted at home. A splendid idea; for as long as one is in Buenos Aires!

We paid our homage to Evita in the Recoleta Cemetery and then decided to explore the old quarters of San Telmo and La Boca. Tango bars resounded to the sound of heavy music and old men danced provocatively with young girls in the open streets. Black and red were the favourite colours of the many tango stars with white flesh occasionally exposed by a passionate young girl as she wrapped a high flung leg around the jacketed waist of her adoring partner.

San Telmo was rich in dusty, treasure-filled antique shops containing priceless heirlooms sold by owners long since past. I bored Anne to tears when I searched from shop to shop admiring hand made navigational instruments, precision range-finders for naval guns, intricate chemical balances, coins, medals, and military regalia. There was so much of interest that I could have filled a container and made a small fortune upon my return to the Bahamas.

In contrast, La Boca's pressed tin houses were painted a rainbow of colours and the side-streets bordering this old sea port were rich in tradition. They were the streets where Diego Maradonna played football as a child and La Boca Juniors, his old team, still played in a large stadium that was approached through avenues of brilliant colour. In the evening, as we walked through one of these streets, a parrot added its own splash of colour as it came to rest beneath the dim light of an old street lamp. Young boys kicking a ball around looked on in amusement as I struggled to take a photograph of this strange intruder.

For all its diversity, the elusive spirit of Argentina is present everywhere in Buenos Aires. It suffered 70 percent devaluation in 2001 and yet there is no evidence of real hardship. The Portenos have made the most of their beautiful city. It is clean, well maintained and the stores are better stocked than any high class boutique in London, Paris or Madrid. Young men and women have very little disposable income, and yet, they wear the most beautiful clothes. Their immense inner beauty, honesty, good nature and friendly demeanour put most Americans and Europeans to shame. It is undoubtedly a city which I would be proud to call my own.

I would be doing a terrible wrong to the restaurants of Buenos Aires if I did not mention the incredible quality of food and wine in their parrillas. When Europeans first settled in Argentina they brought their cattle with them and they thrived on the rich grasses of the Pampas. No hormone shots or special feeds had ever been necessary to make Argentinean cattle into superb breeding stock. The combination of good feed, good climate, plenty of water and wide open spaces produced the finest beef in the world. Nowhere would one find a bigger, better, juicier and more tender steak than in a Buenos Aires parrilla. Following devaluation a couple could order starters, two glasses of sparkling wine, two huge steaks with vegetables, wash it down with a bottle of malbec, tip the waiter and collect change from a 20 dollar bill. Beat that Mr MacDonald!

I wanted to fly down to Tierra del Fuego, but we had missed the short summer season, and then I realized that Anne had never seen any of the world's great waterfalls. She had never been to Victoria, Niagara, Kaieture or Angel Falls, yet just 90 minutes north of Buenos Aires on a local flight were the magnificent Iguaçu Falls. These falls are 269 feet high at the Devil's Throat and 1.7 miles wide; it sounded as though we needed to visit them.

We flew to Iguaçu and were immediately enthralled by the many cataracts that spread in a huge horseshoe across the Iguaçu River. The falls are located just upstream of the confluence with the Parana River where the two form a neat triangle that separates Brazil, Paraguay and Argentina. When I stood above this confluence I was immediately reminded of our visit to the Golden Triangle where I had purchased a bag of uncut sapphires. This time I bought a large polished crystal ball with a break-away section that revealed a fine creamy blue crystalline structure; the seller said that it came from a remote mine in the Andes.

We walked around the falls on the Brazilian side and were astonished by an ant eater which ran across Anne's path. The saying goes that Argentina owns the falls but Brazil owns the view. This is not entirely true because the Argentine side is also stunning. A perfectly symmetrical rainbow spread across the Devil's Throat and a smooth cooling spray soaked our sweating bodies as a friend took our photograph while we stood together in the frame of a multi-coloured rainbow.

Anne joined two girls whom we befriended at the airport and they took a white-water ride into the Devil's Throat. Their wide rubber raft was fitted with four huge outboard motors and it took them beneath one of the cataracts. I carried their handbags and walked for miles through the rain forest. I followed wooden walkways which passed across wide sections of rocky terrain. I walked past several cataracts and they all looked the same; I was lost.

Bananaquits, Flycatchers and Hummingbirds frequented the small bushes around my path while Turkey Vultures and Black Hawks circled in the rising air currents high above my head. The rainforest was incredibly fresh and a delightful fragrance wafted through its leafy folds. Orchids grew from lofty trees and their roots waved in the breeze taking deep gulps of sustenance from the moisture laden air. Snowy Egrets, Striated Herons and Cormorants searched the waters edge for signs of food; 448 types of bird are said to live in the Misiones Region and I wanted to see as many as possible.

Suddenly, as I walked across a long wooden bridge a dinosaur flew by, at least its nearest living relative, a flying beak; more correctly known as a Red Breasted Toucan. Later in the evening I spotted hundreds of Blue Swallows diving through the falls to roost on the rocky ledges within, while dozens of differently coloured Parrots and Parakeets settled in nearby trees. I have travelled throughout Trinidad, Venezuela and Uruguay to see this particular variety of bird and now huge numbers gathered within a few square miles. Anne thoroughly enjoyed her visit and these sightings were the icing on the cake for both of us. They made our trip to Iguaçu a truly memorable occasion.

Following our return to Buenos Aires we continued to explore new neighbourhoods and we visited a different parrilla each evening. We never spent more than $20 and indulged ourselves more than we had ever done before. Anne was not a meat eater but she could not resist such quality. I thought about Anne's brother Henry; he would have enjoyed the restaurants of Recoleta and for one tenth of the price that he was accustomed to in his usual haunts of London's Mayfair.

My back was beginning to trouble me again and this presented the ideal opportunity for Anne to search the high class shops of Florida Avenue. The styles were as good as anything that could be found in Europe. Many of the coats on display were made of fine suede in the best of Argentine's leather workshops. Pullovers were woven from the finest cashmere and scarves from a more unusual but very course lama wool. Anne bought several of each, some for herself and some for Christmas presents. My job was to go shopping for a third and very large canvas bag to carry all of Anne's purchases.

Montevideo

We had a few more days to spare and so we decided to take the

Buquebus from Puerto Madero to Montevideo, which is in Uruguay on the opposite side of the Rio de la Plata. It took our catamaran three hours to make the 100 mile journey. The coastal area around the Rio de la Plata is extremely flat and as we sailed into a huge bay I was surprised to see a small hill standing alone. I called to Anne, "look, I can see a hill". I was later told that in 1516 a Portuguese mariner shouted these very words; "monte vi eu"! Hence the name given to this old sea port, the most southern capital city in the world.

The Montevidean people were not as well dressed as those in Buenos Aires. I asked a young girl the reason for this and she explained that Portenos are city dwellers while in Uruguay everyone is a farmer. Cattle were first introduced to Uruguay in 1602 and they were allowed to roam free across the Pampas; four hundred years later these numbers had increased to 12 million head of high grade cattle and 4 million horses. I suppose it is no surprise that some of the best horsemen in the world live in Uruguay.

The reason that I wanted to visit Montevideo was the Maritime Museum. I wanted to gain more insight into the Battle of the River Plate. This was a very famous battle that took place on 13th December, 1939, between cruisers Exeter, Ajax and Achilles of the Royal Navy and the German pocket battleship Admiral Graf Spee. The Exeter-led hunting group was very fast but it only had 8-inch and 6-inch guns while the Graf Spee was armed with formidable 11-inch guns. Exeter was badly damaged in the initial engagement and she had to retire to the Falklands while the Graf Spee who only suffered superficial damage chose to seek refuge in the neutral port of Montevideo.

The German Navy did not have radar in 1939 and Langsdorff, Captain of the Graf Spee, was a German from the old school; he was not a Nazi. He was only permitted to remain a short time in Montevideo and he had no idea how many warships were waiting for him at the mouth of the River Plate, and fearing for the lives of his crew, he ordered his ship to be scuttled. This was a major boost to the morale of the British people who were suffering terrible losses in the North Atlantic.

The museum was attended by a Naval Warrant Officer and I was very disappointed to find that I was the first and probably the only person to visit the museum on that particular day. It carried letters, uniforms and photographs from many officers and ratings involved in the battle. Several items removed from the Graf Spee were on display along with relics from many other naval encounters. Amongst these were items taken from British ships built at Butlers Yard in the 19th century. I would recommend anyone visiting Montevideo to pay the museum a visit.

On Sunday morning we took a short tour of the city and our noses found a large shed by the docks which had been converted into a covered eating place. Its three storey high roof was blackened with soot from the many log fires that burned below, and an ornate clock tower stood in the centre with large Big Ben type hands stuck at 4:30 pm. It carried the name of Mercado Del Puerto and at lunchtime carnivorous Montevideans flocked through its rather grandiose iron gates to devour huge servings of cholesterol laden meats. They sat at long marble bars that framed the asador who constantly tendered huge amounts of pork, lamb, chicken, and especially beef as it charred to smoky perfection on the parrilla.

Anne enjoyed another really large meal of grilled meat and I did not begrudge her the best part of a bottle of rose Uruguay wine; I felt that she deserved a little tolerance after eating such a good meal. If only I could get her to eat this well in Blighty! Later in the day we sailed back to Buenos Aires where Anne did some more last minute shopping and then we joined our Iberia flight to Madrid and England.

Northern India

Anne's father spent his early years in British India where her grandfather, Sir Arthur McWatters, was 'Chancellor' of the British Indian Empire. A son of the Raj, Stephen returned to England when he was seven years old; his Toupee being blown into the sea as he sailed from Bombay, leaving Aya and Chokidar behind for the rigors of preparatory school at the Dragon, Oxford.

Anne so much wanted to walk in her father's footsteps and to see the things that he told her stories about when she sat on his knee as a small child. She wanted to see the small government bungalow in New Delhi where her father discovered a Krait in his bathtub and the Himalayan foothills where he spent his hot summer months.

We had already travelled much of the world together and so I decided that our next overseas visit had to include these places. The internet had become such a wonderful learning tool and I scanned through its numerous websites while planning my perfect surprise itinerary for an extensive tour through Northern India and Nepal.

We set out on our first ever pre-planned adventure on Tuesday 27th December 2005. It was not the best of starts; Anne had forgotten to do the only thing required of her; to reserve a seat on the airport coach. Even our Virgin Atlantic flight was a terrible disappointment. We were not offered a choice of food, the seats and TV screens were extremely small and the films were started half way through. I was very disappointed. I had always been a staunch supporter of Richard Branson, but on this occasion I felt that his service was not up to scratch.

I had charged Compass India with the task of implementing the practical aspect of my tour arrangements. I cannot commend this company or its contracted employees enough for the excellent service they provided. I divided our tour into four different geographical sections and in each section we were attended around the clock by a friendly driver with a 4-wheel drive vehicle. A local guide waited patiently at each of my chosen destinations and without exception their punctuality and good manners were impeccable.

New Delhi lived up to my expectations. A minority of wealthy Indians lived in opulent luxury serviced by a small middle class. The remainder lived in absolute poverty without the most basic of facilities. Some lived in the most horrendously filthy conditions and appeared to survive by sending their children into the road to beg at traffic lights. What did surprise me was the close proximity and yet sharp segregation of Hindu and Islamic peoples, a powder keg waiting to explode. India has been ruled over the centuries by many different conquering powers and their influence still remains.

The sharp divisions that exist between these different groups emerged on our very first day. We had hoped to visit the Red Fort, once the most opulent fort and palace of the Mughal Empire, but it had been closed following a terrorist attack and so we drove directly to the Jama Masjid; the largest mosque in India. Our morning newspaper reported that the King of Saudi Arabia had just offered a huge sum to facilitate the renovation of this mosque but our guide said that the government would not accept for fear of increasing Islamic influence.

We approached the mosque on foot through slum-like streets crowded with poverty stricken people. Rickshaw boys jogged by with smartly dressed businessmen in tow, young girls wore colourful saris and stinking fly covered cows weaved through narrow streets grazing on piles of rubbish and drinking from open sewers.

After passing through the mosque, shoes in hand, we emerged on the far side and found ourselves in the Muslim quarter. The squalor was no different, but on this side the cows hung from meat hooks and women of unknown beauty covered their faces with an oppressive black hajib. The only similarity between these two proud cultures was their abject poverty; on all other fronts they were poles apart.

After brief visits to the Raj Ghat where Mahatma Gandhi was cremated and the Qutub Minar, another huge historical site where Hindu and Muslim cultures are intertwined, we headed for the more peaceful diplomatic enclave of New Delhi. We drove through an affluent area where white bungalows stood back from a wide tree-lined street. Darkness was not so far away and troupes of monkeys searched for fresh fruit as flocks of green parrots began to roost. This was the street where Anne's father once lived. As we rounded the end of the street we entered a large processional way flanked by huge colonial buildings. I had known what to expect but I don't think Anne was prepared for what she found. The financial buildings that once housed her grandfather were magnificent; their imposing grandeur was beyond her imagination.

Our drive to Jaipur was our first of many long journeys through Northern India and I had to ask our driver Ram to take more care when overtaking. He seemed to have a mistaken belief that the strange mixture of camel trains, elephants, ox carts, donkeys and huge painted lorries would all make way for him in his shiny new vehicle.

Jaipur brought back childhood memories of Errol Flynn and other dashing young British Officers fighting in old movie films on the Northwest Frontier. The city walls, the majestic palace where the Maharaja still resided, and the town dwellings were all plastered and painted a lush pink colour in honour of the visit of Prince Albert, Queen Victoria's consort. The colour and atmosphere remained unchanged and I could still feel the proud spirit of Rajputana.

I stood outside Hawa Mahal, the 'Palace of Winds' and was startled by two snake charmers who chose that moment to release their huge cobras. The snakes lunged several times in my direction. Their fangs were intact and I suspect that their poison glands had not been removed. Usually in these situations the Charmer has encouraged his cobra to strike continually at his flute or 'pungi'. This is painful for the snake and it eventually becomes reluctant to strike. My fear of snakes is overwhelming and I became very uncomfortable when one of them suddenly left its basket and came in my direction. We departed rather swiftly!

Rajasthan is so different to anything else that I have ever experienced. Trains of camels pulling wooden carts trekked along old dusty roads and proud sun scorched men with wrinkled leathery skin sat on their haunches smoking old clay pipes as life passed them by.

The Rajput men wear a distinctive and very huge red turban or 'Dastar', a collarless shirt called a 'Kurta' and a length of material that is draped around their waste and drawn up between their legs to form a 'Dhoti'. The women wear very drab clothing by normal Indian standards. They wear a pleated skirt called a 'Lehanga' and a short blouse or 'Choli' that bares their midriff and much of their back. They drape a length of fine cotton called a 'Dupata' over their heads and in several cases we noticed that the older women used this to conceal their faces.

We visited the Amber Fort which stands in a well fortified position below a ridge of arid hills. From outside, the fort looked very forbidding but once inside the Maharaja's palace thrilled Anne with its beautiful fusion of Mughal and Hindu style architecture. I joined Anne and our rather fastidious guide for an extensive tour through the audience chambers, private rooms and harem, but I only had one thought in mind; where was the Jai Van?

Eventually our guide relented and we drove to the Jaigarh Fort which stands in a commanding position high above the valley. We walked along the ramparts to a bastion where the Jai Van stood in all its splendour guarding the southern approaches. The Jai Van is absolutely huge; pulled by several elephants it is easily the largest muzzle loaded wheel mounted cannon in the world. The craftsmen who built this magnificent artillery piece must have been really proud of their creation, but I guess that its size limited its usefulness as a strategic weapon.

Returning to Jaipur we passed the tallest elephant that I have ever seen. Its head and trunk were painted with yellow, pink and green flowers. It lunged at a casual yet fast moving pace along the middle of the road carrying a bundle of millet stalks. When I stood in the road to take photographs the Mahout invited Anne to stand beside its huge trunk. It stood so tall that Anne could have walked beneath its belly without stooping. I had always thought the Indian elephant to be smaller than the African but this proved otherwise.

Our next stop was the Ranthambhore nature reserve. Covered in hardy dhok climax forest the hilly terrain of the Vindhyas was very difficult to negotiate. We arrived earlier than expected on New Year's Eve and a game drive was just leaving. We managed to share a land cruiser with an American couple and as we drove through the forest our game ranger heard the warning cry of a spotted deer. After ten minutes of careful probing we found a Royal Bengal Tiger crouching in a clump of tall yellow grass. A short while later we found his mate with two young cubs.

Many visit the reserve for as long as two weeks without seeing a single tiger. We were extremely fortunate. Then, to add to our luck, we heard another warning call just before dark and found a lone tiger hunting in a small ravine. We spent the remainder of the old year dancing Ceroc to Indian music over an open barbecue in the grounds of our small game lodge.

This was the last time that we spotted any tigers, but we discovered a large variety of birds, wild animals and reptiles below the steep rocky ridges of the Aravalis Great Boundary Fault. Two long eared owls looked down on us from their perch in the fork of an old tree, and further down the road a spotted deer walked up to Anne and allowed her to hold its antlers while a bright yellow bird with a long black and white tail perched on its rump; neither seemed to hold any fear of humans.

In spite of very severe penalties, tiger skins and tiger animal parts used for traditional medicine command a high price in Tibet and China. Poachers were taking a heavy toll in the area and this problem was further aggravated by the cruel climate which had not produced any measurable precipitation for three long years. I fear that we will have been among the last generation of visitors to find wild tiger in this vast, arid and denuded tract of eastern Rajasthan.

After a few days we set off on another very long drive along remote country roads through Rajasthan and into Madhya Pradesh. We passed more camel trains and dozens of pretty young girls who wore colourful saris and carried huge water gourds on their heads. I was pleased to find no beggars in the farming communities that we drove through, only hard working families who earned a living from the land using the same techniques and implements as their forefathers; perhaps with a little improvisation here and there.

Ram pointed out several homemade lorries loaded with sacks of rice chugging along with a strange put-put sound. It was some time before I realized what he was trying to tell me; their engines were modified borehole water pumps connected to the drive shaft with a thick rubber belt.

We arrived late afternoon in Fatehpur Sikri, a deserted red sandstone capital city built by Emperor Akbar in the late 16th century. The remains of his palace are in pristine condition and it is not difficult to imagine the kind of life that he must have led. Akbar took three wives; Hindu, Muslim and Christian and housed each separately in a building of size and grandeur equal to their relative importance; a rather unique way to encourage religious tolerance.

My visit was ruined by the persistence of a very annoying hawker who continually thrust a chess set into my face; he even followed me into the temple. He was so physically aggressive that I had to refrain from striking him. He was not an old beggar or a young child in rags; he was a relatively well dressed young man who obviously used this tactic with some measure of success. This was perhaps the only occasion when I was disappointed with my local guide; he should have controlled the situation.

A couple of hours later and we arrived in the second great capital city of the Mughal Empire, Dar-ul-Khilafat or 'seat of the emperor'. Now known as Agra this once small village has become a large and very ugly metropolis with its skyline dominated by a huge impregnable red sandstone fort. This fort was also built by Emperor Akbar and it is now occupied by the Indian Army. It holds an impressive position looking down onto the wide slow flowing River Yamuna and some of its more opulent buildings are open to the public.

In the early hours of the following morning we visited a monument that neither of us would ever forget. It was shrouded in a low lying mist, and for a moment, its limp translucent curtain parted, and before us, like the radiant incandescence of a ghost, stood in shining white marble the world's most famous monument to love; the architectural wonder that is the Taj Mahal.

I had waited several years to visit this stunning mausoleum; ever since the time when I sat in the Naqsh-e Jahan Square in Esfahan and stared and stared at the stunning design of the Shah Mosque. It is said that Persian architect Usted Isa designed the Shah Mosque before he was retained to build the Taj Mahal. Now I had an opportunity to examine what was surely his greatest masterpiece.

Commissioned by Emperor Shah Jahan, the Taj is a white marble memorial to his beautiful wife Mumtaz Mahal. It took 22 years to complete and was designed with a stunning balance of structure. Perfectly symmetrical it has elegant domes, intricately carved screens and some of the best inlay work that I have ever seen. The four marble towers standing guard at each corner are testament to the structural integrity of Ustad's work; they slope ever so slightly away from the main building and because of this careful design they will fall safely into the gardens if an earthquake should ever topple them.

Guides have a nasty habit of taking their customers to their favourite tourist traps; factory shops which sell locally produced goods. I normally refuse to enter such establishments, but on this occasion I made a deliberate exception. The intricate practice where semi-precious stones are cut then inlaid into translucent white marble was so exceptional in the Taj Mahal that I decided to purchase a locally crafted example. I bought a very expensive piece to decorate our glass-top table in Bristol. I made my purchase from the same factory that was visited by my favourite American, President Bill Clinton.

The next stop on my self designed itinerary was the holy city of Varanasi in Uttar Pradesh. We closed the triangle and drove back to Delhi where we stayed the night before flying to Varanasi on Jet Airways. We were very sorry to say goodbye to Ram, our faithful companion and driver for so many dusty tiring miles.

Varanasi, better known as Benares or Kashi, is the most sacred of Hindu destinations and the world's most ancient living city. It is an obvious choice on any tourist itinerary but nearby Sarnath was my target. I wanted to visit the place where the great sage Buddha came after attaining enlightenment at Bodh Gaya. It was here in a deer park that he proclaimed his gospel of peace to all humanity and gave his first sermon to five disciples 2,596 years ago.

A small museum with a wealth of ancient exhibits stood close to the ancient stupa that honoured Lord Buddha. At the entrance was the priceless 'Lion of Sarnath'. This is four lions sculptured into a 'capital' that once stood atop a column commissioned by Emperor Ashok in the 3rd century BC. It had been erected by Ashok to mark the place where Buddha proclaimed his gospel of peace.

I found the small village of Sarnath to be restful and could not help but compare it with Nazareth. As with Christianity in Israel, the Buddhist religion has very little following in its country of origin. This was well demonstrated by the nationality of those organisations providing charitable support in the area, and yet, the Lion of Sarnath has been adopted as the national emblem of India. It is carried on bank notes and I recall seeing it on the columns marking the entrance to the Governor's Palace in New Delhi.

After taking time so that I might learn more of the teachings of Buddha, we turned our attention to the Ganges. Old people come from all over India to die on its banks in Varanasi and thousands more bathe their worldly sins away in its cold fast flowing waters. The city boasts a thousand temples to honour their many gods and it was here that Lord Shiva is believed to have lived during the later part of his life 3,500 years ago. It is the city of light and the capital of all Hindu knowledge.

I learned of Lord Krishna, the supreme god who was born in the year 3,228 BC and of the three main Hindu deities; Brahma the creator, Vishnu the preserver and Shiva the destroyer. I found that my information was very sketchy and different sources credited the same deities with totally different powers. I found it all very confusing and in the end satisfied myself in the knowledge that the Hindu religion is at least tolerant of other beliefs. With the possible exception of the Druids at Stonehenge, it is by far the oldest religion practised by modern man.

We visited several temples and I was shocked to hear that goats were still being sacrificed. This barbaric practice paled into insignificance when I discovered that Tantrics in nearby villages were enticing poverty stricken people to sacrifice young children by mutilation to Maha Kali, the wife of Lord Krishna. Kali is the goddess of dissolution, destruction and death. I don't know what she could do for these wretched people except to make things even worse for them; they lived in such squalor that they must have been desperate to try anything in the hope of a better life.

As evening approached our guide walked with us through narrow cobblestone streets to the steep steps of the Daswamedh Ghat. We bought two candle floats and paid a young boy a few rupees to row us in a wooden boat to a good viewing position in front of the Aarti Ceremony. As the sun set below the crumbling temples and decaying palaces that rose in tiers from the waters edge, hundreds of small candles floated out into the central current of the Ganges. We lit our own candles and with a couple of wishes added them to the growing flotilla.

As darkness descended six novice priests mounted six separate and very curiously adorned platforms and began to chant mantras while swinging caskets of burning incense in elaborate patterns before a huge congregation. Similar ceremonies were being performed at many other Ghats along the river bank, and as darkness became total, the holy river could only be identified by hundreds of small pin pricks of light that twinkled in a romantic kind of way as they carried our secret wishes into the distance.

We returned to the same Ghat before daybreak and rowed downstream to the first of the cremation Ghats. As the suns rays brought daylight back into the world of the living, priests shovelled the ashes of cremated bodies into the river. Twenty yards downstream several laundry men washed hotel linen in the polluted water while their women beat sheets and towels against a wall and laid them onto ancient stone drying beds. Twenty yards upstream a dozen pilgrims stripped down to their shorts and immersed themselves fully in the freezing cold water. Every part of the sacred river bank was used.

Anne loved vegetarian food and also had a strong preference for fish. One would consider India to be a gourmet paradise for her. However, after two weeks even she was beginning to have difficulty in digesting the fluidic mixtures of spiced vegetables proffered to her twice every day in a selection of small silver bowls. Now it was time for her to have an even bigger shock to her digestive system. People who died of snake bite or disease could not be cremated. Instead their bodies were weighted and cast into the middle of the river; they were being fed to the same fish that appeared on her lunchtime menu!

As we walked back up the steep banks of 'Ganga' funeral parties carried dead bodies past us on stretchers, sacred cows urinated in the narrow cobbled streets, monkeys scrambled across roof tops, a sacred ram chased a young goat with a huge erection, old men sold fresh bread and small cups of tea, and young children ran bare foot on their way to school. I wondered what kind of diseases proliferated in such an archaic society. I found the complete experience to be physically overpowering, but I respected the strong religious beliefs of these kind people. They were our hosts for a few brief days and their behaviour and eagerness to please was unforgettable.

My visit to Varanasi completed my own very special kind of pilgrimage, a pilgrimage that started thirty four years earlier when I first visited Jerusalem. It has taken me to most of the holy places that are representative of the World's major religions, past and present. I have observed these religions first hand and have been able to form my own constructive judgement upon the relative merits of each. I don't have the benefits of a Cambridge theology education but then I had not been polluted by the misguided opinions of others.

I have considered the evidence available to me from Karnak to Chichen Itsa and Sarneth to Stonehenge. All religions and beliefs but one have resulted in large loss of life. All but one has sacrificed, tortured or mutilated in the name of its deity. One in particular is not tolerant of other religions. It is true that the prophets and disciples of these great religions may have preached differently, but I believe that it was how their followers behaved that matters.

I came to the conclusion that there is only one group of people that are tolerant of others; a group that does not inflict mental or physical pain on any living being, human or otherwise. This group followed the teachings of Buddha; a great sage who was deeply disturbed by the behaviour of mankind towards one-another and, in particular, he condemned the ritual sacrifice of defenceless animals.

I am a Christian and yet I am of the opinion that those who followed the teachings of Buddha over the past two millenia are perhaps more true to the teachings of Christ than those who have purported to represent him. If asked my true faith then I would have to say that I was born a Christian but endeavour to live my life in the ways of Buddha. I must admit that I have often set a rather a bad example from time to time.

Before leaving Varanasi we walked to the remains of the Kashi Vishwanath Temple or Golden Temple as it is commonly known. It is one of the oldest and holiest of temples in India and was destroyed by Mughal Emperor Aurangzeb to make way for the Gaynvapi Mosque, which now stands in its place. Similar to the Wailing Wall in Jerusalem, one of the walls of Kashi Vishwanath remains and forms an integral part of the Mosque. Also, as with the Wailing Wall in Jerusalem, Kashi Vishwanath has become the focal point for religious confrontation in Varanasi. A watch tower stood on each corner, several machine gun nests were positioned on nearby roof tops and policemen wandered around carrying old Lee Enfield rifles. I had a strange foreboding that a terrorist attack was imminent. I was right! An Islamic group detonated several explosive devices shortly after our visit.

Nepal

Wherever I travelled I appeared to attract organised violence of some kind. This trip was no exception. Two days before we were due to fly to Nepal, Maoist insurgents ended their ceasefire and resumed their armed struggle against the royalist forces of King Gyanendra. Our flight from Varanasi to Kathmandu was cancelled.

Our local agent discussed the situation with Compass and they quickly found a solution. We drove north across the remotest areas of Uttar Pradesh until we reached the Himalayan foothills. After securing an entry permit at a primitive border post we crossed into Nepal and caught a local flight with Buddha Air that took us across the first range of mountains and into the Kathmandu Valley. What other travel agent would take such good care of his customers?

We found the atmosphere in Nepal to be much more relaxed than in India. The Nepalese people were poor but they did not beg and they lived in streets that were more open and much cleaner. The police were heavily armed and they toured the streets in armoured vehicles with mounted machine guns at the ready, but they were always courteous to us. We were also encouraged by newspaper reports in which the leader of the insurgents assured tourists that they would not be targeted. Despite this the streets were empty of Europeans and, as always, it was those who earn their living from the tourist trade that suffered first. Just as it was in Luxor so it was in Pokhara.

The Kathmandu Valley, once a separate kingdom and now the commercial hub of Nepal contained three fabled cities; Kathmandu, Patan and Bhaktapur. Each was an artistic exposition of graceful multi-roofed pagodas, ornate palaces and brick paved courtyards, all linked by an intricate maze of brick paved streets to their own Durbar Square.

I had never seen anything that resembled the unusual architecture of these beautiful buildings and I guessed that they were unique to Nepal. Red brick was used to construct the walls and intricately carved wooden beams supported three or more red tiled roofs layered one on top of the other, just like a wedding cake. Stone lions guarded the largest of the Durbar Squares in Kathmandu and a huge cobra was poised threateningly above the head of a young malla king. This entire majesty lay beneath the magnificent white crown of the surrounding snow covered Himalayas.

We walked through quaint narrow cleanly swept streets, such a pleasant contrast with our experience of India. We tasted local dishes, photographed old women making clay pots and we spun prayer wheels. This was another new experience for me and I was surprised by the mechanised way in which people saved time when praying to Buddha. When followers entered a temple they struck several small bells to attract Buddha's attention; then they spun a row of prayer wheels in a clockwise direction. Why clockwise? Each contained prayer scrolls coiled in an anti-clockwise direction. Spinning several wheels enabled a visitor to transmit dozens of prayers to Buddha at the same time. Tourists were easily recognised; they spun the wheels anti-clockwise or walked around the temple in the wrong direction. The most faithful also lit three incense sticks and made a private wish, or they sought a blessing from the head monk.

Anne visited a Hindu shrine and touched red powder to her forehead. She smudged the powder into a rather large mark and young children teased her for the rest of the morning. The children were so friendly; untouched by the outside world they found their own simple pleasures.

During the days of Empire, Britain had been unable to defeat the tribes of this mountain kingdom. They isolated Nepal and it remained a forbidden land, largely by choice under a system of hereditary prime ministers, until a palace revolt in 1951 re-established Crown authority and links with the outside world were opened for the first time. This isolation was blamed for making Nepal one of the most underdeveloped countries in the World. Perhaps it was this isolation that had enabled its peoples to remain so natural and in tune with its unique surroundings.

High above the Kathmandu Valley stands the colossal stupa of Swayambu Nath. This 2000 year old Buddhist shrine stands like a sentinel guarding the valley of the three ancient kings. It is surrounded by several small pagodas and the main temple is crowned with copper guilt. As we walked around its huge base the all seeing eyes of Buddha were always upon us.

We left Kathmandu before daybreak and joined Air Buddha for a special flight along the Himalayan range. It was one of those things in life that is so special that it had to be done regardless of the cost. Our specially trained hostess named each of the peaks as we flew by and then we were invited to the cockpit so that we could get the best possible view of

Everest. I looked at Base Camp where Dave Mellor hoped to take me in October. The terrain was covered with jagged mountain ridges and deep hostile ravines free of all signs of vegetation. Everest looked forbidding and easily recognisable from any direction. To the right of Everest I could see Lohtse and I felt proud when I told the pilot that one of my good friends was the oldest person ever to reach its summit, and alone.

After landing back in Kathmandu another Air Buddha flight took us to Pokhara, a beautiful town lying below the Annapurna massif on the picturesque banks of Lake Phewa; truly the most romantic and most beautiful place on earth. By now we had become attached to the Beechcraft 1900D that Air Buddha used to ferry us through dangerous mountain terrain. We felt very relaxed and safe inside its small pressurised hull and its powerful turboprop engines made light work of the short high altitude runways that we were obliged to use.

We crossed by raft and rope to Fishtail Lodge on the far bank of Lake Phewa and our receptionist gave us a choice of two rooms. The first was very comfortable while the second was very sparse with stone floors and a hard wooden bed. I chose the second because it had a fabulous view of the mountains. My waiter told me at dinner time that I had chosen the same room as Prince Charles when he visited the Annapurnas.

On our first morning I turfed Anne out of bed at 5 am and we ventured into the fresh cold morning air to admire the wondrous scenery before us. Twenty four thousand feet high, the snow capped peaks of Annapurna I to Annapurna IV radiated an incandescent orange glow in the early morning sunlight and this reflected in a perfect mirror image on the still waters of the lake directly in front of us. Machhapuchhre with its fish-tailed pinnacle stood out from all others and resembled the perfect snow-capped needle-pointed mountain that every schoolboy dreamed of conquering; lower in altitude that many of its neighbours, but an impossible challenge to even the very best of mountaineers. Dave don't read this, your pacemaker is not up to it!

Ghorka hill tribes lived in an area north east of Pokhara and it was from this area that the British Army first recruited a fierce mercenary fighting force now known as the proud Ghurkha Regiment. I hoped to find an original kukri and Anne was surprisingly patient as I spent several hours each day examining hundreds of purpose made tourist replicas. Eventually I found a rusty and very old kukri that belonged to a hill farmer. It is about the most ferocious looking thing that I have ever purchased and Brett was stunned when he realised that I had carried it through the customs check point.

The Pokhara Valley is also an ornithologist's paradise and our waiter proved to be a very experienced self educated wildlife guide. I paid him a sizeable sum and he took us birding along the river and into the heavily scented hills above Pokhara. We walked passed old farmers cottages and modern well constructed bungalows where retired Ghurkha soldiers lived; an old stone building had a wooden sign erected which said that it was the British Army pension pay station. This must be the most remote British army outpost in the world.

Three kinds of eagle, two kinds of vulture and several kites soared high above the river. At first they all looked the same but after ten minutes and the careful use of a powerful pair of binoculars our guide taught me how to distinguish each one. Along the river banks we found redstarts, bulbuls, stonechats, warblers and flycatchers, and perched on a fence post watching a group of workers shovelling river gravel was a lone and very colourful kingfisher.

As we climbed into the hills many different birds flitted through the trees beside us, several followed our path for some distance, some burst into song and others chattered noisily in protest of our presence. Our guide carefully named each type for me and eventually I learned to identify many by their call. There were blackbirds, thrushes, mynas, orioles, drongos, magpies, tree creepers, chats and very beautifully coloured sunbirds.

We visited a Tibetan refugee camp and were very impressed with the way that the Nepalese people had opened their hearts and their countryside to these proud people. They had left their Chinese invaders on the far side of the Annapurnas to build a new life in the Pokhara Valley. They are now able to live and to worship as they please and they earn a living by spinning wool, weaving carpets and making small tourist trinkets, which they sell outside hotels in Pokhara; I have no idea what the men do!

A group of Tibetan women sold trinkets on the landing stage opposite our lodge. Their huge toothless grins were a pleasure to behold as we passed from stall to stall ensuring that we bought at least one item from each on our last day. It was a shame that we were the only buyers and it was such a lovely day. Chinese politics in the form of Maoist guerillas had followed them over the Annapurnas to cast a giant shadow across the future of this unspoilt ancient kingdom.

Early one morning we drove up to Sarangkot to enjoy an even better view of the sunrise. We stood in darkness and waited for the first rays of a new sun to strike the snow capped peaks behind us. Hill people brought mugs of hot tea, and then our guide broke into a verbal attack on the King. "He will resign or he will die!" I was surprised by this unguarded and very open statement; hill tribes are peace loving people and they want so little from life. I then discovered how much contempt they had for King Gyanendra.

I was told that Gyanendra ascended his throne in February 2001 after Crown Prince Dipendra had killed the whole of the Nepalese Royal Family in a lovers rage before killing himself. The Crown Prince was well liked by the Nepalese people and they did not believe the official story of events.

Totally separate from the circumstances of Gyanendra's ascent to the throne is an older situation that was inspired by the Chinese revolutionary leader Mao Zedong. Maoist rebels under Prachanda wanted to replace Nepal's monarchy with a communist state. They began their 'Peoples War' on 13th February 1996 with an attack on a police post in mid-west Nepal. Since then 12,500 people had been killed.

I am deeply saddened by this tragic sequence of events and fear that Maoists will one day combine with ordinary people in a popular uprising to overthrow the monarchy; the ancient Kingdom of Nepal would then become a republic; how sad that would be!

Koh Samui

I had hoped to travel on from Kathmandu to Southern Thailand. Anne and I loved this part of the world so much and it was the right time of the year. The monsoon season was over and the islands in the Gulf of Thailand were passing through their coolest period. Anne unfortunately had to return to the grindstone and so after a couple of weeks in Spain and a few more in England I headed off to join Michael Gabor in Koh Samui. Michael was a new friend whom I met in Grand Bahama.

It was a long flight to Bangkok and I arrived very tired in the morning to find that bad weather had closed Koh Samui Airport. Extremely frustrated I purchased a new air ticket to Surat Thani and crossed by ferry from Don Sak to Nathon Pier. This was the fourth air ticket that I had torn up in as many months.

I must admit that it was a novel way to arrive on such a beautiful tropical island. I lugged my suitcase down the gangplank as a driver hailed me from his 'Songtaew', which was drawn up on the dockside. He threw my suitcase on the roof and I climbed into the back of his converted truck-cum-bus with a motley collection of backpackers from Australia. As we hurtled along ill-maintained roads in the general direction of Cheweng a tropical storm raged and I wondered what had happened to the mild weather promised in my on-line electronic tourist brochure.

I jumped down from the tailgate and walked into a small tin-covered open building. A bare-footed Thai welcomed me warmly and carried my suitcase to a spotlessly clean bungalow. My balcony stood on tall stilts above huge granite boulders that formed one side of a beautiful bay. Lush green tree covered hills fell steeply to a small curving beach of white coral sand, which on my arrival, was being beaten mercilessly by huge white crested waves. It was good to be back in Thailand again.

I settled down on my balcony determined to write a couple of chapters for my book. The sound of pounding waves reaching the end of their long journey and the feeling of fresh salt laden wind on my cheeks inspired me and I wrote several pages each day. Sadly, or perhaps not, the sun eventually returned to cast a strong glare across the liquid crystal display of my laptop and I was forced to retreat to the cool sanctuary of my air-conditioned lounge.

As I have already mentioned, political trouble does seem to follow me around. Shortly after my arrival a popular uprising developed against

Prime Minister Thaksin Shinawatra. His family had sold shares in their Telecommunications Company to a Singapore organisation and the Thai People claimed that he ignored ethics and morality and used state mechanisms for his personal benefit. Over the next few weeks the situation deteriorated rapidly and on Friday 24th February 2006 Shinawatra stood down and announced that new elections would take place. He was re-elected on a strong rural vote and then overthrown in a military coup on the 19th September 2006.

Meanwhile Michael arrived from Los Angeles. It was his first ever visit to South East Asia and he was fairly bouncing with excitement. He begrudgingly agreed to rent a 4-wheel drive open vehicle to tour the island. He wanted desperately to ride one of the small motor bikes which every islander seemed to ride. I was reluctant at first because these bikes were notorious for their high mortality rate. Eventually I relented and we hired two bikes for a couple of weeks.

I found mine rather dangerous at first and I insisted upon wearing a crash helmet. Eventually I became over-confident and threw it into my cupboard. It was a small island and I soon learned where the sand traps and deep potholes were. I even set a rather bad example by giving two villagers a lift home. Three on a bike was a first for me; Bophut Fishing Village to the Big Buddha.

Before long Koh Samui became rather small and we took the ferry across to Koh Pha Ngan; famous for the full moon party. Within 10 minutes of landing we had hired two motor bikes and were riding north along the rugged coastline. Koh Pha Ngan is still unspoiled by heavy tourism. It is a beautiful tropical island, covered with coconut trees and steep granite hills that shot straight out of the deep blue waters of the Gulf of Thailand. We struggled over tortuous hills, stopping to push our bikes up the steepest of slopes, and took refreshments at small picturesque fishing villages. Each village had small thatched cottages raised on stilts which could be rented for a few hundred Baht. I loved real Thai food, not the stuff you bought in a posh English restaurant, the kind that you found at the roadside; it was exquisite.

I bought a delicious meal of Pad Thai on the beach and washed it down with fresh coconut milk for less than 40 Baht; a dollar in real money. It was Saturday 25th February 2006 and very nearly my last day on this earth. Late in the afternoon while crossing a high mountain in the centre of the island Michael stopped in front of me. He signalled frantically and when I rode up to him his gesticulations became all the more urgent. He yelled; "there is a cobra under your foot". I looked down and saw a five foot bright green snake. It had a diamond shaped head with a white spot at the centre. It moved quickly and resembled a large white-lipped pit viper; not a cobra but still a very aggressive and dangerous snake. There were no medical facilities nearby and I shuddered to think what might have happened if it had bitten me.

Singapore

After a couple of weeks of paradise Michael moved on to Australia and I took a local flight with Bangkok Airways down to Singapore. Anne had already visited Singapore and I suspected that this would be my only opportunity. Singapore is so heavily steeped in British colonial history that I knew exactly what I wanted to do before I even set foot off the aeroplane.

If one has the money then everything can be found in Singapore. It has beautiful orchid gardens, large butterfly enclosures and incredible aquariums. This small democratic country has even built its own beaches with sand imported from the Philippines. In my short time I was determined to see them all, but only after I had paid my respects to the war dead.

When I trained as a young apprentice many of my workmates were in protected employment. Some had laboured on the Thailand-Burma Railroad; others had been incarcerated in Changi Barracks after the fall of Singapore, or both. I wanted to visit Changi so that I might learn more of the hardships they endured and to pay my respects to those of their friends and comrades who never returned.

I took a guided tour of the area around Changi Prison and was surprised by what I found. I had not known of the Sook Ching massacre when around 50,000 ethnic Chinese were 'cleansed' for their support of Chiang Kai-Shek in the second Sino-Japanese War. Neither had I known that British Singapore capitulated to an outnumbered and poorly equipped Japanese invasion force. It is considered to be the largest and most humiliating defeat in the history of the British Army. The British Government is no different to any other; they are economical with the truth when their information is not good.

Singapore is an incredible city. It really is unique. Its position as a gateway to South East Asia has strengthened enormously since Hong Kong returned to China. New high rise buildings shoot into the sky along the Singapore River. New and old blend together in harmony with each other, as do the different cultures; Chinese, Malay, Indian and European. All of the world's four main religions are fully integrated into Singaporean society. Hindu, Buddhist, Muslim and Christian school children are taught to understand each other's culture so that they will grow into mature adults free of religious bigotry. Perhaps the rest of the world has much to learn from them.

After visiting Changi my first stop downtown was a large hotel just up from the City Hall on the East West Line of the MTR. I sat down at a small French-polished round wooden table and nodded to the waiter. My Simon Templar touch worked and he brought me pen and paper; it was the Writers Bar in the Singapore Raffles Hotel. Singapore Sling on my small round table, a souvenir beer mat in my pocket and a little light-headed I proceeded to write a few notes for my book. I had already enjoyed my first 'Sling' on the Riverside.

I wrote about the Bum Boats, the old cargo lighters that carry early evening tourists down the Singapore River. I wrote about the huge blue-green frogs and blue coloured crabs that were held captive in wire cages on my sidewalk. Chalkboards were marked frogs porridge, baked crab and grilled duck? I had chosen grilled duck earlier; it was one of my favourites but on this occasion I was horrified to be served with the ducks long intestine.

A pianist played a medley of tunes on a drawing grand and I could only marvel at the way her hands danced across the ivory keys. I wished that I had such skill. I took another sip of my Singapore Sling then she stopped and passed by my table to take a short break. I congratulated her on her excellent playing and she promised that she would be back in ten minutes. She wore a long black dress and had a Chinese look about her, but her accent was not discernable. Condensation dripped from the bottom of my uniquely shaped glass. I suppose they had designed its shape to fit with the advertising slogan of this charming cosmopolitan city 'Uniquely Singapore'. This was the same name that the City had given to their entry in the 2005/2006 Clipper Round the World Yacht Race.

Sparrows danced across the floor but there were no breadcrumbs here. Singapore was known by the locals as the 'city of fines'. Littering was strictly forbidden. I suppose even in the Raffles Hotel a few dared to cast a few crumbs across the polished floor. The Piano player returned, smiled across the piano at me and played a cheeky tune. Catch a falling star and put it in you pocket; an old Perry Como favourite. I gave another Simon Templar nod to my waiter and he brought my bill. "Hell, 20 dollars for a Singapore Sling, do I need to leave a tip"?

I left two dollars on the table and moved to the Long Bar on the second floor and ordered a glass of white wine; a bottle of Penfolds was proffered. I took a handful of peanuts from a cone shaped clay pot on the bar top and threw the empty shells across the floor. What was all this nonsense about littering? I asked for more paper but only a bar mat was given; definitely no tip this time.

A half naked girl hung from a nail on the wall opposite and beside her a clock indicated that it was still only 8 pm. The porcelain English bulldog resting beside one of the pump handles reminded me that this was one of the world's famous Colonial watering holes. It reminded me of the Peninsular in Hong Kong, Imperial in New Delhi, Reed in Madeira, Stanley in Nairobi and the Polana in Laurenco Marques. I struggled to think of a similar place in the United States but could only come up with the Queen Mary in Long Beach Harbour, California. Meanwhile, a middle-aged businessman from Chicago was talking bullshit over my right shoulder. He introduced his German girl friend and explained how he, presumably meaning his father's generation, had saved our arses in the Second World War. What the hell did he know? He didn't even realize that his girl friend's father was on the other side. I have so many very good American friends who are friendly hospitable people and I do apologise for commenting upon his behaviour.

Chapter 26

A Pirate's Life for Me

Shiver me timbers lad, it's the real thing, beard and all
A Black Pearl Pirate!

The film 'Pirates of the Caribbean, Curse of the Black Pearl' was such a huge box office success that Disney decided to make 'Pirates of the Caribbean II & III" and to save costs they filmed the battle sequences for both at the same time and in the Bahamas. They opened an office in Port Lucaya and towards the end of 2004 they put out a 'Casting Call' for rough looking sailors with long hair, beards and preferably some form of unusual disfigurement. Nick and I both thought that we fitted that description and so we went along to the casting call; I did cheat a little and submitted photographs that were taken while I was training for the Clipper Race, but Nick had no need to.

We didn't hear anything else until June 2005. I was in Spain and Nick telephoned me and said that he had been contacted by Bradley Grant, who worked in the casting department. I telephoned Bradley and he asked me to resubmit my photographs along with a list of my specialist skills. Two hours later I received a reply inviting me to attend the Bahamas Film Studio for costume fitting. Getting back to the Bahamas was easy; re-growing my beard was another matter.

The Bahamas Film Studio was in the process of being built on the old American Missile Base near to Gold Rock Creek and progress was slow. The Bahamian construction team was months behind schedule and when I visited for my costume fitting the Studio was still a broken shell consisting of several dilapidated buildings. On my first visit a string of green arrows directed me to an old hanger which had been fitted out with small tents to serve as changing rooms.

I completed the obligatory indemnity form which signed my life away and then entered one of these tents. An attractive young woman called Jane followed me in and told me to strip. Rather startled I asked if I was to remove my trousers and she looked at me as if I was stupid. She brought in two pairs of breeches and an armful of coarsely woven shirts. After several attempts she found a combination that fit me. I tried to fasten my shirt and she brushed my hands to one side. I had crossed the union demarcation line; dressing me was her job.

Jane left the tent and came back again with several old but very carefully woven jackets, a long sash to place around my waist, a very thick leather belt with a huge buckle and a leather shoulder strap called a baldric to carry my cutlass. These were a little easier to fit around my rather ample frame. Next Jane brought a huge pair of leather boots that folded over at my hips. She had several attempts to find a pair that would pull over my oddly shaped feet and I was very surprised to find a hand made label stitched inside. It carried the name of a high class Milan leather shop.

My wardrobe must have cost Disney a fortune. Finally a black three-cornered hat was thrust atop my head and then Jane paraded me in front of Penny Rose for her approval. Penny was the head costume designer for Disney and she received the equivalent of an Oscar for her work on the first pirate film. Everyone jumped to attention when she was around and nothing missed her sharp eye for detail. After Penny made several small changes to my costume I was transferred to the hairdressing department.

These young women were a little more patient with me. They decided that my beard was scruffy enough to pass, but my hair was too short. They rummaged through a huge selection of hair extensions and found one that matched my colouring perfectly. They clipped it to the back of my head and then passed me to make-up. The make-up girl took one look at me and decided that I was ugly enough; she passed me on to the photographer who took a series of six photographs in two different profiles.

I had my camera but they would not allow me to take any pictures. I disliked fancy dress balls and I hated to dress-up in strange colourful costumes, but I would have loved to have gone to a party at that particular moment. I definitely looked like the real thing; a Black Pearl Pirate. Filming was due to begin five days later. The film crews and most of the stars had already arrived on the island; but the Colyer Tank was only 60 percent complete. The Colyer Tank was a huge hole in the sand close to the shoreline and reinforced with steel walls. On film this tank blended into the real ocean as if both were one. Wave making machines and huge underwater winches were still being fitted. These were intended to simulate tropical storms while rocking and even capsizing full size sailing ships such as the Black Pearl. It was said to be the largest of its kind in the world. Non-completion of the tank was a difficult situation and one that I thought Disney should have taken into consideration before flying cast and crew into Grand Bahama.

Despite all of these problems I was asked to report to Bradford Docks in Freeport Harbour with my shipmates for sail training on the Black Pearl. It was not real training like on the Clipper Round the World Yacht Race. It was familiarisation with the ship so that we would be comfortable climbing the rattlings and working the lines. Then at lunchtime the production team dropped a bombshell. With no warning to any of the actors or crew they issued a press release putting the film on hold for 10 weeks, they blamed the delay on one of the key English actors who had contracted an ear infection. I suspect that this was just the final straw that broke the camel's back.

We were all terribly disappointed. Nick was so annoyed that he shaved one side of his beard off and left the other side intact. I decided to look for something else to keep me amused and I signed up for a small light hearted film called Eye of the Dolphin.

Eye of the Dolphin

Eye of the Dolphin is about a young girl, played by Carly Schroeder, who visited the Bahamas on holiday with her grandmother, Katharine Ross. While visiting Port Lucaya she found her father, Adrian Dunbar, whom she had thought to be dead, but he was the manager of the Lucaya Dolphin Centre. While getting to know her father again she discovered that she could talk with the dolphins. It is a very simple family film with a simple plot that followed Carly's warm relationship with the dolphins of Lucaya.

Carly is best known for her part as Melina Bianco in Lizzie McGuire and she had just finished the Wrong Element with Harrison Ford. She is a very likeable young girl and she looked much older than she actually was; she was very unpretentious and she mixed easily with the remainder of the cast and crew. I spent a long time talking with Katharine Ross and did not realize that she was the gorgeous young woman that I had fallen in love with so many years ago. She is the girl on the bicycle in Butch Cassidy and the Sundance Kid. She was nominated for an Oscar for her part with Dustin Hoffman in the Graduate. Her list of starring roles is endless and I did not even recognise her; how embarrassing.

My part was only a small one. I was filmed arriving at the Smiths Point Fish Fry with a young woman in a smart party dress; her name was Caraline Joy. Once inside I had to dance with Caraline through the evening and right through the night until 5 am on the following morning. It was a charming location in the open air with a full moon and the waves washing up onto crystal sharp white coral sand. I had a beautiful young women in a nice blue party dress on my arm, what more could I want; perhaps some music would be nice. Yes music, we had to dance for eight hours with no music and with only coloured water to drink. Even the fried fish at our table was imitation.

The director filmed about 30 takes of 5 different scenes. Each time we were given Caribbean music to get us into the beat and then dialogue was called and the music killed. I assumed that music would be added later. First Carly and then Katharine took a careful look at us both and then they walked to the bar. That was about the limit of my stardom. For the rest of the time we were just filling in the background. The whole shoot took 11 hours and we were paid the minimum wage of 75 dollars.

It was an enjoyable evening and I made a lot of friends from California. The Assistant Director was an interesting person. He told me about his most enjoyable films and the people whom he liked working with. He directed the stunt filming on Titanic and worked on a film with Steven Seagal; he said he found Seagal to be a very difficult person and said he would never work with him again. I don't think this surprised me.

As the European Autumn approached my diary became very crowded. Anne and I had been invited by Kevin, Aunt Marjorie's son-in-law, to attend his ceremonial appointment as the new Sheriff of London and on the following day, 17th September, we were invited to the flotilla party in Liverpool for the start of the 2005 Clipper Round the World Yacht Race. Then on the 18th we were scheduled by Disney to re-start filming. I could not be in several places at the same time and so I decided to remain in the Bahamas.

My hair and beard continued to grow and it was very hot and humid, not at all pleasant. I invited Anne to join me for two weeks and she flew out via New York. She had a fabulous time and was not at all put off by my fearsome appearance.

Katrina

A couple of weeks after Anne returned to England we were alerted to the birth of a small tropical depression north of Paradise Island in the Bahamas. This quickly grew into Tropical Storm Katrina which immediately headed straight for Grand Bahama. Low winds were forecast with a considerable amount of rain. No one made any special preparations and I sat on my 8th floor balcony sipping a cup of Ovaltine before retiring at midnight. There was total cloud cover but no wind at all; it was very peaceful.

Two hours later I was awakened by my balcony doors crashing repeatedly against their frames. Lightning flashed and pressure waves hammered against my ear drums. The electric power was already down. I grabbed a torch from my bedside cabinet and then dared to venture into my lounge where Thor himself seemed to be running amok. My old sliding doors were curved inwards, the vibrating glass contained within its uncertain frame of aluminium threatened to burst into huge deadly shards at any moment. Huge objects crashed around on my balcony. I opened the sliding door and tested the strength of the wind before crawling out on my hands and knees to retrieve my plants and furniture before they crashed through my bedroom window.

It was a complete white-out; the buildings on the other side of the harbour were lost in a swirling torrent of airborne seawater. It was as if Neptune, in his anger, had hurled the ocean into the skies to dowse the fire of Thor. The wind came in huge ferocious waves and salt water surged across the lounge floor of my eighth floor apartment picking up my Persian carpets as if Davy Jones himself was trying to ride them to safety.

Walls and gates around Harbour House were ripped away. Huge trees fell across the feeder roads and jeeps in the car park were pushed sideways by the wind until they stacked up against one another. Both elevator shafts filled with salt water and a section of the new hurricane roof, fitted after Frances, ripped off and vanished into a swirling vortex. Water in the harbour far below heaped up against the Bell Channel Inn and short steep waves curled upwards allowing their white tops to be whipped away in the wind. Amidst all of this turmoil small and large boats alike bucked violently against their shorelines fighting for their very survival. Fantasia, a well known party boat, lost its battle and broke loose from its moorings before crashing into two smaller fishing boats tethered nearby.

The US National Hurricane Centre got it wrong. The squalls associated with Katrina battered Harbour House Towers for 12 hours before she swept over Miami and into the Gulf of Mexico. The warm waters of the Gulf then fed her and helped her to develop into a brutal category-5 hurricane. She hit New Orleans on 30th August 2005 like an enraged witch. Her devastating force shattered the lives of millions of people and she went down in history as the strongest hurricane ever to hit the United States mainland.

More than one million people were evacuated from the low lying areas around the metropolitan area and 26,000 people who had no transport took refuge in the huge New Orleans Superdome. Even this refuge could not escape the full wrath of Katrina and she ripped a huge section of the roof off, causing panic amongst those thousands of wretched people seeking refuge on its open playing field. The rest of the story is now common knowledge and when Katrina finally subsided she had taken more than one and a half thousand souls.

Katrina was yet another example of the inability of the United States Government, local and national, to take good care of the safety and wellbeing of its own peoples. The shame of their actions, or lack of, will haunt many US officials for years to come. However, on this occasion, I could not lay any blame at the foot of George Bush; he did not hesitate to make huge resources available to the appropriate authorities.

I blame the police service, the armed forces and all those in authority who were just not up to the job entrusted to them. I lay blame upon those Americans who ignored the plight of desperate people simply because they were the wrong colour. More than once I have heard comments from certain Americans that the niggers decided to stay in New Orleans and so it was their problem. In all my years in Africa I have never come across this kind of racist attitude. For all of the criticism levied against Afrikaaners by the rest of the world, they always looked after their own, white and black alike.

This was not the end of this unfortunate episode. Over the next four weeks Ophelia, Rita and Tammy were born over the Bahamas and it seemed as though we had become the devil's caldron. For the first time in history the National Hurricane Centre in Miami ran out of letters and they had to begin naming storms after the Greek Alphabet. It was the most destructive year on record and because of this oil stocks soared to record prices. Despite what George Bush, alias 'The Ostrich' had to say in Washington about global warming, I am of the firm opinion that the United States should back the Kyoto accord without any further procrastination.

Filming Starts

After months of delay I finally received my call to join the Black Pearl. It was a late morning start and so I set my alarm for 5 am. Yes, that was late in the film business. Soldiers from the East India Militia were being processed first and I was not needed in make-up until 6.30 am. I drove to the set with Nick and Bobby Stone, a young American who was living on a boat and working in the Bahamas on ocean rescue and ship salvage operations. Nick, disorganised as ever, missed his alarm call and eventually rushed out to join us with a bag full of coffee, biscuits, rum and coke. Anyone would have thought that we were setting out on a major journey.

I covered the 20 miles or so to Gold Rock Creek in record time with the speedometer often passing through the 100 mph mark, much to the dismay of my passengers. As it happened, we could not find the costume department and we lost the time we had made up. It was of no consequence, the rest of the Black Pearl Pirates arrived from the Sheraton on their contracted bus at exactly the same time and we all stood in line to sign our contract with Kate Burgess and Bradley Grant, our assistant casting directors.

After signing our lives and commercial rights to Disney we were directed to a huge tent where breakfast was being served. We were all stunned to find several chefs preparing the most incredible arrangement of cereals, fruit, meats and dairy produce. Quantity, quality, diversity and display surpassed even the best of hotels that I have visited in Thailand, Japan or any of my many other exotic destinations. The tent itself was furnished with a dozen rows of wooden benches capable of seating around 200 people in one sitting while huge canvas air-conditioning ducts attempted to keep the heat and humidity of the Bahamas at bay.

After consuming all of Nick's goodies and then a much larger breakfast than normal, I cast a short accusing look at Nick. He shrugged his shoulders with the unsaid response; how was I to know? Then Kate entered the tent and called "Pirates get your clothes on". We shuffled off to the huge make-up tent and met the wardrobe people for the first time. A very likeable and bubbly young English woman called Lizzy took me under her wing and asked for my number. "BP62". She reappeared with three coat hangers and a large blue striped bag containing the course fabric pirate garb that I had been fitted with three months earlier.

Lizzy stood by, unperturbed and unashamed, while I undressed and struggled into my ripped bedraggled pantaloons. Then she helped roll the sleeves up on my shirt and undid the top four buttons to bare my chest. My thigh length leather boots were my greatest challenge and I really struggled to get the last few inches to bridge the top of my foot.

When she was satisfied with my swarthy appearance she placed my own clothes into the striped bag and then showed me how to wrap the handle of the bag around the three coat hangers, pin my BP62 tag to the outside, pass it to the person at the wardrobe counter, and finally get my make-up docket stamped. Standing back with a satisfied look on her face and both hands firmly placed on her hips she said, "that's how it's done, see you remember because tomorrow you will have to do it all by yourself".

Walking along the tented corridor I found myself faced by two short queues, one for make-up, and the other for hairdressers. I chose to stand in line for the next hairdresser; they were all gorgeous looking girls and I am sure they just couldn't wait to get their hands on me. Another young girl guided me to a large pinboard and asked for my number. "BP62". She looked along the board and found a Ziploc bag labelled BP62. It contained 2 photographs taken 3 months ago, my hairpiece, and several beads and trinkets that had to be woven into my hair.

I sat in front of a huge mirror and my hairdresser closed in behind me wearing khaki drill trousers topped with a tight fitting sweat shirt. She had black hair, dark eyes, a neatly trim suntanned body and several hair clips clenched firmly between her pink lips. She, like all of the other hairdressers, was living on less than four hours sleep. What you saw at this time of the morning was what you got. They wore no make-up, their hair was unkempt and they had red-rimmed eyes. But their smiles were genuine and they enjoyed their work; they were gorgeous!

Barbara from LA fitted my hairpiece before spending an inordinate amount of time braiding a sidepiece and fitting the beads and trinkets to match my photographs. After making my hair look rather attractive she then filled her hands with a light oily substance and ruffled the sides until I looked positively scruffy. Standing back she then placed my cocked hat, with its long black feather, on one side of my head, pulled it forward and said "you will do". With that brief cheeky remark she passed me to 'make-up'.

Again I was given a Ziploc bag containing two photographs and again I was placed into a comfortable director's style chair that was placed directly in front of a huge mirror fringed by three sets of incandescent lamps. Dave, a veteran with a dozen movie films on his CV, then set about making me look like my photograph. He fidgeted with his pallet and mixed several shades of black, brown, orange and yellow together with a substance that smelled suspiciously like an addictive substance that had been banned in the United Kingdom.

Dave painted layer after layer on my face. Each layer was a different shade and when he finished my skin looked old and weather beaten. Then he worked on my eyes. "Open your eyes, look down, look up, don't close your eyes". He brushed a dark alcohol based stain onto my open eyelids. This irritated my eyes and as fast as he added the stain my tears washed it away leaving long white and black streaks down my face. Everyone had the same problem and Dave just had to keep going, adding and repairing, until he achieved the look he wanted; an old, weather beaten pirate who looked as though he had just risen from the dead.

Tired and ready for another cup of coffee I was then directed by Kate to 'Props', which was located in three trailers close to the Colyer Tank. I already had my baldric and so I just needed to select a suitable cutlass and then get back to the main tent. As I passed through the lines of 'Movie Makers Caravans' I was approached by a young-looking production assistant called Tasha Prothro; all of the film crew were young and bounding with energy. Tasha looked me up and down and then told me to hurry out to the Pearl and to tell the Assistant Director that I was the stand-in for Mackenzie Crook; the tall skinny one-eyed guy known as Ragetti who is also well known for his part in the UK television series 'The Office'.

On the Black Pearl at last

I boarded one of the Zodiacs at the floating dock and found myself being whisked out to the Black Pearl for the first time. A square section of the hull had been cut out and fitted with two air jacks so that it could be raised and lowered for boarding at sea. Two sets of willing hands were waiting to grasp hold of me as I waited for the next wave to reach its peak. "Pass yer sword" one of them yelled and I quickly pulled it from my baldric before its blunted point pierced the Zodiac's inflatable hull.

I found myself on a very cramped and overcrowded lower deck. The Black Pearl was previously a steel-hulled oil rig supply vessel. She had been stripped completely and fitted with an exterior wooden hull, wooden deck, masts, wheel, and all of the rigging that befits a pirate brigantine of the 17th century. The hull was fitted with gun ports, gun port doors and cannons. Each cannon had a huge air jack to roll it forward into its firing position and then to simulate its recoil when firing a small charge of black powder. In battle the complete scene became alive and very realistic for both cinemagoers and actors alike.

In the forward section below decks were two small and very cramped heads, totally inadequate for the large number of actors, film crew and support personnel carried on board for a typical 10-hour filming session. Beside the heads were makeshift bunks for the 'real' ships crew and a small engineer's panel. The engineer's panel was a laughable excuse for the ship's navigation bridge. I struggled to understand how the US Coastguard could issue a sea going certificate for a ship so poorly equipped.

In the main section, squeezed between both rows of cannon, was a set of makeshift racks that were constantly replenished with fruit, chocolate, cakes, coffee and tea. The floor was covered with large cold boxes filled with ice, water, and various soft drinks and most important of all, cans and cans of Red Bull. The cold boxes were the only seats provided below deck and we spent many days sitting on them over the next four months.

The 80 square foot or so of uncovered lower deck was the resting area, the waiting area, the service area, the operational area and the trades working area. Sound engineers worked amidst the sickening smell of diesel fumes, joiners hammered and drilled as they modified camera platforms, caterers replenished food supplies, actors waited on stand-by and poor John, one of the core pirates from LA, stood at the ramp retching with seasickness. The complete area was organised chaos but everyone to their credit remained patient and co-operative.

Steve Beaupre, the 2nd Assistant Director, took me by my arm and placed me on the port side of the main deck just beside and below a long boat which was partially winched into the air. He gave me a general idea of what was happening and then I rehearsed the scene with four other stand-ins. The idea was to find the best way to hoist and drop the longboat while the camera crew fixed their positions and focal lengths. After about one hour the Zodiac arrived with Johnny Depp, Orlando Bloom, Keira Knightley and five of the supporting actors. I showed Mackenzie Crook what I had been doing and identified the exact position where he must stand for the cameras.

A short while later my shipmates arrived and they were each placed in a key position and told what to do. Some were hoisting sails, others were carrying powder barrels, and a couple helped Mackenzie and Lee to hoist the longboat. I began to feel left out and so I climbed into the rattlings and found a job of my own. This was a mistake, the camera never scanned above deck and having chosen this particular position I had to stick with it through the complete scene, which took several days to shoot.

At noon we were taken off in several Zodiacs and beached at Gold Rock Creek where we could enjoy lunch in relatively cool surroundings within the huge tented restaurant. This was our first experience of the 'pecking order' that we all grew to hate at Disney. Two assistants stood by the ramp and prevented any of the background actors from boarding the Zodiacs. The main actors were taken off first, then the stuntmen, the film crew, the tradesmen and finally the background actors. The fact that we had a Nobel Prize winner, a distinguished mountain climber and several multi-millionaires amongst our group did not matter. To be fair, Disney treated us very well, but this pecking order did make us feel like 'Bilge Rats' and as the days and weeks progressed we began to feel a strong resentment towards it.

After discarding our hats, outer coats, baldrics, swords and flintlocks on a bench in the wardrobe tent we made our way to the restaurant. Again we came foul of the 'pecking order'. A young girl stood in our path and told us that several of the crew still had to be served. She was referring to the electricians, carpenters, hairdressers; all those who were part of the regular team. This was the final straw. I told her that was their problem and not mine; I pushed by her and joined the queue. She was most upset and ran away to report me to the Assistant Director.

The food was incredible. I had heard of the magnificent spread presented by Disney at meal times, but I was still taken aback. Outside the tent stood half a dozen refrigerated trailers, which had been used to ship produce in from the United States. At the entrance a barbecue grilled salmon, huge tee-bone steaks and farmer's sausage. Inside several serving tables were covered with lobster, king prawn, snapper, pork, lamb, vegetables, pasta, fruit, salads, cheeses and sweet deserts. Nothing was wanting and everything was prepared and displayed impeccably.

I took a measured helping of those items I would normally avoid, fully conscious of my weight problem, and looked for an empty seat. I found myself sitting beside a ferocious looking Captain Barbossa; otherwise answering to the name of Geoffrey Rush. I asked him if he was returning to England for Christmas and he looked me straight in the eye and said, "I am from Australia". Well, we all make mistakes!

After dinner Barbara came looking for me and she dragged me away to her lair to repair my braids. John then grabbed hold of me and took me to his very comfortable chair where he brushed another layer of paint over my heavily sweating face. Tasha interrupted his wasted efforts and told me to get my gear back on and to hurry down to the floating dock for re-boarding. I was the last off and the first on giving me the shortest amount of time to eat my food. If I had not pushed past the young assistant who stood in my way I would never have eaten.

The longboat falling scene was repeated several times over the next two days and I began to understand why major films always ran well over budget. Directors of the ilk of Gore Verbinski look for perfection. They take and retake scenes a dozen times and then they repeat everything a few days later. Gore shot film from the foredeck then from the poop deck, from cameras operated by scuba divers and from helicopters passing overhead. Thousands of feet of digitized film was shot and then cut into 10 seconds of cinema footage.

We listened carefully at the end of each take to hear what Gore would say. Hopefully he would look up from his monitor with a smile and say "it's a take". More often than not he would call "reset", and we would return to our starting positions to do it all again. "Reset the reset" became a new pirate call.

The Flying Dutchman rises from the sea

After three days Steve rescued me from the rattlings. He positioned me aft on the main deck close to the Captain's Cabin. The legendary Flying Dutchman surfaced off our port side and Johnny Depp lifted a small barrel above his head singing out and taunting her skipper, Captain Davy Jones. "Hallo! Fish-head, lose something, hah-hah, yoo-hoo, over here, have a look-see". Every one looked at him in utter disbelief and then Johnny's double fell down the poop-deck steps, landing in a heap at my feet. After a few takes Johnny returned and stood directly in front of me. Then he lifted his barrel above the port railings and continued to taunt Davy Jones. In the edited version I can be seen peering over Johnny's shoulder, but only for about two seconds.

The scene continued to develop until Johnny, Orlando and Keira were standing amidships facing the Dutchman. Then the Dutchman opened her starboard gun ports and the cannons rolled out. Panic set in and the Black Pearl Pirates ran to their battle stations. Johnny sauntered across the deck while Orlando and Keira ran towards me to seek shelter in the Captains Cabin. My instructions were very clear. Run between Keira and Orlando blocking them from the camera and then continue to the last cannon. Do not, under and any circumstance, bump into Johnny, Orlando or Keira.

"Pictures Up, quiet please, quiet, quiet, rolling, background action, action". We all ran around the deck for a few seconds doing our thing. "Cut", "cut", "cut" a crescendo of cuts from all corners of the Black Pearl followed by a very loud and clear instruction "cut" ordered by Cotton's parrot.

Anyone who has ever been near to a set during filming will appreciate this sequence of events. Everyone wanted to get into the action. Gore quietly called the shots and then a dozen subordinates on all corners of the ship, looking very important with their headsets and microphones, repeated his commands. The most important one for me was "background action" which I always had to get exactly right, and not always did. The instruction called most often was "quiet", when the only persons making any noise were those repeating Gore's commands around the boat.

The other command always repeated was "cut". When Cotton's parrot joined in and called "cut" everyone was in stitches and Johnny, who always got into the spirit of things, swaggered up, cocked his head and demanded of the parrot; "what". Johnny is an incredibly good actor and he was well liked by everyone. He lived his part; one would swear that he was from the north of England and not Tennessee. During the months that I worked with him as a Black Pearl Pirate he was always Captain Jack Sparrow, on and off set.

Background actors who got their calls wrong, tried to get into the film, looked at the camera or were not playing their part well were sent below deck and very often they were not called in the following day. Usually it was the end of the film for them. I was determined not to be one of these and so I hurled myself into my part.

I asked Keira which direction she was going to run in and then I told her that I would pass on her left hand side. I didn't want my film career to be short lived. After passing Keira and Orlando I had to be careful not to run into Johnny who was still sauntering along with the barrel above his head. Once the main actors were behind me, everyone else was fair play and I found myself confronted by five ugly looking pirates who were running towards me.

Shoulders hunched, head down, I hurtled right through the middle scattering them to my right and to my left. It was with good reason that I played number 8 for Broken Hill Rugby Football Club. Dave Mellor, the mountaineer, came up to me after "cut" was called and said that he was only a little guy. I explained that the shot would not be used if I stopped and said "excuse me". On the next 'take' a gap miraculously appeared when I hurtled towards them.

Steve must have recognised my ruthlessness because all my parts from that moment involved me running from one side of the deck to the other. In one scene I would be carrying a powder keg in another I would be running to man a cannon. He never asked me to remain in a stationary position or to haul on a rigging line.

Early in filming I was told to run with a young lad to the foredeck. The Flying Dutchman was about to open fire with her cannon. I suggested that he should let me go first, but he looked at me, the old guy, and said that he would go first. "Fair enough", I said, "but if I catch you I will run right over you; I'm not stopping". As we reached the last cannon I hurled him to one side and leaped up the steps to the foredeck. I caught him on every single 'take' and still he insisted upon running first. I offered no apology to him because if I had faltered then we would both have hit the cutting room floor. The truth was that I did not like being treated as an old man on the Bristol Clipper and I certainly was not going to stand for it on the Black Pearl.

The cast was a motley lot. Johnny Depp, Orlando Bloom and Keira Knightley were supported by a wealth of distinguished actors including Naomi Harris, Bill Nighy, Stellan Skarsgard, David Bailie, Jonathan Price and Jack Davenport. Then there was Lee Arenberg from 'Startrek', Mackenzie Crook from 'The Office' and Martin Klebba. These three were real down to earth guys and always bought their round if you joined them in Shenanigans, our drinking haunt in Port Lucaya. For me, they were stars when Pirates II hit the big screen, they were outstanding and they helped to make the film the huge box office success that it was.

Johnny had one photo double, Woody Woodcock, a diver with Unexso, two stunt doubles and a hand double; yes, a hand double. In addition there were 20 stunt men and 32 pirates. Eight of the pirates were selected in Los Angeles from 15,000 applicants, all members of the Screen Actors Guild and therefore eligible for union pay and screen credits. The remaining 24 were like me, selected in the Bahamas from people with sailing experience. Everyone in the film business wanted to be part of Pirates of the Caribbean. The stunt men were the best in the business and regular actors from TV series such as Deadwood and Startrek scrambled to get in to the action as a Black Pearl Pirate.

Working background on the Pearl was very different to any other film set. Once on board we were fully involved from sunrise to sunset. There were no director's chairs or any chairs for that matter. Everyone had to find a cannon or a gunpowder barrel to sit on, sacks of sawdust were the best but you had to be quick to find one. Keira preferred to sit on the aft stairs with her back against the railings and a novel in her lap while Johnny preferred to stand by one of the cannons. I never saw him or Orlando sitting down. Keira's mother was always nearby and she was good fun and easy to talk to; a writer of film scripts and plays, she always had a few ideas to share.

At first Keira appeared a little distant, perhaps even shy. I am not sure how happy she was; sitting on the deck of the Pearl in the hot Bahamas sun surrounded by a bunch of rough looking men. I discussed her mother's work with her and found that she was a very interesting person. She was still only 22 years old and perhaps her stardom had forced into a small self-made cocoon where she could hide from those who tried to invade her own private space.

Just before we broke up for Christmas Orlando brought his dog Sidley on board and while he kindly consented to a group photograph with us, he objected to the inclusion of his dog; he said that his dog did not like its photograph to be taken. At first we thought this was a rather strange response, but then on reflection I suspect that he had a very good reason. It must be difficult learning to cope with fame at such a young age.

Giving our all for Disney was not without its dangers. Nick took a fall with three stunt men. They said they would look after him and they did. They all landed on top of him leaving him lying stunned and winded on the deck. The look of dismay on his face when Gore Verbinsky shouted for a re-take was a picture. Later in the same sequence Nick was hit on the forehead by a cannonball. A second cannonball fell down the hatch and stunned one of the director's assistants. Three people were injured by cannonballs that day.

The Kraken attacks

In another scene we were attacked by the Kraken. Several pirates held the monster at bay with long pikes while Nick and three others lifted a heavy grating to expose a cargo net in the main hold. One of the pirates, Colin Davis, hit Nick over the head with his pike and Nick fell forward trapping his hand beneath the grating. Poor Nick lost consciousness and had to be carried below for treatment. A few takes later I took a heavy, but deliberate, fall in front of the camera and cracked a couple of bones in my hand. I had hoped that the editor would recognise the look of sheer agony on my face and use the footage; no such luck.

Almost all of my fellow pirates were injured. Most were hurt when they collided with a part of the boat or, worse still, a rampant stunt man. No one complained and very few reported their injuries for fear of being cashiered. I asked the medic to fix an ice pack to my left hand. Steve Beaupre looked at me several times, I suspect that he knew, but he never asked the question. The ridiculous situation was that our remuneration, which was 75 dollars for an average 14-hour day, did not even cover our doctor's bills. Only one of our group asked for assistance with his medical bills and he was referred to the Bahamas Department of Labour; I don't think that he received any help.

Gore Verbinski gave Lejon, an Afro-Caribbean with long black curly hair a speaking part. He told him to lean out from the starboard rattlings and shout "It's on the starboard side". After several shots Gore Verbinski called it a 'take' and then said, "ladies and gentlemen, I give you Lejon." He was not being facetious; those few words could give Lejon the break that he so desperately needed. Everyone onboard applauded wholeheartedly and wished Lejon well; he was well liked by cast and crew and we hoped to see more of him.

Gore changed tack for a short time and filmed several sequences for Pirates of the Caribbean III. This was probably to suit the availability of Chow Yun-Fat, better known for his leading role in Crouching Tiger, Hidden Dragon. Chow was master of the Sao Feng Pirates on the Pirate Junk, Empress. He looked magnificent in his smart oriental costume and walked along the floating dock every morning to board one of the Zodiacs as if he was the King of Siam; his hands held outwards to protect his long protruding fingernails. His behaviour was similar to Johnny's, a true professional living his part. On reflection, he was the King of Siam in an earlier film. He starred alongside Jodie Foster in Anna and the King.

Our procedure as a background actor remained the same every day. Alarm call at 0315hrs, catch the studio bus from Sheraton to Gold Rock Creek at 0400hrs, sign contract at 0500hrs, take breakfast then pass through wardrobe, hairdresser, make-up and finally props by 0730hrs. Then Tasha hurried us down to the floating dock where we almost always sat on our backsides and watched the sun rise to signal another long and very hot day. Another phrase came into our pirate vocabulary; 'hurry to wait'. So often we were hurried through make-up and then rushed down to the floating dock only to wait for several hours. It didn't matter to the Production Director that he had a dozen pirates sitting around bored to tears. We only cost him 75 dollars a day.

I became a Sao Feng Pirate for 5 days and the make-up people did their very best to make me look like an Asian. It was an impossible task but with some imagination they were able to make me look good enough for long range shots of the attacking Empress. They had sufficient real Chinamen for the close-ups.

On one of my days as a Sao Feng Pirate I sat with others on the floating dock for six hours, then we were taken out to a floating barge where we remained for a further three hours with no protection from the sun and no toilet facilities. We were already four hours past our contracted day of eight hours and, to the best of my knowledge, not a single camera had been pointed in our direction. We didn't mind working the extra hours but we did object to sitting around in the sun with nothing to do. We would gladly have paid the Production Director 75 dollars to be able to go home.

Eventually the barge master told our caretaker, the same bossy young girl that gave us problems at the restaurant, that the conditions were unsuitable and that he was taking us ashore. She stopped him and we had to wait another hour before he finally ignored her and called in a tug to take us to the floating dock. It was 6 pm and the sun was already setting; the young girl jumped off the barge and tried to stop us leaving the dock. She said we could not leave until we had the Production Director's permission. We all brushed by her and returned to the make-up tent where we cleaned-up and collected our 75 dollars. It was the hardest 75 dollars that I ever earned. Yes, 'hurry up to wait' can sometimes be a good description of the background actor's lot.

Money was never the issue but fair treatment was very important to us. Lee Arenberg told me one evening that the Disney Production Team was having difficulty in dealing with the Black Pearl Pirates. He said that they were surprised when they found themselves working with background actors who had already accomplished so much with their lives. I don't know if this was true or if Lee was just being a good diplomat on Disney's behalf but there was much in what he said.

Ron Russell is a distinguished American Marine. He lived for 12 months on the South Pole as part of an isolation experiment in the moon programme and Russell Bay in Antartica has been named in his honour. After receiving two purple hearts in Vietnam he retired into civilian life and worked in the team that received the Nobel Science Prize for discovering the 'Quark'. Ron has artificial hips, yet he overcame his terrible war injuries to become a Black Pearl Pirate.

Dave Mellor is an accomplished mountaineer. He is in the Guinness Book of Records for being the oldest person to climb Lhotse in the Himalayas; one of the most difficult climbs in the world. He also climbed Everest; en-route he found a man frozen to a ledge and later he cut a frozen girl free from the end of a rope. With the summit in reach a sudden change in the jet stream brought a terrible storm and he lost all three of his partners. He survived to become a Black Pearl Pirate.

Walter Kitchen was an oil man. He owned several oil wells in North America and sold them to retire in the Bahamas. He owns the Fortune Hills Golf Club and is one of the top Wahoo fishermen in the islands. He gave up his fishing to become a Black Pearl Pirate.

These are some of the people who became known as the 'Bilge Rats'. Why did they do it? Well, the Production Director may have the answer to that question. I heard a rumour that he, or one of his management team, said that it was not necessary to pay the local background actors more than 75 dollars a day because they would work for bragging rights. If he did indeed say this, then he was right and I was one of them!

Each day brought a new adventure and eventually the day came when Gore was to blow up the long boat. Our battle with the Flying Dutchman was at its height and cannon balls were ripping into the Pearl. Overnight the special effects team had jig-sawed jagged invisible cuts through sections of the long boats hull and they connected these sections with strong thin wires to a large air jack. These wires were hidden from the camera's view by gunpowder kegs and bags of wood shavings. They then connected the air jack through a solenoid valve to a high pressure air reservoir. Finally the armourer primed a small charge of black powder beneath the long boat.

Gore filmed me and several other Black Pearl Pirates in the immediate vicinity of the boat, and then called us back to the safety of the poop deck. "Fire in the hole"; there was a bright flash as the black powder ignited, the solenoid valve opened and high pressure air rushed into the power cylinder. Its steel piston plunged forward and the thin wires attached to its arm ripped the long boat apart. This was one of the few shots that only had one take; the long boat was history. On the big screen it looked as though it had been hit by a cannon shell and everything blended into three seconds of incredible film footage.

Yes, the special effects team had everything under control, or so they thought. As we moved back to our 'start' positions there was a second very loud explosion, more violent than the first. Startled, we stood back and looked around in bewilderment. It was several moments before we realised that the battery used to power the electrical equipment had exploded for real. Presumably it had overheated or become contaminated with salt water; we shall never know. Fortunately no one was injured.

Hurricane Wilma

There really was no end to the run of bad luck that followed Disney. They were already late and seriously over budget when Wilma was born in the Western Atlantic. She swept across Cozumel and up the Yucatan Peninsular leaving a trail of destruction in her wake. She trapped thousands of European holidaymakers in the holiday resort of Cancun. Virgin storm refugees; most found their plight uncertain and incredibly uncomfortable after living the whole of their lives in the protected and relatively stable weather environment of Western Europe.

She struggled out into the gulf and the US Hurricane Prediction Centre tried desperately to do better this time around. They were still suffering terribly from the aftermath of Katrina. A high pressure system moved down from Texas and turned Wilma across southern Florida. The weather gurus in Miami were a little out on their timing, but the point at which they predicted the eye would turn was surprisingly accurate. Wilma then came at us from the West; the worst possible direction for tidal surge. Meanwhile, the Disney production team quickly cobbled together an emergency evacuation plan. To their credit they left nothing to chance; they packed tents away, tied caravans down, secured ships in harbour and then they chartered aircraft in readiness to evacuate all 500 actors and crew to Los Angeles.

The Production Director filmed until the last possible moment and then he called a halt to filming just before lunch on Friday 21st October 2005. Everyone assembled on the main deck of the Black Pearl for last minute instructions. There seemed to be a strange sense of foreboding in the air and many of the stunt men, background actors and film crew thought that they were deserting a sinking ship. They came to shake my hand and they urged me and my fellow pirates based in the Bahamas to stay safe.

Oil stocks in the United States soared again. The offshore oil fields, refineries and oil distribution centres around New Orleans were still under repair after Katrina. The doom and gloom merchants predicted more disruption to supplies and even higher oil futures. I took advantage of this highly volatile market and quickly increased my own holding of oil and gas stocks. Wilma turned later than predicted and then passed quickly across Florida causing unexpected destruction to property in the Fort Lauderdale area. She left United States territory as a category 2 hurricane and then raced north-east picking up momentum as she passed over the warm Gulf Stream.

When she headed away from the United States coast, the Hurricane Prediction Centre lost interest in her and the residents of Grand Bahama thought that no news was good news. I believed otherwise and I prepared my apartment for the worst. Learning from my experience of Katrina I removed both wall-mounted air-conditioning units and clamped plywood across the vacant holes. I brought my plants and patio furniture into my lounge and draped my carpets across my settee. Then I sandbagged both patio doors and reinforced them with pieces of solid wood. Almost all of my damage from Frances came through my ceiling from the apartment above. I gained access to this apartment and made it as secure as possible, also placing sandbags in front of the apartment's patio doors.

I re-stocked my supply of tinned food, candles, batteries and bottled water and then I joined a special meeting of the Board of Directors of Harbour House Towers. I was one of the few Directors on-island and we needed to prepare the building common parts for the arrival of Wilma. We covered all offices windows with plywood, removed records to a safe location, secured boats in the harbour and removed light fittings from the gardens. Several owners who were off-island had left their plants and patio furniture outdoors. Our maintenance staff removed these potentially dangerous missiles and I made a mental note to raise a special resolution at the next AGM.

I was the nominated 'Technical Director' and as such I decided to place the complete building in 'lock down mode'. There was no mention of the storm on BBC World News, CNN or any of the Miami news channels. Many believed from this silence that she was going to pass well to our north and that her effect would be minimal. However, the

Board of Directors supported my decision, and stood by me against the complaints of several residents who were only concerned with their own personal discomfort.

I sandbagged the entrances on all nine floors to each of our two elevators. As fast as I placed my sand bags in position, inconsiderate residents removed them so that they could gain access with their shopping trolleys. I was furious; as the storm approached I moved both elevators to the top floor and isolated their power in the switchgear rooms. Again, several of the residents complained bitterly. I tried to explain that it was better that they used the stairs than risk getting trapped during the storm. I was dumbfounded that some people could be so unreasonable.

I opened the main gate which was on a security lock and then threw its isolator so that it remained in the open position. This ensured that the emergency services would have access during the storm. Finally I switched off the water pumps and opened their isolators. Even more of our residents started to complain. Why was the main gate open? Why was there no water? Why were the elevators not working? Hell, didn't they know that a hurricane was heading towards us; I put the keys in my pocket and went to bed.

Wilma finally hit us on Monday 24th October 2005 at 11 am, a little later than expected. Her eye passed to the north-west of us and by midmorning she had increased to a category 3 hurricane with winds gusting to 145 miles per hour. Her eye was travelling across the sea at an incredible 47 miles per hour. As Bahamians say when they warn of an approaching hurricane, "Hurricane travelling man"; and this one really was travelling.

One of our elderly residents, Virginia Husby, had not evacuated in time. Her intention had been to join her daughter in a more secure location. Unfortunately she had not reckoned on me switching the elevators off. Several policemen came to her aid but Virginia understood the situation and she elected to remain in her apartment. I wished that those who were younger and more able could have followed her excellent example.

When the fury of the storm was upon us I walked around the exterior of the building and ensured that we were in good shape. I took several photographs and in doing so ruined a brand new and very expensive camera that I had purchased in Gibraltar five months earlier. Virginia was coping well although I did have to strengthen her sliding patio door. It was threatening to burst into her small studio apartment. I placed a chair in her bathroom and told her to climb into the bath if all hell broke loose. Meanwhile another director, Naomi Acosta, brought Virginia a couple of rather nice ham sandwiches. I think she enjoyed all of the attention she was receiving. A couple of days later I received a very kindly worded thank-you card from her.

The fury of the storm passed in less than four hours. In this short passage of time the handmaidens of Thor cleaned the pollution of industrialised humanity from the sky and left it fresh, sweet smelling and crystal clear. As the sun began to set, the western horizon gave the most incredible display of colours that I had every witnessed; from golden yellow to orange and then a deep blood red. At the same time different shades of purple spread to both the north and to the south poles before finally converging in one last dazzling display in the eastern sky where the sun re-emerged on a different world; a different Grand Bahama. Thor had done his terrible work for the day.

Pinders Point, Lewis Yard, Eight Mile Rock and several other native communities on the south west coast were wiped out by a huge tidal surge. No one had been warned to evacuate and the villagers were caught in raging flood waters that exceeded 12 feet on exposed beaches. A one year old baby was swept from his mothers arms; everyone was terribly upset but Grand Bahama counted its blessings that all other lives were spared that day.

I drove along the south west coast and was shocked to find that so many people in this area live in such desperate poverty. Many are refugees from Haiti and I suppose they are still trying to establish their families in a new community. Behaving like a rich tourist, driving through their midst with a borrowed camera on my lap, I was too ashamed to even consider taking photographs of their plight. Cars, boats, houses, trees, rubbish, clothing, furniture and mud were all mixed together in one big melée.

Village homes in Pinders Point were constructed mainly from wood with a corrugated iron roof. They stood no chance against the storm surge. Amidst this carnage, in a large open clearing, lay the complete roof of a small church. Its wooden trusses were intact and it had a small decorative bell tower at one end. I looked far and wide, but could not find the sanctuary that this roof once protected. The hand of God surely reached out and placed this roof in a safe place so that it might be used again.

Village homes in Eight Mile Rock had a more solid construction using stone and concrete. Yet they faired no better against such a ferocious onslaught. They were swept away and the only evidence that could be found of several dwelling places was a smooth concrete surface amidst heaps of rubble where a lounge or bedroom once stood. The surge had been so strong in this area that it opened several graves in the village cemetery and decomposed bodies were found beached several miles away; a most gruesome operation for those charged with their recovery and re-internment.

I could not help but draw a comparison between the villagers of Grand Bahama and the urban residents of New Orleans. The simple folk rendered homeless in Pinders Point and Eight Mile Rock put on a brave face and resigned themselves to their situation. This was so different to the behaviour witnessed in and around New Orleans where looting was rampant and aid workers were attacked. It was a great pity that the world media had chosen to show these ugly scenes while ignoring the sad plight of the villagers on Grand Bahama who had set a courageous example to us all.

Grand Bahama benefited from lessons learned during Frances and Jeanne. The cable, water and electric utilities took pre-emptive action and to their credit they were able to re-establish supplies within two days. In the previous year it had taken them almost 2 months. In addition many companies and residents had fitted their buildings with a steel hurricane roof; this reduced wind damage significantly in Freeport and Lucaya.

The big losers were Club Caribe and Bell Channel Club; both lost their entire roof structure for the second time in 12 months. What was left of Pier 1, a long time favourite with tourists, was swept into the sea, taking with it any hope that it may be re-built one day. Jenks from the Sand Bar lost most of his newly repaired house, but he was happy that he and his wife survived. They were plucked to safety by friends who rescued them in a large truck.

As for Harbour House Towers; well my plan of placing everything in 'lock down mode' and sticking to my guns worked. I made a few enemies but no one was hurt, no one was trapped at any time and one hour after the storm passed I was able to re-start all of the electrical equipment. The Board was appreciative and they asked me to record my action plan as a formal 'Hurricane Lock-Down Procedure'.

After the Storm

Disney did not hang around; they had their workers back on-site as soon as the airport re-opened. Damage was not as bad as expected; the construction team had done a pretty good job in closing down the set and protecting the ships. The crew followed a few days later and filming resumed.

Smoking was discouraged on the Pearl, but many sneaked a quick smoke on the foredeck or on the ramp of the lower deck. One day the Production Director gathered everyone together and read the riot act. "Today we are hot", he said. "We will be firing cannon and the powder kegs are filled with black powder. Anyone smoking will be removed from the Pearl immediately". His voice was sharp and his demeanour stern as he tried to ignore a thick plume of smoke which drifted slowly across his shoulder; Gore Verbinski was rarely seen without a smouldering Churchill in his hand, I assume it helped him to concentrate. Before I get hung drawn and quartered I should mention that Gore did succumb to the rules of the day.

I have to admire Gore, he always strived for perfection. I could never understand why he sometimes repeated each 'take' as many as 10 times. I was told that 'costs' were running at 12 dollars per second and my simple mental arithmetic calculated that each set of 'takes' must have cost around 14,000 dollars. He was always the first on to the Pearl and very often the last off; not counting us bilge rats of course. I was impressed with his boundless energy. He was a hands-on man and I often saw him helping carpenters to move props into a new position. He led by example which is so rare in today's world. I was proud when one day he shouted down to me from the poop deck. "Hey you, yes you, Grizzly Adams; look at the Kraken". I had very long hair and a very unkempt, wild looking beard. It was an honour to be addressed by the big man, even if it was a mild rebuke.

As the days progressed a strong camaraderie built up amongst the Black Pearl Pirates. We held 'Pirates Meetings' at Billy Joe's on Port Lucaya beach and swapped stories while downing glasses of rum and coke; one of the few beverages produced in the Bahamas and therefore cheap. The Core Pirates from Los Angeles told us about the 'Curse of the Black Pearl' and I enjoyed listening to Russell's experiences while working on the TV series 'Deadwood'. All of the LA guys had an interesting story to tell but they were struggling to make ends meet. Acting, for most, was not a rewarding career.

Working in the film industry was a very new experience for me. Not only was there this incredibly old-fashioned pecking order, but a rather nasty blame culture existed. The bilge rats always had to take the blame for everything. Most Disney employees were on short term contracts and they were frightened to take responsibility for their own mistakes. A young Director's Assistant was particularly nasty with one of our elderly pirates and the young lad, the one whom I pushed aside in my rush to the foredeck, corrected her and suggested that she should show more respect. Because of this it was rumoured that she had the young lad 'cashiered'; sadly this was not the only story to circulate.

One morning Tasha asked me to run past one of the stuntmen at the same time as he was being racked into the air to simulate a hit by the Kraken. It was a frightening experience. He wore a very tight body harness under his pirate garb and thin wires were attached to three points on his harness. He was then racked 20 feet into the air in less than a second. It was like being fired from a Martin Baker ejector seat. The look of horrible expectation on his face as he stood staring at the Kraken showed real fear; it was not faked for the cameras. Gore had the poor guy racked six times before calling the take, but he limped away several thousand dollars the richer.

Tasha said she would signal when I was to run. She made the call and I knew it was too early. I crossed in front of the camera as the stuntman was racked and I blew 4,000 dollars into thin air. Gore gave the nod, Steve passed his hand across his throat and Tasha came to me and said "you did good; now go below and wait until I call you". Two days later I was still waiting for her call. Tasha had made the wrong call but I carried the can, I was a bilge rat. This blame culture existed at every level in the management structure. Everyone was frightened for their job except us bilge rats. The management style of Disney created, in my opinion, a deliberate pyramid of fear.

Two more pirate calls were introduced; "Trashed by Tash" and if it was a particularly bad day then it was a "Tasha day". This was very unfair of us. Tasha was not responsible for most of the mistakes that we made on set. She was the person who worked closest with us and she was always, in a good humoured way, the nearest person to blame. I served my penance below deck and was eventually brought back when the Kraken resumed its attack on the Pearl. It was a rough day at sea and our hairdressers and make-up guys quickly returned to shore. It was not a day for landlubbers.

"Pictures Up, quiet please, quiet, rolling, quiet, we are hot, we are hot, weapons to full cock, background action, action". Seven 'takes' later and 98,000 dollars lighter the cameras moved to another angle on the same scene and everything started again. Stunt men were fixed to three wires and then they were catapulted into the air. Several fell onto mattresses and others were thrown into the sea where they were quickly retrieved by scuba divers. While this was happening the special effects department created additional mayhem with water cannons which they used to shoot huge volumes of water at us from neighbouring boats and three mortars hurled cork and balsa wood into the air above our heads.

I was issued with a real flintlock which an armourer charged with a small amount of black powder before each 'take'. It was fun but also very dangerous. Several 'dead bodies' lay on the deck covered in blood; cutlasses hung limp from outstretched lifeless hands and eyes stared blankly into the sky. Everyone had to be very careful during a simulated battle for fear of falling on a cutlass or stepping on someone's unprotected face. After each take there was a general call; "is everyone alright". No one ever admitted to an injury but many were seen making a discrete visit to the ice box. Dave Mellor had an enormous shiner, Michael Gabor had a dead leg and poor old Nick, well he was Nick.

One of our scenes caused real problems for Orlando. The 'sides' called for him to run across the main deck calling for the gunpowder barrels to be loaded onto the net in the cargo hold. 'Sides' was the name given to the scripts which were passed to all participants at the beginning of the day. They described each scene in brief detail and gave the words that were to be spoken by each actor in that scene. Orlando only had nine words to remember but one was a real tongue twister and not easy to get right during the mayhem of a huge battle scene. He was really hung up and his embarrassment was evident. When Gore finally called it a 'take' Orlando turned to me and said. "Well, did you get the gunpowder onto the net?"

While it was fun for us bilge rats it was serious work for the stuntmen. One of my friends told me that with 'residuals' he could make 120 thousand dollars for his work on the Black Pearl. He said that he was paid 4,000 dollars for each special stunt and with four takes on each stunt he could do very well. He needed to because the career of a stuntman is never a long one; even their heavily protected torsos can only stand so much punishment.

Towards the end of the month Tasha earned a new nickname, 'The Grim Reaper'. She came to the floating dock and asked for eight pirates. Everyone thought they were being given an important role. Instead they were told to lie face down across barrels, cannons and longboats, and play dead. They stayed in their positions for the whole morning while water cannons fired hundreds of gallons of water above their heads. This mixed with rubbish from several mortars and soaked into every crevice of their bodies. Two of the pirates contracted painful ear infections and as usual, they paid their own doctors bills. This begged the big question; what if one of us should fall from the rattlings or get crushed by the longboat?

After several hours the 'dead pirates' emerged onto the floating dock looking very wet and miserable. They took their clothing off and sat in the sun to dry while costume girls paired up to wring water out of their clothing. When the Grim Reaper called them back to the Pearl no one moved. No one wanted to repeat their miserable ordeal. Meanwhile, Kate Bosworth from 'Superman Returns' sat in the background with a group of friends and looked on in amusement.

Another of our shipmates was pulled away to be a photo double. Woody was already doubling for Captain Jack Sparrow and now Dave Cook was asked to double for 'Bootstrap' Bill Turner. Each had their own dressing room, limousine transport, personal make-up attendant and access to the stars' dressing room. But they still remained on bilge rats pay and did not even get a mention in the credits. Disney really did take its ounce of flesh, but Woody and Dave got a whole load of bragging rights, and we would each have gladly jumped into their shoes.

Michael called a 'Pirates Meeting'

We never knew when Disney would call it a wrap. Closure dates came and went and new schedules lost all credibility before they were printed. We were unable to make any personal arrangements and eventually several of my friends called it a day and left the island. I had to cancel my own travel arrangements and reluctantly I tore up my non-refundable air tickets to England. Bradley, Kate and Tom showed their appreciation by giving me an extra day's pay. This did not go far towards the cost of a new ticket, but their kind gesture made all the difference.

Any casual observer would have thought that the Disney production team was incapable of organising a 'piss-up in a brewery'. I am sure this was not the case. The Disney team moved crew, equipment and supplies with considerable expertise. I suspect the real problem was that they were not keeping us bilge rats fully informed.

Michael Gabor had become a very close friend over the past couple of months and one evening he called a 'Pirates Meeting' at Billy Joe's on Port Lucaya beach. Michael was one of the core pirates and he had good connections on set; his wife Vicky is a vice president of Disney Film Productions. Mike was a good organiser and he kept us bilge rats together as a team. Unfortunately our meeting was rained off and so we reconvened in my apartment at Harbour House Towers. It was such a successful evening that Michael kindly volunteered my home for all further meetings. I was very happy with the arrangement because he supplied the alcoholic beverages and acted as cook for the evening; all I had to do was wash up. These meetings strengthened the pirate bond that existed between us bilge rats and our professional friends from LA. In November we had low Spring Tides and Gore Verbinski flew to the Exumas to film parts of his memorable mill wheel sequence. He waited for several days for the weather to improve and during this time Johnny contracted a serious chest infection which was rumoured to be pneumonia. The other lead actors and the first film crew returned to Los Angeles while he recovered and the second film unit was instructed to get some heavy weather footage of the Black Pearl. The second film unit gave me a 'call' on Sunday 20th November 2005. It was a great day, we worked for 16 hours and stayed at sea until the sun had fallen below the horizon; I enjoyed every minute. Working with the second film unit was a breath of fresh air. The Assistant Director even allowed those who had cameras to take photographs and we were given almost total freedom of the decks when filming was not taking place.

When Gore returned he wanted helicopter footage of the Pearl running from the Flying Dutchman while she fired a full broadside at our port quarter. No balls, chains or shot were loaded; nevertheless, it was still a chilling experience staring into the open barrels of cannon firing at close quarters. In a real battle I would have needed more than a couple of swigs of navy rum to give me sufficient courage to stay at my post.

The skipper manoeuvred the Pearl into position half a dozen times and each time the Dutchman fired her cannon in a full broadside while the helicopter pilot made a high speed pass down the port side of the Pearl. The helicopter pilot flew incredibly close and on the last couple of passes it appeared as if his rotor blades would surely cut through our stays. Marty was hanging from our rattlings and he became more concerned with each pass. His balding head was not in need of a haircut and I pointed this out to him. His face contorted as he looked in the direction of Gore Verbinski and he complained to Gore that the pilot was much too close.

The bilge rats reached boiling point

Later in the week our pent-up frustration reached boiling point and several of us rebelled against the arrogant 'pecking order' that demeaned us so much. We rebelled against the system and not the film crew, because the crew were a great crowd and a privilege to work with.

It was one of those days when we had a heavy sea and the catering department brought hot food to the Pearl. A break was called in filming but we, the bilge rats, had to remain in pecking order. It was this episode that helped me to understand something that had bugged me for a long time. Why were we always the last off the Pearl and why did we always have to stand at the back of a food line? While waiting to be called forward to the food line, one of the stuntmen told me that he received a Screen Actors Guild compensation of 62 dollars for every 15 minutes that he was late in receiving his lunch; almost as much as I received for a full days work. He said that a similar arrangement was in place for all of the actors and crew that were members of the Screen Actors Guild. I don't know how true this was, but it suddenly occurred to me that the reason that we were always the last may have been because we were the only ones not being paid SAG compensation!

It was a long time before the bilge rats were served but it looked really good. My mouth watered as I balanced my plastic container on a stack of wooden props and cut enthusiastically into my huge succulent T-bone steak. Moments later the Assistant Director yelled, "films up". I pushed my container behind a barrel and took my starting position. The camera helicopter made two passes and then the Assistant Director gave us permission to return to our food. As I lifted the lid from my container the helicopter swooped in for another high speed pass. This ridiculous sequence continued several times until our food was unfit to eat; not even by us bilge rats. I eventually threw mine in the garbage bin.

This set the tone for the rest of the day because we were hungry and very, very angry. The Pearl jibed down the coast for most of the day, taking advantage of the wind direction to fill her sails. Eventually the helicopter made her final pass along our eastern beam and a huge red sun sank into a clutch of small fluffy pink clouds that floated menacingly on the distant horizon. Two Zodiacs had been following us during the day. They came alongside and took the film crew off the Black Pearl. They had eaten and Bobby Stone was so furious that he forced himself onboard.

The Pearl then set out for Gold Rock Creek which was now a good two hours sail down the coast. After a while another Zodiac came out of the dark. It was carrying the night shift riggers and it took the day riggers and several large pieces of equipment on board for the return journey. I was furious that pieces of mechanical equipment were taking precedence over us. I grabbed hold of the load master and asked him why a boat had not been sent out to collect us. I was so livid that I almost threw him in the water. I told him in no uncertain words to get another boat alongside and to radio ahead and tell Disney to have a double pay packet waiting for us.

Eventually a boat pulled alongside and the helmsman announced that he would take 16 passengers. There were exactly 16 of us but as we clamoured aboard he stopped the last person and pulled away. The most important thing that I learned on the Round the World Yacht race was to work as part of a team and to look after every single person in that team. I yelled to the other Pirates. "We all leave the Pearl together or none of us leave". I then shouted at the helmsman and told him to return for the remaining person. He knew that our mettle was up and so he put about.

The Pearl refused to lower her ramp and in turn we prevented the helmsman from backing away; we had an infuriating stalemate. Eventually after five minutes the loadmaster threw a large bag of equipment onto our stern. I was beside myself with rage; again equipment was taking precedence over people.

On our return to Gold Rock Creek I stormed past the Movie Maker caravans, the welder's compounds, the joiner's sheds and into the large tent which was home to the stunt men and us background actors. Tasha, the Grim Reaper, was unfortunate to be the first person in my line of fire. I tore into her and told her that one of our group had been left on the Pearl; "it isn't right, it just isn't bloody well right". For the first time since I had met her she was lost for words.

As it happened, our missing bilge rat was taken off by another Zodiac which had passed us in the dark. He was already removing his make-up in the changing-tent. We felt like Japanese soldiers on a remote island; no one had told us that the war was over. Shortly afterwards we were given a double pay packet. I finally got home at 9 pm. I had dinner and turned in at midnight with my alarm set for an early morning call at 3 am. The following day was Tuesday 22nd November, the day we sailed to Freeport Harbour.

I survived Scene 93A

My 3 am alarm call awakened me from a nervous and very shallow sleep which had not satisfied my tired, battle weary body. Davy Jones and the Flying Dutchman were taking their savage toll. The wind was whistling and I had a foreboding that all did not auger well. I brought in my patio furniture and told myself to remember to switch off my kitchen light this time. I wondered if we would be able to shoot today.

At 4 am we boarded our bus at the Sheraton and watched late night revellers stagger back to their hotel rooms after far too many drinks in the Bahama Mama. Amongst them was Brad Fox the barman of the Bahama Mama; a Black Pearl Pirate and one of us! Brad used brief moments between 'takes' to gather whatever sleep he could. The revellers settled into a comfortable rolling bed, rolling in their drunken stupor, while we headed for the Black Pearl which was riding a gently pitching sea; the outer remnants of Tropical Storm Gamma fast approaching from the South West.

The night guard huddled over his torch, trying to keep warm, as we approached his small lean-to at the entrance to Gold Rock Creek. I had sand in my eyes from lack of sleep and could barely make out his black frame in the darkness of the bush as he struggled to raise the wooden barrier that kept press and public at bay.

Get yer breakfast, get yer breakfast, we got to go; we got to hurry to wait. Get on the boat; we got to do a Wayne. Reset the sweat. Reset the re-sweat. We reeled off all of our new pirate expressions and the young girl in blue tried desperately to get us down to the floating dock for an early start but we found it was difficult to take her seriously any more. Disney had done all they could to us and we just didn't care anymore. So we thought! We were told that we were doing scene 93A today. What the hell was that! Everyone was offered seasick pills. Mr Cotton's photo double took a couple but he failed to give one to his parrot; very inconsiderate.

The sun was beginning to rise and Zodiacs were waiting to take us to the Pearl which was moored in the channel and still within the relative protection of the coral reef. Then to my disbelief the Pearl set sail, presumably to beat the tide. Half an hour later each one of us was asked if we were willing to join the Pearl at sea. We were warned that the transfer would be difficult and told that anyone who felt unable should stay ashore. Jim Pappas remained on terra firma and everyone else boarded two Zodiacs and gave chase.

The best we could make into the heavy seas was six knots and we were unable to gain on the Pearl whose skipper continued to sail further away from shore. Eventually he turned back towards us and the first Zodiac closed with the Pearl's ramp which had been lowered on the seaward side; yes the seaward side. The Zodiac fell a good six feet below the ramp as each of the huge waves swept by. Suddenly it slammed with crushing force into the ramp and the loadmaster refused to take any further transfers. Our two Zodiacs circled around the Pearl while her crew looked across in dismay. They just didn't know what to do next.

It took a further half hour for our boat to surf the waves back into the floating dock. Several waves passed straight through the interior of our Zodiac and many of us were soaked to the skin. Poor Lizzy from wardrobe took the brunt of this and she had to change into a dressing gown while her clothing was put through a drying machine.

Two hours later the Pearl came into the floating dock on high tide and we boarded for what turned out to be a very interesting day. The 2nd Unit Assistant Director, Eric Glasser, was in charge that day. Eric had a realistic and very friendly attitude; we all warmed to him and this was just as well because the day did not go as planned.

It should have been a normal day of sailing in fairly heavy seas with the helicopter taking film footage from different angles. We only had the 2nd film unit, the bilge rats and our support staff from hairdressing, make-up and costumes on board. We enjoyed the early part of the afternoon and Eric Glasser allowed us to develop our own sequences. In the first I ran forward past Keira's double to number 1 port gun. Dave Pollard followed. We decided it was unserviceable and ran back to number 3 gun which was amidships and then prepared this for firing. This sequence timed perfectly with the helicopter passing down the port side of the ship.

At other times I ran from the port side of the main deck to the starboard side of the hold carrying a powder barrel on my shoulder. I then passed this to another pirate and ran back to collect another. I always ensured that the barrel was on the opposite shoulder to the side where the helicopter was passing. I also took care to avoid the two mainsails which would have shielded me from the cameras. By now I had become camera savvy.

As the day progressed the weather deteriorated and suddenly the main sheet came loose and looped itself around Colin Davis's throat. I jumped forward and pulled him to safety. In the melée that followed Jim's cocked hat was lost overboard but we counted ourselves very fortunate that Colin was still with us. Unfortunately the weather had deteriorated to the point where we could no longer return to Gold Rock Creek. We found ourselves riding heavy seas in what was really a Hollywood Prop and not a Brigantine Pirate Ship with a deep keel.

After dark our skipper headed for the main harbour at Freeport and then one of our engines failed. We were only making 1.3 knots over the ground and then, to make matters significantly worse, the main sail unfurled and began to push us towards the Lucayan Reef. The sea conditions were horrific but the skipper had no alternative, he asked four of the ship's crew to go aloft, three of them girls, to gather-in the main sail. Just like in the old movies, except this was for real.

Soon our foredeck was burying itself deep into huge seas. Lizzy from wardrobe was so violently ill that I told her to find a central point on the main deck and to lie down and try to sleep. This would prevent her brain from trying to maintain equilibrium, which contributed to her seasickness. The poor girl was so cold that she wrapped her legs and arms in toilet paper; held ingeniously in place by bands of masking tape.

Lizzy was soon joined by several hairdressers and make-up girls. All were cold, frightened and miserably seasick. Those of us who were real sailors and were still active had to be careful not to step on them in the darkness of the storm. Gunpowder barrels and wooden buckets hurtled across the heaving deck threatening to hit the poor girls as they lay inert and riggers had to hurry to secure loose cannons before they joined the melée. The wretched girls remained ignorant to these dangers, not caring if they lived or died. One of the film crew was hurt and her friends voiced their anger when they realised that there was no medic on board to help her.

It took five hours to cover the short distance from a point six miles off Port Lucaya to the Freeport Harbour entrance. I was very worried about the time when we would eventually have to turn into the harbour channel and expose our beam to the heavy seas. When we reached this point the skipper passed orders for everyone to sit down on the deck and to hold onto something. I was the only person to overcome my male ego and put on a lifejacket; I knew there was a serious possibility of broaching.

We made the turn just before midnight and found a huge freighter leaving port. It blocked our passage to safety and our skipper was forced to pass outside the first channel marker with huge surf breaking on the nearby reef. For much of this time the skipper controlled the boat's direction from the poop deck with a hand held remote control unit that was connected to the control desk with a long TRS cable. Given the navigational instruments available the Skipper did a fantastic job. However, many of us with 'Blue Water' sailing experience expressed thoughts on the day's events that are best left unsaid.

We eventually moored safely at Bradford Quay; it was just after midnight. A van full of cold pizzas and a luxury bus waited to take us to Gold Rock Creek for de-robing and clean-up. The regular film support crew struggled down the gang plank with black clouds of anger covering their faces; many swearing never to sail on the Pearl again.

I understand that those who were members of the Screen Actors Guild received very substantial union-agreed compensations for the day. We, the Bilge Rats, were given a double wage packet and a warm apology from Bradley, our casting agent. On the whole it was a great pirate adventure!

As an added twist to the story, Grand Bahama is in the heart of the Bermuda Triangle. Towards the end of the Second World War a squadron of Avengers, known as the Lost Patrol, vanished from radar when approaching the Lucayan Reef. We could so easily have been a further addition to the mysteries of the Triangle, instead we all qualified to wear a new sweat shirt fashioned for the occasion; 'I survived scene 93A'.

The following day I visited the Sheraton to collect my extra pay packet and Kate asked if I remembered Lizzie. Of course I did! Kate told me that Lizzie wanted to thank me for my kind help during the storm. She said that she could not have made it through the night without my help.

I was surprised that she had recognised me in the darkness. She told Kate that she didn't know my name but that I was BP62. Her thanks meant a great deal to me. The make-up, hairdressers and wardroom boys and girls had long since become part of our close knit team and a strong feeling of camaraderie had developed between us. I met many in the foyer of the Sheraton on their way home for thanksgiving. They all rushed over and gave me a big hug. Things had certainly moved on from that first day when we were given our first make-over.

Verizon Radio

Disney called a short break for Thanksgiving and they gave Verizon Radio permission to use the Black Pearl for a TV commercial. I was selected with Bradley, his father and four other Black Pearl Pirates to work with the stunt men. We were all in our second childhood. We stood in line while Penny Rose passed her experienced eye across each one of us and declared us ready to ship out. It was an incredible day and we all had a tremendous amount of fun. None of the Disney restrictions were enforced and we could pretty well do what we wanted.

The TV commercial we were making was to advertise the launch of Verizon's new wireless film service. Three office partitions had been erected in the middle of the Pearl's main deck. In the area bounded by these partitions was a simple office arrangement with a desk, filing cabinet and chairs. Three smartly dressed young executives gathered around a cell phone within this make-believe office and one of them dialled a number. Suddenly a real pirate battle scene erupted around them.

Three mortars on the main deck hurled huge amounts of rubbish into the air while flames leaped from gas burners hidden beneath the Pearl's open hatches. Two machines belched smoke into the air around us and three more smoke-making machines circled on purpose built motor launches.

Film crew, special effects and Verizon onlookers all wore masks for protection while we had to suffer the choking black smoke. My eyes were soon bloodshot and my throat and nostrils became raw with aggravated pain. Amidst all of this make-believe mayhem we fought amongst ourselves, whacking everyone within reach with rubber bottles, shelaghleys and belaying pins.

Several of us teamed together and developed our own battle routines, carefully rehearsing each sequence to reduce the risk of an accident. Not all of our weapons were made of rubber and falling on another person's sword was a real possibility. I improvised with the Pirate Captain and we developed an excellent scene together. I used a real flintlock pistol and I had to be careful not to fire into anyone's face. At one point I spilled black powder on my fingers and it ignited when I fired the pistol.

The stunt men stole all of the best positions from us and we watched and learned as they rehearsed their own routines. They had been given huge battle axes and they looked rather comical as they chased each other across the set. At one point I led a charge across the deck towards the camera. I jumped through flames erupting from the main hatch and fell in front of the pirate horde following me. The stunt men fell on top of me and we all ended up in a huge writhing heap in front of the camera. I don't know if this shot was used but it was very authentic!

As the day drew to a close and the huge red sun finally settled below the horizon I got to die in a macabre looking position hanging from the rattlings. It was a great day and I never once had to sit below deck.

Thanksgiving gave us all a well earned rest from filming and we used this time to catch up on our sleep and to do some deep sea fishing with Walter Kitchen, one of the Tortugas Pirates known in the Bahamas as the King of Wahoo. I caught a 55 pounder after a terrific fight off West End and Michael caught another Wahoo a few hours later off Eight Mile Rock.

This encouraged us to go spear fishing with Barry Thorpe. We dived on the blue hole just off Nick's place and Barry followed angel fish to several coral heads where we found lobsters. He said the angel fish were waiting for us to remove the lobsters so that they could return to their residence, pull out their furniture, roll out the carpet and make themselves back at home. I don't know if Barry was spinning a line but we speared 22 lobsters in less than half an hour.

Well provisioned, Michael purchased a few bottles of wine and invited everyone back to my apartment for another pirates meeting. We feasted on fresh lobster and Wahoo with mushrooms, pasta and rice.

Legs more famous than Marilyn Munroe

The Disney crew returned to Grand Bahama a couple of days after Thanksgiving. All of the core LA pirates and several of the stunt men were missing. I don't know if they were no longer needed or if they were dropped to save money. Their comradeship was sadly missed but the reduced numbers gave more camera exposure to those of us remaining.

Al Romano, one of the core pirates, had a key position lying dead beneath the main mast and I was chosen to take his place. It was silly not to have brought him back because they had to pay top wages for three people to give me a 3-hour make-over each morning. It was very difficult sitting motionless in a canvas chair from 5 am to 8 am every morning while two people built a new beard hair by hair on top of my own. A third person also worked on me to change the very appearance of my face. This was called a make-over as opposed to a make-up. I kept falling asleep in my chair and each time one of the young girls would gently lift up my chin and say. "We are nearly finished love, just a few more minutes".

My costume suited me more than BP62 and my hairpiece was handmade from human hair by a top salon in London. It was valued at 2,000 dollars and it was this last piece of information that persuaded me not to add it to my collection of souvenirs. After my make-over I had to rush down to the floating dock where the Pearl was waiting to put to sea. None of my fellow bilge rats recognised me. Even Steve Beaupre, the Assistant Director, had to admit that hairdressing and make-up had done a tremendous job on me.

The continuity assistant placed me in position below the masthead and to one side of the stairwell. My head lay back on a dirty wet deck with my feathered musketeer's hat falling to one side. My sword lay across the deck with my left hand outstretched towards its hilt. In my lifeless right hand I held a flintlock pistol across my bared chest. One leg sprawled across the deck and the other rested very close to a huge piece of Kraken. It was a precarious position and one which frightened me during takes when the cameramen and armourers trampled around my unprotected body.

I lay in this position with my mouth gaping wide open for four whole days. Each day I was the first into make-up and the last on to the Pearl. I was so tired that sometimes I slept on the deck while they filmed around me. I saw myself in this repose several times towards the end the film.

The scene being shot by Gore was the final one in the movie. Elizabeth gave Jack a long passionate kiss as she pushed him slowly back to the masthead. Distracting him with her searing kiss she manacled him to the masthead and then rushed away to the longboat telling him that the Kraken did not want the ship, it wanted him; it wanted Captain Jack Sparrow.

I lay on the deck looking up at Johnny and Keira for four days as they played out this scene. My legs were never out of camera shot and I was sure that they would soon become more famous than even those of Marilyn Monroe. The bloodied upper torso of Barry Thorpe stretched across one side of the stairwell and the Kraken covered lower torso of Barry Coulton stretched across the other. Together the two Barrys would surely have made a whole. Just before each 'take' the armourer set fire to the pieces of Kraken that lay around me and on one occasion the flames were so huge that a stunt man rushed forward with a fire extinguisher; he thought that I was on fire.

I sometimes chatted with Johnny Depp while we were waiting for the cameras to be moved into a new position. I found that he was interested in my Clipper Round the World Yacht Race and I asked him if he would sign my sailing logbook to cover my days on the Black Pearl. After all, he was the skipper, and my entries had to be countersigned by the master of the vessel. I brought my logbook in on the following day and I asked him to sign it Captain Jack Sparrow. This he did, and then he added his own signature to authenticate his entry.

We were not permitted to ask for autographs and Gore headed menacingly towards us. Johnny casually gave me the logbook and said. "Thanks mate; I am pleased to be working with you, it was an honour to sign your book". Gore seemed to be satisfied and he carried on with what he was doing. It was small things such as this incident that made Johnny very special to all of those who were fortunate to work with him.

Shortly after this we broke up for Christmas and my short film career came to an end. I was privileged to be able to be part of such a large production. Millions would have given anything to be in my place. It was an experience which I have benefited from and I have made considerable use of my bragging rights. I understand that Pirates II & III enjoyed a combined budget of 680 million dollars and that they are the two most expensive films of all time. When 'Pirates of the Caribbean Dead Mans Chest' was released it became the first film to gross 100 million dollars in the first two days and it broke several other box office records. We shall have to wait to see if it receives any Oscar nominations but I don't think that my name will be one of them.

I have achieved almost all of my goals in life and the final one was the realization of a dream; to be a Black Pearl Pirate. Would I do it again? Yes! As Sir Robin repeated so many times during our Clipper Race. "This is the best thing that I have done with my life……so far".

Epilogue

My daughter Michele is still working in her beauty business and she is currently refurbishing a small apartment on the seafront in Bognor Regis; it has a fabulous uninterrupted view across the English Channel. My granddaughters are young adults and they are now finding their own way in life. Hayley works in the office of a music store in Chichester, Fiona is a physical fitness instructor on the Cruise Ship Carnival Princess and Stevi is studying travel and tourism at Chichester College. Toni gave birth to a beautiful baby girl on Thursday the 2nd March 2006 and named her Mia Lucy. Sadly my great-granddaughter caught a streptococcus B infection and passed away in her sleep three and a half months later. She had such a captivating smile and the whole family was devastated.

My son Brett and his long time girl friend Julia married in Schladming, Austria, during their annual snowboarding holiday. Julia gave birth to a baby girl on Monday the 10th July 2006. Sadie Josslyn was six weeks premature. She is doing fine and they hope to move into a new house in Cricklade Road, Bristol next week. Earlier in the year Ron Dennis of Formula One motor racing offered Brett a prestigious position as a design engineer with Maclaren in Woking, but he decided to remain with Dyson in Malmesbury where he is now a senior design engineer.

My wife Anne continues to work hard in her data quality consulting company, Design 21. And me, well I am off to Beijing to play chess with my old friend Ken Philip who has retired in China, and then I plan to look for Giant Panda in the mountains of Sichuan Province before walking the rolling grasslands of the Qinghai/Tibet plateau.

THE END – *For Now*

I started life in a small village community with little opportunity for personal advancement. I decided to change this and I set myself a series of lifetime targets. One by one I achieved each target and in writing my book I hope that I have encouraged others to do the same. Only by following different opportunities in life and by setting goals for each can a person realise their true potential.

Barry Coulton
2 June 2007